WINGS

OF FAME

Aerospace Publishing Ltd
AIRtime Publishing Inc.

Published quarterly by
Aerospace Publishing Ltd
179 Dalling Road
London W6 0ES
UK

Copyright © Aerospace Publishing Ltd
1995

ISSN 1361-2034

Aerospace ISBN 1 874023 68 9
                (softback)
                1 874023 74 3
                (hardback)

Published under licence in USA and
Canada by AIRtime Publishing Inc.,
10 Bay Street, Westport,
CT 06880, USA

Editorial Offices:
WINGS OF FAME
Aerospace Publishing Ltd
3A Brackenbury Road
London W6 0WE UK

Publisher: Stan Morse
Project Editor: David Donald
Contributing Editor: Jon Lake
Sub Editor: Karen Leverington
Editorial Assistant: Tim Senior

Artists: Chris Davey
         Keith Fretwell
         Tim Maunder
         Jonathan Mock
         John Weal
         Iain Wyllie

Origination by
   Chroma Graphics, Singapore
Printed by
   Officine Grafiche DeAgostini,
   Novara, Italy

The editors of WINGS OF FAME
welcome photographs for possible
publication, but cannot accept any
responsibility for loss or damage to
unsolicited material.

The publishers gratefully acknowledge
the assistance given by the following
people:

Herr Hallensleben of JG 71 press office
for his assistance with the Jagdgeschwader
Richthofen article

Jan Keohane and the staff of the Fleet
Air Arm Museum, and Ray Sturtivant
for their help with the Fleet Air Arm
1960-1969 feature

Flt Lt John Hancock, No. 56 Sqn,
RAF, for his help with the 'Firebirds'
article

Thanks to Mustang pilots: Randy
Acord, William Anderson, Lee Archer,
Bud Biteman, Jack Bradley, Devol
'Rock' Brett, Roscoe Brown, Lowell
Bruland, Bruce Carr, Woodrow
Crockett, Ken Dahlberg, Ben Davis,
Bill Ellis, Fred Fazenfeld, Robert
Goebel, Clayton Gross, William H.
Holloman III, Walt Karr, Felix
Kozaczka, George Lamb, Clint Martin,
Charles Magee, Stanley Ordway,
Andrew Ritchie, Mike Rogers, Harry
Stewart, Tom Thacker, Luke Weathers,
Charles White.

Thanks also to: Edward Horkey of the
P-51 design team.

Thanks also to: Hal Andrews, Warren
M. Bodie, Peter M. Bowers, John M.
Campbell, Robert L. Cavanagh, Bill
Crimmins, Michael P. Curphey, Larry
Davis, Lou Drendel, Jeffrey L. Ethell,
Dan Hagedorn, Bill Hess, Brad C.
Hood, Tom Ivie, Kyle Kirby, David
McLaren, David W. Menard, Merle C.
Olmsted, Charles Osborn, Terry
Panapolis, Bruce Potts, Kenn Rust.

**WINGS OF FAME is published
quarterly and is available by
subscription and from many fine
book and hobby stores.**

**SUBSCRIPTION AND BACK
NUMBERS:**

**UK and World (except USA and
Canada) write to:
Aerospace Publishing Ltd
FREEPOST
PO Box 2822
London
W6 0BR
UK
(No stamp required if posted in
the UK)**

**USA and Canada, write to:
AIRtime Publishing Inc.
Subscription Dept
10 Bay Street
Westport
CT 06880, USA
(203) 266-3580
Toll-free order number in USA:
1 800 359-3003**

Prevailing US subscription rates are as follows:
Softbound edition for 1 year:
   $58.00
Softbound edition for 2 years:
   $108.00

Softbound back numbers (subject to availability)
are $19.00 each. All rates are for delivery within
mainland USA, Alaska and Hawaii. Canadian and
overseas prices available upon request. American
Express, Discover Card, MasterCard and Visa
accepted. When ordering please include your card
number, expiration date and signature.

Publisher, North America:
   Mel Williams
Subscription Director:
   Linda DeAngelis
Retail Sales Director:
   Jill Brooks
Charter Member Services
Manager:
   Janie Munroe

WINGS
OF FAME

CONTENTS

Fighter Combat over Korea

PART 1

FIRST KILLS

"Suddenly, all hell broke loose. Colonel Stephens shouted for me to break left. An instant later, two flashing silver aircraft dove into me out of the sun. As they swept by, I gave my F-80 full throttle and tacked onto one's tail, trying to manoeuvre into firing position. It was definitely a MiG and I got a clear look at him when he started to climb back up into the sun. He had no distinguishing markings, just polished aluminium, swept wings and plenty fast.."

"When the MiG ahead of me broke to the left, he made a fatal mistake. He could climb faster than I could, but when he turned I cut him off and got in four good short bursts with my .50-calibres.

"It was difficult to tell if I had hit him. He just rolled over and headed for the deck in a steep dive. I racked my aircraft around and followed him down. My airspeed was indicating over 600 mph, but I could not close the gap. He was still approximately 1,000 ft away, when I gave him another four bursts.

"Black smoke spouted from the right side of his fuselage. I knew it was now or never, so I gave him one long burst. Orange flames licked back over the fuselage and suddenly the entire MiG exploded in the air! After that I don't remember what happened, as I was too busy trying to pull out of my high-speed dive."

Lieutenant Russ Brown, an F-80 pilot of the USAF's 26th Fighter Squadron, but flying with the 16th Fighter Interceptor Squadron, describes a typical dogfight with MiG-15s during the long and bloody war of 1950-53. It was just one of many high-adrenaline and deadly engagements fought between Western pilots and both inexperienced Chinese (and North Koreans) and combat-hardened Russians.

On 25 June 1950, after a secret

With its all-black F-82G Twin Mustangs, the 339th F(AW)S began the war at Yokota, Japan led by World War II ace Major James W. 'Poke' Little. The squadron, using the callsign ANTHONY, escorted a C-54 carrying General MacArthur to Korea on 29 June 1950. Though another Twin Mustang oufit, the 68th, drew first blood, the 339th was in air-to-air action against North Korean Yakovlevs and Lavochkins from the start.

and massive mobilisation of its forces, Communist North Korea crossed the 38th Parallel and invaded the pro-Western and nominally democratic South. The lightly-equipped South Korean army fled in disorder, and US Army. reinforcements rushed in from Japan proved no more effective. The North Korean troops were spearheaded by T-34 tanks and fighter-bombers, and cut through the defences like a knife through butter.

On the day of the invasion, four Yak-9s appeared through the scudding clouds to strafe Seoul's Kimpo airport. Within 24 hours of the attack, it was apparent to US Far East Command that the capital Seoul was in immediate danger of falling to the Communists.

The North Korean's only weakness was in the air, although the country's sole air regiment had been

Carrying 230-US gal 'Misawa' external fuel tanks, Lockheed F-80C Shooting Stars of the 9th Fighter-Bomber Squadron, 49th Fighter-Bomber Wing, line up at Taegu air base, alias K-2, by the Naktong River in South Korea.

The leftover World War II attire is typical for F-80C pilots of the 80th Fighter-Bomber Squadron 'Headhunters', of the 8th Fighter-Bomber Wing, who started the war flying from Itazuke Field, Japan, but moved to Korea after the Inchon invasion. Flying from Japanese bases, the F-80s had very limited range and endurance.

expanded to divisional size and was adequate to deal with any South Korean air power. The Pyongyang regime had to gamble that they would not be opposed in the air.

With the North Korean military juggernaut smashing through South Korean defences, the most pressing necessity was to airlift US citizens

and members of the South Korean government out of the city. Any such airlift would clearly require fighter support. This task was instantly entrusted to the USAF – and formed its first contribution to the UN war effort against the invaders.

The USAF, however, had a major

logistical problem: most of their aircraft were based in Japan with the 8th Fighter Bomber Group at Itazuke, the 35th Fighter Interceptor Wing at Yokota, the 49th Fighter Bomber Group at Misawa and the 51st Fighter Interceptor Wing at Naha, Okinawa (not then part of Japan).

The Start of the War

Korea had been spilt apart into separate countries, North and South, as a direct result of Russia's late and opportunistic declaration of war on Japan on 8 August 1945, when Japan was clearly about to surrender. The USA offered to divide the responsibility for accepting the surrender of Japanese forces in Korea, with the 38th Parallel being used as a convenient dividing line. The same border had been proposed years before, when Russia and Japan discussed dividing the small country. Following the surrender Russia installed Kim Il Sung as leader of the new Democratic People's Republic of Korea on 9 June 1948, while the USA put in Syngman Rhee as president of the Republic of Korea in the South.

By late 1945, the war-weary United States was exhausted and ready to enjoy peace and prosperity. The American population was ready to trade war production for new luxury goods and a better way of life. The last thing anyone wanted was to get involved in another war. The politicians reduced the military down to a dangerously low level.

General of the Army Douglas MacArthur, commander of UN forces, had previously taken the surrender of the Japanese.

American involvement in Korea was limited, and the new nation was not seen as a priority by United States diplomats. This was so much the case that when Secretary of State Dean Acheson listed the countries for which Americans were willing to 'bleed and die' in defence against Communism, he did not think to include Korea.

To North Korea, whose leader saw the unification of the two countries by force of arms as being akin to a holy mission, this seemed like a green light to seize the South and reunify Korea. Kim quickly sought, and gained, the approval of Moscow for his plans. The die was cast for a surprise attack, spearheaded by T-34 tanks and supported by air power.

North Korean documents captured after the war revealed that "Within two months from the date of attack, Pusan should have fallen and South Korea would no longer exist."

The time table for this bold statement also took into consideration the fact that the United States would intervene to help South Korea. With no US intervention, the war was to have been finished in 10 days. Without the intervention of US air power, this timetable might even have been turned into reality.

Key

■ CITIES
● Air Bases

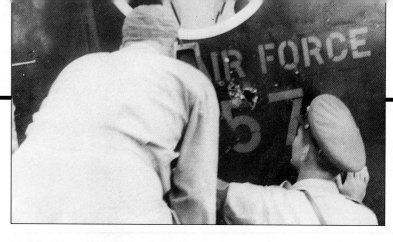

25 June 1950 ■
TWIN MUSTANG GOES TO WAR

Despite its unusual, rather anachronistic appearance, the F-82G Twin Mustang was an excellent aircraft. Essentially a pair of lightweight Mustang fuselages joined by a short centre section (the prototype used XP-51Fs), the aircraft had handed engines and counter-rotating propellers to minimise torque, and a powerful SCR-720C search radar mounted below the centre section. The radar operator sat in the starboard fuselage, with the pilot in the port fuselage.

Fortunately, the F-82G Twin Mustangs also had a remarkable range and endurance. A total of 40 could be made available from the 339th Fighter (All Weather) Squadron at Yokota, the 4th Fighter (All Weather) Squadron at Naha, and the 68th Fighter (All Weather) Squadron at Itazuke. These would provide cover for the C-54 and C-47 transports flying in and out of Seoul's Kimpo airfield. F-80 jet fighters from the 35th, 36th and 80th Fighter Bomber Squadrons at Itazuke, the 16th, 25th and 26th Fighter Interceptor Squadron at Naha, and the 41st Fighter Interceptor Squadron at Yokota would in turn fly cover for the F-82s, although their endurance was such that they would have only a few minutes of time over Kimpo. Moreover, when

the F-80s started flying fighter-bomber sorties, ammunition for their six .50-calibre machine-guns had to be reduced from the maximum 1,800 rounds due to centre of gravity problems. A single reconnaissance squadron, the 8th TRS, equipped with RF-80As, was also based at Yokota.

When the sun set over Itazuke Air Base on the evening of 24 June, all was calm. However, at 04.00 hours the next morning, 68th All Weather Squadron crew, 1st Lt George D. Deans and his radio officer 2nd Lt Marv Olsen, were given the alert. They were ordered to get airborne immediately and check in with 'Moonshine Control' – the radar-control for southern Japan. Lt Olsen remembers the mission vividly.

Tech Sgt Durocher and Lt John P. Kelley of the 68th Squadron check battle damage to Lt Charles Moran's F-82G. Charlie Moran borrowed Lt Rober Bobo's B.O. PLENTY for a 26 June mission, scored a kill on 27 June, and was lost in a Twin Mustang mishap on 7 August 1950.

"Soon after starting our climb, we were given a vector to Seoul. The instructions told us to fly up to the 38th Parallel and report back on any activity seen on the main roads. Far Eastern Air Force had received a report that North Korean forces were moving south towards Seoul. When we arrived in the area, it was overcast with cloud up to 8,000 ft. Lt Deans flew out over the water for a letdown, using our AI radar.

"We broke out at about 2,000 ft, just west of Inchon and proceeded immediately to the airfield at Kimpo, before we took up a northerly heading for the 38th.

About 10 miles south of the line, we saw a huge convoy of vehicles moving south. We counted well over 58 tanks, trucks and assorted vehicles on the road.

"Deans took us back up to 8,000 ft, so we could report back to base... Headquarters ordered us to return to Itazuke immediately, where we were debriefed by a member of General MacArthur's staff."

This F-82G reconaissance flight was recorded as the first fighter combat mission of the Korean War, although an SB-17G with armed turrets had flown from Itazuke to Kimpo and Pusan and back on the evening of 25 June 1950.

26 June 1950 ■
ATTACK AND COUNTER-ATTACK

Air action intensified on 26 June. It was a day of feint and counterfeint, the protagonists testing each other's mettle and taste for combat. That morning, North Korean fighters

ventured down into the Suwon/Seoul area. They had very little knowledge of what the US was doing in the way of air support, and made half-hearted attempts to attack the transports on

the ground at Kimpo. In a sudden change of orders, the F-82s flying cover over Inchon harbour were sent inland to patrol the truck convoys leaving Seoul.

At 13.33 hours, a single Yak-9 came out of the clouds and caught two F-82s by surprise. The American pilots were uncertain whether they should react aggressively and, as the ships in the harbour were not in immediate danger, they took evasive action. The Yak broke off and headed north.

1st Lt George Deans, a pilot in the 68th, recalls more aggressive early encounters.

"Lt William 'Skeeter' Hudson and myself flew the first air patrol over Inchon. The weather was overcast. While we were patrolling the evacuation road from Seoul to Inchon, we spotted a single bandit

Lt. William 'Skeeter' Hudson was credited with the war's first aerial victory flying with the 68th F(AW)S 'Lancers'. His F-82G Twin Mustang (apparently 46-401, though the identity of the first Yak-killer is in dispute) was glossy black overall with red 'buzz' numbers, serial numbers and 'USAF' legend.

astern of us. He had no trouble closing on our aircraft as we were loafing along at 160-180 mph. This was because we were set on long-range cruise speed.

"Hudson's radio officer, Lt Carl Fraser, was the first to spot him and immediately we dropped our fuel tanks and applied full power, starting a sharp turn. It was at that moment that the enemy fighter fired on our F-82. No hits were scored and the bandit disappeared into the overcast... Hudson radioed top cover, but they never saw him. Fraser thought the enemy aircraft was an La-7, but it happened so fast that we couldn't be sure."

Another confrontation soon followed. Lt Hudson takes up the story.

"After going up and down the road a couple of times, we spotted a couple of Russian-made fighters at 11 o'clock high. We were instructed not to fire unless fired upon, so we didn't make any aggressive moves in their direction. They started a wide turn toward us and we started one

Left: This 1950 glimpse of Capt Washatka's F-82G of the 4th F(AW)S accents the enormous centre fairing which carried up to 16 .50-in (12.7-mm) guns on the original Twin Mustang design but which was employed on the F-82G to carry the SCR-720(C) airborne intercept radar. Both propellers rotated toward the centre pod.

Above: An F-82G of the 68th F(AW)S over Itazuke airfield at Fukuoka, Japan in 1951, near the end of the type's combat service. The 68th used the radio callsign VICIOUS. By the end of 1950, number-crunchers asserted that the 68th had flown 566 sorties, dropped 103 bombs, and fired 276,000 rounds of .50-in(12.7-mm) ammunition. In the early days of the war, its long range and endurance made it invaluable.

to keep them in sight.

"Suddenly, the leader tightened up and peeled off at us – his wingman right behind him. When we saw he was going to attack, we dropped our external tanks, poured on the combat power, turned on the gun switches and started climbing toward him...

"We were forced to wait for him to make the aggressive move, but he was either over-eager, or green, because he started firing from too far out, his bullets lagging far behind us for his entire firing pass. His wingman started to make a pass on our wingman, but he wasn't in a good enough position to fire. They broke off and started a turn around on our tails, so we pulled up through the overcast. We figured that, if they came through, we'd be up there in a position to let them have it... They never showed up above the cloud layer."

68th Fighter (All Weather) Squadron

The 68th went to Korea in the F-82G Twin Mustang, but the squadron's lineage pre-dated dark and difficult days in World War II: Constituted on 20 November 1940, the squadron flew P-36s, P-40s, and P-43s before operating Bell P-400 Airacobras in the tropical hell of Guadalcanal. The 'Lightning Lancers' reached VJ Day in the Lockheed P-38 Lightning and operated the P-51 Mustang briefly thereafter. In 1948-49, the 68th flew the the P-61 Black Widow in occupied Japan. In February 1947, the unit became the 68th F(AW)S. When the Korean War began the 68th

was attached to (but not part of) the 8th Fighter-Bomber Wing at Itazuke, Japan. In 1949, the squadron converted from F-61Bs to F-82Gs. Its mission was air defence of the Western Japanese islands – western Honshu, Kyushu, and Okinawa – during inclement weather and at night. Many of the squadron's black Twin Mustangs carried the squadron insignia, the famous 'Lightning Lancers' badge, on the tail. This was a stylized depiction of an armoured knight girding for battle while riding a pair of lightning bolts.

Lt George Deans of the 68th Squadron gives an optimistic thumbs-up from the cockpit of his F-82G, after flying the first mission of the Korean War. The aircraft in the background is an RB-17.

F-82G-NA Twin Mustang 46-383
46-383, nicknamed *Bucket O'Bolts* (though no appellation appears on the aircraft), is usually cited as the F-82G flown by Lieutenant William 'Skeeter' Hudson on 27 June 1950. Squadron records have not survived, memory is unreliable, and 383 was on the scene, but some now aver that Hudson flew 46-401 when he shot down his Yak.

Above: F-82Gs of the 68th F(AW)S at Itazuke in 1951. The butt of an Air Force bar-room ballad, Itazuke was too small and cramped for F-80s and F-82s to 'bed down' together, but there was no ready alternative.

Left: F-82Gs of the 4th F(AW)S over North Korea. The F-82G was a night- and all-weather fighter, as its 'clean' configuration here shows, but in the absence of long-range dedicated fighter-bombers it became the first warplane in Korea to drop a napalm tank, and made much use of 5-in HVAR (high-velocity aircraft rockets).

27 June 1950
FIRST BLOOD

On the next day, 27 June, encounters were actually pressed home by both sides. It proved to be a day of triumph for US fighters: seven enemy fighters were shot down by F-82s and F-80s, with no losses sustained.

The first dogfight was brief but bloody. Increasingly bold North Korean feints throughout the morning left little doubt that they would eventually attempt to press home an attack against the unarmed transports on the ground at Kimpo. Such attacks soon materialised, eventually destroying seven of the infant Korean air arm's 16 aircraft. These losses were quickly replaced by the supply of 10 USAF Mustangs.

At noon, five Yak-type fighters were spotted heading straight for Kimpo airfield. Waiting for them were five F-82Gs from the 68th and 339th. Within minutes, three of the enemy fighters had gone down in flames. Radar operator Lt Carl Fraser remembers the explosive engagement.

"It was while we were circling Kimpo that two North Korean fighters came up out of some low clouds and started after Charlie Moran's ship, which was the No.4 plane in our flight. They managed to shoot up his tail. Meanwhile, my pilot, 'Skeeter' Hudson, slipped around and got onto the tail of their flight leader. When the guy realised that we were there, he pulled up into some clouds and tried to shake us...

"Fortunately, we were so close to him that we could even see him in the middle of the clouds. Our first burst hit the rear of the fuselage and knocked some pieces off. The enemy pilot racked his fighter over in a steep turn to the right and we gave him another burst along his right wing. This set the fuel tank on fire and took the right flap and aileron off.

"By this time, we were in so close that we almost collided with him. I could clearly see the pilot turn around and say something to the observer. Then he pulled his canopy back and climbed out on the wing and once again leaned over to the observer's cockpit. Either the rear seater was wounded or scared – he made no attempt to jump. The pilot pulled his ripcord and was pulled off the wing just as the fighter rolled over and went in.

"The entire fight took place below 1,000 ft. We made a low level run over where the enemy pilot had parachuted and he was surrounded by South Korean troops."

Lt's Hudson and Moran (pilots of the 68th Squadron), and Major James Little (339th CO), all claimed 'kills'; Hudson (flying F-82G 46-383) claimed a Yak-11 and the others claimed their victims as La-7s. Two more pilots of the 339th claimed kills, but these were credited only as probables. It was not until 1953 that Hudson was officially recognised as having scored the first of these – and of the war. More recently, some experts have speculated that Little's kill may have been the first.

FIRST JET KILLS

Another 'first' of the war was the intervention of jet fighters. Lockheed F-80s were responsible for the other four 'kills' made that day. A flight of four Shooting Stars nominally led by Captain Raymond Schilleref, a veteran 9th AF Mustang ace during World War II, was flying a defensive patrol over Kimpo when Il-10s broke through and attempted to strafe transport aircraft on the ground. The details of that action are recalled by Lt Robert E. Wayne of the 35th Fighter Bomber Squadron.

"Our group was fragged to provide cover for the C-54s evacuating US personnel from Kimpo Air Base. My flight, 'C' Flight, had flown on an uneventful mission that morning and was scheduled for another go in the afternoon.

"My flight 'line up' was myself as lead with Lt Ralph G. 'Smiley' Hall as No. 2, Captain Ray Schillereff as element lead and Lt Robert H. Dewald as No. 4. I briefed them that when we arrived in the target area, we would split into elements and set up an orbit between the 38th Parallel on the north and Suwon on the south. We were not allowed to cross the parallel.

"I wanted to have two aircraft always heading north at all times. I don't remember the exact weather, but it couldn't have been too good. We logged 1 hour 45 minutes of weather on the mission. As I remember, the target area was something like 12,000 ft overcast, with a lower broken undercast layer at 5,000 to 6000 ft, and good visibility in between.

"Upon arriving in the target area, we split into elements and started our orbits. We had our power pulled back so that we could spend as much time as possible in the target area. On one of our orbits heading north, as I remember, in the Seoul area, my wingman called out a bogey which I could not pick up. I told Smiley to take the lead and attack.

"As we turned to initiate the attack, I picked up seven prop aircraft in a loose echelon to the right. I would mention here that during our intelligence briefing, we were told that the British had a carrier in the Sea of Japan and that we might see some of their aircraft in the area. Unfortunately, one of the aircraft aboard was the Firefly, a single-engined aircraft with a

This Lockheed F-80C Shooting Star was the aircraft of 35th FBS MiG-killer Robert Dewald, whose exploits are recounted here. It carries HVARs underwing, with enlarged wingtip fuel tanks.

gunner in the rear cockpit. As we closed on the bogies I saw that they matched the description of the Firefly, so I told Smiley to drop back until I had made an identification pass.

"As I approached the No. 6 aircraft, I could see the rear gunner firing at me. I told Smiley to open fire, but he was too close. I broke left and lined up behind No. 1. I fired a few rounds – he exploded. I made a tight 360° turn to the left and lined up behind No. 2 and had the same results! I thought to myself, this is easy – maybe I can get them all!

"I made another 360° turn to the left and rolled out where No. 3 should have been, but they had all disappeared into the clouds below. I looked around the area for a few minutes trying to find any of the

339th Fighter (All Weather) Squadron

The F-82G-equipped 339th F(AW)S of the Korean War dated to 1942. Flying Lockheed P-38 Lightnings in World War II, the squadron claimed, among many other achievements, the shoot-down of the Japanese Mitsubishi G4M carrying Admiral Isoroku Yamamoto, Commander-in-Chief of Tokyo's Pacific Fleet. On the eve of the Korean War the 339th was at Johnson AB, Japan and converted from the Northrop P-61B Black Widow to the F-82G. The squadron was temporarily at Yokota on 25 June 1950 but soon returned to Johnson. World War II ace Major James W. 'Poke' Little scored one of the first aerial victories in early Korean fighting on 27 June 1950. The squadron emblem depicted a silver dragon with red eyeballs, white pupils, and flames of fire jetting from his mouth, rearing upward between two clouds. The F-82G stayed in action with the 339th until 1951 when replaced by the Lockheed F-94B. The squadron remained at Johnson through the 27 July 1953 armistice. It did not score any aerial victories in the F-94B — leaving Little's as its only victory credit during the entire Korean War.

At Johnson Air Base, F-82G Twin Mustangs of the 339th F(AW)S greet the first snowfall of 1950. Korea had the full range of seasons – broiling heat in summer and sub-zero cold in winter. Twin Mustangs never flew from Korean bases but confronted the weather every day, along with the enemy's guns. Maintenance was performed in large well-appointed hangars at the Japanese bases.

five remaining enemy fighters, but to no avail. Being below Bingo fuel, I gathered up my wingman and headed home.

"In the meantime, the other element in my flight had headed north when the bogies were sighted and each pilot got a victory. We returned to Itazuke in elements and of course I had to make a victory roll. After landing it was determined that I had fired 328 rounds of .50-cal, which shows just what devastating results six .50s can provide."

Meanwhile, a two-jet element headed north, piloted by Capt Schillereff and Lt Dewald. They immediately ran into the enemy. Lt Dewald takes up the story.

"Having moved away from the other element slightly to the north of Kimpo, I spotted a dark-coloured aircraft moving on a straight course to the south along

the Naktong River... By the time I was able to get Capt Schillereff lined up on my wing (he had not seen the bogey yet), I found myself high above the North Korean aircraft and going in the opposite direction.

"I was already practically on my back trying to keep the bogey in sight. Pulling straight through, I was in an almost perfect vertical curve of pursuit. As I rapidly closed on the enemy aircraft, I could tell it was shaped like a fighter, but it had a cockpit that seemed to be long enough to have a second crewman behind the pilot.

"Suddenly, I noticed what seemed like a blinking light in the rear of the cockpit. I realised that there was a gunner behind a gun and he was firing at me! I was converging fast and was within range, so I pulled off a long burst with all six 50s firing into the

North Korean's cockpit area. The enemy pilot took no evasive action, flying straight and level. So I pulled up and began to position myself for another firing pass.

"This time, there was no light blinking from the rear gun, so I put another long burst along the fuselage and walked it on up to the engine compartment. Again, there were no apparent results...there was no smoke, the prop was still turning and the aircraft was still in a level, straight flight.

"This called for me to line up for a third pass. I dropped far enough back to allow me to level off and come up behind at point blank range. There was no curve of pursuit, just a long firing pass. Still no evidence of damage – but I noticed that the fighter had started to descend at a significant angle. This observation was made...close behind the bogey.

"Just then, I found my windscreen covered with engine oil. Glancing off to each side, [I saw] the same oil had covered my leading edges and tip tanks. Low on fuel, Schillereff and myself climbed for altitude and rode some good tailwinds back to Itazuke AB.

"After assessing the gun camera film from our F-80s, it was determined that both of us had shot down a North Korean Il-10 bomber. As far as I was concerned, it was a hard-earned victory..."

Robert E. Wayne was credited with two kills, bringing the total to four.

35th Fighter Bomber Squadron

The 35th FBS "Panthers" of the Korean era (part of the 8th FBW) trace its lineage to 1917 – one of the oldest Air Force squadrons. The squadron flew P-39s, P-40s, and P-38s in the Pacific. When the Korean War began, it was at Itazuke. On 27 June 1950 the 35th became the first American jet squadron to down enemy aircraft. F-80Cs led by Capt Raymond E. Schillereff went to Seoul, caught a four-plane flight of Ilyushin Il-10s, and shot all four down. The squadron scored at least three more kills in F-80Cs while flying grueling air-to-ground missions. The squadron made several moves in 1950-51 and briefly flew the F-51D Mustang before settling at Suwon on 24 August 1951, there to remain until the ceasefire. In the F-51D, pilots learned the obvious – that the superb escort fighter which had accompanied Allied bombers to Berlin five years earlier was not the world's

best fighter-bomber and was painfully vulnerable to ground fire, including small-arms fire. Like other F-51D squadrons, the 35th suffered heavy losses – roughly the equivalent of an entire squadron per year. In 1953, the 8th FBW and its squadrons converted from the F-80C to the F-86F Sabre. Though the squadron accounted for no MiGs during the conflict, its pilots shot down three MiG-15s on 10 May 1955 – the final American air victories of the era as well as the last American kills, ever, by the Sabre. The squadron has never come home and now flies F-16C Fighting Falcons at Kunsan.

'Panthers' who scored kills included 1st Lieutenant Robert E. Wayne (two kills); 1st Lieutenant Richard J. Burns (one); Captain Francis Clark (one); 1st Lieutenant Robert H. Dewald (one); 2nd Lieutenant David H. Goodnough (one), and Schillereff (one).

Below: Russ Rogers of the 35th FBS with his F-51D. Beside Rogers are half of his Mustang's six 0.50-in (12.7-mm) machine guns and six 5-in HVARs. The Mustang's liquid-cooled engine made it vulnerable to ground fire.

Robert Dewald, a pilot with the 35th FBS, blasts a North Korean Il-2 from the sky with the combined firepower of his six .50-in machine-guns on 27 June 1950. This was one of the first jet kills of the war.

Iain Wyllie

North Korean air force

The major weakness in North Korea's military was the fact that it included little or no air power. This was to be remedied in late January 1950, when Major General Wang Yong expanded the lone North Korean air regiment into a division, taking the opportunity to modernise the force with fighters delivered from Russia. Early records indicated that the newly expanded unit had a personnel strength of close to 1,700 officers and enlisted men. Of this total some 76 were pilots, several of whom had fought with the Japanese during World War II, and many of whom had received training in the USSR afterwards.

As soon as the air arm began its expansion, the Soviet Union started providing more aircraft, all of which were from Russia's arsenal of World War II surplus. No jet aircraft were included in the package. The most effective fighters in this build-up were the Yak-7 and Yak-9 series, which were broadly equivalent to the P-51 Mustang, lighter, shorter-ranged, but more agile and with heavier-calibre guns.

By June 1950, it was estimated that the NKAF had about 178 aircraft in their inventory. Thirty of these were Po-2 and Yak-18 trainers, 70 were Il-l0 *Shturmovik* ground attack aircraft, and the remainder were split between various fighter types. There is some confusion as to exactly which fighter variants were on charge. Yak-9s and Yak-9Ps were captured when UN forces later overran North Korean airfields, but Yak-3s, Yak-7s and even radial-engined Lavochkin La-7s were reported in combat reports.

When UN forces retook Seoul's Kimpo airport after the Inchon landings, they found this crashed North Korean Ilyushin Il-10. An Il-10 was later tested in the United States, along with at least one example of the Yakovlev Yak-9P.

29 June 1950
RETURN OF THE MUSTANG

The next day (29 June) saw an intensification of the air war. The US government authorised MacArthur to employ air power against military targets throughout the Korean peninsula, and the USAF extended its operations north of the 38th Parallel, although operations north of the Yalu remained forbidden.

At the same time the United Nations, acting despite a Soviet boycott, passed a resolution supporting the defence of South Korea. Sixteen nations committed ground troops, while Australia, Britain, Canada, Greece and South Africa were to send pilots (and in some cases aircraft). The first of these were from Australia, No.77 Squadron, RAAF, who joined the defence of Korea (from their base at Iwakuni, as part of the occupation forces) on 30 June, suffering their first combat loss on 7 July.

Simultaneously, MacArthur was appointed Commander-in-Chief UN Command (CINCUNC). The North Korean air force was taken completely by surprise: F-80s and B-26s flew repeated bombing and strafing sorties over the Parallel, and many North Korean aircraft were destroyed on the ground.

General of the Army Douglas MacArthur visits Kimpo on 1 October 1950. MacArthur used his C-54 Skymaster, the Bataan, for trips to Korea. He also had a Ryan L-17 Navion. Here, he celebrates the Inchon invasion. Six months later, President Truman had him replaced because he felt that MacArthur was overstepping the mark in his public pronouncements.

This survivor of the 1905-1945 Japanese occupation of Korea, apparently a Mitsubishi Ki-54 'Topsy' transport. It was left behind by the North Koreans when they abandoned Pyongyang East, the airfield serving their capital, as the Allies overran Pyongyang and drove north.

Left: A North American F-51D Mustang of Australia's No. 77 Squadron. In Japan as part of the occupation, No. 77 was committed to the Korean action four days after war broke out. After hard fighting in Mustangs, the Aussies swapped their prop-driven fighters for factory-new Gloster Meteor F.Mk 8s, which had little success in air-to-air work but made lethal fighter-bombers.

Right: Japan's Mount Fuji passes behind a Lockheed F-80C of the 36th FBS. The F-80C was too fast and not manoeuvrable enough for dogfights with North Korean Yaks, but pilots quickly discovered that having centreline guns and no prop up front eased their job when supporting ground troops with low-level strafing and bombing runs.

Within four weeks, much of the North Korean air force had been destroyed on the ground, although the 18 Polikarpov Po-2s that would later cause such a nuisance as 'Bedcheck Charlies' escaped unscathed, while Yak-9s and Il-10s continued to operate close to the Yalu – perhaps part of a reserve force based in or resupplied from Manchuria.

That day (29 June) also witnessed the return to combat of one of the great fighters of World War II: the P-51 Mustang. General MacArthur, supreme commander of UN forces in Korea, decided to fly up to Seoul to get an overview of the war situation. To UN high command, this was a risky move as the North Korean air force was still active in the area. F-80s flew a heavy screen over MacArthur's transport and, to play it safe, a number of F-51s covered the route at low altitude.

Four F-51s, flown by seasoned Mustang pilots who had re-converted to the aircraft from the F-80, also patrolled north of Seoul. This formation was the first to draw blood. 2nd Lt Orrin E. Fox of the 80th FBS downed two Il-10s, while Lts Harry Sandlin and Richard Burns each splashed another. Sandlin was officially credited with an La-7, but this was probably due to poor recognition!

These four kills were reportedly witnessed by a VIP, although some sources record a separate dogfight resulting in the destruction of four Yak-9s. No record of such an engagement appears on official kill lists, however.

MacArthur had no sooner arrived at Suwon airfield than the four North Korean intruders roared in through scattered cloud. The series of dogfights described above immediately ensued at low altitude, the noise bringing MacArthur out of his staff room to watch, according to one report, and actually taxiing in between strafing runs according to another. The Il-10s proved to be manoeuvrable, but the superior speed of the F-51s, and the greater experience of their pilots, ensured the destruction of all four enemy aircraft. Two kills had been scored earlier in the day by squadron-mates Lt Roy Marsh, claiming an Il-10, and Lt William T. Norris who downed an La-7.

8th Fighter Bomber Squadron

The 8th FBS 'Black Sheep' dates to 1941 and the Curtiss P-36 Mohawk, and has been part of the 49th Fighter-Bomber Wing (formerly group) throughout its existence, The squadron fought World War II in New Guinea and elsewhere in the Pacific, flying the Lockheed P-38 Lightning. With P-38, P-39, P-40, P-47 and P-51 in its history, the squadron was flying the Lockheed F-80C Shooting Star at Misawa in northern Japan on 25 June 1950. Within hours, the 8th moved to Ashiya, then Itazuke (on 8 July 1950). As with half a dozen other USAF squadrons, the 8th drew the task of blooding the F-80C, the first time Americans went into combat in jet cockpits. Always focused on the air-to-ground mission, the squadron began converting from the F-80C to the Republic F-84E Thunderjet in 1951. On 18 September 1951, Thunderjet pilot 1st Lt William Skliar toted up the 8th's final aerial victory, a MiG-15. The squadron moved to the new airfield at Kunsan, Korea on 1 April 1953 and was there with F-84E and F-84G fighters at the time of the armistice. Today, the world knows the 8th as an operator of the Lockheed F-117A 'Stealth Fighter'. The squadron insignia is a black sheep silhouette, partly enclosed in a black circle, with a white eye visible and a red lightning flash pointing to the left. 8th FBS pilots with aerial victories in Korea included 1st Lieutenant Roy W. Marsh (one), and Skliar (one). Mis-prints in the official kill list resulted in Lts Harry Sandlin and Orrin Fox having been frequently (and erroneously) identified as members of the Eighth, although they actually flew Mustangs with the 80th.

Col Stanton T. Smith, seen on 25 July 1950, was commander of the 49th FBG, and often flew with the 8th Fighter Bomber Squadron, although this aircraft bears the badge of the controlling 49th Fighter Group on its nose. The squadron colour of the 8th FBS was yellow, and the unit applied yellow noses and tailbands to its aircraft. Other squadrons in the wing used red and blue as their unit colours.

30 June 1950 ▮▮▮▮▮
Aggressive Yaks

The following day there was more activity in the air. Two F-80s flown by 1st Lt Charles Wurster and 2nd Lt John Thomas were bounced by a pair of unusually aggressive Yaks. Fortunately, although they were at low level, the F-80s were able to turn the tables, using their superior speed and acceleration. Wurster recalls: "I was flying wing with John Thomas in the vicinity of the Naktong River, when we found ourselves in a scrap with two Yak-9s that had seen us first and initiated the attack... A long burst of fire put the first Yak out of business. An instant later the pilot bailed out near Suwon. He pulled his ripcord, the chute streamed out of its pack, but never opened. It was a streamer. For some reason the pilot never made any attempt to get a bubble of air into the chute, maybe he was unconscious or injured. Realising almost too late that the other Yak was still in the area (the enemy fighter had got onto Lt Thomas's tail), I called for him to break hard, which he did. In a matter of seconds he had manoeuvred his F-80 into position to make a kill. We both watched as the second Yak pilot bailed out. This time the chute opened. Interestingly, the Korean chutes were square. As he drifted down, Thomas safed his guns and made several passes for confirmation with gun camera film. From his reaction, getting into as small a ball as possible, the Korean must have expected to be gunned while he was in his harness." Both Yaks had eventually been downed, but Wurster and Thomas noted that the enemy pilots had fought with skill and daring. This led some to speculate that the Soviet Union had sent pilots to Korea, but it seems more likely that the pilots were Koreans who had flown with the Japanese during World War II, and who had subsequently received extra training at the hands of the Russians.

The USAF in the Far East

General Douglas MacArthur, CINCFE (C-in-C Far East) was overall commander of US occupation forces in Japan, and most of the Pacific, although the handful of troops in Korea actually fell outside his jurisdiction. His air commander was Lt Gen George E. Stratemeyer, head of the US Far East Air Force. Under him was Major General Earle E. Partridge, commander of the constituent Fifth Air Force in Japan. On paper, US air forces in the area looked impressive. The core was provided by seven numbered wings based in Japan and on Guam, part of the Marianas (a US dependency). US Navy air power in the area did not come under FEAF jurisdiction or command, but at any one time could include one or more aircraft-carriers.

USAF units in the area included the 8th Fighter Bomber Group at Itazuke, with the F-80-equipped 35th, 36th and 80th Fighter Bomber Squadrons and the 68th Fighter (All Weather) Squadron with F-82Gs. The 35th Fighter Interceptor Wing at Yokota was similarly equipped, with the F-80s of the 40th and 41st Fighter Interceptor Squadrons, the 339th Fighter (All Weather) Squadron with F-82Gs, and the 8th TRS,

equipped with RF-80As. The 49th Fighter Bomber Group at Misawa consisted of the 7th, 8th, and 9th Fighter Bomber Squadrons, all with F-80s. The final fast-jet unit was the 51st Fighter Interceptor Wing at Naha. This parented the 16th, 25th and 26th Fighter Interceptor Squadrons with F-80s, the 4th Fighter (All Weather) Squadron with its F-82s and the 31st Photo Reconnaissance Squadron, Very Long Range, flying RB-29 Superfortresses.

Johnson AB near Tokyo housed the 3rd Bomb Wing, whose squadrons operated the B-26. Further bomber strength in the region was provided by the 19th Bombardment Wing at Andersen AFB on Guam, equipped with the B-29 Superfortress. Tachikawa Air Base housed two squadrons of C-54 Skymasters, of the 374th Troop Carrier Wing.

Miss Carriage *was an F-82G of the 4th Fighter (All Weather) Squadron based at Naha as part of the 51st Fighter Interceptor Wing, serving alongside three F-80-equipped day fighter squadrons.*

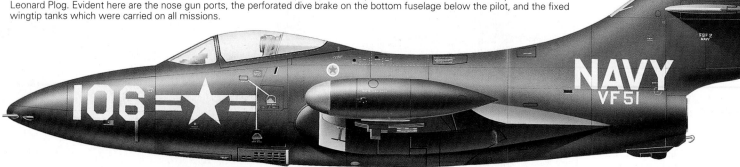

F9F-2 Panther, flown by Lieutenant Leonard Plog VF-51, USS *Valley Forge*
'Happy Valley' was near Hong Kong when the North Koreans invaded, and became the first US Navy carrier to reach the combat zone. The F9F-2 was the first Navy jet to see combat and to rack up an aerial victory. Pilot for the first historic victory was Lt Leonard Plog. Evident here are the nose gun ports, the perforated dive brake on the bottom fuselage below the pilot, and the fixed wingtip tanks which were carried on all missions.

3 July 1950
Carrier strikes begin

A carrier task force consisting of the USS *Valley Forge* (CVA-45) and HMS *Triumph* steamed to their station off the North Korean coast from Okinawa, the USS *Philippine Sea* (CVA-47) following close behind. Before dawn on 3 July, the *Triumph* made history by launching the first non American UN air strike of the war. Nine Griffon-engined Supermarine Seafire F.Mk 47s of No. 800 Squadron and 12 Fairey Fireflies of No. 827 Squadron were launched, these mounting an effective strike against the North Korean airfield at Haeju. At the same time, on the same morning, history of another kind was being made by US Navy aircraft, participating in the conflict for the first time. These attacked the capital of North Korea, Pyongyang. AD Skyraiders and F4U Corsairs of CVG-5 were launched from the carrier USS *Valley Forge*; they were followed soon afterwards by a wave of eight F9F Panthers. The jets were timed to arrive before the main strike force, to counter any attempt by the NKAF to intercept the bombers. Numerous Yak-type fighters scrambled as the Panthers converged on the big airfield complex at Pyongyang and, seconds later, the sky above it was snarled-up in a 'furball' of fierce dogfights.

Lt Leonard Plog, flying a Panther of VF-51, pulled in rapidly behind one of the Yak-types. Before he could line the aircraft up in his gunsight, he noticed another North Korean fighter moving in on him from the flank.

"He had a perfect run on me," Plog recalls, "but, evidently, he had never shot at anything moving that fast before…" Almost immediately,

The Supermarine Seafire F.Mk 47, latter day naval variant of the Spitfire, made one combat cruise aboard Triumph *before the Hawker Sea Fury took over as the Royal Navy's Korean War shipboard fighter. Its origins as a derivative of the Spitfire gave it trickier deck-handling characteristics than the Sea Fury.*

VF-51

VF-51 'Screaming Eagles' owes its lineage to Navy squadrons VF-1, established 15 February 1943; VF-5 of 15 July 1943; VF-5A of 15 November 1946; and VF-51 of 16 August 1948. The squadron's background includes the F4F Wildcat and F6F Hellcat. In post-war years the squadron flew the North American FJ-1 Fury before converting to the Panther. When Korean fighting began, the squadron was embarked on the closest aircraft-carrier, USS *Valley Forge* (CV-45), flying Grumman F9F-3 Panthers. On 3 July 1950, eight F9F-3s of VF-51 escorted a strike on Pyongyang airfield in the first combat sortie, ever, by jet-propelled US Navy aircraft. In the melée over Pyongyang, Ensign E. W. Brown and Lieutenant (jg) Leonard Plog each shot down a Yakovlev Yak-9. Two more 'Screaming Eagles' pilots destroyed North Korean Yaks on the ground. VF-51's first combat cruise as part of Air Group Five on 'Happy Valley' (accompanied by similarly-equipped VF-52) was made from 25 June to 1 December 1950, encompassing the early days of conflict, the Inchon invasion, and the Allied drive north. The squadron made a later cruise in improved F9F-5 Panthers with the same ship and air group from 20 November 1952 to 25 June 1953, in all completing more than 1,100 sorties. In later years, VF-51 flew the F-4B Phantom in Vietnam and subsequently the F-4N Phantom and F-14A Tomcat before being disestablished in an economy move in March 1995. VF-51 pilots who downed enemy aircraft were Brown and Plog – one each.

An F9F-3 Panther from VF-51 on Valley Forge *makes a stop at Kimpo air base, or K-14, in October 1950. To the Air Force at K-14, Navy blue was an infrequent sight.*

another Panther, flown by Ensign E. W. Brown, slipped in behind the Yak and gave it a burst with his four 20-mm cannon. The devastating firepower blew away the Yak's tail assembly. With the threat gone, Plog immediately pursued and destroyed his original target.

With the loss in seconds of two of their aircraft, the remaining North Korean pilots scattered. This allowed the Panthers a chance to strafe the airfield. On the first pass, three more enemy fighters were destroyed on the ground. With enemy air cover annihilated, the main strike force could bomb at will: heavy damage was inflicted on aircraft hangers and a rail complex in the area. Air Group Five returned later that day, wrecking 15 locomotives.

A Fairey Firefly Mk 5 of No. 827 Squadron at Suwon airfield, alias K-13, in 1951. Fireflies first joined the Korean fighting, together with Seafires, when they arrived aboard HMS Triumph in June 1950 with No. 827 Squadron of the Royal Navy. The Firefly was a fast, agile, tough, stable bombing and strafing platform, and Americans greatly envied its British and Australian crews, although the US Navy's Douglas AD Skyraider offered very similar capabilities.

July 1950
The Korean advance continues

The raid on Pyongyang may have been a big step in taking the fight to the North Koreans, but nothing could hide the fact that the war on the ground was going badly for the UN. The North Korean People's Army continued to make major inroads and, by mid-July, had pushed over 100 miles into the south. The 24th Division put up a valiant fight but could not stem the tide, and were pushed back into what became known as the Pusan perimeter.

The situation was so serious that the 80th FBS were put on 24-hour alert in case they had to cover an evacuation. Fortunately, the North Korean air force was not seen as far south as Pusan, since hordes of UN aircraft were active between Pusan and the Koreans' Manchurian bases. The Army and Marines relied heavily on light observation aircraft, initially using Ryan L-17s, and later the Piper L-4 Grasshopper. These slow unarmed aircraft proved something of a magnet for the NKAF's Yaks, and one was shot down by a Yak.

Honours were even, however, since on another occasion an L-4 scored what would today have been termed a 'manoeuvre kill' by suckering the enemy fighter into flying into a hillside. Fortunately,

Right: A red-nosed F-80C of the 9th FBS. An F-80 flying from Japan could remain over Seoul for only 15 minutes. To succeed, the F-80 force had to be shifted to Korea.

UN command of the air was emphasised with each new action. Yak-9s were downed on 15 July by Lt Robert A. Coffin, whose victory was not recorded on the official F-80 kill list, and on 17 July by Captain Francis Clark of the 35th FBS, flying an F-80.

In yellow Mae West and World War II-tan flight coveralls, 1st Lt Frank Clark of the 35th FBS models the no-frills attire of the well-dressed F-80C Shooting Star pilot, circa 1950.

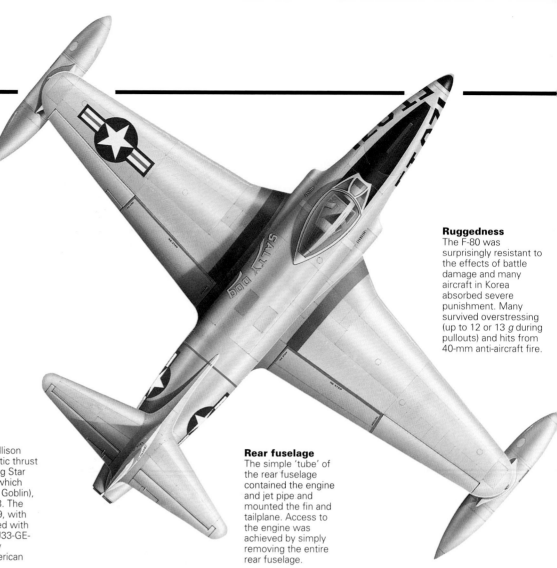

This F-80C was flown by Captain Francis B. Clark who scored an air-to-air victory on 19 July 1950. Apart from being the standard USAF fighter in the Far East when Korea boiled over, the Lockheed F-80C Shooting Star was the first operational American jet. It came within hours of fighting in World War II – examples were in Italy on VE Day – and established numerous speed, altitude, and range records in the post-war 1940s. Deemed too advanced in the early days of Korean fighting when the enemy had only propeller-driven aircraft, the F-80 was outclassed five months later when the swept-wing MiG-15 appeared. Though it fought relentlessly in the air-to-ground role, the F-80s scored many kills, their best-known combat achievement coming in history's first jet-vs-jet battle in November 1950 when Lieutenant Russell Brown downed a MiG-15.

Ruggedness
The F-80 was surprisingly resistant to the effects of battle damage and many aircraft in Korea absorbed severe punishment. Many survived overstressing (up to 12 or 13 g during pullouts) and hits from 40-mm anti-aircraft fire.

Jet power
Late production F-80Cs were powered by the Allison J33-A-21 engine rated at 5,200 lb (23.13-kN) static thrust with water injection. The first prototype Shooting Star had been built around a British Halford engine (which later became the highly successful de Havilland Goblin), but later aircraft used the indigenous Allison J33. The first few had the 3,850-lb st (17.13-kN) J33-GE-9, with the 4,000-lb st (17.79-kN) GE-11 being introduced with the 30th aircraft. Most used the similarly rated J33-GE-17. The J33 was one of the few centrifugal-flow turbojets to reach widespread service in an American warplane.

Rear fuselage
The simple 'tube' of the rear fuselage contained the engine and jet pipe and mounted the fin and tailplane. Access to the engine was achieved by simply removing the entire rear fuselage.

19 July 1950
More kills for the F-80

The next air-to-air kill of the war was scored by Captain Francis B. Clark of the 36th FBS, who downed a Yak-9 on 17 July. Two days later, on 19 July, the same squadron achieved an even more resounding victory.

That day, Lt Robert D. McKee was flying No.3 position in a flight of four F-80s 20 miles northeast of Taejon. Suddenly, the flight was informed by radio that four Yak-types were strafing and bombing Taejon airfield. Within seconds, No. 1 and No. 2 fighters started toward the hot spot, while McKee and No. 4 moved into position to cover them from above and behind. McKee recalls what happened immediately afterwards.

"At approximately 12,000 ft, No. 2 man spotted four Yak-9s in formation headed north at at about 6,000 ft. Lead still did not see the bogies, so No. 2 man took the No. 1 slot. We remained about 2,000 feet behind them and 1,000 feet above them. As we got in behind them and were discovered, two Yaks on our left made a sharp turn to the left and down... The two on the right turned right and up...

"At this time, I noticed my lead pull straight up. Our No. 2 man hit the enemy element that had turned left and down. My element went after the other two Yaks. I used my gyro sight and closed in on the lead ship and started to fire at 15-20° off, slightly above him and at 1,000 ft range. My hits were clustered around the engine, cockpit and left wing root.

"Suddenly there was a fair-sized explosion around the wing root, and he began trailing a white-grey smoke with a small fire on the bottom side of the wing. I broke off the attack by breaking high left and trying to spot No. 1 and No. 2 man of our flight who had taken the other enemy element. At this time, I jettisoned my rockets and tip tanks.

"Completing a quick 360° turn, I came in on another Yak-9. As I opened fire from zero angle-off and approximately 900 feet, I observed hits on both wing roots and in the rear of the cockpit. At that same

Major Dick McNeese of the 36th FBS 'Flying Fiends' on the prowl in an F-80C Shooting Star in July 1950. Everything was difficult in those early days, and fighter pilots knew that American soldiers, hard-pressed by the enemy onslaught, truly needed their help.

Guns
With no engine and propeller up front, the F-80C enjoyed a concentrated package of six .50-in (12.7-mm) Colt-Browning M2/M3 machine-guns with 300 rounds per weapon. Without a lead-computing gunsight and with their small rounds – the MiG-15 fired 23-mm and 37-mm shells – these guns were not ideal in a dogfight, although they were easy to aim.

Rockets
The F-80's most effective air-to-ground weapon was the 5-in (12.7-cm) HVAR (High-Velocity Aircraft Rocket), a weapon especially effective against rolling stock. Ten could be carried. F-80s also delivered bombs and napalm in Korea, and used their .50-in machine guns for strafing.

Tail fin
The configuration of the F-80C was entirely conventional, the plank-like wing providing superb agility. The fin stood 11 ft 3 in (3.43 m) high. Length was 34 ft 5 in (10.49 m). Wing span was 38 ft 9 in (11.81 m). Contrary to legend, all versions of the F-80 had wings of the same area and thickness.

Lockheed F-80C
35th FBS

Tip tanks
The wing tanks of the F-80 evolved with the necessities of war: in Korea, the original 165-US gal (625-litre) "teardrop" fuel tank was hastily replaced by the 200-US gal (757-litre) "Misawa" tank produced by combining this design with the cylindrical centre sections of another Fletcher tank. With 750 US gal (2839 litres) of fuel including early teardrop-shaped drop tanks, the F-80C had a combat radius of 506 miles (814 km) with a typical load of two 1,000-lb bombs or 10 5-in (12.7-cm) HVAR rockets.

Cockpit
The cockpit of the F-80 was gently pressurised, and in the F-80B and F-80C contained a primitive ejection seat. The blown canopy provided an excellent all-round view, but the cockpit was never adequately ventilated or air conditioned, and very high cockpit temperatures could be encountered. The proximity of the canopy to the pilot's head made use of a crash helmet essential!

67th Fighter Bomber Squadron

The 67th FBS 'Fighting Cocks' date to 1940 and flew P-38s, P-39s, and P-51s in New Caledonia and elsewhere in the South Pacific. The squadron moved from Clark Field, Philippines to Taegu, Korea with F-51D Mustangs at the outset of Korean fighting. One of its pilots, Major Arnold 'Moon' Mullins, was understood at the time to have attained four aerial victories in the F-51D although revised Air Force records credit him with just one of the squadron's propeller kills. Part of the 18th Fighter Bomber Wing throughout the war, the 67th converted to the F-86F Sabre in 1953 and produced just one ace, Major James P. Hagerstrom, who had scored his first four victories in a different outfit. The 67th was flying F-86Fs at the new airfield at Osan, Korea, when the war ended. The 67th later became one of the first US squadrons committed to Vietnam in the Republic F-105 Thunderchief. Squadron insignia is a gamecock with boxing gloves, ready for action.

67th pilots who shot down enemy aircraft: Mullins (one), Hagerstrom (8.5), Capt Robert D. Thresher (one), 1st Lt Henry S. Reynolds (0.5), Capt Howard I. Price (1.5), Capt Alma R. Flake (one), Major Howard Ebersole (one), and 1st Lt James B. Harrison (one). Mullins, Thresher, Price, Reynolds, Flake, and Harrison flew the F-51D.

The 67th FBS maintained this 'victory notch pole' to record its successes against various targets, seen here with CO 'Moon' Mullins (left) and Howard Price (right).

67th FBS pilot Price and his crew chief pose in front of a remarkably clean Mustang (with the 40th Fighter Squadron's two-coloured propeller spinner) at K-9 airfield. The code number 42 is a very unusual marking for this squadron, rarely seen in the Korean War.

instant, I noticed tracers zipping between the target and myself. I broke hard left and high. (During this second encounter, I was keeping a wary eye on the first Yak, who was in a steep smoking dive, straight ahead. In seconds he had crashed into a hillside.)

"I then flew up to the enemy aircraft and on his left wing. I was slightly back and about 200 feet out. He was in a slight turn to the right, and the pilot was looking over his right shoulder. He appeared to be wearing a dark brown leather helmet with no goggles. He turned his head toward me and sat up straight as though startled, but took no evasive action.

"As I was beginning to overrun [the enemy aircraft], I made a hard break right and about 50 feet over him and headed toward Taejon where our No. 1 man was having some difficulty... Later, our No. 4 man said he saw the pilot bail out of the first Yak-9 that I had scored some hits on at a very low altitude... Generally, I would say that these four Yak-9s were flown by inexperienced pilots. Their evasive action was nil, and they were never aggressive in any of their attacks..."

This F-80C was flown by Charles Wurster (49-733) at Itazuke in the summer of 1950. Wurster was still regarded as an FNG ('f--king new guy') a mildly derogative epithet applied by older, more experienced F-80 pilots, although he was also one of the few F-80 pilots successful in air combat.

20 July 1950
Taejon falls

On 20 July, Taejon fell to the North Koreans, leaving only the Naktong River between the invaders and the sea. There seemed little hope that Taegu, or even Pusan, could be held. But while things went badly on the ground, 2nd Lt David H. Goodnough and Captain Robert L. Lee of the 35th FBS each shot down a Yak-9. These were to be the last aerial victories

for 103 days, until 1 November. July and early August witnessed a massive mobilisation of US air forces. Although it had been decided that there were sufficient F-82s and F-80s in-theatre, it was felt that there was an urgent need for more F-51Ds for use in the close air support role, not least because the F-80, despite being an excellent, stable gunnery platform, was proving too short-legged and

too fast for effective use in the ground attack role. The Mustang was far from ideal, however, since its liquid-cooled engine and exposed belly-mounted radiator made it enormously vulnerable to ground fire. Serious consideration was given to sending F-47 Thunderbolts to Korea, but the Thunderbolt had been largely withdrawn from use, whereas the Mustang was still available in significant quantities. To achieve an increase in the Mustang force some aircraft were literally

reprieved from scrapping and were pressed back into service, while many F-51Ds were withdrawn from Air National Guard squadrons and were inhibited for the long sea journey. The carrier USS *Boxer* (CVA-21) sailed from the US with

This Grumman F9F-2 Panther, from one of many Reserve squadrons activated for the war, is ready to launch from the hydraulic catapult of USS Boxer (CV-21) in the Sea of Japan. F9F-2, -3, and -5 variants of the Panther fought in Korea, as well as F9F-2P and -5P photo-reconnassance craft.

F-51D-30-NA Mustang 44-757728, flown by Major Arnold 'Moon' Mullins
Mullins was a colourful figure who readily risked North Korean gunfire on close-support and strike missions. The four red stars denote the North Korean Yaks he was credited with at the time, although he is now credited with only one. His F-51D carries HVARs and bombs.

145 Mustangs and 70 experienced pilots, making the crossing in a record eight days and 16 hours.

Naval and Marine air power was similarly expanded, with the wartime vintage F4U Corsair taking an important place on carrier decks for use in the ground attack and close support roles. The US First Marine Aircraft Wing arrived in Japan with three squadrons of F4U Corsairs and helicopters; the USS *Badoeng Strait* (CVE-116), and the USS *Sicily* (CVE-118) catapulted their fighters off the decks for the flight to Itami air base, Japan. These units (VMF-214 and VMF-323) were subsequently carrier-based for their initial operations, whereas VMF(N)-513, with their night-fighting F4U-5N Corsairs, began to operate out of Itazuke for night raids over South Korea. The USS *Philippine Sea* (CVA-47) arrived on station with Air Group 11, consisting of the Panther-equipped VF-111, and VF-112, VF-113 and VF-114 with Corsairs, plus VA-115 with AD-4Q Skyraiders.

Right: **MAC'S REVENGE, named for pilot Major William J. O'Donnell's niece, is an F-51D of the 36th FBS ready, here, for another high-risk trip to treetop level carrying a load of napalm and 5-in HVAR rockets.**

August 1950
Calm before storm

In August the air war went suddenly very quiet. There was a good reason for this: B-26 and B-29 bombers were giving all known enemy airfields a hard pounding.

These operations included the inadvertent strafing of Antung (in China) by two F-51Ds on 27 August, and the bombing of the nearby marshalling yards by a B-29 on 22 September. Worse still, two F-80s later actually strafed a Russian airfield near Vladivostok on 8 October, leading to a court martial for the pilots (who were found not guilty), and to their commander being relieved of his command.

Nevertheless, North Korean forces continued to make large advances on the ground, and the Pusan Perimeter – the last pocket of UN resistance in the South Korean peninsula – was in constant danger of being breached. A major strategic gamble would be needed on the part of UN ground forces if the country was to be saved.

15 September 1950
Landings at Inchon

The dice were thrown on 15 September 1950. In Operation Chromite, the largest sea-to-land operation since D-Day, Army troops and the US Marines came ashore at Inchon and, in a matter of days, had cut off the enemy's supply routes. The landings were a masterpiece of radical strategic thinking and brilliant execution.

The 1st Marine Division went ashore at dawn, landing against one of the roughest, highest tides and storming a 10-ft high sea wall. The port of Inchon was secured before night fell, and heavy equipment began rolling ashore with the Army's X Corps. Kimpo fell to the Marines two days later, and Seoul itself was in UN hands by 18 September. Simultaneously, the 8th US Army began its break-out from the Pusan pocket. The North Korean army faced crushing defeat, and undertook a bitter rearguard action as they withdrew towards and beyond the 38th Parallel.

US Marine Corps pilots of the veteran Vought F4U Corsair usually fought under the same primitive, difficult conditions as the Air Force's Mustang fliers, and the building seen here was an atypical luxury. Most maintenance work was performed out-of-doors. This F4U-5 belonged to VMF-212 'Devilcats'. The Corsair gave the Marines an excellent fighter-bomber with which to support their own ground combat troops – with its tough, radial engine, it was far less vulnerable to small-arms fire than the in-line powered Mustang, and the Corsair remained in factory production until late 1952.

September-October 1950 ■
Turning the tide

On 27 September forces advancing from Inchon under General Almond (X Corps) linked up with the Eighth Army who had broken out from Pusan. The situation for the North Koreans was made worse by a total absence of air cover. US F-80s roamed the skies and strafed retreating North Korean columns without interference. The total number of 'kills' recorded for the month of September was only eight, and none was recorded in

A Marine F7F Tigercat of VMF (N)-542 makes an unusual daytime take-off from K-2 airbase, located at Taegu.

October. This reflected the diminishing status of the North Korean air force: they simply could not put enough planes in the air. November proved to be the last month that their Yak-types were out in significant numbers.

Marine air power was further strengthened in September, with the arrival of VMF(N)-542's night intruder Grumman F7F Tigercats at Kimpo, and by the arrival of the F4U-5 equipped VMF-212 and VMF-312 at the same base. As the North Korean retreat turned into a rout, Wonsan fell to the UN forces on 13 October, becoming a base to Marine Corsairs and Tigercats.

A Grumman F7F Tigercat of the US Marine Corps' VMF (N)-542, at K-2 airfield in October 1950. Too late for World War II, Tigercats had considerable air-to-air success in Korea.

Pyongyang fell one week later, while the main bulk of UN forces had reached the Yalu River. To them, it must have seemed that the war would be over before Christmas.

Right: A Vought F4U-4B Corsair of Marine squadron VMF-214 'Black Sheep' prepares to launch from USS Sicily (CVE-118). Five F4U-4B units alternated between land bases and carriers in the Yellow Sea.

UN dominance of the skies was ensured when USS *Leyte* (CVA-32) and HMS *Theseus* replaced USS *Valley Forge* and HMS *Triumph* on station off North Korea. Leyte embarked VF-31 with Panthers, VF-32 and -33 with Corsairs, and VA-35 with Skyraiders. Aboard HMS *Theseus*, the Hawker Sea Furies of No. 807 Squadron replaced the Seafires of No. 800, while the Fireflies of No. 810 replaced those of No. 827. The Sea Fury represented a considerable improvement over the Seafire, being faster, more rugged, and more agile. It was later destined to win glory in Korea, as will be related in a future issue of *Wings of Fame*.

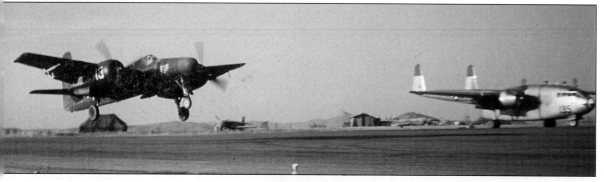

1 November 1950 ■
Mustang versus Yak

Most UN tactical air forces had followed the army and moved their operating bases deep into North Korea. Although the North Korean air force was now obviously severely depleted, it was still prepared to throw everything it had against the UN 'invaders'. This

was the stuff of desperation and, for US pilots patrolling the Yalu River sector, increased the risk factor dramatically. The 18th Fighter Bomber Group, the most experienced Mustang outfit to fly in Korea, had its forward base at Pyongyang. Although the unit was officially tasked with fighter-

bomber duties, one of its squadrons, the 67th, seemed to always be at the right place at the right time for air-to-air action. The squadron had accounted for the three confirmed 'kills' of August, and the first day of November put the 67th in the spotlight once more, as Captain Robert Thresher, (an unscoring) veteran of World War II recalls.

"It was 07.00 and bitter cold.

There was a fresh layer of snow on the ground. The cold Mustang started on the first try and the instrument needles settled exactly where they should be... A good sign! My wingman was Captain A. R. 'Dad' Flake. Minutes later, I was lined up on Flake's wing ready for take-off. The lead element was already halfway down the snow-covered runway. We were armed for close support with .50-cal rounds, six 5-in rockets and two large tanks of napalm slung under the wings. This close support role just did not sit right with most of us old World War II fighter pilots, but we did what we had to do.

"When we reached our assigned area, we picked up the 'Mosquito' (T-6 Forward Air Controller) who had already lined up a strike for us against a roadblock. We lined up and made our runs, blasting the

F-51D squadrons, including the 36th FBS 'Flying Fiends', operated from captured airfields such as K-24 in North Korea while the Allies were driving north. On 1 November 1950, Mustangs became the first UN aircraft to run into the MiG-15.

target and, to our dismay, [there was] no ground fire on any of our passes... Minutes later, the 'Mosquito' pilot called out that he had some ox-carts headed north... I thought to myself that this day was going downhill fast, even the targets were lousy...

"All of a sudden, big orange balls were snapping across my left wing. I yelled 'flak' and broke right. Before I could worry about the

ground fire, a blurred shape flew past me and then I knew that my problem was not what I had thought, but an enemy fighter!

"Being an old P-47 pilot, out of instinct I initiated evasive action. I rolled into a sharp left turn to try and hook up with 'Dad', but he was hot on the tail of another bogie, so I was in this one alone... Squinting into the sun, I knew he was still up there and I did not

want him having another clean shot at me..

"Suddenly, the 'Mosquito' pilot yelled... 'Look out No. 4, he's right on your tail!' I snapped my head around and saw the yellow winking lights of a Yak's two 12.7-mm machine-guns and 20-mm cannon. He had been sitting up there all this time in the sun and now he had the advantage over me. I went into a sharp turn and it took most of the

blood out of my head, making me grey out. I knew the Yak could turn inside me but, in my panic, I held it in, hoping that the enemy pilot would not be able to follow through after his last pass. At 7,000 lb max gross weight, the Russian-built fighter had the turning and climbing edge over any Mustang...

12th Fighter Bomber Squadron

The 12th Fighter Bomber Squadron, one of three F-51D Mustang units in the 18th Fighter Bomber Wing, was constituted on 20 November 1940 and flew Bell P-39 Airacobras at Guadalcanal and New Guinea before graduating to the Lockheed P-38 Lightning. The squadron flew P-47, P-51 and P-80 in post-war years but discarded its early jets to fight in Korea in the Mustang. Claiming just one aerial victory in the Mustang (1st Lieutenant James L. Glessner) but suffering more than 20 aircraft lost to ground fire in the first year of the conflict, the squadron went on to slog through a total of 30 months of gruelling air-to-ground action in the F-51D. In early 1953, together with the other two squadrons in the 18th FBW (67th FBS and SAAF No. 2 Sqn), the 12th converted to the North American F-86F Sabre. The squadron badge shows an eagle armed with a sword and includes the motto IN OMNIA PARATUS (Prepared for all things). In the post-Korea era, the 12th operated the F-100 Super Sabre, F-105 Thunderchief, F-4 Phantom, and F-15 Eagle. The 12th FBS grand total of two aerial victories consisted of Glessner's plus a MiG-15 shot down in 1953 by F-86F Sabre pilot 1st Lieutenant Donald R. Forbes.

P-51 Mustang pilots of the 12th FBS, like Ray Bell (seen here), were fond of their aircraft, but were only too aware that it had many drawbacks, especially in terms of its vulnerability to ground fire.

1 November 1950

"I rolled out to see that the enemy pilot had gone across the top of my Mustang and, taking advantage of his speed, he had pulled into a tight loop. That was all he needed. He was above me with the altitude advantage. If he could come out of the loop right, he would be right on my tail again. Only this time he would have speed to burn! I swung sharp left to pass directly beneath him and he must have been watching me because he kept his stick back too far and stalled out. He spun all the way down from 6,000 ft. I rolled back into a turn, hoping desperately to come out behind him. Actually, he was spinning down the axis of the circle I was making.

"He recovered and I thought for a moment that I should try to tighten my turn and jump him while he was floundering out of his spin, but he snapped the Yak over and got his flying speed back up in a matter of seconds and, due to the light weight of his fighter, went into a steep climb! This time he slacked off at the top of his loop and followed through gently.

"Now the pattern had been established... I was flying a tight circle on the horizontal; he elected to fly his sparring circle on the vertical, snapping at me as we passed each other. We held our turns, I looked for a break and as he picked up speed, I saw that we were getting closer each time we closed on the south side of my circle. More and more rapidly, the two fighters got out of phase. I was able to kick my rudder and snap a shot at him each time now...

"The North Korean pilot saw this. He knew that after another pass, I would be coming in behind him as he began his climb. It unnerved him to the extent that he wobbled at the top of his next loop. I added throttle and waited him out. He fell unevenly this time. I cut wide briefly. At the bottom he recovered and began his pull-up, but luckily my timing was good. I wrapped up my '51 and while I was still in my turn began firing. I saw the tracers converge and pour into his wings. I eased the rudder to the right to keep him in my sight... Then a puff of blue smoke spouted from his wing. He wobbled and fell out of his turn. Slowly, he rolled over and went into a long glide. I watched him go down... A Yak-3. A left-over from the last war, just as my Mustang and I were! But this 'kill' meant a lot to me as I knew I still had what it took to be a fighter pilot..."

Captain Ross Flake remembers his part in the same dogfight.

"My first serious fight with the enemy happened when... we were at low altitude, working ground targets up along the [Yalu] river. Four Yak-type North Korean fighters, in elements of two, crossed the Yalu on a southerly heading,

Below: This F-51D of the 35th FBS, seen at Suwon during late 1950, is loaded with napalm, a popular weapon during the Korean war. Mustangs of the 35th had blue noses and fin tips.

just east of our position. Their movement was called out by Lieutenant Ausman. I ordered the flight to climb at maximum power and assume combat formation.

"Almost immediately, the Yaks began a diving attack on our two elements. I turned my element hard right to meet them head on. As we came around the lead Yak fired a short burst and broke off to his left and down. I proceeded to engage, continuing a maximum right turn. I had lost sight of him momentarily... then picked him up as he pulled out of his dive. He started a left climbing turn and was well below me.

"While I manoeuvred to attack, he apparently lost sight of me, because he continued in an almost gentle climbing turn. This enabled me to gain a firing position from behind and slightly inside his circle. Having expended part of my ammunition against ground targets, I did not want to fire until within optimum range. At a slight overtake speed and estimating about 600 ft range, I pulled the trigger.

"Almost immediately, the Yak began trailing smoke... the pilot levelled the aircraft and bailed out. The Yak spiralled down and crashed. The pilot had a good chute, so he probably survived...

"As I pulled away, there was Ausman, locked right on my wing. Although quite young, he was an excellent pilot and I knew that I had no worries about surprise attacks with him out there. The wingman of the first [North Korean] element circled the area until he saw his leader bail out, then headed north. The other two broke off their attack before coming into range, diving to ground level and crossing the river before our element, in hot pursuit, could catch up. My impression was that these pilots were quite inexperienced and unskilled."

F-51D-30-NT Mustang 45-11736, flown by Lieutenant James Glessner
The shark's teeth were the trademark of the 12th FBS/18th FBW. Not all Mustangs had an anti-glare shield which went around the canopy rails and behind the canopy, but the 'buzz' number, national insignia, and serial-number presentation on the tail were all standard. Glessner flew this Dallas-built 'Fifty One' to glory, becoming one of the few Mustang pilots to claim an aerial victory.

2 November 1950
More encounters

"The next day, near the same area, we were again attacked by four Yak-types. This time, the combat lasted longer and was pursued much more vigorously by both combatants. My opponent this time was very experienced and eager to engage. After passing each other on a head-on pass, I pulled almost vertical to gain altitude while slowing my speed to quicken my turn. At my next sight of him, he was above me, his nose was almost on me and he was closing so fast he would be firing before I could get in position. Rolling and inverting, I headed straight down with an uneasy feeling that he was

close behind me.

"I cannot recall the details of the gyrations that ensued. Knowing that I could not turn with him, I felt my life depended on gaining the airspeed and altitude advantage. I used every ounce of power and speed that my Mustang had to give to overcome his superior manoeuvrablity. It ended in a series of vertical moves, from about 10,000 ft at the top down to the deck and then straight back up.

"He would hold the Yak in the vertical climb until it appeared to stop in mid-air... fall backwards and spin out. The only shots I came close to getting off were when he peaked at the top. I would gain on

him in the top of the climb, but just as I got in range he would tumble back, and you cannot hit a spinning target.

"After three or four such manoeuvres, I apparently got some hits on him as he approached his peak again. He seemed to break out of his climb prematurely and head straight down. He pulled out very low over some rolling hills and headed north. I was able to reach a good position behind him, slightly above and to the right. As I fired, his right wing appeared to pull away at the wing root! The enemy fighter rolled abruptly and crashed, spreading flames and debris over a large area. As I pulled up, I observed another dogfight in progress, with the enemy fighter manoeuvring in much the same way as the one I just fought. It turned out to be Captain Bob Thresher...

"Low on fuel and ammunition, we returned back to base. Our Wing (the 18th) had experienced very little air-to-air combat in Korea, so the victory rolls excited everyone. We were met with much acclaim and I felt very good about the mission. During the rest of my tour I had no further opportunity to engage enemy aircraft."

The 2 November mission saw two Yak-9s fall before James Glessner's guns, and Alma Flake claimed another. Howard Price of the 67th FBS scored one and a half more, with 1st Lieutenant Henry Reynolds claiming the last half of the Yak-9.

In close formation for a photograph, a pair of remarkably anonymous F-51D Mustangs from the 36th FBS fly over North Korea. The Mustang units suffered heavy losses, primarily to ground fire.

26 November 1950
China enters the war

The war might conceivably have been over by Christmas had the UN limited itself to the restoration of South Korea's pre-war borders. Syngman Rhee, the nominally democratic leader installed by Washington, was staunchly opposed to such an inconclusive end to the war, protesting that this would lead only to a temporary peace, while denying him his personal goal of leading a united Korea. Remarkably, and with some reluctance, US President Harry S. Truman agreed that the Communist forces would have to be utterly destroyed, and US forces continued to advance.

On 3 October, Chinese Premier Chou En Lai warned of Chinese intervention if the UN forces advanced north of the 38th Parallel, but this warning went unheeded. By 13 October Kim Il Sung had been forced to relocate his government to China, and still the UN forces advanced. Four B-29 wings had joined the single wing operating from Guam, but two were soon withdrawn. It was judged that the North Korean economy had already been destroyed, and that three B-29 wings were sufficient to keep pounding at the remaining airfields, ports, marshalling yards and troop concentrations. Washington analysts estimated that 39,000 North Korean troops had been killed by the end of the year.

The spectacle of North Korea's total defeat now proved too much for China. In early November its forces entered North Korea and, on 26 November, attacked US units, drastically escalating the war. Chinese 'volunteers' numbered 300 to 400,000 men in some 50 divisions. They struck along the full length of the UN front line, forcing a rapid retreat. MacArthur had categorically ruled out Chinese intervention, and was planning victory celebrations scheduled for Christmas or the New Year.

Bombed and strafed by UN aircraft and then overrun by advancing allied troops, this airfield in North Korea housed a Tachikawa Ki-55 'Ida', a wartime Japanese trainer taken over by the North Koreans.

November 1950
Enter the MiG-15

UN flyers finally found their dominance of the air seriously challenged: the Soviet state-of-the-art swept-wing jet fighter, the MiG-15, had suddenly made its appearance in the skies over the Yalu River. Its arrival changed the character of air-to-air combat, and forced the USAF to reconsider its tactical priorities. Of still greater concern should have been the fact that the new jets were not piloted by 'green' Chinese or North Korean pilots, but by experienced Russians. This was not realised at the time, despite evidence from radio monitoring, and lead many to underrate the enemy jet fighters. Because a US patrol had captured a Chinese 'volunteer' infantryman on the ground, it was widely assumed that the MiGs were piloted by the Chinese too, and that the snatches of Russian conversation heard on air-to-ground frequencies were merely Russian instructors lending a hand with conversion training. In fact, the 29th Fighter Aviation Regiment had been sent under conditions of great secrecy from its base at Kubinka, near Moscow, to China in February 1950. It was joined by the 151st Fighter Aviation Division to form the 64th Fighter Aviation Corps, and the unit was committed to action in November 1950.

Documents recently released by the former Soviet Union offer conclusive proof of this. To lessen the chances of discovery, the MiGs only flew combat missions north of a line drawn between Wonsan and Pyongyang – an area that became known as 'MiG Alley'. Pilots wore Chinese uniforms and flying kit, and were officially banned from using Russian over the radio. Casualties were secretly interred in the Russian cemetery at Port Arthur, alongside the dead from the 1904 Russo-Japanese war. This 'secret war' continued until the summer of 1951, after which select Chinese and North Korean pilots began to augment their Russian trainers.

The weather grew worse as winter closed in, and the attack by Chinese forces in November 1950 made close air support by allied warplanes more important than ever. This F-51D Mustang of the 12th FBS/18th FBW enjoys a moment in the sun, but as Christmas approached it was mostly snow, rain, clouds and slush.

This 25th FIS/51st FIW F-80C at Itazuke was the personal mount of 51st Group commander Lieutenant Colonel Oliver Celini, a leading USAF fighter tactician of the early Korean period and a veteran of action on Guadalcanal.

The 25th FIS 'Assam Dragons' was part of the 51st FIW located on Okinawa when the war began, moving to Seoul's Kimpo airfield following the Inchon invasion with their F-80C Shooting Stars.

6 November 1950
Yak-9s remain main threat

While the arrival of the MiG-15 caused consternation and excitement, enemy piston-engined fighters and heavy, accurate groundfire continued to provide the main threat to allied pilots. On 6 November 1950, for example, Captain Howard I. Price of the 67th Fighter Bomber Squadron encountered Yak-9s while undertaking an armed recce.

"We took off and climbed to altitude. The No. 4 man in the flight aborted soon after. The three remaining Mustangs, armed with rockets, proceeded to the target area. Once we got close to the Yalu we kept an eye on the Antung complex, because we knew that was where the MiGs were coming from. It was easy to see all the dust being kicked up as they prepared to launch. On this day, however, the MiGs stayed on the ground and we were attacked by six Yak-9s which came up at us from the east.

"My wingman, 1st Lieutenant George Olsen, spotted them first and called them out. They were climbing up from our 9 o'clock. I immediately turned into them so I could identify them positively as being hostiles. I did not see any insignia but could identify them as Yaks. Olsen and I dove on the nearest one. The enemy pilot must have spotted us pretty quickly as he panicked, snap-rolled and dove for the deck.

"I picked up the next nearest Yak who turned sharply to the left, away from his leader. I was able to follow him on down and, as he began another turn, I cut inside. This allowed me to give him a long burst. Pieces flew off the Yak and his engine quit. Seconds later the pilot bailed out. I wheeled around hoping to get another one, and all I

A famous World War II veteran, the Yakovlev Yak-9 was the most numerous fighter in the North Korean air arm, and many were captured as UN troops drove toward the Yalu. A Yak-9P similar to this one was later shipped to the US and test-flown at Wright Field.

Ross Flake, whose encounters with Yaks are described above, may have been the first allied pilot to have a 'close encounter', albeit not a conclusive one, with a MiG-15. During late October the 12th and 67th Fighter Bomber Squadrons had operated close to the Yalu, interdicting the Korean road traffic coming south.

"After flying up into this area for several weeks, we started noticing MiG activity. They usually operated in two-ship elements at very high altitude, coming over the Yalu and circling the area that we were working. My first 'almost' aerial combat took place when a pair of MiGs made two passes at the flight I was leading. It happened when we were on a low-altitude search and destroy mission. Our lead element, myself and Lieutenant Harold 'Ace' Ausman, had just climbed to assume top cover and the second element had resumed the low-level search. We were at 2,000 ft when Ausman called two MiGs off our right wing, and quite high. Expecting them to stay high, we made no counter move, but kept one eye on them. Suddenly, both of the MiGs inverted, launching an almost

vertical pass at us. As we started a hard turn, hoping they would continue down and engage, they broke off the pass. Climbing in a circle to the left they began a second pass, this time not nearly so steep. We turned into them, and were almost head-on when they broke it off again. Although I was out of range, I pulled the trigger and continued on them as long as possible, hoping to get them

recorded on my gun camera film. After we returned to base, the film was processed and there were seven frames that clearly showed the new swept-wing fighters. The film was flown to Command HQ, and then on to the UN to confirm that there were indeed Soviet-type jet fighters operating in Korea."

Flake's gun camera film had been taken at extreme range, but a closer glimpse of the new Russian

fighter was afforded by Lieutenant Colonel Clure Smith, commander of the 25th FIS, who closed on a MiG-15 in his F-80 and let fly with his guns, only to find that they had frozen solid and would not fire. Fortunately, his gun camera recorded the incident, giving intelligence analysts their first confirmation that the MiGs were carrying underwing fuel tanks.

saw was our other pilot, Lieutenant Reynolds, chasing a Yak as it made a run for safety. I pushed the throttle wide open in order to catch up with Reynolds. He told me that his guns had jammed, so it was up to me to try and head the straggler off. I slid down and across as Reynolds pulled off. I fired each

of my rockets, trying to save ammunition. Each rocket missed, one going over the Yak and one below it. These rockets were worthless. They had been stored on Guam since 1945 and the propellant had solidified on the underside of the rocket. You never knew whether the rocket would

'hook' or 'slice'.

"I then lined up from slightly below and fired my .50s. I hit him from behind the cockpit all the way forward to the engine, with three or four good bursts. All at once, bluish flames started coming out of his engine. At the same instant, the aircraft nosed over, his guns started

firing and he went down in a very steep dive. I think he must have been dead, because he made no attempt to pull out. I watched him all the way down until he hit the ground near Sinuiju."

Price was credited with one and a half Yak-9 kills, the other half being credited to Reynolds.

8 November 1950
Jet against jet

On 6 November, a flight of F-51Ds from the 8th FBG had been jumped by MiG-15s, but had escaped unscathed. This pattern was repeated on 7 November, when four Mustangs from the 36th FBS were jumped by a similar number of MiGs near the Yalu. While appearances by the MiG-15 remained sporadic, it was clear that a jet-versus-jet confrontation would be inevitable

sooner or later. The first such encounter, between USAF F-80s and the MiGs, took place on 8 November high over the Yalu River. A flight of four F-80Cs from the 16th Fighter Interceptor

Right: The F-80C was the standard USAF fighter in the Far East in 1950, but was unable to hold command of the air in the face of slashing attacks by MiG-15s. This aircraft wears the markings of the 8th FBS.

Above: A Lockheed F-80C Shooting Star of the 80th Fighter Bomber Squadron is seen on the hardstand at K-2. Pilots of the 80th would soon encounter a mysterious jet fighter being flown by adversaries across the Yalu – the superlative MiG-15. The enlarged wingtip fuel tanks devised and manufactured in-theatre are clearly visible.

Left: F-80s of the 80th FBS taxi out for a mission from K-14, each armed with four rockets. The Fairchild C-119 Flying Boxcar (background) was as vital to UN troops as the F-80s. At all Far East airfields ramp space was precious and hard-pressed, so jets and transports often lived together.

An F-80C of the 51st Fighter-Interceptor Wing is seen at Kimpo (K-14) during the wing's brief stay in October-December 1950. It carries a napalm tank on one wingtip. The wing left its 26th squadron on Okinawa but moved to Korea with the 16th and 25th, creating a 40 per cent increase in the size of the F-80 force. The 51st scored the first MiG kill supporting ground troops.

Squadron were on a fighter-bomber mission targeted against anti-aircraft batteries around the airstrip at Sinuiju.

The mission was in support of a B-29 raid, which had F-80s from the 51st FW providing top cover plus F-80s and F-51s suppressing enemy air defences. The senior pilot in one flak-suppression F-80 formation was the 16th's commanding officer, Lieutenant Colonel Evans G. Stephens; on his wing was 1st Lieutenant Russell J. Brown on detached duty from the 26th FIS. It was this element that caught the brunt of the MiG attack, as Evans Stephens recounted.

"After we had successfully delivered our ordnance on target, we took up a heading to the southeast in a low-angle climb to gain distance along with altitude. As flight leader, I used 97 per cent power in order for the rest of the flight to join up after their strafing passes. At this time there was some radio chatter from another flight that stated there were numerous aircraft in the air across the Yalu.

"I started a shallow turn to the left for a better view of the river. I would guess that we were about 4 miles south of it and the No. 3 and No. 4 aircraft in my flight were about a quarter of a mile behind us.

Lieutenant Brown was about 100 yd in my 4 o'clock..."

Lieutenant Russ Brown recalled that Stephens reported sighting eight MiGs north of the river. He also commented that they seemed to be playing around – doing barrel rolls and loops.

"I thought to myself, this has got to be one crazy war when the enemy can practise stunt flying right in front of you!" Brown said later.

Colonel Stephens watched Brown rocket downwards at high speed to attack one of the MiGs.

"I rolled left to see [Brown's] F-80 in a steep dive about 3,000 ft below me. I then looked for the rest of my flight and to see if any other MiGs were in the area... and to see if one was on my tail! I looked back down and found the F-80 starting to pull out of its dive and I saw the impact explosion of the MiG as it hit the ground.

"At the onset of the fight, I did not call for the lead element to drop tanks because it would have put them into the path of No. 3 and No. 4 trailing behind us. Brown did not realise at the time that his high-speed dive had caused some wing twist due to the fuel tanks still being attached."

VF-111

VF-111 'Sundowners' (not the same squadron which served in the US Navy from 4 May 1956) reached the Korean conflict aboard the second carrier to arrive, USS *Philippine Sea* (CVA-47), beginning in 1 August 1950. Aboard *Philippine Sea* was Carrier Air Group Eleven with VF-111 as one of its squadrons, flying the Grumman F9F-2 Panther. The Panther was not initially intended for air-to-ground action but soon found itself conscripted with bomb racks. On 10 November 1950, Lieutenant Commander William Thomas Amen, F9F-2 pilot and squadron commander, shot down a MiG-15, the US Navy's first jet kill. The squadron's first combat cruise ended on 7 April 1951. VF-111 returned to Korea aboard USS *Valley Forge* (CVA-45) as part of Air Task Group One (an ATG was a carrier air group in all but name), for a cruise lasting from 15 October 1951 to 3 July 1952, this time in cannon-armed F9F-2B Panthers. A final Korean cruise with ATG-1, this time with improved F9F-5 Panthers, began on 30 March 1953 aboard USS *Boxer* (CVA-21), although the squadron cross-decked to USS *Lake Champlain* (CVA-39) from 30 June 1953 through the 27 July 1953 armistice. The squadron returned to the US in October 1953. The squadron with the same number and designation flew F-8 Crusaders, F-4 Phantoms (the type operated on two cruises in Vietnam), and F-14 Tomcats before being disestablished in 1994. VF-111 aerial victories were scored by Lieutenant Commander W. Thomas Amen (one), Lieutenant Commander W. E. Lamb (one), Lieutenant R. E. Parker (one), and Ensign F. C. Weber (one).

Grumman F9F Panthers from VF-111 and other Navy squadrons usually flew from carrier decks but were occasionally seen on land. The F9F was also the standard land-based jet fighter for Marine Corps pilots.

9-10 November 1950
MiG-15 victory and losses

The following day, 9 November, MiG-15s attacked an RB-29 and forced it to crash-land, killing five of its crew. One of the gunners exacted some revenge, however, claiming to have downed one of the attackers. Things went no better for the MiG pilots on 10 November. They did down a B-29 but the commander of VF-111 aboard the *Valley Forge*, Lieutenant Commander William Thomas Amen, downed a MiG-15 at low level; this marked the first victory by the plank-winged Panther over the swept wing MiG-15. With its four 20-mm cannon in the nose,

Above: Lieutenant Commander William Thomas Amen, skipper of VF-111 'Sundowners', chalked up the US Navy's first aerial victory against a MiG-15 while flying the straight-winged Grumman F9F-2 Panther.

These F-86A Sabres wear the distinctive black and white stripes of the 4th Fighter Interceptor Wing. They are seen at K-13, Suwon, their home in 1951 after their return to the Korean peninsula.

the Panther packed a significantly heavier punch than the F-86, and its big wing gave it plenty of turn performance.

Smarting from these early skirmishes, the MiG pilots became increasingly aggressive, although the first unit to be rotated to Korea had been ill-prepared for the conflict. They were, however, extremely highly motivated, selective propaganda leading them to believe that they were defending socialist North Korea against aggression by the capitalist, Western-dominated UN forces. Many pilots were taken to witness the effects of UN bombing raids on schools or villages (which had been hit accidentally) before they started flying operations. Fear of failure was another motivating factor, since Russian pilots knew that they would 'lose everything' if taken prisoner, and that their families would not be safe. Moreover, the MiG-15 was superior to any USAF aircraft then in-theatre, and was even superior to the F-86 Sabre in

Carrying just two 5-in rocket projectiles, this F-80C of the 80th FBS 'Headhunters', part of the 8th FBW, is ready for action at K-14. This location was also known as Kimpo air base and was located 14 miles (22 km) from Seoul in late 1950.

some respects, although it was optimised as a bomber-destroyer and had been sent to Korea to stop UN bombing raids rather than to tangle with USAF fighters. Fighter-versus-fighter combat was avoided, except when USAF aircraft prevented the MiGs from reaching the bombers, or where they were encountered accidentally. Sergei Kramorenko commanded a MiG-15 squadron in Korea, and added 13 victories to the 12 he had scored during the Great Patriotic War.

"The Sabre was the most dangerous threat to my friends and me in Korean skies. Our MiG-15 and the F-86 belonged to the same class, similar types with similar performance. The MiG-15 had an advantage in rate of climb at altitude, while the Sabre was

superior in manoeuvring, especially at low level. These advantages could seldom be used. As a rule the fight was decided in the first attack. After a first pass the MiG-15s reached for altitude, while the Sabres rushed for the ground. Each tried to reach the altitude where it held a distinct advantage, and thus battles faded."

The MiG-15 also had greater firepower than the F-86, with two NR-23 23-mm cannon and a single 37-mm N-37 cannon. Slow rate of fire made it difficult to hit a manoeuvring fighter target, but one hit was usually sufficient to down a Sabre, whereas the first MiG-15 shot down in Korea reportedly absorbed almost 1,000 rounds before it succumbed. Top-scoring ace of the war, Yevgeni Pepelyaev, recalled that "the US Browning 0.50-calibre guns acted on our aircraft like peas! It was routine for our aircraft to return home having taken 40 or 50 hits." Since such hits were usually accompanied by clouds of smoke and debris and a frantic steep dive to escape, many MiG-15s were claimed as shot down but actually returned to fight again. The MiG pilot was well protected by armour, an armoured windscreen and effective self-sealing fuel tanks. The MiG-15's primitive gunsight was prone to failure, especially during high-*g* manoeuvres.

Although they were more effective than most of the North Korean pilots, the Russians were

not up to the standard of the USAF pilots they faced and, in recognition of this, an Order of Lenin could be had for the destruction of as few as three enemy aircraft, and rotation home followed only 40 sorties! When subsequent Russian units were rotated in, they were better selected, better prepared and better trained, and proved to be more formidable opponents. Moreover, the MiG-15 did not remain the only threat to UN air superiority.

As has been noted, the MiG-15 was optimised for the bomber-destroyer role, with its heavy-calibre, slow-firing 37-mm cannon and high-altitude performance. The smaller, nimbler Lavochkin La-15 'Fantail' had always been intended as the Soviet Union's primary air superiority jet fighter and, with its greater speed, agility and armament of three 23-mm cannon, was felt to be more than a match for the Sabre. An evaluation unit of 22 La-15s was sent to China for service over Korea. Fortunately for UN fighter pilots, the La-15 proved unable to operate in the primitive conditions encountered in China, and no fewer than four aircraft were written off in landing accidents before the detachment was sent home. This marked the beginning of the end for the La-15 and only about 600 were built, their flimsy landing gear condemning them to second-line duties at well prepared airfields in the Soviet heartland. Frontal

Aviation had no need for such a delicate aircraft!

For the moment, the F-80s and the Navy's F9F could cope with the threat, but the imminent threat was that the USAF could soon lose air superiority. High Command in Washington therefore ordered the 4th Fighter Wing, flying swept-wing F-86A Sabres, to prepare for an immediate move to the Far East. The 4th Fighter Interceptor Wing was probably the best jet fighter unit in the USAF, with many combat veterans from World War II, and was equipped with the latest F-86As off the production line.

Meanwhile, the Chinese Army was putting UN forces under immense pressure; constant bombing raids had to be mounted over North Korea to relieve hard-pressed American and other troops. F-80s were forced to fly cover for the bombers and protect them from the attentions of the MiGs.

12 December 1950
F-80s kill again

On 12 December, 1st Lieutenant Evan Rosencrans, flying an F-80C with the 80th FBS, found himself in a tight spot with a group of MiG-15s.

"As I remember, it was an afternoon mission and our job was to fly top cover for some F-80s that were bombing the Sinuiju airfield just south of the Yalu. We were close to the Chinese side and catching some AAA from the north side of the river.

"From our altitude we watched the MiGs launch from their base at Antung. It wasn't long after they were airborne that all of the anti-aircraft fire stopped. At that moment, I noticed 12 enemy fighters about 3,000 ft above us... four off the left wing, four off the right and four trailing behind us.

"First, the four MiGs off our left side dove in on us and we immediately turned into them. When that flight's No. 4 man passed us, the four MiGs off our right side turned in on us and we turned into them. More than likely this was a training mission for the MiGs, as they were attacking in 'string', one after the other in each flight. Just as soon as that flight finished, the ones in the rear came in, and that is where I got my chance. I locked onto the No. 4 man in the trailing formation and scored hits on him from his intake all the way down to his tailpipe...

"In the meantime, the other MiGs that had made passes had regrouped and were starting their runs all over again. After the second set of passes, the MiGs exited the area for their base at Antung. Several months later, the MiG-15 that I had hit was confirmed to have crashed, so I was credited with a 'kill'."

In fact, according to current records, Rosencrans was actually credited with damaging the MiG.

335th Fighter Interceptor Squadron

The 335th FIS 'Chiefs' did not go to Korea as a squadron during the initial deployment in December 1950, but did provide some of the pilots who first appeared at Kimpo with the F-86A Sabre that month. The squadron eventually returned to, and fought from, Kimpo after the airfield was retaken from the Chinese. Later in the war, the 335th was commanded by Lieutenant Colonel Vermont Garrison, an 11-victory World War II ace who also became a double ace in Korea.

Although aerial victory credits are difficult to assess because of different ways of counting – Air Force records show Colonel James K. Johnson as a 335th pilot even though he was the 4th FIW commander – it appears that 335th pilots accounted for more MiGs than those of any other Sabre squadron. The squadron finished the war with F-86Fs. With a silhouette of a Native American tribal chief as its symbol, the squadron flies the F-15E Eagle today at Seymour Johnson AFB, North Carolina.

The top-scoring air aces of the 335th FIS were Garrison (10 kills), Captain Lonnie R. Moore (10), Captain Clifford D. Jolley (seven), and Major Winton W. 'Bones' Marshall (six and a half).

These North American F-86A Sabres wear the slanted black and white recognition stripes (including vertical black stripes on the fin) which were worn by the 335th and other squadrons of the 4th FIW from December 1950 until late in 1951. At that time, they were replaced by the yellow bands worn by other Sabre units in Korea.

North American F-86A-5 Sabre 334th FIS/4th FIW Kimpo December 1950
49-1281 was flown by Lieutenant Colonel Glenn T. Eagleston, commander of the 334th FIS and a World War II ace who became the second F-86 pilot to bag a MiG (claiming the first of his two MiG-15 kills on 22 December 1950). The windscreen shape and flamingo-coloured air intake lip typify early F-86As. These suffered from maintenance problems and were not as fast as the MiG-15.

10-15 December 1950 ▬
The Sabre arrives

On 10 December, the carrier USS *Cape Esperance* (CV-88) arrived in Tokyo Bay with the 4th Fighter Wing and its F-86A Sabres. The United Nations forces at last had a fighter capable of meeting the MiG-15 on even terms.

Top priority was given to the movement of the Sabres into Korea. Time was critical: the Chinese advance was rolling unchecked and all the territory gained north of the 38th Parallel after the breakout from Pusan was being retaken. There was a distinct possibility that the new MiG-15 could swing the balance of the ground war by gaining control of the skies. The Sabre was the only UN fighter aircraft that could possibly compete with the Russian fighter. Unfortunately, although measures had been taken to protect the F-86s from sea water during their long journey, corrosion had already begun in some areas and had caused problems with wing fuel reading gauges and other electrical equipment. Some aircraft took a week of intensive

The 4th FIW's F-86A Sabres were given a protective coating and shipped across the Pacific in late 1950 aboard the escort carrier USS Cape Esperance (CVA-88).

rectification before they could be flown from Japan to Korea.

It was determined early on that two squadrons of Sabres would operate from forward bases in South Korea, with one squadron in reserve in Japan. Five days after arriving in Japan, an advance party flew to Kimpo to set up shop. Lieutenant Colonel Bruce Hinton flew in the first of an initial seven F-86As. These were the only aircraft to have escaped corrosion damage during their sea voyage. This first unit to arrive at its forward base became known as Detachment A. It was this cadre that would put the F-86 through its paces in its first encounters with the MiGs. The detachment started flying orientation sorties on 15 December, but was grounded by heavy snow the following day, as were the Soviet-crewed MiG-15s at Antung.

17 December 1950 ▬
The first Sabre kill

The following day (17 December) dawned cold and clear over Kimpo airfield. The sun was extremely bright, and flashed off a recent heavy snowfall.

At about 14.00, four F-86As blasted a cloud of fine snow into the air as they powered out of their parking area en route to the primitive airfield's only active runway. They were each equipped with two external 275-US gal (1040-litre) tanks hanging from wing pylons, and armed with 2,000 rounds of .50-calibre HEI (High Explosive Incendiary) ammunition for their six guns. The tanks gave the Sabres a range of 490 miles (790 km), enough to get to the Yalu and back, but giving little endurance for prolonged hassling. The flight was 'fragged' CAP 04 BAKER, callsign CREATURE BAKER. At 14.05 , BAKER 01 and 02 roared down the runway, rapidly followed by BAKER 03 and 04. One of the Sabres experienced some problems retracting its landing gear. This was

due to splashing water from the runway freezing on the oleos; several actuations of the retraction system corrected the problem and the flight headed north toward the Yalu. The US pilots knew that at one of the air bases in Manchuria, several MiG-15 pilots, either on alert or preparing for a scheduled mission themselves, would be scrambling to meet them for a historic confrontation that was now only minutes away. Lieutenant Colonel Bruce Hinton, commander of the forward detachment at Kimpo, was leading the flight from the front.

"As we headed north, we were certainly motivated. We joined up, changed channels, checked in and then I pumped the rudder pedals to fishtail, which was the signal for the flight to go to combat spread. We

In winter, Korea meant snow and freezing winds howling down from Siberia. The 4th FIW arrived at Kimpo just in time for snow to keep its Sabres out of combat for a whole day (16 December). The 4th shared K-14 with F-51s and F-80s, and its mechanics worked out-of-doors.

Right: Squanee was the F-86A assigned to Lieutenant Colonel Bruce Hinton, but not the aircraft he was flying when he claimed the Sabre's first MiG kill in December 1950. In February 1951, ousted from Korea, these jets lined up at Chitose, Japan.

climbed out to 25,000 ft heading on a direct course to Sinuiju which was about 200 nm away. Crossing over Pyongyang at altitude, we test-fired our guns just to be sure that they were working. We had clear blue sky with visibility all the way into Manchuria. It seemed like the entire world was covered with fresh snow, even the ragged mountain ridges and peaks.

"Approaching Sinuiju, we dropped our speed to approximate that of the F-80 at cruise setting, hoping to tease [the MiGs] out. We knew they had radar, and probably with it GCI control. We had wondered the day before the mission how much they knew about us. Were they aware we were in Korea? Did they know anything about the performance of our fighters? Would they come up and fight?

"About 5 miles south of Sinuiju, we turned right in combat spread to patrol parallel with the Yalu River. The sun was high behind us with the ground below an endless expanse of white.

"Suddenly, one of the pilots in our flight called out, 'Bogies at 9 o'clock low, crossing, BAKER 2.' Slightly below us at 20,000 ft and climbing I saw a flight of four swept-wing fighters moving very fast and crossing our track about 1 mile ahead. It was a completely startling sight! They were in a loose fingertip and their wing sweep looked somehow different from the F-86. The snow below them made them look like they had been painted white instead of silver. Their speed was astonishing.

"Punching the mike button, I said 'BAKER, drop tanks now.' A dead transmitter. I tried again...still dead. Again...and it was clear my transmitter had failed. The MiG flight went across to our right side and started a climbing turn back to us. No time to lose, so I punched off my external tanks, with full throttle already on. A hard pull into their turn brought me in at 5 o'clock to them, and closing!

"They were climbing to meet us...we were diving slightly on them. Their No. 3 and No. 4 element was on the right, with No. 2 left of lead. I had picked the lead element to attack. My No. 3 and No. 4 were headed for the remaining element of MiGs. When

I was 4,000 ft and closing, their tanks came off.

"The MiGs' tanks were mounted on the underside of the wings with very little space between the tanks and wing surface. When they separated they twisted sideways, then flipped, trailing a long plume of white spray. I checked my airspeed as I moved into six o'clock on the enemy element. Our aircraft were red-lined at 0.95 Mach and my Mach meter indicated a pretty good gap over the red line. That was the highest speed I had ever flown the F-86.

"At this point, the MiG flight began to spread. Out of the corner of my eye, I saw that the element

No. 3 and No. 4 seemed to be breaking off under their lead element. MiG No. 1 and No. 2 slowly rolled from a right climbing turn into a level left bank with the lead MiG going slightly high.

"That settled it. I picked up the closest enemy, which was MiG No. 2, put my pipper on his left fuselage about where the main fuel tank should be and closed. I was using stadiametric ranging on the gun sight with a 30-ft span set.

"All this time, I could hear my flight talking on the radio, calling my position, calling me (with no answer) and calling their moves against the MiGs. But about now, almost at good gun range, I stopped

hearing them. When it looked like 1,500-ft range, I let go a short burst and saw strikes against the middle left fuselage and from the right wing where the bullet pattern from the six .50-calibres had sprayed

4th Fighter Interceptor Wing

The 4th FIW was, and is, one of the premier combat establishments in the US Air Force, remembered for scoring more than 1,000 aerial victories in Europe in World War II (as the 4th Fighter Group) and known today as an operator of the F-15E Eagle (as the 4th Fighter Wing). In 1950, while most Americans were buying new automobiles and homes for the first time, the 4th was uprooted from Wilmington County, Delaware with a call to war inspired by the appearance in Korea of Chinese troops and of the MiG-15. The wing's F-86A Sabres were shipped to Japan aboard the 'jeep' carrier USS *Cape Esperance* (CVE-88).

The squadrons of the 4th were the 334th 'Pidgeons' (later changed to 'Eagles'), 335th 'Chiefs' and 336th 'Rocketeers'. Its initial component to reach the Korean theatre was a combat group headed by wing commander Colonel George F. Smith, which arrived at Kimpo air base, also called K-14, near Seoul in December 1950. The wing scored the first Sabre victory against a MiG-15 on 17 December 1950, but two weeks later abandoned Kimpo to the advancing Chinese.

Like all American combat wings, the 4th FIW assumed the identity of the World War II group of the same name in 1950 but continued to have a subordinate combat group until 1952. The active-duty Air Force dispensed with combat groups between 1952 and 1993, so that flying squadrons reported directly to wing headquarters.

The wing's 334th FIS began flying from Suwon (K-13) in March 1951, where it was replaced by the 335th FIS in May. In May 1951 the 336th operated from Taegu in a brief, aborted attempt to use the F-86 as a fighter-bomber. The 334th's Captain James Jabara remained behind, flying with the 335th to get his fifth and sixth MiG kills on 20 May 1951, becoming the world's first jet ace.

During August 1951, the 4th FIW returned with its combat group (the 4th FIG, commanded by World War II ace Colonel John C. Meyer). Two squadrons were deployed to Kimpo and one remained in Japan.

On 10 February 1952, Major George A. Davis, 334th FIS commander, was killed after scoring his 14th MiG kill in an action, which made him the only air-to-air pilot awarded the Medal of Honor. The 4th scored the last aerial kill of the war, an Ilyushin Il-12 transport, on the day of the armistice, 27 July 1953.

The 4th FIW produced the second- and third-ranking American aces (Major James Jabara, 15 victories; Captain Manuel J. (Pete) Fernandez, Jr, 14.5 victories). Among wing commanders during the war were Colonels Harrison R. Thyng (five kills) and James K. Johnson (10 kills).

MiG-killer Lt Col Bruce Hinton, 336th FIS commander, swaps notes with NAA Tech. Rep. E. R. Christopherson during a respite from missions to 'MiG Alley'.

across. The holes appeared to cause some kind of leaks from either internal fuel or smoke from the API ammunition I had fired. I waited for a short while. (Time, now that we were engaged, was passing so slowly there was an opportunity to see everything and think it over.)

"The lead MiG had drifted higher, sitting forward at about 45° to the right and about 200 ft higher than his No. 2 man and myself. We were in a left turn diving very slightly banked, about 35°. Could the MiG leader position himself to hit me from where he was? He could be about to work a defensive split, as one of our pilots would do, to draw my attention away, or pull off a high attack on my wingman and me.

"It was at that time I realised that my wingman was not with me. We had initiated a break into the MiGs at the same time my transmitter quit. I had momentarily straightened out to try getting it back. BAKER 2, 3 and 4 had continued a hard break coming around on the MiG element, crossing and separating. My pause had actually caused our separation in the quick manoeuvre. I decided to watch MiG lead, but work on No. 2, who suddenly popped his speed brakes, then retracted them immediately. That momentary drag increased my closure, so I put the pipper on his tailpipe, to get at his engine, thinking the cold air and

non-volatile jet fuel might inhibit burning or exploding of his fuel tanks.

"My airplane abruptly began violent twisting and bouncing in his jet wash, so I slid off to the inside slightly, clearing the turbulence. Range was about 800 ft and I pressed the trigger for a good long burst into his engine. Pieces flew out, smoke filled his tail pipe, then flame lengthened out of the opening. He immediately lost airspeed and I put out my speed brakes, throttled to idle, but still moved in on him.

"We hung there in the sky, turning left, with my Sabre tight

A flight of 4th FIW Sabres breaks into the circuit at Kimpo prior to landing. The Sabres frequently returned to Kimpo having jettisoned their external tanks, and with gunports blackened, but engagements were often inconclusive and in the fog of war both sides over-claimed dramatically.

against his underside in a show formation. We seemed to be about 5 ft apart, giving me a good close view of the MiG. It was a beautiful, sports car of a fighter. The silver aluminium of pure metal was clean and gleaming – no dirt on the underside of the wings from wet mud thrown back by its wheels. The rivets, structure, everything all looked first class.

"He seemed to be slowing even more so, after hanging close there for a long time, I moved out and over him looking for the other MiGs. No one in sight...we were all alone. The MiG was losing altitude very fast in a 45° bank left

at a low airspeed. I moved farther to his inside, about 2,000 ft above, and thought, 'Why doesn't he blow?' His aeroplane was smoking out of several places and fire was still coming out of the tailpipe. In an attempt to finish him off, I made a diving turn, putting the pipper on his forward fuselage. At this point, I fired a very long burst. The API flashed and twinkled on the left and right wingroots and the cockpit area. He rolled on his back and dived, trailing smoke and flaming toward the snow-covered ground.

"My No. 3 and No. 4 were on the radio. They had just broken off a chase of MiGs 3 and 4 when, to our surprise, the MiGs had outrun the F-86s and headed toward the sanctuary of the Yalu River. My No. 3 and No. 4 were talking between themselves about observing the MiG I had killed, going down. My lost wingman, BAKER 2, had joined them. I heard BAKER 2 ask if anyone knew where lead was. No one knew, and I couldn't tell them I was OK. One of them had seen an aircraft go down and they were wondering who it was.

"It seemed a long way back to Kimpo alone in all that brightness.

The tail of a 4th Fighter Interceptor Wing F-86A Sabre in the early days of combat in Korea. 49-1173 is typical of the wing's early A models, not as high-flying or as manoeuvrable as the MiG at high altitude but – with future modifications – soon to be the best in the sky.

Above: Bill Taylor of the 334th FIS flew this F-86A. The Sabre was the only allied fighter capable of meeting a well-flown MiG-15 on anything approaching even terms. Fortunately, many MiG-15s were poorly flown.

Right: A line-up of 4th FIW Sabres. The nearest aircraft was that of Lonnie Moore of the 335th FIS, who went on to score 10 victories, and the yellow-nosed aircraft further down the line belonged to the 336th FIS.

The performance of the MiG-15 had been far better than we were told. The airplane also appeared to be a lot tougher than I had imagined when it came to shooting it down. I brought my Sabre down in a long fast dive to the active runway at Kimpo, levelled out at 500 kt over the field and rolled through a victory roll. It had been a very memorable day!"

Thus, Lieutenant Colonel Bruce Hinton had the honour of being the first F-86 pilot credited with shooting down a MiG-15, even if no-one actually saw the enemy fighter crash. It set the tone for hundreds of future engagements, with Sabres usually emerging victorious and usually claiming a confirmed kill, although post-war revisions made it clear that many

enemy aircraft had limped home. A clue to the MiG's robustness and ability to soak up punishment was the fact that Hinton had exhausted virtually all of the 1,802 rounds of ammunition which his F-86A carried. The Russian fighters rarely came out in small numbers again,

however. Five days after Hinton's famous 'kill', 15 MiGs took on eight Sabres and, later still, 35 of them mobbed l6 US jets. Details of these aerial duels over Korea will be revealed in the next issue of *Wings of Fame*.

Warren E.Thompson

Kills list - 1950

Date	Pilot	Aircraft/Unit	Enemy	Date	Pilot	Aircraft/Unit	Enemy
27.06.50	1st Lt William G. Hudson	F-82, 68th F(AW)S	Yak-11	19.07.50	1st Lt Robert A. Walsh	F-80, 80th FBS	Ground kill
27.06.50	Maj James W. Little	F-82, 339th (AW)S	La-7	19.07.50	1st Lt Robert A. Walsh	F-80, 80th FBS	Ground kill
27.06.50	1st Lt Charles B. Moran	F-82, 68th F(AW)S	La-7	19.07.50	1st Lt Jack D. Watts	F-80, 80th FBS	Ground kill
27.06.50	1st Lt Robert E. Wayne	F-80, 35th FBS	Il-10	19.07.50	1st Lt Jack D. Watts	F-80, 80th FBS	Ground kill
27.06.50	1st Lt Robert E. Wayne	F-80, 35th FBS	Il-10	20.07.50	2nd Lt David H. Goodenough	F-80, 35th FBS	Yak-9
27.06.50	Capt. Raymond E. Schillereff	F-80, 35th FBS	Il-10	20.07.50	Capt. Robert L. Lee	F-80, 35th FBS	Yak-9
27.06.50	1st Lt Robert H. Dewald	F-80, 35th FBS	Il-10	24.07.50	Lt Col William T. Samways	F-80, 8th FBS	Ground kill
29.06.50	1st Lt Richard J. Burns	F-51, 35th FBS	Il-10	25.07.50	Lt Col Harold L. Price	F-80, 8th FBG	Ground kill
29.06.50	2nd Lt Orrin R. Fox	F-51, 80th FBS	Il-10	03.08.50	Capt. Edward C. Hoagland Jr	F-51, 67th FBS	Ground kill
29.06.50	2nd Lt Orrin R. Fox	F-51, 80th FBS	Il-10	03.08.50	Capt .Howard I. Price	F-51, 67th FBS	Ground kill
29.06.50	1st Lt Harry T. Sandlin	F-51, 80th FBS	Il-10	10.08.50	Maj. Arnold Mullins	F-51, 67th FBS	Ground kill
29.06.50	1st Lt William T. Norris	F-80, 9th FBS	La-7	10.08.50	Maj. Arnold Mullins	F-51, 67th FBS	Ground kill
30.06.50	1st Lt Roy W. Marsh	F-80, 80th FBS	Il-10	10.08.50	Maj. Arnold Mullins	F-51, 67th FBS	Ground kill
30.06.50	1st Lt Charles A. Wurster	F-80, 36th FBS	Yak-9	12.09.50	Lt Col Harold L. Price	F-80, 8th FBS	Ground kill
03.07.50	Lt Leonard Plog, USN	F9F-2, VF-51	Yak-9	12.09.50	Lt Col Harold L. Price	F-80, 8th FBS	Ground kill
03.07.50	Ens. E. W. Brown, USN	F9F-2, VF-51	Yak-9	12.09.50	Lt Col Harold L. Price	F-80, 8th FBS	Ground kill
14.07.50	Maj. Vincent C. Cardarella	F-80, 35th FIS	Ground kill	28.09.50	1st Lt Ralph G. Hall	F-51, 35th FIS	Ground kill
14.07.50	Capt. Wen E. Radcliff	F-80, 35th FIS	Ground kill	30.09.50	Capt. Ernest D. Fahlberg	F-80, 8th FBS	Ground kill
15.07.50	1st Lt Robert A. Coffin	F-80, 39th FIS	Yak-9	30.09.50	Capt. Ernest D. Fahlberg	F-80, 8th FBS	Ground kill
17.07.50	Capt. Francis B. Clark	F-80, 36th FBS	Yak-9	01.11.50	Capt. Alma R. Flake	F-51, 67th FBS	Yak-3
19.07.50	2nd Lt Elwood A. Kees	F-80, 36th FBS	Yak-9	01.11.50	Capt. Robert D. Thresher	F-51, 67th FBS	Yak-9
19.07.50	1st Lt Robert D. McKee	F-80, 36th FBS	Yak-9	02.11.50	Capt. Alma R. Flake	F-51, 67th FBS	Yak-9
19.07.50	1st Lt Charles A. Wurster	F-80, 36th FBS	Yak-9	02.11.50	1st Lt James L. Glessner Jr	F-51, 12th FBS	Yak-9
19.07.50	1st Lt Ralph A. Ellis	F-80, 36th FIS	Ground kill	02.11.50	1st Lt James L. Glessner Jr	F-51, 12th FBS	Yak-9
19.07.50	1st Lt Ralph A. Ellis	F-80, 36th FIS	Ground kill	06.11.50	Capt. Howard I. Price	F-51, 67th FBS	Yak-9
19.07.50	Capt. James A. Gasser	F-80, 36th FIS	Ground kill	06.11.50	Capt. Howard I. Price	F-51, 67th FBS	Yak-9 (½)
19.07.50	Capt. James A. Gasser	F-80, 36th FIS	Ground kill	06.11.50	1st Lt Henry S. Reynolds	F-51, 67th FBS	Yak-9 (½)
19.07.50	Capt. Homer K. Hansen	F-80, 36th FIS	Ground kill	08.11.50	1st Lt Russell J. Brown	F-80, 16th FIS	MiG-15
19.07.50	Capt. Homer K. Hansen	F-80, 36th FIS	Ground kill	09.11.50	Sgt Harry J. Lavene	RB-29, 91st SRS	MiG-15
19.07.50	1st Lt Roy W. Marsh	F-80, 8th FBS	Ground kill	09.11.50	Lt Cdr W. T. Amen, USN	F9F-2, VF-111	MiG-15
19.07.50	1st Lt Roy W. Marsh	F-80, 8th FBS	Ground kill	14.11.50	Staff Sgt Richard W. Fisher	B-29, 371st BS	MiG-15
19.07.50	Lt Col William T. Samways	F-80, 8th FBG	Ground kill	28.11.50	1st Lt William P. Dougherty	F-51, 35th FIS	Ground kill
19.07.50	Lt Col William T. Samways	F-80, 8th FBG	Ground kill	17.12.50	Lt Col Bruce H. Hinton	F-86, 336th FIS	MiG-15
19.07.50	Lt Col William T. Samways	F-80, 8th FBG	Ground kill				

Northrop YF-17

The fighter they didn't want

In 1974 Northrop pitched into one of the most famous competitive procurement battles in the history of aviation – the reward was one of the most lucrative contracts ever placed, with enormous spin-off export potential. For a number of reasons, including those both operational and political, the YF-17 lost out to the General Dynamics YF-16, but nothing should be taken away from Northrop's superb twin-engined fighter which ushered in a new era of fighter design with the accent on high-Alpha manoeuvring. This loss was not total for Northrop, as the basic design evolved into the F/A-18 Hornet, but by selling huge numbers to the US Navy it was McDonnell Douglas which reaped the big profits rather than the creators of this beautiful yet highly capable craft.

As it finally emerged, the YF-17 exhibited a futuristic layout which embodied the state-of-the-art in fighter design. The almost straight wings conferred good agility at most speeds, while the long leading-edge root extensions and leading-edge flaps allowed the aircraft to manoeuvre at angles of attack previously only dreamt of. At such low speeds, two fins were needed to provide sufficient directional stability.

Having produced the biggest and heaviest fighter of World War II (the P-61 Black Widow) and one of the biggest-ever jet fighters (the F-89 Scorpion), the Northrop Corporation switched in 1954 to studying light fighters. Northrop raapidly became convinced that the superior agility of small fighters – together with other advantages such as presenting a smaller target, a lower price and potential greater numbers – made them worthy of special study.

This led to the N-102 Fang, a Mach-2 tailed Delta powered by a single GE J79 afterburning turbojet. The engine was fed by a ventral inlet. This design lost out to the Lockheed F-104, which was much less agile and found its true role not as a dogfighter but as a stand-off interceptor and tactical attack and reconnaissance platform. The Fang was succeeded by a less ambitious (Mach 1+) project, with a tapered but unswept wing carrying Sidewinder missiles on the tips, a T-tail and two small engines of superior thrust/weight ratio. With the tailplane moved to the bottom of the fuselage this design became the N-156F and resulted in the T-38 Talon supersonic trainer, the F-5A/B/C/D Freedom Fighter, and the winner of the International Fighter Aircraft competition, the F-5E/F Tiger II. Total production of these twin-jet light fighters and trainers amounted to 3,805, despite little USAF interest being shown in the fighter variants.

Much later, during the 1980-85 period, an outstanding fighter derivative of the F-5E won much respect but failed to find customers. This was the F-5G, later restyled F-20 Tigershark, and was Northrop's last lightweight fighter. Back in 1966, however, flushed with the success of the basic F-5, Northrop had tried to find a market for a completely new next-generation fighter. Company studies, including new aerodynamic research, showed that it would be possible to build a fighter with capabilities that no F-5 could approach. Relaxed static stability promised to improve agility by making the aircraft unstable longitudinally, building in a tendency to pitch nose up. Air-combat manoeuvrability could be dramatically enhanced to the point where the limiting factor would be the human pilot.

A completely unstable aircraft requires a multiplexed flight-control system with several fast computers interposed between the pilot and the control surfaces, because only a computer can make the thousands of tiny control inputs necessary to maintain the aircraft in controlled flight. A human pilot would be unable to 'keep up' and the aircraft would rapidly depart. During the mid-1960s Northrop did not feel that such FBW control systems had reached the required level of foolproof reliability, and elected in their P.530 study to retain a degree of pitch stability (though this was marginal) and to retain conventional mechanically signalled flight controls.

High angle of attack

A second fundamental advance available for a new fighter design was an increasing capability to design for controlled flight at unprecedented AoA (angle of attack). Traditional aircraft had stalled at an AoA of about 16°, and above this even some of the best fighters (such as the P-51 Mustang) suffered violent uncontrolled departures, sometimes rolling outwards through up to 270°. By the 1960s new shapes of wing, with hinged leading edges and large LERXes (leading edge root extensions), were making possible post-stall manoeuvring at AoA exceeding 30°, and later exceeding 40°. This could be of immense advantage in any close-in, slow-speed combat.

A further factor was the unceasing advance in jet-engine technology. One of the leading companies in the field was General Electric (GE), which had provided propulsion for almost all Northrop jets. GE was a dynamic company, and in the 1960s it was determined to provide a new engine to fill the gap between the J85, with an afterburning thrust in the 5,000-lb (22.24-kN) class, and the 25,000-lb (111.21-

Above: Northrop was working on its advanced lightweight fighter from about 1966 under the P.530 programme. This model represents the P.530 design as it stood in 1968, with high-set wings, thin LERX reaching almost to the nose and small, widely splayed twin fins.

Left: The design which eventually emerged as the YF-17 underwent many changes as a result of tunnel testing. This is a model of the YF-17 in nearly its final form, with almost upright fins, broad, curved LERX and nose strakes.

kN) F100. New engines promised greater thrust, greater reliability and improved fuel economy. They were also lighter and with a lower parts count, and therefore offered thrust-to-weight ratios of at least 8:1, compared with 5:1 for engines of the 1950s, such as the J79 used in the F-104 and F-4 and proposed for Northrop's Fang.

Engines take longer to develop than aircraft, so it was crucial that GE should start engine development well in advance of any decision by Northrop to build a new fighter. Several Northrop executives, from President Tom Jones down, visited GE, whose initial response to the P.530's propulsion requirements was to offer a derivative of the existing J97 turbojet, uprated to 8,000 lb (35.59 kN) . By 1968 the thrust of this engine had been increased to 10,000 lb (44.48 kN), but it was evident that newer technology was available. Under the direction of Ed Woll, General Electric's designers worked on a more advanced engine.

By 1971 the P.530 design – named Cobra during the year – was being aimed primarily at NATO nations such as the Netherlands, in whose colours this model is painted. Subsequent events proved that the marketing strategy, at least, was sound. European nations were to buy huge numbers of the F-16, winner of the ACF competition.

Unusual features of the YF-17 were the small strakes added to the nose, which energised the air around the forward fuselage, and the LERX slots, which allowed the dumping of fuselage boundary layer air. The inset depicts airflow across a tunnel model – note the large vortices streaming from the LERX back across the wing.

through the hot core. This did little more than cool the casing of the engine, and the GE15 was jokingly called 'a leaky turbojet'. However, this had important advantages to the P.530 designers in that the engine bays required little cooling and could be made mainly of normal low-cost airframe materials, with a reduced need for thermal protection. Keeping the bypass ratio down held the engine diameter to only 32.5 in (82.5 cm), compared with nearly 40 in (101.6 cm) for the J79 (which was itself considered an outstandingly slim engine in its day).

The thrust of the initial GE15 in maximum afterburner was to be 14,300 lb (63.61 kN), similar to that of early J79s, but there any similarity ended. The contrast in diameter has already been referred to. In length, the J79 was typically 208 in (5.28 m), while the GE15 came out at a mere 145 in (3.68 m). A typical afterburning J79 weighed 3,800 lb (1724 kg), while an afterburning GE15 promised to weigh just half as much, at 1,900 lb (862 kg). Not least, fuel economy promised to be significantly better.

On top of all this, GE adopted a 'design to cost' philosophy from the outset. The designers traded off performance gains against cost, doing everything possible to hold down the price of the GE15 while still making it as competitive as possible against its larger rivals, such as the F100 selected for the twin-engined FX, which was to become the F-15. This was to pay dividends far in the future. For the moment, however, there was still no official requirement for such an engine.

Engine go-ahead

The two leaders of GE aircraft engines, Gerhard Neumann and Jack Parker, visited the then Assistant Secretary for Defense, David Packard. They offered to develop a GE15 demonstrator programme for $10 million. Packard asked the Air Force if it could find the money. Neumann then visited General Glasser and, literally on the back of a brown envelope, mapped out a complete GE15 development schedule, with costs. Fortunately, Glasser's view was that the Air Force could do with an advanced engine filling the gap between the J85 and the F100, though he would have been hard pressed to point to a direct application for such an engine! Thus, in April 1972 GE received its $10 million contract, and the GE15 became the YJ101. Neumann assigned the project to Paul Setze, and handed him the brown envelope he had shown to Glasser as the blueprint for the programme. The engine ran in 1973, and was cleared for prototype flying in February 1974.

With some assurance, but no guarantee, that GE would come up with a suitable engine, Northrop went ahead with engineering design of the P.530 in mid-1966. This was the worst possible time to embark on a lightweight fighter. Despite the fact that aircraft in this class could be highly capable, cost/effective and in virtually all respects – not even excepting range – equal to or superior to larger fighters, the Air Force was about to embark on a programme for a large and powerful fighter, then still known as FX. This

Back in 1969 the J97-derived engine had been replaced by a completely new design designated GE15. It used a core scaled down from the F101 turbofan of the B-1 bomber, but with important differences. Unlike the J85 and J97, the GE15 was a two-spool engine. The advantages of such a configuration included a reduced number of compressor stages, with shorter engine length, and this outweighed the drawbacks of having two shafts and extra bearings. With the J85 eight stages of compression generated a pressure ratio of only 7:1, but with the GE15 10 stages generated a pressure ratio exceeding 20. Eventually the ratio reached 25:1. The very first news of the P.530, in *Aviation Week* for 1 February 1971, described the engines as "turbojets with afterburners derived from the J97....could generate as much as 12,000 to 14,000 lb each."

An unusual feature of the GE15 was that it was not a turbojet but a bypass engine (low-ratio turbofan). Its bypass ratio was only 0.25: the cool airflow expelled down the bypass duct was only one-quarter as great as that going

Assigned the Air Force serial 72-01569, the first YF-17 took to the air on 9 June 1974 with Northrop test pilot Hank Chouteau at the controls. The maiden voyage lasted for 61 minutes, during which time the aircraft was put through basic handling tests, revealing no major flaws. Two days later the aircraft flew again, exceeding Mach 1 in level flight without the use of afterburners, probably the first aircraft to do so.

was considered so vital as to virtually prohibit even the suggestion that there might be room for a lightweight fighter (LWF).

The FX programme led to the F-15, the prototype flying in May 1972. The cost of this aircraft alarmed Congress, and the Air Force pulled out all the stops to get its message across. A popular saying in the Pentagon was "Why settle for a Volkswagen when you can have a Cadillac?" Another, which demonstrated the almost religious reverence with which the F-15 was regarded, ran "The only way a captain can make it to major is by swearing total allegiance to the F-15." In December 1970 the Vice-Chief of Staff, Gen John C. Meyer, asked a Pentagon fighter analyst, Col Riccioni, for his views on fighter procurement. Riccioni explained how exhaustive analysis had thrown up a convincing case for a smaller aircraft with equal performance. On the next working day Riccioni was posted to Korea.

Only too aware that support for the LWF was regarded as being akin to heresy in the Department of the Air Force, Northrop pointed out "We've been here before. The Air Force never wanted the F-5, but by aiming it at export customers we sold over 3,000 of that family." Accordingly, in a vigorous but low-key campaign that was designed to keep on good terms with the Air Force, Northrop gradually assembled a package aimed at a wide spectrum of possible foreign buyers. Prime targets were every air force using the Lockheed F-104. Others included Australia, and several Middle East countries, led by Iran.

Northrop calculated that the P.530 development programme, excluding the engine and using off-the-shelf avionics, would cost $350-400 million. Assuming an eventual total procurement not far short of the F-5 level, they calculated that the flyaway price might be $2 million.

While keeping tight control of the overall design, Northrop proposed to parcel up not only manufacture but even the detailed engineering design of the P.530 among customer countries. These countries could build up their own industrial capability, each being an associate in the overall business project. Whereas the usual practice in large aircraft programmes is to price early batches highly, in order to recoup development cost and then to reduce prices as manufacturing costs fall, Northrop proposed selling every one of perhaps 1,000 P.530s – one-third of a 3,000-aircraft market, worldwide – at the same price. (Had Northrop ever committed to legal agreements, the inflation of the 1970s would have made this a perilous undertaking.)

Northrop investment

Later in 1971 Northrop raised the estimated flyaway price to $3 million. They said at that time that they had already invested $20 million of corporate funds in "design and analytical wind-tunnel work to achieve the highest degree of technical confidence. More than 600,000 engineering man-hours and nearly 4,000 subsonic, transonic and supersonic wind-tunnel hours have gone into determining the basic design, making the P.530 one of the most highly tested aircraft at this stage of its development. A substantial amount of detail design and development work remains to be done in participating countries. The P.530 is designed to counter any air threat that the using nations might face in the 1975-90 period."

But this was still not a good time to propose an LWF, even one aimed nominally at the export market. The much-troubled TFX project (which had evolved into the F-111) was a fighter with a very high wing-loading and a maximum gross weight exceeding 100,000 lb (45360 kg).

From the start of the flight test programme the rival YF-16 was considered by a small margin to be the better aircraft in high-energy fighting undertaken at longer range. Conversely, the YF-17 exhibited excellent close-in dogfighting potential at the lower end of the speed spectrum. When it came to slugging it out in a turning 'knife fight', the YF-17 had the better of any fighter it flew against, and could still challenge today's generation of super-agile fighters such as the MiG-29.

Above and right: Although the YF-17 was not fitted with any sophisticated weapon system, it was assessed for its bombing potential during the LWF evaluation. During November 1974 the first aircraft was fitted with underwing pylons for the carriage of two 2,000-lb (907-kg) Mk 84 bombs, which were released in a steep dive. The aircraft also demonstrated an ability to land carrying both weapons. From the outset the YF-17 always had greater air-to-ground potential than the YF-16.

This tended to make the FX (which became the F-15), at a maximum gross weight around 50,000 lb (22680 kg), seem like quite a lightweight fighter. Moreover, thanks to the new-technology F100 engines and Colonel John Boyd's insistence on a huge wing to confer a very low wing-loading, the F-15 was going to have tremendous inflight performance and outstanding agility. Many saw a lower-cost, lighter-weight alternative as being an unnecessary distraction and an unwelcome competitor, which would inevitably have reduced capability and which might put US lives at risk. Only the best would be good enough!

Boyd was concerned about the size, weight, complexity and cost of the F-15, however. He could show that Mach 2.5 capability was as useless as it was costly, that long-range radar was responsible for a mere 2.8 per cent of all aerial targets acquired in Vietnam, and that long-range missiles were unreliable and inflexible. Together with civilian Pierre Sprey and Colonel Riccioni, he toiled ceaselessly to confirm, demonstrate and convince others that an LWF could outfly the F-15 in most respects. In senior echelons of the Air Force this clique was regarded with suspicion, and was named 'the LWF Mafia'. They appeared to be conspiring to impose an inferior fighter on the Air Force.

In late 1967 the fighter 'Mafia' eventually settled on an FX² (FX-squared) project with about 400 sq ft (372 m²) of wing and a maximum clean gross weight of 25,000 lb (11340 kg). This tallied precisely with the P.530. Ironically the creators of the overweight, over-sized F-111, General Dynamics at Fort Worth, also showed interest and came on

board as enthusiastic converts to the lightweight fighter concept. They had finally had enough of 50-ton fighters with the F-111. But all this remained unfunded heresy. Official USAF interest lay in trying to arrest such work, which threatened to take funds from the F-15 and which might even convince Congress that the big fighter was not needed. It was this political background which forced Northrop to avoid any suggestion that the USAF might buy the P.530, and instead to publicise it purely as "an airplane intended for use by the Free World."

From the outset it was to be twin-engined. Although combat damage that knocks out one engine often (but not always) takes out its companion, Northrop was able to show convincing statistics demonstrating that engine-related major accidents happen more often to single-engined fighters, and that a twin-engined aircraft would suffer lower attrition in peace and war. The single-engined figure per 100,000 flight hours was in all cases more than six, whereas for the twin-engined aircraft it was between zero and four.

From the outset, in late 1966, the P.530 had an unswept wing, tapered mainly on the leading edge and mounted high on the long fuselage with anhedral of 5°. Basic thickness/chord ratio was 4 per cent. This very high lift wing had an area of about 400 sq ft (37 m²), compared with 186 sq ft (17 m²) for the F-5E, so that even allowing for the greater weight the wing-loading was reduced from 133 lb/sq ft for the F-5 to exactly half as much in the P.530. This was fundamental to enhanced manoeuvrability, just as it was in the big F-15.

Other features included a conventional tail, with slab tailplanes mounted below mid-level. The twin J97-derived engines were fed by long ducts from semi-circular inlets with a movable half-cone centrebody ahead of the wing. The Northrop configuration was very similar to Lockheed's rival (F-104 derived) CL-1200 Lancer. This similarity was to fade.

Growth of the LERX

In 1966 the P.530's LERX was a modest triangle little bigger than that of the F-5E, but within one year it had grown dramatically. Tunnel testing had shown that a large LERX could greatly improve lift and stability, especially at extreme AoA. As the AoA increased, so did the size and strength of the vortex shed by the sharp edge of the LERX. This vortex eventually scrubbed over the inner 30 per cent of the upper surface of the wing, increasing local lift, re-energising sluggish boundary layers and preventing what would otherwise have been a sharp spanwise migration of the boundary layer towards the tips, creating high drag. High-speed flow was preserved roughly parallel to the fuselage over the outer wings, enabling conventional ailerons to remain effective.

The combination of a large LERX with a conventional wing behind it is termed a hybrid wing. The LERX themselves generate considerable lift at large values of AoA, their presence adding something like 50 per cent to the lift from the basic wing in such conditions. This not only enhances turn capability but also avoids the destabilising effect of the centre of lift migrating forwards.

Extending the LERX ahead of the engine inlets had a further effect of guiding the airflow into the inlets and presenting the engines with a full flow of relatively undisturbed air at extreme AoA. Airflow into the inlets was further improved by providing a long axial slot in each LERX adjacent to the fuselage ahead of the inlets. Without such apertures, drag in supersonic flight would have been increased by a build-up of air ahead of the inlet. The slots provided an escape route for this air. At the other end of the speed range, at extreme AoA, they provided an escape route for boundary-layer air which scrubbed across the fuselage ahead of the inlet.

The canopy itself was from the start a large frameless moulding with a bulged cross-section giving the pilot unobstructed 360° visibility and good sightlines over the

nose and downwards on each side. It marked a return to a common sense that had been ignored on fighters like the F-8, F-4, MiG-21, MiG-23, Mirage and F-5, where low drag had taken precedence over pilot vision.

In 1968 the LERX were further enlarged, the forward portions being extended ahead as strakes that continued past the windscreen almost to the nose. Outboard of the LERX the wing had always had variable camber, which was favoured by fighter designers as a better form of variable geometry than variable sweep. The camber was provided by hinged flaps along the straight leading and trailing edges, those on the trailing edge stopping a little over half-way to the tip in favour of conventional ailerons. In 1968 the leading-edge flap was divided into front and rear sections to increase lift coefficient in the depressed position. Operation was made automatic according to a software schedule.

The ability of the P.530 to fly at extreme AoA increasingly showed that the tail was inadequate. The vertical surface in particular was blanketed in the wake of the wing. To restore control in extreme conditions the single centre-line fin was replaced by twin fins, each about half as large as the original single surface, canted out at almost 45° to put

them in free-stream flow. To reduce cross-coupling effects in roll, the rudders reached only halfway up the fins. The horizontal tailplanes were also redesigned, being enlarged and moved forward almost under the wing.

Undercarriage and gun

During 1969 engineering design of the structure and systems began. The landing gears could hardly have been simpler, with single shock struts and multi-ply high-pressure tyres which later were enlarged for operation from unimproved surfaces. Surprisingly, it took until 1973 to add an advanced anti-skid braking system. An airfield arrester hook was added, but not a braking parachute. A door-type airbrake was added above the rear fuselage between the fins. Armament comprised Sidewinder missiles on wingtip rails, other stores on three pylons (under each wing and on the centreline), and a gun. At first, the F-5's armament of two M-39 cannon was considered, but these outdated weapons were soon replaced by a single M61. The location of this gun posed problems, but Northrop eventually settled on the centreline under the nose, despite the proximity of the muzzle to the radar antenna.

The second aircraft (72-01570) joined the flight test programme on 21 August 1974. The only major difference between the two was the blue/grey camouflage applied to the second aircraft.

Although it was externally identical to the latest incarnation of the P.530 design, the YF-17 was assigned the company designation P.600 in recognition of its purely experimental status. Here the aircraft is shown firing the M61 Vulcan cannon in low-level strafing runs at Edwards.

Northrop YF-17 No. 2 LWF/ACF Joint Test Force Edwards AFB, California 1974

YF-17 programme – key players

Thomas V. Jones – President of Northrop Corporation
Welko E. Gasich – V-P and General Manager, Northrop Aircraft Division
Lee F. Begin, Jr. – Manager, P.530 Cobra programme
Walter E. Fellows – Manager, P.600 lightweight fighter
Roy P. Jackson – Manager, YF-17 programme (later F-18)
Ward Stewart – Deputy Director, YF-17 programme
John Patierno – YF-17 Deputy Program Manager, Systems
T. R. Rooney – Manager, YF-17 engineering
Henry E. 'Hank' Chouteau – Chief Test Pilot, Northrop
Joseph B. Jordan – Northrop YF-17 test pilot
Paul Setze – original head of project, YJ101
Burton A. Riemer – Manager, General Electric J101 (F404)
Capt (later Lt Col) John R. Boyd – pioneer of fighter analysis
Pierre Sprey – systems analyst, Department of Defense
Lt Gen Otto P. Glasser – USAF VCAS, Research and Development
Col Everest E. Riccioni – Chief, Development Plans and Analysis
Lt Col James G. Rider – Commander, LWF/ACF joint test force
Col William E. Thurman – Deputy for Prototypes, USAF ASD
George Sprangenburg – Director, Evaluation Div, NASC

Test programme
During the LWF/ACF programme the two YF-17s logged 345.5 flying hours (including 13 supersonic) in the course of 288 sorties. This compared with 330 sorties and 417 hours flying for the two YF-16s. During the YF-17 flight trials a sustained AoA of 63° was reached at 50 kt, while sideslip angles of 36° were achieved with 40° AoA. During one period one aircraft flew seven times in seven hours, turnround times averaging 15 minutes.

Control surfaces
The YF-17 featured full-span leading-edge and half-span trailing-edge flaps which altered the wing camber to increase lift at low speed and when manoeuvring. Outboard sealed-gap ailerons provided roll control in conjunction with the differential tailerons, which also provided pitch control. Yaw control was provided by a rudder on each fin, mounted low down to minimise the roll moment caused by the outward canting of the fins.

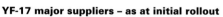

YF-17 major suppliers – as at initial rollout
Airbrake actuator – Asco Machine Products, El Segundo, California
Air data computer – Bendix Corporation, Teterboro, New Jersey
AoA system – Rosemount Inc., Minneapolis, Minnesota
Brakes – Goodyear Tire and Rubber, Akron, Ohio
Canopy – Sierracin Corporation, Sylmar, California
Ejection seat – Stencel Aero Engineering Corporation, Asheville, N. Carolina
Engines – General Electric, Lynn, Massachusetts
Environmental system – Hamilton Standard Division, Windsor Locks, Connecticut
Flap actuators – Datron Systems, Pico Ribera, California
Flight control power units – Parker Hannafin, Irvine, California
Fuel tanks – Firestone Tire and Rubber, Magnolia, Arkansas
Gearboxes – Kelsey-Hayes Company, Springfield, Ohio
Graphite composites – Hercules Inc., Magna, Utah
Gun and ammunition system – General Electric, Burlington, Vermont
Head-up display – JLM International, Cambridge, Massachusetts
Inertial navigation – Litton Industries, Woodland Hills, California
Instruments – Gull Airborne Instruments, Smithtown, New York
Landing gear – Cleveland Pneumatic, Cleveland, Ohio

Cockpit
The well laid-out cockpit was conventional featuring none of the CRT displays of the F-18 development. A simple HUD was incorporated, either side of which the coaming formed a shade over the main instrument panel. Flight instruments were sensibly grouped in the centre, while to the right-hand side were seven duplicated tape gauges for the engine readings.

Linear actuators – Barber-Coleman Company, Rockford, Illinois
                   Plessey Industries, Hillside, New Jersey
Oxygen convertor – Essex Cryogenic Industries, St Louis, Missouri
Radar – Rockwell International, Anaheim, California
Rudder pedal assembly – Grumman Aerospace, Bethpage, New York
Stability augmentor – Sperry Rand Corporation, Phoenix, Arizona
Transponder – Teledyne Electronics, Newbury Park, California

Control column
The centrally mounted stick operated conventionally for pitch control, hinging from the base on the cockpit floor, but for roll control was unusually articulated just below the grip.

Powerplant

The two YJ101s were mounted close together to minimise the asymmetric effects on handling in the event of an engine loss. Northrop always considered these engines as underpowered when fitted to the YF-17s: certainly, they could have provided more power at the time of the ACF fly-off, which might have helped Northrop's cause. Described as 'leaky turbojets' rather than true turbofans (like the YF-16's F100), they suffered from a lower specific range, one of the factors cited in favour of the YF-16 after the 13 January 1975 announcement of the GD fighter's win.

Foreign prospects

After the loss of the ACF competition, Northrop concentrated on trying to sell its F-18L land-based fighter. Technical data export licences were acquired covering Australia, France, Canada, West Germany, Greece, Japan, Spain, Turkey and the United Kingdom. Prior to the Islamic revolution, Iran was also a prospect. Canada and Spain were pursued with vigour, including painting the second aircraft in their colours. However, those nations which purchased US fighters chose either the F-16 or McDonnell Douglas' navalised Hornet. In April 1985 Northrop eventually gave up with the F-18L when it was settled that the entire programme was the responsibility of McDonnell Douglas.

Armament

For the ACF competition, armament was restricted to wingtip AIM-9J Sidewinders and the nose-mounted M61 cannon. Proposed developments would have featured radar with Sparrow capability.

Navy programme

In August 1974 the US Navy's own VFAX programme was cancelled by Congress in favour of NACF, which instructed the Navy to choose from either of the two ACF rivals. McDonnell Douglas, eager to get a share of this Navy contract, studied both aircraft and decided that the YF-17 was a far better option. Their approach to Northrop to develop a navalised version was accepted in October 1974. The first money assigned to what had become the F-18 programme was awarded on 2 May 1975 in the form of a short-term development contract, the second YF-17 being earmarked for development work as the 'F-18 prototype' (the first real F-18 did not fly until November 1978). Northrop retained 30 per cent of Hornet development work, and 40 per cent of production. Full-scale development was authorised on 28 January 1976. By comparison with the F-17, the naval F-18 featured larger wings, more capacious fuselage for greater fuel carriage, sturdier structure and undercarriage for carrying bigger loads and to cope with carrier operations, and a deeper nose housing the APG-65 multi-mode radar.

USAF 01570

Airframe

The semi-monocoque fuselage was largely of light alloy structure, but did include some graphite composites. The dorsal airbrake was constructed in this material. The wing was a multi-spar structure, set at 5° anhedral. The sweepback value at the quarter-chord line was 20°.

Keith Fretwell.

The YF-17 exhibited an extremely sleek shape, but surprisingly suffered from a supersonic drag problem not found on the YF-16. Other areas where the YF-16 enjoyed an advantage – notably roll rate and thrust/weight ratio – could have easily been attended to if the Northrop team had not been hampered by a late start in the competition which disabled them from making any changes to the aircraft.

Northrop technicians work on the second prototype YF-17 to prepare it for an ACF evaluation mission. In order to complete the necessary tests the Northrop ground team had to triple-shift throughout the six months available to them, the first shift preparing the aircraft, the second supporting the daytime flying, and the evening shift bedding-down the aircraft. Inflight refuelling played an important part in the acceleration of the tests, allowing several different test points to be flown during each flight. Around 250 refuellings were undertaken. General Dynamics were able to conduct their programme at a far more leisurely pace, the first YF-16 having preceded the YF-17 into the air by over five months.

In 1969 intensive further refinement resulted in several major changes. The most visible modification was to redesign the tail. The canted fins were approximately doubled in size and moved to a remarkably forward location, partly overlapping the wing. In contrast, the tailplanes were moved as far aft as possible. This process was to continue to late 1970, by which time the outward cant of the fins had been reduced to 18° and the tailplanes further enlarged. Programme manager Walt Fellers said the huge tailplanes, with a span of nearly 22 ft (6.7 m), gave the most powerful possible longitudinal control authority while deflecting only 12°, roughly half the angle that would be needed with tailplanes of normal size. They enabled the centre of gravity to be moved 3 per cent further aft, reducing pitch stability and conferring low trim drag. Moreover, without needing stability augmentation, the P.530 could approach the manoeuvring stability point, at which it was unstable in pitch.

Area rule

A major reason for altering the position of the tail surfaces was to obtain the best compliance with the area rule, distributing cross-sectional area such that a graph would show a smooth curve from nose to tail. This, coupled with a need to further refine the high-AoA lift distribution, led to a further redesign of the huge LERX. These became curved in plan, while in side view they curved up from the wing to level out at a higher level beside the cockpit. Over the previous four years the wing had migrated down from the high to the mid position, and in 1970 the fuselage itself was subtly modified, the entire forward section being raised in relation to the wing and LERX. The leading-edge flap

was by this time in six sections (three front, three rear) on each wing.

By 1970 it was accepted that not even Mach 2 was an essential design objective. This enabled the inlets to be simplified. They were made shorter and brought back further under the LERX. By this time the large LERX so resembled the hood of a cobra that Cobra became the P.530's name. Later in 1971 the half-cone centrebodies were eliminated, and the inlets were separated from the fuselage by a large rectangular splitter plate. Throughout 1971-72 work continued to refine the inlet shape and location, the final shape selected being a canted oval shape with a fixed, slightly rounded edge, with the top some 4 in (10 cm) below the underside of the LERX and with the duct curving back into the fuselage. Immediately behind the duct was the aft-retracting main gear. The boundary-layer air diverted inside the splitter now escaped through a further-enlarged slot in the root of the LERX, while spring-loaded doors above the inlet provided an escape route for excess air at supersonic speed.

Further aerodynamic refinement improved the appearance of the boat-tail at the rear fuselage, and reduced base drag between the engines. From the outset, Lee Begin and his colleagues had taken it for granted that the engines had to be removable straight downwards. With the F-5 it was necessary to remove the boat-tail section before extracting an engine, but the P.530 boldly featured huge doors hung on piano hinges so that an engine could be disconnected straight on to a removal dolly and rolled away. It would have been structurally easier to withdraw engines on rails to the rear, but Northrop had their eye on a possible naval market and even with a short engine only 145 in (3.68 m)

long there would seldom be room to pull an engine out backwards in the crowded hangar deck of an aircraft-carrier.

Throughout this period there was no funding for the P.530, though GE had obtained support for the YJ101 engine. By 1971 this was rated at 15,000 lb (66.73 kN) thrust, and GE produced six engines for flight test. In contrast, Northrop had to spend their own money on refining the Cobra, and never quite succeeded in putting together the hoped-for package of international participants. Having begun in 1966 with West Germany and Canada as likely customers, by 1971 the key nations were seen as the Netherlands and Australia, followed by Iran, Belgium, Norway, Italy, Greece and Turkey.

Cobra delays

On 28 January 1971 the previously unannounced programme was revealed to the world. Northrop invited every significant aviation magazine and air correspondent to their Hawthorne (Los Angeles) factory for a detailed briefing in which the main speaker was Lee F. Begin. All seemed optimistic, but at a further briefing two years later Begin was still unable to announce more than "Our current program goal is a Cobra go-ahead not later than January 1974." But in those two years much had happened within the US.

Smarting at having lost the International Fighter Aircraft programme to Northrop's F-5E, in December 1970 Lockheed's C. L. 'Kelly' Johnson, director of the famed Skunk Works, visited Washington. He saw many Air Force people, starting with the Secretary of the Air Force, Robert C. Seamans. At this time the policy of Total Package Procurement had become discredited by the experiences of the F-111 and C-5A, and Johnson saw that future procurement should rest upon demonstration of flying hardware. He proposed that Lockheed should quickly put together a prototype package based on the CL1200-2, at no cost to the Air Force.

Provided it did not compete with the F-15, his proposal was well received. What Johnson did not expect – and the last thing he wanted – was that it resulted in rival LWF proposals arriving at the Pentagon from Northrop, General Dynamics, Boeing and LTV. Deputy Secretary of Defense David Packard concurred with his advisors that it could do no harm to study the LWF on a purely experimental basis.

Plan for a lightweight fighter

After much further political effort Packard signed a Program Decision Memorandum on 25 August 1971 authorising the Air Force to allocate $200 million to a programme to build and test two competing designs of two dissimilar types of aircraft. One was to be an Advanced Medium STOL Transport, the rivals being the Boeing YC-14 and McDonnell Douglas YC-15. The other was to be an LWF.

When the five proposals were in they were submitted to a scoring process. To Johnson's extreme chagrin, Lockheed were placed last. To the astonishment of many, the General Dynamics Model 401 was placed first, and two prototypes were ordered at a cost of $37,943,000 with the designation YF-16. In second place came the Northrop P.600, and two examples of this were ordered at a cost of $39,878,715 as the YF-17. These contracts were placed on 13 April 1972.

One of the factors which caught the attention of the Air Force and enabled the LWF competition to happen was Colonel Riccioni's success in persuading the Air Force that the Navy was already deep into LWF studies, disillusioned by the escalating cost and technical difficulties being experienced by the F-14. The two projects fed off one another and one of the immediate results of the Air Force LWF programme was to give a huge spur to Navy work, which in the spring of 1974 resulted in the VFAX requirement.

The P-600 was externally almost indistinguishable from the 1971 form of the P.530 Cobra. Despite this, Walt Fellers was appointed to head the P.600 team in a building half a mile from the P.530 operation, which remained under Begin in its original building at Hawthorne. The USAF Prototype Program Office was located in the Aeronautical Systems Division at Wright-Patterson Air Force Base in Ohio, though, of course, the actual flight evaluation would take place at the Air Force Flight Test Center, Edwards AFB, in the California desert.

The fundamental difference between the YF-17 (P.600) and P.530 was that the latter had always been envisaged as a fully operational multi-mission aircraft, with at least the same air/ground capability as an F-4, whereas the YF-17 was a pure air/air demonstrator with no armament except a gun and two Sidewinder missiles mounted on the wingtips. On the other hand, many of the advanced features of the YF-17 were immediately incorporated into the projected P.530. One was a switch to fly-by-wire flight controls, the tail circuits being quadruply redundant but the ailerons being simplex (no fallback) because the aircraft could always be controlled in roll by the tailplanes. At low speeds the latter (moving 30°) provided 10 per cent of rolling power, but this increased with flight speed until at supersonic speeds the tailplanes took over roll authority completely.

Whereas the maximum takeoff weight of the P.530, with air/ground weapons and external fuel, was 40,000 lb (18144 kg), that of the YF-17 was initially only 21,000 lb (9526 kg) (it soon grew to 23,000 lb/10433 kg). Moreover, unlike the YF-17, the P.530 was designed for operation from unimproved airstrips outside the USA. The YF-17 landing gears were simplified, saving considerable weight. A much higher proportion of the structure, to a total weight of 900 lb (408 kg), was of graphite fibre, including the LERX, ailerons, flaps, airbrake, engine doors, fin leading

Both YF-17s were often in the air together, and indeed flew mock combat against each other. Both ACF contenders flew against a wide range of existing fighters, although they never fought each other, or the F-15. The fact that either could trash the Eagle in close-in combat would have been politically unacceptable to the USAF fighter brass for whom the F-15 was their primary concern. In addition to fighting with US fighter types, both YF-16 and YF-17 are reported to have flown air combat with MiG-17s and MiG-21s from the USAF's secret foreign technology squadron which lurked in the Nellis range area.

Above and right: Throughout the ACF competition Navy pilots had favoured the YF-17 for their own service on account of its twin-engined safety, better carrier compatibility and greater multi-role potential. In October 1974, McDonnell Douglas assumed development of the naval version, to be designated F-18. The second aircraft made an appearance at the 1976 Farnborough air show, complete with its Air Force serial rendered in BuAer number style as 201570. Northrop used this show to officially relaunch its Cobra II sales drive for the export F-18L. The YF-17 subsequently appeared in several Navy schemes, including that of the Fighter Weapons School ('Top Gun').

and trailing edges, rudders and many access doors.

Other design changes were the addition of an inflight-refuelling receptacle above the nose, relocation of the M61 gun in a quickly removable pallet in the upper part of the nose instead of underneath, the addition of long but narrow sharp-edged strakes along the sides of the nose, further enlargement of the LERX apertures, and addition of an emergency hydraulic power unit. Northrop had used cannon above the nose in the F-5, and said flash blindness at night was no problem.

Traditional cockpit

In general, the YF-17 cockpit was the same as that planned for the P.530, with traditional electro-mechanical instruments (albeit with vertical tape engine displays) and a conventional centre stick, using the full length for pitch control and with roll control provided by a short pivoted upper portion. In 1973 Northrop contracted with Litton to supply the LN-33 inertial navigation system, but the question of which radar to use was left until 1974. The Air Force specifically wanted to avoid either LWF having a high-power multi-mode radar, such as that fitted to the F-15, and Northrop retained a constricted nose of pointed conical form. Nevertheless, in April 1974 they contracted with Rockwell for a compact radar with a phased-array antenna which this nose could accommodate (though it was not fitted to the two YF-17s as built). As late as November 1974 Northrop selected the IBM System 4/Pi as the YF-17's tactical computer.

Northrop were eager to co-operate with the Air Force and present the YF-17 as "a demonstrator to help define technologies the Air Force might need in future fighter programmes," while at the same time building the YF-17 as virtually an operational aircraft. For example, unwanted by the Air Force, both prototypes had the capability of carrying up to 17,000 lb (7711 kg) of ordnance and fuel on nine external stores stations. As a result, the YF-17 was larger than its rival, whose air-to-ground capability was initially very limited. Of course, everything possible was done to

facilitate rapid turnaround and re-arming, and plans were published for a single-seat F-17A and – again unrequested – for a two-seat F17B.

Largely because it used the same engine as the F-15, the rival GD F-401 (YF-16) ran ahead of schedule. The Northrop YF-17, however, used an engine that had never flown, and which did not pass its PFRT (Preliminary Flight Rating Test) until December 1973. This was a factor in delaying the roll-out of the first YF-17 to 4 April 1974 (when the first flight was already overdue) and delayed the first flight itself to 9 June. From then on the flight programme went well. On Flight 2, on 11 June, Hank Chouteau exceeded Mach 1 in dry thrust, and it was soon clear that the YF-17 could accelerate away from an F-4 in afterburner without using more than military power. The no. 2 aircraft, painted in blue/white camouflage, made its first flight on 21 August.

By this time the Air Force was quietly putting the entire LWF programme into top gear. Until 1974 the Air Force had shown a united front in disclaiming interest in buying an LWF for the inventory. Testimony before Congress (which kept asking why an LWF was needed) stated in 1972 that, "It could be used to modernise our allies, and possibly the Air National Guard." From 1970 it had become the increasingly obvious intention of several large allied air forces to buy a new fighter, to replace such aircraft as the F-104 and F-5. The American LWFs were potential winners, but several European aircraft emerged as rivals, notably the Dassault F1-M53 and Saab's Eurofighter (a Viggen variant).

Whether or not GD and Northrop could by themselves have persuaded the Air Force to regard the LWF not as a mere technology demonstrator but as a fighter for the inventory is doubtful. But in April 1974 the prospect of big business, provided that the European rivals could be beaten, suddenly resulted in the Air Force changing its attitude towards the LWF. Almost overnight it changed the designation from LWF to ACF, for Air Combat Fighter. On 27 April 1974 the Secretary for Defense, James Schlesinger, announced "It is appropriate to consider full-scale development and eventual production of an ACF-type aircraft ."

Sale of the Century

Although there were several other big potential markets, the main one comprised Belgium, Denmark, the Netherlands and Norway. These European air forces formed a consortium to study rival aircraft. On 28 June 1974 this Multinational Fighter Programme Committee visited Edwards and spent a day with the YF-17 programme. This committee announced that it would select the same aircraft for the four air forces and announce its choice in January 1975. If they chose American, it would be whichever aircraft was selected by the Air Force.

Both GD and Northrop were suddenly in a 'winner takes all' situation. The European buy was quickly filling media front pages as 'The Sale of the Century'. Basically, it was a contest between two new-technology aircraft, which could fairly be called the fighter pilot's dream, and two older but more mature and well proven European aircraft. For an American contender to win, the Air Force had to announce its choice by mid-January, which meant that all the flight-test data had to be in by December. This presented few difficulties to GD, but it was a serious problem to Northrop. Because of their later start, they had to compress a 12-month test programme into six months.

This was theoretically just possible, by flying on a round-the-clock three-shift basis seven days per week, and provided that aircraft serviceability remained at what should have been an impossibly high level. The more serious result for Northrop was that it precluded any modification, or even rectification of any deficiencies that might emerge.

On 11 September 1974 the Air Force announced that it would buy 650 examples of whichever ACF it considered

to be the better aircraft. By this time, though the two YF-17s were performing extremely well, it was almost a foregone conclusion that the rival aircraft would win, mainly because of its engine. Whereas the GE engine was immature and would require enormous investment in tooling costs, spare parts and even documentation, the Pratt & Whitney F100 was already in series production and, as the powerplant of the F-15, was on the point of entering service at many Air Force bases throughout the world. Selection of the GD fighter would merely reduce the price per engine, because of the larger numbers involved, and would thus have an effect on F-15 costs. Few could have predicted the serious problems which the engine would run into, grounding the F-15 fleet on a number of occasions and prompting close examination of alternative powerplants.

Weight arguments

There were prolonged arguments regarding two fundamental factors: weight and cost. Northrop's Begin never ceased to stir a hornet's nest by insisting that, other things being equal, a twin-engined fighter could be made lighter than a single-engined one. As far as the engines themselves were concerned, the thrust/weight ratio of the F100 (based on maximum augmented thrust) was $23,100/3,036 = 7.84$, while that of the GE J101 was $15,000/1,900 = 7.89$. In fact, the YF-17s were powered by prototype YJ101 engines, whose T/W ratio was $14,300/1,983 = 7.21$. In any case, the significantly better specific fuel consumption of the bigger engine rapidly dominated the equation, and resulted in the YF-16 having a considerably longer range. (In the Pentagon, Riccioni and Spangenberg caused a storm by showing that the ACF would have a longer range on internal fuel than the F-15, which seemed almost unbelievable, but which proved accurate.)

Where weight of the whole aircraft was concerned, the Air Force cranked in factors to allow for the never-disputed fact that, where big contracts are at stake, contractors 'lie and brag'. Putting it more kindly, an Air Force evaluation officer said "contractors are just overly optimistic." What actually happens is that they report a future weight of an improved and refined aircraft which, in Northrop's case, they never had time to achieve.

One Northrop official admitted "The Air Force did an excellent job. They were right on our real weight of the airplane". [What is harder to comprehend is why the actual completely equipped but otherwise empty aircraft were not simply weighed.]

As the evaluation progressed it became increasingly obvious that the YF-16 had an all-round higher performance, especially in supersonic flight. The overall bulk of the GD aircraft was slightly less, and as test data mounted the margin between thrust and drag was seen to be in favour of the single-engined aircraft, the margin becoming quite large at Mach 0.9 and above. What was less easy to determine was whether this meant poor thrust or high drag. Begin blamed the engines, saying "GE were too conservative with the YJ101. They had it downturned so much [i.e. they adjusted the fuel control to flows below the maximum] that it wasn't putting out the power that we had predicted. We didn't find out until November or December." Northrop were never given credit for the fact that the production engine would have been significantly more powerful, and that many advantages enjoyed by the prototype YF-16 would have been lost had production versions of the rival aircraft been compared.

Marked as the F-18 prototype, the second YF-17 shows the obvious similarities between it and Northrop's earlier lightweight fighter, the very successful F-5E.

In F-18 guise, the YF-17 was displayed at Paris in 1977. When McDonnell Douglas turned the YF-17 into the Hornet, the type acquired true multi-role capability, but only at the expense of its uncompromised excellence at air-to-air combat. A similar fate befell the YF-16, which in its production version lost much of the 'zip' which had helped it win the ACF competition.

Following the devastating loss of the ACF competition, Northrop pushed the YF-17 hard to other potential customers, Canada being seen as a major opportunity. With McDonnell Douglas handling development of the maritime version for the US Navy, Northrop marketed its land-based version as the F-18L. Accordingly, the second prototype was given two versions of a Canadian scheme (above and right). The name Cobra was resurrected for the type, recalling the aircraft's origins as the P.530 export fighter, and it was marked as the 'CF-18L prototype'.

Another way of evaluating aerodynamic drag is to fly straight and level at a selected speed and then suddenly close the throttle(s). According to Fellers, "In supersonic flight...the YF-16 would keep going while the pilot of the YF-17 was practically thrown through the instruments. Everyone said we must have a lot of drag, but...what we found out much later, after the decision was over, was that after throttle chop the F100 engine does not shut down. It decels in its own sweet time," continuing to push out a significant amount of thrust for some time and reducing the deceleration due to drag. At the same time, Begin frankly admitted "We did have a problem with supersonic drag...it is connected with some of the things that have shown up with the F-18...with the LERX slots and the bleed doors...but it was covered up by the prototype engine missing on thrust."

When the evaluation progressed to simulated combat, flying against threat aircraft (but not, according to most reports, against each other, nor against the F-15), the YF-16 again showed some advantages. This was almost entirely because of superior roll rate, especially at Mach 0.8 and above. This was a particularly misleading parameter, as Begin explained. "We had a weak horizontal stabilator. We didn't have enough stiffeners in the fuselage. We needed to put a bigger-diameter [powered-control] piston in. It would have taken three to four weeks. We didn't have time. We would have fixed it in production." It seems beyond doubt that a new taileron actuator would have actually conferred on the YF-17 better roll performance than was enjoyed by the YF-16.

Conflicting reports

Among the toil of hundreds of evaluation staff concerned solely with trying to come up with meaningful cost figures, all four prototypes were flown by an increasing spectrum of contractor, Air Force, Navy/Marine and civilian pilots. According to Boyd, who was unashamedly biased in favour of the single-engined aircraft, "Every pilot who flew both airplanes considered the YF-16 the superior aircraft." This was very far from the truth, since many pilots (ironically including many of those with actual combat experience) expressed a preference for the Northrop aircraft. Virtually all expressed confidence that either LWF could beat any anticipated threat aircraft, although in the crucial low-speed, rolling-scissors type of engagement the YF-17 would win every time. One experienced USN pilot, Commander 'Mugs' McKeown, pointed out that the YF-16 needed its AoA limiter (set at an unimpressive 20°), having been spun unintentionally on three occasions during the evaluation, while the YF-17 exhibited no tendency to depart at all. He was swift to aver that "The YF-17 was probably the simplest jet I have flown. On the very first flight I went to 45° AoA, 90 kt at 40,000 ft, put in full rudder and the airplane just turned around 90°." McKeown represented the general preference for the YF-17 by the Navy's pilots, who appreciated its twin engines and low-speed handling characteristics. "If suckered into a low-speed turning fight, you wouldn't necessarily die in the YF-17," explained one. "You don't have to look inside the cockpit to make sure you are in the proper envelope to prevent some uncommanded manoeuvre, you don't have to spend some of your attention in keeping out of particular areas of the envelope, and that gives you a tremendous advantage in maintaining visual contact with an enemy aircraft at all times." The evaluation was effectively controlled by USAF officers, however, few of whom had seen combat, and many of whom wanted a solution that would lower the cost of the F-15, ignoring other considerations. The Navy was largely ignored. Kent Lee, Navy representative at the evaluation said that "I thought that the board picked the wrong airplane, but I really didn't have a vote. They had their minds made up." On the other hand, a key manager of the YF-17 team, who later went on to work on the F/A-18, stated years later (after the emotions had subsided) that the YF-16 was clearly the better aircraft for the Air Force's needs.

Whatever the relative merits of the YF-16 and YF-17, one fact emerged that was rapidly swept under the carpet, and that was that either contender would have been able to best the F-15 in air-to-air combat. Ironically, the superior load-carrying capability demonstrated by the YF-17 was ignored, although the production F-16 was destined to enter service primarily as an air-to-ground mud-moving fighter-bomber, a role for which it had to be enlarged and greatly modified. "We ripped up the plans, spent $1.5 million in redesign, added 3,000 lb extra weight and came close to doubling the cost. And what was a great fighter became almost great," mourned Pierre Sprey, a member of the original 'fighter Mafia'.

Air Force selection

In the end, the economic advantages of the single-, common-engined YF-16, together with its better roll performance, won out over twin-engined reliability and better low-speed handling and agility. On 13 January 1975 the Air Force selected the GD F-16 as the winner of what had never been intended as a fly-off of rival fighters but merely as technology demonstrators. At the same time it increased its requirement for an ACF to 1,400 aircraft, actually overtaking procurement of the F-15.

This was a very severe setback to Northrop, which could do little to stop its carefully cultivated international market switching their attentions to the F-16. Northrop had, in fact, originally submitted to the LWF programme a single-engined Cobra derivative, the P-610, with the same F100 engine as the YF-16, and which would have almost certainly won the competition. However, all was not yet lost.

For several years the Navy's fighter programme, the Grumman F-14 Tomcat, had been in trouble because of its very high and escalating cost. Grumman was actually building the F-14 at a loss, and was beginning to express an

unwillingness to continue doing so. Several alternatives were studied, including an F-15 armed with the Phoenix missile and long-range AWG-9 radar, and a simpler and cheaper 'F-14X' without this radar/missile combination. By early 1974 a completely new lightweight VFAX was being studied, to complement the F-14 at lower cost and to replace remaining F-4s in the fighter role, and the A-4s and A-7s still active in the attack role.

Projected VFAX designs quickly arrived by the truckload, one being the Northrop P.630, a carrier-equipped Cobra. However, on 28 August 1974 the Congress directed the Navy to select its VFAX from one of the Air Force ACF designs "with minimum modifications." Despite the disastrous experience of commonality in the F-111 programme, the Navy acquiesced to this directive. McDonnell Douglas quickly studied the GD and Northrop ACF aircraft and decided the latter would be the better basis for a VFAX, or Navy ACF. On 7 October 1974 the two companies announced a teaming agreement, under the terms of which McDonnell Douglas would be prime contractor for the Navy version, while Northrop would be prime contractor for the Air Force and allied versions.

Of course, selection by the Air Force of the F-16 left Northrop with nothing of which to be prime contractor. While the McDonnell Douglas F/A-18 Hornet went ahead with Northrop participation, all Northrop could do was to try to market a lighter land-based F-18L version. Despite having a dramatically superior performance to the carrier-based version, this never found a buyer. After years of litigation, Northrop conceded that the Hornet was a McDonnell Douglas aircraft. **Bill Gunston**

An overview of the second aircraft displays the strange scheme applied to the 'CF-18L'. Spain was another natural F-18L customer, and a suitable paint scheme was applied to the YF-17 which was evaluated by Spanish pilots. Having unsuccessfully fought another design in the ACF fly-off, the Northrop aircraft was now in competition with itself (at least the McDonnell Douglas-developed version of it). Both Spain and Canada opted for the navalised F-18, ending Northrop's two best chances of getting the F-18L into production. The fact that Northrop gained a sizeable amount of work as the primary sub-contractor on the F/A-18 programme was of little comfort to the design team.

Flying with the
Firebirds

The original caption for this photo read simply 'Get at that beer!'. Flying the Lightning was exhilarating but could be exhausting, particularly during an aerobatic display.

Right: The 'Firebirds' were justifiably proud of their position as arguably the RAF's premier fighter squadron. Their F.Mk 1As were the most flamboyantly marked of all the Lightnings, featuring not only a large checkerboard and squadron badge, but also a stylised fin-flash and liberal amounts of red paint on spines, fins and leading edges.

The 'Firebirds' five-ship formation pulls over the top of a barrel roll during the 1963 display season. With nine Lightnings the team ranked as one of the noisiest to have ever taken to the air. The following year the official RAF team mantle was adopted by Jet Provosts – one of the slowest and quietest jet display mounts.

For a generation of RAF pilots the ultimate flying tour was on the Lightning, the first and the last Mach 2+ front-line fighter of all British designs. The Lightning was fast, agile and responsive, a real adrenalin machine, albeit primitive and crude, with a cockpit workload that only the best could cope with. Every pilot's ambition was to go single-seat/air defence after training, and join the elite: the Lightning force.

On 4 April 1957, the same day that the government announced that manned aircraft would soon be replaced by missiles, the first P.1 prototype made its maiden flight. On 4 August 1958 the more powerful P.1B took to the air. The Lightning survived, being considered too far developed to cancel, and it promised to be a useful interim interceptor, pending the availability of missiles. Since the Lightning was thought to be only an interim type, it was never sufficiently developed, and the RAF ended up with an aircraft handicapped by a ludicrously short range. Nevertheless, with its IR-homing Firestreak missiles, Ferranti AI.23 Airpass radar and breathtaking performance, the aircraft represented a quantum leap over the subsonic, cannon-armed Hunter, and was eagerly awaited by the pilots of Fighter Command.

Despite its shortcomings, the Lightning was destined to give full value for money, entering service

with the Air Fighting Development Squadron in December 1959 and continuing in front-line service until 1988.

Squadron Leader Henryk Ploszek was a pilot on one of the first Lightning units and went on to fly the Lightning for three operational tours, instructing on No. 226 OCU for a further tour and acting as unit test pilot at the Lightning MU at Leconfield for another.

"After a tour on Hunters with No. 43 Squadron I was posted to Stradishall in September 1960 to join No. 56 Squadron, also with Hunters. The Hunter is a beautiful aeroplane – the queen of the skies – but I was looking forward no end to converting onto the Lightning. When we got the Lightning, in December, there was no two-seat trainer version and only a very basic simulator, so you did the ground school, a couple of sorties in the simulator and then your first Lightning trip, with a chase Hunter tagging along.

Firebirds

Above: As the first unit to get the true operational F.Mk 1A, No. 56 Sqn was the elite of the Air Force, a fact reflected in the esprit de corps of the unit at the time. This proud group is seen at the press day in May 1961, celebrating the full equipment of the squadron. Among the aircrew is 'The Boss' – Sqn Ldr David Seward (fourth from left), narrator Flt Lt Henryk Ploszek (second from right) and Flt Lt Terry Thompson (third from right), a very fortunate RCAF exchange officer.

"The instructor in the Hunter got airborne first and then said 'Right, Go!' You put on full power and took off while he flew over as fast as he could, having picked up enough speed to keep up with you for the first part of the climb. He was there to give you advice if anything went wrong. You'd just do a climb, which took about five minutes, a bit of handling, and then come back for a straight-in approach to land.

First solo

"I was about the sixth or the seventh on the squadron to get converted, and my first solo was on 3 March 1961. On the Lightning the nose gear retracts forwards, and you have to retract it below 220 kts or the airflow will overcome the jack, and there you are with the gear hanging, unable to retract it, climbing away with a nosewheel red. It didn't do the aircraft any harm, but you had to slow down, wait for the gear to come up, and then accelerate again. So every time anybody went off on a first solo everyone went out to watch, and I was

Right: One of the most spectacular manoeuvres of the 'Firebirds' team was the arrowhead bomb-burst. Although the team became the stuff of legend, it was the official RAF display team for only a short while from 1963, having taken over from the Lightning F.Mk 1s of No. 74 Sqn ('The Tigers'). Such were the operational commitments and maintenance headaches encountered in readying at least nine aircraft on one day that they performed relatively few displays during their brief existence.

Below: The F.Mk 1A was the first variant to introduce a refuelling probe, so No. 56 Sqn were given the unenviable task of performing the first trials with the type, including a proving deployment to Cyprus. Here Flt Lt Mike Graydon is plugged into a Valiant B(K).Mk 1 of No. 214 Sqn, with Sicily's Mount Etna looming far below. The relative attitudes of the Lightning and Valiant give some idea of the problems encountered, quite apart from the offset position of the probe.

Main picture: A view not many pilots saw of a Lightning in 1963 as the 'Firebirds' practice their formation routine. With its legendary performance, notably in the climb, the Lightning could escape from any situation it found itself in, while its excellent radar enabled it to manoeuvre into an optimum attacking position long before its quarry could detect its approach.

determined that I was not going to be slow in getting the gear up. I practised on the simulator, and decided that as soon as I got airborne I'd go into a turn to make sure my speed didn't build up, giving me time to get the wheels up. Of course, I got bollocked by the senior officer on the conversion team for that, so I remember my first Lightning solo very well!

"The normal sortie length was about 35 or 40 minutes, and if you got 50 minutes you were really stretching it. If you took off in reheat, did a reheat climb and then accelerated in reheat you could have a 20-minute sortie, and that was fairly typical. If you were using reheat continuously you could run out of fuel in 15 minutes.

"Serviceability was poor initially, and the aircraft were being used for converting the other guys, so we started off flying under 10 hours per month on the Lightning, keeping our hands in on the Hunter, or even the hack Meteor.

"Initially we didn't use the aircraft to its full capability; we used it like a swept-up Hunter, and the only change was having the performance and the Firestreak missiles. At Wattisham, we and Treble-One had the first really operational aircraft, the Mk 1As, because the Mk 1s used by No. 74 only had UHF radios and weren't equipped for inflight refuelling.

Refuelling trials

"On No. 56 we did the first Lightning trials with inflight refuelling, and that turned into a bit of a saga, because no-one in the RAF had done inflight refuelling using a displaced probe.

"The Javelin, the Vulcan and the rest all had probes sticking out in front, but English Electric put the probe under the wing, where you couldn't see it. They sent us to the USAF at Woodbridge to do some inflight refuelling sitting in the back of their F-100 Super Sabres, which had a probe sticking out from under the wing. We found that you couldn't fly the probe into the basket, but just had to line yourself up with the tanker and ease forward, not looking at the probe tip at all. After that we did some tanking with our Lightnings and the Valiant tankers, and we virtually wrote the rule-book on refuelling for the Lightning.

"We did the first overseas deployment. The Boss and John Curry flew two aircraft out to Cyprus with Valiant tankers. Ian Thompson and myself flew out on the support aircraft. We did a quick trip there, then the next day Ian and I flew the aircraft back with the tankers. As we got half way up Italy we could talk to UK on HF. Apparently the weather was very bad, so they launched about another four tankers to top up our tankers and we had to divert to

English Electric Lightning F.Mk 1A
No. 56 Squadron 'Firebirds',
RAF Wattisham, 1963

The 'Firebirds' received their first Lightning F.Mk 1A in December 1960, and by March 1961 were fully equipped, operating XM172 to XM183 inclusive. During the F.Mk 1A period the squadron's markings were at their most colourful. In April 1965 both No. 56 and co-located No. 111 Sqn began transitioning to the F.Mk 3, dispatching the older Lightnings to the OCU and target facilities flights. In April 1967 the squadron moved to Akrotiri for the defence of Cyprus, and while there upgraded to the F.Mk 6 in September 1971. These returned to Wattisham in January 1975, and the squadron officially converted to Phantoms in June 1976.

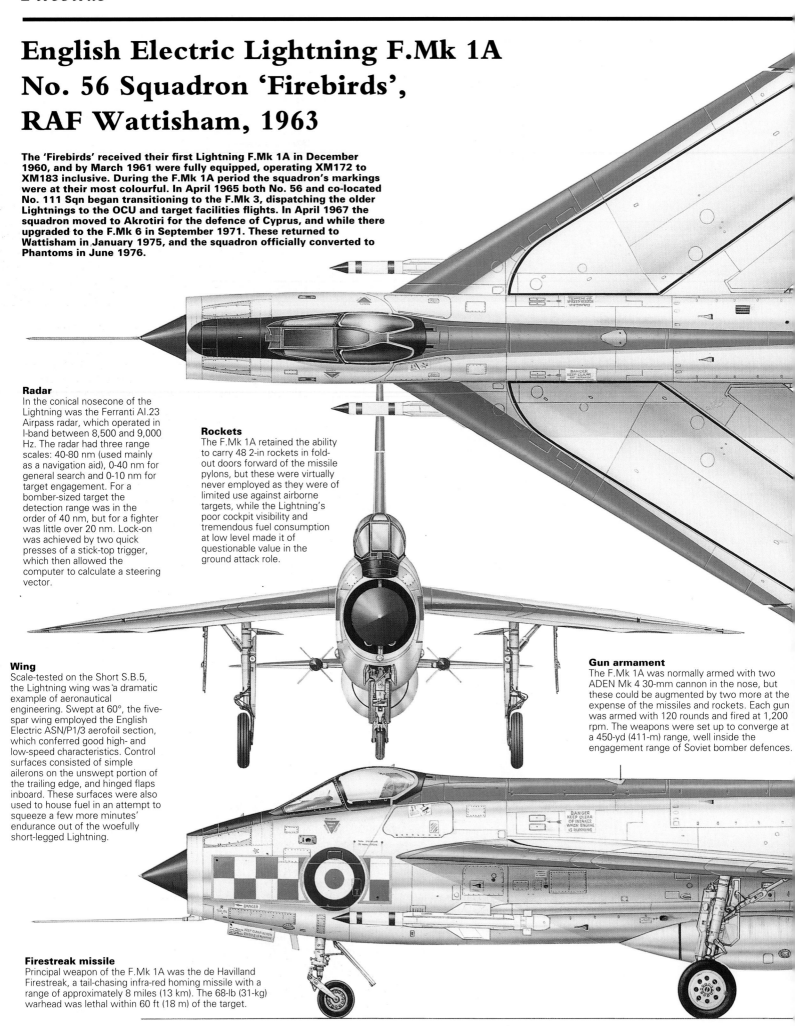

Radar
In the conical nosecone of the Lightning was the Ferranti AI.23 Airpass radar, which operated in I-band between 8,500 and 9,000 Hz. The radar had three range scales: 40-80 nm (used mainly as a navigation aid), 0-40 nm for general search and 0-10 nm for target engagement. For a bomber-sized target the detection range was in the order of 40 nm, but for a fighter was little over 20 nm. Lock-on was achieved by two quick presses of a stick-top trigger, which then allowed the computer to calculate a steering vector.

Rockets
The F.Mk 1A retained the ability to carry 48 2-in rockets in fold-out doors forward of the missile pylons, but these were virtually never employed as they were of limited use against airborne targets, while the Lightning's poor cockpit visibility and tremendous fuel consumption at low level made it of questionable value in the ground attack role.

Wing
Scale-tested on the Short S.B.5, the Lightning wing was a dramatic example of aeronautical engineering. Swept at 60°, the five-spar wing employed the English Electric ASN/P1/3 aerofoil section, which conferred good high- and low-speed characteristics. Control surfaces consisted of simple ailerons on the unswept portion of the trailing edge, and hinged flaps inboard. These surfaces were also used to house fuel in an attempt to squeeze a few more minutes' endurance out of the woefully short-legged Lightning.

Gun armament
The F.Mk 1A was normally armed with two ADEN Mk 4 30-mm cannon in the nose, but these could be augmented by two more at the expense of the missiles and rockets. Each gun was armed with 120 rounds and fired at 1,200 rpm. The weapons were set up to converge at a 450-yd (411-m) range, well inside the engagement range of Soviet bomber defences.

Firestreak missile
Principal weapon of the F.Mk 1A was the de Havilland Firestreak, a tail-chasing infra-red homing missile with a range of approximately 8 miles (13 km). The 68-lb (31-kg) warhead was lethal within 60 ft (18 m) of the target.

Right: Touching down at Wattisham, an F.Mk 1A streams the Irving brake chute. The highly-swept wings conferred good handling qualities at most speeds, but the simple flaps and airbrakes could not stop the aircraft becoming a 'hot ship'. Landing at speeds of 175 mph (280 km/h) on the very thin wheels required a healthy supply of tyres, a problem further exacerbated in crosswind operations.

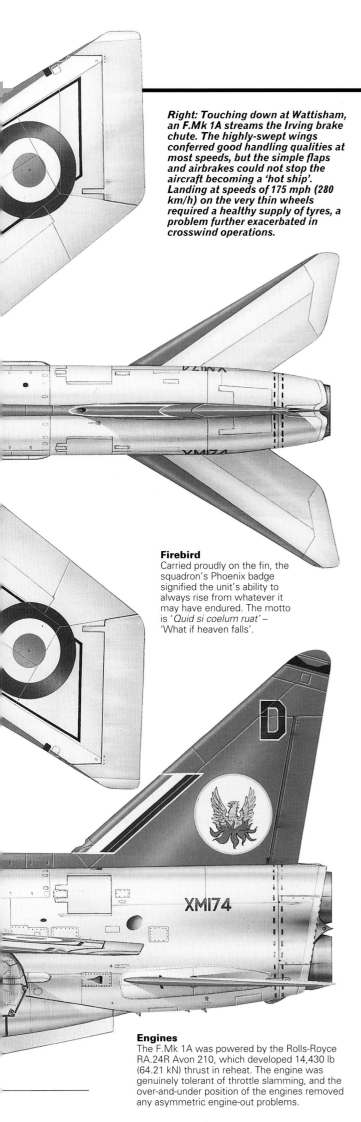

Firebird
Carried proudly on the fin, the squadron's Phoenix badge signified the unit's ability to always rise from whatever it may have endured. The motto is '*Quid si coelum ruat*' – 'What if heaven falls'.

XM174

Engines
The F.Mk 1A was powered by the Rolls-Royce RA.24R Avon 210, which developed 14,430 lb (64.21 kN) thrust in reheat. The engine was genuinely tolerant of throttle slamming, and the over-and-under position of the engines removed any asymmetric engine-out problems.

Warton. We were royally entertained, stopped the night, then flew back to Wattisham the next day.

"We started standing Q [QRA - Quick Reaction Alert] in the early days, virtually as soon as we became operational. It didn't come around that often, because there were quite a few squadrons sharing the commitment. At Wattisham, we were part of Southern Q, shared between us, Binbrook and Leconfield, and we had a fortnight on, then four weeks off. We'd sit on the end of the runway, as we did on exercise, on daytime Q, and the Javelin units had the night-time commitment. We could get airborne very quickly, and from cockpit readiness we could be airborne within a minute and a half.

UFO scramble

"The first live scramble I got on QRA was to intercept a UFO! There had been a number of sightings, very high up, of something flashing in the sky. It was all over the papers. The next day I was on Q and the thing was

seen again, so Fighter Command decided to scramble me. The controller briefed me and said, 'Look, we've got this UFO. I can't see it on radar, but it's been seen by another aircraft at very high altitude, and it's directly over Woodbridge. We'll position you for a high-speed run so that you can accelerate and climb as high as you can to identify it.'

"So they scrambled me, and I went out about 140 miles east, then turned round and accelerated to about [Mach] 1.5 or 1.6, going towards land. That was normally absolutely forbidden. Anyway, I pulled up and climbed to 50-odd thousand and there was the UFO, way, way above me. I identified it as a high-altitude balloon with a gondola swinging beneath it. As I watched, it swung under the light, seeming to change shape from a cigar to a ball, and from the ground it must have looked very strange indeed.

"From very early on, we knew that in 1963 we'd take over the commitment as the Fighter Command Aerobatic Team from No. 74, who were performing with their Lightning F.Mk 1s as the 'Tigers'. We did Paris, and that was the highlight of the Firebirds' display season. I think we went down very well there, and I gather that the audience actually clapped, which was very unusual for anyone except the 'Patrouille de France'!

"We started working up in February 1963, with occasional close formation aerobatics sorties. We had a collision during one practice. On 6 June Mike Cook's wing clipped the missile on

The full nine-ship 'Firebirds' formation performs a loop during practice. The display Lightnings had smoke-making oil injected from a small nozzle into the exhaust from the lower jetpipe.

No. 56 SQUADRON

"The Firebirds"

ROYAL AIR FORCE
FIGHTER COMMAND

Above: This brochure was produced in 1963 to introduce the 'Firebirds' and the squadron.

Left: An unusual formation consists of a Hurricane and two Spitfire PR.Mk XIXs from the Battle of Britain Flight, flanked by two Lightning F.Mk 1As from No. 56 Sqn, with an F.Mk 1 from No. 226 OCU in the slot. The OCU was formed out of the Lightning Conversion Squadron on 1 June 1963. Based at Middleton St George until April 1964, when it moved to Coltishall, it was assigned the 'shadow' identity of No. 145 Sqn. In the early days it operated T.Mk 4 trainers alongside ex-No. 74 Sqn F.Mk 1s.

another aircraft as he rolled out from a break. His aircraft started rolling, because he'd lost his ailerons. He couldn't control it so he ejected. Unfortunately, as he ejected there was a fault in the seat, and as he separated from it, he was pulled out on one side, and his neck whipped around. He landed in a ploughed field and just lay there motionless. I had to direct the ambulances to find him. He'd broken his back, so they had to drive him to Ipswich hospital at about 5 mph, but they could do nothing there and they helicoptered him to Stoke Mandeville the next day. He

survived, but is still in a wheelchair. The other guy landed safely.

Display routine

"The actual display started with a reheat stream take-off, going into a rotation at the end of the runway. Then we joined up into a nine-ship formation for various manoeuvres before splitting into a five and a four, so that we could always keep something in front of the public; as one formation finished a loop the other would come in for a roll. I was No. 3 in the five-ship. We then rejoined for a final break and then landed. It

was a very short display.

"In those days each Command had its own display team, but the Fighter Command team was nominated as the overall Air Force team because we used such a big, impressive, noisy aircraft. It was very expensive to run, and because we had to maintain our operational status we only did five displays in the year, at the end of the season. We'd be doing our normal training throughout the year, using two or three aircraft, and then before each display the ground crew would have a big push to get 10 or 11 aircraft on the line. Serviceability was quite a problem, and we

couldn't have kept it up continuously.

"We were actually the last Fighter Command team and in 1964 the Training Command team, the 'Red Pelicans', was tasked to do the Farnborough show. Its Jet Provosts were very slow after our Lightnings, so when it was found that RAF Valley had an informal and rather illegal team of five yellow Gnats, the 'Yellowjacks', they decided to split the 30-minute Farnborough show slot and give half to the 'Pelicans' and half to the 'Yellowjacks'. That was such a success that the next year they formed the 'Red Arrows' with

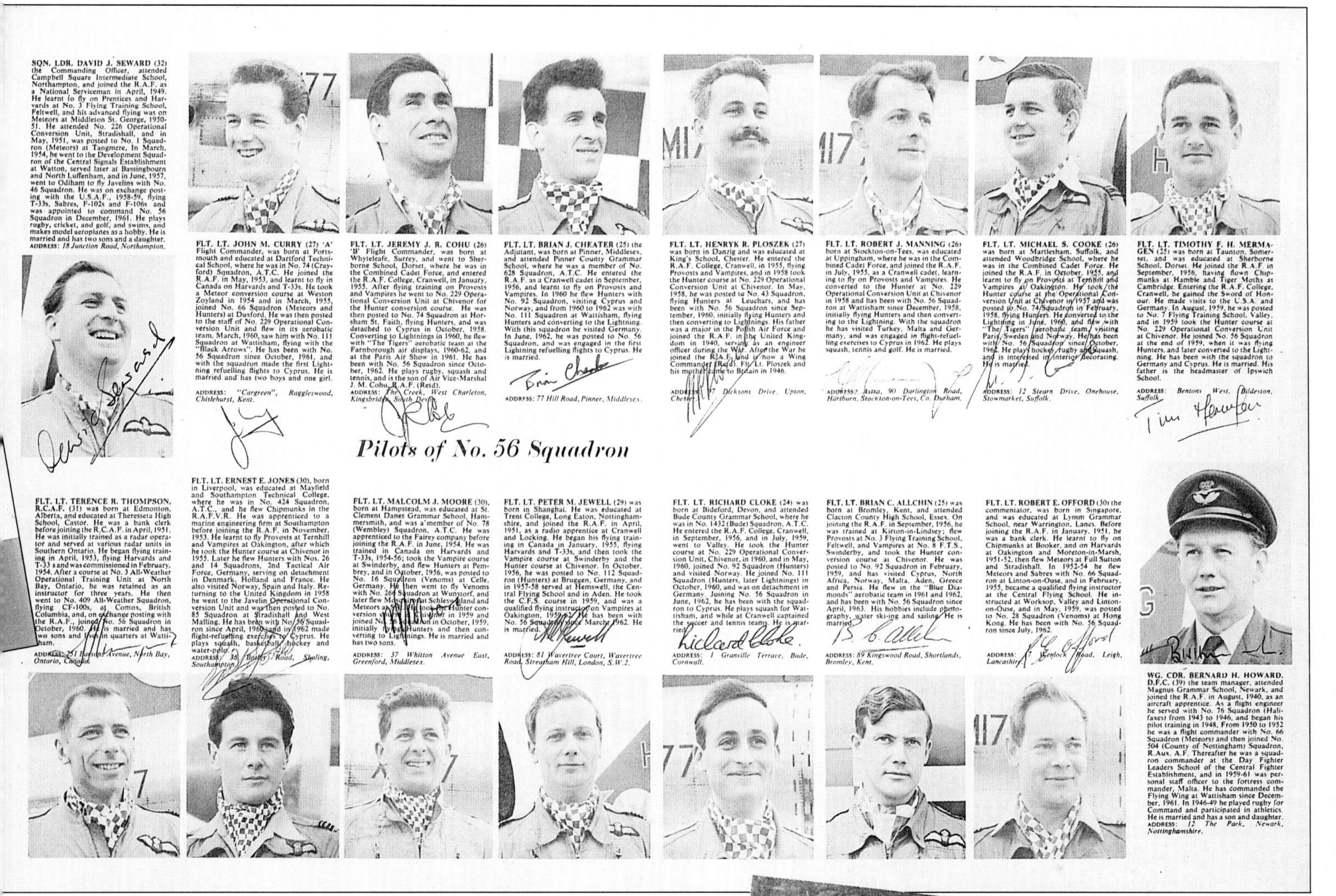

SQN. LDR. DAVID J. SEWARD (32) the Commanding Officer, attended Campbell Square Intermediate School, Northampton, and joined the R.A.F. as a National Serviceman in April, 1949. He learnt to fly on Prentices and Harvards at No. 3 Flying Training School, and his advanced flying was on Meteors at Middleton St. George, 1950-51. He attended No. 226 Operational Conversion Unit, Stradishall, and in May, 1951, was posted to No. 1 Squadron (Meteors) at Tangmere. In March, 1954, he went to the Development Squadron of the Central Signals Establishment at Watton, served later at Bassingbourn and North Luffenham, and in June, 1957, went to Oldham to fly Javelins with No. 46 Squadron. He was on an exchange posting with the U.S.A.F. 1958-59, flying T-33s, Sabres, F-102s and F-106s and was appointed to command No. 56 Squadron in December, 1961. He plays rugby, cricket, and golf, and swims, and makes model aeroplanes as a hobby. He is married and has two sons and a daughter.
ADDRESS: 18 Junction Road, Northampton.

FLT. LT. JOHN M. CURRY (27) 'A' Flight Commander, was born at Portsmouth and educated at Dartford Technical School, where he was in No. 74 (Crayford) Squadron, A.T.C. He joined the R.A.F. in May, 1953, and learnt to fly in Canada on Harvards and T-33s. He took a Meteor conversion course at Weston Zoyland in 1954 and in March, 1955, joined No. 66 Squadron (Meteors and Hunters) at Duxford. He was then posted to the staff of No. 229 Operational Conversion Unit and flew in its aerobatic team. March, 1960, saw him with No. 111 Squadron at Wattisham, flying with the "Black Arrows". He has been with No. 56 Squadron since October, 1961, and with the squadron made the first Lightning refuelling flight to Cyprus. He is married and has two boys and one girl.
ADDRESS: "Cargreen", Ragglesswood, Chislehurst, Kent.

FLT. LT. JEREMY J. R. COHU (26) 'B' Flight Commander, was born at Whyteleafe, Surrey, and went to Sherborne School, Dorset, where he was in the Combined Cadet Force, and entered the R.A.F. College, Cranwell, in January, 1955. After flying tuition on Provosts and Vampires he went to No. 229 Operational Conversion Unit at Chivenor for the Hunter conversion course. He was then posted to No. 74 Squadron at Horsham St. Faith, flying Hunters, and was converting to the Lightning in October, 1958. Converting to Lightnings in 1960, he flew with "The Tigers" aerobatic team at the Farnborough air displays, 1960-62, and at the Paris Air Show in 1961. He has been with No. 56 Squadron since October, 1962. He plays rugby, squash and tennis, and is the son of Air Vice-Marshal J. M. Cohu, R.A.F. (Retd.).
ADDRESS: The Creek, West Charleton, Kingsbridge, South Devon.

FLT. LT. BRIAN J. CHEATER (25) the Adjutant, was born at Pinner, Middlesex, and attended Pinner County Grammar School, where he was a member of No. 628 Squadron, A.T.C. He entered the R.A.F. as a Cranwell cadet in September, 1956, and learnt to fly on Provosts and Vampires. In 1960 he flew Hunters with No. 92 Squadron, visiting Cyprus and Norway, and from 1960 to 1962 was with No. 111 Squadron at Wattisham, flying Hunters and converting to the Lightning. With this squadron he visited Germany in June, 1962, he was posted to No. 56 Squadron, and was engaged in the first Lightning refuelling flights to Cyprus. He is married.

FLT. LT. HENRYK R. PLOSZEK (27) was born in Danzig and was educated at King's School, Chester. He entered the R.A.F. College, Cranwell, in 1955, flying Provosts and Vampires, and in 1958 took the Hunter course at No. 229 Operational Conversion Unit at Chivenor. In May, 1958, he was posted to No. 43 Squadron, flying Hunters at Leuchars, and has been with No. 56 Squadron since September, 1960, initially flying Hunters and then converting to the Lightning. His father was a major in the Polish Air Force and joined the R.A.F. in the United Kingdom in 1940, serving as an engineer officer during the War. After the War he joined the R.A.F. and his mother came to Britain in 1946.
ADDRESS: 7 Dickson's Drive, Upton, Chester.

FLT. LT. ROBERT J. MANNING (26) was born at Stockton-on-Tees, and attended Woodbridge School, where he was in the Combined Cadet Force. He joined the R.A.F. in October, 1955, and learnt to fly on Provosts and Vampires at Oakington. He took the Hunter course at the Operational Conversion Unit at Chivenor in 1957 and was posted in No. 74 Squadron in February, 1958, flying Hunters in June, 1960, and flew with "The Tigers" aerobatic team, visiting Paris, Sweden and Norway. He has been with No. 56 Squadron since December, 1958, initially flying Hunters and then converting to the Lightning. He plays squash, tennis and golf. He is married.
ADDRESS: Astra, 90 Darlington Road, Hartburn, Stockton-on-Tees, Co. Durham.

FLT. LT. MICHAEL S. COOKE (26) was born at Martlesham, Suffolk, and attended Woodbridge School, where he was in the Combined Cadet Force. He joined the R.A.F. in October, 1955, and learnt to fly on Provosts at Ternhill and Vampires at Oakington. He took the Hunter course at the Operational Conversion Unit at Chivenor in 1958 and has been with No. 56 Squadron at Wattisham since December, 1958. The squadron he visited Turkey, Malta and Germany, and was engaged in flight-refuelling exercises to Cyprus in 1962. He plays squash, tennis and golf. He is married.
ADDRESS: 12 Stearn Drive, Onehouse, Stowmarket, Suffolk.

FLT. LT. TIMOTHY F. H. MERMAGEN (25) was born at Taunton, Somerset, and was educated at Sherborne School, Dorset. He joined the R.A.F in September, 1956, having flown Chipmunks at Hamble and Tiger Moths at Cambridge. Entering the R.A.F. College, Cranwell, he gained the Sword of Honour. He made visits to the U.S.A. and Germany. In August, 1959, he was posted to No. 7 Flying Training School, Valley, and in 1959 took the Hunter course at No. 229 Operational Conversion Unit at Chivenor. He joined No. 56 Squadron and flew with the squadron to Germany and Cyprus. He is married. His father is the headmaster of Ipswich School.
ADDRESS: Bentons, West, Bildeston, Suffolk.

Pilots of No. 56 Squadron

FLT. LT. TERENCE R. THOMPSON, R.C.A.F. (31) was born at Edmonton, Alberta, and educated at Theresetta High School, Castor. He was a bank clerk before joining the R.C.A.F. in April, 1951. He was initially trained as a radar operator and served at various radar units in Southern Ontario. He began flying training in April, 1953, flying Harvards and T-33 s and was commissioned in February, 1954. After a course at No. 3 All-Weather Operational Training Unit at North Bay, Ontario, he was retained as an instructor for three years. He then went to No. 409 All-Weather Squadron, flying CF-100s, at Comox, British Columbia, and, on exchange posting with the R.A.F., joined No. 56 Squadron in October, 1960. He is married and has two sons and lives in quarters at Wattisham.
ADDRESS: 231 Harwood Avenue, North Bay, Ontario, Canada.

FLT. LT. ERNEST E. JONES (30), born in Liverpool, was educated at Mayfield and Southampton Technical College, where he was in No. 424 Squadron, A.T.C. and he flew Chipmunks in the R.A.F.V.R. He was apprenticed to a marine engineering firm at Southampton before joining the R.A.F. in November, 1953. He learnt to fly Provosts at Ternhill and Vampires at Oakington, after which he took the Hunter course at Chivenor in 1955. Later he flew Hunters with No. 26 and 14 Squadrons, 2nd Tactical Air Force, Germany, serving on detachment in Denmark, Holland and France. He also visited Norway, Spain and Italy. Returning to the United Kingdom in 1958 he went to the Javelin Operational Conversion Unit and was then posted to No. 85 Squadron at Stradishall and West Malling. He has been with No. 56 Squadron since April, 1960, and in 1962 made flight-refuelling exercises to Cyprus. He plays squash, basketball, hockey and water-polo.
ADDRESS: 30, Bowley Road, Sholing, Southampton.

FLT. LT. MALCOLM J. MOORE (30), born at Hampstead, was educated at St. Clement Danes Grammar School, Hammersmith, and was a member of No. 78 (Wembley) Squadron, A.T.C. He was apprenticed to the Fairey company before joining the R.A.F. in June, 1954. He was trained in Canada on Harvards and T-33s, 1954-56; took the Vampire course at Swinderby, and the Hunter course at Pembrey, and in October, 1956, was posted to No. 56 Squadron (Venoms) at Celle, Germany. He then went to the Venoms to No. 266 Squadron at Wunstorf, and later flew Meteors at Schleswigland and Meteors and was posted to No. 85 Squadron on Hunter conversion and joined No. 56 Squadron in October, 1959, initially flying Hunters and then converting to Lightnings. He is married and has two sons.
ADDRESS: 81 Whitton Avenue East, Greenford, Middlesex.

FLT. LT. PETER M. JEWELL (29) was born at Shanghai. He was educated at St. John's College, Long Eaton, Nottinghamshire, and joined the R.A.F. in April, 1951, as a radar apprentice at Cranwell and Locking. He began his flying training in Canada in January, 1955, flying Harvards and T-33s, and then took the Vampire course at Swinderby and the Hunter course at Chivenor. In October, 1956, he was posted to No. 112 Squadron (Hunters) at Bruggen, Germany, and in 1957-58 served at Hemswell, the Central Flying School and in Aden. He took the C.F.S. course in 1959, and was a qualified flying instructor on Vampires at Oakington, 1959-62. He has been with the squadron since March, 1962. He is married.

FLT. LT. RICHARD CLOKE (24) was born at Bideford, Devon, and attended Bude County Grammar School, where he was in No. 1432 (Bude) Squadron, A.T.C. He entered the R.A.F. College, Cranwell, in September, 1956, and in July, 1959, went to Valley. He took the Hunter course at No. 229 Operational Conversion Unit, Chivenor, in 1960, and on May, 1960, joined No. 92 Squadron (Hunters) and visited Norway. He joined No. 111 Squadron (Hunters, later Lightnings) in October, 1960, and was on detachment in Germany. Joining No. 56 Squadron in June, 1962, he has been with the squadron to Cyprus. He plays squash for Wattisham, and while at Cranwell captained the soccer and tennis teams. He is married.
ADDRESS: 1 Granville Terrace, Bude, Cornwall.

FLT. LT. BRIAN C. ALLCHIN (25) was born at Bromley, Kent, and attended Clacton County High School, Essex. On joining the R.A.F. in September, 1956, he was trained at Kirton-in-Lindsey; flew Provosts at No. 3 Flying Training School, Feltwell, and Vampires at No. 8 F.T.S., Swinderby, and took the Hunter conversion course at Chivenor. He was posted to No. 92 Squadron in February, 1959, and has visited Cyprus, North Africa, Norway, Malta, Aden, Greece and Persia. He flew in the "Blue Diamonds" aerobatic team in 1961 and 1962, and has been with No. 56 Squadron since April, 1963. His hobbies include photography, water ski-ing and sailing. He is married.
ADDRESS: 89 Kingswood Road, Shortlands, Bromley, Kent.

FLT. LT. ROBERT E. OFFORD (30) the commentator, was born in Singapore, and was educated at Lymm Grammar School, near Warrington, Lancs. Before joining the R.A.F. in January, 1951, he was a bank clerk. He learnt to fly on Chipmunks at Booker, and on Harvards at Oakington and Moreton-in-Marsh, 1951-52, then flew Meteors at Full Sutton and Stradishall. In 1952-54 he flew Meteors and Sabres with No. 66 Squadron at Linton-on-Ouse, and in February, 1955, became a qualified flying instructor at the Central Flying School. He instructed at Worksop, Valley and Linton-on-Ouse, and in May, 1959, was posted to No. 28 Squadron (Venoms) at Hong Kong. He has been with No. 56 Squadron since July, 1962.
ADDRESS: 12 The Park, Newark, Nottinghamshire.

WG. CDR. BERNARD H. HOWARD, D.F.C. (39) the team manager, attended Magnus Grammar School, Newark, and joined the R.A.F. in August, 1940, as an aircraft apprentice. As a flight engineer he served with No. 76 Squadron (Halifaxes) from 1943 to 1946, and began his pilot training in 1948. From 1950 to 1952 he was a flight commander with No. 66 Squadron (Meteors) and then joined No. 504 (County of Nottingham) Squadron, R.Aux. A.F. Thereafter he was a squadron commander at the Day Fighter Leaders School of the Central Fighter Establishment, and in 1959-61 was personal staff officer to the fortress commander, Malta. He had commanded the Flying Wing at Wattisham since December, 1961. In 1946-49 he played rugby for Command and participated in athletics. He is married and has a son and daughter.
ADDRESS: 12 The Park, Newark, Nottinghamshire.

Above: The inside of the 'Firebirds' brochure depicted the flying members of the squadron, complete with short autobiographies. Thirty years later the idea of publishing the home addresses for front-line operational pilots is unthinkable!

Gnats, and the rest is history!

"I was with No. 56 for about three years and then I was posted to No. 74 Squadron at Leuchars, where they still had the old F.Mk 1s, but were re-equipping with the new F.Mk 3. The F.Mk 3 was a swept-up version, with bigger engines, Red Top missiles, but no guns. It had slightly higher fuel consumption but retained the original small belly tank, so it was shorter-legged. The F.Mk 3 had the better AI.23B radar as well.

Red Top and rapid start

"The Red Tops had more sensitive seekers, and theoretically they could home onto the infra-red energy generated by the leading edge of a supersonic target, which allowed us to make head-on or beam attacks. Having worked out the geometry, the computer generated a steering dot in the gunsight and you just had to follow that. The F.Mk 3 had a gang bar too, and if you pulled that you turned on the starter switches,

instruments, fuel pumps and pitot heater in one fell swoop. Then you pressed the two starter switches and you were off.

"On No. 74 the Boss made us fly in the partial pressure suit and pressure helmet all the time, even for medium-level exercises. It was cumbersome, if you weren't used to it, and could have been a bit of a flight safety hazard, but if you wore it every time you soon didn't notice it that much. After the 'Tigers' I had a ground tour out at Steamer Point, Aden, for a year, and then came back to the Lightning OCU at Coltishall. That was mainly QWI courses, and I was also involved in converting the Saudis onto the Lightning, using their T.Mk 55s. That was a lovely aeroplane, a T.Mk 5 with a big wing and a big tank, like a two-seat F.Mk 6. Then I had another ground tour, going back to flying in September 1975, flying Lightning F.Mk 6s with No. 56 Squadron in Cyprus."

Sqn Ldr Henryk Ploszek

The Firebirds meet the fashion birds...

CHECKMATE!

What, you might well wonder, have the Firebirds, the RAF's crack aerobatic jet squadron, in common with a fashion mode? The answer, as you'll see if you look closely at the picture, is — CHECKS. Big, bold bold-dazzling checks that appeal to both the Firebirds AND the fashion birds.

The Firebirds — No. 56 Squadron Fighter Command — have adopted bold checkerboard checks in red and white as their motif.

This explains why the chosen checks are splashed all over their helmets, on their neck scarves and even on the side of their 1,500 mph Lightning fighters.

The fashion birds have made the check-clad scene — thanks to the designers who are using similar bold geometric patterns for the first of the autumn styles just zooming into the shops.

SECURITY NOTE: There was no breach on anyone's part. It is a mere coincidence that fighter pilots and fashion models are wearing roughly the same eye-catching gimmick at the same time.

Bringing the Check Set together: Mirror cameraman Bob Hope, who took these pictures on the squadron's base at Wattisham, Suffolk.

Fashion birds meet Firebirds. Shared motif — the checkerboard checks.
HIS checks: On helmet, neck scarf and the plane.
HER checks, left to right in the picture: a black and white sweater by Jaeger 5½ gns., a suit by Mr. Sherman (also seen separately in the picture on the right) and a handwoven and washable wool dress by Donald Davies 11½ gns.

On the tarmac: Fashion bird in a scarlet, black and white suit with its own matching polo-necked sweater, in the background, checkerboard fuselage of a Firebird Lightning fighter. Suit 11½ gns. by Mr. Sherman of London.

The 'glamorous' life of the 1960s fighter pilot occasionally extended beyond the cockpit or the bar, and publicity stunts such as this certainly boosted the 'Fifty Six' image. Henryk Ploszek is the seated pilot.

In many pilots' eyes, the P-51B with the British Malcolm hood was the best of all Mustangs. Lighter, faster and with crisper handling than the bubble-hooded P-51D, the Malcolm hood actually gave better all-round view. The only disadvantage lay in the armament – four instead of six guns – which proved more prone to jamming. Modifications soon solved this problem, and many aces regarded aircraft like this one as the ultimate Mustang. The Iowa Beaut was assigned to the 355th Fighter Group's 354th Fighter Squadron, and has had its topsides camouflaged in two shades of dark green, probably using locally available RAF shades.

North American P-51 Mustang

The fighter that won the War

Designed and built for the British Royal Air Force as an alternative to NAA-built P-40s, for use in the tactical reconnaissance and fighter-bomber roles, the P-51 Mustang rapidly demonstrated such prowess that it was adopted by the USAAC. Transformed by the addition of the Rolls-Royce Merlin (to meet an RAF requirement), the Mustang became a more useful aircraft, a long-range air superiority escort fighter capable of taking the bombers all the way to Berlin. Bomber losses dropped, and it was the turn of the Luftwaffe's fighter arm to take a mauling. The Mustang's contribution to winning the war cannot be overstated.

First of the breed. The NA-73X is seen during a test flight, probably in spring 1941 after being rebuilt following a 20 November 1940 crash landing. Though not a US Army aircraft, it wears Army-style red/white fin colours.

Quality workmanship is evident in the NA-73X prototype (NX19998), seen with no markings or anti-glare shield prior to its first flight, just 186 days after the start of the design. This aircraft later crashed and was rebuilt and painted to more closely resemble a US Army Air Forces craft, although it was of course built as a new fighter design for Britain's Royal Air Force. The three-bladed propeller was retained by the Mustang I, XP-51 P-51A, A-36A, and F-6A Mustang variants.

AG345 was the first production Mustang I for the RAF and made its maiden flight on 23 April 1941, piloted by Louis Wait. Retained by North American for tests, this ship has the short carburettor air scoop atop its nose cowling – later extended to coincide with the propeller hub.

After World War II, Reichsmarschall Hermann Göring, former No. 2 in the Nazi hierarchy and supreme commander of the mighty Luftwaffe, said, "When I saw Mustangs over Berlin, I knew the war was lost." He had earlier proclaimed that "no enemy bomber will cross the Reich Frontier", and without the P-51 Mustang escort fighters his boast might to all intents and purposes have been proved true, at least in daylight hours. It is almost impossible to overstate the importance of the P-51 Mustang to the US war effort, particularly when used as a long-range escort fighter. Having flown 600 miles (965 km) from its bases in Britain, Italy or the Pacific, the Mustang could successfully engage in head-to-head combat with enemy fighters and come out on top. And today, despite some major faults and drawbacks, the Mustang has become a legend, the most famous fighter of World War II.

The eventual largest customer for the fantastically successful P-51 was initially by no means sure that the North American company could even build the superior fighter aircraft they promised, and refused to place an order for the aircraft that became the Mustang. Hostility to the new type persisted even when the British Royal Air Force ordered it as an alternative to licence-built Curtiss P-40s. The US Army Air Corps initially failed even to send a test pilot or engineer to collaborate with the designers. The USAAC thought it had all the fighters it needed, and so showed no interest in the aircraft being built for Britain. Like the RAF, the USAAC initially failed to see the Mustang's true air-to-air combat potential. When it did at last place an order it was for a version tailored specifically to ground attack and dive bombing.

Another quirk in the tale is that the Mustang familiar to every enthusiast today – the bubble-hooded, Merlin-engined P-51D – is a totally redesigned version of the basic Mustang which played a major role only in the final year and a half of the war. From 1941 until the winter of 1943-44, the Mustang served in every theatre of war in versions which looked very different, early versions of which might hardly be recognised by the uninitiated if they were to appear at one of today's air shows.

Genesis

Between the world wars the British aircraft industry included over 50 companies which designed and built aeroplanes. Twenty of these were world famous. The idea that they should collaborate with a foreign partner, or that the RAF might ever need to buy from abroad, was unthinkable. By 1937, however, the growing possibility of war with Hitler's Germany quite suddenly threw not only Britain but France into a panic. Both countries went shopping for aircraft in the United States.

Both went to North American Aviation (NAA), and placed substantial orders for the NA-16 advanced trainer, which the RAF named the Harvard. NAA was quite a small team. Formed in 1934 with 75 employees, it searched for a place to build a factory and selected Inglewood, Los Angeles. Work began there only a year earlier, in 1936, and they took any work they could get, such as building seaplane floats for other manufacturers. But NAA had ambitions, and had the potential to grow fast. They were in the right place, surrounded by an economy that was once again booming, and which was to a high degree based on high-technology aviation. They had engineers who were skilled in the design of advanced all-metal stressed-skin aircraft. Their management, led by President James H. ('Dutch') Kindelberger, took rapid and correct decisions. And they set out to build aeroplanes for war, which they could see would sell like the proverbial hot cakes in Europe.

Sir Henry Self of the British Purchasing Commission was posted to New York to see how American industry could help his country's war needs. Barely had he arrived when Self began seeing terms like 'urgent' and 'high priority' in despatches reaching him from home.

The team of British purchasers found only two American fighters which might be of some use to the Royal Air Force. Neither was ideal. The Bell P-39 Airacobra and Curtiss P-40 Warhawk were not up to the standards of performance of the latest British and German fighters, but they were the best that America had to offer. They promised to be useful ground-attack machines, allowing the precious

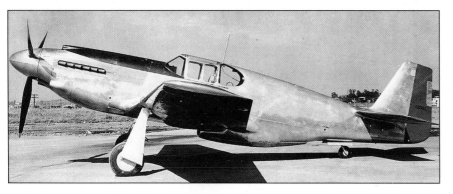

Development and Prototypes

Contrary to the legend of the Mustang, the British never set a 120-day, or 180-day, or 186-day deadline for completion of the prototype. The only dates set forth in the contract were January 1941 for initial delivery and 30 September 1941 for completion – both handily exceeded by North American's energised team.

Although design leader Edgar Schmued, aerodynamicist Edward Horkey and others had access to material on the Curtiss XP-46 fighter, all say that they made minimal use of Curtiss documents in creating the Mustang. Curtiss engineer Fredric Flader, among others, insisted that the XP-46 and the prototype NA-73X were "strikingly similar." When Vance Breese flew the NA-73X on 26 October 1940, it was evident that this was an advanced design mirroring ingenuity and innovation.

AG345, the first production ship for Britain, was ready in April 1941. Breese conducted test flights, with British pilots making spot checks. AG346 became the first ship to reach Britain, in October 1941, a year after the maiden flight. Testing and development was remarkably smooth, as was the US Army's evaluation of the 4th and 10th production RAF Mustang Is, which became XP-51s.

Right: This XP-51 (41-038), the first of two pulled from RAF production for the US Army, arrived at Wright Field on 24 August 1941. This fourth Mustang I (AG348), far from being ignored as reported, was wrung out by test pilots.

Left: The unarmed Curtiss XP-46A 'looked' right but progressed at a glacial pace, not making its initial flight until 15 February 1941, which was still ahead of the armed XP-46. The Mustang programme picked up momentum, while the XP-46 and XP-46A were left behind by history.

Spitfires and Hurricanes to be used for air defence.

The British and French governments placed orders in 1940 for 1,740 Curtiss P-40 Hawk pursuit ships, but neither nation was satisfied with the performance of these aircraft. The British also purchased small numbers of Airacobras. In April 1940, Sir Henry, wanting more and better planes, concluded that the manufacturers he had talked to, so far, had no more production capacity to offer him.

New design

Among Self's contacts was manufacturer North American Aviation (NAA) in Inglewood, which was doing a superb job of building trainers (including NA-16 Harvards for Britain) but had no track record in the design and construction of warplanes. Self's 1939 discussions with the NAA's 'Dutch' Kindelberger, coupled with a December 1939 visit to Inglewood to agree to further contracts for NA-16 trainers, marked the start of events which led to the design of the North American P-51 Mustang. In essence, Self asked North American whether it could build P-40s for the RAF, to augment the flow from Curtiss. The P-40 had its roots in a design of 1933, and NAA's obvious answer was, in so many words, "Yes, if we must, but we could design you a much better fighter ourselves."

'Dutch' Kindelberger had visited the Heinkel and Messerschmitt aircraft factories in 1938 and had taken notes on how the Germans were developing fighters with liquid-cooled engines. Kindelberger convinced the British that instead of gearing up to build P-40s, North American should embark on a more dramatic course. The British purchasing team was briefed on North American's proposed NA-73X by Kindelberger, Vice-President Lee (J. Leland) Atwood, Chief Engineer Ray Rice and a preliminary design team led by Edgar Schmued.

The aircraft that was proposed was a totally new and uncompromised design. According to some accounts, which are now seriously disputed, Kindelberger made the claim, up front, that the prototype could be flying four months from go-ahead. The legend persists that North American Vice President Atwood and a masterful design team (led by Schmued and Rice) cooked up the Mustang from scratch and created it at lightning speed. In fact, Atwood spent months working with the British and, at British insistence, because NAA had no fighter experience, with the Curtiss firm. Curtiss designer Don Berlin had created another sleek fighter called the XP-46 and Atwood was ordered by the British to secure all current data from Curtiss on P-40 developments, including this aircraft.

It requires no graduate diploma in engineering to see that while the XP-46 and P-51 looked similar, they were philosophically miles apart. Even so, the effect of the sale of data and the full magnitude of the Curtiss/Don Berlin contribution to the Mustang remain in dispute to this day. Claims that the Mustang was a copy of the XP-46 are somewhat facile, since the Curtiss aircraft shared only a similar radiator/oil-cooler configuration with the P-51, and did not

Remarkably, the first XP-51 (41-038) has survived. Rebuilt by Darrell Skurich, it flew in the 1970s before being put on display at the Experimental Aircraft Association's Museum in Oshkosh, Wisconsin.

EW998 was the sole example of the NA-97 Invader (the USAAF's A-36) to reach the United Kingdom. This dive-bomber variant, here carrying two 500-lb (227-kg) bombs, was ideally suited to the army co-operation role, but was not pressed into service by the Royal Air Force. The Mustang I, IA and II remained in RAF use until well after D-Day, by which time the surviving airframes were becoming very long in the tooth.

The Mustang was simply too slick for the dive-bombing role, and rapidly built up speed in the dive. To stay at slower, more controllable speeds in very steep dives, more drag was required. Here the RAF's only A-36 Invader (EW998) shows off its fence-style, mid-wing dive brakes. A USAAF report called the A-36 an excellent attack aircraft but an 'inferior' dive bomber, and urged that the dive brakes be deleted. The RAF felt that the A-36 offered no major advantage over the Mustang I, although its Mustang IIs were effectively A-36s without dive brakes.

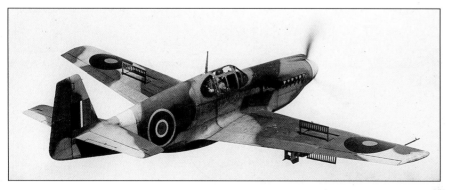

have laminar flow wings. It did, however, use automatic leading-edge slats similar to those of the Bf 109, and had various other innovative features that were wisely ignored by the North American team. Cynics suggest that the XP-46 data was most useful in suggesting directions not to follow! Moreover, development of the XP-46 lagged behind that of the Mustang, and prototypes were not ready to fly until February 1941. Furthermore, preliminary design of the P-51 was completed before NAA gained access to the Curtiss material. In addition to the Curtiss material upon which it was later alleged to have drawn so heavily – although there have been convincing denials by Schmued and aerodynamicist Edward Horkey – NAA drew upon the latest aerodynamic research by NACA (National Advisory Committee for Aeronautics).

Timescale

Atwood and Kindelberger presented the British with a preliminary design less than four months after the blueprints were approved by the British Purchasing Commission. The British also suggested that a timescale of 120 days, from approval of drawings (or from the date of the order, according to some sources) to prototype roll-out (or first flight according to some), would be a good target, although this legendary timescale has since been misinterpreted and consequently denied ever since.

Britain's request was made in April 1940, and the preliminary design was approved by Sir Henry Self, Air Vice-Marshal G. B. A. Baker and Mr H. C. B. Thomas on 4 May. The British order was placed on 29 May 1940. Final assembly and engine installation began on 9 September (127 days after approval, 102 days after the British order), and ground running of the engine on 11 October. The first flight followed on 26 October.

Some 78,000 engineering hours and 127 days went into the first prototype, which was rolled into the sunlight at Mines Field in Los Angeles on 9 September 1940. So hastily had the new fighter been assembled that it had no engine (until 7 October) and, in the absence of the new disc brakes, the aircraft was rolled out on wheels borrowed from an AT-6 trainer.

The delay in receiving an engine was due to the fact that, as a private venture, the NA-73X was given 'government furnished equipment' on an as-available basis, and was

not accorded a high priority by comparison with P-40s rolling off the production lines for the Army Air Corps. The 1,150-hp (862-kW) Allison V-1710-F3R engine was eventually installed, and freelance test pilot Vance Breese made a successful first flight on 26 October.

The company also had to seek Army Air Corps permission for its plant to be thus committed to a foreign contract. This was granted, but in return the Army requested that two examples of the NA-73 should be supplied without charge for testing at Wright Field. The fourth and 10th production aircraft off the line were delivered to Wright Field as XP-51s and were evaluated, although no orders were initially placed by the USAAC.

NAA went into top gear and hired almost anyone who wanted a job, to work not only on the new fighter but also on the existing trainers and on the series of advanced twin-engined bombers which was already in design, and which culminated in the B-25 Mitchell. They settled down to working two eight-hour shifts, seven days a week. Ironically, at this time British industry was still mainly working a single shift, while the German industry – considering the war already won – was working a single shift at about half its potential output.

Description

Predictably, the NA-73X was 'clean as a hound's tooth'. The aerodynamics were as modern as the hour, with the wing, fuselage and cooling system all being more advanced in design than any other fighter at that time. Most notably, the wing was the first fitted to any production aircraft to have a so-called 'laminar' aerofoil profile. Whereas traditional wings had the maximum thickness about one-fifth of the way back from the leading edge, and almost all the camber (surface curvature) on the upper surface, the NACA/NAA profile adopted for the NA-73X had maximum thickness almost half-way back, and nearly as much camber underneath as on top.

This shape forced the air to keep accelerating over almost the entire front half of the wing, so that the favourable pressure gradient (from higher pressure to lower) kept the flow smooth and laminar, whereas in other aircraft it would almost immediately break down into local turbulence, causing extra drag. The drawback was marginally poorer behaviour at lower speeds. The new fighter was going to weigh more than a typical Spitfire, because of a slightly heavier structure and far greater fuel capacity. Because it would have only 233.19 sq ft (21.66 m²) of wing area compared with 242 sq ft (22.48 m²), it was important to make the wing work as well as possible. One result was to fit particularly powerful slotted flaps.

The fuselage was designed with extreme care, and the result was noticeably slimmer than that of rival American fighters. For minimum drag, even at the cost of the weight and combat vulnerability of long piping, the engine coolant and oil radiators were grouped in a long profiled duct under the rear fuselage. During the course of development it was eventually found possible not merely to eliminate the usual drag of radiators but to make the duct give propulsive

Left: Mustang I AM106, wearing a yellow 'P' for prototype enclosed in a yellow circle, served as the trials aircraft for the British S gun. A white stripe on the fuselage was a camera calibration marking for firing trials of the new gun.

A Mustang I of the RAF's No. II Squadron overflies British countryside in July 1942. No. II used Mustang Is to replace its Curtiss Tomahawks, like many Army Co-operation Command units. The national insignia seen here were adopted in August 1941.

Allison-powered Brits

The Allison-powered Mustang was found by British pilots to be faster below 25,000 ft (7740 m) than the Spitfire V, but the RAF never regarded it as primarily an air-to-air fighter. The Mustang was delivered to the Army Co-operation Command of the RAF, as well as Fighter Command, for service as a low-level tactical fighter.

From the time the first Mustang I in England (AG346) was assembled at Burtonwood in October 1941, the RAF moved deliberately to make its best use of the new warplane. The Mustang was a fine replacement for the Curtiss Tomahawk which had been employed until 1942 on Army co-operation duties.

Britain had intially acquired the new fighter with two 0.50-in (12.7-mm) calibre machine-guns in the nose and two more in the wings, plus four 0.30-in (7.62-mm) calibre guns. On the Mustang IA, this familiar armament was replaced by four 20-mm cannons, which was also the initial armament 'set' tried by the USAAF.

By the time the Mustang I flew its first sortie against the French coast near Berck-sur-Mer on 10 May 1942, there was tremendous confidence in this new fighter-bomber. Plenty of changes still lay ahead, however. Mustang Is began to acquire camera ports in their left rear cockpit area. All the way through to VE-Day, the RAF never found a more effective reconnaissance aircraft than the Allison-powered Mustang.

At a display of what were described as 'certain American aircraft soon to be seen in numbers in this country', the fifth Mustang I for Britain (AG349) poses at Burtonwood with a Curtiss Kittyhawk I, a Lockheed Hudson and several Douglas Bostons. The location was an assembly area where aircraft arriving via sea were assembled, made airworthy and air-tested.

Left: Since the first Mustang I stayed at the factory, the second ship (AG346) was the first to reach the UK. AG346 suffered minor damage en route when the ship carrying it was bombed, but it eventually arrived intact on 24 October 1941.

As a lend-lease version of the USAAC P-51, the Mustang IA introduced four wing-mounted 20-mm cannons, but deleted the nose-mounted machine-guns. It retained the Allison engine and the familiar three-bladed propeller. This example has early flame-dampening exhaust stacks which were later replaced by a neatly-arranged row of exhausts.

thrust, by adding heat energy to the air and expelling it at high velocity.

The new fighter was not only outstanding aerodynamically, but it was also the first production aircraft to be designed almost entirely on the basis of conic sections: straight lines, circles, parabolas and hyperbolas. These can be exactly expressed in simple algebraic terms, facilitating the production of drawings, tooling and detail parts. Not only were the leading and trailing edges of the wing and tail as far as possible straight lines but the underlying structure was outstandingly simple, and easy to make and assemble accurately. The man-hours required to make a wing soon fell below two-thirds of the figure for a Spitfire V wing and below half that of a Hurricane or Typhoon wing. Structurally the entire aircraft was Alclad light alloy, all exterior skins being flush-rivetted. The wing was made in left and right halves joined on the centreline. Each had two spars far enough apart for a 0.5-in Browning gun to fit between them with only the barrel projecting through the front spar. Each spar was straight, with plate webs and extruded top and bottom booms, simple ribs pressed from sheet with flanged lightening holes and extruded spanwise stringers to carry the large skin panels.

Fuselage structure

The fuselage was made in three sections, which could be separated by undoing bolts. One joint sloped from the leading edge to just ahead of the windscreen, while the other was vertical immediately in front of the tailwheel. All control surfaces were metal-skinned, and had trim tabs, the rudder and elevators having square mass-balances. The main landing gears were elegantly simple, and with a track of almost 12 ft (3.66 m) made taxiing much simpler than in most fighters. The retracted main wheels were housed in the wing roots, the leading edge being kinked forward to provide room. The retracted wheels were covered by doors hinged near the aircraft centreline, closed again by their own jacks when the landing gears were fully extended. The steerable tailwheel, linked to the rudder, retracted on pivots into a compartment with twin doors.

The Allison engine was carried on rubber blocks on two Y-shaped bearers, made like the wing spars from aluminium sheet and extrusions, attached to the steel firewall at the bolted joint between the front and centre fuselage. The propeller was a three-bladed Curtiss Electric, the hub incorporating an electric motor and reduction gearbox to alter the pitch of the blades. It had a diameter of 10 ft 6 in (3.22 m), with constant-speed and feathering capability. The carburettor was fed by a long duct from an inlet above the cowling about 2 ft (0.6 m) behind the propeller.

The port, cockpit-area camera installation retrofitted in Britain is evident behind the pilot of AL995, the 358th Mustang I, which belongs to the RAF's No. II Squadron.

Fuel was housed in two self-sealing cells between the wing spars, one in each inboard wing. Total capacity was no less than 180 US gal (150 Imp gal; 681 litres), almost double that of a Spitfire. Oil was housed in a 12-US gal (10-Imp gal; 45.5 litre) tank squeezed between the engine and firewall. The engine-cooling radiators were in the form of a giant circular drum behind the cockpit, filling the lower half of the fuselage at this point. The centre of the matrix cooled the oil, and the outer ring the Prestone (glycol) coolant for the cylinders. Warm air for the cockpit could be taken from the duct downstream, which was controlled by a large exit flap driven by a jack behind the pilot's seat.

The comfortable cockpit was directly above the inner ends of the fuel tanks. Behind the spring-mounted seat was a bulkhead reinforced to serve as a crash pylon, to protect the pilot's head should the aircraft overturn on the ground. This frame surrounded a slab of armour to protect the pilot from the rear. The canopy consisted of two fixed windows on the right, a frame on the left with two windows (the front one sliding open to the rear) which could be hinged out and down for access, and a transparent roof which hinged open to the right. After studying a blown Plexiglas windscreen it was decided to meet RAF requirements with a flat 5-ply bullet-proof front screen sloping at 40°. The control column carried a US-style handgrip, rather than a British spade-grip and, again following American practice, the brakes were pedal-operated.

Though electric actuation was common an American aircraft at this time, the new fighter was made essentially all-hydraulic. The engine-driven pump supplied sub-systems at various pressures not only for the landing gear and flaps but also for the brakes. On the other hand, armament control was electric. NAA took care to ensure that the fighter could carry a bomb under each wing if necessary, but the initial armament was guns only. Thanks to British influence, far heavier armament was selected than that common in US Army fighters at this time, although

Mustang I No. 26 Sqn RAF Gatwick 1942

AM101 was the 364th Mustang I for Britain. This aircraft served with No. 26 Squadron, based at RAF Gatwick, where it commenced operations in January 1942. The squadron's main task was flying 'Rhubarbs' (fighter sweeps over occupied France) and 'Poplars' (photographic reconnaissance flights over the French coast).

On moonlit nights the squadron flew 'Rangers' (night fighter-bomber sorties) against rail targets. It participated in Operation Jubilee, the ill-fated Dieppe raid.

The Mustang I served with 24 squadrons of Army Co-operation Command. In October 1942, RAF Mustang Is made their historic raid against the Dortmund Ems canal, becoming the first RAF single-engined fighters to operate over Germany.

Installation of an F24 camera behind the pilot on the port side of the aircraft was a step taken after the Mustang I was in service, performed in the field. This occurred in parallel with the USAAF decision to modify 55 of its initial 150 P-51s as photo-reconnaissance aircraft, using an installation which originated at the NAA plant.

AG357, the 13th Mustang I, carries out a trials flight with rocket projectiles mounted on rails – a potentially ideal weapon for the army co-operation role. The size of the cockpit is evident in this aircraft, which has early flame-damper exhaust stacks.

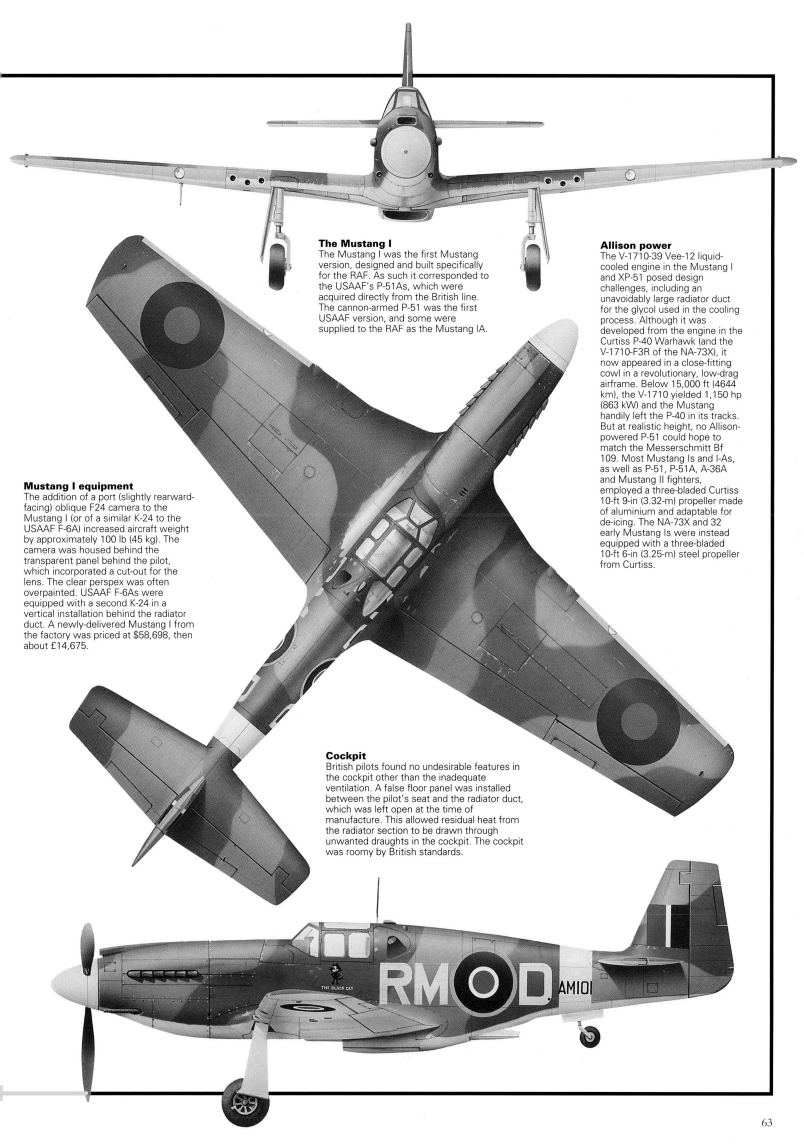

The Mustang I

The Mustang I was the first Mustang version, designed and built specifically for the RAF. As such it corresponded to the USAAF's P-51As, which were acquired directly from the British line. The cannon-armed P-51 was the first USAAF version, and some were supplied to the RAF as the Mustang IA.

Allison power

The V-1710-39 Vee-12 liquid-cooled engine in the Mustang I and XP-51 posed design challenges, including an unavoidably large radiator duct for the glycol used in the cooling process. Although it was developed from the engine in the Curtiss P-40 Warhawk (and the V-1710-F3R of the NA-73X), it now appeared in a close-fitting cowl in a revolutionary, low-drag airframe. Below 15,000 ft (4644 km), the V-1710 yielded 1,150 hp (863 kW) and the Mustang handily left the P-40 in its tracks. But at realistic height, no Allison-powered P-51 could hope to match the Messerschmitt Bf 109. Most Mustang Is and I-As, as well as P-51, P-51A, A-36A and Mustang II fighters, employed a three-bladed Curtiss 10-ft 9-in (3.32-m) propeller made of aluminium and adaptable for de-icing. The NA-73X and 32 early Mustang Is were instead equipped with a three-bladed 10-ft 6-in (3.25-m) steel propeller from Curtiss.

Mustang I equipment

The addition of a port (slightly rearward-facing) oblique F24 camera to the Mustang I (or of a similar K-24 to the USAAF F-6A) increased aircraft weight by approximately 100 lb (45 kg). The camera was housed behind the transparent panel behind the pilot, which incorporated a cut-out for the lens. The clear perspex was often overpainted. USAAF F-6As were equipped with a second K-24 in a vertical installation behind the radiator duct. A newly-delivered Mustang I from the factory was priced at $58,698, then about £14,675.

Cockpit

British pilots found no undesirable features in the cockpit other than the inadequate ventilation. A false floor panel was installed between the pilot's seat and the radiator duct, which was left open at the time of manufacture. This allowed residual heat from the radiator section to be drawn through unwanted draughts in the cockpit. The cockpit was roomy by British standards.

Red the Wrecker III was a cannon-armed P-51, the initial USAAF variant, and was probably seen in Italy. The forward location of the squadron identity codes is noteworthy.

Below: Carrying M-10 smoke tanks (used to dispense smoke screens and tear gas), this trio includes 43-6237 (foreground), the 234th of 310 P-51As. The national insignia with a narrow red surround was only authorised for use between June and August 1943, although examples were still seen months later. The white nose-band was unusual on US-based aircraft.

contemporary British fighters were still largely equipped with the rifle-calibre 0.303-in machine-gun. In the underside of the nose, beside the engine crankcase, were two 0.5-in M2 Browning guns, synchronised to fire past the propeller blades and canted over so that they could be fed from magazines fitting neatly in the bottom of the nose, with case and link collector boxes on their outboard sides. The left gun was staggered ahead of the right so that the magazines could lie one behind the other. Two similar guns were mounted upright inside the wing, outboard of the landing gears. Farther outboard were four Browning guns of 0.30-in calibre, each inboard gun of this calibre (thus, the middle of the group of three) being mounted lower so that its muzzle was below the leading edge. Ammunition for all the wing guns was in three long spanwise boxes outboard of the guns, so that the 0.5-in feed was immediately behind the front spar.

Flight test

The NA-73X prototype was completely unpainted, except for six black aperture shapes painted on the leading edge to show where the guns would be installed. These marks are retouched out in many reproductions of the most famous early photographs of the aircraft. The faired holes for the nose guns were present, however, and in the only other pre-flight photograph commonly seen of the NA-73X the photographer arranged for the left nose gun aperture to be hidden behind the wing tip. Later, the upper fuselage ahead of the cockpit was painted with anti-dazzle black, and later still the registration NX19998 was applied. In one company photograph issued to the press, US Army Air Corps tail stripes were drawn in, though of course they were not painted on the actual aircraft.

Confident of a production order, NAA began producing tooling and collecting material as early as June 1940, and when the initial order for 320 aircraft was signed three months later there was already the beginning of a produc-

tion line. Fortunately, even on the first flight on 26 October test pilot Vance Breese was delighted with the new fighter. The initial flying was all done from Mines Field, adjacent to the plant, which later grew into LA International Airport.

Breese made four flights, after each of which minor modifications were made. The most important was to redesign the forward part of the radiator duct so that the inlet stood entirely away from the underside of the fuselage ahead. The gap ensured that turbulent and sluggish boundary-layer air did not enter the radiator duct. It took about two months, with several aircraft, before the production standard was agreed, with the external form of the duct less bulging and with the inlet moved several inches forward. A more immediately obvious change was to extend the carburettor inlet duct right forward to the nose, immediately behind the propeller. The first four aircraft were all thus modified.

Crash causes delays

From flight No. 5 the test pilot was to be Paul Balfour. Most unfortunately, on his very first familiarisation flight, on 20 November, Balfour made an error in switching fuel-feed and the engine went dead at a critical moment. Balfour had no time to attempt a re-start before aircraft and ground came together. The NA-73X piled up in an upside-down wreck. Unhurt, Balfour was more annoyed than worried as he clambered out of the inverted fighter. A major delay had just been introduced into the Mustang development programme, although the NA-73X did, in fact, resume flying on 11 January 1941 and continued to operate as part of the initial development programme until being retired on 15 July 1941. After Balfour, subsequent testing was headed by R. C. (Bob) Chilton.

With its Wright Field 'arrowhead' marking, pre-war rudder stripes and silver finish, 41-039 was the second RAF Mustang I turned over to the US Army under the terms which enabled Britain to purchase the aircraft. Designated as XP-51s, these aircraft found and solved many problems, including a need for minor changes in the Mustang aileron design.

This P-51A was photographed while pausing at the B-24 base at Kurmitola, India, for repair to minor damage from Japanese gunfire. Allison-powered P-51s, much-needed in the China-Burma-India theater, served first with the 530th FBS of the 311th Fighter Bomber Group from October 1943. They were used in the air-to-ground and air-to-air roles.

In USAAF service

Long after the decision was taken to install the Merlin engine in the Mustang, Allison-powered fighters poured off the NAA production line and showed up in combat groups from one end of the globe to the other.

The A-36A and P-51A were superior to other USAAF pursuit ships – indeed, at low altitude, the Allison Mustang remained in most respects the top-performing fighter of the war – and they were sorely needed everywhere.

It took time to get North American's famous craft into battle. Although British Mustang Is were seeing action by mid-1942, by as late as New Years Day 1944 only half a dozen USAAF combat groups had made the transition to the new fighter. Thereafter, of course, change came with the speed of a tidal wave.

On the home front, Allison-powered Mustangs performed test, training, and developmental work and tested everything from the V-1710 to one-off colour schemes and Arctic skis.

Above: P-51A Mustangs wear the distinctive white stripes of the 1st Air Commando Group over Burma in 1944. Group commander Lt Col Philip 'Flip' Cochran pilots 43-6189 in the background, flying wing on Mrs Virginia (foreground) which displays no serial.

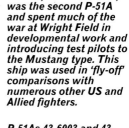

43-6004, or Slick Chick, was the second P-51A and spent much of the war at Wright Field in developmental work and introducing test pilots to the Mustang type. This ship was used in 'fly-off' comparisons with numerous other US and Allied fighters.

P-51As 43-6003 and 43-6005 went to Ladd Field, Alaska, where Lt Col Randy Acord and other pilots flew them with retractable skis. Few problems were found, but after Japan's early thrust at the Aleutians the war produced no further use for a 'Ski Fifty One'.

Above: This early, cannon-armed P-51 Mustang sports a camera blister behind the pilot and a dramatic, 'disruptive' camouflage scheme which was tried briefly at Wright Field.

In December 1940, having toyed with the name Apache, the RAF decided to call its new fighter the Mustang. The NA-73X was later repaired and resumed test flying, but the programme was seriously delayed by Balfour's accident. Indeed, the second aircraft – the first production Mustang, with British serial AG345 – did not fly until 1 May 1941, four months after NAA was contracted to begin deliveries. Moreover, a considerable amount of work remained to be done to bring the Mustang I to an operational standard.

AG345 was initially unpainted apart from having the black anti-dazzle panel and the serial painted by hand, in US style, under the left wing and above the right wing and on a coloured rudder. Later it was given RAF camouflage and markings, armament, a landing light in each wing leading edge, a camera gun in the outer leading edge, the longer carburettor inlet, the definitive radiator inlet and a vertical mast for HF radio. The second series aircraft, AG346, was painted from the outset in RAF day-fighter camouflage, and was the first to be accepted and paid for. It arrived by sea at Liverpool and was flown from RAF Burtonwood on 24 October 1941. On the following day it was flown to the Aeroplane & Armament Experimental Establishment at Boscombe Down, where it was quickly fitted with standard British TR.1133 v.h.f. radio, Mk II★ reflector gunsight, British oxygen connectors and other combat equipment. The instrument panel and compass were wholly American.

First Mustang for England

This first Mustang to reach England was a test ship for many to follow. Although service ceiling at this time was limited to 30,000 ft (9288 m), British pilots were pleased with the fighter, noting only that camouflage paint slowed its maximum airspeed by some 8 mph (13 km/h). Initial test results showed that the American fighter could reach a speed of 375 mph (604 km/h) at 15,000 ft (4644 m), as compared to the British Spitfire Mk V which topped out at 340 mph (548 km/h) at the same height.

To say that AG346 made a favourable impression is a considerable understatement. At all heights up to over 20,000 ft (6096 m) it was faster than any fighter in service with the RAF. At 13,000 ft (3965 m) the speed was measured at 382 mph (615 km/h), and from 7,000 to 20,000 ft (2133 to 6096 m) the margin of speed over the Spitfire V was always greater than 28 mph (49 km/h). Rate of climb, acceleration, speed in a dive, stability, handing in all configurations, rate of roll and radius of turn were all rated satisfactory to outstanding, and in one regard – range – the Mustang 'rewrote the book'. While Spitfires had a range of some 400 miles (640 km) and endurance of two hours, the Mustang could be flown by a pilot unfamiliar with it for four to five hours, covering over 1,000 miles (1600+ km).

On the minus side of the ledger, the Spitfire could climb to 20,000 ft (6192 m) in seven minutes, while the Mustang required 11. Both the Spitfire and Messerschmitt Bf 109 were deemed more nimble at higher altitude. The Mustang, which weighed about a third again as much as a Spitfire, was considered to be underpowered. This was not felt to be a significant problem for the fighter reconnaissance role.

The only major shortcoming, and it was a serious one, was that the Allison F3R engine was supercharged for best performance at low levels. Above about 13,000 ft (3960 m) performance fell away increasingly rapidly, so that at 20,000 ft (6096 m) it was overtaken by the Spitfire V. Of course, the forthcoming Spitfire IX promised from about mid-1942 to fly rings round both, while the latest Bf 109 and Fw 190 variants already could!

A P-51A Mustang (43-6246) in post-August 1943 national insignia with the nose 'plane in group' number of a stateside training squadron. Army olive-drab, weathering, and a certain warlike look all typified USAAF aircraft serving at home.

Bronx Cheer *displays features unique to the A-36A Invader, including its lattice-like aluminium dive brakes, early flame-damping engine exhaust stacks, and paired lights on the port leading edge. It carries 500-lb (227-kg) bombs hung from early-style shackles underwing. The 27th Fighter Bomber Group operated A-36As in North Africa, Sicily and Italy, some with nose guns removed. Ironically, the speed of the Mustang was a hindrance in the dive-bombing role but the aircraft without dive brakes performed well as level bombers.*

This was one of 500 A-36A Apaches or Invaders built by NAA. The aircraft belonged to the 27th FBG in Italy and, in keeping with group practice, originally had its two-letter code applied on the fin. It was flown by Michael Russo, the only A-36 ace. His status was briefly celebrated by the application of a huge skull and crossbones on the fin, but when this was overpainted so were the code letters.

Two swastikas on the nose behind the spinner commemorate air-to-air victories scored by this A-36A Invader of the 86th Fighter Bomber Group. It is seen here undergoing maintenance amid the mud and muck which were a constant challenge to the Allies at forward airfields in Italy. The aircraft's tail is crudely propped up on an oil drum.

Thus, reluctantly, the RAF decided the Mustang would have to go to Army Co-operation Command for use in the tactical reconnaissance role. When the Command's No. 26 Squadron at Gatwick took delivery of its first Mustang Is in January 1942, British pilots finally had an aircraft which – unlike the Curtiss Tomahawk IIA they had been flying – gave them the means to snap back and fight for real if they were bounced by Messerschmitt Bf 109s.

Camera fit

While retaining the full US armament, the Mustang I entered operational service in February 1942 with No. 26 Squadron, carrying an F24 reconnaissance camera fitted immediately behind the seat looking out obliquely to the rear behind the left wingtip, through the fixed window behind the cockpit. Very soon a second camera was installed vertically ahead of the tailwheel, for photography from higher altitudes.

Although the Command's mission was low-level reconnaissance, the RAF had already found that this could usefully be combined with fighter sweep and fighter-bomber roles, and it was soon discovered that the Mustang I excelled at both. The aircraft was a match for any Bf 109 or

Fw 190 at low level, and could deliver bombs with formidable accuracy. By a remarkable chance, the first victory credited to the Mustang was claimed by P/O Hollis H. Hills, an American volunteer (in the Royal Canadian Air Force) from the same state of California whence the aircraft came. He downed an Fw 190 during the Dieppe raid on 19 August 1942, and later joined the US Navy and flew F6F Hellcats. Several other RAF reconnaissance pilots gained victories in the Allison-engined Mustang I, including Duncan 'Bitsy' Grant who scored three victories. On one occasion a pair of RAF Mustang Is downed five enemy aircraft on a single sortie.

More important, but less glamorous, was the Mustang's ability to range far into enemy territory. In October 1942, Mustang Is became the first RAF single-engined fighters to fly over Germany, during a raid on the Dortmund Ems Canal. By this time the RAF had received the 320 NA-73s and most of a second batch of 300 designated as NA-83s, which were almost identical apart from having broad fishtail ejector exhausts. Individual aircraft were used for various test programmes, including underwing rockets, large flush-fitting ferry tanks and (on AM106) two 40-mm Vickers S anti-tank guns. Perhaps the most extraordinary thing about the Mustang I, Mustang IA and Mustang II in RAF service was their astonishing longevity. On D-Day, No. 168 Squadron's active Mustangs included the RAF's second aircraft, AG346. The last front-line RAF Allison-engined Mustangs were phased out in early 1945.

Lend-Lease Mustangs

In March 1941 President Roosevelt signed the Lease-and-Lend Bill, and this resulted in the work of the DPC being supplanted by US funding for war material supplied freely to Allies (i.e. Britain) as long as the war lasted. The first Lend-Lease Mustangs for the RAF were a batch of 150 designated as NA-91s. For contractual purposes they were purchased by the US Army Air Corps under the designation P-51, and the F3R engine received the War Department designation V-1710-39. These aircraft differed from the previous batches mainly in having the even more powerful armament of four Hispano-Suiza M2 20-mm cannon in the wings, with the long barrels projecting far ahead of

A-36A Apache

The A-36A Apache was the US Army Air Forces' derivative of the Mustang I and is sometimes loosely compared to the Junkers Ju 87 'Stuka' which was larger, slower, sturdier, and more specialised. The A-36A was supposed to give the Army a high-speed dive bomber to support ground troops, but it was never terribly effective delivering bombs in a dive.

The A-36 was armed with four 0.50-in (12.7-mm) calibre guns in the wing and two more in the nose, although the latter pair

was often removed in service. Bomb shackles were installed under the wing but not at the usual Mustang bomb station. The guns were moved closer to the main landing gear strut to minimise stress under taxi and take-off conditions.

As for the name, everyone who saw these aircraft called them Mustangs. An effort was made to change the Apache's name to Invader following the successful invasion of Italy. All were used, but Mustang stuck.

Above: A row of North American A-36A Apache dive bombers of two unidentified training squadrons (with red and yellow propeller hubs) is seen at a Stateside base. The aircraft wear the red-bordered US national insignia used only between June and August 1943.

Above: Wearing the yellow-bordered, pre-June 1943 national insignia of 'Torch' landings in North Africa, an A-36A (42-83807) awaits action that month at Sousse, Tunisia.

fairings attached to the leading edge. Deliveries began in July 1942, with RAF designation Mustang IA, but 57 of the 150 were retained in the USA, 55 of them by the Army Air Force (as the Air Corps had by then been renamed).

Looking back, some American observers debate whether Britain needed so many Mustangs so early, when the Spitfire was on its way to becoming more numerous (22,000 built) than any American fighter of the war. When Sir Henry Self's purchasing team contracted for the Mustang, the Battle of Britain was not yet joined, its outcome by no means assured. 'Worst case' thinking had to include Germany taking over the United Kingdom, including its production facilities, with the RAF exiled to foreign shores to press on with the fight. A more optimistic view might have looked ahead to the Allies turning the tide and invading occupied Europe. Either way, the Spitfire never had the range or load-carrying capability of the Mustang and was never ideal for long-distance escort missions, nor for the low-level reconnaissance role at which the early Mustangs

excelled.

In 1941 NAA duly supplied the fourth and 10th aircraft off the British production line to the Army Air Corps, which designated them XP-51. NAA bestowed the name Apache, but the Army eventually settled for the British name Mustang. The two evaluation aircraft, 41-038 and -039, were unpainted except for US Army insignia and, once they had reached Wright Field, sported the usual WRIGHT arrowhead emblem on the fuselage and the serial repeated in large figures on the nose.

At this time the Army's fighter programme was based entirely on Bell, Curtiss, Lockheed and Republic, and the Wright Field test pilots were grossly overworked with a large and growing fleet of prototypes from these and several other companies. The XP-51 had to take its turn, and as with many other types there were various problems, both contractual and technical, while North American was an unproven quantity. Thus, although the excellence of the NAA fighter was evident from the start, it took until early

An A-36A Apache of the 311th Fighter Bomber Group at Myitkyina, Burma in August 1944. USAAF statisticians determined that A-36As flew 23,373 sorties in all theatres during the war, accounting for 86 enemy aircraft despite their air-to-ground role.

A-36A Apaches first went into combat with NAAF (Northwest African Air Forces) in mid-1943, marked with chordwise yellow bands similar to the markings worn by RAF Mustangs and 15th Air Force P-51s.

AL963 was one of five Mustang Is diverted to Rolls-Royce, Hucknall, for trials with the Merlin 65 engine and four-bladed propellers. The front chin scoop was one of several features which underwent change as flight tests proceeded.

Merlin Mustangs

The Merlin and the Mustang were a match that had to happen. Rolls-Royce's in-line engine had proven itself in the Hurricane, Lancaster and Spitfire. Named after a small European falcon (not the legendary wizard), the Merlin incorporated such advances as the first use of fuel injected directly into the blower. Packard acquired rights to produce it long before the US entered World War II, and the Merlin became the V-1650 to the US Army.

The supercharger design was the real key to Merlin performance. A two-speed, two-stage design, it kept atmosphere inside the induction system equal to sea level pressure. It did this with such remarkable

success that a Merlin developed more horsepower at 26,000 ft (8049 m) than the Allision did at full power on take-off at sea level. To make the system work, an elaborate cooling system was necessary and at times the Mustang's radiator was its Achilles' heel, at least when facing gunfire at low altitude.

The Merlin/Mustang combination had been discussed by many on both sides of the Atlantic. Both the RAF and USAAF flew Merlin-powered test ships, one of which became NAA's P-51B prototype.

As had been obvious, the Merlin significantly improved Mustang performance at high altitude.

Re-engined and named Mustang X, the five Merlin 65 trials aircraft each featured improved engine installations. The No. 2 prototype, AM203, with a smoother chin scoop and angled cowling louvres, reached 422 mph (679 km/h) at 22,000 ft (6811 m).

The final configuration of the production Merlin-powered P-51B/C and Mustang III was quite clean. This black P-51B at Wright Field tested a paint finish for night fighters on 21 February 1944, and is a fine illustration of the smooth and flowing lines of the Merlin-driven fighter.

1942 for any aircraft of this basic design to be ordered for use by the USAAF.

Accordingly, the first P-51s – indeed, the only aircraft with this designation – to reach the AAF were the 55 held back from the RAF's Lend-Lease Mustang IA batch. They were retrofitted with two K24 cameras in the rear fuselage for the tactical reconnaissance role, and were then officially designated as F-6As, although the designation P-51, or P-51-1, was also retained. They went to Peterson Field, Colorado, to the newly established aerial reconnaissance school, and then to the 12th Air Force in Tunisia, where 41-137328 of the 154th Observation Squadron flew the first USAAF Mustang mission of the war, a recce over Kairouan airfield. Ironically, in view of the fact that the F-6As were actually diverted from an RAF Lend-Lease

batch, the RAF's No. 225 Squadron frequently borrowed Mustangs from the same group to augment its shorter-range Spitfires. The F-6A proved extremely successful in service, but also pointed to many difficulties which would be experienced as the Mustang became more widespread. Not the least such problem was the type's similarity in shape to the German Bf 109. The 154th's first combat loss was the result of this similarity when friendly AAA failed to notice the differences, with fatal results.

On 16 April 1942 NAA received the first contract to build aircraft specifically for the Army inventory. The contract covered 500 NA-97 ground-support dive bombers, and because of the nature and extent of modifications involved they received the attack designation A-36A. The engine was the V-1710-87 (F21R), rated at 1,325 hp (994 kW) at 3,000 ft (914 m). The four 0.30-in guns were replaced by a single extra 0.5-in gun in each wing, making the gun armament six of the heavier calibre (four of them in the wings), and a rack was added under each wing for a 500-lb (227-kg) bomb, or a 75 US-gal (62-Imp gal; 284-litre) drop tank, or smoke-curtain equipment. Large slatted-fence dive brakes were added above and below the wings outboard of the bombs, normally recessed into the wing but opened to 90° by a hydraulic jack to hold speed in quite steep dives to about 250 mph (400 km/h).

A-36A into service

The A-36 went to war in April 1943, with the 27th Fighter Bomber Group based at Rasel Ma in French Morocco. Here it was called the Invader, but the seldom-used official name was the Apache epithet rejected by the RAF. The first operational sortie was flown on 6 June 1943, during the mass fighter-bomber assault on Pantelleria. This island was captured and became the base for two A-36 groups during the assault on and invasion of Sicily. One of the pilots of the 27th Fighter Bomber Group, Lieutenant Michael T. Russo, became the only ace in the Allison-engined Mustang, although several of his colleagues also scored aerial victories (totalling 84 enemy aircraft). The only other A-36 user was the 311th Fighter Bomber Group in India. The A-36s were used intensively and 177 were lost before the type was withdrawn, to be replaced by newer, younger airframes. The type's relatively brief service life should not camouflage the fact that it made a major contribution to the Allied war effort in both North Africa and Burma.

The first version bought by the Army for the fighter role was the NA-99, of which 310 were ordered in August 1942 as P-51As. These were essentially A-36As without the dive brakes or fuselage guns, and with the V-1710-81 (F20R) engine rated at 1,125 hp (843 kW) at 18,000 ft

One of the early P-51Bs is seen in RAF camouflage and carries an RAF fin flash and serial number (FX883), although marked with the short-lived, mid-1943 US national insignia. Such markings were applied temporarily for test flying in the USA. This aircraft is on a routine flight along the West Coast from Inglewood. Several of these early aircraft were handed over to the USAAF on arrival in Britain.

(5490 m) to give better performance at over 20,000 ft (6096 m). This engine was fitted with a new supercharger which further enhanced low-level performance. A larger-diameter propeller was also fitted. Maximum speed rose to an excellent 409 mph (658 km/h) at 11,000 ft (3353 m), faster at medium altitudes than any other fighter then in service. The magazines were enlarged, two for 280 and the others for 350 rounds, but as in the A-36A the guns lay almost on their sides and the belt feed tended to jam under severe *g* loads. Of the 310, 50 went to the RAF as Mustang IIs. FR893 was tested at Boscombe Down, and demonstrated a best rate of climb of 3,800 ft (1158 m) per minute (at 6,000 ft/1828 m), with a full-throttle climb allowing the aircraft to reach 20,000 ft (6096 m) in 6.9 minutes and 34,000 ft (10363 m) in 24 minutes.

Nearly all of the USAAF P-51As served in the CBI (China-Burma-India) theatre and in North Africa. The first P-51A group was the 311th Fighter Bomber Group in India. USAAF P-51A operations began on Thanksgiving Day, 1943 (23 November) with an escort mission by eight P-51As from Chennault's 23rd Fighter Group, for B-25s attacking a Japanese airfield near Shinchiku. When production of the Allison-engined Mustang ended, some 1,580 had been built.

Enter Rolls-Royce

The point has already been made that, having for the first time ever agreed that a foreign company should produce a wholly new design of aircraft for the RAF, the purchasing commission at first appeared content to let that company get on with it. Whether or not the result was successful, the need for fighters had by 1940 become so pressing that the initial contract for 320 would probably have been allowed to stand anyway. The remarkable thing is that no attempt was made by the purchasing commission to apply the detailed provisions of Air Publication 970, the 'Manual of Design Requirements', so that the Mustang emerged with an apparently haphazard arrangement of instruments instead of the standardised RAF blind-flying panel, an American single-grip stick, entirely American accessories and ground-support equipment, and 0.30-calibre guns firing rimless ammunition, incompatible with the 0.303-in cartridges fired by almost every other British military aircraft.

It also had an American engine known to fall away in power at high altitudes to a much greater degree than the British Rolls-Royce Merlin used by aircraft like the Spitfire and Hurricane. The gear-driven supercharger of the

V-1710-F3R fitted to the Mustang I provided a full-throttle rated altitude of 11,800 ft (3597 m), above which power diminished quite rapidly. Although plans had been laid for the Merlin to be made in the USA by Ford, which was later replaced by the Packard Motor Co., no engines from this source were available in quantity until 1942, and then they were needed for the P-40, Lancaster and Mosquito, and even for the Spitfire and Hurricane.

In the absence of any alternative, the decision to stick with the Allison was inevitable. NAA carefully considered fitting a turbosupercharger, which in the P-38 gave a very similar V-1710 excellent high-altitude performance, but decided against it. Had a turbo been fitted, there is little doubt that every Mustang would have been Allison-powered. Indeed, at the end of the war some of the fastest versions reverted to the V-1710, and similar engines powered the production P-82 Twin Mustang for post-war use.

History records that the P-51 Mustang was most successful in its later form, powered by the Rolls-Royce Merlin. Although the Merlin-engined P-51B and P-51D (and their Dallas-built equivalents, the P-51C and P-51K) were used to greatest effect by the USAAF, the impetus to re-engine the aircraft was again provided by the British.

Rolls-Royce Merlin 60

The switch to the British engine was spurred by the urgent development of the Merlin 60 series. This new family was originally produced for an aircraft that made almost no impact on the war, the pressurised, high-flying Wellington VI. To obtain power at the greatest possible altitude the Merlin was fitted with two superchargers in series, both on the same shaft geared up from the crankshaft. Because of

The smooth finish of the Mustang's laminar-flow wing is clear in this portrait of a brand new production P-51B. The aircraft is seen purring along over California powered by its Packard V-1650. The fighter wears mid-1943 national insignia. It had not yet been turned over to a USAAF squadron which would add codes and other necessary identification markings.

The second XP-51B prototype (41-37421), unlike the first, retained cannons. Both were drawn from among 57 out of 157 RAF Mustang IAs left behind in the US. North American's corporate emblem (the word 'logo' had yet to be invented) did not appear on the first ship but is readily apparent on the fin of this one.

Above: With its bulbous Malcolm hood pulled back, this Inglewood-built P-51B (43-6706) of the 380th FS/363rd FG taxis past emergency vehicles; the crew chief on the left wing guides the pilot. The type performed well on rough surfaces.

Phyllis was a Malcolm-hooded F-6C photo ship of the Ninth Air Force, seen here landing at a forward airstrip. The black and white invasion stripes were adopted to enable Allied warplanes to recognise each other quickly amid the frenzy of combat, and initially encircled wings and fuselage. The wide track of the Mustang's main landing gear is readily apparent here.

Wearing familiar Army olive-drab, with light grey undersides, 43-6706 was a P-51B of the 380th Fighter Squadron, 363rd Fighter Group, part of the hard-working Ninth Air Force. White wing bands have been retained, but the nose band has been repainted in the squadron colour, blue in the case of the 380th. This unit evolved into the 160th Tactical Reconnaissance Squadron of the redesignated 363rd TRG, with P-51s and F-6s. By mid-1944 the British-developed Malcolm hood was common on surviving P-51Bs and P-51Cs in the ETO.

the compression, and resultant heating of the air to 205° C (401° F) (more than twice the boiling point of water), an intercooler was inserted in the delivery duct to the engine. Although the Wellington VI saw only very limited service, the obvious home for the new engine was the Spitfire, where it was matched with a four-bladed propeller to absorb the power at high altitude, and an extra underwing radiator for the intercooler. The result was the Spitfire VIII, but to rush the extra performance into service quickly the new engine was put into basic Mk V airframes, the result being the Mk IX, intended to be an interim type but actually more numerous than the fully refined Mk VIII.

On 30 April 1942, when the Spitfire Mk IX was about to enter service, Ronald Harker made a 30-minute flight in a Mustang at the Air Fighting Development Unit at Duxford. He found the aircraft every bit as good as he had been led to believe, and in addition to the outstanding speed at low level and unrivalled range and endurance he noted the high rate of roll, even at high airspeeds, where the Spitfire rolled increasingly sluggishly. Harker was no ordinary wartime pilot. His life career had been with Rolls-Royce, testing cars and aircraft, and he had been intimately involved with the development of the Spitfire with the Merlin 66 engine.

He immediately flew back to Hucknall, drove to Derby and earnestly argued the case for a Merlin-powered Mustang before General Manager Ernest (later Lord) Hives. Hives called Air Marshal Sir Wilfred Freeman, and a few days later the Hucknall establishment was beginning conversion of three Mustangs. Later, two more were added. All five aircraft were powered by the Merlin 65, which in comparison with the Mk 66 had a lower full-throttle height (21,000 ft; 6400 m) but gave higher powers at lower altitudes. This is not to suggest it was just like the Allison V-1710; power at 20,000 ft (6096 m) was 205 hp (154 kW)

higher and at 25,000 ft (7620 m) it was 490 hp (356 kW) higher.

The conversion was authorised on 12 August 1942. By this time the Rolls-Royce performance office had calculated that, powered by the single-stage Merlin XX (an engine available in quantity from Packard in the USA), the speed would reach 400 mph (643 km/h) at 18,600 ft (5486 m), broadly similar to the existing Mustang II, but that fitting an engine of the Mk 60 series would result in a speed of 441 mph (710 km/h) at 25,500 ft (7770 m).

All five Rolls-Royce conversions were designated Mustang X. The differences between them were often significant, but the first two had a deep-jowled nose because a large inlet under the nose served the duct to the updraught carburettor and the radiator for the intercooler. This was the simplest way of installing the new engine, the original radiator and duct being left unaltered or modified only slightly. Captain R. T. Shepherd flew the first Mk X (AL975) on 13 October 1942, initially with a regular Spitfire IX Rotol propeller and later with a larger propeller designed specially. The second ship (AL963) flew on 13 November 1942, the third (AM121) on 13 December. This aircraft went to the AFDU at Duxford, for service evaluation, and the fourth and fifth aircraft, completed in January and February 1943, were evaluated by the USAAF in full USAAF markings, with VQ codes. The success of this evaluation led to an immediate merger of the British and American Merlin Mustang programmes.

Surprisingly, the tailor-made propeller gave little improvement in performance, but there was never any doubt of the excellence of the re-engined aircraft, level speed being measured by Boscombe Down at 433 mph (697 km/h) at 22,000 ft (6700 m). One of the few adverse features was that yaw (directional) stability was degraded by

P-51Bs of the Ninth AF

The first Merlin Mustangs arrived in England in September 1943 and on 11 November began to reach the 354th Fighter Group at Boxsted under Lieutenant Colonel Kenneth R. Martin. Mustangs reaching the UK were assigned to the Ninth Air Force, reorganised from North Africa and assigned to support Operation Overlord, the coming Allied invasion of German-occupied France. But Major General William Kepner, fighter boss for the embattled Eighth Air Force, sorely needed the P-51B and P-51C Mustangs to escort bombers, and 'borrowed' them for that purpose.

The Ninth Air Force's 100th Fighter Wing consisted of the 354th, 357th and 363rd Fighter

Groups, each with three squadrons of 16 aircraft. As late as February 1944, these still came under the Ninth AF, even though the Eighth had essentially pirated them. The Eighth AF only gained its own P-51s when it exchanged its 358th (P-47) Fighter Group with the Ninth's 357th (P-51) Fighter Group.

Before the change, still with the Ninth, 357th commander Lt Col James Howard became the only fighter pilot in Europe awarded the Medal of Honor for an 11 January 1943 assault on Bf 110s attacking a formation of B-17 Flying Fortresses.

Top-scoring Ninth AF ace was 1st Lt Glenn Eagleston, with 18½ aerial victories (to which he added two MiGs in Korea).

Green Hornet of the 363rd Fighter Group taxis down a temporary pierced steel planking runway, with pilot John Stricker being guided by his crew chief. Having a 'scanner' seated on the wing became a routine method of easing the taxiing workload, obviating the need for constant weaving.

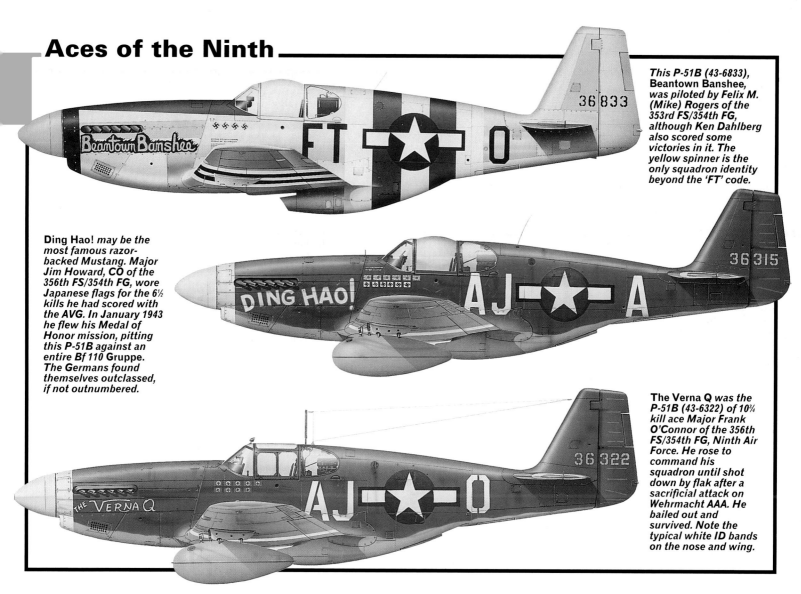

This P-51B (43-6833), Beantown Banshee, was piloted by Felix M. (Mike) Rogers of the 353rd FS/354th FG, although Ken Dahlberg also scored some victories in it. The yellow spinner is the only squadron identity beyond the 'FT' code.

Ding Hao! may be the most famous razor-backed Mustang. Major Jim Howard, CO of the 356th FS/354th FG, wore Japanese flags for the 6½ kills he had scored with the AVG. In January 1943 he flew his Medal of Honor mission, pitting this P-51B against an entire Bf 110 Gruppe. The Germans found themselves outclassed, if not outnumbered.

The Verna Q was the P-51B (43-6322) of 10¾ kill ace Major Frank O'Connor of the 356th FS/354th FG, Ninth Air Force. He rose to command his squadron until shot down by flak after a sacrificial attack on Wehrmacht AAA. He bailed out and survived. Note the typical white ID bands on the nose and wing.

the increased side area of the nose, and various schemes were proposed to fit a taller or broader fin or (as was done) add a dorsal fin.

Rolls-Royce planned quickly to produce 500 Merlin Mk 65 engines to re-engine most of the RAF's Mustangs to Mk X standard. The difficulty was that there seemed to be nowhere not already working around the clock where the conversions could be done. In any case, even with Merlins being produced at Derby, Crewe and Glasgow, and by the Ford Motor Co. at Manchester, another 500 could not be fitted into the existing programme. In the USA, however, there was no such problem.

The American Merlin

It has already been mentioned that Packard was licence-building the Merlin engine for the Canadian-built Hurricanes, Lancasters and Mosquitos, and for the P-40F. As soon as it became known that the two-stage Merlin 60 series was taking shape, Packard began discussions about extending its licence to cover the series. This proposal was soon accepted, and Packard began production of the Merlin 68, with two-stage supercharger and intercooler, as the V-1650-3. Additional orders were placed with Continental Motors.

Mention should also be made of a remarkable alternative scheme proposed by Ray Dorey, manager of the Hucknall test establishment. He proposed fitting the even more powerful two-stage Griffon 65 engine amidships, resting on a completely new truss structure and driving the propeller reduction gear via a long shaft as in the Airacobra, the cockpit being where the engine had previously been. Calculations showed that about 500 mph (805 km/h) would be attained, and a superb metal mock-up was built (with a 'bubble' canopy), but a go-ahead was withheld.

Lieutenant Colonel Thomas (Tommy) Hitchcock, US Assistant Military Attache at the American embassy in Lon-

don, had already flown the Mustang, and was an enthusiastic supporter of the type. Rolls-Royce had informally told Hitchcock of their plans to re-engine the aircraft with the Merlin. He immediately conveyed his enthusiasm for the idea to both NAA and Wright Field.

In late 1941, when they heard unofficially about the two-stage Merlin 60 series, NAA had looked at the work that would be involved in switching to the British engine. The task appeared to be entirely feasible, and instead of adopting the simplest answer, as had been necessary in the virtually simultaneous programme being undertaken at Hucknall, Schmued's project staff began scheming an ideal conversion, though essentially as a spare-time occupation almost on the back of the proverbial envelope. On 25 July 1942, however, NAA received a signal authorising the conversion of two aircraft into XP-78s, powered by Merlin 65 engines sent from England.

The two aircraft were NA-91-12013 and -12082, the extra pair of P-51s not allocated to USAAF units from the 57 left in the USA from the Lend-Lease batch of 150 Mustang IA fighters, with four 20-mm cannon. Serialled 41-37352 and -37421, they were painted olive drab and became NA-101s, and NAA pulled out all the stops to

Peg O'My Heart of the 354th FG was the mount of George Bickell, and shows the earliest Ninth Air Force markings, before the introduction of white recognition bands on nose and wings to distinguish the Mustang from the Messerschmitt Bf 109. The aircraft name was applied on both sides, which was atypical.

The P-51B named Little Bitch *was flown by Captain Dave Perron of the Eighth Air Force's first Merlin Mustang unit, the 357th FG. It has white ID bands, a Vargas-style pin-up, vertical bombs used as mission markers, and swastikas to represent air-to-air victory claims.*

After D-Day (6 June 1944) many P-51B/C Mustangs of the Eighth and Ninth Air Forces were detached to forward airstrips in France. Here a mixed bag of P-51s ready themselves for take-off for a fighter sweep over the beaches. The nearest is from the 361st Fighter Group, but the second is from the Ninth AF's 363rd FG.

The Merlin-powered Mustang reached the Eighth Air Force in January 1944 when the 357th Fighter Group shifted to the Eighth to escort bombers over Europe.

The 363rd FG came next, followed by the 4th FG commanded by Colonel Donald Blakeslee. The 4th became dispersed on the first planned Berlin raid on 3 March 1944, but Blakeslee's P-51s escorted American bombers over the German capital on 4 March. The arrival of North American's spirited aircraft over Berlin's rooftops marked a turning point for the Third Reich – the beginning of the end.

Gradually, other Eighth AF squadrons converted to the Mustang, not just the razorback P-51B/C but also the bubble-canopied P-51D. The Eighth became the most decorated military formation in US Air Force history and the war was pressed relentlessly against Hitler's *Festung Europa*. Bomber crews all but worshipped the 'little friends' in Mustangs who finally had the reach to go with them all the way to the target.

From mid-1944, Eighth AF Mustangs began to dispense with olive-drab camouflage, thereby gaining about 5 mph (8 km/h) in air speed. Air opposition never waned and the weather over Germany never improved, but Mustang pilots fought on: on 7 October 1944, 1st Lt Urban Drew of the 376th FS shot down two of the new Me 262 jet fighters, the first of dozens to fall. A few P-51Ks arrived to cap off the job in 1945.

achieve the optimised aircraft. The work even involved testing various modifications on the actual aircraft in the recently commissioned 80-ft (24-m) wind tunnel at the NACA Ames Laboratory at Moffett Field.

Despite the additional 'plumbing', and possibly higher weight and combat vulnerability, for minimum drag the answer was clearly to provide a small 'chin' inlet for the carburettor, and to pipe the intercooler circuit through a radiator added in the original radiator duct under the fuselage. After six weeks of working around the clock a definitive rectangular radiator matrix was devised, totally unlike the drum used in previous Mustangs and in fact transferring heat at a considerably greater rate. Like the Rolls-Royce engines, the V-1650 was cooled by a 30/70 mix of glycol and water. The new radiator was fitted into a redesigned duct. A major advantage of the aft location of the intercooler heat-exchanger was that it left the nose changed only superficially, with little change to directional stability and little increase in drag.

The XP-78 becomes the XP-51B

The first conversion was 'about an 80 per cent job', with an improved but still interim radiator installation and many

other features which were far from final. Bob Chilton flew it on 30 November 1942, by which time the designation XP-78 had been replaced by XP-51B. It was soon followed by the second aircraft, which retained its four 20-mm guns but had almost the production standard of engine installation, driving a specially designed Hamilton Standard propeller with four broad blades with a diameter of 11 ft 2 in (3.4 m). It also had the definitive radiator duct with a sharply sloping inlet standing further away from the belly ahead of it. It was at this point that the so-called Meredith effect, in which the radiator was made to give a major amount of propulsive thrust, first became fully obtainable.

Even before the predicted performance of the conversion could be confirmed, the USAAF moved into top gear. In August 1942, 400 P-51Bs were ordered on the basis of NAA's performance predictions, even before the XP-51B could make its maiden flight. Almost overnight the Mustang changed from being just another tactical attack/reconnaissance aircraft into the most important fighter in the entire Allied armoury. The results of the Hucknall tests, and the USAAF's evaluation of the Mustang Mk X, came in early 1943, in time for the production Merlin Mustang to take advantage of various lessons, and prompting the RAF to order a massive 1,000 P-51Bs as the Mustang Mk III.

Thus, as 1943 dawned, the Mustang programme suddenly expanded enormously. Engines were to be no problem, with massive production from both Packard at Detroit and Continental at Muskegon. Under instructions from the

The 352nd FG was in combat with Eighth Air Force from 9 September 1943 to 3 May 1945. This P-51B (42-106709) Snoot's Sniper *was flown by 5½-kill ace Francis W. Horn of the 328th FS. D-Day stripes were removed from top surfaces soon after the invasion.*

Above: **Texas Terror III** was a P-51B Mustang of the 354th FS/355th FG. This was about as 'standard' as a Mustang could be – stock Army olive-drab, white wing, tail and nose bands adopted in-theatre for recognition, but deleted from the fin, and an American-style radio mast.

By September 1944 when this Malcolm-hooded P-51B of the 353rd FG was photographed, most Mustangs had shed their camouflage. This hack bore a 'war weary' WW tail designator.

Above: This P-51B/C was one of several which fell into Luftwaffe hands. Most of these were operated by Zirkus Rosarius, as Germany called its captured-aircraft evaluation and demonstration unit. This P-51 was flown from Oranienburg in October 1944.

Suzy G was a P-51B of the 375th FS/361st FG, flown by 1st Lieutenant Leonard H. Mottis on combat sorties from RAF Little Walton. Note the disparate sections of olive drab paint applied to the upper surfaces in the field.

Left: Although no two-seat Mustang came off the production line, many were created in the field for training and hack duties. One flew General Dwight D. Eisenhower over France in July 1944.

Aces of the Eighth

Patty Ann II was a Malcolm-hooded P-51B (42-106872) flown by 1st Lieutenant John F. Thornell, Jr, of the 328th Fighter Squadron, 352nd Fighter Group in July 1944. It has a late-style swept radio mast.

P-51B (42-106448) The Hun Hunter from Texas was flown by 1st Lieutenant Henry Brown, a 14½-victory ace of the 354th Fighter Squadron, 355th Fighter Group, in April 1944. Brown was shot down by flak in October 1944 and became a prisoner of war in Germany.

This P-51B (43-24824) was one of several craft named **Old Crow** and flown by Captain Clarence 'Bud' Anderson of the 362nd Fighter Squadron, 357th Fighter Group in May 1944. Anderson chalked up 16½ air-to-air kills and destroyed one more Luftwaffe aircraft on the ground.

The 31st Fighter Group returns to its Italian base after a 1944 mission. When the sun was shining, Italy was gorgeous. Much of the time, however, even with the pierced steel planking seen here, mud was the real enemy.

A trio of ground crew members of the 325th FG 'Checkertail Clan' who travelled to the Soviet Union aboard a B-17 confers with a Russian soldier in front of a P-51B (42-103387) flown by Lieutenant William Adams of the 318th FS.

Captain Andrew Turner, a squadron commander in the all-Negro 332nd FG at Foggia and pilot of Skipper's Darlin', describes an encounter to a fellow pilot in front of his 'red-tailed' P-51B in the autumn of 1944. Although he scored no confirmed victories, Turner was widely respected.

Fifteenth Razorbacks

The Fifteenth Air Force was formed in November 1943, initially with three P-38 Lightning groups to escort Allied bombers. On 2 April 1944, the Spitfire-equipped 31st Fighter Group received P-51Bs, the first in the Fifteenth, and escorted a 21 April raid on Ploesti, downing 17 aircraft. The 52nd and 325th Fighter Groups became the next Mustang operators. Next, in June 1944, came the all-Negro 332nd FG in P-51Cs with red tails and noses from Foggia, Italy.

On 31 August 1944, the 52nd FG attacked the Luftwaffe airfield at Reghin in Romania and destroyed over 150 enemy aircraft as the P-51s flew pass after pass over the devastated area.

The men of the 332nd FG demonstrated again and again that being black was no impediment to being a fighter pilot. To a

degree, the top brass saw the Med as an area of secondary importance – in the tenor of the times, a reason for stationing the Negro combat group there. At times, black P-51D pilots battled discrimination and the Third Reich at the same time: top-scoring pilot Lee Archer had his fifth kill snatched away so as not to be recognised, at the time, as an ace.

Still, the Tuskegee airmen of the 332nd performed well in every combat situation into which a P-51 could be thrown, and took enormous pride in never losing a single bomber in their charge.

Fighting the war from Italy meant coping not just with the Luftwaffe, but with mud, muck, rain and weather which was often every bit as grim as the murk which vexed pilots in England.

Rattlesnake was a typically colourful P-51B flown by the Negro-manned 332nd Fighter Group. Its proudest claim was never to have lost a bomber in its charge – a unique feat.

A mix of P-51B/C and P-51D Mustangs belonging to the 332nd FG beats up the airfield at Foggia at the beginning of a combat mission in late 1944 or early 1945. Despite discrimination, hostility and ignorance, the black fliers proved courageous and extremely highly motivated.

USAAF, NAA could make plans for the greatest possible increase in rate of output. The already huge Inglewood plant was greatly extended, and devoted entirely to the Mustang, the B-25 Mitchell programme being progressively transferred to Kansas City. Output of the AT-6 and related trainers had already been transferred to the giant new facility at Dallas, and the USAAF instructed NAA to expand this Texas plant even further as a second source for Merlin Mustangs.

By the end of January 1943 the production standard for the P-51B had been agreed. To make full use of the greater power the airframe was restressed in detail, and the opportunity was taken to match this restressing with the ability to operate at weights considerably greater than previous versions. The wing racks were eventually cleared to carry bombs of 1,000 lb (454 kg) each, or a wide range of other stores including drop tanks or triple rocket tubes.

The engine installation was further refined, with a rectangular filtered-air inlet in each side of the carburettor duct, visible on each side of the cowling, and the exhausts expelled through individual ejector stubs projecting through a slim fairing. The ailerons were modified aerodynamically and structurally, although this was visible externally only by the fact that the tabs were of plastic. The armament selected was simply four 0.5-in Browning MG53-2 in the wings, the fuselage guns being abandoned. This armament, similar to that of the P-51A, was judged to be the best compromise between weight, firepower and duration of fire, the magazines holding a total of 350 rounds for each inboard gun and 280 rounds for each of the outer weapons. Late in the production of the P-51B and C, a new six-gun armament was introduced, as explained later.

A contract for the P-51B

Testing with the XP-78s had by the end of 1942 shown a maximum speed of 442 mph (711 km/h) at 24,000 ft (7315 m), or some 70 mph (113 km/h) faster than previous Mustangs at this height. Rate of climb and combat ceiling were also of a totally new order, the best climb at sea level rising from 1,900 to 3,520 ft (579 to 1073 m) per minute. When the magic figure '442' was cabled to Washington, NAA received an immediate contract for 400 P-51B-1 fighters, to which the company assigned charge-number NA-102. P-51B procurement was completed by orders totalling 1,588 for the NA-104 models, called P-51B-5, -10 and -15. A further contract for 1,350 was placed with Dallas. These aircraft, called NA-103 and designated P-51C by the customer, differed only in very minor details, as did further blocks of P-51Cs with charge-number NA-111.

In the course of production of the P-51B-10 and P-51C-1, the decision was taken to omit the olive-drab camouflage and deliver aircraft in natural metal finish. It had become an objective to try to bring the Luftwaffe to battle, rather than to try to hide from it, and the move saved weight, cost and drag. Camouflage was later reapplied to upper surfaces at field level, and was subsequently

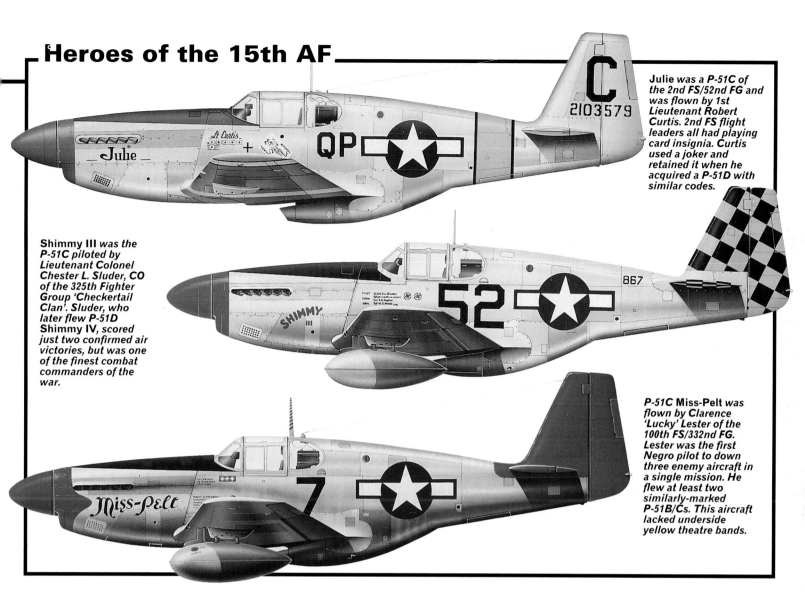

Julie was a P-51C of the 2nd FS/52nd FG and was flown by 1st Lieutenant Robert Curtis. 2nd FS flight leaders all had playing card insignia. Curtis used a joker and retained it when he acquired a P-51D with similar codes.

Shimmy III was the P-51C piloted by Lieutenant Colonel Chester L. Sluder, CO of the 325th Fighter Group 'Checkertail Clan'. Sluder, who later flew P-51D *Shimmy IV*, scored just two confirmed air victories, but was one of the finest combat commanders of the war.

P-51C *Miss-Pelt* was flown by Clarence 'Lucky' Lester of the 100th FS/332nd FG. Lester was the first Negro pilot to down three enemy aircraft in a single mission. He flew at least two similarly-marked P-51B/Cs. This aircraft lacked underside yellow theatre bands.

removed again after D-Day. RAF aircraft, however, stayed in day-fighter camouflage until almost the end of the war, when they followed suit.

Most significant of the developments during P-51B/C production was the initially bold decision to add a third internal fuel tank immediately behind the pilot's seat. Although the Mustang already offered outstanding range, further extended by drop tanks, the expanding operations in both the European and Pacific theatres demanded still more. After testing the Fisher XP-75, which had been planned as the escort for the AAF's heavy bombers, Colonel (later General) Mark Bradley decided something else had to be devised, and fast. He told Kindelberger to put an extra tank in the back of a Mustang. Calculations showed that a tank of 85 US gal (71 Imp gal; 322 litres) could be fitted between the seat armour and the radio bay, giving an internal capacity of 269 US gal (224 Imp gal; 1108 litres), or 419 US gal (349 Imp gal; 1586 litres) with two drop tanks. The decision was bold because the aft shift in CG (centre of gravity) would make directional stability (which was already marginal) almost non-existent, so that combined with the ponderous weight on take-off the aircraft would need extremely careful piloting until a lot of fuel had been burned off.

Inglewood sent the three-tank P-51B to the AAF at Wright Field, and Bradley made a careful take-off with maximum internal and external fuel. He flew to Albuquerque, New Mexico, circled the city and flew back. There was no need to look further for a bomber escort, because he had just done the equivalent of England to Berlin and back. (He searched in vain for somewhere to put extra fuel in the P-47, so that fighter never managed to escort bombers on their longest missions.) The third tank went into the final 550 P-51Bs, which became P-51B-7, and into P-51Cs which became Block 3 aircraft. It was retrofitted to many existing aircraft, and of course became

standard on future production, but unfortunately the tricky handling at maximum aft CG resulted in an order to put only 65 US gal (54 Imp gal; 246 litres) in the fuselage tank. With later Mustangs this was still enough for escort missions to Berlin, however.

In the course of production of the P-51B and C several further modifications were introduced. The P-51B-15 and all P-51Cs from Block 5 onwards were powered by the V-1650-7 instead of the Dash 3. The latter was rated at 1,400 hp (1050 kW) at take-off, with war emergency rating of 1,620 hp (1215kW) at 16,800 ft (5120 m), whereas the Dash 7 engine gave 1,450 hp (1087 kW) for take-off and had emergency ratings of 1,695 hp 1271 kW) at 10,300 ft (3139 m) and 1,390 hp (1042 kW) at 24,000 ft (7315 m).

Under Lend-Lease provisions the RAF received 274 P-51Bs and 636 P-51Cs, these becoming Mustang Mk IIIs. In AAF service 71 Bs and 20 Cs were fitted with cameras in

Below: This aircraft is a rather mysterious Mustang. Many references have described this photo as depicting this Mustang (apparently coded 'CL') as belonging to No. 5 Squadron, part of the SAAF's No. 7 Wing. Certainly photographed in Italy in late 1944, the aircraft's true identity remains unknown. While South African pilots took the Mustang to war five years later, in Korea, records suggest that the P-51 was not used by the SAAF during the World War II.

the rear fuselage for the reconnaissance role, becoming F-6C-NA or F-6C-NT, respectively. The usual fit was two oblique K24s, as in the F-6A, or a K24 and a K22. In each case the cameras were immediately in front of the structural break ahead of the tailwheel, looking out to the left side.

The first P-51B was flown for the first time on 5 May 1943, and the first P-51C followed on 5 August. The first combat unit to be equipped with the P-51B was the 354th Fighter Group in October 1943.

Surprisingly, the first Merlin-powered P-51Bs to become operational in England belonged not to the Eighth Air Force which needed them for bomber escort but to the Ninth Air Force, which was charged with air-to-ground responsibilities to support the expected invasion of occupied Europe. The 354th Fighter Group at Boxted under Lieutenant Colonel Kenneth Martin was the first unit in the ETO (European Theatre of Operations) to receive Mustangs. The group, consisting of the 353rd, 355th and 356th Fighter Squadrons, remained under the jurisdiction of Ninth Air Force but was immediately ordered to support bomber operations by the Eighth Air Force.

In the Merlin Mustang's first USAAF combat mission, an 11 December 1943 bomber escort to Emden, not much happened. A few days later, however, Lieutenant Charles F. Gumm shot down a twin-engined Messerschmitt Bf 110 for the first aerial victory by an American Mustang group. The days in which the Luftwaffe could use its heavily armed but unwieldy twin-engined *Zerstörer* in daylight over Germany were coming to an end. More worrying, for the Luftwaffe, was the fact that the new Mustangs could also outfight the agile single-seat, single-engined Bf 109 and Fw 190. By the end of the month, the 354th FG had shot down eight Luftwaffe aircraft, including four more rocket-carrying Bf 110s, but had lost eight Mustangs, most due to technical problems. While this was going on, the group's pilots were adjusting to what amounted to a new kind of warfare. Now, the Mustang pilots were facing four- to five-hour missions. This kind of flying imposed new demands on the pilot, creating all kinds of discomfort, but it was even worse on the aeroplane. The Mustang was prone to coolant loss at high altitude where engines overheated and eventually seized. Coolant, oil, and oxygen problems needed to be resolved.

First P-51 ace

On 11 January 1944, Major James H. Howard of the 354th repeatedly risked his life to defend bombers from Luftwaffe fighter attack. Separated from his flight, Howard was alone near a B-17 bomber formation which came under attack from six to eight twin-engined German fighters. There were dozens of Luftwaffe fighters not far away but Howard unhesitatingly went into harm's way and shot down, in quick succession, a twin-engined ship, a Focke Wulf Fw 190 and a Messerschmitt Bf 109. Moments later, he shook another Bf 109 off the tail of an American aircraft. Howard continued fighting aggressive and persistent Luftwaffe pilots for half an hour thereafter, becoming the first P-51 ace, and the first ETO 'Ace in a Day'. His ship during the engagement was 43-6315, nicknamed 'Ding Hao'. A soft-spoken figure who wrote up a report of the incident without mention of his own heroism, Howard received the highest American award for valour, the Medal of Honor. Significantly, Howard's aircraft performed this feat with a dwindling number of guns, ending the engagement with only one gun working, as a result of icing and jams due to *g* forces.

The 357th Fighter Group, also initially assigned to the Ninth Air Force but quickly transferred to operational control of the Eighth for bomber escort, flew its first P-51B Mustang mission on 11 February 1944, with Major Howard (on loan from the 354th) in the lead.

On 23 February 1944, the 363rd Fighter Group became the third P-51B Mustang operator in the European theatre,

flying from Rivenhall. That month, the 4th Fighter Group at Debden, under Colonel Donald Blakeslee, also began converting to the P-51B. While the Merlin Mustang began to enter service with UK-based USAAF squadrons in the bomber escort role, RAF deliveries went to re-equip fighter and fighter-bomber squadrons operating early mark Spitfires. The Mustang III formally entered service with the RAF's No. 65 Squadron at Gravesend in December 1943.

During April 1944 Merlin Mustangs began replacing Spitfires with the 31st and 52nd Fighter Groups, which transferred from the 12th to the 15th Air Force. The 31st flew its first big mission on 21 April 1944, when its Mustangs escorted B-24s attacking the oil refineries at Ploesti, Romania. Two more 15th Air Force Groups, including the Negro-manned 332nd, later converted to P-51Bs and P-51Cs.

Despite its lack of an experienced cadre, and in the face of obstacles imposed by segregation, the 332nd built up an enviable reputation during its brief service with the Mustang. The red-tailed 332nd Fighter Group, which shifted from the Thunderbolt to the P-51D Mustang in June 1944 at Lesina, Italy, was the only Negro pursuit group in the segregated Army. Lee A. Archer was the group's top-scoring pilot with five air and six ground victories, although one aerial victory was later re-allocated to another pilot to prevent him becoming an ace. One day, Archer and Wendell O. Pruitt went rushing into a formation of Messerschmitts which outnumbered them six to one. Each American scored two kills and came through the fight unharmed.

Commonwealth Merlin Mustangs

Merlin Mustangs also equipped RAF and Commonwealth units in the MTO. The first RAF squadron in Italy to equip with Mustangs was No. 260, which received Mustang IIIs at Cutella in April 1944. The 14th Air Force in Burma began receiving P-51Bs in February and March 1944, and the type also equipped the USAAF 5th and 20th AF in China and the Pacific.

Some 3,738 P-51Bs and P-51Cs were produced, and some of these served with front-line units until the end of hostilities, while other, older, war-weary aircraft were converted as two-seat trainers and hacks. Although the later bubble-hooded P-51D was better known, it was the intervention of the P-51B/C that swung the balance of the bomber war over Germany, and changed the tide of the war. Many aces opened their scores on the P-51B and P-51C, and some preferred it to the later variant. Although the early bomber escort missions were not very successful, things soon began to change as tactics were refined and experience began to build. P-51Bs began escort missions on

Captain Andrew Turner typified the 332nd's pilots. Highly motivated despite the obstacles and discrimination which they faced, they gained an impressive combat record.

P-51C-10-NT 302nd FS 332nd FG, 15th AF Foggia, Italy 1944

Lee 'Buddy' Archer's P-51C *Ina the Macon Belle* was adorned with the red tail and spinner of the 332nd FG, the USAF's only Negro-manned group. A caricature of a zoot-suited hepcat was also found on the Mustang flown by Archer's partner, Wendell Pruitt. Originally named simply *The Macon Belle*. Archer's aircraft gained the name *Ina* when his 'friends' discovered the name of the pilot's sweetheart. Archer and Pruitt were nicknamed the 'Gruesome Twosome'. Both were viewed as sophisticated 'city boys', so the hepcat moniker was inevitable.

Belle had a single yellow band around each wing in the position normally associated with P-51s and A-36s, although red wingtips and red-outlined codes were also worn.

With an official score of four but widely recognised as having more than five kills, Archer is the only African-American ace. He is reluctant to make a fuss about it, half a century after the war, so the official record will continue to show no 332nd aces.

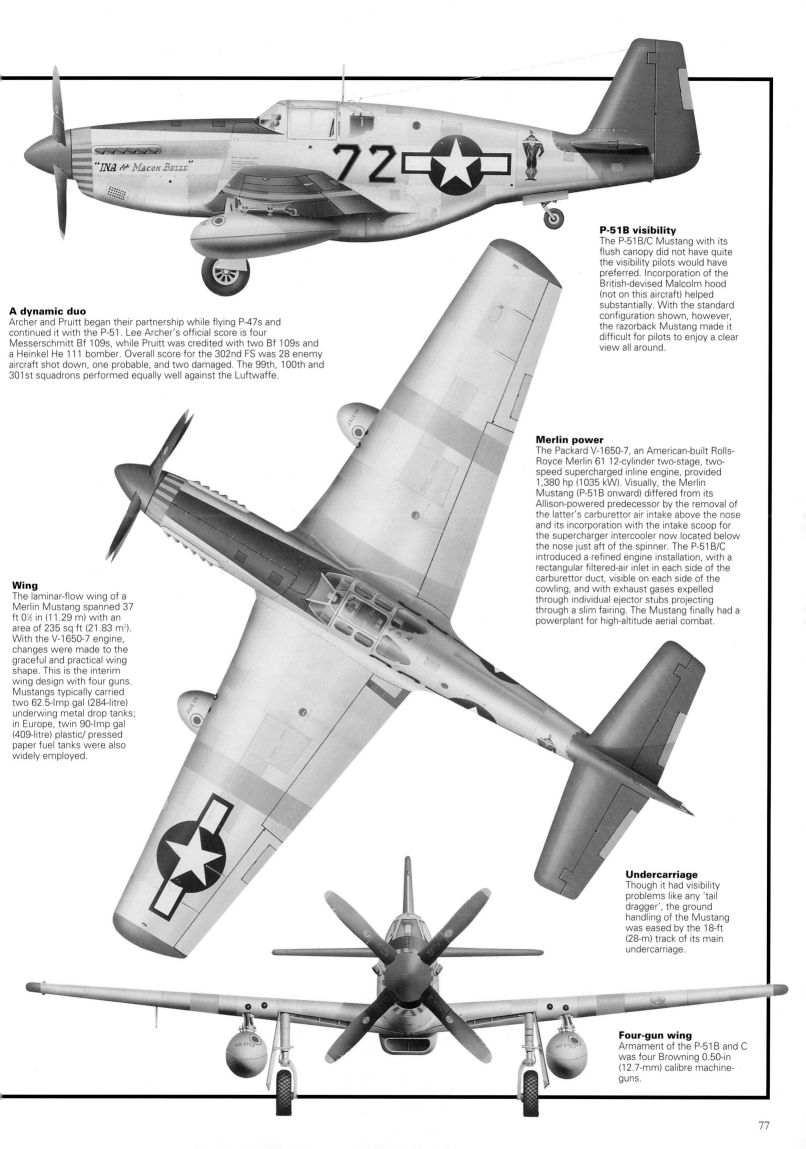

P-51B visibility
The P-51B/C Mustang with its flush canopy did not have quite the visibility pilots would have preferred. Incorporation of the British-devised Malcolm hood (not on this aircraft) helped substantially. With the standard configuration shown, however, the razorback Mustang made it difficult for pilots to enjoy a clear view all around.

A dynamic duo
Archer and Pruitt began their partnership while flying P-47s and continued it with the P-51. Lee Archer's official score is four Messerschmitt Bf 109s, while Pruitt was credited with two Bf 109s and a Heinkel He 111 bomber. Overall score for the 302nd FS was 28 enemy aircraft shot down, one probable, and two damaged. The 99th, 100th and 301st squadrons performed equally well against the Luftwaffe.

Merlin power
The Packard V-1650-7, an American-built Rolls-Royce Merlin 61 12-cylinder two-stage, two-speed supercharged inline engine, provided 1,380 hp (1035 kW). Visually, the Merlin Mustang (P-51B onward) differed from its Allison-powered predecessor by the removal of the latter's carburettor air intake above the nose and its incorporation with the intake scoop for the supercharger intercooler now located below the nose just aft of the spinner. The P-51B/C introduced a refined engine installation, with a rectangular filtered-air inlet in each side of the carburettor duct, visible on each side of the cowling, and with exhaust gases expelled through individual ejector stubs projecting through a slim fairing. The Mustang finally had a powerplant for high-altitude aerial combat.

Wing
The laminar-flow wing of a Merlin Mustang spanned 37 ft 0½ in (11.29 m) with an area of 235 sq ft (21.83 m²). With the V-1650-7 engine, changes were made to the graceful and practical wing shape. This is the interim wing design with four guns. Mustangs typically carried two 62.5-Imp gal (284-litre) underwing metal drop tanks; in Europe, twin 90-Imp gal (409-litre) plastic/ pressed paper fuel tanks were also widely employed.

Undercarriage
Though it had visibility problems like any 'tail dragger', the ground handling of the Mustang was eased by the 18-ft (28-m) track of its main undercarriage.

Four-gun wing
Armament of the P-51B and C was four Browning 0.50-in (12.7-mm) calibre machine-guns.

The contrast between the P-51B/C and the teardrop-canopy P-51D was never more apparent than in this view of Arrow Head and Swede. The P-51D defined the North American Mustang for most of the world, and offered 33 per cent more firepower.

Big friend, little friend: A B-17G Flying Fortress of the 385th Bomb Group gets a boost from a P-51D Mustang of the 357th FG. Other pairings failed to shield bombers from the Luftwaffe throughout their long missions, but the Mustang proved to be the answer.

Eighth Air Force P-51D Mustangs shoot up a German airfield. Many argue that the radial P-47 was a better strafer than the Mustang, with its glycol coolant so vulnerable to ground fire – yet P-51D pilots made short work of numerous ground targets during 1944-45.

P-51D in Europe

One of the early combat missions by the new P-51D with the bubble canopy was the 29 June 1944 strike on Leipzig, escorted by the 357th FG. Lt Col Tommy Hayes fought a prolonged dogfight with a Bf 109 and shot it down, but came to the conclusion that he preferred the razorback P-51B/C. The B and C models remained in service all the way to VE-Day and some pilots, like Hayes, swore by them.

Many, however, welcomed the definitive Mustang. All P-51Ds (and similar P-51Ks, which entered combat in Europe in January 1945) were manufactured with six 0.50-in (12.7-mm) calibre machine-guns, cut-down rear fuselage, dorsal fin (from the D-5 onward), a host of minor refinements, and the best visibility that any Mustang could enjoy, including those flying razorbacks with the vaunted Malcolm hood.

The build-up in P-51 strength occurred later in the war than is generally recognised, but it had gained full steam by mid-1944. In that year, more than 9,000 Mustangs emerged from the factory, most of them with the teardrop canopy.

The Mustang, begun as an export for Britain (which employed the P-51D as the Mustang IV), had now reached maturity as the Americans' own top fighter of the war, a status hotly contested by P-38 and P-47 veterans, yet unassailable: The Mustang stands alone in being consistently cited as the US's best.

1 December 1943, and crossed into German airspace for the first time on 15 January 1944. Early problems when the escorts left their charges to go chasing after Luftwaffe fighters were gradually resolved, although only one group (the 332nd) could claim never to have lost one of its charges to enemy fighters. The first escort mission to Berlin in March 1944 proved the Mustang's 'legs' but was not a big success: as many men in B-17s died as did Germans on the ground. Things soon got better, however.

Two British companies made significant improvements to the operational effectiveness of the P-51B and C, F-6C and Mustang III. Pytram Ltd mass-produced drop tanks which, although they held 90 Imp gal (108 US gal; 409 litres), were lighter than the metal kind, cheaper to produce and, dropped by the thousand over Germany (output was 24,000 per month), did not provide the enemy with aluminium as they were made of impregnated paper. After having been familiar with the Mustang for three years the RAF belatedly decided that the cockpit canopy was "not acceptable for European operations". R. Malcolm Ltd devised a bulged aft-sliding hood of blown Perspex which

in a modest number of man-hours could replace the unsatisfactory hinged canopy. The result transformed the cockpit, not only giving extra space but most importantly effecting a dramatic improvement in view, especially to the rear and obliquely down to the front and over the sides. Many pilots expressed a preference for the Malcolm-hooded P-51B over the later bubble-hooded P-51D, especially insofar as visibility was concerned. Several Eighth Air Force and Ninth Air Force groups obtained Malcolm hoods for their P-51Bs and P-51Cs, but the modification was primarily a British one, and was unknown in the USAAF's Mediterranean and Far East squadrons.

In June 1944, the 10th Tactical Reconnaissance Group picked up the 12th and 15th Reconnaissance Squadrons, equipped with F-6B and F-6C Mustang photo-reconnaissance aircraft. F-6s served with the Eighth, Ninth, Twelfth and Fifteenth Air Forces, and with the Fifth Air Force in the Far East. The F-6s retained four .50-calibre (12.7-mm) machine-guns and frequently scrapped with Luftwaffe fighters. Captain Clyde East of the 15th Squadron became the war's top-scoring reconnaissance pilot with 15 aerial victories.

The P-51D and K

The Mustang design was now close to a level of maturity which would back its claim as the finest fighter to come out of World War II. Steady improvement of every facet of the aeroplane's design, from radiator to supercharger and from armament to electrical systems, had produced a better and better fighter. There remained a handful of final changes to create what has come to be regarded as the definitive Mustang, including a change of armament from

Ridge Runner, flown by Major Pierce 'Mac' McKennon of the 335th FS/4th FG, taxis at Debden, England. The aircraft is festooned with two non-standard rearview mirrors, evidence that bubble-canopy visibility could be improved.

P-51D Mustangs of the Eighth Air Force peel off to land as the B-17 Flying Fortresses they escorted over Europe pass overhead. Wartime censors disclosed only that these 'big friends' and 'little friends' were coming home from a target used for supplying German troops fighting in Belgium.

A welcome view for the crew of a damaged B-17 is provided by this P-51D from the 356th Fighter Group.

European Theatre of Operations P-51D aces

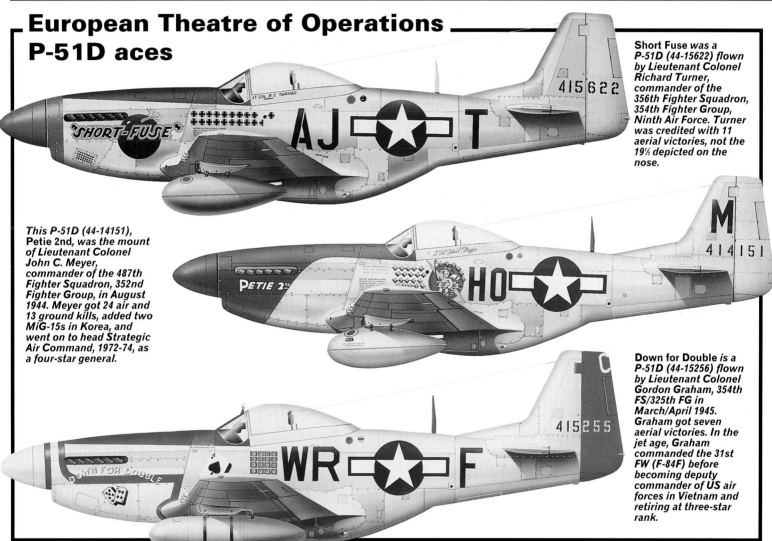

Short Fuse was a P-51D (44-15622) flown by Lieutenant Colonel Richard Turner, commander of the 356th Fighter Squadron, 354th Fighter Group, Ninth Air Force. Turner was credited with 11 aerial victories, not the 19½ depicted on the nose.

This P-51D (44-14151), Petie 2nd, was the mount of Lieutenant Colonel John C. Meyer, commander of the 487th Fighter Squadron, 352nd Fighter Group, in August 1944. Meyer got 24 air and 13 ground kills, added two MiG-15s in Korea, and went on to head Strategic Air Command, 1972-74, as a four-star general.

Down for Double is a P-51D (44-15256) flown by Lieutenant Colonel Gordon Graham, 354th FS/325th FG in March/April 1945. Graham got seven aerial victories. In the jet age, Graham commanded the 31st FW (F-84F) before becoming deputy commander of US air forces in Vietnam and retiring at three-star rank.

four to six guns, with increased ammunition, strengthened underwing pylons and the addition of a cut-down rear fuselage and a bubble canopy.

Colonel Bradley made a further major improvement to the P-51. In January 1943 he had been sent to England, and while there he had seen how the newly invented 'bubble' or 'teardrop' canopy had given the Spitfire and Typhoon pilots unobstructed 360° vision. He returned to Wright Field in June and immediately set about getting

such canopies on AAF fighters. Republic put one on a P-47 in record time, and Bradley then flew it to Inglewood to show it to Kindelberger. NAA quickly schemed a surprisingly large teardrop, with a blown bubble of Plexiglas held in a strong aluminium frame, sliding back over a slightly lowered rear fuselage.

Two P-51Bs (43-12101/12102) were taken from the assembly line and converted into proof of concept vehicles for the P-51D, although they retained camouflage and

These P-51D Mustangs (44-63228, left) at Mt Farm, England carry 7th Photo Group markings of blue spinner and red cowl stripes. By 1945, P-51Ds began escorting the group's F-5 Lightning photo ships.

Lieutenant Colonel M. P. 'Mike' Curphey taxis a P-51D (44-13964) of the 385th FS/364th FG in 1945. The teardrop-canopy P-51D (and the P-51K which joined it at this time) was slower than razorback models but, on balance, better liked.

P-51Ds in Italy

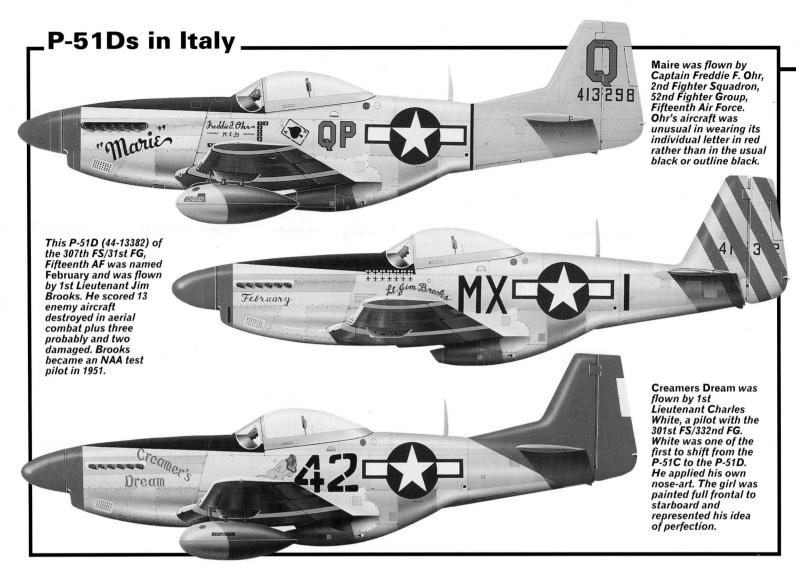

Maire was flown by Captain Freddie F. Ohr, 2nd Fighter Squadron, 52nd Fighter Group, Fifteenth Air Force. Ohr's aircraft was unusual in wearing its individual letter in red rather than in the usual black or outline black.

This P-51D (44-13382) of the 307th FS/31st FG, Fifteenth AF was named February and was flown by 1st Lieutenant Jim Brooks. He scored 13 enemy aircraft destroyed in aerial combat plus three probably and two damaged. Brooks became an NAA test pilot in 1951.

Creamers Dream was flown by 1st Lieutenant Charles White, a pilot with the 301st FS/332nd FG. White was one of the first to shift from the P-51C to the P-51D. He applied his own nose-art. The girl was painted full frontal to starboard and represented his idea of perfection.

lacked the dorsal fin added to most Ds to restore directional stability. In the first of these, referred to at the time as an XP-51D, Chilton made the first flight of a bubble-canopy Mustang at Inglewood on 17 November 1943. Two prototype P-51D aircraft (company NA-106) from Inglewood (42-106539/106540) also came from the P-51B line. The bubble canopy was instantly popular, although not universally so, as has been mentioned.

Plans were made to introduce not only the new canopy but also the new armament briefly mentioned earlier. NAA had never regarded the P-51B/C armament as satisfactory, partly on the ground of limited firepower (half that of a P-47, and with much less effect than four 20-mm) and partly because of the need for the guns to lean over at quite large angles, so that the belt feeds had to make sharp bends which under combat loads often jammed. After much

Far right: Ralph J. 'Doc' Watson in the cockpit of one of his P-51Ds. Watson flew with the 5th Fighter Squadron before flying as a wing staff officer. As such, his aircraft carried a fin diamond bearing the colours of all four 15th Air Force Mustang groups.

P-51D (44-13464) of the 307th FS/31st FG, fighting from Italy in late 1944. Flown by Major Samuel J. Brown, a 15½-victory ace, 464 wears the same code as the later Dorothy VII, the mount of 2nd Lieutenant John T. Nelson who was credited with two kills in the Mediterranean.

Miss Rogers is a P-51D (44-13485) of the 4th Fighter Squadron, 52nd Fighter Group. This was the second combat group in Fifteenth Air Force to acquire Mustangs. The all-yellow tail was the trademark of the 52nd and was one of the most easily recognised unit markings of the war.

Mediterranean P-51Ds

The 31st, 52nd, 325th and 332nd Fighter Groups in the Mediterranean theatre made the transition from the P-51B/C to the P-51D gradually, and in some squadrons not until early 1945. The definitive, teardrop-canopy Mustang made an enormous contribution during the final fighting in this region, including some truly marathon missions escorting bombers to their targets.

Although it faced even greater distances than the Eighth AF in England, the Fifteenth escorted B-17 and B-24 bombers on missions deep into Germany. They made the 1,500-mile (2414-km) round trip to Berlin on 25

March 1945. This mission, which involved all four fighter groups, saw Colonel William Daniel, commander of the 308th Fighter Squadron, 31st Fighter Group, prevail over a Messerschmitt Me 262, the first victory by Fifteenth Air Force P-51Ds over the German jet. That day, six others fell, including three claimed by the 332nd.

The P-51Ds of the Fifteenth had very colourful markings, which were extended over a larger surface of the aircraft in the winter of 1944-45. One of the most prominent was the 52nd's yellow empennage, which was stretched to cover the entire rear fuselage.

ting, and in the European theatre alone USAAF P-51s were credited with 4,950 victories in aerial combat (more than half the AAF total), almost all by the B/C/D/K versions.

The first aircraft built as P-51Ds were 42-106539/106540, taken from the middle of the P-51B-10 block and designated XP-51D, later P-51D-1. The production aircraft incorporated further small modifications, including wingroots extended forward to give a lower thickness/chord ratio and a more obvious kink in the leading edge. By the time the D appeared, in late spring 1944, the production lines at Inglewood and Dallas were really rolling. Even though the war had only a year to run, far more of these versions were built than of all preceding versions combined, and they are the only Mustangs commonly seen today.

Above: With victory in the Mediterranean nearly in their grasp, Mustangs from the 52nd Fighter Group displays their fabled yellow tails on a flight over Italy in early 1945. The Italian theatre offered up a diversity of missions, a few of which, when they involved escorting bombers to Berlin, covered greater distances than sorties from England.

experimentation NAA devised a superior installation with three MG53-2 guns close together in each wing, all upright. The outer gun in each wing was fed from a 270-round magazine behind the front spar, the middle gun from a similar box lying on top of the first, the feed arching across the outer gun, and the inner gun was mounted further back, drawing ammunition from a 400-round box lying behind the first pair. Users had the option of removing the middle guns and providing the outer guns with 400 rounds like the inner guns.

The old B/C wing armament was later improved by adding ammunition feed boosters scavenged from other aircraft types, and this made them less prone to jamming. With modified guns and a Malcolm hood, the P-51B was arguably a better aircraft than the D, with better visibility, lower weight, and without the structural problems which afflicted early Ds. Its departure characteristics were also more benign.

P-51D/K gunsight

A further modification in the D and K (see later) versions, which made a tremendous difference to combat effectiveness, was that the N-3B reflector gunsight was replaced, first by the N-9 and then by the K-14. The N-9 merely had a larger aiming ring, with the 'pipper' aiming mark in the centre, but the K-14 was the US-built version of the British (Ferranti) gyro sight. This was considered almost miraculous when it appeared. The K-14 was fitted almost from the start of P-51D production, ahead of all other US aircraft, the P-51K receiving this sight from mid-1944. It required the pilot to dial in the target wingspan and, via a roller-grip on the throttle lever, the approximate range. Everything was then done by an inbuilt computer. This sight made a major difference between missing or hit-

Major Herschell Green, an ace of the 325th Fighter Group 'Checkertail Clan', seems unaware that the American flag is displayed backwards on his shoulder (the union, or blue shield containing stars, should face forward). Full coloured tail units were used by all of the 15th AF Mustang groups.

Classic Warplanes

The first large P-51D production order, known by the company designation NA-109, constituted some 2,500 aircraft, and the D/K series eventually outnumbered all other Mustangs put together, with a total production of 9,603. The company epithet NA-110 went to 100 similar ships which went to Australia for assembly by Commonwealth. The manufacturer's terms NA-111, NA-122, and NA-124 covered further contracts for P-51D production which totalled 6,502 aeroplanes built in Inglewood and 1,454 built at Dallas.

Inglewood delivered 6,502 P-51Ds, ordered as the NA-109 (D-1 to D-10), NA-111 (D-15 and D-20) and NA-122 (D-25 and D-30). Dallas built 1,454, as the NA-111 (D-5 to D-20) and NA-124 (D-25 and D-30). In addition, the Texas plant delivered 1,500 P-51Ks, all on the NA-111 charge. These differed mainly in having an Aeroproducts propeller of 2-in (5-cm) smaller diameter (i.e. exactly 11 ft/3.353 m).

Lend-lease

Of this total, 281 Ds and 594 Ks were supplied under Lend-Lease to the RAF, which designated them Mustang Mk IV. The reduced side area of the rear fuselage finally degraded yaw stability with maximum fuel below acceptable limits, and during the D-10 block a dorsal fin was introduced, subsequently retrofitted to most existing P-51Ds, and even to some earlier aircraft. The final 1,100 P-51D-25-NA and all P-51K-10-NT and subsequent K aircraft were fitted with stubs under each wing for zero-launching of 5-in HVARs (high-velocity aircraft rockets); 10 could be carried, or six plus tanks or bombs. As noted earlier, some aircraft had previously been fitted with triple 'Bazooka'-type tubes for the M8 rocket of 4.5-in calibre. There were a few field conversions to special armament fits, and in the CBI (China/Burma/India) theatre some almost became standard, examples including two tanks and six 100-lb (45.4-kg) bombs, four 100-lb bombs plus 36 fragmentation bombs, or four 75-Imp gal (16.5-litre) drop tanks. CBI aircraft also usually had a direction-finding loop antenna ahead of the fin.

In 1944 the Australian government obtained a licence for manufacture of the P-51D, to be powered by engines from Packard. To launch the programme Packard supplied 80 V-1650-3 engines, and NAA 100 sets of airframe parts for assembly by Commonwealth Aircraft (CAC) at Fishermen's Bend, Melbourne. The resulting 80 CA-17 fighters were called Mustang XX (post-war Mk 20), and they were followed by 40 CA-18 Mustang 21s with the V-1650-7, 14 Mustang 22s with the British installation of an F24 camera behind the cockpit, and finally 66 Mustang 23s with Rolls-Royce Merlin 66 or 70 engines. CAC also produced a derived fighter, the CA-15, powered by a two-stage Rolls-Royce Griffon 61. Too late for service in the war, the CA-15 flew on 4 March 1946 and was tested for four years before being scrapped.

Photo aircraft

The figure for P-51D production includes 136 aircraft completed as F-6D photo aircraft, equipped in the same way as the F-6C. Likewise the figure for P-51K production includes 163 similarly completed as F-6Ks. Later, a few P-51Ds were converted to this standard, becoming successively FP-51Ds and RF-51Ds, some being fitted with a second seat with the designation TRF-51D.

In 1944-45 there were several instances of standard D or K aircraft flying with a second man (usually being rescued) sitting on top of the pilot. As many of these rescues went wrong as succeeded, and the practice was officially discouraged. There were also several field conversions (usually of war-weary P-51B or P-51C aircraft) with a passenger seat in place of the original radio bay. By 1945 there were an increasing number of NAA-designed conversions to TP-51D standard, with full dual controls. In 1948 these became

TF-51Ds. One example, 44-14017, was fitted with a sting-type hook for shipboard testing in December 1944, subsequently receiving a P-51H-type fin and becoming the sole ETF-51D. It was retained by the USAF, unlike an early P-51 (41-37426) which became the only Mustang transferred to the Navy, as BuNo. 57987. Other post-war developments are listed later.

As P-51Ds and Ks began pouring off the assembly lines they were used to equip new groups, and to replace tired P-51Bs and P-51Cs. In the Eighth Air Force, the Mustang allowed a move towards greater standardisation, as P-47- and P-38-equipped fighter groups transitioned to the new type. The new variant was considerably better equipped for air-to-ground operations and this became important during the later part of 1944, when the German fighter force was 'on the run' and when close support of the advancing Allied armies became a more important priority. During the war, the Eighth Air Force actually counted aerial and strafing victories equally, and many Eighth Air Force pilots built up huge scores with a mix of air and ground kills.

The P-51D began to appear in Eighth Air Force groups during the early summer of 1944, and by June four groups had re-equipped. P-51Ds were delivered (albeit at a slower rate) to the Fifteenth Air Force at the same time. With the P-51D, Mustang groups began flying regular shuttle missions, escorting bombers to Russia, where they were rearmed and turned around before flying another mission home to England or Italy.

In RAF service, there was less of a rush to replace the Mustang III (P-51B/C) with the Mustang IV (P-51D/K), and the type did not enter service until September 1944. Mustang IIIs remained in front-line use, and the new aircraft allowed the steady enlargement of the RAF's Mustang force.

The last RAF Mustangs

The final RAF squadron to receive Mustangs during the war was No. 611, which began to re-equip in January 1945 at Hawkinge. The squadron received Mustang IV (P-51D) and Mustang IVA (P-51K) variants. As the war progressed into 1945 and Allied troops moved across Europe, No. 611's pilots, like their USAAF Eighth, Ninth and Fifteenth Air Force counterparts, encountered the enemy's exotic jet and rocket fighters, and the latest versions of the Bf 109 and Fw 190. While there were still a handful of highly experienced Luftwaffe pilots eager to further increase their scores, the majority of enemy fighters were poorly flown and were

**P-51D-15-NA
352nd FS
353rd FG,
8th AF
Raydon, UK
1945**

Alabama Rammer Jammer was flown by Lieutenant Arthur C. Cundy of the 352nd Fighter Squadron, 353rd Fighter Group. It was named after the Alabama University student newspaper.

Cundy's aircraft wears typical early 352nd FG markings with the black recognition stripes retained. The nose chequers were extended aft during November 1944 to avoid confusion with the black and white chequered Mustangs of the 52nd FG.

From November 1944 to March 1945, Cundy chalked up a tally of six enemy aircraft destroyed, including three in a single day on 2 March 1945, and they were all shot down in this P-51D. Cundy was killed on 11 March 1945 after a coolant leak outbound over the North Sea led to an engine fire. His wingman on his last mission recalled later "I remember it very vividly, it was my first combat mission. I was assigned to fly Arthur's wing, and knew I was lucky, as he was our squadron's hottest pilot."

Lieutenant Arthur C. Cundy and B-17 aircrew pose in front of his **Alabama Rammer Jammer.** *The 353rd FG converted from P-47D to P-51D in late 1944, and also flew the P-51K while flying from Raydon, England.*

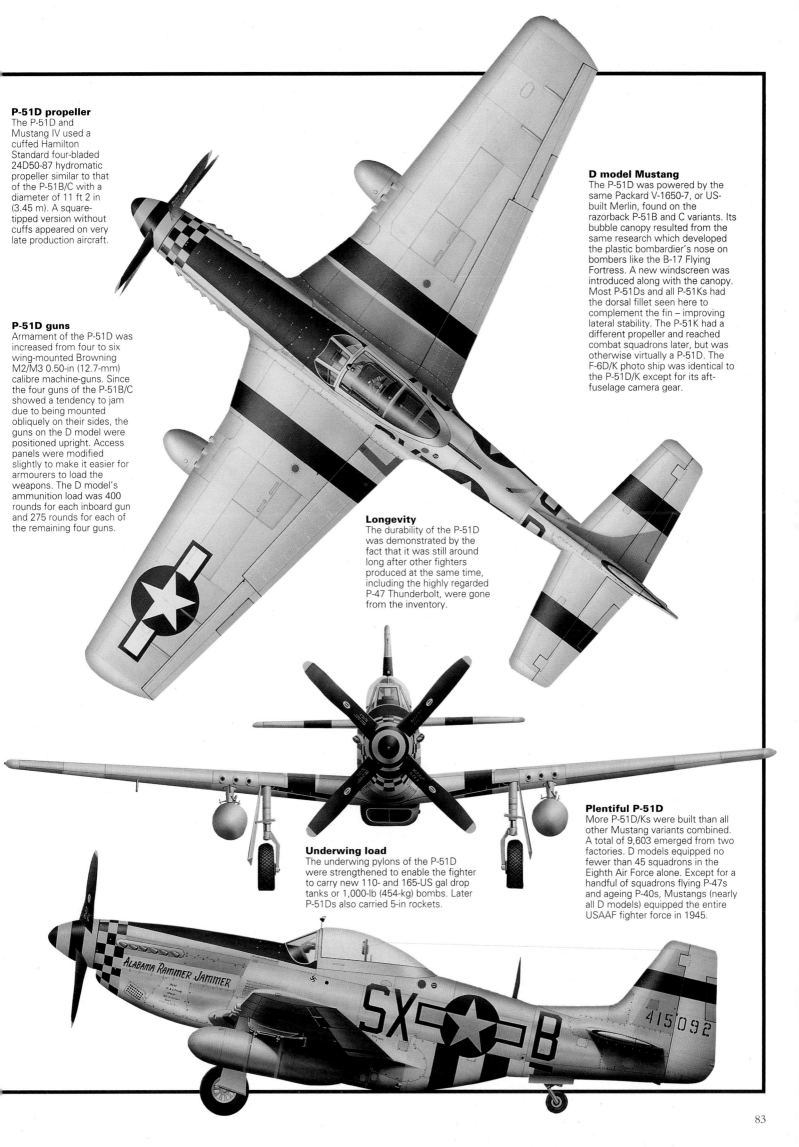

P-51D propeller
The P-51D and Mustang IV used a cuffed Hamilton Standard four-bladed 24D50-87 hydromatic propeller similar to that of the P-51B/C with a diameter of 11 ft 2 in (3.45 m). A square-tipped version without cuffs appeared on very late production aircraft.

P-51D guns
Armament of the P-51D was increased from four to six wing-mounted Browning M2/M3 0.50-in (12.7-mm) calibre machine-guns. Since the four guns of the P-51B/C showed a tendency to jam due to being mounted obliquely on their sides, the guns on the D model were positioned upright. Access panels were modified slightly to make it easier for armourers to load the weapons. The D model's ammunition load was 400 rounds for each inboard gun and 275 rounds for each of the remaining four guns.

D model Mustang
The P-51D was powered by the same Packard V-1650-7, or US-built Merlin, found on the razorback P-51B and C variants. Its bubble canopy resulted from the same research which developed the plastic bombardier's nose on bombers like the B-17 Flying Fortress. A new windscreen was introduced along with the canopy. Most P-51Ds and all P-51Ks had the dorsal fillet seen here to complement the fin – improving lateral stability. The P-51K had a different propeller and reached combat squadrons later, but was otherwise virtually a P-51D. The F-6D/K photo ship was identical to the P-51D/K except for its aft-fuselage camera gear.

Longevity
The durability of the P-51D was demonstrated by the fact that it was still around long after other fighters produced at the same time, including the highly regarded P-47 Thunderbolt, were gone from the inventory.

Underwing load
The underwing pylons of the P-51D were strengthened to enable the fighter to carry new 110- and 165-US gal drop tanks or 1,000-lb (454-kg) bombs. Later P-51Ds also carried 5-in rockets.

Plentiful P-51D
More P-51D/Ks were built than all other Mustang variants combined. A total of 9,603 emerged from two factories. D models equipped no fewer than 45 squadrons in the Eighth Air Force alone. Except for a handful of squadrons flying P-47s and ageing P-40s, Mustangs (nearly all D models) equipped the entire USAAF fighter force in 1945.

CBI Mustangs

In most respects, the China-Burma-India theatre (CBI) was a backwater — located at the end of the logistics train where pilots and maintenance men struggled under primitive conditions, improvised without adequate supplies, and carried out gruelling sorties over long distance against an experienced and entrenched Japanese enemy.

It began with the Flying Tigers, the over-rated American Volunteer Group which fought in P-40s in 1941-42 and, contrary to myth, never came near a Japanese 'Zero'. The principal wartime formations were the Tenth and Fourteenth Air Forces.

The 311th FG of the Tenth AF introduced the Mustang to the CBI with its A-36As and P-51As from October 1943. Soon, the 1st and 2nd Air Commando Squadrons and the 23rd Fighter Group (which evolved from the AVG) appeared with Mustangs, including P-51B/Cs and P-51D/Ks, They were joined in the region by the 51st FG.

Unlike Europe, where the emphasis was on air-to-air action, the 23rd based at Kwelin, China flew strafing and bombing attacks on shipping and land targets. On 8 December 1944, Mustangs successfully raided Hong Kong with 500-lb (227-kg) bombs.

P-51Ds were scattered around China on VJ-Day. Some were flown by the Kuomintang air force.

Above: Captain James J. England in the cockpit of his war-worn P-51A, Jackie. England was an ace who flew with the 311th FG's 330th SS.

Princess is a Fourteenth Air Force P-51C (42-103896), seen here escorting a C-47 Skytrain over China on 24 July 1945. The yellow-tailed Mustang hails from the 530th FS/311th FG. The ADF (aerial direction-finder) antenna on this P-51C is a vital navigation tool in the CBI.

Below right: Gonzales was an F-6D Mustang photo ship of the 2nd Air Commando Group, seen on a combat sortie in the China-Burma-India theatre in early 1945.

Below: In front of the Curtiss P-40 Warhawk it replaced, a 311th P-51B Mustang awaits action at an airfield in China in early 1945. By this time, Merlin-powered P-51B/Cs and P-51Ds had replaced the A-36A and P-51A in the 311th. This ship belongs to the 529th FS. Group and squadron were part of the Tenth Air Force.

easy meat for the Mustangs. After several years of combat flying, even some of the *Experten* were exhausted, their morale shattered, and many fell to the guns of relatively novice Allied pilots during the closing months of the war. Moreover, fuel and ammunition shortages frequently grounded the opposition, and it became difficult for ambitious Allied pilots to find foes, let alone score kills. When the enemy did make an appearance, the results became steadily more predictable, and even the swept-wing, jet-engined Me 262 found itself hunted by the Mustangs.

The Mustang also saw extensive service in the Far East, in both the China/Burma/India theatre and in the Pacific. With the Fifth Air Force, 3rd Air Commando Group began operations with the P-51D in December 1944, flying from the Philippines. The 348th FG converted from the P-47 in January 1945 and the 35th FG traded P-47s for P-51Ds in March 1945. The F-6D and F-6K entered service with the 82nd and 110th TRS of the 71st TRG in late 1944, replacing P-40s.

On 11 January 1945, Major William A. Shomo of the 82nd TRS was at the controls of F-6D 'Snooks 5th' (and not his famous P-51D Mustang (44-72505), the 'Flying Undertaker') on a mission over northern Luzon in the Philippines. Attacked by a swarm of Japanese fighters including Ki-44 ('Tojo') and Ki-61 ('Tony') fighters, Shomo pulled off the unprecedented feat of shooting down seven Japanese warplanes in a single mission. For this achievement, he became the second Mustang pilot of World War II to be awarded the Medal of Honor.

Almost all Fifth Air Force Mustangs wore broad black/white/black bands (narrowly edged in yellow) around the fuselage and wings. The Mustangs of the Fifth were used in support of the invasion of the Philippines, and the assaults on Bataan and Corregidor. They also escorted bombers against targets in Borneo, Formosa, Hong Kong and Canton, before moving to Okinawa and Ie Shima for the final assault on Japan.

Mustangs on Iwo Jima

It was that tiny crag of rock, the island of Iwo Jima, invaded by US Marines on 19 February 1945, which eventually became home for a massive P-51 force. The Seventh Air Force had no Mustangs until the P-51Ds of the 15th Fighter Group began arriving at Iwo Jima's South Field on 6 March 1945, followed by the 21st FG, and (in late April) the 506th FG. Soon P-51 Mustangs, usually carrying two 165 US-gal (137-Imp gal; 625-litre) drop tanks, began escorting B-29 Superfortresses in the final campaign against the Japanese home islands. They also undertook long-range fighter and fighter-bomber sweeps. The Merlin Mustang also served with the 14th Air Force, with P-51Bs and P-51Ds equipping the 23rd FG and 51st FG, often replacing Allison-engined P-51As and A-36s.

The P-51D/K was the version that saw the war out, and is the version familiar to air show crowds today. Thousands of pilots who flew it probably thought it the best fighter in the sky, but it is important for every fighter pilot to feel the same about whatever he flies. To try to settle arguments, in 1991 a limited flight-test programme was flown in the USA on surviving examples of four classic types of fighter: a North American P-51D-30-NT (45-11586, lent by Harry Tope of Mount Pleasant, Michigan), a Republic P-47D-40 (45-49181) and two Navy fighters, a Grumman F6F-5 Hellcat (BuNo. 79683) and a Goodyear FG-1D Corsair (BuNo. 92509), the last-named being a licence-built Vought F4U. The report by John M. Ellis and Christopher A. Wheal was published by the Society of Experimental Test Pilots.

A modern evaluation

The objective was to try to evaluate each of the four on an equal footing. One problem is that today such aircraft

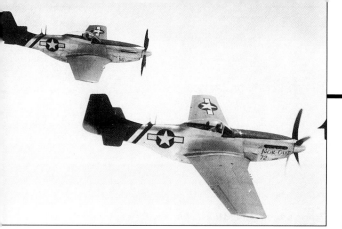

Nok Out *of the 75th FS/23rd FG leads a nameless P-51D on a mission in China late in the war. The 23rd took over the mantle of the Flying Tigers but applied shark's teeth to 76th FS P-51s only. The 51st FG, not linked to the Tigers, had teeth on most of its Mustangs.*

are valuable and almost irreplaceable, they are no longer young, and they have each been subjected over many years to various modifications. The only really serious modification was that the P-47 no longer had a turbosupercharger, which significantly degraded its high-altitude performance, although this was minimised by concentrating on performance at 10,000 ft (3050 m) or below. Because of their age, the airframes were not subjected to stresses exceeding 6g, while non-availability of wartime 115/145-grade fuel resulted in manifold pressures being limited to those appropriate to today's 100LL, which fractionally reduced power of the three aircraft powered by the R-2800 Double Wasp engine.

The fascinating report listed good and bad features under various headings. On the score of Cockpit, the P-51 was an easy winner, with the greatest comfort. The high pedals and inclined seat "gave the feeling of sitting in a high-class sports car", and the fully automatic engine cooling was praised. Such a cockpit was deemed especially important because, unlike the Navy fighters, "by the time battle was joined the [P-51] pilot had already been in the air several hours." (Surprisingly, the most cramped and uncomfortable cockpit was that of the big P-47.)

For taxiing, the P-51 was again top, with its steerable tailwheel linked to the rudder; the freely castoring tailwheels of the rivals forced the pilot in a crosswind "to ride the downwind brake, increasing wear and possibly leading to brake overheating." Take-off came out roughly even, all needing right rudder trim and only the F6F needing right rudder in addition. On Climb, the F6F did best, although the need for sustained right rudder proved tiring; the Mustang's V-1650-9 ran roughly at 4,000 ft (1219 m), resulting in power being reduced, or otherwise it might again have come out on top.

Stalling and spinning

Investigating Stall characteristics was an eye-opener. In combat a pilot is dead if he does not fly to the very limits, and this repeatedly means nudging the stall in the tightest of turns and pull-outs. The P-47 and F6F were easy, and guns could still be aimed accurately well into pre-stall buffet. The Corsair generated severe buffet even in a steady 3g turn, and could rapidly lead into unpredictable motions and sudden departure. The P-51 could manoeuvre well until, with essentially no warning, it would depart violently "with complete loss of control, on occasion rolling through 270°... losing 500 ft... with aileron snatch violent enough to take the stick out of the hand of an unprepared pilot." In practice, it was felt the two-handed stick forces needed to cause departure were so high that a stall/flick was unlikely in combat, although "there are plentiful accounts of Mustangs spinning out of combat engagements."

In testing Turn Performance there was little to choose between the four aircraft, although for both sustained and instantaneous turn the F6F was best; on the other hand, while the P-47 was into buffet at 4.8g and the F6F at 6g, the Mustang and Corsair were buffet-free at 6g up to their maximum level speeds. In manoeuvring stability the Mustang's much higher stick forces in wind-up turns at VMAX

made it a two-handed aircraft, tiring in sustained combat. Measures of static lateral/directional stability gave the Mustang good marks, while roll put it roughly second to the FG-1, and second to the P-47 when rolling under 3g. It came top in dynamic stability, but in a 30° dive and pull-out it was just pipped by the P-47.

Final 'proof of the pudding' tests were mixed. In g-capture and hold the Mustang and FG-1 overshot by 0.5g, and in a 180° turn under high power the FG-1 took 8.5 seconds while the rest were all about 10. Air-to-air tracking was marred by the Mustang's high longitudinal stick force

A wartime censor's caption places this razorback at 'a South China Fourteen Air Force base which was evacuated and blown up on 19 November 1944 under pressure from the Japanese'. This Merlin Mustang looks weathered, as if the pressure is very real.

Left: Major John B. 'Pappy' Herbst, commander of the 23rd FG's 74th FS, scored 18 victories, 14 of them in Mustangs. His vanquished enemies included such types as Ki-43 ('Oscar') and Ki-44 ('Tojo') fighters, two D3A ('Val') dive-bombers, and a DC-2 ('Tess') transport. His P-51B, named Tommy's Dad, *carried an impressive scoreboard, consisting largely of Japanese flags.*

A Merlin-powered, shark-mouthed P-51B/C in China. Many China-based Mustangs wore shark-mouths, following the example of the AVG's Curtiss Hawks.

The location: the costliest chunk of rock ever taken by the US Marines. P-51Ds of the 458th FS/506th FG prepare to escort B-29s to Japan from one of five airfields on Iwo Jima. The 'Zebra' stripes are black and natural metal.

Me Darlin was piloted by Major Morgan R. Beamer, Jr of the 41st FS, who was credited with one aerial victory in November 1944. The unsung 41st served with the equally little-noticed 35th FG, and ended its Pacific war fighting in the Philippines.

and propensity to flick away at about 4.5g, although view ahead was good. In air-to-ground tracking the Mustang was again hampered by high stick forces, although rudder forces were lower. Finally, the automatic radiator controls and fast-reacting propeller made life for the Mustang pilot by far the easiest on the score of power management, eliciting the comment "It is surprising more effort was not given to developing similar systems for other aircraft."

The Conclusions said, in full, "The objective...was to decide which was the best US fighter of World War II. For general all-round comfort, field of view and ease of operation, the Mustang was a hands-down winner. It also scored high in performance, was well suited to long-range escort missions and would do well intercepting non-manoeuvring targets. However, its extraordinarily high stick forces, totally inadequate stall warning and vicious departures make it quite unsuited to the air-combat manoeuvring environment. It is a tribute to the adaptability of the pilots who flew them that Mustangs scored so many kills against the opposition."

Lightweight Mustang

Although the Mustang was a thoroughbred from the start, almost from its inception engineers and pilots spoke of creating a lighter-weight version. A fair amount of funding

Right: P-51D Mustangs of the 45th FS/15th FG head from Iwo Jima toward an escort mission over Japan. The slash on the fin was green.

Below: A black-trimmed P-51D of the 457th FS/15th FG is lightered via barge from an aircraft-carrier to the hard-won airfield near Red Beach One on Saipan.

and design work went into this effort. The real impetus, as with the original design, came from the British.

As noted earlier, the original NA-73 had been designed to higher load factors than the British Air Publication 970 demanded. As a result, the structure was significantly heavier than, for example, a Spitfire. In January 1943 NAA suggested to the USAAF that they should build a special lightweight Mustang, designed to British load factors and also incorporating every possible weight-reduction feature. Edgar Schmued had travelled to England and inspected Supermarine factories, as well as captured Messerschmitts and Focke-Wulfs. The proposal was sanctioned, two XP-51Fs being ordered with a company charge number of NA-105.

The result resembled earlier Mustangs in general appearance only, hardly a single part being common. The wing had a later 'laminar' profile, and was slightly increased in area, to 235 sq ft (21.8 m²), by making the leading edge straight. The fuselage was redesigned, with an integral cradle for the V-1650-7, which drove a lightweight Aeroproducts Unimatic propeller with three hollow steel blades. The cockpit had the standard British panel, and was covered by a relatively gigantic canopy. The radiator duct was again redesigned, the main landing gears were new, with very small wheels with disc brakes, the fuel comprised just two 102-US gal (85-Imp gal; 386-litre) wing tanks, and the four guns had 440 rounds each. The contract was amended to five aircraft, three being XP-51Fs and two XP-51Gs.

The first flight of the XP-51F was made by Bob Chilton on 14 February 1944. Three were built (43-43332/43334). One posed for portraits for record purposes on 10 April, although the pictures apparently were not released until later.

Disappointing performance

Considering that the equipped empty weight was 1 US ton (2,000 lb; 907 kg) less than that of a D or K, the performance was perhaps slightly disappointing, level speed being 466 mph (750 km/h) at 29,000 ft (8839 m). The third example was shipped to England as the Mustang Mk V, FR409. Weighing a mere 7,855 lb (3580 kg) in interceptor trim, it was regarded very highly apart from poor directional stability, which was recognised as a shortcoming of many variants.

The final two lightweight prototypes were completed as XP-51Gs, retaining the NA-105 charge number. They differed mainly in having British-supplied Merlin Mk 145 (RM.14SM) engines, rated at 1,910 hp (1432 kW), driving a Rotol propeller with five densified-wood blades very similar to that used on the Spitfire XIV.

The first flight of the XP-51G appears to be a matter of some dispute. Most sources say the maiden flight was made 10 August 1944 by Edward W. Virgin, who later directed North American operations in Washington, DC. A document from the manufacturer, however, credits Chilton with the first flight on 12 August, while Mustang expert Paul Coggan (below) tells us that pilot Joe Barton may have achieved this honour on 9 August.

Two XP-51Gs were built (43-43335/43336). The second ship went to Boscombe Down and flew with the RAF as FR410, strangely called a Mustang IV, though utterly unlike the standard aircraft of this mark. British priorities

War in the Pacific

Although long range made it ideal for Pacific island-hopping, the Mustang did not reach General George C. Kenney's Fifth Air Force until late 1944, when F-6Ds joined the 82nd TRS/71st TRG in the Philippines. Captain William A. Shomo flew an F-6D on 11 January 1945 when he downed *seven* Japanese aircraft on one sortie, becoming the second Mustang pilot awarded the Medal of Honor.

By the end of the war, three fighter groups were at work in the Philippines. In January 1945, the 3rd Air Commando Group received P-51Ds. The Mustang came into its own in the Pacific after 19 February 1945 when US Marines landed on Iwo Jima to secure fighter bases at a price of 24,000 casualties in the costliest battle to Americans since Gettysburg.

Bloody Iwo had three airfields plus two coral diversion strips. Here the 15th, 21st and 506th FGs with P-51Ds (plus the 507th with P-47Ns) readied for Operation Olympic-Coronet, the invasion of Japan slated for February 1946. First, Mustangs escorted B-29s. The March 1945 firebombing of Tokyo sealed it, and Hiroshima and Nagasaki capped it: the Pacific war was resolved, in its final throes, not by more beach landings but by air power – B-29s helped by P-51s.

Hel-Eter was a P-51D of the 457th FS/506th FG from Iwo Jima. It is seen here circling with a B-29 at a rendezvous point off the coast of Japan in July 1945. Its trim was insignia red. Mustangs and Superfortresses still faced credible opposition even at this late stage in the war.

Tiny Gay Babe and Three of a Kind belonged to the 72nd FS/21st FG and were caught up in combat missions from Iwo Jima in early 1945. Over-water navigation rapidly became a major challenge to the single man in the P-51 cockpit.

apparently had changed, however, and the fate of FR410 is unclear after the end of test flying in February 1945. The first XP-51G with a five-bladed Dowty Rotol propeller was used only once on a 20-minute flight and deemed a failure. Contrary to what most sources have told the world, all other flying was apparently carried out with more conventional Aeroproducts Unimatic A-542-B1 four-bladed propellers.

Remarkably, this first, very rare XP-51G fighter has survived. The book 'Mustang Survivors' by Paul A. Coggan recounts the efforts in the 1980s by John Morgan of La Canada, California to restore and fly 43-43335. Morgan's task was not easy, for the XP-51G has parts not interchangeable with heavier, mass-produced Mustangs. It also has a different centre of gravity.

In any event, the XP-51G was clearly the 'hottest ship' ever built by NAA, with a speed of 485 mph (780 km/h) at 20,750 ft (6329 m), even at the higher weight of 8,879 lb (4031 kg), and one pilot at Boscombe Down claimed a speed of 495 mph (796 km/h) with it in February 1945, although NAA's own figure for the other G was 472 mph (759 km/h) at the same height.

XP-51J

For comparative purposes, NAA added to the NA-105 programme two aircraft designated XP-51J. These reverted to one of the latest versions of the engine fitted to all the earlier Mustangs, the Allison. The V-1710-119 gave 1,500 hp (1125 kW) for take-off, and no less than 1,720 hp (1290 kW) with water injection at 20,700 ft (6309 ft). A dorsal fin was fitted, and in an attempt to reduce drag the inlet to the injection-type carburettor was in the roof of the radiator duct, to give a perfectly streamlined nose. First flown on 23 April 1945, by Joe Barton, the first XP-51J weighed 7,550 lb (3435 kg) and had been predicted to reach 491 mph (790 km/h), but the engine was not yet cleared for full-power operation, so no performance measurements could be taken.

After the war, Bob Chilton was asked why no inflight photos of the XP-51F, XP-51G and XP-51J have survived. Chilton said that, to his knowledge, none were taken. Pilots and others were too busy with testing programmes to schedule photo sessions. In later years, North American's Gene Boswell looked for a photographic record of these experimental lightweight Mustangs in the air, but his search was in vain.

While the lightweight Mustangs were not superior in every aspect of mission performance – they were not as easy to maintain and were ill-equipped to operate from rough airfields – the XP-51F, G and J out-performed other Mustangs. In time, they led to a production ship which incorporated mature thinking on how to build a light-

weight Mustang, namely the P-51H.

From early 1943 it had been evident that a great deal could be done to improve the mass-produced D/K, and that the NA-105 was an excellent basis. Accordingly, and under considerable pressure, the NAA advanced design staff, now grown to a strength of many hundreds of engineers, worked on a derivative aircraft specifically intended to be the future baseline fighter. The USAAF allocated the designation P-51H.

A very important advance was the availability from Packard and Continental of a further-uprated production Merlin, the V-1650-9. Cleared to operate on 150-grade fuel, this engine gave 1,380 hp (1035 kW) for take-off at sea level, but as it climbed the power increased until, with water/methanol injection, the war emergency power peaked at 2,218 hp (1663 kW) at 10,200 ft (3109 m) and 1,900 hp (1425 kW) at over 20,000 ft (6096 m). This fitted

Jumpin Jacques was a Dallas-built P-51D (44-64076) of the 3rd Air Commando Group. It had a Bugs Bunny badge below its cockpit. The spinner, nose flash, tail and nickname were in medium blue. Fuselage and wing stripes are black and white. The 3rd fought in the Philippines in 1945.

Mustang Colour Schemes

United States Army Air Force

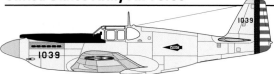

Prototypes
(Second XP-51-NA, 41-39, Wright Field)
Wearing the pre-war neutrality stripes on the tail and simple white stars (without bars, but with red centre dots), this aircraft typifies the colours worn by USAAC fighters in 1940-41.

P-51 initial USAAF scheme
(41-37452, c.August 1942)
The type 2 insignia, without red central dot, was introduced on 18 August 1942. Mustangs initially carried a 40-in diameter version. The first production USAAF P-51s were camouflaged.

A-36A initial USAAF scheme
(42-84067, c. December 1942)
A-36s had a slightly different camouflage demarcation line between top surface and underside colours. The fuselage insignia was reduced to 30-in diameter and moved forward to give more space for the radio call number and unit codes.

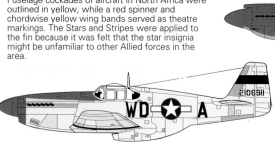

P-51 North Africa
(41-3722, 154th OS, c. April 1943)
Fuselage cockades of aircraft in North Africa were outlined in yellow, while a red spinner and chordwise yellow wing bands served as theatre markings. The Stars and Stripes were applied to the fin because it was felt that the star insignia might be unfamiliar to other Allied forces in the area.

A-36A North Africa, post-June 1943
(42-8390, 27th FBG, August 1943)
The star and bar was introduced on 29 June 1943, and was initially outlined in red. This sometimes displaced the call number to the fin. Two-digit unit codes were usually in white on the fin, sometimes side-by-side, sometimes vertical.

P-51B early ETO c. 1944
(43-6928, 358th FS, 355th FG)
The danger of confusing ETO Mustangs with Bf109s was such that chordwise white bands were applied to the fin, tailplanes and wings, with a white nose and spinner. The star and bar lost its red outline from 17 September 1943.

Identification bands were applied in black on natural metal aircraft.

P-51B ETO May 1944
(42-106911, 355th FS, 4th FG)
Natural metal finished ETO Mustangs had their identification markings in black. Many 8th and 9th Air Force Mustangs had their black or white nose bands and spinners repainted in the group colour. Two-letter unit codes and a single-letter individual code were separated by the star and bar, RAF-style.

P-51B ETO May 1944
(42-106924, 354th FS, 4th FG)
The chordwise identification stripe across the fin was quickly deleted because it was judged to break up the distinctive outline of the Mustang's fin. Some 4th FG and 9th AF aircraft had it overpainted in red as an additional group marking.

P-51B ETO June 1944
(43-6928, 362nd FS, 357th FG)
Before D-Day, many natural metal Mustangs had their top surfaces recamouflaged, necessitating the reintroduction of white recognition bands on the tops of the tailplanes and wings. Fins were sometimes camouflaged, and sometimes left in natural metal. D-Day invasion stripes initially encircled the entire fuselage and wings.

P-51D ETO August 1944
(44-13305, 354th FS, 355th FG)
D-Day stripes were removed from the top surfaces of Allied aircraft soon after D-Day (in July), to help reduce conspicuity on the ground, especially on forward airfields. Wing stripes were removed from September 1944 and underfuselage stripes disappeared in early 1945.

When the white identification bands were applied in the field, they were often ragged and not of constant width.

P-51D Mediterranean 1943/44
The initial recognition marking for MTO-based Mustangs was an 18-in yellow band whose outer edge was 9-in from the flap/aileron junction on the trailing edge.

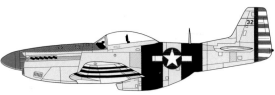

P-51D MTO 1945
(44-15569, 100th FS, 332nd FG April 1945)
Mustangs in the MTO used a red spinner and yellow wing bands as their theatre identification markings. Entire tail units were painted in group colours, after an initial brief period in which more discrete markings were used.

P-51D Pacific 1945
(39th FS, 35 FG, April 1945)
Mustangs in the Pacific and China/Burma/India theatres had no overall theatre markings. The Fifth Air Force did use broad black bands as seen here. The pre-war type rudder stripes were a group marking, with the spinners reserved for squadron colours.

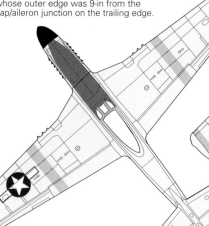

P-51D Mediterranean 1945
The original mid-wing yellow stripe was moved inboard to the wingroot, and was often augmented by a narrower (10 in) stripe at the wingroot.

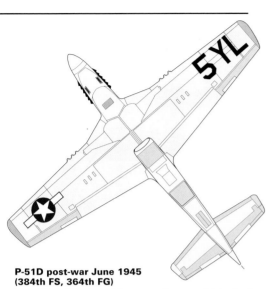

P-51D post-war June 1945
(384th FS, 364th FG)

Incredibly, within days of the war ending, complaints about low flying began to be heard. The USAAF repeated unit and aircraft codes under the port wing in an effort to make identification of low-flying aircraft easier. When the USAAF gained its independence as the USAF in 1947, the legend USAF was applied under the port wing, above the starboard wing and on the fuselage sides. The fuselage inscription was later changed to read 'US AIR FORCE' on some aircraft. Air National Guard aircraft had the abbreviated name of their unit in the same place. From about 1950 most regular P-51s had buzz numbers consisting of two letters (FF for F-51s and RF for recce aircraft) and three numerals (the last three of the serial).

Mustang III RAF 1944
(FB201, No. 19 Squadron, February 1944)

RAF Mustang IIIs used the same white identification bands as USAAF ETO-based Mustangs, and most also had standard RAF yellow wing leading-edge bands. The bands around the fin and tailplanes were very soon removed, leaving only those around the wingroots and on the nose.

Royal Australian Air Force

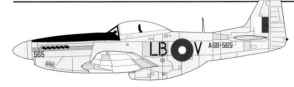

P-51K FEAF 1945
(A68-565, No. 84 Squadron, July 1945)

RAAF Mustangs based in Northern Australia and Labuan during the closing stages of the war (and just after) wore blue and white SEAC-style roundels and fin flashes, and A68- prefixed serials. RAAF Mustangs in Europe were actually borrowed from the RAF and wore standard RAF colours.

Royal New Zealand Air Force

P-51D early RNZAF
(NZ2423, No. 1 Repair Depot, August 1952)

Delivered in USAAF markings, New Zealand's Mustangs initially retained their US serials, and had roundels applied directly over the US star, leaving the blue and white bars visible.

United States Army

F-51D US Army 1970s
(O-72990, Edwards AFB, 1977)

The three Army Mustangs used as chase aircraft wore the olive drab and white colour scheme used by other less unusual Army fixed-wing types, with a black cheatline and red wing and fin tips. The serial prefix was O (not 0) for 'obsolete'.

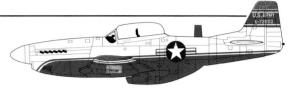

Royal Air Force

Mustang I RAF 1944
(AG366, No. 26 Squadron, May 1942)

The RAF's first Mustangs were delivered in brown and green camouflage with sky undersides. Non-standard Type A1 roundels were applied, with broader white and yellow rings. Sky spinners and fuselage band were *de rigueur* on RAF single-engined fighters. Because ocean grey paint was in short supply some aircraft had a locally-mixed alternative, using medium sea grey and black.

Mustang I RAF 1944
(AG550, No. II Squadron, July 1942)

The dark green and brown camouflage useful for camouflaging aircraft on their airfields was replaced when the RAF went on the offensive, and Mustang Is were among the first aircraft to be repainted in ocean grey and dark green.

Mustang I RAF 1944
(AM148, No. 26 Squadron, August 1942)

The similarity in shape between the Mustang and the Bf 109 led to the addition of yellow chordwise bands on the upper surfaces of the wings. Simultaneously, all RAF fighters received yellow leading edges as a recognition feature head-on.

Mustang III RAF 1944
(No. 126 Squadron, late 1944)

Many of the Mustangs flying anti-diver patrols had their white identification markings and yellow leading-edge stripes removed.

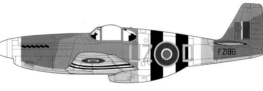

Mustang III RAF 1944
(No. 126 Squadron, 1944)

D-Day invasion stripes were introduced on 4 June 1944.

P-51D British Commonwealth Occupation Force.
(A68-808, No. 76 Squadron, 1946)

Full-colour roundels and fin flashes were reinstated soon after the war. This basic colour scheme was used for the rest of the Mustang's RAAF career, with variations in spinner colours between the various squadrons.

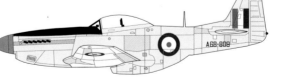

While RAF Mustang IIIs used white stripes like those applied to USAAF ETO P-51s, earlier aircraft used a 12-in yellow band like that originally applied to MTO P-51s, in the same mid-span position.

P-51D RNZAF
(NZ2414, No. 1 Squadron)

The four RNZAF squadrons used checkers as unit markings, placed over the old USAAF bars. No. 2 Squadron used black and yellow, No. 3 black and red and No. 4 blue and yellow.

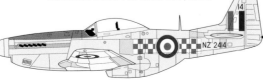

P-51D RNZAF alternative marking style
(NZ2429, No. 4 Squadron, 1953)

One of the RNZAF squadrons initially used a chevron and bar insignia instead of checkers, but this did not last long.

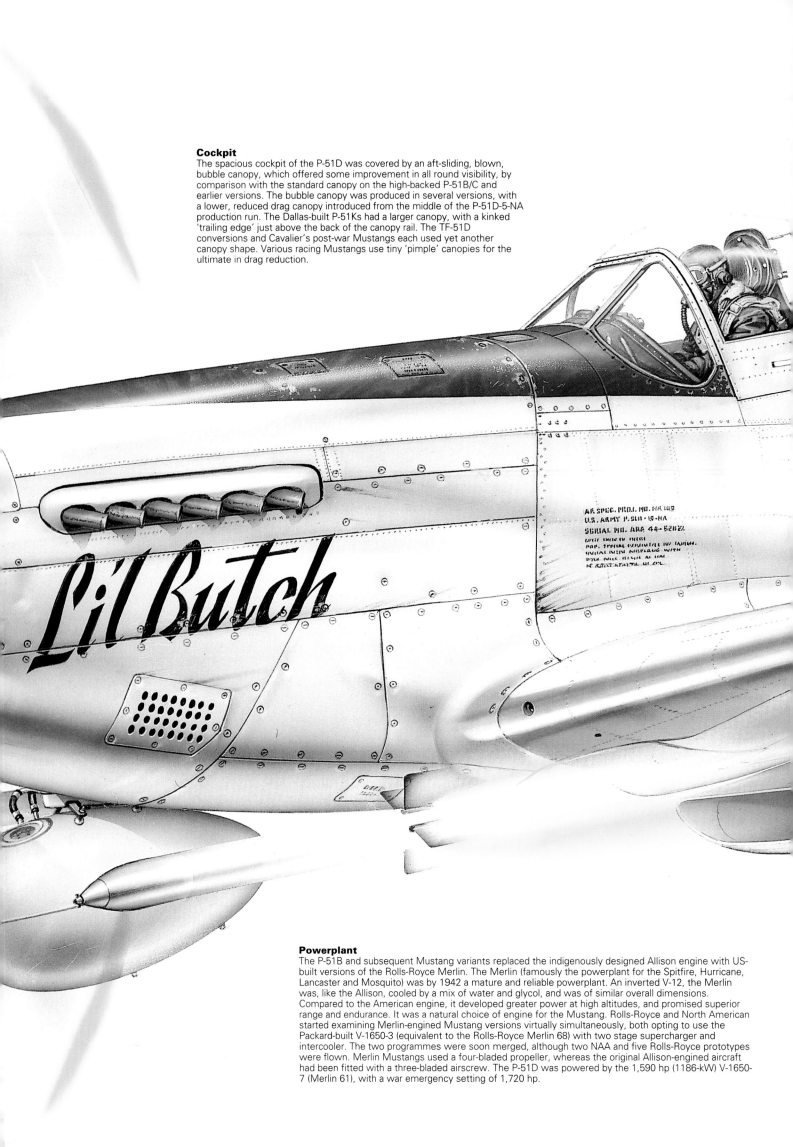

Cockpit

The spacious cockpit of the P-51D was covered by an aft-sliding, blown, bubble canopy, which offered some improvement in all round visibility, by comparison with the standard canopy on the high-backed P-51B/C and earlier versions. The bubble canopy was produced in several versions, with a lower, reduced drag canopy introduced from the middle of the P-51D-5-NA production run. The Dallas-built P-51Ks had a larger canopy, with a kinked 'trailing edge' just above the back of the canopy rail. The TF-51D conversions and Cavalier's post-war Mustangs each used yet another canopy shape. Various racing Mustangs use tiny 'pimple' canopies for the ultimate in drag reduction.

Powerplant

The P-51B and subsequent Mustang variants replaced the indigenously designed Allison engine with US-built versions of the Rolls-Royce Merlin. The Merlin (famously the powerplant for the Spitfire, Hurricane, Lancaster and Mosquito) was by 1942 a mature and reliable powerplant. An inverted V-12, the Merlin was, like the Allison, cooled by a mix of water and glycol, and was of similar overall dimensions. Compared to the American engine, it developed greater power at high altitudes, and promised superior range and endurance. It was a natural choice of engine for the Mustang. Rolls-Royce and North American started examining Merlin-engined Mustang versions virtually simultaneously, both opting to use the Packard-built V-1650-3 (equivalent to the Rolls-Royce Merlin 68) with two stage supercharger and intercooler. The two programmes were soon merged, although two NAA and five Rolls-Royce prototypes were flown. Merlin Mustangs used a four-bladed propeller, whereas the original Allison-engined aircraft had been fitted with a three-bladed airscrew. The P-51D was powered by the 1,590 hp (1186-kW) V-1650-7 (Merlin 61), with a war emergency setting of 1,720 hp.

Colour scheme

The USAAF initially painted its Mustangs olive drab overall, with grey undersurfaces. This gave way to a natural metal finish. In Europe, upper surfaces were again camouflaged during 1944, before overall natural metal was reintroduced. Many aircraft actually had their wings painted silver, while the fuselages were left in bare metal finish. The top decking forward of the cockpit was painted matt olive drab to serve as an anti-dazzle panel. National markings were without red centre discs or stripes, in order to avoid any confusion with the Japanese 'meatball'. Various schemes were used to avoid misidentification – P-51s in Europe wearing white (or black on silver aircraft) noses and stripes on wings and tails, while some aircraft in the Far East had equally prominent black bands, though these were never completely standardised.

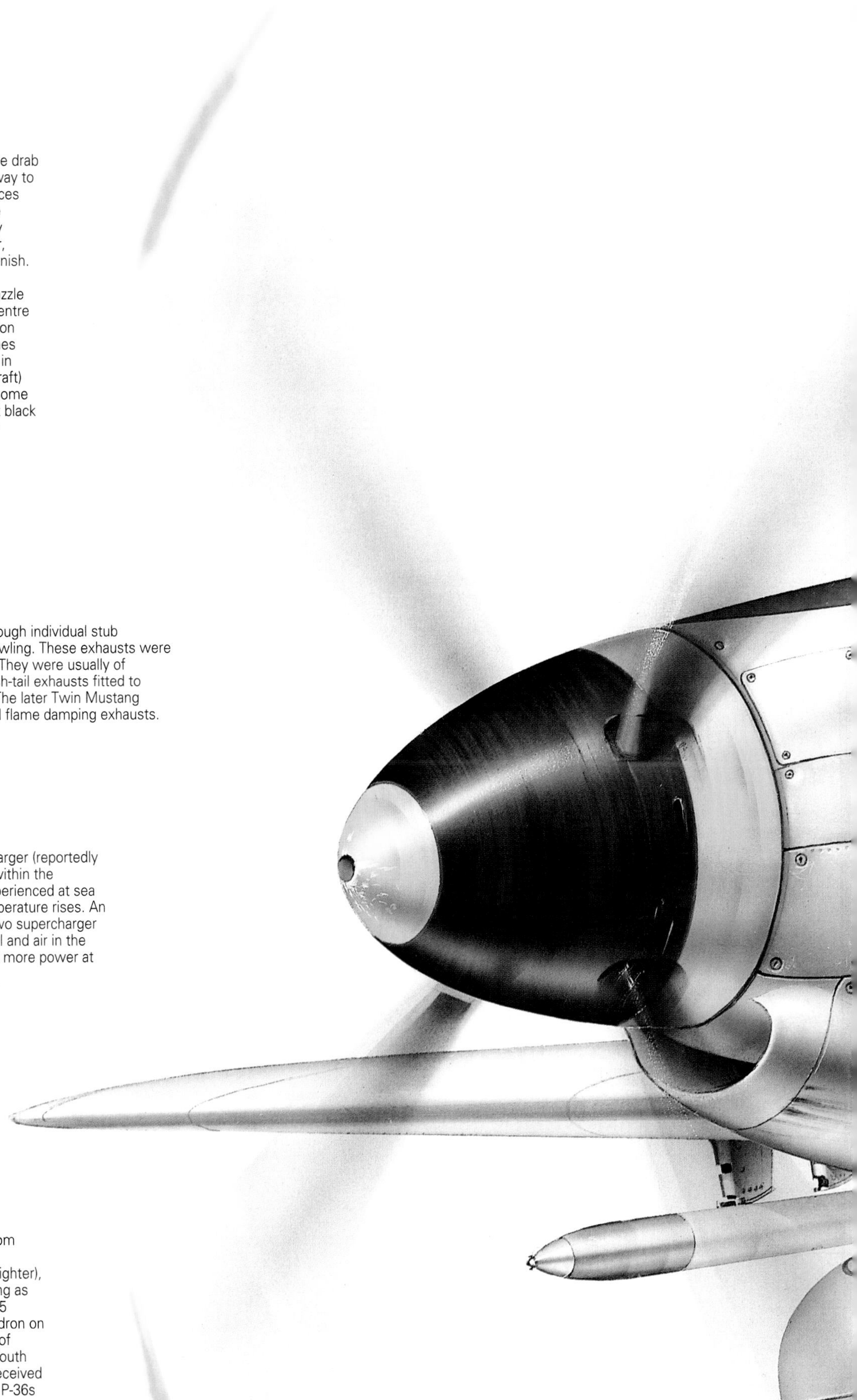

Exhausts

The Merlin's twelve cylinders exhausted through individual stub exhausts projecting from the sides of the cowling. These exhausts were often faired in, with a shroud, as seen here. They were usually of circular cross-section, unlike the flattened fish-tail exhausts fitted to many of the earlier Allison-engined aircraft. The later Twin Mustang (which was also Allison-powered) introduced flame damping exhausts.

Supercharger

The Merlin's two-speed, two-stage supercharger (reportedly designed by Wright) maintained pressures within the induction system equal to the pressures experienced at sea level. When any gas is compressed, its temperature rises. An intercooler is therefore used between the two supercharger compressors, giving a denser mixture of fuel and air in the cylinder. The supercharged Merlin produced more power at 26,000 ft than the Allison did on take off.

The 47th Fighter Squadron

Today an AFRes squadron flying the A-10 from Barksdale, the 47th Fighter Squadron was constituted (as the 47th Pursuit Squadron (Fighter), USAAC) on 22 November 1940, redesignating as the 47th Fighter Squadron (Interceptor) on 15 February 1942 and as the 47th Fighter Squadron on 15 May 1942. After moving around a series of airfields in Hawaii, the squadron moved to South Field, Iwo Jima in February 1945. The unit received Mustangs in 1944, after flying P-26s, P-40s, P-36s and P-47s. The squadron received a Distinguished Unit Citation on 7 April 1945. One of the squadron's fellow units in the 15th Fighter Group, the 45th Fighter Squadron had a similar history, while the other had a longer tradition, dating back to 1918! The 15th Fighter Group supported the invasion of Iwo with bombing and strafing missions, flying similar sorties against enemy targets in the Bonin Islands in March. It flew its first mission to Japan on 7 April, escorting B-29s which pulverised the Nakajima plant near Tokyo. The Group transferred to the 20th Air Force during the Summer of 1945. The Group inactivated on 15 October 1946 after moving back to the States in November 1945.

Propeller

Most examples of the P-51D were fitted with a four-bladed J-6523A-24 or K-6523A-24 Hamilton Standard propeller, with drag reducing 'cuffs' at the roots. Such cuffs were often removed in service, especially after the war. Some later aircraft used a square-tipped 'paddle-bladed' Model 6547A-6 Hamilton Standard prop, while P-51Ks had an 11ft 2 in diameter, four-bladed A20-156-24M Aeroproducts propeller.

Royal Canadian Air Force

P-51D early RCAF
(9566, EPE, c.1946)
Post-war, the RCAF adopted a maple leaf as the centrepiece of its roundel. This was initially tactical style, without the centre white ring.

Mustang IV RCAF
(9569, No. 402 Squadron, c. 1950)
The maple leaf roundel was soon replaced. Colourful markings became common, especially on reservist units.

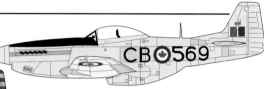

Mustang IV later RCAF
(9569 Trenton station flight)
RAF-style three-letter codes were replaced by USAF-style buzz numbers during the early 1950s. Mustangs did not survive long enough to replace their fin flashes with the Canadian ensign, however.

South African Air Force

F-51D SAAF
(334, No. 2 Squadron, 1951)
South Africa's borrowed Mustangs received SAAF serials and full national insignia, while flying with the USAF's 18th FBW in Korea.

Royal Netherlands Air Force

P-51D Netherlands East Indies AF
(H-315, No. 121 Squadron, 1945)
When supplied to the Dutch at the end of the war, the Mustangs carried simple markings which recalled the Dutch flag.

P-51D Netherlands East Indies AF
(H-322, No. 121 Squadron, 1949)
The two Mustang squadrons of the Netherlands East Indies AF wore red and blue spinners, respectively for Nos 121 and 122 Squadrons. Dutch roundels reappeared very soon after the end of the war.

Chinese Nationalist Air Force

P-51B Chinese Nationalist Air Force
(serial and unit unknown, c. 1945)
China's Mustangs wore a variety of colour schemes, depending on their origin. Many were extremely well-worn. P-51Bs and Cs tended to have over-large national insignia.

P-51B Chinese Nationalist AF
(unit unknown c. 1946)
Few Chinese Mustangs carried codes or unit markings, many even omitted serials. Blue and white rudder stripes became part of the national insignia.

P-51D Chinese Nationalist Air Force
(P-14371, unit unknown c. 1946)
Unusually, this P-51D has both its Chinese serial and its former USAAF identity on its tailfin. It has the small national insignia common (but far from standard) on the P-51D.

Indonesian National Armed Forces – Air Force

P-51D Tentara National Indonesia –
Angkatan Udara (F-319, 1950)
On its ex-RNEIAF Mustangs Indonesia simply applied its own national flag, replaced the Dutch roundel with a long hyphen and changed the serial prefix.

P-51D Tentara National
Indonesia – Angkatan Udara
(F-303, c. 1956)
Indonesia soon devised its own national insignia, but retained the old Dutch East Indies serialling system.

Republic of Korea Air Force

F-51D Republic of Korea Air Force
(18, 1st Fighter Squadron, 1951)
The Korean Mustangs were transferred directly from USAF stocks and retained their USAF colours, with a new centre for the star and bar, a large K on the tail (later increased in thickness) and with a two-letter code on the forward fuselage.

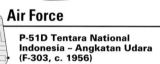

Armée de l'Air

F-6D Armée de l'Air
(44-7207, GC II/33, 1946)
At the start of their service lives, French Mustangs carried rudder stripes (replaced by modest fin flashes), and carried only a single-code letter.

F-6C Armée de l'Air
(44-10889, GC II/33, 1951)
French Mustangs were delivered from USAAF stocks and retained USAAF serials, with full French national insignia and three-digit codes.

F-6D Armée de l'Air
(44-14743, GC II/33, 1951)
Most French Mustangs carried a squadron badge on the fin, but this was always fairly small. Some later had badges below the cockpit, at the end of their service lives.

Flygvapen

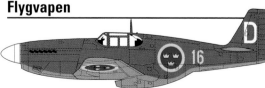

P-51B interned & impressed
(26001, F16 c. 1945)
Mustangs interned by Sweden generally retained the colour schemes in which they had arrived. When impressed into Swedish air force service they were repainted and received full national insignia.

P-51D Flygvapen
(26003, F16, c. 1946)
Two P-51Ds wore green and grey camouflage. The first was an interned aircraft which had always been thus painted, but the second was repainted in service.

P-51D Flygvapen standard scheme
(26097, F8, c.1953)
Swedish P-51s carried the wing number in yellow next to the fuselage insignia, with an individual-letter code on the fin. The HQ flight used white, the first squadron red, the second blue, the third yellow and the fifth green. F8 was a liaison unit and applied all codes in green.

North American P-51 Mustang

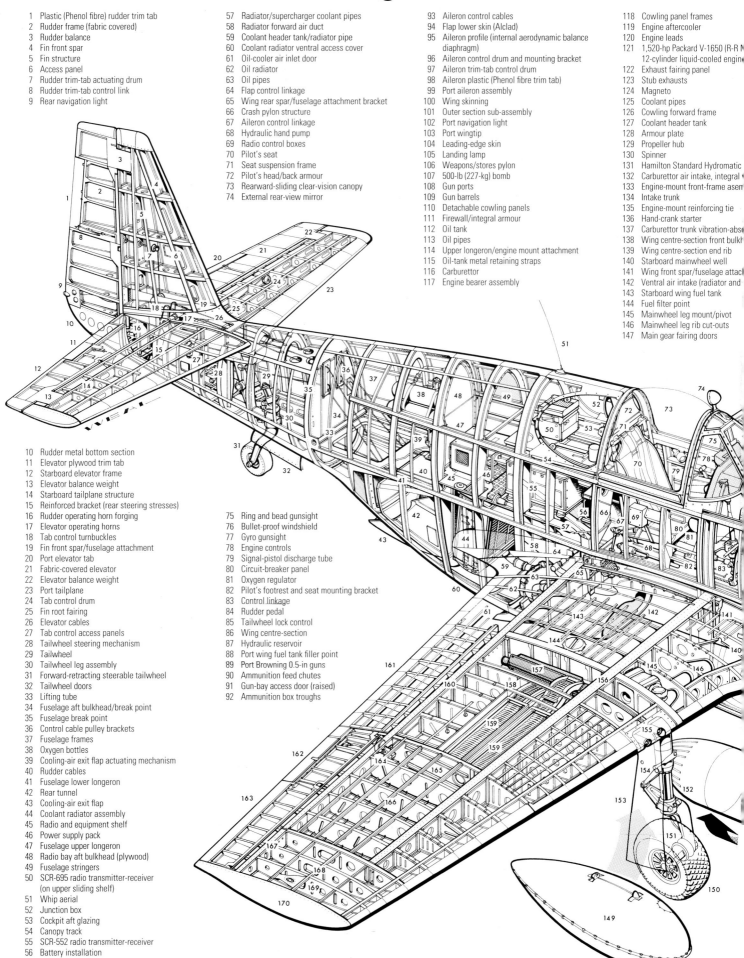

1 Plastic (Phenol fibre) rudder trim tab
2 Rudder frame (fabric covered)
3 Rudder balance
4 Fin front spar
5 Fin structure
6 Access panel
7 Rudder trim-tab actuating drum
8 Rudder trim-tab control link
9 Rear navigation light
10 Rudder metal bottom section
11 Elevator plywood trim tab
12 Starboard elevator frame
13 Elevator balance weight
14 Starboard tailplane structure
15 Reinforced bracket (rear steering stresses)
16 Rudder operating horn forging
17 Elevator operating horns
18 Tab control turnbuckles
19 Fin front spar/fuselage attachment
20 Port elevator tab
21 Fabric-covered elevator
22 Elevator balance weight
23 Port tailplane
24 Tab control drum
25 Fin root fairing
26 Elevator cables
27 Tab control access panels
28 Tailwheel steering mechanism
29 Tailwheel
30 Tailwheel leg assembly
31 Forward-retracting steerable tailwheel
32 Tailwheel doors
33 Lifting tube
34 Fuselage aft bulkhead/break point
35 Fuselage break point
36 Control cable pulley brackets
37 Fuselage frames
38 Oxygen bottles
39 Cooling-air exit flap actuating mechanism
40 Rudder cables
41 Fuselage lower longeron
42 Rear tunnel
43 Cooling-air exit flap
44 Coolant radiator assembly
45 Radio and equipment shelf
46 Power supply pack
47 Fuselage upper longeron
48 Radio bay aft bulkhead (plywood)
49 Fuselage stringers
50 SCR-695 radio transmitter-receiver (on upper sliding shelf)
51 Whip aerial
52 Junction box
53 Cockpit aft glazing
54 Canopy track
55 SCR-552 radio transmitter-receiver
56 Battery installation

57 Radiator/supercharger coolant pipes
58 Radiator forward air duct
59 Coolant header tank/radiator pipe
60 Coolant radiator ventral access cover
61 Oil-cooler air inlet door
62 Oil radiator
63 Oil pipes
64 Flap control linkage
65 Wing rear spar/fuselage attachment bracket
66 Crash pylon structure
67 Aileron control linkage
68 Hydraulic hand pump
69 Radio control boxes
70 Pilot's seat
71 Seat suspension frame
72 Pilot's head/back armour
73 Rearward-sliding clear-vision canopy
74 External rear-view mirror
75 Ring and bead gunsight
76 Bullet-proof windshield
77 Gyro gunsight
78 Engine controls
79 Signal-pistol discharge tube
80 Circuit-breaker panel
81 Oxygen regulator
82 Pilot's footrest and seat mounting bracket
83 Control linkage
84 Rudder pedal
85 Tailwheel lock control
86 Wing centre-section
87 Hydraulic reservoir
88 Port wing fuel tank filler point
89 Port Browning 0.5-in guns
90 Ammunition feed chutes
91 Gun-bay access door (raised)
92 Ammunition box troughs

93 Aileron control cables
94 Flap lower skin (Alclad)
95 Aileron profile (internal aerodynamic balance diaphragm)
96 Aileron control drum and mounting bracket
97 Aileron trim-tab control drum
98 Aileron plastic (Phenol fibre trim tab)
99 Port aileron assembly
100 Wing skinning
101 Outer section sub-assembly
102 Port navigation light
103 Port wingtip
104 Leading-edge skin
105 Landing lamp
106 Weapons/stores pylon
107 500-lb (227-kg) bomb
108 Gun ports
109 Gun barrels
110 Detachable cowling panels
111 Firewall/integral armour
112 Oil tank
113 Oil pipes
114 Upper longeron/engine mount attachment
115 Oil-tank metal retaining straps
116 Carburettor
117 Engine bearer assembly

118 Cowling panel frames
119 Engine aftercooler
120 Engine leads
121 1,520-hp Packard V-1650 (R-R M 12-cylinder liquid-cooled engine
122 Exhaust fairing panel
123 Stub exhausts
124 Magneto
125 Coolant pipes
126 Cowling forward frame
127 Coolant header tank
128 Armour plate
129 Propeller hub
130 Spinner
131 Hamilton Standard Hydromatic
132 Carburettor air intake, integral
133 Engine-mount front-frame asem
134 Intake trunk
135 Engine-mount reinforcing tie
136 Hand-crank starter
137 Carburettor trunk vibration-abso
138 Wing centre-section front bulkh
139 Wing centre-section end rib
140 Starboard mainwheel well
141 Wing front spar/fuselage attac
142 Ventral air intake (radiator and
143 Starboard wing fuel tank
144 Fuel filter point
145 Mainwheel leg mount/pivot
146 Mainwheel leg rib cut-outs
147 Main gear fairing doors

Tail unit

The Mustang's tail unit was little changed during the course of production. A dorsal fillet was added during the manufacturing run of the P-51D, and was subsequently retrofitted to many early Ds and even some P-51Bs and P-51Cs. This added keel area and restored stability lost when the rear fuselage upper-decking was cut down and the bubble canopy was introduced. Many Mustangs incorporated AN/APS-13 tail warning radar, and these had an array of rod and linked-rod antennas projecting at right angles from the sides of the fin. The tail unit was entirely conventional, with a single fixed fin and full-height internally mass-balanced rudder and fixed horizontal tailplanes with no dihedral. The rudder was fabric covered, with a metal skinned trim tab, while the elevators were metal skinned as well as their trim tabs. All variants, from the first prototype NA-73X onwards, had a fully-retractable tailwheel which was covered by a pair of narrow doors when it retracted forwards into the rear fuselage. The Mustang's nose and tailfin were the usual sites for the display of squadron and group insignia. These included simple group-coloured rudders (sometimes with trim tabs picked out in a squadron colour), stripes, checkers and geometric shapes. Sometimes the entire tail unit would be painted in the group's colours. The permutations were almost endless, and were sometimes duplicated in different theatres.

Keith Fretwell

Wing

The one-piece wing was built around two main spars, with a smaller auxiliary spar at the leading edge. It accommodated two fuel tanks in the centre section, each containing 92 US gal (348 litres) of fuel. The fuselage tank contained a further 85 US gal (321 litres). The wing of the Mustang changed little in planform from the NA-73X to the P-51K, but changed in almost every detail. The gun bays were altered to accommodate various weapons, from the four 0.30-in and two 0.50-in guns of the original P-51 (which had two more 0.50 calibres in the nose), to the four 20-mm cannon of the Mustang IA (P-51A), the four 0.50-in Brownings of the P-51B/C or the six 0.50 calibres of the P-51D. The A-36A incorporated dive brakes on the upper and lower surfaces of the wings. All production Mustang versions had underwing hardpoints plumbed and wired for the carriage of fuel tanks or weapons.

North American P-51D-20-NA Mustang
7th Fighter Squadron, 15th Fighter Group
Seventh Air Force
US Army Air Force
Iwo Jima, 1945

This Inglewood-built P-51D-20-NA of the 47th Fighter Squadron wears the unit's distinctive yellow-edged black wing and fuselage bands and fin triangle, and black-banded yellow spinner. Other squadrons in the group used diagonal green stripes edged in black on wings, tail and fuselage, and black and yellow fin, wing and tailplane tips. These very large and prominent markings allowed easy differentiation between Mustangs and enemy fighters. Although it had Mustangs for only a relatively brief time (its aircraft arrived at Iwo Jima from 6 March 1945), the 15th Fighter Group notched up an impressive record. The 47th Fighter Squadron alone notched up 36 kills during its brief Mustang era. This was no mean achievement, since while the quality and experience level of the average Japanese fighter pilot was declining, his morale and commitment was not, and 'easy kills' were few and far between. While primarily tasked with escorting bombers (mainly B-29s) en route to Japan, the Group's three squadrons also flew fighter sweeps and even strafing missions, although in the Far East as in Europe, the Mustang's forte was long-range escort, its comfortable cockpit, easy engine handling and long range making it perfect for long duration missions. For the long haul to Japan, aircraft usually carried a pair of 165 US gal (624.5 litres) tanks, although smaller tanks were sometimes substituted. The Mustang served for slightly longer with the Fifth Air Force (initially from bases in the Philippines) and was an important type in the USAAF's 14th Air Force in the forgotten war in the CBI (China, Burma, India) theatre. In the end, though, the Mustang really won its spurs in the skies over Germany, with the Eighth, Ninth and Fifteenth Air Force fighter groups who escorted vulnerable USAAF heavies to targets at the very heart of Nazi Germany. They were the only fighters that could routinely go to Berlin and back, and as such their value was incalculable. Could the bomber offensive against the Third Reich have been won without the Mustang? The answer will never be known, though it is certain that without P-51 escort fighters, the battle would have been even costlier.

462822

150

Armament

In its primary fighter escort role, the P-51D relied on its internal armament of six Browning M2 0.50 calibre machine guns, three mounted side by side in each wing, together with 400 rounds for each inboard gun and 270 rounds for the other four guns. Every fifth round was usually a tracer, but the mix of tracer and Armour Piercing or incendiary ammunition varied according to Command and even Group. Spent ammunition cases were simply ejected through rectangular ports on the underside of the wing. The guns were mounted upright, eliminating many of the jamming problems encountered in the four-gun P-51B and P-51C. The Mustang also had underwing hardpoints for an external fuel tank or bomb (500 lb, or from the P-51D, 1,000 lb). This pylon could even mount a 'bazooka' type three-tube M10 launcher for 4.5 in rockets. The standard P-51D tank (seen here) was made of metal, and contained 75 US gal (284 litres), a larger tank of similar shape contained 110 US gal (416 litres). In an effort to save metal, and to avoid littering Germany with useful aluminium which could be recycled, a 108-US gal (409-litre) tank of impregnated paper construction was used by Eighth Air Force Mustang units. Redundant fuel tanks were often converted to serve as Napalm containers. The aircraft could also be fitted with zero-length launchers for unguided 5-in rocket projectiles (seen here). These launchers were simple streamlined mini-pylons, to which rockets were directly clipped. With no rocket rail they represented a remarkably low-drag weapon mount.

Intake

The Mustang's liquid-cooled Merlin engine relied on a complex air-cooled radiator. This was mounted in the belly, aft of the wing trailing edge. The radiator was 'fed' with air by a massive ventral airscoop. This was a low-drag solution to the cooling problem, but the radiator's location made it vulnerable to ground fire. The intake of the Merlin Mustang, like that of the A-36, was fixed, while the P-51 and P-51A had articulated intakes, with opening lips to admit more airflow under certain conditions, especially on the ground. The mouth of the intake was of considerably greater cross-sectional area than that fitted to Allison-engined aircraft, reflecting the Merlins increased requirement for cooling air. All Mustangs had an opening rear vent, downstream of the radiator itself. In certain circumstances, the expulsion of hot air from this duct actually gave a slight improvement in performance. The first British Merlin Mustang conversions had a chin-type air intake, dramatically altering the aircraft's appearance.

North American P-51 Mustang

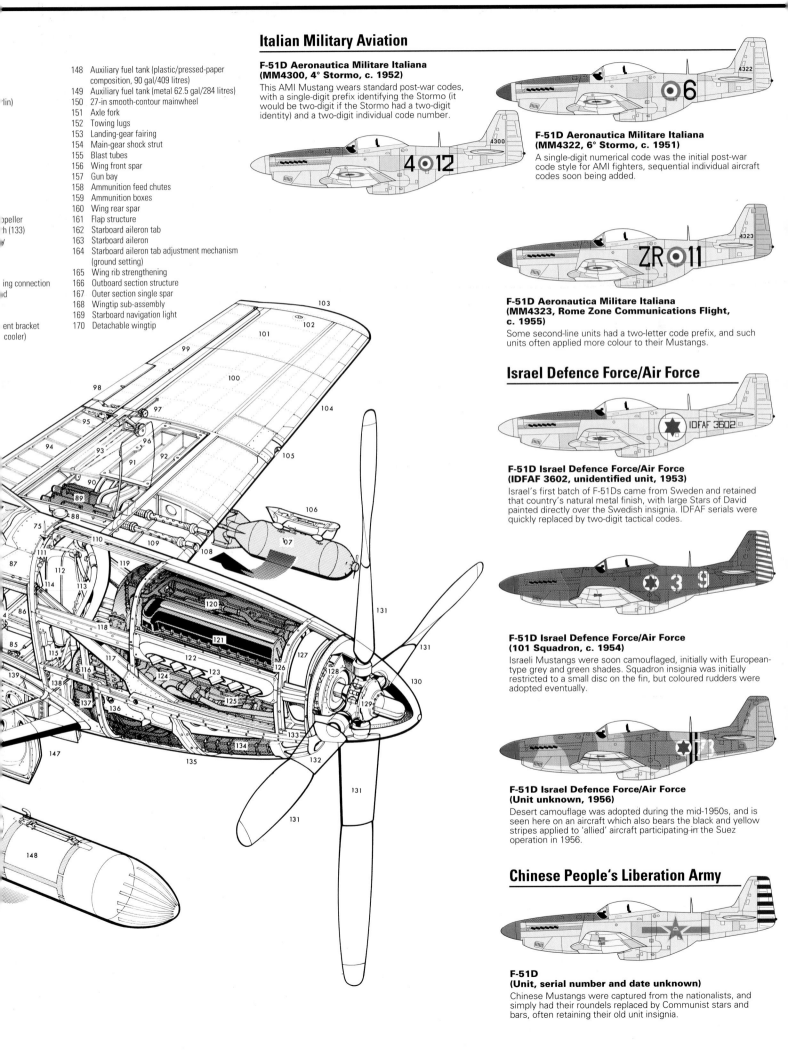

148 Auxiliary fuel tank (plastic/pressed-paper composition, 90 gal/409 litres)
149 Auxiliary fuel tank (metal 62.5 gal/284 litres)
150 27-in smooth-contour mainwheel
151 Axle fork
152 Towing lugs
153 Landing-gear fairing
154 Main-gear shock strut
155 Blast tubes
156 Wing front spar
157 Gun bay
158 Ammunition feed chutes
159 Ammunition boxes
160 Wing rear spar
161 Flap structure
162 Starboard aileron tab
163 Starboard aileron
164 Starboard aileron tab adjustment mechanism (ground setting)
165 Wing rib strengthening
166 Outboard section structure
167 Outer section single spar
168 Wingtip sub-assembly
169 Starboard navigation light
170 Detachable wingtip

Italian Military Aviation

F-51D Aeronautica Militare Italiana (MM4300, 4° Stormo, c. 1952)

This AMI Mustang wears standard post-war codes, with a single-digit prefix identifying the Stormo (it would be two-digit if the Stormo had a two-digit identity) and a two-digit individual code number.

F-51D Aeronautica Militare Italiana (MM4322, 6° Stormo, c. 1951)

A single-digit numerical code was the initial post-war code style for AMI fighters, sequential individual aircraft codes soon being added.

F-51D Aeronautica Militare Italiana (MM4323, Rome Zone Communications Flight, c. 1955)

Some second-line units had a two-letter code prefix, and such units often applied more colour to their Mustangs.

Israel Defence Force/Air Force

F-51D Israel Defence Force/Air Force (IDFAF 3602, unidentified unit, 1953)

Israel's first batch of F-51Ds came from Sweden and retained that country's natural metal finish, with large Stars of David painted directly over the Swedish insignia. IDFAF serials were quickly replaced by two-digit tactical codes.

F-51D Israel Defence Force/Air Force (101 Squadron, c. 1954)

Israeli Mustangs were soon camouflaged, initially with European-type grey and green shades. Squadron insignia was initially restricted to a small disc on the fin, but coloured rudders were adopted eventually.

F-51D Israel Defence Force/Air Force (Unit unknown, 1956)

Desert camouflage was adopted during the mid-1950s, and is seen here on an aircraft which also bears the black and yellow stripes applied to 'allied' aircraft participating in the Suez operation in 1956.

Chinese People's Liberation Army

F-51D (Unit, serial number and date unknown)

Chinese Mustangs were captured from the nationalists, and simply had their roundels replaced by Communist stars and bars, often retaining their old unit insignia.

Swiss Air Force

**F-51D, Schweizer Flugwaffe
(J-2113, unit unknown, 1953)**
A handful of Mustangs remained in service long enough to receive roundel-type national insignia.

**F-51D, Schweizer Flugwaffe
(J-2003, Überwachungsgeschwader, 1946)**
Swiss Mustangs were delivered in natural metal finish with white crosses on their red rudders and on broad chordwise wing bands. Squadron markings were not used.

Dominican air force

**F-51D Fuerza Aérea Dominicana
(1912, Escuadron de Caza, 1975)**
For the last 10 years of their lives, until retirement in 1984, the Dominican P-51s wore subdued brown and green camouflage, with toned-down national insignia.

**F-51D Fuerza Aérea Dominicana
(1936, Escuadron de Caza 'Ramfis', 1953)**
The Dominican Mustangs initially retained the natural metal finish they had worn in Sweden. They later received coloured noses and flashes on the cowlings, and had garish sharkmouths.

Haitian air force

**F-51D Corps d'Aviation d'Haiti
(44-14826, unit unknown, 1963)**
Haiti's Mustangs were eventually painted light grey, this scheme's adoption perhaps being applied during an in-country modification programme by Cavalier.

**F-51D Corps d'Aviation d'Haiti
(44-14826, unit unknown 1954)**
Haiti's F-51s were unarmed, their guns locked in the Presidential armoury in case of a coup! The pilots were purged before Duvalier took over, but the F-51s remained, flown by mercenaries.

Guatemalan air force

**F-51D Fuerza Aérea Guatemalteca
(Escuadron de Ataque y Reconicimiento, 1968)**
During their twilight years, the Guatemalan aircraft wore camouflage, some with sharkmouths.

**F-51D Fuerza Aérea Guatemalteca
(Escuadron Costa Atlantico, 1958)**
Like most Latin American operators of the Mustang, Guatemala initially operated its aircraft in natural metal finish. Coloured spinners were used at one stage to identify squadrons.

Bolivian air force

**F-51D Fuerza Aérea Boliviana
(511, Escuadron de Caza, 1971)**
Refurbished Mustangs delivered from Cavalier had Bolivian markings (including sharkmouths) applied over a glossy grey finish.

**F-51D Fuerza Aérea Boliviana
(511, Escuadron Tactico, 1956)**
Bolivian Mustangs were originally delivered in natural metal, and had national insignia above the port wing and below the starboard, USAF-style.

Costa Rican air force

**F-51D Fuerza Aérea Costaarricense
(1, 1956)**
Costa Rican Mustangs were delivered direct from the Texas ANG and retained their original red spinners. The national insignia was obtained by simply removing the blue ball and white star!

Cuban air force

**F-51D Fuerza Aérea Revolucionaria
(FAR-401, 1959)**
Cuba's anti-government forces used three ex-civil Mustangs, these probably being flown unmarked until after Castro's victory, when these markings were applied.

Philippine air force

**F-51D
(421, unit and date unknown)**
Philippine air force Mustangs followed 1950s USAF colour scheme styles, with a three-digit 'buzz number' on the forward fuselage. Some later gained squadron badges on the fin, sharkmouths, and command stripes.

Uruguayan air force

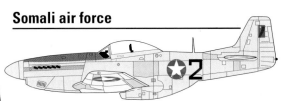

**F-51D Fuerza Aérea Uruguaya
(FAU265, Grupo de Aviacion No. 2 (Caza), 1960)**
Uruguay's Mustangs carried an adaptation of the national flag on the rudder, with roundels of similar design above and below the wings.

Somali air force

**F-51D Somali air corps
(Unit unknown, 1959)**
The Somali aircraft were inherited from the Italian air force, which had operated aircraft based in Somalia. They retained natural metal finish, and had their Italian insignia overpainted.

Nicaraguan National Guard

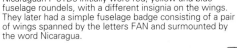

F-51D Fuerza Aérea de la Guardia Nacional de Nicaragua (GN 84, 1957)
Nicaraguan F-51Ds initially wore red, yellow and blue fuselage roundels, with a different insignia on the wings. They later had a simple fuselage badge consisting of a pair of wings spanned by the letters FAN and surmounted by the word Nicaragua.

**F-51D Fuerza Aérea Boliviana
(511, Escuadron de Caza, 1976)**
Bolivia's Mustangs adopted a USAF-style three-tone camouflage during the 1970s, but national markings and sharkmouths remained unchanged.

Salvadorean air force

**F-51D Fuerza Aérea Salvadorena, 1969
(411, unidentified fighter squadron)**
This D wears the yellow identification bands applied to all FAS Mustangs during the Soccer War. A former US civilian Mustang, it wears non-standard camouflage. The Cavalier Mustangs delivered in 1968 had USAF-type camouflage.

virtually the same nose as in the D/K, and it drove an Aeroproducts Unimatic propeller with four blades reduced in weight compared with those of the P-51K.

The P-51H airframe was very similar to that of the F, except that the fuselage was lengthened to make the aircraft 33 ft 4 in (10.16 m) overall. A small dorsal fin was added, and from the 21st production aircraft the vertical tail was increased in height, which once and for all eliminated the snaking (yaw instability) problem. The fuselage was also made slightly deeper amidships, raising the cockpit to give the pilot an 8° depressed gunsight line looking down the straight top line to the spinner. The cockpit canopy was

much smaller than that of the F, being similar to that on late D/K Mustangs but with the highest point further forward.

The radiator installation was revised yet again. The matrix was enlarged, increasing the depth of the inlet duct, the inlet itself being vertical as in the previous lightweight versions, and the bottom line downstream being almost straight instead of bulged. The fuselage tank was restored, although its capacity was reduced to 50 US gal (42 Imp gal; 191 litres). Armament reverted to six 0.5-in guns, access to both the guns and ammunition bays being improved and the belts being housed in removable boxes which could be

44-64164 was the fifth P-51H Mustang. The production H model, although lighter than the D, was larger around its middle. P-51Hs succeeded in the USAAF, the newly independent US Air Force and the post-war Air National Guard.

Lightweight P-51s

Although the Mustang was more than able to hold its own against just about any adversary, North American was under some pressure to trim weight from the basic P-51 to produce a better-climbing, more nimble fighter with performance like that of the Spitfire and Bf 109 (neither of which had the Mustang's range).

The manufacturer and the USAAF invested heavily in a lightweight fighter study and in an ambitious development and test programme which produced three experimental Mustangs, the XP-51F, XP-51G, and XP-51J. The XP-51F was constructed to a goal of trimming overall weight by 5,700 lb (2585 kg) as compared with the P-51D/K. Among features which contributed to this goal were a thinner wing cross-section, a redesigned teardrop canopy, a smaller landing gear strut and wheels, and a three-bladed Aeroproducts propeller of lighter weight.

The XP-51G incorporated these features but was powered by an experimental Rolls-Royce RM-14SM engine which proved cantankerous. Mechanical problems were greater than could be accepted in an operational environment but, when the XP-51G was in top form, it was clocked at 495 mph (796 km/h). The XP-51J was a stretched lightweight built around the new Allison V-1710-119, which also suffered from technical difficulties.

None of the trio was produced, but all contributed knowledge which led to the P-51H, essentially an XP-51F with a 13-in (33-cm) stretch to the fuselage and powered by a Packard V-1650-9 of 1,380 hp (1035 kW) at 3,000 rpm. Although 370 P-51Hs reached USAAF squadrons by August 1945, the H model never saw combat in any war. It served valiantly, but was the only Mustang never to be exported.

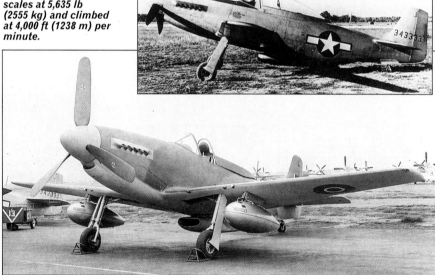

Right: The XP-51F (three built, of which 44-43333 was the second) tipped the scales at 5,635 lb (2555 kg) and climbed at 4,000 ft (1238 m) per minute.

Above: Rarely seen in photos, 44-64160 was the first P-51H (there was no XP-51H model) and is portrayed here at the Inglewood factory, with NAA emblem on its tail.

Above: In RAF markings (but still at the factory, before delivery to Boscombe Down), FR 409 was one of three XP-51F test ships and was flown by British pilots. Had the G model been chosen by Great Britain, it would have become the Mustang V.

Left: The attractive XP-51G (two built) was powered by a Rolls-Royce RR 145M engine driving a five-bladed Rotol propeller. Apart from the powerplant, the G model was identical to the XP-51F.

pre-loaded and then quickly installed in the aircraft. Under-wing stores were as for late-model D/K.

Orders were placed for 2,000, to be made at Inglewood under charge number NA-126, and for 1,629 to be made at Dallas as P-51Ms, under charge number NA-124. The M was to differ in having the Dash 9A engine, with a lower war-emergency rating caused by deletion of the water/methanol injection system.

The P-51L (company NA-129) was to have been a Dallas-built Mustang identical to the P-51H model. Some 1,700 P-51Ls were ordered but the contract was cancelled before any could be built or flown. A further variant from Inglewood was the P-51M (company NA-124) with a V-1650-9A engine. One of these was built (the final P-51D, redesignated) and 1,628 subsequently cancelled.

The P-51H (later, F-51H) served valiantly in the US Air Force and Air National Guard but never saw combat. The P-51H was faster in level flight and in a dive than other Mustangs. In fact, with the ability to brush up close to the landmark speed of 500 mph (805 km/h) under certain circumstances, it was arguably the fastest propeller-driven fighter ever to attain operational service.

Bob Chilton flew the first P-51H, 44-64160, on 3 February 1945. At a clean gross weight of 9,500 lb (4313 kg) it achieved 487 mph (784 km/h) at 25,000 ft (7625 m), making it the fastest production aeroplane of World War II, apart from the Me 262 and He 162 jets. A single H was supplied to the RAF for evaluation as KN987, but after VJ-Day in August 1945 contracts were slashed. Only 555 aircraft were retained, the last being completed in November 1945, and the remaining 1,445 were cancelled. Only one P-51M-1-NT (45-11743) was completed, the remaining 1,628 being cancelled. All 1,700 P-51Ls were cancelled, as were contracts for all versions of the V-1650 engine.

Post-war

Production by Inglewood and Dallas amounted to about 15,575 Mustangs of all versions. Other sources give other totals − Gruenhagen suggests a total of 15,582, and another total given is 15,684. An additional 100 were assembled in Australia. At the war's end the USAAF had 5,500 P-51s and F-6s on strength, almost all being D or K or derived versions. A few units re-equipped with the H, but these were soon replaced by the P-80 jet, and in the interests of standardisation − and also in the belief that they were more robust in the ground attack role than the H − the USAAF standardised on the D and K post-war. It also supplied about 700 of these earlier variants to the newly formed Air National Guard. The same versions found customers in at least 26 foreign air forces.

The US Air Force became an independent service branch on 18 September 1947. On 11 June 1948, the 'P' for 'pursuit' designation was changed to 'F' for 'fighter.' The Mustang was now the F-51. The Twin Mustang (below) became the F-82. Photo-reconnaissance Mustangs (the F-6 series) became RF-51s.

The F-51D/K was the first model assigned to the Air National Guard, the F-51H being initially preferred for service with regular squadrons. Six hundred F-51Ds were removed from permanent storage at Newark, New Jersey − they were new (but for test and ferry time) and had been

44-64164, the fifth P-51H, is seen on an early proving flight over southern California. The P-51H might have seen combat had it been necessary to invade Japan, but when the war ended the first examples were only beginning to reach USAAF squadrons.

This XP-51J (44-76027), the first of two built, was powered by an Allison V-1710-119 in place of the Merlin but was otherwise the same aircraft as its bantam-weight companion, the XP-51F.

This operational F-51H (the P for pursuit designation was changed to F for fighter in July 1948) belongs to the 'Copperheads' of the 197th Fighter Bomber Squadron, Arizona Air National Guard. 44-64455 served at Phoenix until the 197th converted from F-51H to F-51D in 1952.

F-51D Mustangs of the 35th FBW receive attention at K-16 Seoul airport, on Yoi island in the Han River, on 29 April 1951. At the time, Mustangs were providing close support missions for the US 3rd Infantry Division, then caught up in a big fight with Chinese forces.

An F-51D of the 18th FBW, already hauling 5-in HVAR (high-velocity aircraft rockets) taxis to the loading area to have napalm tanks hung under its wing in September 1951. By this time, the USAF had lost more F-51Ds than the batch of 145 initially sent to Korea.

stored after the war – and these went to the Guard. The remaining 100 were absorbed from the active-duty force.

Air National Guard service

The pre-war National Guard (whose air component became the Air National Guard with the passage of the 1947 National Security Act which also created the Department of Defense and the US Air Force) had never operated anything more aggressive than a North American O-47 observation craft. But from 1946 Guard units flew B-26 Invaders, F-47 Thunderbolts and, particularly, Mustangs.

It appears that the first ANG operator of the F-51D was the 120th Fighter Squadron, Colorado ANG, at Buckley Field in Aurora near Denver. This unit took delivery of its first 'Fifty-One' on or about 30 June 1946. The second F-51D user, the 110th Fighter Squadron, Missouri ANG, Lambert-St Louis Municipal Airport (a P-51 operator while activated during the war) initiated the F-51D beginning about 23 September 1946.

Backbone of the Guard

The Mustang was assigned to more ANG squadrons than any other aircraft and served for an unprecedented (at the time) 11 years. No fewer than 75 Guard squadrons were equipped with Mustangs at one time or another. Of these, 44 used the F-51D as their first mission aircraft, 29 converting from other types to F-51D/Hs, and seven using RF-51Ds (the former F-6Ds). An ANG fighter squadron typically had an authorised strength of 25 fighters, and often

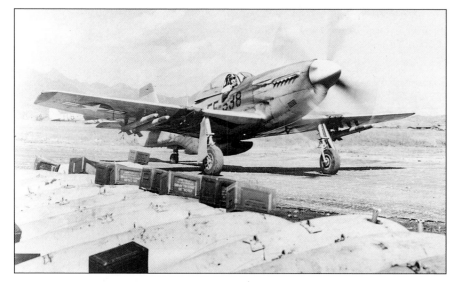

An F-51D taxis through standing water on a Korean airfield, loaded with bombs and rockets. Conditions at some of the airfields in Korea were very primitive, and the F-51Ds proved better able to cope than the first jets.

had additional aircraft on charge for spares and support.

The Korean War disrupted the ANG's re-equipment with the P-51, beginning in July 1950 when 145 of the Guard's 754 Mustangs were uprooted from Guard service and rushed to Korea aboard the carrier USS *Boxer* (CV-21) for use by regular forces. (More than one F-80 Shooting Star pilot complained that his jet was "too fast" to dogfight effectively with North Korean Yaks and Lavochkins.) These were eventually replaced by more Mustangs pulled from storage.

Just about everybody who fought in Korea was involuntarily recalled through one process or another and veteran Mustang pilots were no exception. Beginning on 10 October 1950 when 15 squadrons were called to active duty, a total of 67 ANG squadrons was called for 21 months of federal service. Many relieved active-duty squadrons in other parts of the world so they could fight in Korea. Guard units which actually went to Korea converted from Mustangs to F-84E Thunderjets.

Six units were still operating Mustangs at the end of 1956. The 167th Fighter-Interceptor Squadron, West Virginia ANG in Martinsburg, relinquished the last F-51Ds employed operationally as fighters in March 1957. The F-51D had thus outlived the later F-51H, since the last of these 'Super Mustangs' had been retired from the 112th FS, Ohio ANG, in April 1956, and the 182nd FS, Texas ANG, in August 1956.

The Twin Mustang

Chronologically, the first military rebuild was also by far the most dramatic. During World War II there was a general belief that for long bomber-escort missions a fighter needed two engines and a crew of two. Although the P-51D effectively disproved this in the European theatre, the Pacific theatre and the range of the B-29 made even this aircraft's radius of action inadequate. In late 1943 NAA proposed a novel solution: join two P-51 fuselages by a common wing and tailplane!

The USAAF quickly ordered four prototypes designated XP-82, built under charge number NA-120. Two were cancelled, and the first XP-82, 44-83886, made its first flight at Inglewood on 15 April 1945. It was basically made up of two XP-51G fuselages, with an extra section inserted ahead of the tail, joined by a new rectangular tailplane/elevator and a new rectangular centre wing. The outer wings were modified to house larger tanks but to omit the provisions for landing gear and armament, the guns being installed in the middle of the centre section. The two main undercarriage units each retracted inwards across a fuselage

War in Korea

When the Korean War began, the Lockheed F-80 Shooting Star was the standard USAF fighter in the Far East. Confronting a North Korean air arm with propeller-driven warplanes, the USAF rushed 145 Mustangs to Korea as deck cargo on the carrier USS *Boxer* (CV-21). The Mustang and its F-82 derivative made short work of the NKAF but faced a greater challenges carrying out air-to-ground work. Some officers felt the F-47N Thunderbolt was less vulnerable to ground fire, but not enough 'Bolts were on inventory so the F-51D kept its job.

On 5 August 1950, Major Louis J. Sebille, commander of the 67th Fighter Bomber Squadron, 18th Fighter Bomber Wing, lost his life diving an F-51D into a ground target. It was a heroic action which made him the third and final Mustang pilot to be awarded the Medal of Honor.

Mustangs served with the 18th and 35th FBWs. Photo-reconnaissance RF-51Ds (the former F-6Ds, redesignated in July 1948) served with the 45th TRS. In addition to the Americans, the F-51D was flown in combat in Korea by pilots of the Royal Australian Air Force's No. 77 Squadron and the South African Air Force's No. 2 'Cheetah' Squadron. The F-51D also became the first combat aircraft of the Republic of Korea Air Force (RoKAF).

Captain G. B. 'Lippy' Lipawsky of the South African Air Force's No. 2 'Cheetah' Squadron heads aloft in his F-51D on 17 December 1950. The SAAF Mustangs were borrowed from the USAAF, but were painted with SAAF three-digit serials and full national insignia. The squadron converted to F-86F Sabres in 1953.

to stow the wheel in the leading edge immediately inboard of it. The engines were a V-1650-23 and a V-1650-25, differing in the direction of rotation, such 'handed' propellers greatly improving handling and ease of control.

The Twin Mustang resulted from a compelling need. The P-51 had extraordinary range: it could fly escort from England to deep into the Third Reich and over Czechoslovakia, northern Italy and Poland. But this was not enough, as even greater range was required for the final campaign against the Japanese home islands. The P-82 with twin engines, two pilots and a huge fuel capacity was the answer. Later versions transformed the second crew member, on the starboard side of the Twin Mustang, into a radar operator.

The P-82 proved entirely successful. With 576 US gal (480 Imp gal; 2180 litres) of internal fuel, the XP-82 could still reach 482 mph (766 km/h), and combat radius with four drop tanks easily exceeded 1,000 miles (1610 km). (In 1947 a P-82B flew non-stop from Hawaii to New York, a distance of 5,051 miles/8129 km.) Manoeuvrability was not significantly worse than that of the single-seater. The AAF quickly ordered 500 P-82Bs, purely for escort, with the right-hand cockpit fitted only with flight controls and sufficient instruments for relief or emergency operation of the aircraft. In the event, with the war's end only 20 were built, and 480 cancelled. They led to production of 100 P-82E (from 1948 F-82E) day fighter/bombers, able to drop four 1,000-lb (454-kg) bombs or other stores. The aircraft were powered by 1,900-hp (1425-kW) Allison V-1710-143/145 engines, licence-production of the Merlin having terminated with the end of the war.

Night-fighter Mustangs

The 10th and 11th P-82Bs were converted into night-fighters, with the pilot on the left and the navigator/radar operator on the right. The first became the XP-82C with an SCR-720 radar in a giant pod under the centreline, and the second the XP-82D with the smaller APS-4 radar. These led to 100 P-82F night fighters with APG-28 radar and 50 P-82Gs.

The only aircraft in this series which began life with an 'F for fighter' rather than 'P for pursuit' designation ship was the F-82H, the final version of the Twin Mustang. This designation applied to the last nine P-82Fs (46-496/504) and five selected P-82Gs (46-384/388) which were 'winterised' for service in Alaska. From the first P-82E onward, all Twin Mustangs were powered by 1,600-hp (1200-kW) Allison V-1710-143/145 engines

with opposite rotation. The P-82F, P-82G and F-82H all had the same engines as the E, and could even fly attack missions, but with only a 2,000-lb (907-kg) bombload.

F-82F and F-82G Twin Mustangs were operated by Air Defense Command as interceptors, replacing the F-61B/C Black Widow. The F-82E served as a long-range escort with Strategic Air Command from 1948 to 1950. F-82Gs and F-82Hs served in the Korean War as, of course, did F-51D and RF-51D Mustangs.

Raiding the Guard squadrons

At the beginning of the Korean War, only a handful of Mustangs were in American units in the region and none belonged to 'line' fighter squadrons. Steps were taken immediately to rush Mustangs to the Korean theatre, but not every officer in the Far East approved. Some felt that the Mustang was not the best warplane in which to be fighting down near the deck. The Mustang, with its belly-mounted radiator and reliance on liquid coolant, was dangerously vulnerable to ground fire.

At Iwakuni on the main Japanese island of Honshu, the Royal Australian Air Force's No. 77 Squadron's F-51D Mustangs were ordered on 30 June 1950 to join the defence of South Korea. On 7 July, the Australians suffered their first combat loss when Squadron Leader G. Strout failed to return from an armed reconnaissance mission along the coast of North Korea. Strout's Mustang (A68-757) apparently was hit by ground fire while searching for targets of opportunity.

From the time the decision was made to go to war, American officers wanted more prop-driven fighters available to them. On 23 July 1950, the aircraft-carrier USS *Boxer* (CV-21), serving as a cargo ship for the moment, arrived at Yokosuka, Japan with 145 North American F-51D Mustang fighters for the US Air Force's command in the region, known as FEAF (Far East Air Forces) and pronounced to rhyme with 'leaf'. *Boxer* had made the Pacific crossing in a record eight days, 16 hours.

These Mustangs of the Royal Australian Air Force's No. 77 Squadron are ready to join the USAF's 35th FBW in the largest F-51 attack of the Korean War, on 29 January 1951. RAAF Mustangs in Korea were replaced by Meteor Mk 8 jet fighters in May 1951.

F-51D Mustangs of the Republic of Korea Air Force (RoKAF) taxi out on ubiquitous PSP, or pierced steel planking, which seemed to be everywhere in Korea. South Koreans began the war with nothing more lethal than a T-6 Texan, although some of the pilots had flown for the Japanese in World War II.

The Mustangs were a mixed blessing to the embattled Allies who were making a stand in a corner of Korea and facing the prospect of being pushed into the sea. True, the Mustang was more manoeuvrable and had greater endurance than the F-80 (at least until enlarged wingtip tanks were developed for the F-80), but some airmen had doubts. Like their Navy counterparts, they viewed a liquid-cooled powerplant as vulnerable during low-level operations. For a time, serious consideration was given to fielding a squadron of Republic F-47N Thunderbolts (the former P-47), with air-cooled engines, in Korea. But the US Air Force did not have enough F-47s in inventory.

On 5 August 1950, Major Louis J. Sebille, commander of the newly-arrived 67th FBS/18th FBW, in an F-51D Mustang (44-74394), flew straight into the concentration of enemy troops where his Mustang exploded in their midst. For sacrificing his life to help friendly ground troops, Major Louis J. Sebille posthumously became the first Air Force member amid a raging air-ground battle, and the first flier in Korea to be awarded the Medal of Honor.

South Africa also supported the UN action in Korea with No. 2 Squadron 'Flying Cheetahs', which served as part of the USAF's 18th FBW. Their first mission was flown on 19 November 1950.

Foreign users

The number of overseas operators of the Mustang increased dramatically in the post-war years, eventually including 28 nations. During the war, the only major Mustang operators had been the USAAF, the British RAF, and the various British Commonwealth air forces which fought alongside America and Britain. These included Australia, while Canadian and Polish squadrons operating within the Royal Air Force also flew Mustangs.

Before VJ-Day, the Netherlands received 40 P-51Ds for use by the Netherlands East Indies Air Force. In the East Indies, there was a strong nationalist movement which made itself felt in sporadic fighting between the Dutch Colonial authorities and native Indonesians. Here, the Netherlands Army Air Corps was operating three fighter squadrons: No. 120 with Curtiss P-40N Warhawks and Nos 121 and 122 Squadrons with P-51D Mustangs. The Mustangs frequently flew in combat during the upheaval which belatedly led to the formation of Indonesia on 21 December 1949. When Indonesia became independent on 27 December 1949, its air arm (AURI-Angkatan Udara Republik Indonesia) was slated to receive two squadrons of F-51D Mustangs from the departing Netherlands air arm. On 21 June 1950, the Netherlands Indies Air Force was

A P-51H of Colonel David Schilling's 56th Fighter Group at Selfridge Field, Michigan in 1946. The fabled 56th changed from the P-51H to the P-80B Shooting Star early in 1948.

disbanded and its airfields and aircraft were turned over to the Dutch, including F-51Ds which equipped No. 1 Squadron. By 1955, this was part of a composite air group equipped with Mustangs, B-25 Mitchells, C-47s and other types. The AURI used F-51D and F-51K Mustangs in several internal conflicts in the post-war years, and later received a number of Cavalier Mustangs.

China, another ally in the war against Japan, also received P-51D Mustangs from the US before the end of World War II. These were later used by the Nationalist air arm in the 1946-49 civil war against the Communists. A few may also have been operated by the Communist side. A significant number of F-51D Mustangs reached Taiwan in 1949 and, as late as the mid-1950s, one of the Chinese Nationalist Air Force's five fighter wings was equipped with F-51Ds and RF-51Ds.

Enemy and neutral Mustangs

A handful of forced landings by US and British Mustangs also resulted in some unusual operators, including the German Luftwaffe. Of 10 Mustangs which were interned after they made emergency landings in Sweden during the war, four aircraft (two P-51Bs and two P-51Ds) were pressed into Swedish service under the designation J26. Even before VE-Day, Sweden ordered 50 P-51Ds from the US, a figure which rose to 157, the first arriving in April 1945 and the last in March 1948. These, too, were designated J26. Thus, 161 aircraft served in Sweden. Twelve later became S26 photo-reconnaissance aircraft.

The first Swedish Mustangs were allocated to F16 in Uppsala. Sweden began re-equipping its fighter units with de Havilland Vampires (Swedish designation J28) and with the Swedish-manufactured Saab J 29 'Flying Barrel'. Sweden disposed of most of its Mustangs, 25 going to Israel in

F-51H-10-NA 131st FIS Massachusetts ANG Barnes Field 1951

44-64570 wears typical Air National Guard (ANG) markings. In addition, the spinner, fintip, wingtips, and diagonal squadron commander stripes are the traditional 'Polish Guard' red associated with the 131st squadron.

A healthy rivalry exists between two Massachusetts ANG combat squadrons. During the 1950s, the 101st FIS was based in Boston, a city with a large Irish-descent population, whereas the 131st was organised in the southwestern part of the state where Polish ancestry prevails. The 101st became known as the 'Irish Guard' and adopted kelly green for its aircraft markings, while the 131st became the 'Polish Guard' with insignia-red markings.

The F-51H Mustang was well liked by pilots and was possibly the most manoeuvrable as well as the fastest-climbing version of NAA's famous fighter. Its service was important as the Cold War unfolded. The F-51H was never deemed quite as sturdy as the F-51D and was not considered for combat operations in Korea.

F-51H of the 112th Fighter Bomber Squadron, 180th Fighter Bomber Group, Ohio Air National Guard at Akron-Canton Municipal Airport in 1953. The H model Mustang served until early 1959. The squadron later flew F-100s.

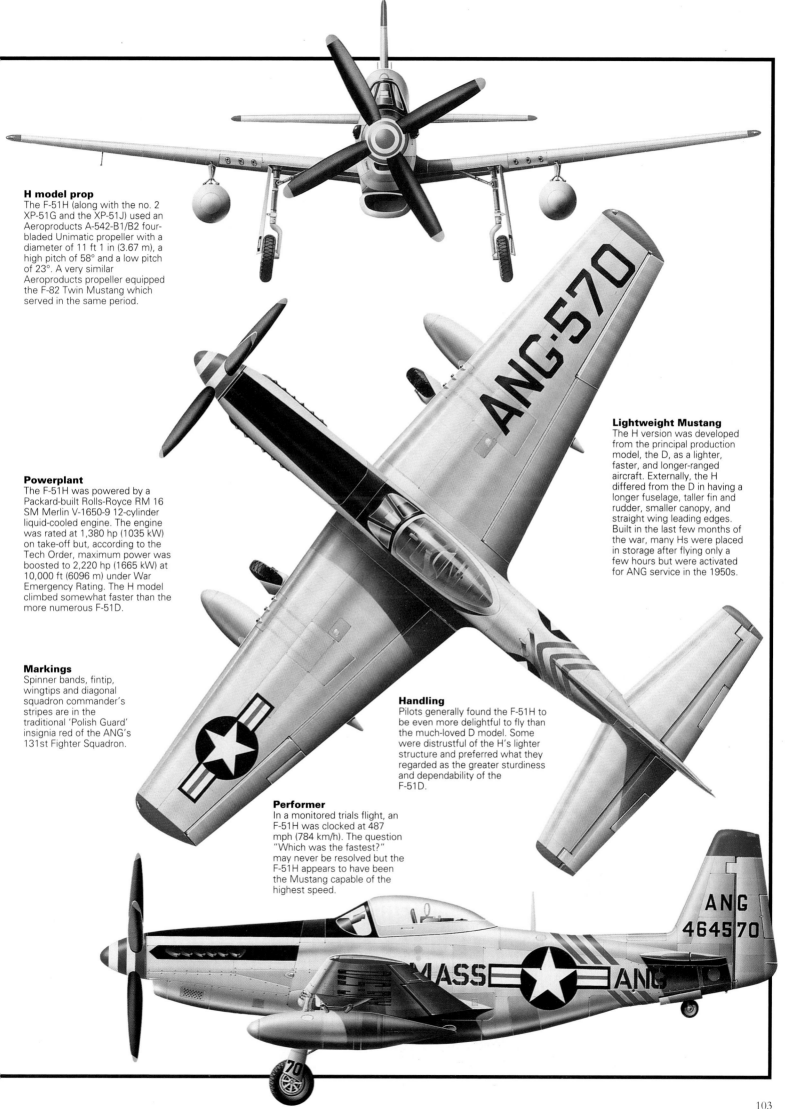

H model prop
The F-51H (along with the no. 2 XP-51G and the XP-51J) used an Aeroproducts A-542-B1/B2 four-bladed Unimatic propeller with a diameter of 11 ft 1 in (3.67 m), a high pitch of 58° and a low pitch of 23°. A very similar Aeroproducts propeller equipped the F-82 Twin Mustang which served in the same period.

Powerplant
The F-51H was powered by a Packard-built Rolls-Royce RM 16 SM Merlin V-1650-9 12-cylinder liquid-cooled engine. The engine was rated at 1,380 hp (1035 kW) on take-off but, according to the Tech Order, maximum power was boosted to 2,220 hp (1665 kW) at 10,000 ft (6096 m) under War Emergency Rating. The H model climbed somewhat faster than the more numerous F-51D.

Markings
Spinner bands, fintip, wingtips and diagonal squadron commander's stripes are in the traditional 'Polish Guard' insignia red of the ANG's 131st Fighter Squadron.

Lightweight Mustang
The H version was developed from the principal production model, the D, as a lighter, faster, and longer-ranged aircraft. Externally, the H differed from the D in having a longer fuselage, taller fin and rudder, smaller canopy, and straight wing leading edges. Built in the last few months of the war, many Hs were placed in storage after flying only a few hours but were activated for ANG service in the 1950s.

Handling
Pilots generally found the F-51H to be even more delightful to fly than the much-loved D model. Some were distrustful of the H's lighter structure and preferred what they regarded as the greater sturdiness and dependability of the F-51D.

Performer
In a monitored trials flight, an F-51H was clocked at 487 mph (784 km/h). The question "Which was the fastest?" may never be resolved but the F-51H appears to have been the Mustang capable of the highest speed.

44-73257 is an F-51D of the 175th FIS, South Dakota ANG, at Sioux Falls. The 175th went from P-47D to the P-51D to the all-weather Lockheed F-94A/B interceptor. Mustangs served at Sioux Falls from 1946 to 1954. A C-82 Packet in visible in the background.

This F-51H Mustang, Lindy Lou II, of the 182nd Fighter Interceptor Squadron, served at Brooks AFB, Texas, in 1954. In flight, the F-51H often flew with tail wheel locked down because of problems with the retraction system.

Seen high over San Francisco Bay on a typically foggy day, this F-51D is one of those serving with the 194th Fighter Squadron of the California Air National Guard. The squadron was located at nearby Hamilton Field. After a move to Fresno, the 194th transitioned to the F-86A Sabre.

A 109th FIS Minnesota ANG F-51D at Holman Field, St Paul, in 1956. Master Sergeant Jim Frantesl runs the aircraft up prior to squadron participation in the last of several annual 'Mustang round up' events held at Volk Field, Michigan. Later, the 109th acquired the T-28 as an interim aircraft.

Air Guard Mustangs

The Air National Guard took on its duty as an operational and combat arm of the Reserve component in the immediate post-war years, and by 1947 was building up to 74 fighter squadrons each with 25 aircraft. Initially, ANG units were equipped with Mustangs on the West Coast and in the hinterlands and Thunderbolts on the East Coast.

Always professionals, Guardsmen were 'weekend warriors' only in the sense that drill weekends, which included their part-time members, took place on Saturdays and Sundays. Guardsmen have been pressed into service in every crisis, and the 1950-53 Korean conflict was no exception.

In the first hours of the Korean War, the ANG transferred 145 of its 764 F-51Ds to the active-duty force (which also reclaimed many individuals) and filled the gap by pulling from storage lightweight F-51H Mustangs which had been stored since World War II.

Ultimately, Mustangs – including the often overlooked F-6/RF-51 reconnaissance and TF-51D training variants – wore Air National Guard colours for just less than a dozen years. The first had been delivered in 1946 while plans for the post-war force were still being sketched out. The last was retired in March 1957 when Wham Bam an F-51D of the 167th Fighter Interceptor Squadron, West Virginia Air National Guard, Martinsburg, made its final flight.

The final total was 75 operational squadrons equipped with Mustangs, including 18 which employed the F-51H.

1952-53, 26 to Nicaragua in 1953, and 42 to the Dominican Republic in 1954.

Switzerland acquired 100 surplus F-51D Mustangs in 1948 while awaiting the delivery of de Havilland Vampire FB.Mk 6 jet fighters. Arrival of the Mustangs permitted retirement of the Flugwaffe's last surviving Messerschmitt Bf 109Es in 1949. The Mustangs remained in service until 1956 when re-equipment with the Vampire was completed. Elsewhere in Europe, a few ex-USAAF P-51 and F-6 Mustangs were acquired by France's Armée de l'Air shortly after VJ-Day, and in Italy 48 F-51D Mustangs were operated between 1948 and 1953.

Last Commonwealth Mustangs

The RAF had more than enough Spitfires to equip its fighter squadrons after the war, while waiting for the Meteor and Vampire jets, and rapidly retired the Mustang after VJ-Day (the aircraft were Lend-Lease equipment and were thus due to be returned, although in fact they were simply scrapped). The last RAF Fighter Command Mustangs had disappeared by the end of 1946. Canadian Mustang I squadrons had already re-equipped with Spitfires before the end of the war, and the re-equipment of Nos 442 and 443 Squadrons with Mustang IIIs and IVs was not completed. In 1945, however, the RCAF purchased 100 ex-USAAF P-51D Mustangs. These equipped both regular and auxiliary fighter squadrons and training units until declared obsolete at the end of 1956. The Polish Mustang squadrons lingered on in the RAF until 1947, when they disbanded.

Other Commonwealth air forces kept or acquired the P-51 after the war was over. The Royal Australian Air Force fighter-bomber squadrons operating in the Mediterranean had followed the example of RAF Desert Air Force units, and had started to trade their ageing P-40s for P-51s during the last part of the war. These were British-supplied aircraft, paid for by the treasury, and wore RAF serials. Only No. 3 Squadron actually re-equipped completely, and operated the type from November 1944 until May 1945. They were returned to the RAF for disposal. Beginning in 1945, however, Australia had taken delivery of its first of 214 American-supplied, direct Lend-Lease P-51D Mustangs and 84 P-51Ks. The RAAF also chose the P-51D Mustang for licence-production to meet its need for a long-range fighter for the southwest Pacific. Australia acquired a complete aircraft and 100 assembly kits, 80 of which were assembled by Commonwealth as the CA-17 Mustang Mk 20, powered by the Packard V-1650-3 Merlin engine. Commonwealth then manufactured 14 Mustang Mk 22 reconnaissance aircraft. Thereafter, the manufacturer delivered 40 CA-18 Mustang Mk 21s in two batches powered by the V-1650-7 engine, and 66 Mustang Mk 23s with British-built Rolls-Royce Merlin 70s. Original plans had been for the production of 170 CA-18s alone.

Australian Mustang production

The total number of Mustangs produced in Australia was a modest 200, rather than the 690 which had once been foreseen. The RAAF for a long time had far more fighters than it needed, and the 200th indigenous Mustang was not delivered until April 1951, five years after the first. First RAAF units to receive the Australian-serialled Mustangs were Nos 84 and 86 Squadrons at Townsville, Queensland, which disbanded in January 1946.

During the occupation of Japan, Australia's P-51Ds equipped Nos 76 and 82 Squadrons, which remained in Japan until 1949 when they were withdrawn to Australia. No. 77 Squadron remained at Iwakuni when the Korean War began in 1950.

Operating first from Iwakuni, Japan and later Pohang, Korea, the RAAF Mustangs served in Korea until 6 April 1951, after which the squadron converted to the Gloster Meteor F.Mk 8. In 3,800 Mustang sorties during the Korean War, No. 77 Squadron lost 18 aeroplanes and eight pilots. Other squadrons to re-equip with the Mustang included Nos 3 and 4 in the reconnaissance role (serving until 1952). The Citizen Air Force was reformed after a 1948 decision, with one squadron based in each state capital. All five were equipped with the P-51D and were No. 21 ('City of Melbourne'), No. 22 ('City of Sydney'), No. 23 ('City of Brisbane'), No. 24 ('City of Adelaide'), and No. 25 ('City of Perth'). These squadrons re-equipped with Vampires between 1952 and 1956, with the exception of No. 24, which soldiered on until June 1960, at which time all five squadrons were axed. Civil-registered Mustangs served on as target tugs with Illawarra Flying Services into the 1970s.

In 1945 negotiations between US and New Zealand led to a decision by the Royal New Zealand Air Force (RNZAF) to acquire 370 Mustangs. These were expected to complement the RNZAF's Vought F4U Corsairs in the final battle against Japan, before that war was cut short by the dropping of the atomic bombs. The first batch was to consist of 30 P-51D-25-NT aircraft. The remaining 137 of an initial batch of 167 fighters (to be followed later by 203 more) were to be P-51Ms.

Kiwi Mustangs

The end of the war in the Pacific made a 370-plane Mustang purchase superfluous, but the first 30 were already en route. These 30 P-51D-25-NT Mustangs were delivered to the RNZAF in 1945 but were not introduced into service. The Mustangs were stored until New Zealand decided to breathe new life into its Territorial Air Force (TAF), a reserve component which was revived after the war. The TAF's No. 4 Squadron received its first four Mustangs in late 1951. Mustangs remained in service with TAF squadrons until August 1955, when mounting problems of landing gear weakness and coolant system corrosion forced their withdrawal. Four Mustangs had a brief, second life in a drogue-towing role until they were retired in 1957.

The South African Air Force (SAAF) committed its No. 2 'Cheetah' Squadron to the United Nations' effort in the

Korean War. Although the SAAF's fighter units flew Spitfires at home, the 'Cheetahs' were issued with F-51Ds and formed part of the US Air Force's 18th Fighter-Bomber Wing. Operations began when five SAAF Mustangs began missions from K-9 airfield near Pusan, Korea, on 19 November 1950. At this juncture, the Allies occupied most of North Korea and the 'Cheetahs' soon moved to K-24 airfield at Pyongyang. China's entry into the Korean War reversed the Allies' fortune and No. 2 Squadron, with its parent wing, withdrew to K-13 airfield at Suwon and then to K-10 airfield at Chinhae at the southernmost tip of Korea. This remained the permanent home base for the 'Cheetahs' but air-to-ground missions were flown from forward locations at K-9, K-16 airfield at Seoul, and K-46 airfield at Hoengsong.

It was a dirty, low-level war for Mustang pilots in Korea, who were given the close support mission and who were expected to strike enemy targets with rockets, napalm and bombs in the face of heavy ground fire. Two SAAF Mustangs were shot down by MiG-15s, but the painful magnitude of the 'Cheetahs' casualties can be understood only when we remember that of the 95 Mustangs loaned to No. 2 Squadron, 74 were lost in combat or in non-combat mishaps. The SAAF's Mustangs flew 10,373 sorties in

F-51D Mustangs of the 104th Fighter Interceptor Squadron, Maryland ANG, fly formation near Glenn L. Martin Airport in Baltimore in 1955.

Lieutenant Colonel Ed Bollen, boss of the Pennsylvania ANG's 146th FBS, flies an F-51H (44-64622) with the F86A and F-84F that would replace the Mustang in mid-1955.

O-1553 of the Texas ANG is headed for film stardom, part-way to being painted in Korean markings to serve as Rock Hudson's mount in Battle Hymn, the story of Colonel Dean Hess who helped form the RoKAF. Texas Guardsmen flew 'combat' against T-28 'Yaks' in the movie.

A J26 Mustang of the Swedish air force's F16 wing at Lulea. This particular aircraft was formerly a USAF P-51D (44-72406). Sweden also operated S26 photo-reconnaissance aircraft (converted from stock P-51Ds) which wore numerals instead of letters as codes. Sweden purchased 161 Mustangs and also operated a few USAAF aircraft that were interned during the war.

Below: This F-51D is now at the Italian Air Force Museum, Vigna di Valle and is understood to be the only surviving Mustang in Italy. The country operated 173 of the fighters from September 1947 until 1958. The type served with 3°, 4°, 5°, 6° and 51° Stormi, and with a number of schools and liaison units.

Above: This IDF/AF F-51D was photographed while being flown by Bernard Lurie in 1953. Israel had only one F-51D Mustang during its 1948 fight for independence, but by the mid-1950s the numbers had grown. Twenty-five Swedish Mustangs were sold to Israel in 1952-53.

Above: Canadian pilots excelled in the Mustang during World War II, the Allison-engined versions equipping three RCAF squadrons in Europe. Canadian pilots also flew with various RAF units. In 1945 the Royal Canadian Air Force purchased 100 ex-USAAF P-51Ds like this one. Until declared obsolete in 1956, the F-51Ds equipped regular and auxiliary RCAF squadrons, being replaced by de Havilland Vampires and Canadair-built Sabres.

Korea with 12 pilots killed in action, 30 missing or captured, and four wounded. The Mustang story ended on 31 December 1952 when the 'Cheetahs' stood down temporarily to re-equip with F-86F Sabres. Reports suggest that a handful of South African Air Force units flew small numbers of Mustangs during World War II, but this cannot be confirmed.

The Mustang also played a part during the 1948-49 struggle for Israel's independence. They used a mix of aircraft, including Czech-built Avia S-199s (licence-produced Messerschmitt Bf 109s) and Spitfire LF.Mk IXs. Most of the aircraft and flight training for Israeli and foreign pilots came from Czechoslovakia. The Israeli Defence Force/Air Force designated its fighter outfit as No. 101 Squadron and soon received two P-51D Mustangs. The first P-51 combat was flown by Gideon Lichtman, an American flying with the IDF/AF who had previously flown P-51s in the Pacific. In October 1948, pilot Lichtman flew a reconnaissance mission to Beirut and Damascus. Near the end of the mission, Lichtman was attacked by an Arab fighter which he sought to engage, but his guns jammed. The Mustang pilot came home without having fired a shot.

The pair of Mustangs belonging to the fledgling IDF/AF flew several dozen combat missions and toted up at least one aerial kill before the 1948-49 war ended. In September 1952, Israel took delivery of 25 F-51D Mustangs from Sweden and these arrived between November 1952 and June 1953.

IDF/AF F-51D Mustangs saw plenty of action during the Suez Crisis which began with Israel's attack on Egypt on 29 October 1956. Two Mustangs were assigned to cut

45-11573 was a late F-51D Mustang typical of those flown by the Philippine air force. Few details have emerged of the role of the F-51D in the early 1950s fight against the Hukbalahap guerrillas. F-51Ds were replaced by F-86Fs.

Foreign Fifty-Ones

The warplanes which wrested victory from Germany were junked, scrapped, and discarded by the thousand but, despite this wholesale destruction, more P-51 Mustangs survived after the war than the US needed. The USAF had already begun its gradual shift to an all-jet force.

It was inevitable that the best-known and most numerous American fighter, now plentiful in storage and mothballs, would be available for export. The onset of the Cold War, and the perceived need to arm allies, added impetus. Almost immediately, starting with 1945 acquisitions by Canada and New Zealand, the US began providing P-51s to overseas users.

Some nations were logical choices. It was easier to provide Mustangs to France than to ship them home from French soil. Sweden had become familiar with the Mustang when it impressed into its air force examples which had sought refuge during the war and, based on this experience, was ready to buy.

Other nations were less likely. Israel acquired its Mustangs indirectly. South Korea became a user of the redesignated F-51 when hurled into a 1950 conflict that few had foreseen. Bolivia and the Dominican Republic flew the P-51 and became the last nations with operational aircraft.

The Dominican Republic snapped up 42 Mustangs from Sweden, obtained more elsewhere, and finally picked up Cavalier-built machines under the US Military Assistance Program (MAP). Dominican F-51s served from 1952 to 1983, the fighter's longest continuous military use.

Left: Dominican F-51Ds line up in the colours of Escuadron de Caza 'Ramfis', as the country's F-47- and F-51-equipped fighter unit was designated between 1952 and 1961. The nearest Mustang joined the US civil register in 1984.

Egyptian phone lines using special hooks trailing from long cables: when these devices failed to work, the Mustang pilots did the job with their wing leading edges and sustained only minor dents.

Mustangs were quietly retired from Israeli service in the late 1950s and a few have been salvaged as warbirds.

When the Republic of Korea, or RoK, was established on 15 August 1948 south of the 38th Parallel, its military aircraft were L-4 Cub and T-6 Texan trainers. When the Korean War began, Korean pilots with wartime operational experience were given conversion courses in Japan on the F-51D Mustang. These men formed the first operational squadron of the RoK Air Force, commanded by Colonel Kim Shin, who had fought in China with General Chennault's volunteer group, the Flying Tigers. The South Korean Mustangs were initially used for defensive purposes but, in the autumn of 1952, the first RoKAF wing was formed with additional Mustangs and began flying close support missions.

Also in Asia, the Philippines was embroiled in conflict with its Hukbalahap guerrillas. F-51D Mustangs, together with C-47 transports, were employed in the campaign against the Huks. By the mid-1950s, the Philippines began disposing of its small force of F-51D Mustangs and these were dispersed to various other countries.

Latin American operators

Despite a US preference to equip friendly nations in Latin America with the F-47, the Mustang was destined to see widespread and long-lasting service in South and Central America.

Dominica became the first mainland Latin American Mustang user during the reign of Rafael Trujillo. Early Dominican Mustangs consisted of a mixed bag of six P-51A, P-51C and P-51D fighters acquired in 1948, with one crashing on its delivery flight. These augmented eight surviving P-38/F-4s, 10 newly delivered Bristol Beaufighters and five new Mosquitos. The Cuerpo de Aviacion Militar subsequently purchased 44 F-51D Mustangs from Sweden in October 1952, along with a batch of de Havilland Vampire F.Mk Is, while 25 F-47s were acquired from the USA under MAP provisions. At least one more Mustang was obtained from unknown sources.

In the mid-1950s, the Dominican Army Aviation Corps had two fighter squadrons, one with F-51D Mustangs and the other operating both F-47D Thunderbolts and Vampires, with four T-33s never officially handed over from the USAF mission, which left in 1958, prompting the sale of the F-47s. Plans to replace the propeller-driven fighters with new or surplus F-86F Sabres, in the face of threats from Castro, never materialised, and the US asked Britain to withhold delivery of the Hawker Hunters ordered by Trujillo. The restoration of links with the US allowed the rebuild of at least 27 Mustangs by Cavalier and these aircraft were intensively used during the 1965 Civil War, two being shot down by AAA. Under Project Peace Hawk, 15 Mustangs were refurbished and upgraded by Cavalier, with some other aircraft being given to the Florida-based company in part-payment. The last Vampires were withdrawn in 1970, leaving the Mustangs to soldier on, with the surviving Haitian aircraft being acquired for spares in 1972. The last 12 aircraft were still flying from Santo Domingo in 1984, when they were retired and sold off to private owners for $300,000 each – the last operational Mustangs in the world.

When the US government decided to standardise all

This highly polished F-51D (FAG 315) belonged to the Guatemalan air arm. This Mustang was apparently one of a batch of ex-Canadian aircraft to reach the Fuerza Aérea Guatemalteca, which operated the fighter until 1972.

Right: During the late 1960s the US Army employed rebuilt Cavalier Mustangs as chase aircraft at Edwards AFB, mainly in support of the AH-56 Cheyenne helicopter test programme. These had tall tails and wingtip fuel tanks.

Above: N451D was one of the first Mustangs rebuilt and customised by David B. Lindsay, Jr's Trans Florida (later Cavalier) firm. Tip tanks and all, this ship went to Indonesia as F-360 and crashed in central Java on 24 June 1975.

The Cavalier Mustang III replaced the Merlin with a Rolls-Royce Dart turboprop. Several attempts were made to produce a turboprop version of the Mustang but none led to an aircraft with strong civil or military sales potential.

N4222A was a Cavalier Mustang II with six 0.50-in (12.7-mm) guns and six LAU-3/A pods containing a total of 114 rocket projectiles. This was a company-financed aircraft and was examined but not bought by the USAF. Cavalier's modification with wingtip tanks and tall fin proved popular, particularly among Latin American air forces.

friendly Latin American nations on the F-47, while the F-51 continued in ANG service, Uruguay turned down what would have been virtually free fighters and held out for Mustangs, which it received in 1950. Uruguay employed a squadron (Grupo 2) of 25 F-51D Mustangs as fighter-bombers until 1960, when they were replaced by F-80C Shooting Stars. The eight best survivors were 'sold' to Bolivia for $1 each. Fuerza Aérea Uruguaya pilots underwent training in the United States.

The Haitian Corps d'Aviation, a branch of the Garde d'Haiti, received four F-51D Mustangs in 1951. These formed part of a composite squadron at Bowen Field, Port-au-Prince, and were used for internal policing. The last was retired in 1973-74, and passed to the Dominican Republic.

First Central American use

The Fuerza Aérea Guatemala acquired its first three F-51D Mustangs on 27 July 1954, making it the first Central American operator of the type. Attempts by the Arbenz and Arévalo governments (viewed by the United States as Communist) in 1950 and 1953 to acquire F-51Ds were foiled by a refusal to grant export licences. A proposed purchase from Sweden was quashed by American intervention. The CIA supported Castillo forces then seeking to take over the country from the supposedly Communist Arbenz government, and two F-51Ds were clandestinely supplied to the rebels via Nicaragua and Honduras along with three F-47s. The fighters actually operated, without markings, from Managua Las Mercedes. When Castillo invaded Guatemala his air power proved decisive, and after he had seized power a batch of three F-51Ds was supplied to the FAG by the United States, reaching Guatemala on 20 December 1954. Batches of three and seven Mustangs followed from the USA, together with a single TF-51, and the air arm also obtained the ex-Castillo rebel aircraft. Another 14 Mustangs, many of them ex-Canadian, fol-

lowed from 1957. The final official tally was 30, which made up portions of four composite squadrons, although more aircraft may have been acquired for cash from Israel. The Mustangs remained in service until 1972, some of them equipping one five-aircraft section of an aerobatic display team which also included six T-33As and four T-6Gs. Two Mustangs were lost in a collision in 1972, and this prompted the sale of the remaining six airworthy aircraft. During their service the Guatemalan aircraft saw intensive action in the COIN/internal security role.

Bolivian Mustangs

The Fuerza Aérea Boliviana was destined to be one of the last users of the Mustang. During July 1954, the FAB (purged and weakened after the 1952 revolution) acquired three Mustangs (two F-51Ds and a TF-51D), although one of these crashed on its delivery flight. The two survivors, with a single P-47 and a single P-38, formed the Bolivian fighter force, although a replacement Mustang was eventually delivered and T-6/SNJ trainers were on charge to keep pilots current. In 1960, Bolivia received eight former MAP Mustangs from Uruguay for $8.00 in what was virtually a MAP redeployment. Six more F-51Ds were acquired on the civilian market during 1966, in time for use against Che Guevara's attempts to ferment a people's war by the peasantry. With a real Communist enemy, US assistance increased, and, as late as 1967, Trans-Florida (renamed Cavalier that same year) received a US Air Force contract for 'new build' F-51D Mustangs to be delivered to several Latin American countries. Bolivia was to be one of those nations, and, over time, nine of the remanufactured Cavalier Mustangs – six F-51Ds and three TF-51Ds – were added to the FAB's order of battle under operation Peace Condor. The 25 aircraft delivered formed a Mustang force which survived until 1978, with a peak strength of 12 airworthy aircraft. Five were lost in mishaps. Several of the ex-Bolivian Mustangs found their way on to the US civil register as part of the burgeoning warbird community in the United States, exchanged by the FAB with a Canadian dealer for T-33 jet trainers.

The Guatemalan rebel (Castillo) Mustangs operated from Nicaragua and were coveted by the Somoza regime. When it became apparent that these aircraft would have to be handed over to Guatemala, the Fuerza Aérea de Nicaragua acquired 26 ex-Swedish F-51Ds to equip one fighter squadron, operating alongside a fighter-bomber squadron equipped with F-47D Thunderbolts. The F-51Ds arrived in January 1955 and were augmented by two ex-USAF TF-51s and at least seven ex-ANG aircraft. The majority

were sold in 1961, but three were loaned to Cuban exile forces during the Bay of Pigs invasion (they were not used). Two survived as gate guards until the fall of the Somoza regime in 1979, and in 1980 an example was reported, airworthy and in Sandanista markings, at Managua.

Nicaraguan support of incursions into Costa Rica included the provision of unmarked aircraft, and in January 1955 Costa Rica acquired four F-51Ds directly from the Texas ANG, paying $1 per aircraft under the terms of the Reimbursable Aid Program. One aircraft was lost, and the other three landed in Nicaragua where they were briefly interned. On return they were little used, and remained in storage apart from occasional training and demonstration flights during which one more was lost. The two survivors were sold in March 1964.

Final Latin American buy

The last Latin American nation to acquire the Mustang was El Salvador, although the country first sought approval for the supply of Mustangs in 1953. FG-1D Corsairs arrived in 1957, but by the early 1960s these were plainly in need of replacement, and El Salvador took advantage of the US-sponsored programme in which Cavalier sold remanufactured Mustangs to a range of Latin American countries. Five single-seat Mustang IIs, with tip tanks and tall tails, were augmented by a single TF-51D, all delivered in early 1969. One crashed soon after delivery and was quickly

replaced. The hunt for additional P-51s continued apace.

Although a few US Air Force officers wanted to use the Mustang in Vietnam, its last conflict was the El Salvador/Honduras 'Soccer War' (Guerra de Futbol) of July 1969. The conflict erupted after the two nations played three bitterly contested matches in the World Cup. Behind it lay other grievances. Spurred by riots against Salvadorean immigrants (who formed one-eighth of the Honduran population) and by long-standing territorial ambitions, El Salvador opened hostilities on 14 July 1969 after mistreatment of its national football team. A ceasefire took effect four days later but El Salvador took further action until the Organization of American States threatened sanctions on 29 July. The 'Soccer War' is listed in one encyclopedia as 'costing thousands of lives' but the actual number may be as few as a dozen; a peace treaty was not signed until 1980.

Honduras' air arm consisted mainly of Vought F4U Corsairs, while El Salvador possessed Goodyear FG-1D Corsairs and a handful of C-47s used as bombers, in addition to the new fleet of Mustangs. Another F-51D had been a pristine

A Cavalier Mustang F-51D Mk 2 (foreground) and TF-51D Mk 2 overfly Sarasota, Florida before being delivered to Bolivia. They wear full US Air Force markings for their delivery flight. The last true USAF Mustang was a P-51D of the West Virginia ANG, retired to the Air Force Museum at Wright Field on 27 January 1957. The TF-51D was written off by the FAB in July 1970.

N482PE shows off the initial configuration of the second-series Piper PA-48 Enforcer (first flown 9 April 1983), with a test probe projecting from its port tip tank.

Upgrades & Derivatives

Many efforts were made to modernise the Mustang in the post-war era. The pioneer in this effort was David B. Lindsay, Jr, who created Trans Florida Aviation, later called Cavalier Aircraft. He actually sold dozens of refurbished Mustangs, initially to wealthy private owners and then, from 1967, to selected MAP recipients.

Project Peace Condor saw the upgrade of some Mustangs to Cavalier standards for Bolivia and El Salvador. Later aircraft went to Indonesia, and to the Dominican Republic. Cavalier's new Mustangs appeared in several variants, many with tall tails and wingtip fuel tanks. Two Cavalier two-

seat Mustangs and a P-51D rebuilt by Aero Sport were used by the US Army as chase aircraft, and the D became the last US military Mustang, being retired in February 1978.

Lindsay's efforts to market a turboprop Mustang met with no success, but Piper thought enough of the idea to buy Lindsay out and to offer two generations of Piper PA-48 Enforcers, working to persuade the USAF that this F-51 derivative belonged in the modern world. It had modern plastic armour, self-sealing tanks and compatability with a range of new weapons. The PA-48 was offered in the 1968-70 competition which produced the A-10.

Below: N481PE was the first aircraft of the second pair of Piper PA-48 Enforcers. The PA-48 was 15 in (42 cm) longer than the standard F-51D Mustang and had a new cockpit canopy, new spars (good for 14,000 hours), a larger fin and rudder, and new ailerons.

Above: The Allison-engined Mustang has never been common on the warbird and racing circuit. Racing number 2 was assigned to one of the rare Allison ships in the Unlimited races, an A-36A (42-83665) registered as N39502 and now in the USAF Museum at Wright-Patterson.

John Crocker's Mustang Sumthin Else *(44-74502, N51VC) finished in first place in the 1979 Reno race with an average speed of 422.302 mph (679.627 km/h). The aircraft had previously raced as* Miss Foxy Lady, *owned by Ken Burnstine. Many Mustang racers were modified with various styles of flush canopy in an effort to add speed to the bubble canopy P-51D.*

N1204X was an F-6C (42-103831) owned by Hollywood stunt-flier Paul Mantz and flown by T. J. Mayson in the 1946 Bendix Trophy Race from Van Nuys, California to Cleveland. This ushered in the brief post-war resurrection of Unlimited Air Racing in the United States. The aircraft now belongs to the Weeks air museum, in Florida.

RAF pilot. Most F-51Ds, however, were flown by FAS regular and reserve pilots.

Documentation is lacking, but it appears that five Mustangs were lost in action in a conflict which saw virtually all aircraft hit by friendly and hostile fire. Two Mustangs were lost to a mid-air collision, and two to fuel starvation. No Salvadorean pilot claimed an air-to-air victory while flying an F-51, but at least one FAS F-51D was shot down by a Honduran F4U Corsair – and some sources say two were. The final Mustang ever to be lost in an air-to-air engagement was piloted by FAS Captain Humberto Varela and was shot down on 17 July 1969 by an F4U-5 flown by Honduran Major Soto, who also downed an FG-1D.

Final combat honours

At the end of the 'Soccer War' El Salvador had 10 flyable Mustangs, and the very last combat laurels ever to be won by this famous fighter. After the war El Salvador continued to try to increase its Mustang force, resulting in the arrest of several US citizens who tried to smuggle aircraft to the country. In the wake of the war, Honduras re-equipped with F-86s and Super Mystères, and this forced the retirement of the Salvadorean Mustangs in favour of Ouragan jet fighters. The last Mustangs were sold in 1974.

Reports that Honduras used a small number of F-51Ds until 1959 and that they were replaced by F4U-5 Corsairs are totally without foundation, although the country did briefly examine the possibility of acquiring 22 (ex-French) F-51Ds in 1953. Similarly, reports that Cuba received some F-51Ds in 1947 as military assistance from the United States under the terms of the Rio Pact are erroneous. The Fuerza Aérea Ejercito de Cuba (as the country's former Aviation Corps, or Cuerpo de Aviacion, was renamed in a 1955 reorganisation) never had Mustangs. Cuba's Fuerza Aérea Rebelde (later Fuerza Aérea Revolucionaria) did, however, illegally acquire three civilian-registered Mustangs in 1958, and these remained nominally in service with the Cuban Military Air Force until replaced with Soviet equipment in the early 1960s, although serviceability was very poor. The

warbird owned by local businessman and engineer Archie Baldocchi. His aircraft was impressed in the only known occurrence of a civil aircraft being recalled for combat: Baldocchi became an advisor to the Fuerza Aérea Salvadorene (FAS) on Mustang operations, removing the tanks from the Mustang IIs and devising quick prop repairs and other modifications. He taught fuel-management techniques and devised ingenious new drop tanks. Eleven more standard F-51Ds were purchased from various sources in the USA. Some of these were unarmed, and were used only for carrying bombs and napalm. Sr Baldocchi designed, built and installed reflector sights for some of the new aircraft which did have guns, but which had long ago been stripped of sights. He also assisted the FAS in building a two-seat TF-51 from stock aircraft using parts from attrited Mustangs. Alas, this replacement for the TF-51D held in Guatemala crashed before it had an opportunity to be useful. The sole TF-51D diverted to friendly Guatemala when it ran low on fuel on a combat mission and was interned for the duration of the war (alongside a Honduran Corsair).

On a typical mission, Salvadorean C-47s and FG-1Ds carrying bombs were escorted by 'clean' F-51D Mustangs performing escort duty like that at which they had excelled in the war in Europe. Ranges were short, however, and the Mustangs went into battle with minimal fuel loads, except on the occasional deep strike to Tegucigalpa. The FAS had help from some colourful mercenaries who flew some of the Mustang sorties, including 'Red' Grey, a 7-ft former

Inset left: Known as RB-51 (for Red Baron), N7715C was a highly modified Griffon-engined F-51D which performed well in Unlimited racing at Reno and Homestead year after year, and which set a piston-engined speed record of 499.018 mph (803.069 km/h).

Racing Revival

The P-51 Mustang was one of several World War II veterans which spearheaded the late 1940s attempt to recreate the golden age of Unlimited Air Racing which had graced the US in the years before the war. But *Beguine*, a P-51C flown by the legendary Bill Odom, ended the revival when it crashed at Cleveland in 1949, killing Odom, a mother and a child.

Due almost solely to the efforts of Bill Stead, Unlimited racing was again resurrected in 1964 at Reno, Nevada's 'biggest little capital in the world', also known because of legal gambling as the home of the high rollers. An F-51D Mustang flown by Korean War ace Bob

Love surpassed Mira Slovak's F8F-2 Bearcat to win the 1964 event with an average speed of 366.82 mph (590.33 km/h). No Unlimited race has been flown without participation by Mustangs since.

The enterprising spirit of the men who lead the way in air racing has resulted in many Mustangs being modified almost beyond recognition, as more and more performance is wrung out of the same basic fighter design. *Sumthin Else*, *Red Baron* and *Tsunami* among others, have given the Mustang new shapes, new speed, and an entirely new purpose. Unlimited racing thrives today thanks in part to the P-51.

Batista air force are reported to have used some against Fidel Castro's revolutionary forces (who also had, but did not use, Mustangs) in 1959. A single Mustang was traded to Venezuela as part of the deal by which Bolivia acquired surplus FAV Sabres and Mitchells.

Air races

More than any other aircraft of World War II, the Mustang was the subject of post-war modifications for civilian use, either as high-speed executive playthings, for record-breaking or racing. Some were extremely technically interesting, with a host of modifications, mostly to reduce drag. These included cut-down canopies, clipped wings and even relocated radiators. One greatly modified P-51D, with a V-1650-9 boosted to 3,000 hp (2250 kW), held the piston-engined speed record at just over 517 mph (832 km/h).

The ink was scarcely dry on the Japanese surrender when the first P-51 joined the US civil register. For a time, it was possible to purchase a Mustang for almost nothing – prices as low as US $100 (then about £25) – have been reported. While some owners simply wanted to fly a 'warbird' (a new term in post-war aeronautical jargon, meaning a restored military aircraft and first coined in the 1970s), aircraft like the P-51 were not really suitable for private use by the average pilot, and almost all a gas-guzzling 400-mph (643-km/h) Mustang was really good for, in the post-war world, was racing. Many hoped to see the Mustang and its like at the vanguard of a resurrected era of air racing like that of the 1930s.

The dream of matching the golden age of the 1930s was never to be attained, but the National Air Races were resurrected at Cleveland and enjoyed a brief heyday from 1946 to 1949. All the contestants were ex-military aircraft, and almost all were unmodified but for eye-catching colour schemes and a serious amount of polish (and sometimes

filler), and with heavy military equipment, armour and oxygen removed. In the 1946 races at Cleveland there were seven Mustangs, five P-63 Kingcobras, four P-38 Lightnings and three P-39 Airacobras, together with a single FG-1D. The pre-war circuit record was 297.99 mph (479.55 km/h), which was soon broken by the big fighters, a P-39Q taking the honour with a speed of 409.09 mph (659.65 km/h). All except four entrants broke the existing record during qualification. For the Thompson Trophy, a P-39 gained first place, with Tony Levier's P-38 coming an unexpected second, chased by the various Mustangs. Mustangs gained the top three places in the first Sohio Trophy pylon race, the winner, Dale Fulton, averaging 352.78 mph (567 72 km/h).

For the Bendix transcontinental race that started in Los Angeles there were four P-51s, 15 P-38s, a P-63, a B-26 and an FG-1D. The first four positions were won by converted Mustangs. Paul Mantz' P-51C racer was placed first at an average speed of 435 mph [700 km/h] with an elapsed time of four hours, 42 minutes and 14 seconds (topping the

Allison-powered Mustangs have been rare on the air racing circuit, although the Chino-based Planes of Fame P-51A (43-6251), a couple of others, and at least two A-36A Invaders have been seen rounding the pylons

Clay Lacy, record-breaking United Airlines pilot and owner of a specialist aerial photography business, is also a long-time Mustang owner. For many years his mount was this purple machine, in which he won at Reno in 1970.

Left: Another view of the remarkable RB-51, the Red Baron, alias 'the world's most modified Mustang', which was a sensation at Reno but which nearly killed veteran pilot Steve Hinton when it went down during the 1979 Unlimited event. The aircraft was rebuilt to virtually stock P-51D configuration using parts from an ex-Indonesian air force P-51D. It is now painted in pseudo 357th FG markings.

Above: Seen on an unknown date before July 1959, this civil-owned P-51D pre-dated the widespread use of the word 'warbird' to refer to an airworthy veteran under civil ownership. Apart from new radio gear (note the non-standard aerial), this is a stock NAA D model. It was owned for many years by Dr Mark Foutch, before passing to John Dilley, who repainted it as Lou IV of the 361st FG.

Above: Lefty Gardner's N6169C Thunderbird (formerly 44-73704) is seen on the American registry prior to July 1959. In 1976 it came first at Reno. The practice of painstakingly applying accurate wartime markings had yet to take hold.

Registered N51MR and seen at Reading, Pennsylvania, this stock Mustang once wore the race number 4 and was named Minuteman, although success eluded it. This P-51D was an ex-USAAF and ex-RCAF aircraft which has enjoyed a long civilian career with a variety of owners and wearing a succession of registrations.

In civilian hands

The first civilian to own a Mustang may have been a rancher in Kingman, Arizona, who discovered that he could cart away – and destroy, for its scrap metal value – the top American fighter of World War II upon payment of a mere $25. By then, hundreds if not thousands of Mustangs had already been destroyed by the United States Army Air Force itself. Many, deemed surplus, were blown up in Germany by explosive charges set by hired veterans of Hitler's defeated Wehrmacht.

Fortunately, even in the immediate post-war years when other priorities beckoned, a few visionaries saved examples of victorious warplanes for display in museums. The role of museums was still evolving at that time, and incredible strides have been made in the fields of restoration and display techniques ever since.

And flying? With the revival of air racing came a new and unprecedented phenomenon: the 'warbird movement', which encouraged ownership and above all actual flying of the military aircraft of the just-concluded conflict. No one knows when the word 'warbird' was coined to mean a restored, flyable military aircraft,, but the movement has grown and prospered.

Despite the passage of time since the P-51 was operational, more Mustangs are being flown by civil owners today than at any juncture in the five decades since the war.

And the price tag? Not even the most skimpily-equipped Mustang can be purchased today for less than 10,000 times the price shelled out by that unwitting rancher.

out of his P-40, foreshadowing safety problems which would later kill off the National Air Races.

The 1948 Bendix Air Race from Long Beach, California to Cleveland saw Mantz enter two converted Mustangs. The first four places were taken by Mustangs. In the 1948 Thompson Trophy race, the Mustang at last triumphed, but it was a hollow victory; all of the powerful F2Gs and the P-63 and P-39 dropped out, leaving only three aircraft in the running. The record seemed to give the P-51 a commanding lead in distance events, but the type proved weak in the 'down in the dirt' scrapping around the pylons.

Mantz was noticeably absent when 1949 Bendix Air Race aspirants lined up to launch, but his two F-6s were entered with Stanley Reaver and Herman 'Fish' Salmon doing the honours. Competitor Joe DeBona had been backed by actor Jimmy Stewart to beat Mantz and chose a comparable F-6 in preference to the P-51D he had flown in prior races, stripped to the bone in an attempt to out-speed Mantz's craft. The take-off from Rosamond Dry Lake in the Muroc military reservation was to be the only racehorse start of the post-war contests. DeBona's gloss-blue No. 90, 'Thunderbird', came in first at more than 470 mph (756 km/h). Reaver and Salmon cinched the second and third slots.

In the 1949 Thompson Trophy race, a plethora of P-51A, C, D and K fighters challenged the P-39 and F2Gs. F2Gs took first, second and third, but a Mustang took the headlines. William Odom flew Floyd Odom's P-51C No. 7, modified to incorporate wingtip radiators (resembling

previous record by 153 mph/246 km/h and two and a half hours). Jacqueline Cochran came in second with 421 mph [678 km/h]. The 1946 Thompson Trophy contest also saw numerous Mustang entries.

The January 1947 All-American Air Maneuvers included a similar pylon race to the Thompson, and this was won by a Mustang, which averaged 308 mph (496 km/h) around the shorter course.

Bendix and Thompson races

In 1947, the Bendix Trophy race was won by Mantz for the second year when his bright red converted F-6C clocked an average speed of 460 mph (740 km/h). Joe DeBona's P-51D, 'Magic Town', was only 2 mph (3.2 km/h) behind Mantz. Around the pylons in the Thompson Trophy race, re-engined F2G Super Corsairs set the pace, one setting a record of 396.131 mph (637.49 km/h) (with one lap clocked at 404.5 mph/650.96 km/h), with the highest-placed Mustang 10 miles (16 km) behind in fourth place. One of the F2Gs crashed when its pilot fell victim to carbon monoxide poisoning, and another pilot had to bail

By October 1988, the Confederate Air Force was a leader in the warbird world, and accurate markings had become de rigueur. At Harlingen, Texas, N5428V flies the lead, painted to represent an aircraft of the 343rd FS/55th FG, and is trailed by a Mustang painted as an aircraft from the 352nd.

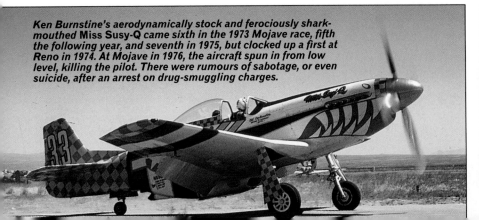

Ken Burnstine's aerodynamically stock and ferociously shark-mouthed Miss Susy-Q came sixth in the 1973 Mojave race, fifth the following year, and seventh in 1975, but clocked up a first at Reno in 1974. At Mojave in 1976, the aircraft spun in from low level, killing the pilot. There were rumours of sabotage, or even suicide, after an arrest on drug-smuggling charges.

ram jets) in place of the belly scoop. The radiators required inflight ram air to cool the overboosted engine. Inexperienced at pylon racing, Odom stalled on the number 2 pylon and crashed into a residential area. Odom and a mother and child lost their lives. The loss of fabled Odom and, in particular, of innocent victims, led to a withdrawal of sponsorship which led to the end of the National Air Races which ended unlimited air racing for a decade and a half – but the Mustang was to return to the pylons in the 1960s.

From 1949 to 1960 only Midgets (Formula One racers with 190-cu in/3113-cm³ engines) were raced in the US, and there was no National race meeting at all. After a major accident in Indiana, from 1960 to 1963, there were no races at all.

Air races return

Bill Stead of Reno, Nevada – safely on the high desert, far from populated areas – dreamed of recreating the National Air Races, and set about realising his dream, drumming up sponsorship and TV coverage. 'Big time' air racing began at the Reno Sky Ranch with the first event on 12-20 September 1964, including an unlimited transcontinental race and an unlimited pylon race, together with the first US aerobatics championship and the US Hot Air Ballooning Championship and a range of other pylon races. Winner of the 1964 unlimited transcontinental race was Wayne Adams' P-51D Mustang, one of eight competing Mustangs. For the unlimited pylon race there were five Mustangs and three F8F-2 Bearcats. A new innovation was the introduction of the flying start, with contestants flying in line abreast, with a pace aircraft which would then pull up to signal the acceleration which would start the race. Bob Hoover flew the first Mustang pace aircraft, and opened the 1964 event with the immortal words "Gentlemen, you have a race!" Mira Slovak won the championship, in a Bearcat, although Bob Love's Mustang actually won the main race. Since then, Reno has been the centre

of the world for racing by wartime fighters, although multi-lap races were also staged at Clearwater, FL, Boulder City, NV, and Lancaster, CA in 1965 and at Lancaster in 1966. P-51Ds won most of these races, but Darryl Greenamyer's Bearcat kept them off the top spot at Reno for both years, and indeed until 1970.

The early Reno races – the pioneer events that paved the way for today's unlimited events – drew increasing crowds and saw Mustangs repeatedly clocked at well over 400 mph (643 km/h), usually dominating the field. In the 36 races at Reno, Denver, Sherman, Hamilton, Homestead, Mojave, Miami and Cape May, Mustangs continued to be the most popular racing aircraft (sometimes being the only type in the field, and often challenging only one example of another type) and won exactly half of them, sometimes taking second place to a Bearcat (10 victories), F2G or Sea Fury.

As the warbird movement expanded in the United States and ownership of restored World War II warplanes increased from dozens to hundreds – Mustangs from about 10 in 1955 to about 50 in 1968 and over 200 today – the P-51 continued to excel at the Reno races. Merely racing a

At least two and possibly more warbirds have been painted to represent the second Old Crow flown by Colonel Clarence 'Bud' Anderson, a 16½ victory ace of the 362nd FS/357th FG. This example, correctly marked with serial 44-14450 and codes 'B6-S', beats up Tico in March 1987.

Australian-built CA-18 Mustang Mk 22 G-HAEC is a superb restoration by Mark Hannah's Old Flying Machine Co. Once on Australia's register as VH-FCB, this aircraft moved to the United Kingdom in the 1970s.

Left: P-51D (44-73877), registered N167F, is here flown by Ward Wilkins of Unlimited Aero, Fort Collins, Colorado, after restoration by Darrell Skurich. The markings are an incomplete representation of those worn by the Mustang flown by 'Bud' Anderson of the 357th Fighter Squadron, 363rd Fighter Group. The name Old Crow is missing from the cowling, and D-Day stripes have yet to be applied.

Above: This warbird was painted to represent the mount of Lieutenant Arval J. Roberson of the 357th FG. High gloss is common on warbirds, being easier to keep clean and offering better protection against erosion and corrosion.

These are two of the three Old Flying Machine Co. P-51Ds which were used in the making of the blockbuster film treatment of J. G. Ballard's semi-autobiographical novel Empire of the Sun. They wear the markings of the 118th TRS, based in China during the war.

Captain William Whisner, a 16-victory ace, later added 5½ to his score flying F-86s in Korea. His wartime mount inspired this remarkably faithful recreation of the original. The colour schemes on restored Mustangs have become more and more realistic.

stock Mustang had once been a thrill. Gradually, it became even more thrilling to improve on the Mustang. Souped-up engines were installed from the start, and drag reduction became steadily more popular as time passed, first with clipped wings and later with more radical modifications.

Typifying the aircraft which retained a standard P-51D appearance have been 'Miss America', in patriotic red, white and blue, with clipped wings, and with its Merlin honed to perfection, something not possible in a World War II fighter group with 78 planes caught up in a heavy surge of operations, each one of which had to run reliably to Berlin and back, day-in, day-out. 'Miss America' was routinely clocked at 460 mph (740 km/h). Another seemingly standard P-51D was 'Georgia Mae', which performed well but remained, in all important respects, a low-drag Mustang. Then there were the aircraft with tiny low-drag canopies which barely protruded out of the Mustang's spine, including aircraft like 'Miss Foxy Lady' (later renamed 'Sumthin' Else'), 'Specter' (formerly 'Leeward Air Ranch Special', 'Galloping Ghost', 'Miss Candace' and 'Jeannie'), 'Dago Red (holder of the piston-engined straight-line speed record at 517.06 mph/832.10 km/h), its replacement, and 'Strega' (winner in 1987). More radically modified was the similar looking 'Stiletto', which deleted the Mustang's characteristic underbelly air scoop in favour of leading edge radiators.

A tremendous contrast is provided by more heavily modified aircraft like 'Precious Metal', created over five years by the Whittington brothers. The aircraft started with

square-cut wingtips and a tall P-51H-type fin, with a slightly lower canopy. It then gained refinements, including a revised low-drag cockpit with a well-sloped windscreen faired into the upward-hinging canopy, and an aerodynamic turtleback. Most importantly, the engine was swapped for a Rolls-Royce Griffon driving three-bladed, contra-rotating propellers. This brought the aircraft to almost the same configuration as the Griffon-engined 'Red Baron', which set an absolute propeller-driven speed record of 499.018 mph (803.06 km/h) at Tonopah in 1979, and which had proved a devastatingly effective competitor at earlier Reno races. Similarly dramatic was 'Vendetta', built from a wreck and using the wing and horizontal tail of a Learjet 23, with a souped-up Merlin and the usual racing Mustang aerodynamic refinements. Pointing the way to the future was the dramatic 'Tsunami', a new design inspired by the most dramatically modified of the racing Mustangs, with tiny laminar-flow wings, a pushed-back cockpit, and a frontal cross-section only 77 per cent of that of the P-51. Unfortunately, the aircraft was lost before it could really prove itself in unlimited competition, winning only the 1990 race at Sherman, Texas. The potential for improving on the Mustang with fin de siecle technology has probably only been breached, and perhaps even greater enhancements to the basic design will appear.

Other rebuilds undertaken during the 1960s were for military purposes.

Temco, Cavalier and Piper Mustangs

In the 1950s, Temco Aircraft received a contract to convert 15 F-51D Mustangs into two-seat conversion trainers, designated TF-51D. In World War II, a number of Mustangs were converted to dual controls in the field by enterprising fighter squadron mechanics. The Temco aircraft differed in having two distinct cockpits, separated by a centre console, as well as a full set of dual instruments and controls.

In 1967 the US Air Force ordered an additional batch of Mustangs from Cavalier Aircraft Corp., which acquired design rights from North American. These new-build aircraft were intended for delivery to South American and Asian nations through the Military Assistance Program but were delivered in American markings with new serial numbers (67-14862/14866; 67-22579/22582; 72-1536/1541). Rebuilt from existing airframes, they were fitted with V-1650-7 engines, new radios, the tall P-51H-style fin, and a strengthened wing.

In 1968, the US Army employed a vintage F-51D (44-72990) as a chase aircraft for the YAH-56 Cheyenne battlefield helicopter. It was so successful that the Army ordered two Cavalier F-51Ds (68-15795/15796) as chase aircraft. Following the end of the Cheyenne programme, these Mustangs were briefly used for other purposes and one (68-15795) was fitted with a 106-mm recoilless rifle and used to evaluate the weapon's value in attacking fortified ground targets.

In 1968, Cavalier flight-tested a modified F-51 as the Turbo-Mustang III, powered by a 1,740-shp (1305-kW) Rolls-Royce Dart 510 turboprop engine. The aircraft was presented in October 1968 for evaluation by the US Air Force in its AX close-support competition, one of several attempts to sell a Vietnam-era version to the service. A similar conversion was toyed with, the following year, in Australia. Among many ex-RAAF Mustangs found on Australia's civil registry was a CA-18 Mustang Mk 23 (A68-187) which was purchased in 1969 by Sydney businessman Hockey Treloar with the intention of converting the aircraft to use a Rolls-Royce Dart turboprop engine. No Dart-powered Mustang ever proved successful.

Two other Mustangs were converted with 2,455-shp (1841-kW) Lycoming T55-L-9 engines. This version was known as the Enforcer and made its first flight on 19 April 1971, the same year Piper acquired design rights from Cav-

The 353rd Fighter Group decorated its Mustangs with black and yellow checkerboard noses, as seen on this modern warbird, which represents a typical wartime member of the group.

A Spitfire and a Pilatus P-2 (painted to represent a Bf 109) lead an attractive but rather less than authentic P-51D warbird. The USAF legend was a post-war innovation and the black and white checkers and nose stripes do not represent any known front-line fighter group in World War II.

alier. Tests of these aircraft in the early 1970s failed to arouse much interest on the part of Air Force officers, but Congress kept pushing the Enforcer. In September 1981, a contract was placed with Piper for two new-built PA-48 Enforcer airframes, the first of which made its maiden flight on 9 April 1983. The USAF evaluated the two PA-48 prototypes exhaustively before retiring them from flight status in 1986. Barely recognisable as Mustangs, the two 'new-build' Enforcers are included in our total for aircraft manufactured while the two converted aircraft (which did not acquire new serials) are not.

What could possibly be a better candidate for authentic markings than Big Beautiful Doll, P-51D 44-72218 flown by Colonel John Landers of the 78th Fighter Group. In real life, this warbird is P-51D 44-72811, registered as N268BD, an ex-Israeli Defence Force fighter placed on the warbird circuit by Bob Byrne of Bloomfield, Michigan.

Today's warbirds

Today, the Mustang is perhaps best known as a warbird, and there are large numbers of P-51s (particularly D models) in private hands, being used for air display, and film work, and even simply for pleasure. The Mustang's long post-war service ensured that large numbers of aircraft survived the mass-scrappings of 1945, and nurtured the growth of a cottage industry to support the aircraft, at first consisting of companies supporting those aircraft being used by minor nations in Latin America, and later supporting the racing fraternity. Today, it is possible to buy almost any component for the P-51D, newly built and at a relatively

reasonable price, and this will ensure that the type continues to be more popular and more common than other wartime fighter types. With such large numbers of warbirds commemorating the Mustang's wartime achievements, it is little wonder that the aircraft has become the most famous fighter of the conflict.

Bill Gunston and Robert F. Dorr

This one-time California Warbirds P-51D is painted to represent Straw Boss (44-14111) but is actually 44-72192. Markings are those of the 328th Fighter Squadron, 352nd Fighter Group, in the European theatre of operations, circa 1944.

Navy Phantoms in Vietnam

Above: The 'Freelancers' of VF-21 made no fewer than seven cruises to the combat zone. This aircraft is seen early in the war, bombing South Vietnamese targets in 1965. Air wings usually worked up in the South when they arrived in-theatre, followed by a move north to Yankee Station and operations against North Vietnam.

No aircraft dominated the air fighting over Vietnam more than the McDonnell F-4 Phantom. Those of the US Navy flew on the first official US missions of the war after the Tonkin Gulf incident, and covered the final evacuation from Saigon. In between, the Navy F-4 pounded targets in both the North and South, but it is as a fighter that it is best remembered. A long list of MiG kills was racked up, but the Phantom force suffered heavily from ground defences.

From 5 August 1964 until 30 April 1975 – for four thousand eleven days and nights – the carrier-based F-4 Phantom fighter squadrons of the US Navy waged war against North Vietnam. For Americans, it was a time when a nation lost its faith, cities turned to fire, and a population was thrown into upheaval, events which had not happened since the Civil War a century earlier. For the attack carriers which were now the capital ships of the US Navy – and the largest objects ever built by man – it was a time of stress and surge, of maximum sacrifice devoted to limited ends, and of a long, terrible journey toward losing a war for the first time.

If there was a sailor on any carrier who was not amazed by the Phantom, he was difficult to find. Brilliant in its two-tone Navy grey/white scheme, two men buttoned down under what looked like a jerry-rigged afterthought of canopies, the Phantom was at once both sleek and ugly, both powerful and costly, both sturdy and complex. Men who spent 12 to 16 hours a day around the aircraft, week after week, month after month, never failed to turn their heads each time the choreography of a jet launch kicked off anew – taxi up to the spot, raise the ship's slab-like JDBs (jet blast deflector), exercise controls, make sure wings are locked, turn on lights at night, make tension on the pullback, go to full power...

Navy F-4s undertook their fair share of mud-moving, especially in the south. With only one Sparrow and one Sidewinder fitted for self defence, this VF-96 aircraft carries two pods of 5-in (127-mm) Zuni rockets.

The big General Electric J79 engine designed for the Convair B-58 Hustler had only a single shaft, but multiple variable-incidence stator vanes assured a high pressure ratio. Two of them on full afterburner for launch meant a stabbing dagger of flame going back eight or ten feet from the burner cans and a power rating of about 34,000 lb thrust (150 kN). At a combat weight of around 41,900 lb (19005 kg) for a fleet intercept mission, a Phantom being hurtled aloft by one of a carrier's four C13 or C13-1 steam catapults had approximately the kinetic energy of a railroad boxcar being hurled off a cliff – but not with the same result. Other carrier planes always dipped, sometimes vanished completely beneath the horizon of the carrier's prow, and seemed certain to plough into the waves before, somehow, righting and picking up momentum to ascend. The Phantom never did this. No matter how much fuel or how many missiles were hung under it – and, soon, bombs – the Phantom went off the 'cat', remained level for a short distance, then bounded for the sky.

For the men who maintained, repaired, serviced and flew the McDonnell F-4 Phantom – the finest combat aircraft in the world, although not without annoying and sometimes fatal flaws – the 11-year journey in Vietnam brought never an instant when anybody figured out how to defeat them. Usually outgunned and outnumbered, sent

*Launching from **Connie's** waist cat, a VF-92 Phantom heads for North Vietnam during the first Linebacker campaign. This was the Navy Phantom's finest hour, hitting back against the North Vietnamese MiGs in a hectic bout of air combat.*

*VF-151 was another stalwart squadron of the Vietnam War, usually paired with VF-161 (both ended up as the last carrierborne F-4 squadrons flying from **Midway**). For their first war cruise in 1964, the 'Vigilantes' were accompanied in **Coral Sea** by a Crusader squadron rather than a second Phantom unit.*

McDonnell F-4B Phantom II
VF-142 'Ghostriders'
USS *Constellation*, 1968

Typical of the Phantoms that carried the war to North Vietnam throughout the conflict from carrier decks, this F-4B wears the markings of VF-142, one of the stalwart squadrons of the Southeast Asia war. Alongside its sister squadron VF-143, the 'Ghostriders' were involved in the very first Navy strikes of the war, and in total undertook seven combat cruises. Four were with the F-4B, followed by three with the F-4J. During the course of these the squadron scored five confirmed kills: four MiG-21s and a single MiG-17.

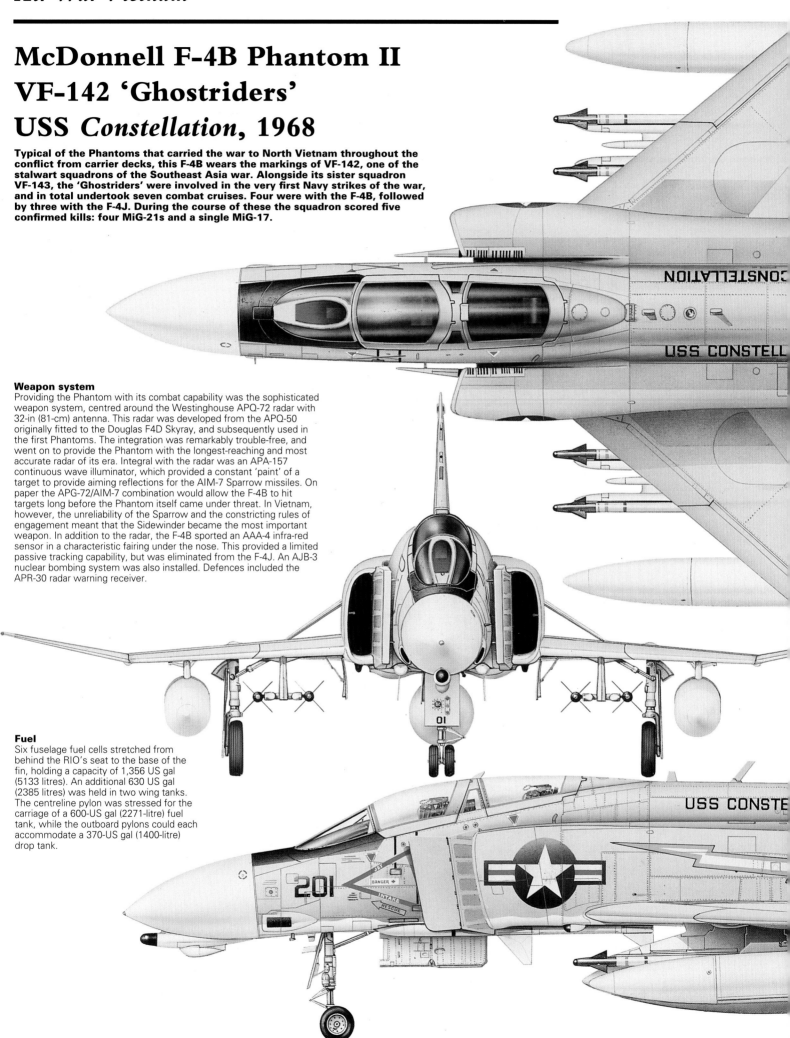

Weapon system
Providing the Phantom with its combat capability was the sophisticated weapon system, centred around the Westinghouse APQ-72 radar with 32-in (81-cm) antenna. This radar was developed from the APQ-50 originally fitted to the Douglas F4D Skyray, and subsequently used in the first Phantoms. The integration was remarkably trouble-free, and went on to provide the Phantom with the longest-reaching and most accurate radar of its era. Integral with the radar was an APA-157 continuous wave illuminator, which provided a constant 'paint' of a target to provide aiming reflections for the AIM-7 Sparrow missiles. On paper the APG-72/AIM-7 combination would allow the F-4B to hit targets long before the Phantom itself came under threat. In Vietnam, however, the unreliability of the Sparrow and the constricting rules of engagement meant that the Sidewinder became the most important weapon. In addition to the radar, the F-4B sported an AAA-4 infra-red sensor in a characteristic fairing under the nose. This provided a limited passive tracking capability, but was eliminated from the F-4J. An AJB-3 nuclear bombing system was also installed. Defences included the APR-30 radar warning receiver.

Fuel
Six fuselage fuel cells stretched from behind the RIO's seat to the base of the fin, holding a capacity of 1,356 US gal (5133 litres). An additional 630 US gal (2385 litres) was held in two wing tanks. The centreline pylon was stressed for the carriage of a 600-US gal (2271-litre) fuel tank, while the outboard pylons could each accommodate a 370-US gal (1400-litre) drop tank.

Configuration

The unmistakable shape of the Phantom evolved from conflicting requirements of high performance and carrier compatibility. The 'bent' wing provided dihedral for roll stability but kept the main wing straight. The outer panel had a large dogtooth on the leading edge to preserve lateral control and avoid pitch-up at high AoA. The aircraft needed a huge keel area, so the fin was very long. However, the constraints of the hangar deck dictated fin height, and the fin was not adequate for directional stability. The tailplanes were consequently given substantial (23.25°) anhedral to provide additional keel area.

Powerplant

The highly successful J79 employed only a single shaft, but introduced multiple variable-incidence stator vanes to produce a very high pressure ratio. These vanes were mounted in front of the first seven rotating compressor stages, mounted on pivots and linked externally to two rams which positioned them for optimum compression at various engine speeds. This significantly reduced fuel burn and provided a greater thrust/weight ratio compared to a similar engine with fixed stator vanes. Furthering the efficiency of the engine was the world's first fully variable supersonic inlets. The outer edge had a sharp fixed lip, while the inner wall consisted of a large ramp held proud from the fuselage to avoid ingestion of boundary layer. The inlet featured movable walls to vary the throat area for maximum air capture efficiency at any speed.

Specification

Powerplant: two General Electric J79-GE-8A/B turbojets, rated at 17,900 lb (879.65 kN) thrust with afterburning
Performance: maximum speed Mach 2 at altitude; service ceiling 71,000 ft (21640 m); combat radius (interceptor) 900 miles (1450 km); ferry range 2,300 miles (3700 km)
Weights: take-off (clean) 46,000 lb (20866 kg); maximum take-off 54,600 lb (24766 kg)
Dimensions: wing span 38 ft 5 in (11.71 m); length 58 ft 3 in (17.75 m); height 16 ft 3 in (4.95 m); wing area 530 sq ft (49.24 m²)

Flight control

All surfaces were fully powered. Pitch control was provided by the powerful stabilators which could move through 40°. Yaw control came from the simple rudder, which at low speeds was interconnected with the ailerons to cancel yaw inputs. Roll control was provided by ailerons on the outboard section of the trailing edge inboard of the wing-fold. These only deflected downwards, being augmented by spoilers on the upper surface of the wing forward of the ailerons. The entire leading-edge of the wing was taken up with three sections of drooping flaps. These, and the simple trailing-edge flaps, were blown with compressor air. All surfaces were untabbed.

Armament

The decision to delete guns from the original Phantom designs came to be regretted in Vietnam, but an internal cannon was never fitted to Navy Phantoms. For air-to-air work the aircraft relied on up to four AIM-9B/C/D Sidewinders carried on shoulder rails from the inboard pylons, with up to four AIM-7C/E Sparrows carried in semi-recessed bays under the fuselage. Air-to-ground stores covered a wide variety of free-fall bombs and unguided rockets.

Keith Fretwell

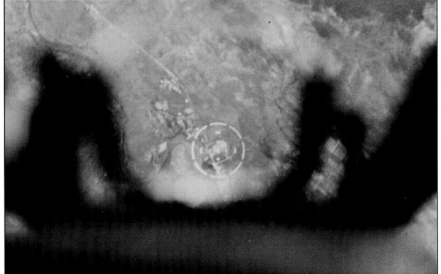

into battle at enormous disadvantage under a mind-boggling banner of handicaps and restrictions, the F-4 squadrons of the attack carrier force set a record for courage and performance that may never be matched. When they drew the final job of evacuating Saigon on the last day, they had been betrayed by circumstance. They had never been – not for a single moment – defeated.

In the shops, on the elevators, and spotted about the deck of USS *Constellation* (CVA-64) churning out of Alameda Navy Yard on 5 May 1964 and slipping under the Golden Gate Bridge to embark on that seminal Southeast Asia cruise, the McDonnell F-4B Phantom was a marvel of engineering. It was a superb fleet defence interceptor, brilliantly equipped with powerful radar and air-to-air missiles to guard the US Navy at sea. Never mind the clichés – it had bent wings because somebody had stepped on the blueprints, it had two seats, two engines, and no guns because an F-8 Crusader pilot had sabotaged the blueprints – the Phantom was a thing of beauty, high-decibel testimony to what many called the 'American century', to a nation which led all others in science and technology, a people who could do anything, a government travelling a righteous

path with the unwavering trust of its citizens. The dominance of America in the world, the leadership, and in particular the trust, were to be swallowed up in the rain jungles of Southeast Asia. But not yet. To get out of San Francisco Bay, *Connie* had to pass Berkeley, where the first anti-government demonstration of the 1960s was taking shape, but no one understood its significance. Americans, F-4B Phantom crews among them, were proud, confident, and so innocent that it seems impossible, today, to remember what it was like then.

Viewing it as just one variant of a famous fighter, the F-4B (at first designated F4H-1) was the first definitive production version of the Phantom and, in keeping with the Phantom as perceived in its early days, was optimised for use as a fleet defence interceptor although it also had air-to-ground capability.

The F-4B was powered by two 17,900-lb (79.63-kN) thrust General Electric J79-GE-8A and -8B engines and equipped with AN/APQ-72 radar and Lear AJB-3 nuclear bombing system. The F-4B was equipped with AN/ASA-32 Automatic Flight Control System (AFCS) used to provide a number of Mach/altitude automatic-pilot relief modes. The aircraft had folding wings, tail hook, probe air refuelling receptacle, semi-submerged fuselage well mountings for four AIM-7C Sparrow III semi-active radar homing missiles, and wing hardpoints which could be employed for two more Sparrows (though the Phantom rarely flew with six) or AIM-9B Sidewinders. The 651 aircraft completed in the F-4B series included 12 delivered as F-4G datalink aircraft

Half of *Connie*'s Phantoms wore a lightning bolt on the fuselage, then the marking of the 'Ghostriders', alias squadron VF-142. The other half featured the clawed black gargoyle silhouette of the 'Pukin Dogs' of VF-143 – not, as was to be widely reported, Puking as in vomiting but, rather, Pukin as in a Chinese place-name from the Boxer Rebellion. In the wardrooms and ready rooms under *Connie*'s steel deck, pilots and backseaters were ready to defend their supercarrier, but unsure whom they would defend against – North Vietnam having not, as yet, mustered more than a token MiG force. When *Constellation* pulled out of Alameda and eased under the Golden Gate Bridge on 5 May 1964 to begin the Phantom's war, the buzz among fliers was that the Navy might eventually take this fine, clean, beauti-

En route to North Vietnam in 1968, these VF-21 F-4Bs carry four low-drag Mk 82 500-lb bombs apiece. Unusually, the aircraft are not fitted with the inboard pylons which normally mount AIM-9 Sidewinders.

ful fleet interceptor and actually hang bombs under it (this was an obscenity in the view of some), changing it from a single-purpose warplane to a multi-role craft. A few remembered that an early Phantom had dropped 28 bombs at once in a withering demonstration of firepower staged for the recently martyred President Kennedy. The pilot of that Phantom had said that he could bomb anybody, anytime, so long as he was asked to fly no farther than a mile and a half. And so, with interceptors, and with vague speculation about the unexpected duty of bombing, the 'Ghostriders' and 'Pukin Dogs' sailed west...

The aircraft they brought to the Pacific was a marvel of technology for the age. The definitive Westinghouse AN/APQ-72 radar with a 32-in (81-cm) dish was a step forward in technology. This made extensive use of minaturised tubes (valves) in its design, conserving weight and optimising the radar for detection at distances up to 60 miles (90 km), or about twice the distance of previous sets. The radar intercept officer (RIO) in the rear seat was provided with target-acquisition and tracking data. The radar and its associated Sparrow missiles had been found in tests to be superior to the F-106A Delta Dart and its MA-1 fire-control system.

The Phantom's weapons were not guns but missiles. The Raytheon AIM-7E Sparrow III, 12 ft (3.66 m) long and powered by a Thiokol pre-packaged liquid rocket motor, had been developed in 1960 and was accommodated in ventral trays with target illumination by the Phantom's own radar. The radar-guided AIM-7 Sparrow gave the Americans a BVR capability at distances up to 28 miles (44 km) but was negated by the despised ROE (rules of engagement) which rarely permitted a 'missiles free' BVR launch.

The AIM-9 Sidewinder had been blooded as early as the Taiwan Straits crisis (1958) by Chinese F-86F Sabres and became standard for USAF and US Navy fighters. The Sidewinder was 9 ft 5 in (2.87 m) long and had a range of about 12 miles (19 km). Its infra-red seeker head had to be cooled before it could lock onto a target, but this was a straightforward process. Ultimately, the Sidewinder scored more aerial victories in the conflict than any other weapon.

Carrier forces

When the Phantom's war began, the capital ship of the Fleet was the 'big deck' attack carrier, or CVA – a series begun in the late 1950s with USS *Forrestal* (CVA-59). Nine

With the exception of the 1965 experimental camouflage, the Navy Phantoms retained their bright colours throughout the war. VF-111 'Sundowners' had among the most spectacular markings. The aircraft in the background is from sister squadron in **Coral Sea**, *VF-51 'Screaming Eagles', who featured a stylised eagle on their aircraft .*

Two views aboard **Kitty Hawk** *show the little-known F-4G variant. After a brief spell serving in the experimental dark green camouflage (above), the aircraft was subsequently returned to standard VF-213 colours (right).*

An attack carrier was commanded by an O-6 (Navy captain), who was a naval aviator and had got his sea legs by commanding a smaller vessel first. On 'big deck' carriers, as many as 4,500 men were aboard (about 3,000 on the 'Midways') during a combat cruise which lasted as much as seven months and might include weeks at a time 'on the line', running combat operations between brief port calls. Of these, all but about 1,500 sailors were part of ship's company, working under division heads who reported to the exec and the skipper.

The Navy's carrier-based combat formation was the carrier air wing, known as a CVW and commanded by an O-5 (Navy commander) who was known as CAG and reported to the ship's captain. His title was a holdover to the days when the wings were called groups, and CAG (rendered like a surname, without a descriptive 'the') was the undisputed boss of every man on the ship who flew in, maintained, repaired, and armed the aircraft. Within the carrier air wing were squadrons, usually headed by an O-5 but at times an O-4 (Navy lieutenant commander). An F-4 Phantom squadron was known as a fighter squadron, or VF, and usually had 12 aircraft, 30 officers, and 270 men.

A cruise by an aircraft-carrier during the Vietnam era – a time when the US maintained a conscript, 'citizen' force – was often as long as eight or nine months, or about 50 per cent longer than those undertaken today. The time spent on a cruise was measured from departure from home port in the United States until return. Some time after departure, a carrier 'chopped' to, or came under the jurisdiction of, the US Pacific Fleet and Task Force 77. Still later, the carrier reached the combat zone and began its 'line periods'. Actual time spent on the line – in combat – was usually about three weeks, followed by a port call, followed by a return to the line. Thus, Phantom crews and carrier sailors were away from home for up to nine months at a time and spent about half-a-dozen periods of three weeks each in combat. The number of carriers committed simultaneously to the war in Southeast Asia ranged from just one in early 1964 to six during the height of Linebacker operations in 1972.

The F-4 Phantom was an exceedingly versatile warplane, employed initially as an interceptor and fighter-escort but before long used to carry bombs. Phantom missions came to be described using terms that had evolved in Navy jargon – among them, BARCAP, TARCAP and MiGCAP. To 'cap' somebody, whether it was a man down on the ground or a strike force flying a mission, meant simply to fly a combat air patrol overhead, providing fighter cover.

of these floating cities at sea were to be available to the Atlantic and Pacific Fleets during the Vietnam War, including four 'Forrestal'-class, four 'Kitty Hawk'-class and the nuclear-powered *Enterprise*. Of the nine only one, USS *John F. Kennedy* (CVA-67), would fail to make a cruise in the combat zone. These ships were *Forrestal*, *Saratoga* (CVA-60), *Ranger* (CVA-61), *Independence* (CVA-62), *Kitty Hawk* (CVA-63), *Constellation*, *Enterprise* (CVAN-65), *America* (CVA-66) and *Kennedy*.

Phantoms on the 'Midway'-class

In addition, F-4 Phantoms were to operate from the three 'Midway'-class flattops completed just after the end of the World War II. These were *Midway* (CVA-41), *Franklin D. Roosevelt* (CVA-42), and *Coral Sea* (CVA-43). The Navy's six wartime, short-hull 'Essex'-class attack carriers were also to participate in the Southeast Asia conflict but without F-4s on their smaller, and in some cases wooden, decks. Four more anti-submarine carriers generally operated no jets at all.

McDonnell F-4G Phantom
VF-213 'Black Lions'
USS *Kitty Hawk*, 1965

Datalink
Otherwise similar to the F-4B, the F-4G incorporated an ASW-21 datalink set in place of the No. 1 fuel tank behind the rear cockpit. The fitment of this equipment was intended to link the F-4, AEW assets and ship radar into a common system by which the interceptor could be controlled from the carrier's operation centre without voice control. VF-213 undertook the only combat cruise with this variant, all of which were demodified and returned to F-4B status during 1966.

Automatic landing
The datalink allowed the F-4G to make fully automatic carrier landings. A radar reflector was mounted near the nosewheel to allow ship-mounted radar to track the aircraft.

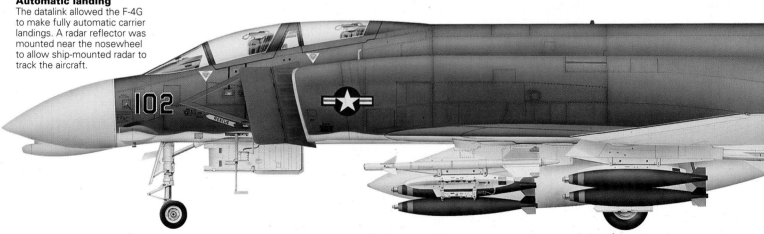

The terms most frequently used:

BARCAP: Barrier Combat Air Patrol. In the words of backseater John Lillard, "You set up a defensive barrier between the threat and whatever you want to protect." In Vietnam, BARCAP usually meant staking out a region of sky and guarding it. This usually was a short-range mission to protect the carrier battle group and meant the Phantom flying in relatively 'clean' configuration. Typically for short- to medium-range BARCAP, a Phantom might carry two 370-US gal (308.4-Imp gal.) under-wing fuel tanks ('bags', in pilot talk) on outer pylon stations, four AIM-7E Sparrow IIIs in recessed wells under the fuselage, and two or four AIM-9D Sidewinders on inboard weapons pylons. For this kind of mission the Phantom would be relatively light and could easily have an endurance up to four hours, although fighter crews did not usually fly patrols for this long.

TARCAP: Target Combat Air Patrol. This term has always been something of a misnomer, since it actually referred to a fighter escort mission. The Phantoms would escort the strike package – the collection of air-to-ground combat planes proceeding against a particular target or targets. The Phantom flight leader was charged with setting up a CAP station on or near the target, and remaining on the prowl for enemy aircraft. The primary purpose was not to shoot down enemy aircraft but to deter them from reaching and interfering with the strike package. The weapons load would typically include the same pair of 370-US gal droptanks, four Sparrows, two or four Sidewinders and the Phantom's ubiquitous 600-US gal centreline 'bag'. Slightly heavier for the TARCAP mission, the Phantom might easily be expected to be aloft for four minutes or longer.

MiGCAP: The pure air-to-air mission which is the stuff of legend and Hollywood film, the MiGCAP sortie divorced the Phantom crew from both carrier and strike package, leaving them free to search out and engage the enemy's fighter force. Describing the MiGCAP mission, backseater Lillard remembered a famous quote from World War I ace Baron Manfred von Richthofen: "The fighter pilots rove in the area allotted to them and when they see the enemy they attack and shoot him down. Everything else is rubbish." For a MiGCAP mission, the configuration would also consist of fuel and missiles. In fact, very few MiGCAP missions were actually flown.

SUCAP: Surface Combat Air Patrol. On occasion, F-4 Phantoms would escort an A-4 Skyhawk or A-7 Corsair II flight engaging North Vietnamese surface vessels – usually small patrol boats – which were rarely direct threats to the fleet. Phantom configuration was often missiles only, with no tanks or bombs.

An F-4B of VF-21 enters the pattern of Midway, *its arrester hook deployed for checking by the ship. The date is 1965, and also on board are the F-8D Crusaders of VF-111. This was one of two war cruises where a single Phantom squadron was partnered by one of the Vought fighters. Of note parked by the island is an EA-3B Skywarrior, used for electronic intelligence by VQ-2.*

A final air-to-air mission was the point defence of the carrier itself (as distinguished from the outer defence afforded by a BARCAP flight). This was provided by the 'alert five birds' – the Phantom configured for short-range, air-to-air combat charged with being available to launch on five minutes' notice.

In real life, few 'pure' missions conveniently filled the definitions established by these terms. Even in the pure air-to-air role, Phantom crews were hamstrung by a myriad of rules and restrictions, including the likelihood of Air Force or Marine Corps strikes taking place nearby, preventing a weapons-free or BVR environment. Employed briefly solely as an interceptor and air-to-air fighter, by 1965 the Phantom was combining these missions with carrying bombs, rockets, and missiles – as intended, in the design, from the outset – for close air support, interdiction, and what amounted to strategic bombing in the on-again, off-again campaign against North Vietnam. The Phantom became what would be known as a dual-role warplane today. To paraphrase its manufacturer, it blew up what was down and shot down what was up. The Phantom was cleared for all bombs in Navy inventory, including all of the Mk 80 series.

By the late 1960s, the decision whether to employ the Phantom to carry bombs was left to the discretion of the squadron commander who, of course, had to satisfy CAG that he could carry out the required job in addition to dropping ordnance. Some F-4 squadron COs converted themselves into bomber units because a Phantom armed with Mk 20 Rockeye cluster bombs was effective at defence suppression of AAA sites (any defence suppression mission, whether against AAA or SAMs, was called an Iron Hand flight). The mission of taking out an AAA installation was often added – in an aircraft with seemingly unlimited fuel capacity and loiter time – to the other duties to be performed, such as TARCAP. On other missions the Phantom was capable of handling a variety of air-to-ground ordnance with a typical maximum bombload of around 16,000 lb (7258 kg). Depending on the mission and combat radius, the F-4B could carry up to eight 1,000-lb (454-kg) Mk 83 iron bombs, four AGM-12C Bullpup B air-to-surface missiles, or 15 packs of 2.75-in FFAR (folding-fin aircraft rockets).

In addition to summarising the missions flown by the Phantom, to understand the Phantom's war it is also useful to be reminded of the major campaigns in which it fought:

5 August 1964 **Operation Pierce Arrow** – A one-day effort against targets in North Vietnam.

2 March 1965-31 October 1968 **Operation Rolling Thunder** – The first and longest campaign of air operations against North Vietnam.

1 November 1968-8 May 1972 **Bombing Halt** – No air operations 'up north', with some limited or temporary exceptions.

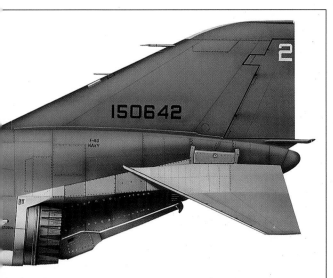

Camouflage
In an effort to make Navy aircraft more suitable for tactical operations, some from the air wings of *Kitty Hawk*, *Constellation* and *Enterprise* were given this dark green scheme in late 1965. The camouflage proved of limited tactical effect, while rendering the aircraft difficult to see at night on deck. The scheme was abandoned after a short while.

As full burner is applied, the hold-back takes the strain waiting for the catapult to fire. Within milliseconds the VF-92 F-4J will be hurled into the air on the first leg of a mission into North Vietnam in May 1972 during the Linebacker II campaign.

26-30 December 1971 Operation Proud Deep Alpha – A five-day limited air effort against some North Vietnamese targets despite the bombing halt.

6 April 1972-7 May 1972 Operation Freedom Train – Renewed but limited air operations against North Vietnam.

8 May 1972-23 October 1972 Operation Linebacker – The second major campaign of air operations against North Vietnam.

18-29 December 1972 Operation Linebacker II, also called The Eleven Day War. The final air effort against North Vietnam spearheaded by massive B-52 bombing 'up north'.

Throughout the Vietnam War, beginning in 1960, the US also fought in Laos. Early on, much of this related to internal disputes but by 1965 Operations Steel Tiger and Barrel Roll were directed against the NVA (North Vietnamese Army) in Laos. Beginning in the late 1960s, US airmen also fought in Cambodia. This continued, beyond the 27 January 1973 end of the Vietnam war, until 15 August 1973.

Unable to grasp anything foreign, Americans ignored hard-to-pronounce names like Xom Bong and Vinh Linh, hardly apt for radio chatter in the heat of combat, and divided North Vietnam into Route Packages, or RPs. Pilots talked of flying to RP One or to Pak Six. Roman numerals were supposed to be used (Route Package VI) but rarely were. The region around Hanoi and Haiphong, where North Vietnam's heaviest defences were concentrated, was Route Pack Six.

The US Navy kept aircraft-carriers at Dixie Station in the South China Sea for operations over South Vietnam, and at Yankee Station in the Gulf of Tonkin for strikes against the North.

The names derived from the north and south in the American Civil War (1861-65). Yankee Station, originally dubbed Point Yankee, was in the Gulf of Tonkin southwest of Hainan, north of the mis-named DMZ (Demilitarized Zone) which divided the two Vietnams, and east of the North Vietnamese coast. The intent was to place carrier aircraft in range of targets in North Vietnam, but this was also the launch point for unpublicised missions over Laos. Yankee Station was moved north in April 1966, cutting the distance aircraft had to fly to reach their targets, moved south again with the 1968 bombing halt, and returned to the northerly location in 1972.

Dixie Station was located in the South China Sea about

Steam rises from the bow cats as a VF-96 'Fighting Falcons' F-4J launches from the waist cat. The paired squadrons VF-92 and VF-96 together undertook the most war cruises of any F-4 units, notching up eight. VF-96 emerged as the most successful of the squadrons in air-to-air fighting, with eight victories.

McDonnell F-4J Phantom VF-96 'Fighting Falcons' USS *Constellation*, 1972

Radar
The AN/AWG-10 weapon system of the F-4J featured the APG-59 radar. The new radar could track both high and low targets.

Powerplant
Power for the F-4J was provided by the J79-GE-10 engine of 17,900 lb (79.66 kN) thrust. These were identifiable by having longer afterburner 'turkey feathers'.

100 miles (161 km) southeast of Cam Ranh Bay, within easy range of the coastal areas of South Vietnam: this southern launch point for carriers was the result of a 1965 request by the US field commander, General William C. Westmoreland, that a carrier be available to back up land-based Air Force and Marine Corps warplanes in supporting combat actions inside South Vietnam. In 1965-66, one carrier was routinely on the line at Dixie Station, two or three at Yankee Station. This was usually accomplished by having a carrier begin its combat tour in the south, then move north – so to speak, 'summering' in the south and 'wintering' in the north. After 1966, carrier operations (including some to targets in South Vietnam) at Dixie Station were terminated, allowing the Navy to keep three or four carriers on Yankee Station at all times, though operations were resumed over the south during the 1968 Tet offensive and 1972 spring offensive.

Marine Corps aviation flew from land bases during the Vietnam conflict as part of the Marine aviators' principal *raison d'être*: to support their troops on the ground. However, Marines have always been charged with the capability to conduct carrier operations. F-4B and F-4J Phantoms were in the war from beginning to end (the first arriving in March 1964, the last departing in August 1974), but all flew from land except for *America*'s 1972-1973 cruise, when VMFA-333 'Shamrocks' was embarked on ship with F-4Js and, among other things, scored the Marines' only MiG kill.

The enemy

In South Vietnam, Phantoms were shot down by everything from rifles to debris from their own exploding ordnance. But the compelling danger to Navy Phantom crews lay 'up north' – above the 17th Parallel – where North

Vietnam grew into a fortress.

The Russian-made SA-2 'Guideline' radar-guided surface-to-air missile (SAM) completed Hanoi's 'triad' of air defence weaponry – equipping an air defence network which began modestly in 1965 but was soon to become one of the most formidable the world had ever seen. The SAM threat expanded rapidly with 180 firings during 1965, claiming 11 US aircraft altogether.

Initially, the SAMs were deployed around a 30 to 40 mile (48 to 64 km) circle centred on Hanoi. While the Air Force was quick to introduce ECM (electronic countermeasures) pods which helped to confuse Hanoi's air defence radars and thus make the SAMs' job more difficult, the Navy was slower to do so and was not to have a true electronic warfare capability until the Grumman EA-6B Prowler was introduced very late in the war. Meanwhile, Phantom crews worked to devise tactics to counter these flying 'telephone poles'. The basic situation was that if you could detect a SAM firing in time, you could evade the missile with abrupt manoeuvring.

As for AAA (or 'Triple A', meaning anti-aircraft artillery), North Vietnam began with a few dozen guns (or 'tubes' in Army parlance) but by the late 1960s was to have thousands, ranging from small, mobile 37-mm rapid-fire cannons to 120-mm weapons capable of reaching as high as 35,000 ft (10836 m). Most of the larger guns were radar-guided, which made them very accurate but also vulnerable to ECM. By itself, the huge arsenal of guns guarding North Vietnam might not have been too difficult to cope with, but the principal benefit of missiles and MiGs was that they drove US warplanes into regions where gunfire (or flak, the World War II term) was witheringly accurate.

On top of all this came the MiG force – a handful of

F-4Js on the prowl: a pair of VF-96 aircraft loaded with Sidewinders are seen during the 1972 cruise in which the squadron scored seven victories (five by Cunningham and Driscoll and two by Connelly and Blonski). Crews trusted the short-range Sidewinder more than the Sparrow, and the carriage of the latter was often restricted to one or two in the aft bays.

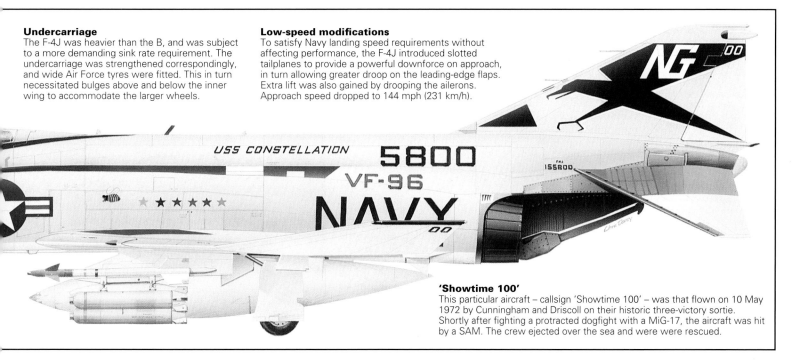

Undercarriage
The F-4J was heavier than the B, and was subject to a more demanding sink rate requirement. The undercarriage was strengthened correspondingly, and wide Air Force tyres were fitted. This in turn necessitated bulges above and below the inner wing to accommodate the larger wheels.

Low-speed modifications
To satisfy Navy landing speed requirements without affecting performance, the F-4J introduced slotted tailplanes to provide a powerful downforce on approach, in turn allowing greater droop on the leading-edge flaps. Extra lift was also gained by drooping the ailerons. Approach speed dropped to 144 mph (231 km/h).

'Showtime 100'
This particular aircraft – callsign 'Showtime 100' – was that flown on 10 May 1972 by Cunningham and Driscoll on their historic three-victory sortie. Shortly after fighting a protracted dogfight with a MiG-17, the aircraft was hit by a SAM. The crew ejected over the sea and were were rescued.

*Phantoms from VF-92 and VF-6 launch from **Constellation** for a Linebacker raid. The F-4 had a large power margin over its MiG rivals, but was not as nimble. While MiG-17s attempted to draw Phantoms into slow, turning fights, the MiG-21s attempted slashing attacks under strict ground control. In the final analysis, the old adage that 'energy is king' won out, backed up by sound training.*

*Far right: Marine Corps Phantoms served a long and gruelling war from shore bases, but one squadron undertook one combat cruise (VMFA-333 in **America**). During the course of this deployment one MiG was claimed. This F-4J is seen in 1975, by which time the squadron was operating from **Nimitz**.*

and kept some on alert.

Phantom crews soon learned that the best way to fight a MiG-17 was to kill it at long distance. The Phantom's radar and radar-guided missiles were still the standard against which all others in the world were measured and, while the AIM-7 Sparrow malfunctioned more than it should have, it was the best way to dispose of a MiG-17 early in the fight. The infra-red AIM-9 Sidewinder could also nail a MiG-17 before he got into gun range, but when the air contest became a 'furball' – a manoeuvring contest at close range – the Phantom was no longer obviously superior.

Introduced in 1966, the MiG-21 was a simple, nimble, lightweight craft designed for the air-to-air role. Limited in range and payload, and not easy to learn to fly, the MiG-21 was far from perfect but it had a twin-barrelled 23-mm GSh-23 cannon and it could also carry up to four KA-13 (AA-2 'Atoll') missiles, North Vietnam's closest equivalent to the Sidewinder.

Powered by a 16,500-lb (33.36-kN) thrust Tumansky R-25 turbojet with afterburner, the MiG-21 could fly at 1,320 mph (2125 km/h) or Mach 2 at 36,000 ft (11000 m). Air-to-air combat in North Vietnam readily demonstrated that speed was not an important attribute when you were trying to out-fight a Phantom, but the 'Atoll' missiles provided a capability not usually fielded by the MiG-17 (although neither MiG ever operated with radar-guided missiles like the Sparrow). The MiG-21 was advanced enough to worry naval aviators considerably, even if it did not become the favourite mount of the enemy's best fighter pilots.

Examined up close, the MiG-21 was a remarkably crude-looking aircraft and gave the impression of having been cobbled together under lax Third World working conditions by people who did not care if the wings matched exactly. Older MiG-21s were held together by relatively crude rivets. The cockpit was narrow and cramped. It was thus tempting to dismiss the MiG-21 with a kind of snobbish disdain. On the other hand, American fighters – the Navy F-4 Phantom at the top of the list – had the drawback of being too expensive, too complex, and equipped with too many secondary systems which added to weight and eroded performance.

Phantom into battle

It was coincidence that the first combat mission by the F-4 Phantom was flown on a significant date, 5 August 1964. This was the day of Operation Pierce Arrow, the air strikes flown in retaliation for real and alleged Vietnamese torpedo boat attacks on US vessels in the Gulf of Tonkin.

In retaliation for the PT boat attacks, President Lyndon Johnson ordered aircraft from Constellation and USS Ticonderoga (CVA-14) to attack four major torpedo boat bases along the North Vietnamese coastline. Constellation had just arrived on the line and was introducing to Southeast Asia a new aircraft type, the F-4 Phantom, which was beginning to take its place as the standard fleet interceptor on the big decks of the larger, 'Forrestal'-class carriers. But the 65 sorties were flown by F-8 Crusaders, A-1 Skyraiders, and A-4 Skyhawks. The Phantoms flew cover.

MiG-17s in 1965 which became an armada of about 380 MiG-17s, MiG-19s and MiG-21s by the end of the war. Though Navy Phantom crews remained more nervous about landing on a carrier at night than about confronting missiles, MiGs and triple-A – roughly half of all Phantoms which failed to return from Vietnam were non-combat losses, victims of the very intense and risky world of carrier operations – North Vietnam's defences became increasingly potent.

The MiG-17 was in many ways dated, little more than an upgrade of the MiG-15 which had been a technical triumph in its day and had overwhelmed the Allies in Korea, but was old stuff by 1965. The MiG-17 was highly manoeuvrable and, unlike the Phantom, armed with guns. Early production MiG-17s were powered by the same VK-1 engines as the MiG-15, but the main production aircraft introduced the 7,500-lb (33.36-kN) thrust Klimov VK-1F with a simple afterburner. Capable of 710 mph (1145 km/h) at 10,000 ft (3048 m), the MiG-17 was armed with three NR-23 23-mm cannons.

North Vietnam's fighter tacticians always enjoyed enormous advantages over the Phantom crews who came from the sea to strike at their nation. It became clear early in the war that the infamous rules of engagement (ROE) devised by Defence Secretary Robert S. McNamara and others were going to prevent the Americans from waging a sustained campaign against Hanoi's airfields. Free from all but occasional attacks on their airdromes, the North Vietnamese kept MiG-17s readily visible in revetments on their fields

Above: VF-114 'Aardvarks' undertook six combat cruises, these F-4Js being seen shortly after their return following the last of these in 1972. From August 1973 the war in Southeast Asia was officially considered to be over, although cruises were still made to the region after this date. In 1975 Phantoms (and Tomcats on their first cruise) were called upon to cover the final evacuation from Saigon.

Left: An F-4J and deck crew enjoy a rare moment of tranquility during operations in the Gulf of Tonkin. Without the sterling efforts of the deck crews, the US Navy's Phantom force would not have enjoyed the successes it achieved.

Billed as a 'limited and fitting response' against 'gun boats and certain facilities of North Vietnam', the strikes partly fulfilled a long-standing recommendation by the Pentagon's Joint Chiefs of Staff that an aerial campaign be mounted against the heartland of North Vietnam which, until now, had been immune from American air power. For eleven years to follow, warriors were to risk their lives in 'limited' combat.

The F-4B Phantoms from USS Constellation (CVA-64) which flew top cover for those Gulf of Tonkin air strikes were a marvel of American technology. Every Navy carrier had two fighter squadrons on board. The Phantom now made up just less than half of the US Navy's carrier-based fighter force, the other half comprising the Vought F-8 Crusader which could operate from World War II 'Essex'-class warships. The F-4 flew from the post-war 'Midway'-class (which in two instances put to sea with one squadron each of F-4s and F-8s) and the post-war 'Forrestal'-class or later flattops.

To single-seat, single-engined, cannon-armed F-8 Crusader jocks, the Phantom was an interceptor and their aircraft, loved by pilots in a way no Phantom ever was, was a fighter. In fact, the Phantom had better radar and Sparrow capability while sacrificing little in manoeuvrability.

Robert F. Dorr

F-4 Vietnam combat cruises by squadron

SQUADRON	MODEX	CRUISE PERIOD	VARIANT	CARRIER	SQUADRON	MODEX	CRUISE PERIOD	VARIANT	CARRIER
VF-11	AA 1xx	16 Jun 67 to 14 Sep 67	F-4B	Forrestal		NH 2xx	6 Nov 70 to 17 Jul 71	F-4J	Kitty Hawk
VF-14	AB 1xx	21 Jun 66 to 21 Feb 67	F-4B	Roosevelt		NH 2xx	17 Feb 72 to 28 Nov 72	F-4J	Kitty Hawk
VF-21	NE 1xx	6 Mar 65 to 23 Nov 65	F-4B	Midway	VF-142	NK 2xx	5 May 64 to 1 Feb 65	F-4B	Constellation
	NE 1xx	29 Jul 66 to 23 Feb 67	F-4B	Coral Sea		NK 2xx	10 Dec 65 to 25 Aug 66	F-4B	Ranger
	NE 1xx	4 Nov 67 to 25 May 68	F-4B	Ranger		NE 2xx	29 Apr 67 to 4 Dec 67	F-4B	Constellation
	NE 1xx	26 Oct 68 to 27 May 69	F-4J	Ranger		NK 2xx	29 May 68 to 31 Jan 69	F-4B	Constellation
	NE 1xx	14 Oct 69 to 1 Jun 70	F-4J	Ranger		NK 2xx	11 Aug 69 to 8 May 70	F-4J	Constellation
	NE 1xx	27 Oct 70 to 17 Jun 71	F-4J	Ranger		NK 2xx	11 Jun 71 to 12 Feb 72	F-4J	Enterprise
	NE 2xx	16 Nov 72 to 22 Jun 73	F-4J	Ranger		NK 2xx	12 Sep 72 to 12 Jun 73	F-4J	Enterprise
VF-31	AC 1xx	11 Apr 72 to 13 Feb 73	F-4J	Saratoga	VF-143	NK 3xx	5 May 64 to 1 Feb 65	F-4B	Constellation
VF-32	AB 2xx	21 Jun 66 to 21 Feb 67	F-4B	Roosevelt		NK 3xx	10 Dec 65 to 25 Aug 66	F-4B	Ranger
VF-33	AE 2xx	10 Apr 68 to 16 Dec 68	F-4J	America		NE 3xx	29 Apr 67 to 4 Dec 67	F-4B	Constellation
VF-41	AG-1xx	10 May 65 to 13 Dec 65	F-4B	Independence		NK 3xx	29 May 68 to 31 Jan 69	F-4B	Constellation
VF-51	NL 1xx	12 Nov 71 to 17 Jul 72	F-4B	Coral Sea		NK 3xx	11 Aug 69 to 8 May 70	F-4J	Constellation
	NL 1xx	9 Mar 73 to 8 Nov 73	F-4B	Coral Sea		NK 1xx	11 Jun 71 to 12 Feb 72	F-4J	Enterprise
VF-74	AA 1xx	16 Jun 67 to 14 Sep 67	F-4B	Forrestal		NK 1xx	12 Sep 72 to 12 Jun 73	F-4J	Enterprise
	AJ 1xx	5 Jun 72 to 24 Mar 73	F-4J	America	VF-151	NL 1xx	7 Dec 64 to 1 Nov 65	F-4B	Coral Sea
VF-84	AG-2xx	10 May 65 to 13 Dec 65	F-4B	Independence		NL 1xx	12 May 66 to 3 Dec 66	F-4B	Constellation
VF-92	NG 2xx	5 Aug 64 to 6 May 65	F-4B	Ranger		NL 1xx	26 Jul 67 to 6 Apr 68	F-4B	Coral Sea
	NG 2xx	26 Oct 65 to 21 Jun 66	F-4B	Enterprise		NL 1xx	7 Sep 68 to 18 Apr 69	F-4B	Coral Sea
	NG 2xx	19 Nov 66 to 6 Jul 67	F-4B	Enterprise		NL 1xx	23 Sep 69 to 1 Jul 70	F-4B	Coral Sea
	NG 2xx	3 Jan 68 to 18 Jul 68	F-4B	Enterprise		NF 2xx	16 Apr 71 to 6 Nov 71	F-4B	Midway
	NG 2xx	6 Jan 69 to 2 Jul 69	F-4J	Enterprise		NF 2xx	10 Apr 72 to 3 Mar 73	F-4B	Midway
	NG 2xx	10 Apr 70 to 21 Dec 70	F-4J	America	VF-154	NE 4xx	29 Jul 66 to 23 Feb 67	F-4B	Coral Sea
	NG 2xx	1 Oct 71 to 1 Jul 72	F-4J	Constellation		NE 1xx	4 Nov 67 to 25 May 68	F-4B	Ranger
	NG 2xx	5 Jan 73 to 11 Oct 73	F-4J	Constellation		NE 2xx	26 Oct 68 to 27 May 69	F-4J	Ranger
VF-96	NG 6xx	5 Aug 64 to 6 May 65	F-4B	Ranger		NE 2xx	14 Oct 69 to 1 Jun 70	F-4J	Ranger
	NG 6xx	26 Oct 65 to 21 Jun 66	F-4B	Enterprise		NE 2xx	27 Oct 70 to 17 Jun 71	F-4J	Ranger
	NG 6xx	19 Nov 66 to 6 Jul 67	F-4B	Enterprise		NE 1xx	16 Nov 72 to 22 Jun 73	F-4J	Ranger
	NG 6xx	3 Jan 68 to 18 Jul 68	F-4B	Enterprise	VF-161	NL 2xx	12 May 66 to 3 Dec 66	F-4B	Constellation
	NG 1xx	6 Jan 69 to 2 Jul 69	F-4J	Enterprise		NL 2xx	26 Jul 67 to 6 Apr 68	F-4B	Coral Sea
	NG 1xx	10 Apr 70 to 21 Dec 70	F-4J	America		NK 2xx	29 May 68 to 31 Jan 69	F-4B	Constellation
	NG 1xx	1 Oct 71 to 1 Jul 72	F-4J	Constellation		NL 2xx	23 Sep 69 to 1 Jul 70	F-4B	Coral Sea
	NG 1xx	5 Jan 73 to 11 Oct 73	F-4J	Constellation		NF 1xx	16 Apr 71 to 6 Nov 71	F-4B	Midway
VF-102	AE 1xx	10 Apr 68 to 16 Dec 68	F-4J	America		NF 1xx	10 Apr 72 to 3 Mar 73	F-4B	Midway
VF-103	AC 2xx	11 Apr 72 to 13 Feb 73	F-4J	Saratoga	VF-213	NH 1xx	19 Oct 65 to 13 Jun 66	F-4B/G	Kitty Hawk
VF-111	NL 2xx	12 Nov 71 to 17 Jul 72	F-4B	Coral Sea		NH 1xx	5 Nov 66 to 20 Jun 67	F-4B	Kitty Hawk
	NL 2xx	9 Mar 73 to 8 Nov 73	F-4B	Coral Sea		NH 1xx	18 Nov 67 to 28 Jun 68	F-4B	Kitty Hawk
VF-114	NH 4xx	19 Oct 65 to 13 Jun 66	F-4B	Kitty Hawk		NH 1xx	30 Dec 68 to 4 Sep 69	F-4B	Kitty Hawk
	NH 2xx	5 Nov 66 to 20 Jun 67	F-4B	Kitty Hawk		NH 1xx	6 Nov 70 to 17 Jul 71	F-4J	Kitty Hawk
	NH 2xx	18 Nov 67 to 28 Jun 68	F-4B	Kitty Hawk		NH 1xx	17 Feb 72 to 28 Nov 72	F-4J	Kitty Hawk
	NH 2xx	30 Dec 68 to 4 Sep 69	F-4B	Kitty Hawk	VMFA-333	AJ 2xx	5 Jun 72 to 24 Mar 73	F-4J	America

1. Gulf of Tonkin
5 August 1964–1 March 1965

- **5 August 1964–21 November 1964**
  5 May 1964–1 February 1965 VF-143 'Pukin Dogs' (NK 3xx) and VF-142 'Ghostriders' (NK 2xx) CVW-14 USS *Constellation* (CVA-64) F-4B
- **8 September 1964–12 April 1965**
  5 August 1964–6 May 1965 VF-92 'Silver Kings' (NG 2xx) and VF-96 'Fighting Falcons' (NG 6xx) CVW-9 USS *Ranger* (CVA-61) F-4B
- **1 February 1965–14 October 1965**
  7 December 1964–1 November 1965 VF-151 'Vigilantes' (NL 1xx) CVW-15 USS *Coral Sea* (CVA-43) F-4B (with VF-154 'Black Knights' (NL 4xx) flying F-8D)

In the wake of the Gulf of Tonkin incident – a real attack on 2 August 1964 and an imagined attack two days later by North Vietnamese P-4 patrol boats against US warships on a Desoto intelligence-gathering patrol – the US Navy ordered *Constellation* to sail from Hong Kong, where it was en route to the Southeast Asia conflict.

The possibility of bombing North Vietnam had been discussed in the Pentagon and White House since the first handful of American advisors began helping the South Vietnamese in September 1960. President Lyndon Johnson had tasked the Joint Chiefs of Staff (JCS) to prepare a plan to blunt North Vietnam's infiltration into the south with a bombing campaign. The proposal, approved by the JCS on 17 April 1964, listed 94 of the most important targets in North Vietnam. These included marshalling yards, port facilities, truck parks, petroleum oil lubricant (POL) storage centres and major bridge spans, including the Thanh Hoa Bridge which was nicknamed the 'Dragon's Jaw' and the Paul Doumer Rail and Highway Bridge near Hanoi. The plan was apparently shelved for a time but the notion of employing air power against the North Vietnamese heartland remained very much in public and private minds.

The idea was based on a refusal by the American brass to understand what was happening in South Vietnam. The Viet Cong guerrillas in the south were, themselves, *South* Vietnamese – a part of the population of the south. Though the 1964 State Department white paper *Aggression from the North* charged that these guerrillas would be unable to fight on without supplies and support from

North Vietnam, the premise was dead wrong. Had the Viet Cong overrun Saigon and won the war in 1964, they would have retained a separate regime. The American notion that the Cong were puppets of the North Vietnamese was to become a self-fulfilling prophecy. The desire of the JCS to bomb the north reflected a mind-set in American military doctrine and strategy: bombing, some believed, would solve any problem.

As if to get a foot in the door, Johnson authorised a 'limited and fitting' response to the torpedo boat attacks. Operation Pierce Arrow, mounted from the decks of *Ticonderoga* and *Connie*, was on 5 August 1964. *Connie*'s air wing, CVW-14, struck the PT boat bases at Hon Gai and Loc Chao – 20 Skyhawks, Skyraiders, and Phantoms striking the former, 12 warplanes attacking the latter. One Skyraider was downed and its pilot killed, one Skyhawk also shot down and its pilot captured – the Navy's first casualties. The losses may be due to the decision to launch in late afternoon, a choice dictated by *Constellation*'s arrival on the line. The role of the Phantom in Pierce Arrow lacked drama. F-4B crews flew TARCAP. They guarded the strike aircraft en route to, and over, their targets.

The first inklings of anti-war sentiment were barely brewing at home (the protests of the 1960s began with the Free Speech Movement at Berkeley, California that month, August 1964). The American public, press, and Congress seemed favourably disposed to the swift strike by carrier-based warplanes in retaliation for North Vietnamese provocation. On 10 August 1964, Congress passed the historic Gulf of Tonkin Resolution – a blank cheque

enabling the President to commit forces without constitutional process. The total damage to American forces inflicted by North Vietnam during the Gulf of Tonkin provocation consisted of one dent made by one bullet in the hull of one Navy destroyer, inflicted by a torpedo boat using more haste than precision – which was exactly what Congress did, as many saw it later, with the resolution that opened the floodgates. When the resolution was passed, there were 21,000 American troops in Vietnam. A year later, there would be 181,000, three years thereafter 541,000.

Pierce Arrow was billed as a 'one of a kind' event, although the JCS still argued not for a single day of strikes but for a sustained campaign. On 18 September 1964, *Ranger* arrived on the line where it would spent 103 days with interruptions between then and 12 April 1965. Aboard were VF-92 and VF-96 with F-4Bs.

---

13 November 1964: An F-4B (151412) of VF-142 was lost in a non-combat mishap aboard *Constellation*. The crew of two was recovered.

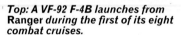

Top: A VF-92 F-4B launches from **Ranger** *during the first of its eight combat cruises.*

Above: The 'Pukin Dogs' were on **Constellation** *for the first combat cruise of the war. Note the line of dogs across the fin-tip.*

Coral Sea spent her first day on the line (of 167 to follow) on 7 December 1964. This carrier had an unusual makeup to its two fighter squadrons which was to be repeated just once more in the Vietnam War: VF-151 was flying F-4B Phantoms and was accompanied by VF-154 with F-8D Crusaders. *Coral Sea* was to lose eight Skyhawks and four Crusaders as the war widened and expanded in 1965 – but no Phantoms. The F-4B was still viewed largely as an interceptor and escort fighter and was not yet flying into harm's way on a daily, sustained basis.

While a debate over whether to bomb North Vietnam produced more heat than light, President Johnson confronted three major options: purely retaliatory air strikes like Pierce Arrow – a swift and heavy offensive against targets of military significance; or a gradual, escalating campaign designed to demonstrate to the enemy that punishment would be linked to his own actions. Around the beginning of 1965, Johnson approved the retaliatory option, although the deteriorating state of the Saigon government delayed its execution. The first retaliatory air strikes since the Gulf of Tonkin affair were those of Flaming Dart I, retaliating for an attack on American troops at Pleiku on 7 February 1965. Next came Flaming Dart II, provoked by a similar attack on Qui Nhon on 10 February 1965. The Pentagon brass wanted a 'fast/full squeeze' – a massive and immediate campaign against everything in North Vietnam, including irrigation dykes which, if breached, would flood the entire country. Johnson, however, shifted from retaliation to the worst of the three options. The 'slow squeeze', dubbed Operation Rolling Thunder, was launched on 2 March 1965.

In addition to missiles, these VF-142 F-4Bs, seen in mid-1964, carry 5-in Zuni rocket pods with frangible nosecones.

2. Rolling Thunder I
2 March 1965–18 May 1965

> ● **10 April 1965-4 November 1965**
> 6 March 1965-23 November 1965 VF-21 'Freelancers' (NE 1xx) and
> CVW-2 USS *Midway* (CVA-41) F-4B (with VF-111 'Sundowners' (NE 4xx)
> flying F-8D)

Ever after, men would say that it was not thunderous and did not roll. Rolling Thunder began with Air Force strikes; the Navy joined the fray on 15 March 1965 when CVW-9 from *Ranger* lost a pilot and an aircraft (an A-1 Skyraider) during a mission against the Phu Qhi ammunition dump.

9 April 1965: The first American air-to-air kill of the war was a bizarre sidelight and began with a Rolling Thunder mission but did not involve the North Vietnamese. F-4B Phantoms from *Ranger* battled four Chinese MiG-17s near Hainan Island. The Phantom (BuNo. 151403/NG-602) piloted by Lt (jg) Terence M. Murphy of VF-96 'Black Falcons' shot down a MiG-17 but was then lost in action. The Chinese claimed that Murphy was shot down by an AIM-7 Sparrow missile fired by his wingmen. Backseater Ensign Ronald J. Fegan also perished.

9 April 1965: a second F-4B (151425) of VF-96 is listed as a non-combat loss.

The unusual pairing of different fighter types aboard *Coral Sea* was repeated when *Midway* reached the line on 10

Below: VF-21 (illustrated) and VF-111 in Midway *arrived on the line in April 1965, bringing their F-4Bs. The squadrons were particularly active over South Vietnam.*

April 1965 with VF-21 in F-4Bs and VF-111 in F-8Ds.

The Navy's participation in Rolling Thunder began slowly and evolved over

Above: A Phantom from VF-21 drops cluster bombs on suspected VC positions in seemingly featureless jungle in 1965. At relatively low level the effect of these weapons would create a carpet of destruction across a wide area. Unfortunately the chances of there being any VC in the vicinity by the time of the bombing was slim.

time. Eventually, the overall air commander in Saigon came to the prescient conclusion that carrier-based warplanes could be most effective in

coastal regions. Route Package VI, which included Hanoi and Haiphong, was eventually parcelled up to give the Navy a crack at the area around the latter city. Air refuelling had long since become *de rigeur* in carrier operations. With it or without it, the Phantom had the reach for almost any target in North or South Vietnam.

3. Rolling Thunder II
18 May 1965–31 January 1966

> ● **27 June 1965-11 November 1965**
> 10 May 1965-13 December 1965 VF-41 'Black Aces' (AG-1xx) and VF-84 'Jolly Rogers' (AG 2xx) CVW-7 USS *Independence* (CVA-62) F-4B
> ● **26 November 1965-22 May 1966**
> 19 October 1965-13 June 1966 VF-213 'Black Lions' (NH 1xx) (F-4B/G) and VF-114 'Aardvarks' (NH 4xx) and CVW-11 USS *Kitty Hawk* (CVA-63) F-4B
> ● **2 December 1965-5 June 1966**
> 26 October 1965-21 June 1966 VF-92 'Silver Kings' (NG 2xx) and VF-96 'Fighting Falcons' (NG-6xx) CVW-9 USS *Enterprise* (CVAN-65) F-4B
> ● **15 January 1966-5 August 1966**
> 10 December 1965-25 August 1966 VF-142 'Ghostriders' (NK 2xx) and VF-143 'Pukin Dogs' (NK 3xx) CVW-14 USS *Ranger* (CVA-61) F-4B

17 June 1965: First American crew to down a North Vietnamese MiG were Cdr Thomas C. Page and Lt John C. Smith, Jr of VF-21 'Freelancers' flying an F-4B (151488/NE-101) of VF-21 from *Midway* near Haiphong. A second MiG-17 was claimed by the F-4B (152219/NE-102) flown by Lt Jack E. D. Batson, Jr and LCdr Robert B. Doremus

But the war was not going well. In an earlier outing against the Air Force, MiG-17s had run up a two-to-nothing score in their favour. On 24 July 1965, a USAF F-4C Phantom became the first American warplane downed by a SAM. Much of what transpired was the prosaic, everyday stuff of carrier operations.

In addition to operating the 12 F-4Gs, the 'Black Lions' of VF-213 also flew a pair of standard F-4Bs during its 1965 combat cruise on **Kitty Hawk.**

28 July 1965: a non-combat mishap aboard *Midway* claimed an F-4B (150646) of VF-21. Both crew members were recovered.

24 August 1965: an F-4B (152215/NE-21) of VF-21 from *Midway* was shot down by a SAM over North Vietnam. Cdr F. A. Franke and LCdr R. B. Doremus were provided with lodging by the North Vietnamese.

6 October 1965: a MiG-17 was shot down by an F-4B (150634/NL-107) of VF-151 from *Coral Sea*, flown by LCdr Dan MacIntyre and Lt (jg) Alan Johnson.

17 October 1965: *Independence* suffered the painful loss of three Phantoms over North Vietnam (followed by two more a week later). The first F-4B (151515/AG-205) of VF-84 was hit by AAA; LCdr S. E. Olmstead was killed and Lt (jg) P. A. Halyburton captured. The second F-4B (151494/AG-210) of VF-84 was claimed by

AAA; Ensign R. E. Gaither and Lt (jg) R. A. Knutson became POWs. Possibly attempting to 'cap' one of these losses, yet another F-4B (150631/AG-105) of VF-41 fell to small-arms fire; Lt R. L. Mayer and Lt (jg) D. R. Wheat also became prisoners.

Gaither and Knutson were apparently the first carrier-based Phantom fliers to be provided with long-term accommodations by the 'Hanoi Hilton', a term used by Americans to refer to all POW camps in North Vietnam although prisoners used the term for one specific location. The treatment of POWs was to be one of the major issues of the war from start to finish. The North Vietnamese tried everything to break these men, including torture, intimidation, deprival of medical treatment and isolation. Some died in captivity. With the possible exception of a single Phantom crew member who accepted early release from his captors, all resisted their captors. One naval aviator who flew a different aircraft was awarded the Medal of Honor for valour as a prisoner.

VF-92 and VF-96 (illustrated) returned for their second combat cruise in October 1965, having switched ships from **Ranger** *to* **Enterprise***. VF-96 were unusual in having a Modex number starting with '6'. It was standard practice for fighter units to use '1xx' or '2xx'.*

Below: Batson and Doremus pose proudly in the cockpit of their F-4B on 17 June, the day they shot down a MiG-17. On 24 August Doremus was himself shot down and taken prisoner.

Above: VF-21 claimed the first two kills of the war against North Vietnamese aircraft on 17 June 1965. The two crews are seen together in the ready room after the mission – (from left to right) Lt Jack Batson, Cdr Thomas Page, LCdr Robert Doremus and Lt John Smith.

25 October 1965: an F-4B (151505/AG-208) of VF-84 was downed by AAA over North Vietnam; Lt G. G. Ericksen and Lt (jg) J. L. Perry were rescued.

28 October 1965: an F-4B (150526/AG-104) of VF-41 was downed by small-arms fire over Laos. LCdr A. M. Lindsey and Lt (jg) R. W. Cooper were rescued.

An F-4G from VF-213 takes on fuel from a KA-3B during operations in the South China Sea in late 1965. The datalink-equipped Phantoms were used in the same role as other Phantoms, and their operational use led to many of the features being incorporated in the F-4J.

Above and right: On occasion carriers were drawn in from the Atlantic Fleet to bolster forces on the line. The first such cruise was by Independence, *which took the F-4Bs of VF-41 and VF-84 with it. The aircraft above is from the 'Jolly Rogers', being prepared for launch for a CAP mission.*

2 December 1965: an F-4B (151409/NG-206) of VF-92 was blown out of the air by its own Mk 82 bombs. The exact cause of this mishap is unclear, but both the Navy and Air Force lost some warplanes when bomb proximity fuses detonated prematurely. In this incident over South Vietnam, *Enterprise's* Lt T. J. Potter and Lt (jg) D. W.

Schmidt were recovered. It was a bad day for the Navy's sole nuclear-powered carrier: a second F-4B (149468) of VF-96 was lost in a non-combat mishap, though both crewmen were recovered. It was also a bad day aboard nearby *Kitty Hawk*, which suffered its first combat loss of the war when an F-4B (152220/NH-412) of VF-114 was lost to unknown causes over North Vietnam and Cdr C. B. Austin and Lt (jg) J. B. Logan were killed.

8 December 1965: an unknown cause resulted in the combat loss of an F-4B (151412/NG-203) of VF-92 over Laos. The bombings in Laos were, of course, a secret from the public if not from the North Vietnamese. Cdr E. A. Rawsthorne and Lt A. S. Hill lost their lives. This was the same day that F-4B (151438) of VF-96 was lost in a non-combat accident; both crew members were recovered.

4. Rolling Thunder III
31 January 1966–1 April 1966

Rolling Thunder IV
1 April 1966–14 February 1967

- **14 June 1966-9 November 1966**
  12 May 1966-3 December 1966 VF-151 'Vigilantes' (NL 1xx) and VF-161 'Chargers' (NL 2xx) CVW-15 USS *Constellation* (CVA-64) F-4B

- **10 August 1966-27 December 1966**
  21 June 1966-21 February 1967 VF-14 'Tophatters' (AB 1xx) and VF-32 'Swordsmen' CVW-1 (AB 2xx) USS *Franklin D Roosevelt* (CVA-42)

- **12 September 1966-31 January 1967**
  29 July 1966-23 February 1967 VF-21 'Freelancers' (NE 1xx) and VF-154 'Black Knights' (NE 4xx) CVW-2 USS *Coral Sea* (CVA-43) F-4B

- **4 December 1966-22 May 1967**
  5 November 1966-20 June 1967 VF-213 'Black Lions' (NH 1xx) and VF-114 'Aardvarks' (NH 2xx) CVW-11 USS *Kitty Hawk* (CVA-63) F-4B

- **18 December 1966-20 June 1967**
  19 November 1966-6 July 1967 VF-92 'Silver Kings' (NG 2xx) and VF-96 'Fighting Falcons' (NG 6xx) CVW-9 USS *Enterprise* (CVAN-65) F-4B

In the Second Battle of Ia Drang Valley in October 1965, the US First Air Cavalry Division defeated a larger force of North Vietnamese regulars. Never again were Hanoi's forces to win a major battle on the ground. Had Vietnam been a traditional war, this triumph by untested Air Cavalrymen against Vo Nguyen Giap's seasoned regulars would have marked the turn of the tide. But Americans were already forgetting that, in addition to veteran troopers from the North, they were fighting against a major segment of the population in the South. Asked what might prevent a global superpower from achieving victory against his fellow insurgents, a Viet Cong prisoner explained, "We live here."

In addition to North Vietnam's air force of Soviet-supplied MiGs, Hanoi was encircled by the largest number of anti-aircraft artillery (AAA) batteries ever implanted in one place. North Vietnam introduced the SAM to battle. None of this weaponry was at the cutting edge of technology, nor were its users better-trained than the Americans.

Air-to-air combat, in the final analysis, was of secondary importance in a war where Phantoms were tasked to deliver ordnance. By early 1965, all three

services were using the F-4 to deliver bombs. The dominant mission of American combat aircraft in the theatre became interdiction – the harassment and destruction of enemy surface forces and supply routes. There was no front line in the accepted sense of the term, and some Phantom pilots were providing close air support to embattled soldiers throughout South Vietnam while others were carrying bombloads north.

A sidelight was the US Navy's F-4G Phantom, taken into battle by VF-213 'Black Lions' aboard *Kitty Hawk*. These Phantoms looked little different from the F-4B but had come off the production line with a two-way data link system installed behind the rear cockpit which could relay information from the carrier concerning the status of a battle under way. The AN/ASW-21 datalink was complemented by a system which allowed the pilot to make a 'hands off' approach to his carrier. Only 12 F-4Gs served, but the Navy was to use some of their features in a newer Phantom model, the F-4J.

Aboard *Kitty Hawk*, A-4 Skyhawks, RA-5C Vigilantes, A-6 Intruders and F-4G Phantoms were painted in an experimental dark green camouflage

Navy Phantoms in Vietnam

Left: The second Atlantic Fleet carrier to deploy to the theatre was Franklin D. Roosevelt, which carried VF-14 and VF-32. This 'Swordsmen' F-4B is launched in the South China Sea in 1966, armed with AIM-9s.

Below: VF-92 and VF-96 (illustrated) made a total of three combat cruises aboard Enterprise with F-4Bs between October 1965 and July 1968. The 'Fighting Falcons' lost more than their share of Phantoms in early 1967, with four lost between February and April.

scheme. It was apparently not a good idea, and it led to logistics problems, of which the Navy had plenty already. When *Kitty Hawk* drew near to the end of this cruise and was running out of numerous items which could not be resupplied – including bombs, which were in scandalously short supply during this period – the camouflage experiment was judged a failure. Indeed. the green was dangerous on a crowded flight deck during the hours of darkness, while grey/white aircraft could be readily seen.

31 January 1966: North Vietnamese gunners in Laos shot down an F-4B (152233/NH-402) of VF-114. Lt W. F. Klumpp II and Lt (jg) J. N. Stineman were recovered.

18 February 1966: a North Vietnamese SAM took down an F-4B (152297/NG-201) of VF-92. Lt (jg) J. T. Ruffin was killed and Lt (jg) L. H. Spencer became a POW.

1 March 1966: an F-4B (150443/NK-310) of VF-143 was lost in combat to unknown causes in North Vietnam; Lt W. D. Frawley and Lt (jg) W. M. Christensen were killed.

5 March 1966: a Phantom was lost in South Vietnam when it was hit by target debris during an air-to-ground sortie. The F-4B (152224/NH-413) of VF-114 was lost but LCdr M. N. Guess and Lt R. E. Pile were recovered.

20 March 1966: an F-4B (151410/NG-202) of VF-92 was downed by AAA over North Vietnam. Lt (jg) J. S. Greenwood was recovered and Lt (jg) R. R. Ratzlaff captured.

26 April 1966: the 'Aardvarks' suffered their second loss in a few weeks to a Phantom hit by debris from its own target, this time in North Vietnam. F-4B 152255/NH-414 of VF-114 was a combat loss but Lts (jg) W. W. Smith and R. Blake were rescued.

15 June 1966: an F-4B (152251/NK-310) of VF-143 was downed by AAA over North Vietnam. Lt C. W. Bennett and Ensign D. W. Vermilyea were recovered.

11 July 1966: an F-4B (152262) was lost in a non-combat mishap. Both crew members survived.

28 August 1966: North Vietnamese AAA claimed an F-4G Phantom (150645/NH-111) of VF-213. Lt R. A. Schiltz and Lt (jg) D. C. Lewis were recovered.

18 May 1966: anti-aircraft fire in Laos shot down an F-4B (152257/NH-113) of VF-213. LCdr C. N. Sommers II and LCdr W. K. Sullivan were recovered.

23 June 1966: a non-combat mishap claimed a VF-151 F-4B (152324); both crew members were killed.

13 July 1966: *Constellation* toted up her first aerial victory when Lt. William M. McGuigan and Lt (jg) Robert M. Fowler shot down a MiG-17 while flying an F-4B (151500/NL-216) of VF-161.

19 September 1966: a SAM claimed a *Coral Sea* VF-154 F-4B (152085/NE-451) over North Vietnam, killing Lt (jg) D. B. Parsons, Jr and Lt (jg) T. H. Pilkington. That

day, for the second time during this cruise by *Constellation*, a non-combat accident cost a VF-151 F-4B (152315) and both crew members.

20 September 1966: due to unknown cause, F-4B 152073 NE-101 of VF-21 was lost in combat over North Vietnam; LCdr J. R. Bauder and Lt (jg) J. B. Mills were listed as missing in action and have since been presumed dead.

5 October 1966: an accident aboard *Franklin D. Roosevelt* resulted in the loss of an F-4B (152238) of VF-32. Both crewmen survived.

9 October 1966: an F-4B (152093/NE-452) of VF-154 was downed by AAA over North Vietnam. LCdr C. N. Tanner and Lt. R. R. Terry were captured.

22 October 1966: AAA claimed an F-4B (151009/NL-214) of VF-161 over North Vietnam; pilot LCdr. E. P. McBride and Lt (jg) E. U. Turner were recovered.

Below: Armourers aboard Roosevelt carefully load a four-round launcher pod for 5-in (12.7-cm) Zuni rockets on to the wing pylon of a VF-14 F-4B. The accurate and hard-hitting Zuni was widely used by Navy Phantoms.

3 November 1966: an F-4B (148433/NE-461) of VF-154 was shot down by AAA in North Vietnam. Lt R. W. Schaffer and Lt (jg) J. P. Piccoli were recovered. That day, an accident aboard *Franklin D. Roosevelt* claimed an F-4B (151018) of VF-14. Both crew members were recovered.

2 December 1966: an F-4B (151014/NE-461) of VF-154 was downed by AAA over North Vietnam. Lt (jg) D. E. McRae was killed, Ensign D. G. Rehman taken prisoner.

Of memorable strike missions flown by the 'Swordsmen', one on 14 December 1966 set a bizarre kind of record. LCdr Herbert L. Schmell, division leader of a flight of four F-4Bs, led his wingmen through an unprecedented number of surface-to-air missiles – 19 were counted – as well as heavy anti-aircraft fire to score direct hits on a target.

20 December 1966: Navy Phantoms' only encounter with the North Vietnamese Antonov An-2 'Colt' biplane. One An-2 each was shot down by the crews of Lt. H. Dennis Wisely/Lt (jg) David L. Jordan and Lt David McCrea and Ensign David Nichols flying, respectively an F-4B (153022/NH-215) of VF-114 and an F-4B (153019/NH-1100 of VF-213.

4 January 1967: an F-4B (152974/NE-451) of VF-154 was downed by AAA over North Vietnam. Lt A. M. Van Pelt and Ensign R. Morris were rescued.

19 January 1967: a non-combat mishap cost *Kitty Hawk* an F-4B (153029) and the lives of both crew members.

4 February 1967: *Kitty Hawk* sustained a battle loss when an F-4B (153007/NH-102) of VF-213 was hit by AAA over North Vietnam. Lt D. E. Thompson and Lt A. P. Collamore were killed.

12 February 1967: a non-combat mishap on *Enterprise* claimed an F-4B Phantom (152219) of VF-96. Both crew members were killed.

25 February 1967: an F-4B (156298) of VF-96 was lost in a non-combat mishap, *Enterprise's* second on this cruise. Both crew members were recovered.

Left: Photographed in June 1966, VF-14 Phantoms launch from Roosevelt for a training mission prior to arriving on the line.

Above: A VF-92 F-4B crew prepares to trap aboard Enterprise. The huge belly tank gave the Phantom an impressive combat radius.

5. Rolling Thunder V
14 February 1967–3 January 1968

- **8 May 1967-11 November 1967**
  29 April 1967-4 December 1967 VF-142 'Ghostriders' (NE 2xx) and VF-143 'Pukin Dogs' (NE 3xx) CVW-14 USS *Constellation* (CVA-64) F-4B
- **25 July 1967-29 July 1967**
  16 June 1967-14 September 1967 VF-11 'Red Rippers' (AA 1xx) and VF-74 'Be-devilers' (AA 2xx) CVW-1 USS *Forrestal* (CVA-59) F-4B
- **28 August 1967-20 February 1968**
  26 July 1967-6 April 1968 VF-151 'Vigilantes' (NL 1xx) and VF-161 'Chargers' (NL 2xx) CVW-15 USS *Coral Sea* (CVA-43) F-4B
- **3 December 1967-9 May 1968**
  4 November 1967-25 May 1968 VF-21 'Freelancers' (NE 1xx) and VF-154 'Black Knights' (NE 4xx) CVW-2 USS *Ranger* (CVA-61) F-4B
- **23 December 1967-1 June 1968**
  18 November 1967-28 June 1968 VF-213 'Black Lions' (NH 1xx) and 'VF-114 Aardvarks' (NH 2xx) CVW-11 USS *Kitty Hawk* (CVA-63) F-4B

A dramatic photograph captures Ensign James Lainge successfully ejecting from his crippled VF-114 F-4B on 24 April 1967. The pilot, LCdr Southwick, followed moments later and both were picked up at sea.

20 February 1967: an F-4B (150413/NG-614) of VF-96 was shot down by AAA over North Vietnam. Major R. C. Goodman was killed, Ensign G. L. Thornton captured.

4 April 1967: The record does not reveal exactly how *Enterprise* lost two Phantoms in its third and fourth non-combat mishaps with F-4Bs, but it is a safe guess that they somehow collided with each other. 150453 and 150994 belonged to VF-92. One crewman aboard each was killed, one rescued.

6 April 1967: a non-combat incident claimed an F-4B (152990) of VF-114; both crew members were recovered.

Below: VF-213 flew three combat cruises with the F-4B during 1966/69. This aircraft is seen in late 1967/early 1968, at the end of Rolling Thunder V. The weapons are standard low-drag bombs, dropped from medium level, an inaccurate tactic unless the Phantoms were led by an A-6 Intruder.

8 April 1967: an F-4B (152978/NG-610) of VF-96 was shot down by AAA over North Vietnam; Lt J. R. Ritchie and Ensign Frank A. Schumacher were rescued.

24 April 1967: typical of days of heavy fighting which cropped up from time to time. Lt. Charles E. (Ev) Southwick of VF-114 'Aardvarks' flew into battle in an F-4B Phantom (BuNo. 153000/NH-210) and shot down a MiG-17 using a Sidewinder, scoring the war's 48th MiG kill. Squadron mate, Lt. H. Dennis Wisely (who had shot down an Antonov An-2 on 20 December 1966) manoeuvred a second F-4B Phantom (BuNo. 153037/NH-100) to the point where he was able to rack up a MiG-17 kill using a Sidewinder. This time, Wisely's backseater was Lt (jg) Gareth L. Anderson.

Southwick, however, had actually been hit by AAA over Kep *before* downing his MiG and had continued through the battle nursing an aircraft suffering from indeterminate damage. He was able to fly the F-4B eastward and so go "feet wet" (get out over water) before it became abundantly clear that 153000 had fought its last

Below: An 'Aardvarks' F-4B cavorts near its 'homeplate' (Kitty Hawk). F-4Bs were modified with new radar warning receivers which added extra antennas to the fin-tip.

battle. The AAA damage made it impossible for Southwick to transfer fuel, and therefore impossible to get back to *Kitty Hawk*. He and his backseater ejected and were rescued.

8 May 1967: a non-combat mishap claimed an F-4B (152997) of VF-114. One crew member was killed, one recovered.

14 May 1967: luck turned sour for LCdr C. E. (Ev) Southwick of VF-114 who had previously downed a MiG, been shot down, and got rescued. This time, Southwick's Phantom (153004/NH-201) fell from the sky of North Vietnam after a collision with its own Zuni rockets. Southwick and Lt D. J. Rollins became POWs.

19 May 1967: a SAM bagged an F-4B (152264/NG-604) of VF-96 over North Vietnam. Cdr R. Rich was listed as missing, later as killed; LCdr W. R. Stark became a prisoner. In addition to this shoot-down of an *Enterprise* Phantom, a second combat

Left: Lt (jg) Bob Hickey climbs from the cockpit of the F-4B in which he and RIO Lt (jg) Jeremy Morris had just shot down a MiG-21. The pair were assigned to VF-143, flying from Constellation.

loss was sustained by *Kitty Hawk* when a SAM took down an F-4B (153004/NH-204) of VF-114. Lt (jg) J. C. Plumb and Lt (jg) G. L. Anderson also became POWs.

21 May 1967: North Vietnamese AAA claimed an F-4B (153040/NH-213) of VF-114. Antonov and MiG killer Lt. H. Dennis Wisely and backseat MiG-killer Ensign J. W. Laing were rescued.

19 June 1967: an F-4B (150439/NK-207) of VF-142 was shot down by North Vietnamese AAA. LCdr F. L. Raines and Ens C. L. Lewnes were recovered.

28 June 1967: an F-4B (152242/NK-301) of VF-143 was downed by AAA over North Vietnam. Cdr W. P. Lawrence and Lt (jg) J. W. Bailey became prisoners.

USS *Forrestal* (CVA-59) began launching missions against targets near Hanoi and Haiphong. This wartime cruise was cut short when a fire swept the deck of *Forrestal*, killing people, wrecking aircraft, and forcing the carrier to retire for repairs. It happened on 29 July 1967 after the carrier which set the standard for the modern Navy had been on the line for just five days.

For a ship at sea, nothing is more dangerous than a fire. The *Forrestal* blaze was a deadly inferno: 134 men died and 62 were injured. Among 21 aircraft lost valued in the hundreds of millions of dollars were seven F-4B Phantoms: 153046, 153054, 153060/153061, 153066, 153069, and 153912.

Above: A pair of VF-114 F-4Bs heads for North Vietnam on 16 April 1967, armed with Mk 82 Snakeye retarded bombs carried on multiple ejector racks. No AIM-9s are carried, but a pair of Sparrows provide some self-defence capability.

Tragedy struck the carrier force on 29 July 1967 when a rogue Zuni caused a fire which swept across the deck of Forrestal. *Fatalities totalled 134, while seven F-4s were lost.* Forrestal *had deployed from the Atlantic Fleet shortly before with VF-11 and VF-74 aboard.*

10 August 1967: good day for VF-142 which claimed two MiG-21s in air combat. Lt Guy H. Freeborn and Lt (jg) Robert J. Elliot were flying F-4B 152247/NK-202. LCdr Robert C. Davis and LCdr Gayle O. Elie were flying 150431, with an unrecorded side number.

21 August 1967: an F-4B (152247/NK-202) of VF-142 was downed by AAA over North Vietnam. Cdr R. H. McGlohn and Lt (jg) J. M. McIlrath were recovered. It was a bad day 'up north': three A-6 Intruders also from *Constellation* were downed by MiGs and SAMs.

23 August 1967: a North Vietnamese SAM knocked down an F-4B (149498/NK-205) of VF-142; LCdr T. W. Sitek and Ensign P. L. Ness were killed.

8 October 1967: an accident aboard *Coral Sea* destroyed an F-4B (150474) of VF-161. One crewman was killed, one recovered.

24 October 1967: the ubiquitous SA-2 'Guideline' surface-to-air missile took two victims, the first being an F-4B (150421) of VF-151. Cdr C R Gillespie and Lt (jg) R C Clark were both seized by the North Viet-

namese. Gillespie was released with other POWs at war's end while Clark died in captivity. The second casualty was another F-4B (150995) from the same *Coral Sea* squadron. Lts (jg) Robert F. Frishman and E. G. Lewis, Jr. became POWs. Frishman was later to gain notoriety as one of only eight POWs – and the only Navy F-4 crewman – to accept premature release from his captors, against orders from the American prison camp commander.

26 October 1967: Lt (jg) Robert P. Hickey and Lt (jg) Jeremy G. Morris of VF-143 shot down a MiG-21 while flying F-4B 149411.

30 October 1967: *Constellation*'s Phantom squadrons racked up their second aerial victory in four days when LCdr Eugene P. Lund and Lt (jg) James R. Borst of VF-142 downed a MiG-17 while flying an F-4B (150629/NK-203). But a few minutes later, Lund and Borst had to eject when their Phantom was hit by one of their own AIM-7E Sparrow missiles. Both men were recovered.

16 November 1967: VF-151, suffering heavy losses on *Coral Sea*'s 1967-68 cruise, lost its third Phantom to a SAM

over North Vietnam. LCdr D. E. Hernandez and Lt (jg) S. Vanhorn were recovered,

27 December 1967: an F-4B (153005/NH-205) of VF-114 was lost in combat to an unknown cause. LCdr L. M. Lee and Lt (jg) R. B. Innes were both listed as missing in action and later found to have perished.

29 December 1967: an F-4B (150449/NL-203) of VF-161 was claimed by AAA over North Vietnam but Lt J. F. Dowd and Lt (jg) G. K. Fliont were recovered.

when an F-4B (152987/NL-104) was downed, causing LCdr F. H. Schultz and Lt (jg) T. B. Sullivan to join the growing population in North Vietnamese prisons.

17 November 1967: an F-4B (151488/NL-207) of VF-161 was downed by North Vietnamese AAA; Cdr W. D. McGrath and Lt R. G. Emrich were killed.

19 November 1967: hard-hit VF-151 lost two Phantoms. An air-to-air missile from a MiG shot down an F-4B (150997/NL-110) of VF-151. LCdr C. D. Clower and Lt (jg) W. O. Estes II became POWs. MiGs also claimed a second F-4B (152304/NL-115) and the POW roster was joined by Lt (jg) J. E. Teague and Lt (jg) T. G. Stier.

16 December 1967: an F-4B (151492/NE-101) of VF-21 was shot down by AAA

VF-142 had a good day on 10 August 1967, with two crews shooting down MiG-21s. Shown above, in front their aircraft, are LCdr 'Swede' Elie (RIO, left) and LCdr Robert Davis (pilot, right), while at left, explaining their kills, are LCdr Robert Davis again (left) and Lt Guy Freeborn (right), pilot of the second MiG-killing aircraft. Freeborn's RIO was Lt (jg) Robert Elliot.

6. Rolling Thunder VI
3 January 1968–31 October 1968

- **22 February 1968-26 June 1968**
  3 January 1968-18 July 1968 VF-92 'Silver Kites' (NG 2xx) and VF-96 'Fighting Falcons' (NG 6xx) CVW-9 USS *Enterprise* (CVAN-65) F-4B

- **31 May 1968-29 October 1968**
  10 April 1968-16 December 1968 VF-102 'Diamondbacks' (AE 1xx) and VF-33 'Tarsiers' (AE 2xx) CVW-6 USS *America* (CVA-66) F-4J

- **28 June 1968-27 December 1968**
  29 May 1968-31 January 1969 VF-142 'Ghostriders' (NK 2xx) and VF-143 'Pukin Dogs' (NK 3xx) CVW-14 USS *Constellation* (CVA-64) F-4B

- **10 October 1968-30 March 1969**
  7 September 1968-18 April 1969 VF-151 'Vigilantes' (NL 1xx) and VF-161 'Chargers' (NL 2xx) CVW-15 USS *Coral Sea* (CVA-43) F-4B

The US Navy introduced a new Phantom, the F-4J, with VF-33 'Tarsiers' and VF-102 'Diamondbacks' aboard *America* beginning in 1968.

The F-4J Phantom incorporated improvements gained from US Navy experience with F-4B/G models and was

heavier than previous Phantoms and designed to operate at lower speeds on approach to the carrier. The F-4J was powered by 17,900-lb (79.63-kN)) thrust J79-GE-19 engines and incorporated drooped ailerons and slotted stabilator which reduced approach speed from 137 to 125 kt (253 km/h to 231 km/h).

The F-4J was equipped with AN/APQ-59 radar with 32-in (81-cm) dish and AWG-10 pulse-Doppler fire control system which permitted the detection and tracking of high- and low-altitude targets. The F-4J also incorporated the

VF-154's cruise aboard Ranger *covered the end of Rolling Thunder V, and the early phase of Rolling Thunder VI. Here a 'Black Knights' aircraft lets fly with Mk 82 Snakeyes.*

The Atlantic Fleet's America *was heavily involved in Rolling Thunder VI. Here a mixed formation of VF-102 F-4Bs and VA-82 A-7s head for Vietnam for an interdiction mission. Partnering VF-102 was VF-33 'Tarsiers'.*

one-way AN/ASW-25A datalink system which resulted from the two-way system tried on the F-4G. Also on the F-4J were improved TACAN, upgraded AN/AJB-7 bombing system, and APR-32 radar warning receiver. 522 F-4Js were built.

10 January 1968: a non-combat accident claimed an F-4B (153036) of VF-114. Both crew members were recovered. It

was even worse aboard *Ranger* where two F-4Bs (151506 and 151499) of VF-154 were lost in a non-combat mishap, presumably a collision, though all crewmen were recovered.

18 January: *Kitty Hawk* suffered a non-combat mishap which claimed an F-4B (153055) and cost the lives of both crew members.

A fine study of a VF-114 F-4B during the early part of Rolling Thunder VI. The aircraft carries AIM-9D missiles with more pointed seeker heads.

5 April 1968: a non-combat mishap cost VF-96 an F-4B (150463). Both crew members were recovered.

14 April 1968: a non-combat mishap claimed an F-4B (150644) of VF-154. Both crew members were recovered.

15 April 1968: *Kitty Hawk* lost two F-4Bs (153002 and 153043) of VF-114 in a non-combat mishap; all crew members were recovered.

20 April 1968: *Kitty Hawk* suffered a painful fifth non-combat loss of a Phantom on a single cruise (as compared with just one combat loss) when an F-4B (153003) of VF-114 was lost. Both crew members were recovered.

28 April 1968: an F-4B (153014/NE-103) of VF-21 was shot down by AAA over North Vietnam. LCdr D. E. Hernandez and Lt (jg) D. J. Lortscher were recovered.

7 May 1968: an air-to-air missile from a MiG shot down an F-4B (151485/NG-210) over North Vietnam. LCdr E. S. Christensen and Ltr(jg) W. A. Kramer were recovered.

9 May 1968: a MiG-21 was shot down

by an F-4B (153036) of VF-96 flown by Major John P. Hefferman, USAF and Lt (jg) Frank A. Schumacher. It had to be a satisfying moment for RIO Schumacher, who on *Enterprise*'s previous cruise had been shot down and rescued (on 8 April 1967). Air Force exchange officer Hefferman was to suffer the indignity of seeing his name omitted from his own service's roster of aerial victories.

4 June 1968: North Vietnam's AAA claimed one of the 'Tarsiers' new F-4J models (155554/AE-204). Lt E. P. Price was killed, Lt (jg) W.A. Simmons rescued.

2 June 1968: a non-combat mishap on *Enterprise* destroyed an F-4B (150453) of

VF-92. Both crew members were rescued. The squadron suffered its second such mishap five days later, losing F-4B 150994 and, again, both crewmen survived.

10 July 1968: Lt Roy Cash, Jr of VF-33, flying the F-4J (155553/AE-212) shot down a MiG-21. Cash's back-seater was Lt Joseph E. Kain, Jr.

16 June 1968: a MiG firing a missile shot down an F-4J (155548/AE-101) of VF-102. Cdr W. E. Wilber became a prisoner of war. Lt (jg) B. F. Rupinski was killed.

24 July 1968: AAA fire over North Vietnam claimed an F-4J (155551/AE-203) of VF-33 but both Phantom crewmen were rescued. Another F-4J of VF-102 (155540AE-112) was claimed by AAA the following day with one crewman killed, one captured.

17 August 1968: an F-4B Phantom (151504/NK-206) of VF-142 was downed by one of its own AIM-9D Sparrow missiles. Lt (jg) M. L. Gartley and Lt W. J. Mayhew became prisoners of war.

24 August 1968: a non-combat mishap claimed an F-4B (150434) of VF-143. One crew member was killed, one recovered.

16 September 1968: an F-4B (149443) of VF-143 was destroyed in a non-combat accident; both crew members survived.

7. Bombing Halt
31 October 1968–6 April 1972

- **29 November 1968-16 April 1969**
  26 October 1968-27 May 1969 VF-21 'Freelancers' (NE 1xx) and VF-154 'Black Knights' (NE 2xx) CVW-2 USS *Ranger* (CVA-61) F-4J

- **28 January 1969-16 August 1969**
  30 December 1968-4 September 1969 VF-213 'Black Lions' (NH 1xx) and VF-114 'Aardvarks' (NH 2xx) CVW-11 USS *Kitty Hawk* (CVA-63) F-4B

- **31 March 1969-16 June 1969**
  6 January 1969-2 July 1969 VF-96 'Fighting Falcons' (NG 1xx) and VF-92 'Silver Kites' (NG 2xx) CVW-9 USS *Enterprise* (CVAN-65) F-4J

- **12 September 1969-17 April 1970**
  11 August 1969-8 May 1970 VF-142 'Ghostriders' (NK 2xx) and VF-143 'Pukin Dogs' (NK 3xx) CVW-14 USS *Constellation* (CVA-64) F-4J

- **27 October 1969-1 June 1970**
  23 September 1969-1 July 1970 VF-151 'Vigilantes' (NL 1xx) and VF-161 'Chargers' (NL 2xx) CVW-15 USS *Coral Sea* (CVA-43) F-4B

- **17 November 1969-12 May 1970**
  14 October 1969-1 June 1970 VF-21 'Freelancers' (NE 1xx) and VF-154 'Black Knights' (NE 2xx) CVW-2 USS *Ranger* (CVA-61) F-4J

- **26 May 1970-8 November 1970**
  10 April 1970-21 December 1970 VF-96 'Fighting Falcons' (NG 1xx) and VF-92 'Silver Kites' (NG 2xx) USS *America* (CVA-66) F-4J

- **21 November 1970-17 May 1971**
  27 October 1970-17 June 1971 VF-21 'Freelancers' (NE 1xx) and VF-154 'Black Knights' (NE 2xx) CVW-2 USS *Ranger* (CVA-61) F-4J

- **8 December 1970-23 June 1971**
  6 November 1970-17 July 1971 VF-213 'Black Lions' (NH 1xx) and VF-114 'Aardvarks' (NH 2xx) CVW-11 USS *Kitty Hawk* (CVA-63) F-4J

- **18 May 1971-10 October 1971**
  16 April 1971-6 November 1971 VF-151 'Vigilantes' CVW-5 (NF 2xx) and 'VF-161 Chargers' (NF 1xx) CVW-5 USS *Midway* (CVA-41) F-4B

- **16 July 1971-24 January 1972**
  11 June 1971-12 February 1972 VF-143 'Pukin Dogs' (NK 1xx) and VF-142 'Ghostriders' (NK 2xx) CVW-14 USS *Enterprise* (CVAN-65) F-4J

- **4 November 1971-13 June 1972**
  1 October 1971-1 July 1972 VF-96 'Fighting Falcons' (NG-1xx) and VF-92 'Silver Kites' (NG 2xx) CVW-9 USS *Constellation* (CVA-64) F-4J

- **14 December 1971-30 June 1972**
  12 November 1971-17 July 1972 VF-51 'Screaming Eagles' (NL 1xx) and VF-111 'Sundowners' (NL 2xx) CVW-15 USS *Coral Sea* (CVA-43) F-4B

On 31 October 1968, the bombing of North Vietnam (and the Rolling Thunder campaign) ended. Along with Lyndon Johnson's decision not to seek re-election came a 'bombing halt' which was to endure for nearly four years.

Rolling Thunder failed for two reasons. Those who advocated persuasion by bombing had both underestimated North Vietnam's determination and overestimated its vulnerability. No worthwhile strategic targets existed in the nation: there was nothing comparable to the synthetic fuel plants upon which Germany had depended during World War II. The North Vietnamese were able to survive the loss of thermal power plants and even of their only steel mill. They were prepared to make such sacrifices. Furthermore, the bombing campaign created exactly the situation the United States had already claimed was in effect: differences between Communist North Vietnam and the Communist Viet Cong in the South – which had been significant at the start – broke down and vanished.

After one cruise with the new F-4J in Constellation, *VF-143 moved to* Enterprise *for a cruise in 1971.*

Infiltration from the North – not a factor at the beginning – increased.

The difficulties of the Rolling Thunder period (1965-68), as well as the problems of operating sophisticated warplanes in a tropical backwater, did not escape American planners. US Navy Captain Frank Ault visited every combat unit in the fleet and came up with hundreds of suggestions, in his Ault Report, to improve performance in air-to-air combat. One of the recommendations called for DACT (dissimilar air combat training) and led to the creation of the US Navy's Fighter Weapons School, known as 'Top Gun'.

The bombing halt was a good time to tote up the results of the rivalry between the F-8 Crusader, which was near the end of its career, and the F-4 Phantom, which was not far from the beginning. In terms of numbers of aircraft deployed, the 'mix' of F-4s and F-8s was roughly

Right: Seen in 1969, this VF-154 F-4J is launched from Ranger. Despite the bombing halt on the North, limited raids were still undertaken against positions in South Vietnam, hence the Mk 82 bombs.

Below: Action on Ranger's deck as the carrier launches VF-21 F-4Js and VA-56 A-7s. The first of three cruises for the 'Freelancers' with the F-4J began in October 1968.

Left: VF-96 transitioned to the F-4J in late 1968, in time for two more cruises in 1969/1970. In October 1971 the squadron joined Constellation for another cruise.

Below: Sheer muscle power can overcome many obstacles: deck crew on Coral Sea manoeuvre a VF-151 F-4B in 1969.

Above: VF-111 'Sundowners' had previously flown the Crusader, but transitioned to the F-4B for their first Phantom combat cruise in late 1971. This lasted until July 1972, and took in significant action during the Linebacker campaign.

Below: Fully armed and ready to go, a VF-151 F-4B waits on the deck of Coral Sea for its launch time. In addition to the AIM-9D Sidewinders, the aircraft is armed with M117 bombs with extended fuzes. These 'daisy cutters' exploded above ground ensuring maximum blast effect across a wide area. The carrier (with VF-151 and VF-161 aboard) made two cruises during the bombing halt period, later embarking VF-51 and VF-111.

50-50 in 1965, but by 1968 had fallen to about 80-20 in favour of the Phantom. Carrier-based Crusaders flew almost no air-to-ground missions, so could not be compared with the Phantom in the 'mud-moving' arena. In air combat, when the fighting 'up north' ended in October 1968, if only Navy victories were counted, the Crusader had bagged 19 MiGs compared with the Phantom's 13, an advantage of about 50 per cent. There were too many variables for this to have any significance. Ironically, at a time when there was universal agreement that fighters needed guns, the Crusader had not got a single kill with its cannons, though in two instances some shooting had been done after a missile administered the *coup de grâce*: every F-8 kill belonged to the Sidewinder.

14 January 1969: while en route to the Southeast Asia combat zone, *Enterprise* suffered a catastrophic fire near Hawaii. Some 27 men died, 344 were injured, and 15 aircraft were lost.

17 February 1969: VF-21 lost an F-4J (155760) in an accident on *Ranger*. Both crew members survived.

20 February 1969: VF-21 suffered its second non-combat loss of an F-4J (155763). One crew member was killed, one rescued.

Phantoms continued to bomb North Vietnamese troops in Laos. Under limited circumstances, some missions could *still* be flown into North Vietnam. Reconnaissance missions were routine. Bombing missions were called 'Type III limited duration, protective reaction air strikes'. These strikes were ordered after North Vietnamese AAA shot down a USAF RF-4C Phantom on 5 June 1969.

25 March 1969: Marring *Coral Sea's* 1968-1969 combat cruise in which no Phantoms fell in combat, an F-4B (150447) of VF-151 was lost in an accident; both crew members survived.

13 March 1969: a non-combat mishap claimed an F-4B 153018 of VF-114; both crew members were recovered.

3 July 1969: a non-combat mishap destroyed an F-4B (153015) of VF-213. Both crew members were recovered.

22 November 1969: North Vietnamese AAA shot down an F-4J (155889/NK-110) of VF-143 over Laos. Lt (jg) H. C. Wheeler was rescued and Lt (jg) H. J. Bedinger became a POW.

11 January 1970: a non-combat accident resulted in the loss of an F-4J (155750) of VF-154. Both crew members were killed.

25 February 1970: When *Coral Sea* returned to the war zone, the carrier began a second combat cruise in which no Phantoms were to be lost in combat. However, the first of three non-combat mishaps claimed a VF-161 F-4B (152286). Both crew members were recovered.

9 March 1970: on *Ranger*, VF-21 lost an F-4J (155775) in a non-combat incident. Both crew members were lost.

28 March 1970: In a rare, air-to-air engagement during this period when US planes were not regularly bombing North Vietnam, on , Lt Jerome E. Beaulier and Lt Steven J. Barkley flying a VF-142 F-4J (155875/NK-201) shot down a MiG-21.

5 April 1970: an F-4B (152325) of VF-151 was lost in a non-combat mishap; one crew member was recovered, one lost.

17 May 1970: F-4B (152239) of VF-161 was lost in an accident. One crew member was recovered, one lost.

20 May 1970: an F-4J (155738) of VF-92 was lost in a non-combat mishap. The crew was recovered.

5 January 1971: a non-combat mishap claimed an F-4J (155577) of VF-21 on *Ranger*. One crew member was recovered, one killed.

27 February 1971: a non-combat mishap on *Ranger* cost the Navy a VF-21 F-4J (155884). One crew member was recovered, one lost.

Between 27 November 1970 and 6 July 1971, *Kitty Hawk* completed a Vietnam cruise without losing a single Phantom to combat or non-combat causes.

Further strikes, by VF-92 'Silver Eagles' and VF-96 'Fighting Falcons' F-4J Phantoms from *Constellation*, pounded North Vietnam in December 1971. They were joined by VF-51 and VF-111 from *Coral Sea*. Though President Richard Nixon's administration was beginning a measured withdrawal, the war was far from over. That month, Navy Phantoms supported a five-day campaign of bombing above the 17th Parallel, dubbed Proud Deep Alpha.

30 December 1971: an F-4B (150418/NL-203) of VF-111 was hit by a SAM. LCdr D. W. Hoffman and Lt (jg) N. A. Charles became POWs.

Apart from Proud Deep, there were plenty of combat sorties to be flown from Dixie Station over South Vietnam. Still, *Enterprise* survived her 1971-72 cruise without losing a single Phantom.

A pair of VF-111 jets airborne from Coral Sea on a training mission. The 'Double Nuts' Modex on the nearest aircraft signifies that it is the 'CAG-bird', nominally assigned to the Air Wing commander.

19 January 1972: The bombing halt was still in effect when a VF-96 Phantom crew, covering a reconnaissance mission code-named Blue Tree, ran into a heavy barrage of SAMs, dodged them, and shot down a MiG-21 with a Sidewinder. Lt Randall H. (Duke) Cunningham, front-seater of the F-4J Phantom, was a 'Top Gun' graduate. Cunningham and Lt William Driscoll had racked up the 122nd MiG kill of the war and the first in nearly two years. On this mission, the pair was flying F-4J 157267 (NG-112).

6 March 1972: Lt Garry L. Weigand and Lt (jg) William C. Freckelton of VF-111 shot down a MiG-17 while flying an F-4B (153019/NL-201).

8. Freedom Train
6 April 1972 – 7 May 1972

9. Linebacker
8 May 1972 – 23 October 1972

- **8 March 1972-4 November 1972**
  17 February 1972-28 November 1972 VF-213 'Black Lions' (NH 1xx) and VF-114 'Aardvarks' (NH 2xx) CVW-11 USS *Kitty Hawk* (CVA-63) F-4J
- **30 April 1972-12 February 1973**
  10 April 1972-3 March 1973 VF-161 'Chargers' (NF 1xx) and VF-151 'Vigilantes' (NF 2xx) CVW-2 USS *Midway* (CVA-41) F-4B
- **18 May 1972-17 January 1973**
  11 April 1972-13 February 1973 VF-31 'Tomcatters' (AC 1xx) and VF-103 'Sluggers' (AC 2xx) CVW-3 USS *Saratoga* (CVA-60) F-4J
- **14 July 1972-28 February 1973**
  5 June 1972-24 March 1973 VF-74 'Be-devilers' (AJ 1xx) and VMFA-333 'Shamrocks' (AJ 2xx) CVW-8 USS *America* (CVA-66) F-4J – only Marine deployment

203). Lt J. G. Greenleaf and Lt C. McKinney were both killed in action.

27 April 1972: an F-4B (153025/NL-102) was hit by a combination of fire from MiGs and SAMs and went down over North Vietnam. Lt A. R. Molinare and LCdr J. B. Souder ejected and became POWs.

6 May 1972: a MiG-17 was shot down by a VF-51 F-4B 150456 (NL-100) flown by LCdr Jerry B. Houston and Lt Kevin T. Moore. Two MiG-21s fell to VF-114 Phantom crews from *Kitty Hawk*, namely Lt Robert G. Hughes/Lt (jg) Adolph J. Cruz and LCdr Kenneth W. Pettigrew/Lt (jg) Michael J. McCabe flying F-4Js 157249/NH-206 and 157245/NH-201 respectively.

10 May 1972: the Linebacker campaign's third day, yielded the war's largest air-to-air score, eleven MiGs shot down – eight by Navy Phantoms, three more by the Air Force. At 0830 hours, Lieutenant Curt Dose launched in a two-aircraft F-4J Phantom division from *Constellation*. Meanwhile, heavy 'strike packages' from every F-4 wing in SEA were driving north

Demonstrating 'buddy-bombing', with an A-6 providing the accurate navigation and release commands, is a pair of F-4s from Saratoga. Both VF-31 and VF-103 F-4Js are represented here, supporting an Intruder from VA-35.

toward targets in the Hanoi region.

Curt Dose's flight 'beat up' Kep airfield. Flying an F-4J (157269/NG-211) with RIO LCdr James McDevitt, Dose used a Sidewinder to shoot down a MiG while at supersonic speed and tree-top level. As the morning unfolded, Phantoms struck the Paul Doumer Bridge and other targets in the Hanoi-Haiphong region.

Randy Cunningham's squadron mate Lt Michael J. Connelly, flying a VF-96 F-4J Phantom (BuNo. 155769/NG-106) shot down two MiG-17s. His back-seater was Lt Thomas J. J. Blonski. Another Phantom crew from the same *Constellation* squadron, headed by Lt Stephen C. Shoemaker, despatched another MiG-17 with a Sidewinder. Shoemaker and Lt (jg) Keith V. Crenshaw were flying F-4J 155749/NG-111. Cunningham and Driscoll claimed one MiG-17, then rescued a

18 February 1972: North Vietnamese AAA in Laos shot down a VF-92 F-4J (157266/NG-207) Lt B. P. Rowe was killed, Lt (jg) D. E. Spence was recovered.

3 March 1972: an F-4B (150417) of VF-51 was lost in a non-combat incident; both crew members survived.

Another round of fighting 'up North' was brewing. The prolonged bombing halt, years of diplomacy, every effort to find some way solution in Vietnam; all of it had failed. The United States had created a self-fulfilling prophecy. Eight years after the US first accused North Vietnam of invading the South – it did.

Hanoi launched a full-scale invasion, often referred to as the spring offensive, on the night of 29/30 March 1972 when

12 divisions supported by armour and artillery invaded South Vietnam. Invading North Vietnamese forces captured the provincial capital of Quang Tri on 2 April. In the new round of fighting, the US decided to reinforce the very forces it was withdrawing, and the debate resumed about bombing the north.

On 6 April 1972, President Nixon resumed limited bombing of North Vietnam, in a campaign named Operation Freedom Train.

6 April 1972: The Navy's Duke Cunningham scored a second MiG kill, a MiG-17, again flying F-4J 157267/NG-112 with Lt (jg) William P. Driscoll.

14 April 1972: over South Vietnam, hostile gunfire claimed an F-4J (157252/NH-

Lt Robert Hughes is congratulated on his return to Kitty Hawk after he and RIO Lt (jg) Adolph Cruz had downed a MiG-21 on 6 May 1972. Theirs was one of two kills on that day for the 'Aardvarks' of VF-114.

Lt (jg) Tinker and Lt Vaughn Hawkins (pair at left) celebrate with LCdr James McDevitt (RIO) and Lt Curt Dose (pilot, right) after the latter pair had scored a MiG-21 victory over Kep airfield on 10 May 1972. All were assigned to VF-92.

On 18 May 1972 VF-161 tangled with the rare MiG-19, scoring two kills. The victorious crews are seen back in the ready room, comprising (from left) Lt Oran Brown (RIO) and Lt 'Bart' Bartholomy (pilot), with Lt Patrick Arwood (pilot) and Lt Michael Bell (RIO).

Above and left: VF-31 'Felix' flew in the Linebacker campaign from Saratoga. The squadron's sole victory came courtesy of pilot Cdr Sam Flynn and RIO Lt Bill John on 21 June 1972, shown here after the victory in their jet.

Right: A VF-92 F-4J blasts of Constellation's waist cat on 9 May 1972.

wingman by using a Sidewinder to bag another, their second kill of the day and fourth of the war. As the day continued to unfold. Randy Cunningham and William Driscoll fought a close-quarters battle with a MiG-17 and shot it down, their fifth kill – making them the first aces. Soon afterward, their F-4J Phantom (BuNo. 155800/NG-100), callsign SHOWTIME 100, was hit by a SAM. The pair ejected and was rescued at sea.

The busy day of 10 May 1972 saw no air-to-air successes against Navy Phantoms by MiG pilots, but in addition to Cunningham's craft. Cdr H. L. Blackburn and Lt S. A. Rudloff were shot down by AAA while flying F-4J 155797/NG-212; both men became POWs.

Most of the attention on 10 May 1972 focused on *Constellation*'s carrier air wing, but *Coral Sea* managed to claim the third MiG kill of its 1971-72 cruise. Flying an F-4B (151398/NL-111), Lts Kenneth L. Cannon and Ray A. Morris Jr. of VF-51

shot down a MiG-17.

18 May 1972: one of the occasions when the Phantom came up against the twin-engined MiG-19 fighter, employed only in small numbers by Hanoi. Two VF-161 crews claimed a MiG-19 kill each, namely Lt Henry A. Bartholomay/Lt Oran R. Brown and Lt Patrick E. Arwood/Lt James M. Bell flying F-4Bs (153068/NF-110 and 153915/NF-105).

21 May 1972: a *Midway* F-4B (153032) of VF-151 was lost in a non-combat mishap. Both crew members were recovered.

23 May 1972: a Phantom crew racked up an unusual double victory. Flying an F-4B (153020/NF-100) of VF-161, LCdr Ronald E. McKeown and Lt John C. Ensch bagged a pair of MiG-17s.

11 June 1972: *Coral Sea* claimed the

Right: Partnering VF-31 in Saratoga was VF-103 'Sluggers'. The squadron scored the carrier's second kill on 10 August 1972 (LCdr Robert Tucker and Lt (jg) Stanley Edens).

With their memorable three-kill mission of 10 May 1972, Lt Randy Cunningham (pilot) and Lt (jg) Willie Driscoll (RIO) became the Navy's only aces of the war. The aircraft they were flying was the CAG-bird (right), which was downed by a SAM on the return from the North.

Left: VF-74 from the Atlantic Fleet had previously undertaken one combat cruise, and returned in June 1972 with the improved F-4J to take part in both Linebacker campaigns. The squadron was partnered by VMFA-333 on board America.

A VF-114 'Aardvark' manoeuvres through cloud and AAA during a Linebacker raid.

fourth and fifth MiGs of its 1971-1972 cruise. One MiG-17 each was shot down by Cdr Foster S. Teague and Lt Ralph M. Howell in F-4B 149473/NL-114 and Lt Winston W. Copeland and Lt Donald R. Bouchoux in F-4B 149457/NL-113. Both crews were from VF-51.

18 June 1972: North Vietnamese AAA shot down an F-4J (157273/NH-107) of VF-213. LCdr R. Cash and Lt R. J. Laib were both recovered.

After two more Mediterranean cruises, VF-14 'Tophatters' and VF-31 'Felix' transitioned from F-4B to F-4J. Several more Med cruises followed. In 1972, the spring invasion by North Vietnamese forces thrusting into South Vietnam caused *Saratoga* to be diverted from its usual ocean. VF-31 flew extensive air-to-ground missions.

21 June 1972: MiG kill by pilot Cdr Sam Flynn and backseater LT Bill John, one of the few East Coast crews to achieve an aerial victory in Vietnam. Flynn and John were flying an F-4J (157293/AC-101) of VF-31.

10 July 1972: the date of a combat loss over North Vietnam of an F-4J (155803) of VF-103. Downed by a MiG, Lt R. I. Randall and Lt F. J. Masterson ejected and became POWs.

10 August 1972: an F-4J crew of VF-103

shot down a MiG-21 to be credited with *Saratoga*'s second aerial victory of the war. LCdr Robert E. Tucker, Jr and Lt (jg) Stanley B. Edens were flying an F-4J (157299/AC-296).

16 August 1972: over North Vietnam, a SAM shot down an F-4J (157262/NH-211) of VF-114. Cdr J. R. Pitzen and Lt O. J. Pender, Jr were listed as missing and later found to have died.

25 August 1972: a SAM shot down an F-4B (153020/NF-100) of VF-161 over North Vietnam. LCdr N, W. Doyle and MiG killer Lt John C. Ensch became POWs.

27 August 1972: Two days after suffering one combat loss, *Midway* experienced another when an F-4B (151013/NF-210) of VF-151 was downed over North Vietnam by a SAM. Lt T. W. Triebel and Lt (jg) D. A. Everett joined the ranks of 'new guy' POWs.

8 September 1972: North Vietnam's AAA claimed an F-4J (157302/AC-202) of VF-103. Cdr P. P. Bordone and Lt J. H. Findley were recovered.

11 September 1972: the only air-to-air victory by a Marine Corps crew in the Vietnam war: flying an F-4J Phantom (155526/AJ-201) of VMFA-333 'Shamrocks', Major

Lee T. Lasseter and Captain John D. Cummings bagged a MiG-21. It was a costly credit, for Lasseter and Cummings and a second Marine Corps crew were downed by SAMs and rescued. The other F-4J (154784/AJ-206) was flown by Capt A. S. Dudley and 1st Lt Brady.

13 September 1972: a non-combat loss claimed an F-4J (153854) of VF-74. One crewman was killed, one rescued.

29 October 1972: F-4B (153031) on *Midway* was lost in a non-combat mishap, apparently in a collision with an A-6A Intruder which was also lost.

Although they served throughout the war from shore bases, it was not until 1972 that the Marine Corps deployed a Phantom squadron aboard a carrier. The unit was VMFA-333 'Shamrocks', also known as 'Triple Trey', which sent its F-4Js aboard America. One MiG-kill was achieved.

20 November 1972: a SAM over North Vietnam shot down an F-4J (157288/AC-210) of VF-103. LCdr V. E. Lesh and Lt (jg) D. L. Cordes were recovered.

23 December 1972: the hard-pressed Marines of VMFA-333 suffered their third combat loss when an F-4J (153885/AJ-201) was downed by North Vietnamese gunfire.

A pair of immaculate VF-114 F-4Js are seen shortly after the squadron's return from the 1972 cruise which included Linebacker operations. The 'Aardvarks' made a total of six combat cruises.

10. Interregnum
23 October 1972–18 December 1972

- **3 October 1972-28 May 1973**
  12 September 1972-12 June 1973 VF-143 'Pukin Dogs' (NK 1xx) and VF-142 'Ghostriders' (NK 2xx) CVW-14 USS *Enterprise* (CVAN-65) F-4J

Now, the Linebacker campaign ended. The Nixon administration believed that Hanoi was ready for a settlement. Secretary of State Kissinger proclaimed that, "Peace is at hand." Accordingly combat operations north of the 20th parallel were suspended to give Hanoi a chance to draft its peace terms.

Linebacker had been very different from Rolling Thunder. On the enemy

side, the SA-7 man-portable missile had been introduced and the MiG-19 had belatedly joined other members of the MiG stable. However, the US had sharply refined their tactics, and had introduced far more advanced ECM which largely negated the Vietnamese advances.

The expected move towards peace talks did not occur, so Nixon looked to another, heavier air campaign.

11. Linebacker II
18 December 1972–29 December 1972

> - **9 December 1972-31 May 1973**
>   16 November 1972-22 June 1973 VF-154 'Black Knights' (NE 1xx) and VF-21 'Freelancers' (NE-2xx) CVW-2 USS *Ranger* (CVA-61)
> - **31 January 1973-15 August 1973**
>   5 January 1973-11 October 1973 VF-96 'Fighting Falcons' (NG 1xx) and VF-92 'Silver Kites' (NG 2xx) CVW-9 USS *Constellation* (CVA-64)

There was yet another round of fighting, Linebacker II or the 'Eleven Day War'. Very close to a settlement, Nixon finally decided that North Vietnam must be subjected to one final show of force. Between 18 and 29 December 1972, B-52 Stratofortresses finally went to Hanoi and Haiphong, flying 714 sorties and encountering a record 1,293 SAM firings. F-4 Phantoms and other allied warplanes supported this final spasm of fighting.

28 December 1972: on the penultimate day of Linebacker II, *Enterprise* scored an aerial victory when an F-4J (155846/NK-214) of VF-142 shot down a MiG-21.

The 1972 Linebacker campaigns against North Vietnam produced a six to one 'kill ratio' and had inflicted a sound defeat on North Vietnam's MiG force.

VF-96's eighth and final combat cruise began in January 1973, shortly after the conclusion of the Linebacker II effort. America, Enterprise, Midway, Ranger and Saratoga were on the line during Linebacker II.

The creation of the US Navy's 'Top Gun' school, followed in due course by the USAF's 'aggressor' squadrons assured that future fighter pilots would be better prepared. The heavy, two-man, twin-engine F-4 Phantom reigned supreme as the best all-around fighter in the world. A few mavericks in the Pentagon argued that the US needed a 'lightweight' fighter. In the same year that the Vietnam war ended, the USAF flew the F-15 Eagle and the F-14 Tomcat, both very large, heavy, sophisticated fighters ideally suited to American needs. Until these came along, the Phantom was to remain the dominant fighter in the world.

12. End Game
30 December 1972–15 August 1973

> - **31 March 1973-8 August 1973**
>   9 March 1973-8 November 1973 VF-51 'Screaming Eagles' (NL 1xx) and VF-111 'Sundowners' (NL 2xx) USS *Coral Sea* (CVA-43) F-4B

12 January 1973: The 197th and last MiG kill of the war took place when Lt Victor T. Kovaleski of VF-161 'Chargers' aboard USS *Midway* (CV-41) used a Sidewinder to shoot down a MiG-17. Thus, *Midway*'s Phantoms scored the first and last kills of the war. Lt Kovaleski also suffered the indignity of piloting the last aircraft to be lost over North Vietnam when his Phantom was shot down two days later on 14 January. Pilot and backseater were rescued.

27 January 1973: the truce agreement took effect, but on that last day, an F-4J (155768/NK-113) of VF-143 was downed by AAA over South Vietnam; Cdr H. H. Hall and LCdr P. A. Kientzler became POWs.

VF-111 made two combat cruises to the South China Sea, both with the F-4B. One subsequent non-combat cruise covered the Mayaguez incident in May 1975, when this photograph was taken.

29 January 1973: *Ranger* lost two F-4Js (158361 and 158366) in a non-combat accident. Both crew members in the first aircraft were lost. Those in the second were recovered.

The combat records of the US Navy stop with the end of American participation in the Vietnam War in January 1973 – meaning that Phantom losses, if any, for *Coral Sea*'s 1973 cruise are not readily available.

Though the Vietnam War ended 27 January 1973, fighting persisted in Cambodia until 15 August 1973. Phantoms continued to fight in Cambodia until this date while American forces trickled out of Southeast Asia.

VF-92 (left) and VF-96 (right) stayed together on Constellation long after the official end of the war. These carrier ops were photographed in the South China Sea during July 1974.

Throughout the remainder of 1973 and 1974 the South was left to defend itself. A major offensive in 1975 swept the Communists through to Saigon. The final Frequent Wind evacuation of US and some Vietnamese personnel was undertaken during April 1975, when Communists completed the invasion of the South. Vietnam was officially united as one nation on 1 May. Of course US Navy carriers remained in the theatre throughout and after this period, Phantoms providing fighter cover.

The F-4Js of VF-21 'Freelancers' were still in the Gulf of Tonkin in March 1973 when this aircraft was photographed. The cruise had taken in operations during Linebacker II.

Signalling the end of an era in more ways than one, the 1975 cruise by the *Enterprise* not only covered the Saigon evacuation, but was also the first to carry F-14 Tomcats in place of the war-weary Phantoms.

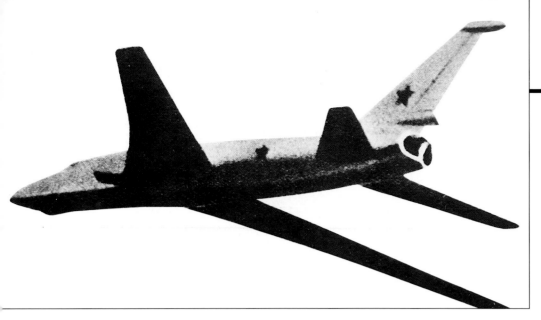

Tupolev Tu-98 'Backfin'
An unknown experimental

With the end of the Cold War, details of contemporary Russian military aircraft have become widely available. Details of historic aircraft remain more deeply hidden, and archives are only now beginning to yield up their treasures.

In June 1956 a top-level delegation of Western aviation leaders, headed by General Nathan F. Twining, USAF Chief of Staff, walked past a marvellous collection of previously unseen Soviet prototypes and production aircraft lined up at Kubinka airfield, Moscow. One might have expected a detailed appraisal to have appeared of each type seen. Any schoolboy enthusiast could have done as much. No such analysis ever appeared, and all that was published in the West was a mere list, and even this was full of mistakes.

One of these hitherto unknown types was an impressive supersonic bomber, which the Allied Standards Co-ordinating Committee decided to call 'Backfin'. It was at first said to be the Ilyushin 140, but this was later 'corrected' to Yak-42. In fact, it was the Tupolev 98, developed by the OKB (experimental construction bureau) led by Andrei N. Tupolev. It has taken nearly 40 years for the West to learn any more about this elusive aircraft. Even now there is argument over whether a second prototype was ever completed.

The requirement for the aircraft was issued by the VVS (Soviet air force) at the end of 1952, shortly before Stalin's death. Partly because it had learned of the project to build the Convair XB-58 supersonic bomber, the demand was for a bomber to carry a bombload of at least 4000 kg (8,820 lb) over an operating radius of at least 1500 km (930 miles) and to be able to accelerate to supersonic speed over the target area. In 1952, this was a considerable challenge.

Two submissions were accepted, both based on Arkhip M. Lyul'ka's large turbojet which, in 1952, was designated TR-7 and which was later redesignated AL-7 in its designer's honour. The Ilyushin Il-54 used two of these engines slung under swept wings. The Tu-98 was larger and heavier, and used two of the more powerful afterburning AL-7F engines inside the rear fuselage. Like the rival Ilyushin aircraft, the bomber required solutions to many new problems although the design was largely conventional and based on previous Tupolev practice.

Design solutions

For example, the wing had a profile in the SR-12s series, but a thickness/chord ratio of only 7 per cent at the root and 6 per cent at the tip. In turn, this meant that the wing skins had to be extremely thick in order to achieve the necessary strength and torsional rigidity. The latter factor was a challenge, because sweep on the leading edge was no less than 58° yet the powered tabbed ailerons were mounted outboard, where their effect was considerable. On each wing a full-chord fence separated the aileron from the huge one-piece slotted flap, which could be lowered hydraulically to 55° for landing. Static anhedral was -5°.

The fuselage was waisted according to the Area Rule, with two fixed oval inlets standing well away on each side at the top of the forward fuselage and leading to ducts which swept inwards across the wing. Ahead of the inlets was the pressure cabin for the crew, the navigator/bomb-aimer occupying the conical glazed nose, with an OPB-11 sight linked to the *Initsiativa* (initiative) radar. Behind him were the pilot and radio-operator/gunner. All three crew

A Mikoyan MiG-21 lends scale to the Tu-98 in this rare airborne view of the unusual bomber prototype. The two aircraft represented a triumph for Soviet aerodynamacists.

were on the centreline in forward-facing KT-1 seats arranged to eject upwards. Under the floor were the radar in a low-drag blister, the hydraulically-steered nosegear with two 660 x 200-mm tyres and, on the right, a fixed AM-23 cannon. Immediately behind the flat vertical pressure bulkhead was a camera bay, behind which was the No. 1 fuel cell.

A structural break then led to the main section of fuselage. At the extreme front was the wing, at mid level, housing integral fuel tanks No. 2 left and right. Above were the air ducts, and under the wing fuselage tanks 3 and 4. Behind the rear spar the space under the ducts was occupied by the 3.68-m (12 ft 1 in) bomb bay, housing a thermonuclear bomb or four FAB-1000 bombs weighing 1000 kg (2,205 lb) each.

Landing gear

Next, under the front of the down-sloping engines, was the bay housing the retracted main landing gears, each with four disc-braked wheels carrying 900 x 275-mm tyres. Behind this bay was No. 5 fuel cell, completing the fuel system at 23500 litres (5,169 Imp gal), or about 19500 kg (43,000 lb). At the extreme rear, separated from the afterburners by a fireproof insulated plate, were the fully powered horizontal tailplanes, which featured tabbed elevators to increase camber. Their span was 7.7 m (25 ft 3 in) and the leading-edge sweep was again 58X. The large fin, also swept at 58X, carried a powered tabbed rudder, a pitot tube and, at the top, an *Argon* aft-facing radar to direct the fire of the remotely sighted defensive barbette with twin AM-23 guns fed by magazines filling the fairing ahead.

Hydraulic systems powered the flight controls, flaps, landing gear, bomb doors and the doors under the rear fuselage for the twin braking parachutes. Attachments were provided for assisted take-off rockets, but there were no airbrakes or flight-refuelling probe. Although the wheelbase was 10.9 m (35 ft 9 in) and the maximum permissible ground angle was 11°30', the track between the bogie centres was only 2.5 m (98 in).

The prototype made its first flight in the summer of 1955. The pilot was Valentin F. Kovalyov, shortly to be transferred to the Tu-104. He was accompanied by navigator/engineer K. l. Malthasyan, who had come from the Tu-91 turboprop attack aircraft. They found the Tu-98 to be a superb aircraft to fly, apart from the narrow-track landing gear, but the fuel consumption in afterburner reduced the radius of action drastically.

OKB testing was completed in 1955, without serious incident. The Tu-98 would then normally have proceeded to NII-VVS (air force state scientific test institute) testing, but in 1956 it

Below and right: The Tu-98 prototype was rebuilt to serve as a development aircraft for the Tu-128 interceptor programme. It almost certainly ended its days after this landing accident, and few photos of the Tu-98 in interceptor configuration have ever been seen.

was one of several programmes abruptly terminated by N. S. Khruschchev. It was following the cancellation that this aircraft was shown to the Western delegation.

That appeared to be the end of the story, although it was known that two Tu-98 prototypes had been ordered. In the spring of 1995, photographs emerged showing a considerably modified Tu-98 sitting forlornly on its belly, at the LII (Flight Research and Test Institute) airfield at Zhukhovskii. The obvious conclusion was that this was the No. 2 prototype, but Tupolev archivist V. Rigmant insists that the second Tu-98 was never completed.

Documentary evidence is lacking, but it seems that the former bomber was converted into a flying testbed to support the Tu-28-80/Tu-128 interceptor programme. This huge interceptor was very similar in size and power to the Tu-98, but much faster. It was designed around an integrated radar/missile system called *Kompleks-80*, and this was first flown in the rebuilt Tu-98.

The small glazed nosecone was replaced by a radome covering the huge RP-5 radar developed by the F. F. Volkov KB as part of the *Smerch* (Whirlwind) fire-control system. Pylons were added under the wings to carry the awesome K-80 air-to-air missiles which formed the weapon part of the '80' system. Two versions of this missile were developed by the Biesnovat

KB to be carried by the Tu-128, with service designation of R-4R (radar) and R-4T (infra-red), and the NATO reporting name of 'Ash'.

The crew of two sat in modified cockpits having canopies similar to those of the Tu-128. All guns were removed, the vertical tail was replaced by a new fin of greater height and sweepback, with the thickened root faired off to a rear knife-edge and the *Argon* radar replaced by a flat dielectric antenna.

Photos of the reconfigured Tu-98 show it after a landing accident. The aircraft might have made a very heavy landing or it may have proved impossible to extend the landing gear, although a belly landing would probably not have caused such severe damage to the left main-gear doors and left wingtip. The flaps can be seen to be fully down, with the tailplanes at maximum negative angle and the roof hatches closed.

We do not yet know the cause of the accident, nor whether the Tu-98 was repaired. It has not appeared in the big outdoor park at Monino VVS Museum. Meanwhile, observer Malthasyan teamed up with Mikhail V. Koziov to test the Tu-128 interceptor, the 28-80 prototype of which at last flew on 18 March 1961. Designed for Dobrynin VD-19 engines, it had to be urgently redesigned to have the old AL-7F, the same engines as the Tu-98.

Phoenix Twice Risen

With its roots in the 'Flying Circus' of World War I, the Jagdgeschwader Richthofen is arguably the most famous fighter unit of all time. It is currently in its third incarnation as a stalwart of NATO airpower, having compiled an enviable combat record in two World Wars, chiefly against the well-trained and well-equipped Royal Air Force.

In 1911 Manfred, Freiherr von Richthofen joined the 1st Uhlan Regiment, a cavalry reconnaissance unit. Granted a lieutenancy in 1912, Manfred fought on both Western and Russian fronts in the early part of World War I before joining the Air Service in May 1915 as an observer. He scored one uncredited kill from the rear cockpit of an Albatros. A chance meeting on a train with Oswald Boelcke fired Manfred with new ambition, and in late 1915 he learned to fly. Initially flying Albatros two-seaters (in which he shot down a Nieuport, again without credit), von Richthofen was then sent to the Russian front, where he was subsequently hand-picked by Boelcke to join him in Jasta 2, a new élite fighter unit on the Western Front. Under Boelcke's tutelage, von Richthofen soon showed his potential, scoring his first kill on 17 September 1916 over an F.E.2. His first 16 kills were scored in the Albatros D II, and the photograph at left shows Manfred (with binoculars) standing in front of this successful fighter with other Jasta 2 pilots, including Leutnant Hans Immelmann (centre left). In late January 1917, von Richthofen adopted the D III, and at the same time assumed command of Jasta 11. For a while in February he flew a Halberstadt D II, but returned to the Albatros D III shortly after, moving on to the D V in June.

Ground crew relax in front of a Bf 109E-1 of 8./JG 2 in late May 1940 at an advanced airfield in France. All three Gruppen of JG 2 accompanied the lightning move through France, scoring some 235 kills by the time the campaign ended in mid-June.

Today's proud upholders of the Richthofen tradition are JG 71, whose two squadrons (711 and 712) fly F-4Fs from Wittmund. This aircraft commemorated the 25th anniversary of JG 71.

April 1917 – 'Bloody April' – saw Imperial Germany's Army Air Service, the Luftstreikräfte, in virtual control of the skies along the Western Front. In those 30 terrible days the RFC (Royal Flying Corps) alone lost 140 machines, and over 300 pilots and observers. But aerial supremacy, once attained, has to be retained; and this can often prove to be the harder of the two. Just as the advent of the D.H.2 and the Nieuport 17 had written *finis* to the 'Fokker scourge' some 12 months earlier, so a new generation of Allied scouts, including the S.E.5 and the Sopwith Triplane, was even now beginning to show signs of wresting the initiative from the Luftstreikräfte's Albatros D IIIs.

With little on the stocks from its own manufacturers (other than an improved, reworked Albatros scheduled to enter service the following month) with which to counter this latest threat, a hitherto surprisingly complacent Idflieg (Inspectorate of Flying Troops) had suddenly to seek other remedies in order to maintain its fighters' hard-won ascendancy. One immediate solution presented itself. The Luftstreikräfte had recently completed a major expansion programme which, since the end of the previous year, had seen the number of its single-seat fighter squadrons (Jagdstaffeln; more commonly abbreviated to Jastas) rise from nine to 37. Before the end of April four of these Jastas (Nos 3, 4, 11 and 33) were flying together as a group in an attempt to ensure local air superiority over enemy fighter patrols. Despite an early encounter with the RFC, which resulted in almost equal losses to both sides, the experiment was deemed sufficiently successful to justify the permanent amalgamation of four such squadrons into the world's first fighter wing, or Jagdgeschwader.

Official activation took place amid a flurry of telegrams during the last week of June 1917. On 24 June Crown Prince Rupprecht, Army Group Commander, ordered that Jastas 4, 6, 10 and 11 were to be established in the area of the 4th Army, with immediate effect, as Jagdgeschwader Nr. 1 (JG 1). The following day a signal from the Commanding General of the Air Service (Kogenluft) appointed Rittmeister Manfred, Freiherr von Richthofen, currently the Staffelführer of Jasta 11, as Kommandeur of JG 1. Finally, on 26 June, a second telegram from Kogenluft formally defined the new unit's role with the following words: "Jagdgeschwader Nr. 1 to comprise Jastas 4, 6, 10 and 11 (stop) The Geschwader is a self-contained unit (stop) Its function is to achieve and ensure aerial supremacy on decisive sectors of the front (end)."

The 25-year-old officer selected to command

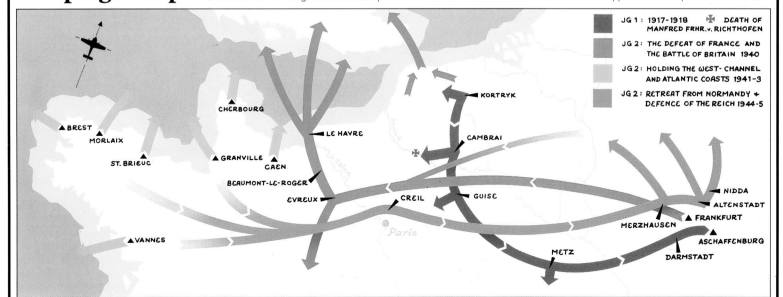

JG 1 and JG 2 campaign map

During both World Wars, the Richthofen Geschwader fought most of its battles in northern France, and for the most part its chief opponents were the RAF and its predecessors, now staunch allies within the NATO framework. In 1940 the Geschwader swept into France with the victorious German army, and remained there until D-day. Along with JG 26, the Geschwader held up the RAF until the overwhelming force of Allied operations forced them back to defend the Reich. II. Gruppe also had a spell in North Africa.

JG 1 : 1917-1918 ✠ DEATH OF MANFRED FRHR. v. RICHTHOFEN

JG 2 : THE DEFEAT OF FRANCE AND THE BATTLE OF BRITAIN 1940

JG 2 : HOLDING THE WEST-CHANNEL AND ATLANTIC COASTS 1941-3

JG 2 : RETREAT FROM NORMANDY & DEFENCE OF THE REICH 1944-5

BREST
MORLAIX
ST. BRIEUC
CHERBOURG
LE HAVRE
GRANVILLE
CAEN
BEAUMONT-LE-ROGER
EVREUX
VANNES
CREIL
Paris
GUISE
KORTRYK
CAMBRAI
METZ
NIDDA
ALTENSTADT
FRANKFURT
MERZHAUSEN
ASCHAFFENBURG
DARMSTADT

Above: Manfred converses with Leutnant Kurt Wolff, one of his key officers in JG 1. Wolff flew with von Richthofen in Jasta 11, and took over the squadron when the Rittmeister was elevated to command JG 1. On 15 September 1917, three days after having been promoted to Oberleutnant, Wolff was killed while flying von Richthofen's first Fokker Triplane (F I 102/17), shot down by a No. 10 (Naval) Squadron Sopwith Camel. He had 33 victories to his name.

Lined up at Douai, the Albatros D IIIs of Jasta 11 display a wide variety of colour schemes. The second aircraft in the line is Manfred's all-red aircraft, known to the RFC as le petit rouge. Von Richthofen was probably the first German pilot to introduce individual colours, a practice which spread rapidly. The plethora of colours in Jasta 11 led to the RFC nickname of 'Flying Circus'.

Right: A group of Jasta 11 pilots with Manfred in the Albatros cockpit and his brother, Lothar, seated cross-legged. Lothar joined Manfred in March 1917, and amassed 40 victories. Among his official credits was the S.E.5 of Captain Albert Ball, No. 56 Sqn, RFC, Britain's most famous fighter pilot of the time. However, the exact nature of Ball's last fight is open to question.

JG 1 had begun his military career as a lancer with the 1st Regiment of Uhlans 'Kaiser Alexander III' in 1911; hence his rank, in June 1917, of Rittmeister (Cavalry Captain) rather than the Air Service's more usual Hauptmann. He had transferred to the air arm in May 1915. In January 1917, with 16 victories to his credit and newly decorated with the coveted *Pour le Mérite*, he was promoted to Staffelführer of Jasta 11. In just five months, under his expert leadership and tutelage, Jasta 11 – which had yet to score a single victory at the time of his arrival – rose to become the most successful squadron on the Western Front; in the process the Rittmeister added a further 38 to his own tally of enemy aircraft destroyed.

By 2 July 1917, JG 1's component Staffeln had taken up residence on their assigned bases around the Flanders town of Courtrai (Kortryk) on the Ypres front: von Richthofen's wing HQ and Jasta 11 (Leutnant Kurt Wolff) at Marcke, Jasta 4 (Oberleutnant Kurt von Doering) at Cuene, Jasta 6 (Oberleutnant Eduard Ritter von Dostler) at Bisseghem, and Jasta 10 (Oberleutnant Ernst, Freiherr von Althaus) at Heule.

Despite their intended mobility – implied in the closing sentence of the 26 June signal from Kogenluft, and evidenced by their generous establishment of motorised transport and tented accommodation and hangarage – the situation on the ground, with Britain's 1917 Flanders offensive (the Third Battle of Ypres) lasting from July right through to November, dictated that JG 1 were to spend the first five months of their existence of Kortryk. They quickly began to make their presence felt. Each Jasta had

brought with it to the Geschwader its own particular colour scheme; Jasta 11's was predominantly red, whereas Jasta 10 favoured yellow, and Jastas 4 and 6 wore black and white spirals and geometrics. These schemes, combined with a growing predilection on the part of the pilots to sport colourful personal markings on their machines, soon led to the formation becoming known as 'von Richthofen's Flying Circus'. Considering the amount of time the unit spent under canvas when on the ground, the description was not altogether inapposite.

JG 1's first success

The first victory credited to the Geschwader was an observation balloon destroyed by Jasta 6's Oberleutnant von Dostler north of Ypres on 5 July 1917. In those days of wireless infancy such balloons, the 'eyes' of a ground army, played a vital role in battlefield intelligence gathering. Their positions were often ringed by heavy anti-aircraft defences, and their destruction – no easy task – ranked on a par with that of an enemy aircraft.

On the following day, however, the Kommandeur himself was to suffer a serious head wound. A single round from a burst loosed off at extreme 275-m (900-ft) range by an observer of a No. 20 Sqn F.E.2d creased von Richthofen's skull. Regaining consciousness to find himself in a vertical dive scarcely more than 150 m (492 ft) above the ground, he nevertheless managed to crash-land his Albatros D V near Wervik (Wervicq) on the Franco-Belgian border. He would be out of the battle for the next six weeks.

This aircraft was the second production Fokker F I (later Dr I), and was the first machine assigned to von Richthofen. In it he scored his 60th kill – and Wolff subsequently met his end.

Stung by this blow, JG 1 claimed nine Allied aircraft destroyed on 7 July. This was also the date on which a 19-year-old Leutnant named Carl-August von Schoenebeck was posted to Jasta 11 from Fliegerabteilung (A) 203, a 1st Army artillery co-operation unit. Although overshadowed by higher-scoring contempo-

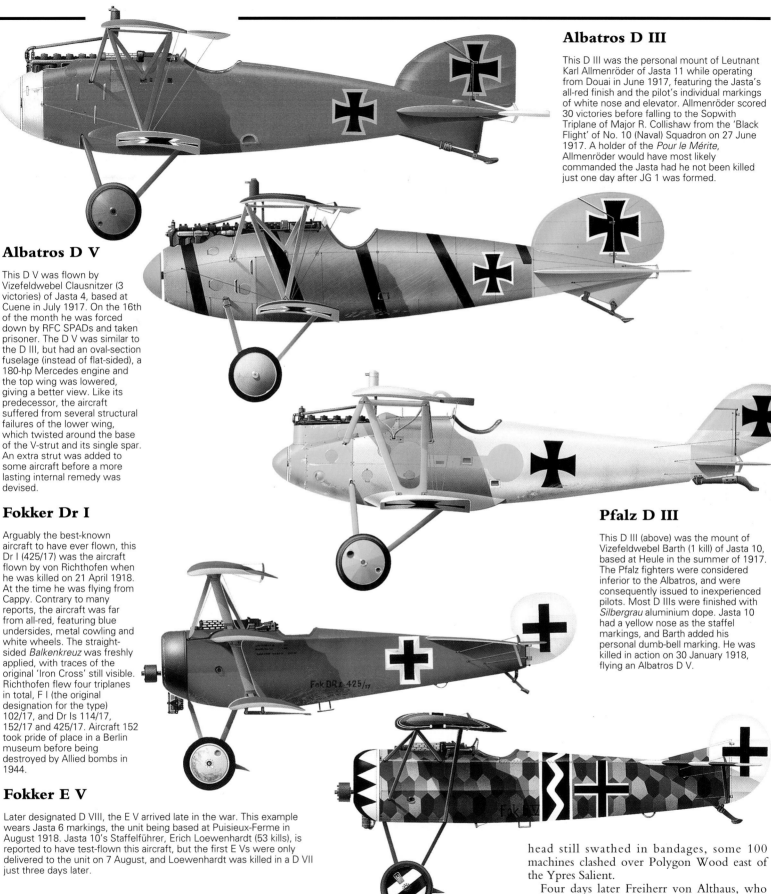

Albatros D III

This D III was the personal mount of Leutnant Karl Allmenröder of Jasta 11 while operating from Douai in June 1917, featuring the Jasta's all-red finish and the pilot's individual markings of white nose and elevator. Allmenröder scored 30 victories before falling to the Sopwith Triplane of Major R. Collishaw from the 'Black Flight' of No. 10 (Naval) Squadron on 27 June 1917. A holder of the *Pour le Mérite*, Allmenröder would have most likely commanded the Jasta had he not been killed just one day after JG 1 was formed.

Albatros D V

This D V was flown by Vizefeldwebel Clausnitzer (3 victories) of Jasta 4, based at Cuene in July 1917. On the 16th of the month he was forced down by RFC SPADs and taken prisoner. The D V was similar to the D III, but had an oval-section fuselage (instead of flat-sided), a 180-hp Mercedes engine and the top wing was lowered, giving a better view. Like its predecessor, the aircraft suffered from several structural failures of the lower wing, which twisted around the base of the V-strut and its single spar. An extra strut was added to some aircraft before a more lasting internal remedy was devised.

Fokker Dr I

Arguably the best-known aircraft to have ever flown, this Dr I (425/17) was the aircraft flown by von Richthofen when he was killed on 21 April 1918. At the time he was flying from Cappy. Contrary to many reports, the aircraft was far from all-red, featuring blue undersides, metal cowling and white wheels. The straight-sided *Balkenkreuz* was freshly applied, with traces of the original 'Iron Cross' still visible. Richthofen flew four triplanes in total, F I (the original designation for the type) 102/17, and Dr Is 114/17, 152/17 and 425/17. Aircraft 152 took pride of place in a Berlin museum before being destroyed by Allied bombs in 1944.

Pfalz D III

This D III (above) was the mount of Vizefeldwebel Barth (1 kill) of Jasta 10, based at Heule in the summer of 1917. The Pfalz fighters were considered inferior to the Albatros, and were consequently issued to inexperienced pilots. Most D IIIs were finished with *Silbergrau* aluminium dope. Jasta 10 had a yellow nose as the staffel markings, and Barth added his personal dumb-bell marking. He was killed in action on 30 January 1918, flying an Albatros D V.

Fokker E V

Later designated D VIII, the E V arrived late in the war. This example wears Jasta 6 markings, the unit being based at Puisieux-Ferme in August 1918. Jasta 10's Staffelführer, Erich Loewenhardt (53 kills), is reported to have test-flown this aircraft, but the first E Vs were only delivered to the unit on 7 August, and Loewenhardt was killed in a D VII just three days later.

raries during his seven months' service with the Staffel, the young von Schoenebeck was to play a unique part in the history of JG 1.

Meanwhile, the RFC was fighting back, not only in the air but on the ground. On 11 July the Geschwader suffered the first of a series of bombing raids when Bisseghem was attacked and three of Jasta 6's tented hangars were destroyed. In the air, JG 1's new Albatros D V was not delivering the decisive supremacy

expected of it; worse, it was found to retain the suspect lower wing of the earlier D III models. Accidents continued to occur, and soon pilots were being advised not to dive too steeply. Hardly an encouraging caveat just as the dogfighting was beginning to increase in frequency and ferocity. On 26 July, for example, the day von Richthofen returned from hospital with his

head still swathed in bandages, some 100 machines clashed over Polygon Wood east of the Ypres Salient.

Four days later Freiherr von Althaus, who had been in action since the outbreak of war and whose eyesight was now failing, left to take up a training post. The man von Richthofen requested as his replacement at the head of Jasta 10 was Leutnant Werner Voss, arguably an even greater 'natural' in the art of aerial combat than the Kommandeur himself. The two had served together in the Jasta Boelcke the previous winter. Now, into their hands was about to be placed the one fighting machine which, above

Jagdgeschwader 'Richthofen'

General Ludendorff, chief architect of the German military campaign, visited Courtrai on 18 August 1917 to review Jagdgeschwader 1. Here von Richthofen presents Jasta 11 to the general, with an Albatros D V in the background.

all others, will forever be associated with the name of von Richthofen.

Fokker's Dr I resulted directly from the Sopwith Triplane. In April 1917 the Dutch manufacturer had visited Jasta 11 at the front, where he had been shown a captured specimen of the British machine and had been regaled with the account of a single Sopwith attacking, and outmanoeuvring, 11 of the Staffel's Albatros D IIIs. Fokker returned to his Schwerin factory and briefed chief designer Reinhold Platz on what he had seen and heard. Within weeks three F I prototype triplanes had been completed. The first was tested to destruction at Adlershof. The other two, Nos 102/17 and 103/17, were delivered to JG 1 at Courtrai on 21 August. Their success was short-lived but spectacular.

Von Richthofen first flew 102/17 on 1 September, scoring his 60th kill: an R.E.8 over Zonnebeke. Shortly, thereafter, the

Kommandeur departed on belated convalescent leave, and several other pilots flew this machine before Oberleutnant Kurt Wolff, Staffelführer of Jasta 11, was killed in it on 15 September. In the meantime, Voss had virtually appropriated 103/17 as his own personal mount. It was he who had scored the triplane's first success, downing a British machine on 30 August.

Voss meets Fifty-six

Over the next three weeks Voss gained a further 20 victories, bringing his final score to 48, before meeting his death on 23 September. In what has been described as *the* epic dogfight of World War I, the silver-blue triplane, with the distinctive white face painted on the front of its black cowling, was engaged by seven S.E.5as of No. 56 Squadron led by Captain James McCudden. For 10 minutes hunters and hunted gyrated wildly about the sky before the guns of Lieutenant Rhys-Davies brought to an end the life and career of Voss, the 'Flying Hussar'.

The Geschwader had thus lost two Staffelführer in the space of eight days. Their places were taken by Leutnant Hans Klein (Jasta 10) and Leutnant Lothar, Freiherr von

Richthofen (Jasta 11). Lothar, the Kommandeur's younger brother, was returning to the front after recovering from wounds received six months earlier.

In mid-October the first six production Fokker Dr Is arrived at JG 1; before the month was out two fatal crashes, caused by faulty workmanship in the wings, led to the immediate grounding of the remainder. The restriction would not be lifted until the end of November when the type, suitably modified, finally entered full-scale operational use. Meanwhile, JG 1 soldiered on with its Albatros D Vs and the newly delivered Pfalz D III. The latter machine, a Bavarian design not altogether suited to the air-to-air combat role, was used primarily by Jastas 4 and 10.

On 15 November Leutnant Hans Adam, who had assumed command of Jasta 6 after the death of Ritter von Dostler on 19 August, was himself killed in action. His place was taken by Oberleutnant Wilhelm Reinhard. By this time the Third Battle of Ypres had finally foundered to a halt in the mud of Passchendaele. But on 20 November fresh danger suddenly erupted as British tanks breached the Hindenburg line at Cambrai.

JG 1 was at last in a position to fulfil its intended function. Orders were immediately cut releasing it from the 4th Army for transfer south to the threatened sector. New airfields were assigned: HQ, Jastas 6 and 11 to Avesnes le Sec; Jastas 4 and 10 to Lieu St Amand and Iwuy respectively. But at this point the organisation broke down. The Geschwader was ready to go, but the fields were unprepared, lacking refuelling facilities, armouries and other necessities. While these shortcomings were being

The Rittmeister, with walking stick, stands in front of Jasta 11's Triplanes with Vizefeldwebel Scholz (7 victories – on left) and Leutnant Mohnicke (9 victories – in centre). Von Richthofen appreciated the Triplane's excellent agility, but he was not the adoring fan of the type which the popular press portrayed. The greatest exponent of the Dr I was Werner Voss, brought in by von Richthofen as commander of Jasta 10. He took the third production Triplane, F I 103/17, applied a bright blue scheme and painted a face on the cowling, and used it to rapidly score his final kills, bringing his total to 48. He fell on 23 September 1917, fighting one of the epic air battles of the war with no less than seven SE.5s from JG 1's main RFC rivals: No. 56 Squadron.

"Who killed the Red Baron?" – shown at right is Captain 'Roy' Brown's combat report of von Richthofen's final action (the abbreviation H.O.P. stands for high offensive patrol). Brown was credited by the RFC with the kill, but several Australian gunners had an equally strong claim to have fired the single fatal shot. Von Richthofen's place as JG 1 commander was taken by Hauptmann Wilhelm Reinhard (above), and the Geschwader continued to prosper despite the loss of their inspiration. Reinhard was killed on 3 July 1918, flying a new fighter type, the Zepp. (Lindau) D I, in trials at Adlershof.

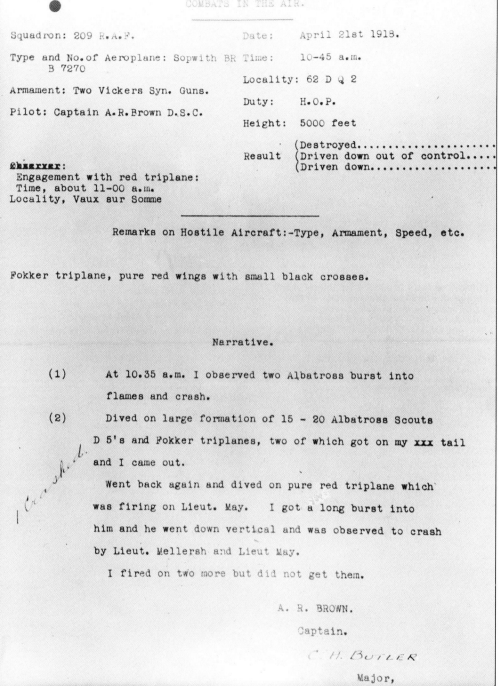

remedied the Geschwader was housed temporarily at Valenciennes, a training establishment some 32 km (20 miles) behind the front.

Thus, within 48 hours of the tanks' breakthrough, elements of JG 1 were in action on the Cambrai front. Reinforced by Jastas 5 and 15, the Geschwader became heavily embroiled over Bourlon Wood where German machine-gunners, who were holding up the British advance, were themselves under attack from ground-strafing aircraft of the RFC. The Kommandeur himself, flying an Albatros, claimed one such close-support D.H.5 shot down into the south-eastern corner of the wood on 23 November. A week later he was to add the first of only three S.E.5as to appear on his list of victories.

Lean times

With the British failing to consolidate their tanks' initial gains, the Battle of Cambrai petered out at the end of the first week in December. The resulting lull in ground activity was reflected in the air. Throughout that month JG 1 flew some 750 sorties for a grand total of just five kills. The opening weeks of 1918 remained equally quiet. The two von Richthofen brothers went on leave, and a combination of bad weather and an understrength pilot establishment kept Geschwader activities to a minimum. Their main task was a spate of balloon-busting, whose purpose was to screen from prying British eyes rear-area preparations for Germany's forthcoming great spring offensive. By mid-March these preparations were all but complete. On 12 March von Richthofen had claimed his first victory in almost three and a half months. Eight days later the Geschwader sent an advanced detachment to the airfield at

Awoingt, south-east of Cambrai.

At 0445 hours on 21 March the Germans attacked on a front 50 miles wide. Nearly one million men, supported by 82 squadrons of aircraft, advanced on either side of the Somme; their aim was to split the British and French armies and drive the former back to the coast. Mist and poor visibility hampered JG 1's part in this, the 'Kaiser's Battle', for the first three days. It was not until 24 March that they were able to mount over 100 sorties. And these netted only one victim: the second S.E.5a of the Kommandeur's career. The following day von Richthofen was again the only pilot to score, on this occasion downing a ground-strafing Camel.

On 27 March the Geschwader's tactics switched from the direct support of their own infantry to those of combatting the ground-attack units of the RFC. This was also the day

they moved forward to Lechelle, a field only recently evacuated by the reconnaissance R.E.8s of 15 Squadron, RFC. By this stage, however, the first phase of the German offensive was losing steam.

After only five days at Lechelle (during which time the RFC had metamorphosed into the RAF), JG 1 moved down to Harbonnières, south of the Somme, on 2 April. Six days later, during a prolonged spell of bad weather, they transferred to Cappy, a village on the Somme some 20 km (12 miles) downstream from Peronne. From here von Richthofen daily awaited the summons which would direct the Geschwader northwards in support of the second phase of the German offensive along the Lys river west of Lille. But the expected call did not come. Instead, an easing of the weather permitted limited operations out of Cappy, and on the evening of 20 April – after a showery

Jagdgeschwader 'Richthofen'

Leutnant Ernst Udet joined JG 1 in March 1917 at von Richthofen's behest, and rapidly became a star pupil. This was his personal D VII, painted in red and marked with the monogram 'Lo!' in honour of his fiancée. He acted as Geschwader commander for just one day when Reinhard left for Adlershof, before being replaced by Loewenhardt, and later took brief command in August 1918 when Göring was away. Udet ended the war with 62 victories as Germany's second-ranking ace, and later became the head of the RLM's technical section. He took his own life in June 1941, having been continually used as a scapegoat for Luftwaffe failures by his professed friend but devious rival Göring.

Members of Jasta 10 await a 'scramble' in full flying gear. The three pilots marked on the picture are, from left to right, Leutnants Grassmann (left – 10 kills) and Heldmann (15 kills), and Offizier Stellvertreter Aue(10 kills).

day – the Kommandeur claimed a brace of Camels from No. 3 Squadron, RAF. These, his 79th and 80th victories, were to be his last.

The Red Baron falls

21 April 1918 dawned cloudy, with a promise of clearance later. In mid-morning six machines took off, two of them piloted by von Richthofens: the Kommandeur in Fokker Dr.I no. 425/17, and his cousin Wolfram, whose first operational patrol this was to be. Only five returned. It fell to Vizefeldwebel Edgar Scholz to report the unthinkable: the Kommandeur had last been seen going down behind Allied lines.

It appears that von Richthofen had not heeded his own oft-quoted maxim "Do not become trapped low beyond enemy lines and fall prey to ground fire," for so intent had he been in chasing a No. 209 Squadron Camel flown by Second-Lt W.R. 'Wop' May – its guns jammed – at low level westwards along the Somme valley, that he failed to realise the danger he was himself getting into. He even chose to ignore, or was oblivious to, another No. 209 Camel on his tail for part of the way. The 5-km (3-mile) steeplechase at tree-top level along the floor of the Somme valley only ended as the two aircraft were forced to climb to clear the ridge west of Vaux. Their course took them over an

Australian field artillery battery whose gunners, having had a grandstand view of the machines' approach, directed a hail of machine-gun fire at the conspicuously marked triplane. It came down, its pilot dead – or dying – at the controls, near an abandoned brickworks on the crest of the ridge. Rittmeister Manfrèd, Freiherr von Richthofen was buried with full military honours at Bertangles cemetery the following afternoon. Controversy has surrounded his death to this day, for while modern research points to his indeed having fallen victim to Australian ground fire, many still believe the mortal blow was delivered by the Camel on his tail in its one diving pass midway through the chase. No. 209 Squadron, at least, were sufficiently convinced later to select 'a red eagle falling' as their official crest.

Back at Cappy, despite the profound shock at losing their leader, life perforce went on. Geschwader-Adjutant Oberleutnant Carl Bodenschatz opened the sealed envelope containing his Kommandeur's last will. On a single sheet of paper, dated 3 March 1918, was just one sentence, hurriedly scrawled in pencil: "Should I fail to return, Oblt. Reinhard (Jasta 6) to assume leadership of the Geschwader. Frhr. von Richthofen, Rittmeister." Even in death, von Richthofen's word was law, and on 23 April Reinhard duly took command of JG 1.

By mid-May the Geschwader had recovered its equilibrium. On 15 May JG 1 mounted 137 sorties, claiming 13 Allied aircraft destroyed without loss; one of their most active, and successful, days ever. On 20 May the Geschwader

finally departed Cappy (and the 2nd Army) for the Guise area in readiness for the 7th Army's imminent Aisne offensive. Prior to their departure a telegram had been received from General von Hoeppner, Commander of the Army Air Service, conferring upon them the honour title "Jagdgeschwader Frhr. von Richthofen Nr. 1".

It was during their first days at Guise that the Geschwader completed re-equipment, begun by Jasta 10 the previous month, with Fokker's latest, and perhaps best, design: the redoubtable D VII. Early on 27 May, the opening morning of the Aisne offensive, JG 1 gathered on their advanced landing-ground at Puisieux-Ferme, some 5 km (3 miles) north-east of Laon. Their opposition was now mainly French, and in the days that followed they exacted a steady toll of Aviation Militaire aircraft and balloons before moving forward to Beugneux-Cramaille on 1 June. However, this third major German offensive in as many months was destined to collapse in the face of stiffening French, and now also American, resistance along the Marne.

A second commander dies

Kommandeur Wilhelm Reinhard, promoted to Hauptmann, was ordered to Berlin-Adlershof on 18 June to participate in the second fighter competition (the first such gathering back in January, attended by the late von Richthofen, had resulted in the selection of the Fokker D VII then entering service in increasing numbers). One of the new prototypes now awaiting testing by experienced frontline fighter pilots was Dornier's advanced, and unorthodox, D-I. On 3 July the D-I was successfully flown by one Oberleutnant Hermann Göring, Staffelführer of Jasta 27. Next to take it up was Hauptmann Reinhard. After climbing steeply to 1000 m (3,280 ft), a strut suddenly snapped, the top wing collapsed and the machine crashed to the ground, fatally injuring Reinhard.

Despite a wealth of talent within the Geschwader – notably Leutnants Erich Loewenhardt and Ernst Udet, recently appointed Staffelführer of Jastas 10 and 4 respectively –

The Fokker E V (later known as the D VIII) arrived in August 1918, but was initially unpopular as its structural integrity was not trusted by the pilots following a series of crashes. The best known unit to receive the type was JG 1's Jasta 6, identified by the black and white markings on the cowling.

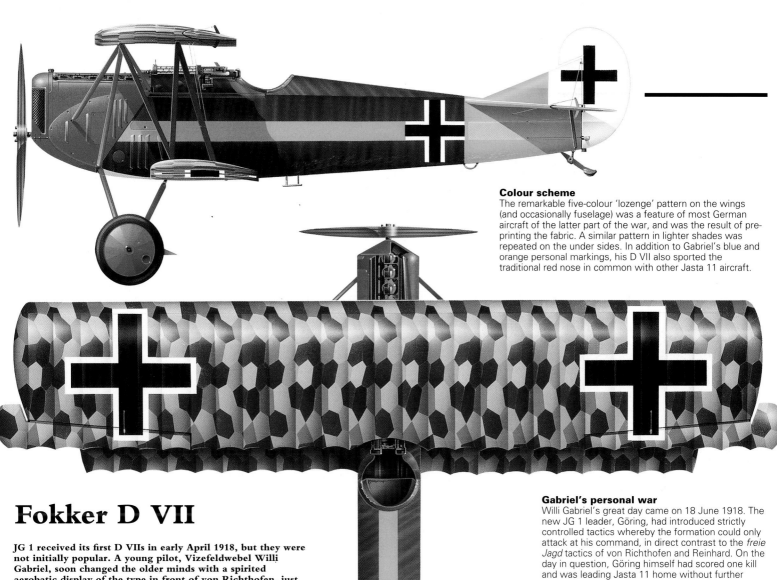

Colour scheme

The remarkable five-colour 'lozenge' pattern on the wings (and occasionally fuselage) was a feature of most German aircraft of the latter part of the war, and was the result of pre-printing the fabric. A similar pattern in lighter shades was repeated on the under sides. In addition to Gabriel's blue and orange personal markings, his D VII also sported the traditional red nose in common with other Jasta 11 aircraft.

Fokker D VII

JG 1 received its first D VIIs in early April 1918, but they were not initially popular. A young pilot, Vizefeldwebel Willi Gabriel, soon changed the older minds with a spirited aerobatic display of the type in front of von Richthofen, just days before the Rittmeister's death. His flamboyant style was matched by the gaudy tail surfaces carried by his personal aircraft, depicted here while based at Braisne in July 1918. The D VII lost some of the agility of the Dr I, but emerged as one of the best fighters of the war. One of its specialities, as demonstrated by Gabriel during his display in front of the Baron, was the *Kavalierstart*, whereby the aircraft took off steeply and hung from the propeller, slowly climbing. This climbing ability, matched to the good speed, adequate manoeuvrability and fine handling of the type, made the D VII a formidable foe, especially in the hands of the expert fighters concentrated in Jagdgeschwader 1.

Construction

The fuselage of the D VII was built of steel tube with internal wire bracing. The one-piece lower wing sat flush with the underside of the fuselage, necessitating a cut-out section in the lower longerons to accommodate the wing carry-through. The high-lift upper wing was attached with steel-tube interplane and centre-section struts, and had horn-balanced ailerons. Both wings had a strong two-spar structure. Further lift was gained from the small aerofoil section covering the mainwheel axle.

Gabriel's personal war

Willi Gabriel's great day came on 18 June 1918. The new JG 1 leader, Göring, had introduced strictly controlled tactics whereby the formation could only attack at his command, in direct contrast to the *freie Jagd* tactics of von Richthofen and Reinhard. On the day in question, Göring himself had scored one kill and was leading Jasta 11 home without further battle. As the aircraft began to land at Beugneux, Gabriel, incensed at these restricting tactics and reflecting the mood of the Geschwader as a whole, opened up the throttle and set off back for the front alone. To illustrate fortune favouring the brave, Gabriel became embroiled in a scrap with several French SPADs but emerged unscathed and with three of the aircraft to his credit. Upon landing a severe and public reprimand from Göring awaited him for his insubordination. That was not the end for Gabriel, for later in the day French Breguet 14s appeared over the airfield. Still smarting from his dressing-down, Gabriel jumped into his D VII and rapidly climbed after the Breguets. After three firing attempts, one fell to his guns, the first time a JG 1 member had scored four kills in one day. This time Göring met him with just a cold order to never again start without a direct command. While he could not further discipline a senior NCO without recourse to a higher command (who would find it difficult to punish a man for scoring four victories!), Göring arranged the ignominy of a transfer to a maintenance aircraft park, so robbing the Geschwader of one of its brightest young hopes, who had amassed 11 kills at the time of his posting.

Powerplant and fuel

The D VII was initially produced with the Mercedes D IIIa engine uprated to 170 hp (127-kW) output. Later aircraft appeared with a 185-hp (138-kW) BMW III engine. Aircraft powered by the latter had considerably better performance, notably in the climb. The fuel tank behind the engine held 20 gallons (91 litres) which, with the 4-gallon (18-litre) oil tank gave an endurance of about 105 minutes.

Cockpit and armament

The D VII pilot had a standard stick control, incorporating a firing button and an auxiliary throttle. The main throttle was located on his port side. Ahead of him were the two 7.92-mm (0.31-in) Maxim LMG 08/15 machine-guns, belt fed from two 500-round ammunition tanks situated between the cockpit dash and the fuel tank.

Jagdgeschwader 'Richthofen'

the officer selected to become JG 1's third and final Kommandeur was the same Oberleutnant Göring who had so narrowly escaped Reinhard's fate in the Adlershof competition. Assuming command on 14 July, Göring proved to be the archetypal new broom. In front of a formal assembly of his pilots, the new Kommandeur expounded his views: no more 'free-for-all' *freie Jagd* operations as had been their wont to date. In future *he* would lead and control in the air as well as on the ground. In short, the Kommandeur would tell the Geschwader where, when and what to engage. Four days later he had the opportunity so to do when he first led Jasta 11 into an attack on an escadrille of French Spads. Well in the van, Göring claimed one unsuspecting victim, but effectively scattered the others before the rest of the Jasta – trailing behind in faithful attendance – could get into firing position. The new regime was not to everybody's liking. Vizefeldwebel Willi Gabriel achieved notoriety, and the unspoken admiration and sympathy of the rest of the Geschwader, by defying Göring's orders and scoring four kills during two unsanctioned *freie Jagd* escapades which earned him a severe reprimand from the Kommandeur and a posting to a rear-echelon disposal unit.

Allied counter-attack

18 July, the day of Gabriel's 'insubordination', saw the launching of the Allied Aisne-Marne counter-attack. This soon led to JG 1 abandoning Beugneux and retiring to two fields near Monthussart-Ferme: Braisne (Jastas 4, 10 and 11) and Courcelles (Jasta 6). It was on 25 July that Lothar von Richthofen scored his first victory since his return to the front after being wounded a second time on 13 March. This kill was also the Geschwader's 500th victory since its formation.

By this time, however, Allied counter-offen-sives were gaining momentum. On 29 July JG 1 fell back again, to Puisieux-Ferme. On 8 August it was the British turn to attack; their storming of Amiens became known as the 'Black Day of the German Army'. All along the front German forces were in retreat. On 9 August the Geschwader was sent up to defend the Somme bridges, the troops' main routes of escape, only to suffer heavily in the process. The following day they moved to Ennemain in the 2nd Army area. Forty-eight hours later they were ordered to transfer to Bernes.

On 13 August Lothar von Richthofen was wounded for a third time. His was far from being the only loss sustained during the bitter fighting taking place between the frequent moves of recent days and, with a shortage of replacement pilots, the Geschwader now found itself down to one-quarter of its strength, or that of a single Jasta.

One slight ray of hope had been the arrival at Jasta 6, on 7 August, of half-a-dozen of Fokker's brand-new E V cantilever monoplanes. This hope was quickly dashed. By the end of the month three mid-air wing failures, all with fatal results, pointed to a repetition of the Dr I's poor workmanship and material problems. This time, in fact, there was even talk of criminal proceedings being instituted against Fokker. But once again the shortcomings were resolved and production was resumed in late September, with the first modified examples,

With a cavalcade of ciné photographers following, Hitler reviews JG 132's Heinkel He 51s at Döberitz. Like the Arados, the He 51s initially wore civilian registrations.

**Both Gruppen of JG 132 received He 51s in 1935.
I. Gruppe (right) remained at Döberitz while
II. Gruppe flew from Jüterbog-Damm (initially as
the Fliegergruppe Damm). I. Gruppe aircraft
carried individual names just above the
undercarriage strut.**

redesignated as the D VIII, arriving at the front on 24 October.

In the interim, JG 1 had continued its nomadic existence, moving to Busigny (Wing HQ , Jastas 6 and 11) and Escaufort (Jastas 4 and 10) at the end of August, and thence to Metz on 25 September, this latter move in response to the US Army's St Mihiel offensive. On 9 October another move took them to Marville. The following day they mounted 69 sorties, no mean achievement under the prevailing conditions. One formation of some 10 Fokker D VIIs clashed with three times that number of Spad S.13s of the American 1st Pursuit Group, led by Captain 'Eddie' V. Rickenbacker, which was out on a balloon-busting mission. Although assisted by the arrival of another German group, JG 1's pilots were nonetheless lucky to escape with only one aircraft shot down.

Now, with fuel and rations short, with spares becoming ever more difficult to obtain and with the Americans advancing on Marville, JG 1's fortunes were at a very low ebb. The first week of November brought a final flurry of action. On 3 Nobember they scored eight victories on the wounding of Leutnant Heinrich Maushake, Jasta 4's Staffelführer of just one week's standing. Forty-eight hours later JG 1 suffered their last casualty of the war with the loss of Leutnant Kirst of Jasta 10. That day was also marked by the eighth and final victory of Leutnant Wolfram von Richthofan.

On 6 November the Geschwader fought its last engagement, against a formation of Spads, claiming three without loss. Landing back at Marville, they were ordered to retire immediately to Tellancourt. It was here that they first learned of the civil and military unrest raging in the Fatherland. Two days later came the order to demobilise. Rather than hand over their aircraft to an American receiving unit as instructed, Göring resolved to lead the Geschwader back to Germany. On 12 November they took off for Darmstadt, where they found a soldiers' council in control of the field. The revolutionaries proceeded to impound the aircraft as they landed, until an enraged Göring delivered his ultimatum – release the confiscated machines at once, or he would give the signal for the remainder to attack. His fighters were returned forthwith.

Having escaped the Americans, Göring was now ordered to lead the Geschwader to Aschaffenburg for surrender to a French com- mission. This he proceeded to do, first taking care to assure his pilots that no-one would be reprimanded for a heavy landing. The resulting controlled crashes as the Geschwader arrived at Aschaffenburg left the French with little to do other than pick up the pieces.

So ended the "Jagdgeschwader Frhr. von Richthofen Nr. 1". In its 17-month lifespan the wing had amassed 644 aerial victories since Ritter von Dostler's luckless balloon went down near Ypres on 5 July 1917. The price it had paid was 56 pilots killed and 52 wounded.

Once risen

Despite the turmoil of post-Versailles Germany, Lothar von Richthofen managed to get back into aviation, only to die in an air crash at Hamburg-Fuhlsbüttel on 4 July 1922. It therefore fell to the youngest of the three von Richthofen brothers, Bolko – Manfred's junior by 11 years – to negotiate for the return of his brother's body. The Rittmeister's remains had been re-interred in Fricourt military cemetery shortly after the Armistice. And it was from here that the body was borne back to Germany for re-burial in Berlin's Invaliden cemetery in November 1925.

Meanwhile the last Kommandeur of JG 1 had discovered politics. Two years earlier, on 9 November 1923, Hermann Göring had marched shoulder-to-shoulder with his leader and mentor, Adolf Hitler, in the abortive Munich putsch. And although this first bungled attempt to seize parlimentary control came to naught, others were already at work circumventing the severe conditions imposed on German aviation in the Treaty of Versailles.

Thinly-camouflaged 'civil' flying schools were already in existence by the mid-1920s, and by the end of 1930 the first three military aviation units proper had been established. These were disguised to the outside world as Reklamestaffeln (advertising squadrons), a name chosen deliberately to imply their being used for commerical aerial-advertising purposes. And it was the central German squadron, based at Berlin-Staaken, which provided the nucleus for the Reichswehr's first covert Jagdgruppe, which was to be set up at nearby Döberitz-Elsgrund. In the event, formal – albeit still clandestine – activation did not take place until 1 April 1934.

The officer chosen to command the Gruppe was 41-year-old Major Robert Ritter von Greim, holder of the *Pour le Mérite* and World War I Staffelführer of Jasta 34. Initially, the new unit's complement of a dozen civil-registered Arado Ar 65s preserved some semblance of secrecy by operating under the title of Fliegergruppe Döberitz. This method of designation, simply specifying the home base and thus affording no clue as to a Gruppe's function or its position within the Luftwaffe organisation as a whole, would remain in force until June 1936.

Rebirth of the Geschwader

On 26 February 1935 Hitler and Göring, by now firmly ensconced in power, signed the Reichsluftwaffe decree. This officially proclaimed the Luftwaffe (although the term 'Reichsluftwaffe' was strictly more accurate, it never found public favour) as a third, separate arm of the Wehrmacht. Just over a fortnight later, on 14 March, an emotional Führer christened the Luftwaffe's one and only Jagdgruppe as the new Jagdeschwader Richthofen: "I announce this edict secure in the knowledge and belief that the Jagdgeschwader Richthofen – imbued with the lofty ideals of the honour and tradition hereby accorded – will prove itself forever equal, both in spirit and performance, to its holy obligations."

There now began a succession of frantic expansion programmes as Germany sought to rebuild its air power. In April 1935 Ritter von Greim's place was taken by Major Kurt von Doering, the original Staffelführer of Jasta 4 back in June 1917. That same month, a cadre departed to set up a second Gruppe at Jüterbog-Damm under Major Johann Raithel.

Bf 109B-1s arrived in early 1937, this scene at Jüterbog-Damm depicting II. Gruppe. Gruppe's new fighters with the old He 51s in the background, all carrying the unit's horizontal bar marking. After a rapid conversion, many II. Gruppe personnel were dispatched to Spain.

Jagdgeschwader 'Richthofen'

JG 132 was the first unit to convert to the Bf 109, and its aircraft participated in many trials and exercises. The Geschwader also supported Hitler's Austrian Anschluss and Czechoslovakian annexation programmes.

In keeping with then-current policy, Raithel's unit was initially known as Fliegergruppe Damm (the cover-title Fliegergruppe Jüterbog having already been allocated to an on-site supply depot). Between the two Jagdgruppen there soon grew up a good-natured but intense rivalry. Döberitz was undoubtedly the premier showpiece station, its modern mess hall, or Kasino, dominated by a life-sized portrait in oils of the legendary Rittmeister. Consequently, all the greater was the satisfaction felt by Raithel's pilots – still roughing it on their as-yet unfinished base outside Jüterbog – upon learning that they were to receive the first production models of Heinkel's new He 51 fighter.

During the summer months both Gruppen converted completely to the Heinkel. And the ongoing spirit of competition (expressed on one memorable occasion by Raithel's pilots flying across to Döberitz in full suits of armour to challenge the residents to a tournament, losers to pay the bar bill!) quickly led to a high degree of proficiency. On official, more hidebound, circles, however, there existed a clear-cut division of labour; Döberitz was responsible for the

testing of weapons and ancillary equipment, and for conducting trials with the ground organisation; Damm was charged with perfecting the tactics of aerial pursuit and interception, and the carrying out of the initial experiments for the 'heavy' fighter (the later *Zerstörer*) concept.

After a busy autumn and winter thus spent, Döberitz was called upon to provide a second cadre, which was detached on 24 February 1936 to become Fliegergruppe Lippstadt. Twelve days later all three Fliegergruppen found themselves at the sharp end of the Führer's first exercise in sabre-rattling when, on 7 March 1936, Germany reoccupied the de-militarised zone of the Rhineland.

The pilots had taken off before sunrise. Once aloft, they opened sealed orders which instructed them to land on forward fields just short of the Rhine: "immediately refuel, and cover the advancing ground columns against enemy reconnaissance and attack from the air." Fliegergruppe Döberitz's patrol area extended across the Rhineland-Palatinate from Karlsruhe up to Koblenz. Raithel's Fliegergruppe Damm was to protect the adjoining sector northwards from the Rhine's confluence with the Moselle

up to the Ruhr. Fortunately, they encountered no Allied response whatsoever; few of the Heinkels were, in fact, armed!

The success of this episode led to a trio of new Gruppen being formed: two from nuclei provided by Damm, another from Döberitz. At the same time, a Geschwaderstab was set up for the two Richthofen Gruppen, their first Kommodore being Oberstleutnant Gerd von Massow. Further changes saw the promotion and posting of von Doering and Raithel, their places at Döberitz and Damm being taken by Major Carl Vieck and one Carl-August von Schoenebeck respectively. Finally, on 1 June 1936, the blanket title Fliegergruppe was discarded and the Döberitz and Damm units were at last revealed as I. and II. Gruppen of the Jagdgeschwader Nr. 132 'Richthofen'.

The existence now of six Jagdgruppen meant that the expansion programme of spring 1937 did not bear too heavily on JG 132. They were obliged to provide cadres for only two of the planned six new Gruppen. Any depletion that they did suffer was more than compensated in the weeks that followed by JG 132 being selected as the first recipient of Professor Willy Messerschmitt's latest Bf 109 monoplane fighter. (The irrepressible II. Gruppe reportedly hit upon a unique method of celebrating the arrival of their new machines with 109 bottles of beer. Whether their successors in their later wartime guise of I./NJG 1 were able to welcome their re-equipment with the Heinkel He 219 in a similar fashion has not been recorded!)

Exercise and experiment

In the early autumn of 1937 JG 132 participated in the large-scale manoeuvres held across northern Germany. The performance of the two Bf 109 Gruppen, the backbone of 'red' force, was followed with keen interest by the many foreign observers attending the exercises. II./JG 132 also took part in trials of a more discreet nature shortly thereafter. These involved rudimentary night-fighter experiments using searchlights, an early venture into the *helle Nachtjagd* type of operation which was to meet with some success at the beginning of World War II.

In March 1938 1./JG 132 played a minor role in the annexation of Austria, the Staffel's duties proving to be nothing more onerous than escorting Hitler's Ju 52 during the Führer's triumphant return to the land of his birth. Then, on 21 April 1938, the 20th anniversary of von Richthofen's death, Döberitz acted as host to its Commander-in-Chief when Generalfeldmarschall Göring unveiled a memorial stone to the fallen hero. Flanked on the one side by a red Fokker triplane, and on the other by one of the Gruppe's dark-green Bf 109Bs bearing the unit's official badge – a red script 'R' on a silver shield – the stone was dedicated as a symbol of the bond between past and present.

With Austria safely under his belt, Hitler's

In the winter of 1938, the Richthofen Geschwader, then designated JG 131, converted to the Bf 109C. This variant featured a deeper radiator bath beneath the nose.

Aircraft types of JG 132 and JG 2, 1935 to 1940

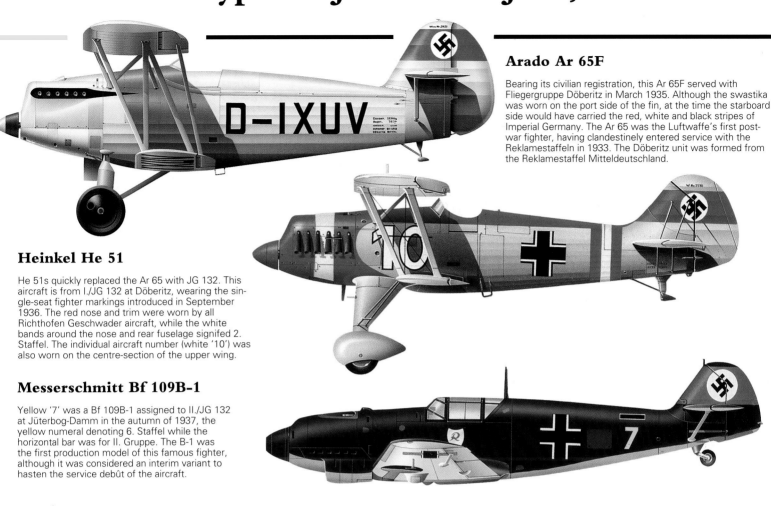

Arado Ar 65F

Bearing its civilian registration, this Ar 65F served with Fliegergruppe Döberitz in March 1935. Although the swastika was worn on the port side of the fin, at the time the starboard side would have carried the red, white and black stripes of Imperial Germany. The Ar 65 was the Luftwaffe's first post-war fighter, having clandestinely entered service with the Reklamestaffeln in 1933. The Döberitz unit was formed from the Reklamestaffel Mitteldeutschland.

Heinkel He 51

He 51s quickly replaced the Ar 65 with JG 132. This aircraft is from I./JG 132 at Döberitz, wearing the single-seat fighter markings introduced in September 1936. The red nose and trim were worn by all Richthofen Geschwader aircraft, while the white bands around the nose and rear fuselage signifed 2. Staffel. The individual aircraft number (white '10') was also worn on the centre-section of the upper wing.

Messerschmitt Bf 109B-1

Yellow '7' was a Bf 109B-1 assigned to II./JG 132 at Jüterbog-Damm in the autumn of 1937, the yellow numeral denoting 6. Staffel while the horizontal bar was for II. Gruppe. The B-1 was the first production model of this famous fighter, although it was considered an interim variant to hasten the service debût of the aircraft.

Arado Ar 68E

Possessing excellent handling qualities and better manoeuvrability than the He 51, the Ar 68 entered service (as the BMW-powered Ar 68F) with some fighter units in mid-1936. The Jumo 210-powered Ar 68E was the main production model. This example was used by III. Gruppe/JG 132, flying from Fürstenwalde in October 1938. The dark green/black green camouflage was standard for the period. In November the unit was redesignated II./JG 141, and later became I./ZG 76. The Ar 68E remained in Richthofen Geschwader use until after the outbreak of war, flying on night-fighter duties defending the capital with 10.(Nacht)/JG 2.

Heinkel He 112B-0

One of the Geschwader's more unusual types, this Heinkel He 112B-0 served with IV./JG 132 at Mährisch-Trübau in October 1938. The marking for IV. Gruppe, a solid circle, is missing, but the aircraft wears the yellow numeral of 12. Staffel. The He 112 entered service thanks to the Sudeten crisis, which necessitated the prompt requisition of the second batch of 12 fighters destined for Japan. However, with the Munich agreement signed, the crisis passed and the He 112s were returned to Heinkel for export.

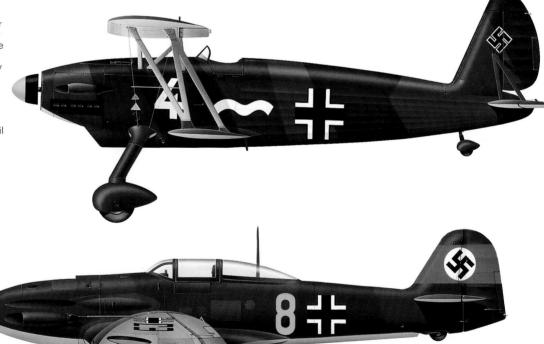

Messerschmitt Bf 109D-1

Seen as it appeared in January 1940 while operating from Langeoog (an island in the East Frisian chain), this Bf 109D served with 10.(Nacht)/JG 2 on night-fighting duties. Instead of IV Gruppe markings, the aircraft wears the letter 'N' (for Nacht) in the staffel colour, and the unit's owl badge. The IV Gruppe also had 11.(N) Staffel on strength, and later absorbed 10.(N)/JG 26 to achieve full status. IV/JG 2 flew night defence for northern Germany into late 1940, being the last front-line unit to use the Bf 109D. The 'Dora' was essentially similar airframe-wise to the C, but was powered by a Daimler-Benz DB 600.

Jagdgeschwader 'Richthofen'

During the Battles of France and Britain, Oberstleutnant Harry von Bülow-Bothkamp was Geschwaderkommodore. Here he bids farewell to III/JG 2 in September 1940, having been unfairly forced to 'resign' his command by Göring.

attention was now focussed on the Sudeten territories of Czechoslovakia. As part of a large-scale military build-up, JG 132 suddenly found itself doubled in size; III. and IV. Gruppen were both activated on 1 July 1938. With six other Jagdgruppen forming on the same date, it was impossible suddenly to equip them all with the Bf 109. And, in fact, III./JG 132 was flying Arado Ar 68s when it departed Jüterbog-Damm for Fürstenwalde. Even more exotic, IV./JG 132 at Werneuchen numbered among its Staffeln one equipped with a dozen Heinkel He 112B-0s requisitioned from an export order at that time being readied for the Imperial Japanese Naval Air Arm. But the quantity, if not the uniform quality, of the arms backing Hitler's latest demand proved more than adequate. On 30 September the Munich Agreement ceded the Sudetenland to the Greater German Reich.

It was on 11 November 1938 that extensive organisational changes were introduced throughout the Luftwaffe. Part of these changes entailed dividing the existing fighter force into 'light' and 'heavy' wings, the latter ultimately evolving into the wartime Zerstörer arm. The Jagdgeschwader Richthofen lost two of its four Gruppen in this reshuffle; II. and III./JG 132 became I. and II./JG 141 respectively. At the same time IV./JG 132, whose perambulations during the Sudeten crisis had taken them from

Views of Helmut Wick's Bf 109E depict the yellow nose and 3. Staffel 'Horrido' pennant (right), and the JG 2 badge and hastily applied mottling (below). Wick was the Geschwader's brightest star in the Battle of Britain.

Werneuchen to Mährisch-Trübau (an ex-Czech base inside the newly-ceded territory) was there redesignated I./JG 331. This effectively left Oberstleutnant von Massow with but à single Gruppe under his control as titular Kommodore of a Geschwader which, as part of the same reorganisation process – but to complicate matters even further – now bore the number JG Nr. 131 Richthofen.

Night-fighter detachment

During the winter that followed, Stab and I./JG 131, both still at Döberitz, converted to the Bf 109C. In February 1939 a small, short-lived Ar 68-equipped night-fighter detachment, which had been set up at Döberitz under Oberleutnant Blumensaat during the height of the Sudeten crisis, was revived under the designation 10.(N)/JG 131. If the nocturnal defence of Berlin was once again exercising the minds of those in high places, could another of the Führer's 'last demands' on some neighbouring territory be far behind?

Predictably, I./JG 131 soon found themselves heading south to take part in the second and final act of Hitler's clinical dismemberment of Czechoslovakia. Shortly afterward the Gruppe returned to Döberitz for re-equipment with the latest model Bf 109E. It was here, on 1 May

1939, and in accordance with the greatly simplified block system of unit designation (the block system allocated numbers 1-25 to units serving under Luftflotte 1, 26-50 to Luftflotte 2, 51-75 to Luftflotte 3, and 76-99 to Luftflotte 4), that they finally emerged as Jagdgeschwader 2 'Richthofen'. This was still to be the composition of the Luftwaffe's premier Jagdgeschwader exactly four months later on the outbreak of World War II: namely, one Geschwaderstab, one single operational Gruppe, and one Staffel of 'night-fighter' biplanes!

Apart from a brief involvement by one Staffel midway through the 18-day *Blitzkrieg* against Poland, JG 2 played no part in this first campaign of the war. Instead the Geschwader, reinforced by I./JG 20, was retained in the home-defence role protecting the German capital. The wisdom of such a measure seemed fully justified on the very first evening of the war, when Berlin's sirens sounded at 1831 hours. The whole of I./JG 2 was scrambled, only to discover the 'attackers' were Heinkel bombers returning from a raid on Warsaw airport.

Despite the complete absence of Allied daylight activity against the heart of Hitler's Reich (Berlin's sirens would not sound again by day, in fact, until 28 August 1940; another false alarm), the Geschwader's guardianship of the capital was to cost them their first casualties of the war. On the night of 16/17 September 1939 two aircraft – a I. Gruppe Bf 109 and an Ar 68 of 10.(N)/JG 2 – both crashed, killing their pilots who had been blinded by searchlight glare.

On 15 November JG 2 departed Döberitz for the Rhineland. Based at Frankfurt-Rebstock, they were reinforced by I./JG 76, another ex-metropolitan defence Gruppe recently arrived from Vienna, and now housed nearby – quite literally – in the cavernous Zeppelin shed which dominated Frankfurt's civil airport. Exactly one week after their arrival at the front, JG 2 opened their score against the western Allies – their principal opponents in the coming five and a half years – when, on 22 November, Leutnant Helmut Wick and Oberfeldwebel

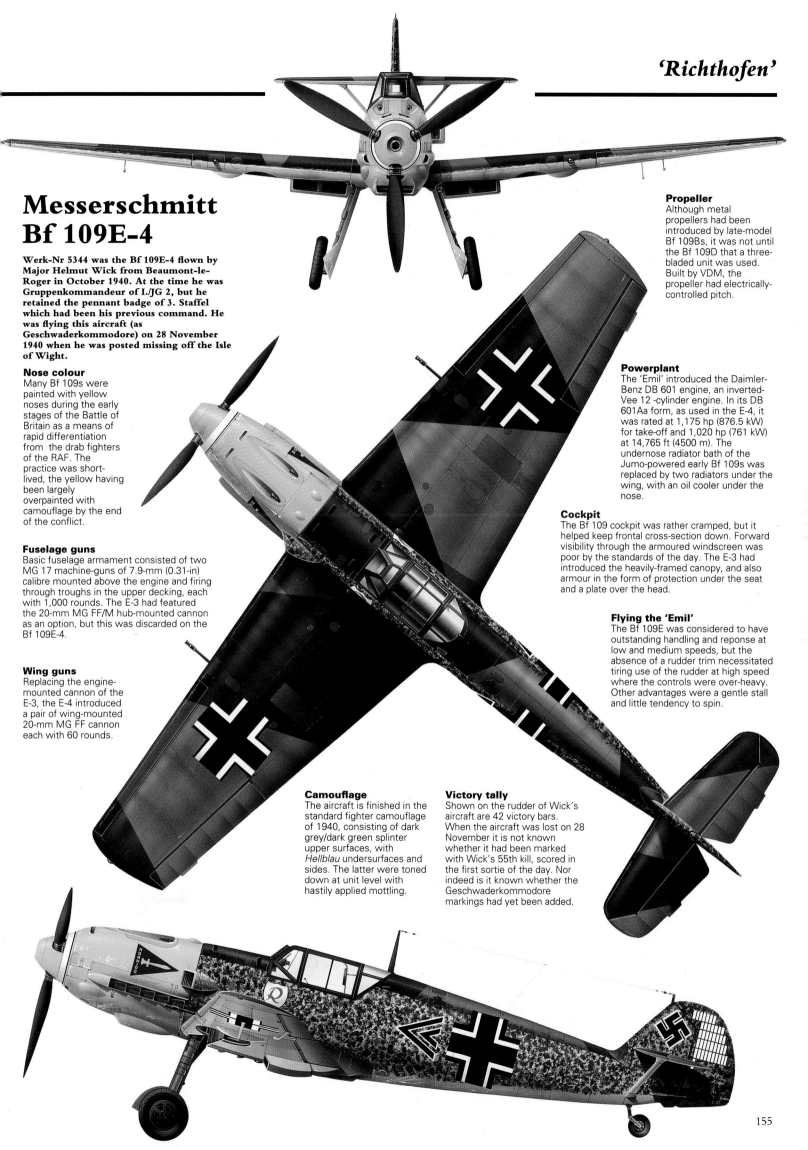

Messerschmitt Bf 109E-4

Werk-Nr 5344 was the Bf 109E-4 flown by Major Helmut Wick from Beaumont-le-Roger in October 1940. At the time he was Gruppenkommandeur of I./JG 2, but he retained the pennant badge of 3. Staffel which had been his previous command. He was flying this aircraft (as Geschwaderkommodore) on 28 November 1940 when he was posted missing off the Isle of Wight.

Nose colour
Many Bf 109s were painted with yellow noses during the early stages of the Battle of Britain as a means of rapid differentiation from the drab fighters of the RAF. The practice was short-lived, the yellow having been largely overpainted with camouflage by the end of the conflict.

Fuselage guns
Basic fuselage armament consisted of two MG 17 machine-guns of 7.9-mm (0.31-in) calibre mounted above the engine and firing through troughs in the upper decking, each with 1,000 rounds. The E-3 had featured the 20-mm MG FF/M hub-mounted cannon as an option, but this was discarded on the Bf 109E-4.

Wing guns
Replacing the engine-mounted cannon of the E-3, the E-4 introduced a pair of wing-mounted 20-mm MG FF cannon each with 60 rounds.

Propeller
Although metal propellers had been introduced by late-model Bf 109Bs, it was not until the Bf 109D that a three-bladed unit was used. Built by VDM, the propeller had electrically-controlled pitch.

Powerplant
The 'Emil' introduced the Daimler-Benz DB 601 engine, an inverted-Vee 12 -cylinder engine. In its DB 601Aa form, as used in the E-4, it was rated at 1,175 hp (876.5 kW) for take-off and 1,020 hp (761 kW) at 14,765 ft (4500 m). The undernose radiator bath of the Jumo-powered early Bf 109s was replaced by two radiators under the wing, with an oil cooler under the nose.

Cockpit
The Bf 109 cockpit was rather cramped, but it helped keep frontal cross-section down. Forward visibility through the armoured windscreen was poor by the standards of the day. The E-3 had introduced the heavily-framed canopy, and also armour in the form of protection under the seat and a plate over the head.

Flying the 'Emil'
The Bf 109E was considered to have outstanding handling and reponse at low and medium speeds, but the absence of a rudder trim necessitated tiring use of the rudder at high speed where the controls were over-heavy. Other advantages were a gentle stall and little tendency to spin.

Camouflage
The aircraft is finished in the standard fighter camouflage of 1940, consisting of dark grey/dark green splinter upper surfaces, with *Hellblau* undersurfaces and sides. The latter were toned down at unit level with hastily applied mottling.

Victory tally
Shown on the rudder of Wick's aircraft are 42 victory bars. When the aircraft was lost on 28 November it is not known whether it had been marked with Wick's 55th kill, scored in the first sortie of the day. Nor indeed is it known whether the Geschwaderkommodore markings had yet been added.

Jagdgeschwader 'Richthofen'

Major Helmut Wick accomplished the most meteoric rise of any Luftwaffe fighter pilot. During 1939/40, he rose from a line pilot to command the Geschwader, scoring 56 kills in the process. He was lost off the Isle of Wight.

Hauptmann Hans 'Assi' Hahn was the flamboyant leader of the Geschwader's III. Gruppe. He scored most of his 108 victories with the unit, and introduced the cockerel Gruppe badge, the name Hahn translating as 'cock'.

Oberstleutnant Kurt Bühligen was the last wartime leader of the Geschwader, serving from just before D-day to VE-day, the period during which the unit was in full retreat to defend the Reich. His personal tally was 108 kills.

Kley each claimed a French Curtiss Hawk destroyed.

The following month von Massow's strength was bolstered by the activation of a long-awaited II. Gruppe. This was commanded by Hauptmann Wolfgang Schellmann, an experienced 'Legion Condor' veteran. But it would be March 1940 before the Geschwader was brought up to full establishment by the creation of III./JG 2 under Hauptmann Dr. Erich Mix, an ex-World War I pilot.

In the meantime, Hauptmann Blumensaat's Ar 68 Staffel had assimilated the similarly-equipped 10.(N)/JG 26 and 11.(N)/LG 2 to become IV.(N)/JG 2. Flying Bf 109Ds (reportedly with the cockpit roof glazing removed to reduce reflected searchlight glare – a lesson learned from the night of 16./17 September?), the Gruppe was initially headquarterd at Jever, with Staffeln and smaller detachments deployed along the North Sea and Baltic coasts. It also played a minor part in the Norwegian campaign. On the night of 20/21 April 1940, with the destruction of a Fairey Battle of the AASF over Crailsheim, Oberfeldwebel Schmale scored the Luftwaffe's first ever night-fighter kill. Two months later the now Major Blumensaat's IV.(N)/JG 2 departed the ranks

of the Jagdgeschwader 'Richthofen' to join the night-fighter arm proper as II./NJG 1.

March 1940 also saw the departure of the Geschwader's two senior-most commanders. Oberst Gerd von Massow was promoted to Jafü 3. His place was taken by Oberstleutnant Harry von Bülow-Bothkamp, one-time Staffelführer of the Jasta Boelcke. And I. Gruppe's Major Carl Vieck, of almost equally long standing, left to take command of JG 3. He was replaced by Hauptmann Roth. It was thus a predominantly untried Jagdgeschwader 'Richthofen' – some two-thirds of its pilots only a matter of weeks out of training school; two of its four commanders, by contrast, dating back to World War I – which now prepared itself for the attack on France and the Low Countries.

At 0530 hours on 10 May 1940 tanks of the 1st Panzerdivision entered Luxembourg. By evening they were across the Duchy and into Belgium. Forty-eight hours later the leading Panzers had reached the banks of the Meuse. I. and III./JG 2's initial task was to protect these spearheads; doing so cost them seven Bf 109s over the Sedan bridgehead on 14 May, but the armoured thrust was unstoppable. By 20 May it had reached the Channel coast. I. and III. Gruppen covered the vanguard all the way without further loss, their own score rising to top the 100 mark.

II./JG 2 meanwhile, operating temporarily under the control of JG 26, was helping push

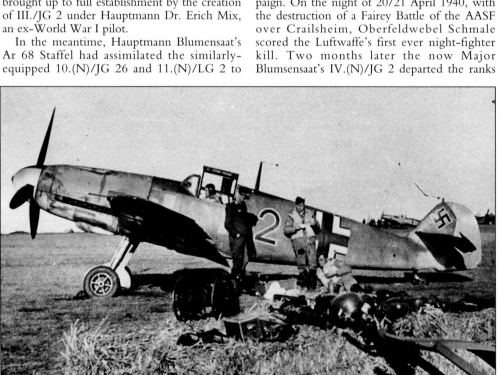

Crews rest after a mission at a French airfield. The Bf 109F-1 arrived in JG 2 service in March 1941, this variant introducing the DB 601N engine in a reprofiled nose, rounded wingtips, smaller rudder and a return to the engine-mounted MG FF/M 20-mm cannon in place of the wing guns

Geschwader insignia

The script 'R' of the Geschwader was rarely worn after the early days of the war, but remained the official insignia of JG 2 as a whole. Most aircraft wore the staffel badges, although those of III. Gruppe were inspired by their leader, 'Assi' Hahn, to wear the cockerel badge. Notable among the badges were the 'Bonzo' character of 1. Staffel, von Winterfeld family crest of 8. Staffel, and the owl and cat representing the Nacht units.

Jagdgeschwader 2

III Gruppe/Jagdgeschwader 2

1. Staffel/Jagdgeschwader 2

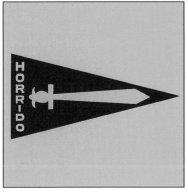

3. Staffel/Jagdgeschwader 2

7. Staffel/Jagdgeschwader 2

8. Staffel/Jagdgeschwader 2

9. Staffel/Jagdgeschwader 2

10. (Jabo) Staffel/JG 2

10. (Nacht) Staffel/JG 2

11. (Nacht) Staffel/JG 2

12. Staffel/Jagdgeschwader 2

the BEF (British Expeditionary Forces) back across central Belgium. Rejoining the Geschwader after the fall of Dunkirk, all three Gruppen now directed their attention to the bulk of the French forces still massed south of the Somme. By the time of the French surrender, their combined number of Allied aircraft destroyed stood at 235.

Significantly, their own final fatality of the campaign – Leutnant Grubel, who was killed on 19 June – coincided with the Luftwaffe's first bombing raid of any strength against the United Kingdom. For with the Battle of France over, the Battle of Britain was about to begin.

JG 2 took up position along the line of the Seine; Stab at Evreux, I. and II. Gruppen at Beaumont-le-Roger, and III. Gruppe on the coast at Le Havre-Octeville. Easternmost of the three Jagdgeschwader currently controlled by Jafü 3, they found themselves operating alongside the Stukas of VIII. Fliegerkorps – commanded by General der Flieger Wolfram von

Richthofen – whose job it was to close the Channel to British shipping.

The Geschwader's first major involvement in the Battle, on 11 August, proved a far from auspicious introduction to cross-Channel campaigning: eight fighters lost and five pilots missing, including Oberleutnant Rempel, Staffelkapitän of 6./JG 2. Over the next few weeks the 160-km (100-mile) stretch of Channel separating the Seine from the Solent was to become very familiar to JG 2's pilots as they flew numerous sweeps along the Dorset, Hampshire and Sussex coastlines, and escorted bombing raids over the Portsmouth and Southampton areas.

At the end of the month they transferred briefly to Jafü 2. Based between Calais and Dunkirk (I. and II./JG 2 at Mardyck; III./JG 2

at Oye-Plage), they ventured over the unfamiliar territory of the Thames Estuary, taking part in a series of attacks on Fighter Command sector stations in the south-east.

Soon, however, they were back over the Isle of Wight area; the scene of most of their engagements. By early September 1940 the ini-

'Assi' Hahn, in the white jacket, holds court in front of III./JG 2's headquarters at Beaumont-le-Roger in 1941. The three constituent Staffel badges are mounted on the building behind.

Jagdgeschwader 'Richthofen'

Between November 1941 and July 1942, Hauptmann Frank Liesendahl led the newly-created 10.(Jabo)/JG 2 on daring low-level raids against British shipping with Bf 109F-4/Bs. The Staffel badge depicted a fox with a ship in its mouth (above), while his tally (right) stood testimony to the effectiveness of these raids.

tiative was beginning to slip from Germany's grasp. In his Berchtesgaden retreat, the Führer was already seeking a scapegoat to blame for his 'inability' to launch the long-delayed cross-Channel invasion. But the only solution Reichsmarschall Göring could offer as a remedy for his fighters' lack of aggression – as he interpreted it – was to replace those 'old men' still leading his Jagdgeschwader with younger, more dynamic personalities.

Displaying a fine disregard for the real root causes of his problems – causes ranging from overall strategy right down to the rigid imposition of individual tactics (shades of 1918!) – Göring made a clean sweep of all his longer-serving Kommodore. One of the last to go, on 2 September, was Oberstleutnant von Bülow-Bothkamp. The new Geschwaderkommodore was to be Major Schellmann, Kommandeur of I./JG 2.

Schellmann's seven-week tenure of office (he departed on 19 October to take over JG 27) saw the Battle reach its climax. For most historians it came to an end on 31 October, but there are many in Germany who would dispute this arbitrary date. None more so, perhaps, than Oberleutnant Hermann Reifferscheidt, Staffelkapitän of 1./JG 2, who was brought down by Hurricanes over Sussex on 1 November. Prior to his capture, the Geschwader had suffered the loss of 22 pilots killed or missing from all causes during the 'official' period of the Battle. To set against this they had claimed the destruction of 281 British aircraft!

JG 2's greatest loss was to occur in November. By then the same Leutnant Wick who had been instrumental in opening the Geschwader's scoreboard 12 months earlier had been promoted – via Schwarmführer, Staffelkapitän and Gruppenkommandeur – to take over from Major Schellmann as Geschwaderkommodore. The meteoric rise of the 25-year-old Major was unparalleled in Luftwaffe history.

By mid-afternoon of 28 November Wick had already scored one kill over the Solent, his 55th. Later in the day he led his fighters back to the same area to claim another. But in doing so,

The Fw 190A arrived with JG 2 in April 1942, heralding an upsurge in the unit's fortunes. While fellow Western front campaigner JG 26 was completely re-equipped, JG 2 retained some Bf 109s until almost the end of the war.

he allowed himself to cross the sights of a steeply turning Spitfire. The one split-second burst must have done mortal damage to the heavily-mottled Messerschmitt, for Wick lost no time in jettisoning his canopy and baling out. His parachute was last seen drifting down into the Channel south-west of the Needles. But despite exhaustive air-sea search, no further trace was ever found.

After the battle

The appointment of Hauptmann Greisert as caretaker Geschwaderkommodore for the next three months is indicative of the hiatus which followed the tailing-off of the daylight phase of the Battle. It was not until 16 February 1941 that Major Wilhelm Balthasar assumed command. For JG 2 the early months of 1941 were occupied by equipping with the Bf 109F. As the year progressed the RAF began to 'lean' more heavily into occupied France. Daylight sweeps by strongly escorted bombers, code-named 'circuses' – strangely apt in view of the identity of the opposition – and designed specifically to inflict casualties on the Luftwaffe fighter force, probed ever deeper inland. And when, at the end of May – as Hitler prepared for his attack on the Soviet Union – the Luftwaffe in north-west Europe was reduced from 22 Jagdgruppen to just six, it clearly marked a turning-point from an offensive to a defensive posture. Of the two Jagdgeschwader remaining in the west, JG 26 was to be responsible for the

protection of Belgium and north-east France; JG2's bailwick took in the whole of the French coast west of the Seine, from Normandy to the Atlantic. Thus, with but minor variations, were the battle-lines drawn up for the next three years of increasingly bitter fighting.

One of the earliest casualties was the Kommodore himself. On 3 July Major Balthasar was killed in combat with RAF Spitfires when a wing broke off his Bf 109F. This time there was less delay in providing a replacement: Major Walter Oesau, one of the Luftwaffe's leading aces, arrived on 20 July from command of III./JG 3 in Russia to assume control.

Throughout this period of retrenchment the Geschwader had also been mounting small-scale tip-and-run raids along the south coast of England, but it was not until 10 November that a specialised fighter-bomber Staffel was formed. 10.(Jabo)/JG 2, commanded by Hauptmann Frank Liesendahl, disdained the high-altitude, almost indiscriminate hit-and-run tactics favoured by their predecessors. Liesendahl's pilots flew in fast and low under the coastal radar screen to attack Britain's offshore shipping. By the end of their first six months of operations, they had claimed over 60,000 tons sunk.

While one part of the Geschwader was thus engaged in destroying enemy shipping, another was intent on protecting its own. The battle-cruisers *Scharnhorst* and *Gneisenau* had been holed up in Brest harbour since March, the target of a whole series of raids by both Bomber and Coastal Commands. In February 1942 Hitler decreed that they should be brought back to the safety of home waters ...... via the English Channel! The historic 'dash' which resulted was protected by a continuous aerial umbrella, provided by both JGs 2 and 26 in turn, as the fleet progressed up-Channel through the Straits of Dover. Allied air and surface attacks cost the defenders a total of 17 fighters, but the ships got through.

JG 2 began re-equipping with the radial-engined Focke-Wulf Fw 190A in April 1942. The Geschwaderstab was still flying its Bf 109Fs when, late in the afternoon of 17 April, a dozen unescorted Lancasters roared low over their Beaumont-le-Roger dispersal, en route for the M.A.N. factory at Ausburg. Quickly giving chase, JG 2 claimed four of the bombers. The one brought down by Unteroffizier Pohl was

Aircraft types of JG 2, 1940 to 1945

Messerschmitt Bf 109E

Three 'Emil' sub-variants were flown by JG 2, this being a Bf 109E-3 wearing the thumb on top hat badge of 7. Staffel. The aircraft is depicted how it would have appeared in June 1940, during the Battle of France, in which JG 2 figured prominently.

Messerschmitt Bf 109F

Quite apart from the fighter 'Friedrichs', JG 2 also flew the F-4/B model with its 10.(Jabo) Staffel. The fighter-bomber variant had a centreline bomb rack for hit-and-run raids capable of carrying a single SC 250 bomb of 250 kg/550 lb). This aircraft was flown by the Staffelkapitän, Oberleutnant Frank Liesendahl, fron Caen-Carpiquet.

Messerschmitt Bf 109G

Wearing the badge of 1. Staffel, this Bf 109G-1 flew from Liègescourt in France in April 1942. The 'Gustav' introduced the uprated DB 605 engine, and the first sub-variant had a pressurised cabin. The G-1s of 1./JG 2 formed a dedicated high-altitude fighter unit. Other JG 2 units converted to the unpressurised Bf 109G-2 from the Fw 190 as the scarce Focke-Wulf fighters were desperately needed in Russia and North Africa.

Focke-Wulf Fw 190A-3

Flying from Cherbourg-Théville in July 1942, this A-3 was assigned to III. Gruppe. The elaborate eagle marking was applied to cover up the oil stains from the engine. The head portion on the cowling was later removed in favour of the cockerel badge, but the stylised wings and tail behind the exhaust slots remained. The early Fw 190As of JGs 2 and 26 caused a considerable shock to the RAF, while A-4/U1 fighter-bombers serving with the Jabo Staffeln of both Geschwaders were used to devastating effect during the Dieppe raid in August 1942.

Focke-Wulf Fw 190A-8

Carrying few markings and showing obvious signs of a recent overpainting, this Fw 190A-8 served with 2./JG 2 from Merzhausen in December 1944. I. Gruppe was active from this base during the Ardennes offensive, chiefly supporting the ground forces. The Fw 190A-8 was the last and most numerous of the radial-engined versions, introducing an optional MW 50 water-methanol boost kit. Armament consisted of four 20-mm MG 151 cannon in the wing roots and outer wings, and two MG 131 13-mm machine-guns in the upper fuselage. The fitment of the latter gave rise to the characteristic bumps ahead of the windscreen.

Messerschmitt Bf 109K

Featuring the better visibility canopy, tall wooden fin, underwing aerial and revised nose profile, the Bf 109K equipped II./JG 2 in late 1944. This K-4 aircraft is seen in January 1945 when based at Nidda, carrying the yellow-white-yellow Reichsverteidigung (RV-Defence of the Reich) band assigned to JG 2. The K-4 featured a pressurised cabin and an engine-mounted 30-mm MK 108 cannon, although some later aircraft had the more powerful 30-mm MK 103.

Focke-Wulf Fw 190D-9

The 'Langnasen-Dora' served with Stab, I. and III./JG 2 from December 1944. This unmarked example took part in Operation Bodenplatte, the Luftwaffe's last organised mass attack against Allied airfields.

159

A group of JG 2 Fw 190A-4s line up at their French airfield. From 1942 the Americans became the Geschwader's principal enemy, the Fw 190s exacting a toll from the daylight bomber formations and their fighter escorts.

Based along the French coast, the Gruppen of JG 2 were in the front line against the 8th Air Force's daylight bombing raids. The 94th Bomb Group B-17F (above left) was shot down on 14 July 1943 by Major Egon Mayer, JG 2's early bomber specialist with 25 bomber kills out of a total of 102 at the time of his death. Shown at right is the pole-mounted B-17 model used by 6. Staffel for sighting practice – in the foreground is a Reflexvisier ('Revi') sight as carried by the Fw 190.

With an Fw 190A-8 in the background, Oberstleutnant Kurt Bühligen (centre) describes his 100th kill to the officers of Stab/JG 2. Bühligen was the last wartime Kommodore.

the Geschwader's 1,000th victory. Major Oesau's victim provided the 1,0001st, and was his own 101st kill. Having been automatically banned from further combat flying after his 100th victory the previous October, Oesau had a ready explanation for his superiors: he was up on a test flight when the Lancaster suddenly appeared, and he had had no other option but to shoot it down in self-defence!

On 17 July 10.(Jabo)/JG 2 lost its Staffelkapitän when Hauptmann Liesendahl failed to return from an attack on a freighter off Brixham. On the last day of the month the Staffelkapitän of 1./JG 2, Hauptmann Rudolf 'Rudi' Pflanz, who had been with the Jagdgeschwader 'Richthofen' since 1938, fell victim to Spitfires near Abbeville. July also witnessed the first appearance of the United States 8th Air Force over France. It was a modest beginning, in just six Boston bombers on loan from the RAF, but in time the Americans would become the Geschwader's major adversary and ultimate nemesis.

August was dominated by the ill-starred landings at Dieppe. Again, both western-based Jagdgeschwader, JGs 2 and 26, were heavily engaged; III./JG 2's Hauptmann Josef 'Sepp' Wurmheller claimed seven kills on that 19 August, despite having a broken leg and suffering from brain concussion at the time! The two Jabostaffeln, 10.(Jabo)/JG 2 now commanded by Oberleutnant Fritz Schröter, were also in action against surface units, damaging destroyers HMS *Berkeley* and *Calpe*, the former so badly that she had to be sunk.

In November 1942 JG 2 undertook one of its few forays out of north-western Europe when II. Gruppe's Fw 190s, accompanied by the Bf 109Gs of 11./JG 2 – a special high-altitude unit formed out of 1. Staffel the previous May – transferred southwards to Sicily. While 11. Staffel was incorporated into II./JG 53, Oberleutnant Adolf Dickfeld's II./JG 2 staged

onwards across the Mediterranean to Tunisia, where they were to remain until March 1943. During their sojourn in North Africa II. Gruppe would claim some 150 Allied aircraft for the loss of 18 of their own.

Menawhile in northwest Europe, action and losses continued to escalate throughout 1943. Then, on 2 March 1944 Oberstleutnant Mayer was killed in action against American P-47 Thunderbolts near Montmedy. Twenty-five of Mayer's 102 victories were four-engined bombers, making him – at the time of his death – the Luftwaffe's most successful *Viermot-Spezialist*. His replacement, Major Kurt Ubben, also fell victim to P-47s the following month. In May Major Kurt Bühligen, who had joined the Geschwader in July 1940, became its ninth and last Kommodore.

Since the beginning of 1944 the bulk of the Geschwader, after withdrawal from the Normandy coastal belt, had been concentrated on two fields north of Paris: Cormeilles (Stab and III./JG 2) and Creil (II./JG 2). I. Gruppe joined them at Cormeilles upon its recall from Aix in May.

This was the position when the Allies invaded Normandy on 6 June 1944. Despite the Luftwaffe's contingency plans for the dispatch of 19 additional Jagdgruppen into the threatened area, Anglo-American air superiority was – and remained – absolute. Hunted in the air and harried on the ground, the Jagdgruppen in Normandy, residents and incomers alike, suffered appalling losses. By the last week in June the entire Jagdgeschwader 'Richthofen', which had had 115 fighters on strength one month earlier, had congregated at Creil with just 15 serviceable Fw 190s and 17 Bf 109Gs (the latter deployed by II. Gruppe, which had re-equipped with the Messerschmitt after its Tunisian venture).

By July I./JG 2 had been withdrawn from the Normandy front altogether. Major Bühligen led the remainder back to Germany shortly afterwards. By November 1944, after some eight weeks spent re-equipping (in III. Gruppe's case at Königsberg in East Prussia), the Geschwader was dispersed on three fields north of Frankfurt: Nidda (Stab and II./JG 2), Merzhausen (I./JG 2) and Altenstadt (III./JG 2).

From here, they embarked upon their last campaign: the Defence of the Reich. Their twin responsibilities – covering ground operations on the western front, as well as combatting the almost daily incursions by American

On 23 June 1942, Oberleutnant Arnim Faber, adjutant of III./JG 2 (note cockerel badge) presented the RAF with one of its greatest prizes of the air war. During a tangle with some Spitfires which had attacked his base at Morlaix, he became disorientated and mistook the Bristol Channel for the English Channel. Faber then landed at Pembrey in Wales, thinking it to be a Luftwaffe base in France. His Fw 190A-3 was exhaustively analysed by the RAF.

Camouflage
Standard fighter camouflage of the period consisted of pale blue-grey undersides with medium-grey upper surfaces, the latter mottling into the former along the fuselage. The pale grey swastika was standard at this period of the war.

Markings
The chevron and double bars on the rear fuselage were applied for a 'Major beim Stab' (major of the staff flight). JG 2 was a *Reichsverteidigung* (Defence of the Reich) unit, and most of the aircraft wore RV bands forward of the tail, JG 2 being assigned yellow-white-yellow.

Canopy
Early Fw 190Ds, including the prototypes, Fw 190D-0s and a few D-9s, featured the standard angular canopy inherited from the Fw 190A. Most production D-9s, however, were fitted with the blown hood introduced by the Fw 190F-2 and subsequent *Schlachtflieger* aircraft, which provided better visibility and more room for the pilot to move his head.

Offensive capability
In addition to the cannon, the Fw 190D-9 was provided with a centreline ETC 504 bomb rack which could carry a single SC 500 bomb. Provision was made for two ETC 71 or ETC 503 bombracks under the wings.

Gun armament
The standard gun armament of the 'Langnasen-Dora' consisted of two MG 131 13-mm machine-guns in the upper fuselage with 475 rounds per gun, and two MG 151 20-mm cannon in the wingroots with 250 rounds each.

Powerplant
Powering the Fw 190D-9 was a Junkers Jumo 213A-1 12-cylinder engine, rated in standard form (without MW 50) at 1,776 hp (1325 kW) for take-off and 1,600 hp (1195 kW) at 18,000 ft (5486 m). The engine was installed as a complete 'power egg' attached to the forward fireproof bulkhead. Two semi-circular radiators surrounded the propeller shaft at the front in an annular arrangement, giving the engine the appearance of a radial. Behind the radiators were thermostat-controlled cooling gills. The three-bladed propeller was a VS 111 constant-speed unit.

The 'Downstairs Maid'
This nickname was applied to the D-9 on account of its lack of cabin pressurisation and high-altitude potential. Intended only as an interim pending the fielding of the Ta 152, the Fw 190D-9 nevertheless performed exceptionally in the desperate defence of the Reich.

Focke-Wulf Fw 190D-9

While II. Gruppe/JG 2 remained with Bf 109s until almost the war's end, the Stab, I. and III. Gruppen converted to the Fw 190D-9 in December 1944. The staff flight was based at Merzhausen, from where this aircraft took part in sorties in support of the Ardennes counter-offensive. On 1 January 1945 it participated in Operation Bodenplatte against Allied airfields in Belgium. It was hit by US Army ground defences near Liège, the pilot being taken prisoner. Despite the fact that it carries staff markings, it was flown that day by Feldwebel Werner Hohenberg of 4./JG 2.

Water/methanol injection
The 'Dora-9' had provision for the MW 50 system, which boosted power to 2,240 hp (1671 kW) at sea level, but this was fitted to only a few aircraft, the remainder having extra fuel in place of the MW 50 system. MW 50 could not be used for take-off, and was intended to give extra boost for a maximum of 10 minutes at a time up to 16,500 ft (5030 m). Enough water/methanol mixture was carried for 40 minutes' use.

Fuel
Two tanks under the pilot's seat held 523 litres (115 Imp gal). Non-MW 50 aircraft also had an additional 114-litre (25-Imp gal) tank aft of the cockpit.

Jagdgeschwader 'Richthofen'

Above: JG 71's first commander was Lt Col Erich Hartmann (left), the highest-scoring ace of World War II (with 352 victories). It was not until 21 April 1961 – the 43rd anniversary of the Rittmeister's death – that Hartmann received the coveted 'Richthofen' title and sleeve band on behalf of the wing.

heavy and medium bombers – inflicted a steady toll on the young, sketchily-trained and inexperienced pilots now making up the majority of the Geschwader. In December, whenever the weather permitted, they lent their weight to the Ardennes offensive. That month also heralded

Although the Geschwader's 'JA' code (denoting the first unit in the fighter series) remained unchanged, the aircraft were recoded from the '1xx' series (seen above on a preserved example) for 1. Staffel and '2xx' for 2. Staffel to '3xx' embracing all of the wing's aircraft (below).

the arrival of two new aircraft types: the Fw 190A-8 Gruppen receiving the first of their D-9 'long-noses', while II./JG 2, still faithful to their late variant Bf 109G-10s and G-14s, started to add some Bf 109K-4s.

On 1 Janury 1945 JG 2 took part in Operation Bodenplatte (baseplate), the last desperate throw of the Jagdwaffe to knock out selected Allied airfields in France and the Low Countries. For the Jagdgeschwader 'Richthofen', above all others, it was a gamble that failed. Some 90 fighters took off from their three fields to rendezvous over Koblenz. From here their course led them along the northern slope of the Ardennes – where they were joined between Aachen and Liége by 50-plus Fw 190F-8s of the ground-assault Schlachtgeschwader 4 – straight to their objective: St Trond.

The first casualties had already occurred before they crossed the front lines, but it was over the target itself, its anti-aircraft defences forewarned of the raiders' approach, that the

Sabres initially flew in natural metal, with the addition of Hartmann's stylised tulip marking to nose and tail. Red nose and tail trim was adopted by 1. Staffel (both pics), yellow by 2. Staffel .

carnage took place. After the survivors had straggled back, the cost was counted: 23 pilots killed or missing (some to this day), 10 captured and four wounded. These were the highest losses sustained by any of the 11 Jagdgeschwader involved in the operation, and they effectively dealt a death-blow to JG 2 as a cohesive fighting force.

True, efforts were made to make good the losses. II. Gruppe was pulled out to re-equip with the Fw 190D-9, on which the whole Geschwader now standardised, and by mid-January I. and III./JG 2 were back in limited action, but continual Allied pressure, coupled with the mounting number of accidents due to inexperience and unfamiliarity with their new mounts, kept their numbers low. Throughout March and April the entire Geschwader could rarely muster more than 20 serviceable aircraft between them.

Late in April two Gruppen of JG 2 retired across central Germany into northern Bohemia. Based at Eger (Stab and II./JG 2) and Karlsbad (I./JG 2), their new task – on paper – was the protection of the dozen or so Me 262 jet fighters still deployed by JG 7 at Prague-Ruzyne to the east of them. Reality was different. When instructions arrived ordering the disbandment of the Geschwaderstab and I. Gruppe, and the transfer of II./JG 2 into Prague itself – and into the path of the advancing Red Army – these were quietly ignored. Faces, and machines, were instead pointed southwards, to Straubing on the Danube. Here, as the first American Sherman tanks nosed their way towards the field, the torch was put to the last dozen Focke-Wulfs of JG 2. The end of the second

On 1 January 1968 the Luftwaffe introduced a permanent serial system. Consequently, the F-104Gs, which had initially flown with the unit's 'JA' codes (right), received new codes in the 2x+xx series (above).

Jagdgeschwader 'Richthofen' may not have been as spectacular as Göring's pilots wiping off their undercarriages in a defiant succession of crash-landings, but it was just as effective.

Twice risen

Post-war Germany lay in ruins, but the political climate was very different to that of 1918. The ideological differences between East and West which – in the recent conflict – had been subjugated to the cause of defeating a common enemy, were now given full rein. The East German Länder evolved into little more than a Soviet fiefdom. In the West, the economic miracle brought with it civil stability and commercial prosperity.

This time there was no need for the secrecy and duplicity which had attended the birth of the Reichsluftwaffe. The West German government was actively encouraged to takes its place within the NATO organisation and establish its own armed forces ready and willing to participate in the defence of Western Europe. For the founding of the new Bundesluftwaffe there was none of the beflagged pageantry as had surrounded the unveiling of the Jagdgruppe Döberitz. In a low-key ceremony at Fürstenfeldbruck on 24 September 1956, three training aircraft – each resplendent in the new 'pate cross' markings reminiscent of World War I – were symbolically handed over, and 10

recently-retrained ex-World War II pilots were presented with their 'wings'.

It was to be more than another two years before Luftwaffe Activation Order No. 110 heralded the formation of Jagdgeschwader 71, comprising two Staffeln, at Ahlhorn on 15 January 1959. Four days later Major Erich Hartmann was appointed Kommodore. The still youthful-looking Hartmann had amassed an amazing 352 victories during his time with JG 52 on the Eastern Front in World War II, the highest total ever of any fighter pilot. His Bf 109 had carried a distinctive black 'tulip leaf' pattern on its nose. When JG 71's first operational aircraft – in the shape of Canadair Sabre

Mk 6s – arrived at Ahlhorn the following month, it was decreed that they, too, should be marked in a similar manner, the design being repeated on the tailfin. These markings, combined with additional coloured trim – red for 1. Staffel, yellow for 2. Staffel – would make the Sabres worthy successors to the original eye-catching 'Circus' when the time came for them to don the Richthofen badge.

By mid-1959 the Geschwader had received its full complement of Sabres, and one year later it took its place within the NATO framework. Fittingly, it was on 21 April 1961, the anniversary of the death of Rittmeister Manfred Freiherr von Richthofen, that Bundespräsident

Geschwader memorabilia

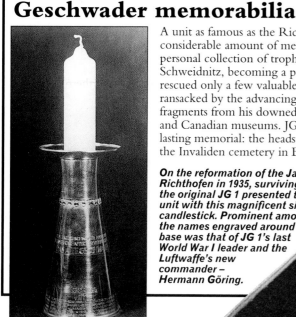

A unit as famous as the Richthofen Geschwader has inspired a considerable amount of memorabilia. Much of the Rittmeister's personal collection of trophies was sent to the family home in Schweidnitz, becoming a public museum. From here his mother rescued only a few valuable items before the house was ransacked by the advancing Russian army. A handful of fragments from his downed Triplane are in Australian and Canadian museums. JG 71 was presented with a lasting memorial: the headstone from his grave in the Invaliden cemetery in Berlin.

On the reformation of the Jagdgeschwader Richthofen in 1935, surviving members of the original JG 1 presented the new unit with this magnificent silver candlestick. Prominent among the names engraved around the base was that of JG 1's last World War I leader and the Luftwaffe's new commander – Hermann Göring.

The Richthofen arm cuffs were proudly worn by (from left to right) ex-members of JG 1 (introduced in 1935), all JG 2 personnel from World War II and post-war JG 71.

Assigned to NATO's 2nd ATAF, JG 71's Phantoms occasionally intercepted Soviet aircraft over the North Sea and Baltic. Here an F-4F, with Bodenseewerk AIM-9L Sidewinders and ALQ-101 ECM pod, shadows a Tu-95 'Bear-A'.

Heinrich Lübke conferred the honour title 'Jagdgeschwader 71 Richthofen' upon the unit. In an interview after the presentation, Oberstleutnant Hartmann unwittingly paraphrased a more emotional speech, delivered just over a quarter of a century earlier, when he said, "The name of Manfred von Richthofen, who was recognised as a chivalrous and fair fighter even by his opponents, will obligate the Geschwader to continue to uphold this tradition in a fair, clean and decent manner." Later that same year, during June and July at Leeuwarden in the Netherlands, JG 71 took part for the first time in a seven-nation NATO gunnery competition, coming a creditable fifth against its long-established competitors.

On 29 May 1962 Hartmann relinquished command to Major Günther Josten, another World War II pilot, previously of JG 51. Eleven months later the Geschwader moved to Wittmundhaven (more commonly known locally as Wittmund), a base whose longer runways would be better suited to JG 71's new equipment. They had been chosen as the first

Jagdgeschwader to receive Lockheed's revolutionary F-104 Starfighter. The difficulties – and the losses – which beset the Luftwaffe while introducing and operating the Starfighter are now notorious. Unlike JG 1's weak-winged Fokkers, or the suspect tail units of JG 2's early Bf 109Fs, this time there was no quick-fix remedy. The problems, like the F-104 itself, were too complex: pilots and ground-crew alike were unprepared for the quantum leap forward into the Starfighter era; the machines were unsuited to the rigours of outdoor dispersal and maintenance in the depths of a north German winter. Aviation history abounds with examples of air forces' bemoaning the arrival of new equipment as being "too little, too late." The Bundesluftwaffe must be very nearly unique in suffering even greater hardship from "too much, too soon."

Arrival of the Starfighter

JG 71's first two Starfighters landed at Wittmund on 9 April 1963. Although the Geschwader was inevitably to suffer its share of losses, the razor-winged F-104 gave sterling service for the next 10 years, performance and reliability being greatly enhanced when the new hangars came into use in the autumn of 1966. The previous year JG 71 had undertaken the

first of its squadron exchanges with its NATO partners, and these exchanges have played a useful and welcome role in the Geschwader's itinary ever since.

On 21 April 1968, the 50th anniversary of the death of von Richthofen, JG 71 celebrated by instituting the first of its hugely successful open days. These annual *Richthofentreffen* (Richthofen meets) not only gave the opportunity for ex-members of the two previous Jagdgeschwader 'Richthofen' – the 'Eisgrauen' ('Ice-greys') of JG 1, and the 'Döberitzers', as all personnel who served with JG 2 are familiarly known – to get together, they also became popular with the local community and attracted visitors from far and wide. These meets, too, have become an important part of the Geschwader's calendar.

JG 71's third and fourth Kommodoren, Oberstleutnant Horst Dieter Kallerhoff and Ulrich Pieper, were both World War II veterans, having served with JGs 3 and 77 respectively. They took the Geschwader into the 1970s. But just as the old guard commanders of World War I vintage had slowly disappeared from the ranks of JG 2 in the early 1940s, so too, now, were wartime members of the present Bundesluftwaffe reaching the end of their service careers.

Oberst Hans-Juergen Rentel assumed command of JG 71 on 10 October 1972. While still deeply conscious of its past history – a monument to the fallen of all three Jagdgeschwader 'Richthofen' was unveiled in April 1973 – JG 71 was about to take another major step forward. At the end of August of that year the first

F-4Fs were initially delivered in grey/green camouflage. To satisfy political constraints, the F-4F was a special version for Germany with reduced tankage, without tailplane slats or medium-range missile capability.

Commanders of Jagdgeschwader Richthofen

Jagdgeschwader 1

24.06.17 – 21.04.18	Rittmeister Manfred, Freiherr von Richthofen,
22.04.18 – 03.07.18	Hauptmann Wilhelm Reinhard
08.07.18 – 11.11.18	Oberleutnant Hermann Göring

Jagdgeschwader 2

09.06.36 – 31.03.40	Oberstleutnant Gerd von Massow
01.04.40 – 02.09.40	Oberstleutnant Harry von Bülow-Bothkamp
03.09.40 – 19.10.40	Major Wolfgang Schellmann
20.10.40 – 28.11.40	Major Helmut Wick
29.11.40 – 15.02.41	Hauptmann Karl-Heinz Greisert (acting)
16.02.41 – 03.07.41	Major Wilhelm Balthasar
20.07.41 – 30.06.43	Oberst Walter Oesau
01.07.43 – 02.03.44	Oberstleutnant Egon Mayer
10.03.44 – 27.04.44	Major Kurt Ubben
00.05.44 – 08.05.45	Oberstleutnant Kurt Bühligen

Jagdgeschwader 71

19.01.59 – 29.05.62	Oberstleutnant Erich Hartmann
30.05.62 – 01.04.67	Oberst Guenther Josten
02.04.67 – 25.09.70	Oberst Horst Dieter Kallerhoff
26.09.70 – 09.10-72	Oberst Ulrich Pieper
10.10.72 – 15.09.76	Oberst Hans-Jürgen Rentel
16.06.76 – 19.09.76	Oberstleutnant Otto Braasch (acting)
20.09.76 – 02.10.79	Oberst Erwin Willing
03.10.79 – 30.09.83	Oberst Lothar Kompch
01.10.83 – 31.03.87	Oberst Klaus Eggert
01.04.87 – 30.06.89	Oberst Dirk Böcker
01.07.89 – 26.03.93	Oberst Heinz Gred Nowak
26.03.93 – 30.03.95	Oberst Dierk Peter Mecklinghaus
30.03.95 – to date	Oberst Wolfgang Fahl

Jagdgeschwader 'Richthofen'

Canadair CL-13B Sabre Mk 6

The Sabre served with JG 71 from June 1959 until 1964. The Luftwaffe procured 225 Sabre 6s (and 75 Sabre 5s) from Canadair to equip three fighter wings. JG 71 was established at Ahlhorn but moved to Wittmundhafen in November 1960 to make way for JG 73. The Sabre 6 was a version of the F-86E and consequently featured an all-flying tail. Powered by the 7,275-lb (32.37-kN) thrust Orenda 14, it was widely regarded as the best dogfighter of its era.

Lockheed F-104G Starfighter

JG 71 was the first Luftwaffe unit to receive Starfighters from Fokker production, serving from 1964 to 1973. In addition to the internal cannon, the F-104G carried the AIM-9 Sidewinder as its main armament. In addition to the F-104G mission aircraft, JG 71 also operated the F-104F, Dornier Do 27, Lockheed T-33 and Piaggio P.149 for liaison and training.

McDonnell F-4F Phantom

Following promising early experience with the RF-4E Phantom, the Luftwaffe ordered 175 F-4F fighters in August 1971. The Richthofen Geschwader was the first recipient, officially beginning training on the type at George AFB, California, on 1 January 1974. The first aircraft arrived at Wittmundhafen on 7 March, and the unit was declared combat-ready on 1 July 1975. Following the *Peace Rhine* update to the aircraft, which added a digital weapons computer, Maverick capability and other improvements, JG 71 had a secondary attack tasking for most of the 1980s, but this was dropped on 1 July 1988.

The current wing badge features the NATO star. Both constituent squadron badges sport the famous red Triplane.

two McDonnell Douglas F-4F Phantom IIs arrived at Wittmund for ground technician training. The first pair of fully operational aircraft – already bearing the now familiar red script 'R' superimposed on the NATO star – touched down on 7 March 1974. And on 1 July the following year the lengthy process of re-equipment was finally complete; the Geschwader resumed its NATO 'combat ready' status as of that date.

For the first time in its history the Jagdgeschwader 'Richthofen' was flying a two-seat front-line fighter, a machine it continues to operate to this day. In the intervening years successive Kommodoren have helped put JG 71 at the very forefront of Western Europe's defences. The constant round of exercises and practice scrambles from Wittmund, combined with the annual deployment to Decimomannu in Sardinia for air combat training, and to Goose Bay, Canada, for low-level flying experience (a practice now frowned upon in an environmentally-sensitive Germany), has ensured that it remains there.

In 1988 the Geschwader was relieved of its long-standing secondary fighter-bomber attack role. The sudden easing of East-West tension two years later, and the subsequent disintegration of the Soviet Union, means that the occasional 'live' scramble and intercept of an inquisitive Russian Tu-95 'Bear' has also become a thing of the past. One of the most unexpected outcomes of the new European order was perhaps the presence at Wittmund in May 1991 of five ex-East German MiG-29 'Fulcrum' interceptor fighters. For three weeks the former 'opposition' was tested for possible integration into the NATO air defence system.

Whatever the future may hold, the Jagdgeschwader 'Richthofen' is determined to retain its links with its past. In 1975, in the middle of the Phantom re-equipment programme, the headstone from the Rittmeister's grave in Berlin's Invaliden cemetery – a gift from the von Richthofen family – was set up as a permanent memorial at Wittmund. But, sadly, one increasingly tenuous human link was finally broken on 4 September 1989 when Carl-August von Schoenebeck, the last surviving member of the original Jagdgeschwader Frhr. von Richthofen Nr. 1, and later Kommandeur of Fliegergruppe Damm in the mid-1930s, passed away, aged 91.

Since the Rittmeister's day the aircraft have changed, the demands made of the men who fly them have changed – indeed, the world itself has changed – but the tradition, and the spirit, live on. **John Weal**

The F-4F fleet was repainted in the 'Norm 81' low-visibility camouflage, although later a lighter all-over grey scheme was adopted. The ICE update programme added AIM-120 missile capability and exchanged the original radar for the APG-65 – ICE aircraft having a grey radome. JG 71 was the first recipient.

Conceived as a long-range fighter to accompany Strategic Air Command bombers, the F-88 never reached production status, yet did provide the basis for the later F-101 Voodoo. This aircraft was also initially designed as a strategic fighter, yet it saw service in three other major roles: nuclear bomber, tactical reconnaissance platform and defender of North American airspace. In the latter tasking, the Voodoo survived into the 1980s in the hands of the Canadians. Difficult to fly and maintain, the Voodoo's sleek looks and blistering performance were nevertheless guaranteed to generate excitement.

The McDonnell F-101 Voodoo evoked superlatives. It was bigger, faster. Pilots who took the RF-101C to Hanoi flew higher and faster than anything around them, challenged formidable air defences, and succeeded at high-risk, daytime combat reconnaissance. Crew chiefs who fussed over the F-101B interceptor assailed by Arctic winds on an icy, outdoor flight line cursed the aircraft for being nearly impossible to work on, but became excited when both afterburners were lit and the huge Voodoo was hurtling skyward. The F-101 Voodoo was also, arguably, the most dangerous, difficult-to-fly aircraft ever admitted into squadron service. From the beginning of its career to the end, the Voodoo had a reputation for forgiving no one, ever.

Coming from a manufacturer which excelled with Banshee and Phantom fighters, the Voodoo gave new meaning to the notion of

Although it was unsuccessful, the XF-88 was instrumental in establishing McDonnell as a major supplier of fighters to the Air Force. Here the very first Voodoo is parked outside the St Louis works – later to become the birthplace of the world-beating F-4 Phantom and F-15 Eagle. The XF-88 exhibited state-of-the-art features for a late 1940s jet fighter, such as lateral wingroot-mounted intakes, bulbous fuselage and wings swept at 35°. Speed performance was poor: the two engines did not provide nearly enough power.

McDonnell F-88/F-101 Voodoo Variant Briefing

Main picture: Of the weapons associated with the F-101, the most impressive was the AIR-2 Genie. Often called a missile, it was unguided and was thus more correctly a rocket. Its mission was to destroy enemy aircraft, especially incoming bombers, and it made up for its lack of guidance by way of a 1.5-kT yield nuclear warhead. This was exploded in the general proximity of the bombers, the aim being to place it in the centre of a formation. The explosion and resulting shock waves were lethal over a wide radius, necessitating immediate evasive action by the F-101 once the Genie was on its way.

brute force. Conceived as a 'penetration fighter', a post-war term for the escort function in which P-51 Mustangs excelled over Berlin, the Voodoo became not just a tactical reconnaissance collector and long-range strategic interceptor, but also an atomic bomber, supersonic propeller testbed, and crew trainer. For all that, Voodoo's imprint on our world was perhaps less than it might have been. The aircraft is remembered today with respect but without universal fondness.

Only the RF-101C 'recce' version got into combat, consistently flying the fastest combat sorties ever flown (with the special exception of the SR-71 Blackbird), daily challenging North Vietnam's missiles, MiGs and Triple-A at speeds greater than those of the F-4, F-8 or F-105. In its interceptor version, the Voodoo wore both 'stars and bars' and Canada's maple leaf, and evolved with difficulty into an exceedingly

potent weapon. The interceptor never won the accolades men bestowed on the prettier, more manoeuvrable (and slightly later) Convair F-106A Delta Dart. Furthermore, the interceptor Voodoo was worth having only after protracted difficulties with its fire-control and weapons systems were resolved.

In all of its versions, the Voodoo had a pitch-up problem caused by the manner in which air flowed over its wings and under its high tail.

There was no prototype of the second-generation Voodoo as such, but this F-101A (53-2418) was the first of the production aircraft and served as an evaluation airframe along with other early machines. Weapon systems were not carried initially, and the nose mounted a long air data probe for the duration of the aerodynamic trials. Here it is seen during its 29 September 1954 first flight from Edwards AFB, with Robert Little at the controls. On this sortie the F-101 became the first aircraft type to achieve supersonic flight on its maiden voyage.

The tendency to jerk into a nose-high attitude, unexpectedly and at the worst of times, killed several pilots, among them air ace Major Lonnie Moore who repeatedly prevailed over the MiG-15 in Korea but, like many, could not win out over the F-101 Voodoo in America. A pitch inhibitor, or 'stick knocker', installed in mid-life, did little to resolve the problem.

We have to remember that the F-101 Voodoo was "not just big", as one pilot described it, "but seriously big." An F-101B,

From 1961 the CF-101 provided Canada's main contribution to NORAD's defensive shield. The survivors of the initial batch of 66 were swapped for a second similarly-sized batch in 1971, and these veterans served until replacement by the CF-188 in 1984/85.

fully-armed, standing alert with a load of fuel tanks topped off, ready to launch against Soviet bombers streaming down from the polar north, swayed the scales at 54,650 lb (24790 kg). Its twin J57 turbojet engines on full afterburner kicked back a combined thrust of over 32,000 lb (142.34 kN), a figure without precedent. With an internal fuel capacity of 2,341 US gal (8862 litres), the Voodoo held five times the 435 US gal (1647 litres) of an F-84D Thunderjet. The fuselage of an F-101B with its length of 71 ft 1 in (22.02 m) was almost 10 ft (2 m) longer than a DC-3 transport. Designer Edward M. ('Bud') Flesh and others who created the F-88 and F-101 series at the McDonnell Aircraft Company in St Louis were thinking big

The F-101's first true mission was a nuclear bomber with the 81st TFW (an aircraft of the 92nd TFS being depicted here). The single nuclear weapon was usually released in a LABS Immelmann, the bomb being lobbed upwards to about 22,000 ft (6705 m), thus giving the Voodoo time to escape. From about 1963 the LADD (low-angle drogue delivery) supplanted the LABS profile, using parachute-retarded weapons.

from the start. They had no choice because their aircraft was conceived for the purpose of accompanying B-36 bombers deep into Soviet territory.

For James S. McDonnell, a pioneer in both aviation and business, the F-101 marked a turning point because it was his company's first sale to the US Air Force.　　**Robert F. Dorr**

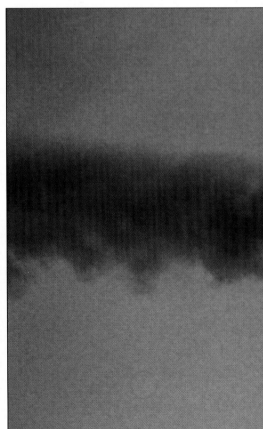

Above: **Photographed from its wingman, an RF-101C makes a high-altitude dash across the North Vietnamese MiG base at Kep. The RF-101C, popularly called the 'Long Bird', was the only Voodoo variant to see combat.**

Right: **Gear down and brakes out, an F-101B of the 29th FIS crosses the Missouri as it prepares to land at its base at Malmstrom AFB, Montana.**

Below: **The Canadian government officially neither confirmed nor denied the existence of nuclear weapons in its inventory, but this spectacular Genie shot from a CF-101B during a William Tell exercise certainly proves the capability.**

McDonnell F-88/F-101 Voodoo Variants

XP-88

On 1 April 1946, McDonnell Aircraft Company in St Louis, Missouri began design work on the company's Model 36 to meet a US Air Force requirement for a 'penetration fighter' to escort long-range bombers to their targets. The US Army Air Forces were planning to fight as they had during World War II, with fighters accompanying bombers and guarding them deep inside enemy territory. Early efforts to develop escort

fighters combining the speed of jet propulsion with the endurance of piston-engined warplanes, like the Consolidated Vultee XP-81 with a turboprop engine in the nose and turbojet in the tail, produced disappointing results. Consequently, in 1946, the USAAF levied a requirement for a pure-jet fighter with a combat radius of 900 miles (1450 km) and performance over the target good enough to cope with anticipated enemy opposition. USAAF planners knew nothing of the MiG-15, which made its first flight on 30 December 1947, but realised the Soviets were developing jet-propelled

aircraft. They anticipated serious air opposition.

On 20 June 1946, the USAAF awarded McDonnell a contract for two XP-88 pursuit aircraft (serial nos 46-525/526). In September 1946, before the P-88 design was finalised, McDonnell's tentative concept looked like the ship which finally emerged but had a butterfly, or Vee-shaped tail.

The XP-88 was first submitted to the US Air Force (which became a service branch on 17 September 1947) with the butterfly tail. The objective was to reduce the number and improve the nature of tail intersections

where compressibility effects were likely to give trouble. Early in wind tunnel tests, however, engineers encountered adverse rolling moments due to rudder action and insufficient longitudinal stability near the stall. A conventional tail was tested in the tunnel and was chosen when found largely free of aerodynamic faults. The V-tail remained in vogue for some years (successful on the Beech Bonanza, it was tested on the Republic XF-91), but McDonnell engineers dropped it early in their design work.

XF-88

On 1 July 1948, nine months after gaining its independence, the US Air Force changed its 'P' for pursuit designation to 'F' for fighter. The first of two McDonnell fighters then nearing completion was redesignated XF-88. The second became the XF-88A and is described separately. The nickname 'Voodoo', consistent with McDonnell's tradition of spirit-like apparitions, was given to the F-88 series.

Rolled out on 11 August 1948, the single-seat XF-88 (48-525) was a low/mid-wing aircraft characterised by 35° swept wings and tail surfaces and a lengthy fuselage to house fuel for its penetration mission. Powerplant was two 3,000-lb (13.35-kN) thrust Westinghouse XJ34-WE-13 turbojet engines mounted in the lower centre fuselage.

McDonnell chief test pilot Robert M. Edholm made the first flight of the XF-88 on 20 October 1948 at Muroc Dry Lake, California. Phase II flight tests were carried out 15-25 March 1949. Tests showed that the XF-88 was disappointingly slow, and led to the decision to add afterburning to the second Voodoo built, which became the XF-88A (below). The sole XF-88 was itself brought up to XF-88A standard with 52-in (130-cm) afterburners. Later, this ship was converted to become the XF-88B turboprop testbed.

Early test-flying at Lambert Field and Muroc Dry Lake revealed that, despite its ultra-thin swept wing, the XF-88 Voodoo was too slow for its intended mission. This was largely due to the low power rating of the engines and the bulky fuselage.

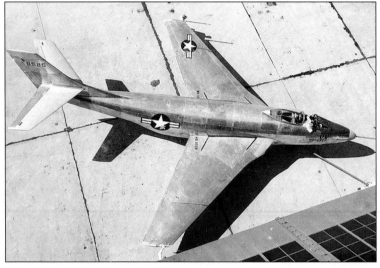

After exhaustive studies into a butterfly tail, the XF-88 finally emerged with a standard tail unit, albeit with the tailplane held part way up the fin to keep it in undisturbed airflow. The wing-sweep of 35° was largely determined by the result of German wartime research, most of which involved data at this setting. Any less was considered at the time as being not worth the effort: any more would be too risky. Originally McDonnell planned the F-88 with engines carried in the wingroots, but this proved unfeasible, and they were located in the lower fuselage where they could be easily reached and dropped out for maintenance. The fuselage was necessarily long and bulky to accommodate sufficient fuel for the escort fighter mission.

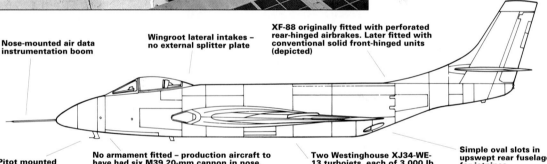

Nose-mounted air data instrumentation boom

Wingroot lateral intakes – no external splitter plate

XF-88 originally fitted with perforated rear-hinged airbrakes. Later fitted with conventional solid front-hinged units (depicted)

Pitot mounted below chin

No armament fitted – production aircraft to have had six M39 20-mm cannon in nose. Installation tested on ground nose section.

Two Westinghouse XJ34-WE-13 turbojets, each of 3,000 lb (13.35 kN) thrust

Simple oval slots in upswept rear fuselage for jetpipes

XF-88A

The second of two 'penetration fighter' prototypes from McDonnell, the XF-88A (46-526) made its first flight at St Louis on 26 April 1949. This fighter was identical to the earlier XF-88 except that it was equipped with afterburners for improved J34-WE-22 engines. In its 318-hour test flight programme, the XF-88A exceeded Mach 1 in dives and otherwise performed well, but the programme was curtailed by funding problems. This was a major disappointment, because the XF-88A was the winner in a vigorous 'penetration fighter' competition with the Lockheed XF-90 and North American YF-93A (F-86C).

This original XF-88A ended up at Langley AFB, Virginia where it was used for parts for the turboprop XF-88B, described separately.

Both aircraft in the F-88 series were eventually scrapped at Langley. The original XF-88A was turned over to base salvage on 7 July 1958. The designation XF-88A also applies to the first XF-88 when it was belatedly modified with afterburners, and before it was further modified to become the XF-88B.

XF-88A serial: 48-526

Nose cannon fitted to XF-88A later. XF-88A used to test underwing armament of two 1,000-lb (454-kg) bombs and six HVAR unguided rockets

Rudimentary McDonnell afterburners fitted to jetpipes. These were designed to be very short due to severe limitations imposed by ground clearance on rotation. XF-88A powered by J34-WE-22 engines of 4,100 lb (18.25 kN) thrust. Production F-88s to have featured Westinghouse J46-WE-2 engines of 5,920 lb (26.34 kN) thrust

Conventional speedbrake fitted in place of perforated brakes

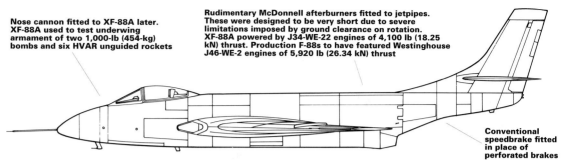

In this configuration the XF-88A was representative of the intended production fighter, lacking the nose instrumentation boom and featuring the cannon and afterburners. The first machine was also brought up to a similar standard, and both set impressive performance figures, including a level speed some 20 mph faster than the contemporary absolute speed record (held by a Sabre).

XF-88B

The XF-88B was the XF-88 (the first airframe, which meanwhile had been brought up to XF-88A standard) modified to become a research testbed for high-speed propellers. The USAF ordered this modification on 25 July 1949. McDonnell converted the aircraft between August and November 1952. The XF-88B 'tri-motor' first flew on 14 April 1953.

A 2,500-shp (1875-kW) Allison XT38, or company Model 501 F-1, turboprop engine was installed in the nose. Fuel tanks in the forward fuselage were removed, leaving about 300 US gal (1135 litres) for the two J34 turbojet engines with afterburners, plus the turboprop, making for very short flights. The engine installation also required that the nose landing gear be mounted about 18 in (45 cm) off centre, but this did not affect ground handling. Because the XT38's turbine was directly behind the pilot's seat, armour plate was installed under the seat.

Propeller gearbox ratios provided three prop speeds of 1,700, 3,600, and 6,000 rpm. The design was be compatible with propellers of 4, 7 and 10 ft (1.2, 2.1 and 3.0 m). With the largest of these, ground clearance was a paltry 6.7 in (17 cm). The XF-88B was designed to take off with the propeller feathered and in an 'X' position to keep it from hitting the ground.

The USAF's Air Research and

Three supersonic propeller configurations tested in flight, consisting of four-bladed (illustrated), three-bladed and three-bladed with 'turnip' spinner. Sensor rigs often carried either side of nose

Allison XT38 turboprop mounted in nose, using fuel from main system. Nosewheel redesigned to accommodate engine

Standard XF-88 airframe used (after upgrading to XF-88A configuration with standard airbrakes and afterburner

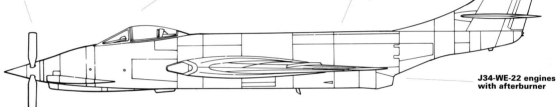

J34-WE-22 engines with afterburner

Development Command (ARDC) embarked on tests of the XF-88B in early 1953 in collaboration with the US Navy's Bureau of Aeronautics and the National Advisory Committee for Aeronautics. The XF-88B's maiden flight was revealed only months after it happened. An Air Force pilot first flew the XF-88B on 23 June 1953 following 16 test flights by McDonnell pilots.

The XF-88B was flown by Capt. John M. 'Fitz' Fitzpatrick to NACA's Langley AFB, Virginia, facility where it was flown with various propeller configurations by NACA project pilots John P. (Jack) Reeder and William L. Alford. The XF-88B made 43 test flights.

Fitzpatrick remembers of the XF-88B that "one obvious test objective was to see how fast it would go. After accelerating to maximum speed, about 0.91 Mach, with full power on both jets and the turboprop, I would put it into a slight dive. On each flight I steepened the dive angle. The Mach meter would get to about 0.96 and stick there. The McDonnell engineers tried to convince us that with their airspeed corrections I was actually supersonic. I may have been, but we had a rule in the Fighter Section that unless you actually indicated supersonic speed, with the accompanying altimeter jump, you could not claim to have done so." On 27 June 1953, Fitzpatrick exceeded

Mach 1.0, possibly the first measured supersonic flight by a propeller aircraft.

The USAF later pursued its fascination for the supersonic turboprop with the Republic XF-84H, although it is hard to see why. A test pilot recalls that, "the propeller lab people were running our R&D programme." These aircraft produced so much noise and vibration that ground crewmen became ill. The XF-88B contributed significantly to aeronautical knowledge, but its successor the XF-84H flew only a few hours. Eventually, the XF-88B was flown by NACA at Langley Field. It was turned over to salvage crews to be scrapped on 16 September 1958.

XF-88B serial: 46-525

Seen prior to its first flight in June 1953, the XF-88B stands outside the St Louis factory, displaying the initial four-bladed propeller installation.

The XF-88B often had to be towed to the runway to conserve fuel, as all three engines ran off the fuel system, which itself was much reduced by the fitment of the turboprop. After take-off with the propeller feathered, it was started for about 20 minutes for tests.

F-88

Several versions of the F-88 Voodoo were proposed by McDonnell engineers:

Navy F-88: On 30 June 1948, McDonnell proposed a US Navy carrier-based XP-88 (redesignated XF-88 the next day). At the same time, the company made changes in US Air Force XF-88 to make it more attractive for naval operations: these included deleting the 350-US gal (1325-litre) wingtip tanks integral to the type's design, which were fitted on the second ship (the XF-88A) prior to its first flight, but were

never flown because wind tunnel tests predicted stall problems. The fuselage nose forward of the cockpit pressure bulkhead was equipped with hinges to rotate the nose section. Wing-fold mechanism and hinges and a strengthened undercarriage for carrier operations were added. The US Navy chose to proceed with the carrier-based McDonnell XF2D-1 Banshee (later XF2H-1) instead, neither the first nor the last time the Navy selected a straight-wing aircraft, and delayed getting into the swept-wing jet fighter business.

Two-seater: In 1948, a concept by McDonnell's H. N. Cole sketched out a

production F-88 with a two-man crew in tandem seats. No contemporaneous documents have survived, but it is likely the manufacturer was still thinking of the escort-fighter role. The design was not proceeded with, but a two-seat configuration evolved separately for the F-101B/F interceptor.

Production USAF version: The production F-88 was to be powered by two 5,920-lb (26.33-kN) Westinghouse J46-W-2 engines. This is the thrust rating of the Westinghouse engine without afterburning (the company's J34, J40, and J46 were used in a series of aircraft deemed underpowered). The production warplane

would have had reheat, although its burner cans still would have been limited to 52 in (130-cm) in length, lest the aircraft scrape the ground when rotating on take-off.

RF-88A: Not an official designation, RF-88A was McDonnell's term for a version with an interchangeable nose which would enable a single airframe to be quickly field-modified, flying as a fighter on one mission, and a photo-gatherer on the next. Studies on an F-88A/RF-88A which could shift roles on short notice contributed to the manufacturer's later work on the YRF-101A.

F-101A

The F-101 was conceived as an escort fighter but the first model to appear, the F-101A, enjoyed only a brief career in different job status as a one-way, single-mission atomic bomber. The F-101A and C fighters were also known as Weapon System WS-105A in Pentagon jargon of the mid-1950s, though the practice of assigning a 'WS' designation to tanks, ships and aircraft lasted only a couple of years.

After determining that the Westinghouse J46 powerplant of the mooted production F-88 offered insufficient thrust, the McDonnell design team under Edward M. ('Bud') Flesh contemplated the Allison J71 as powerplant for the twin-engined F-101. Instead, the aircraft was completed with two Pratt & Whitney J57-P-13 turbojet engines rated at 10,200 lb (45.38 kN) thrust, a figure which rose to 15,000 lb (66.73 kN) with afterburning. The '-13' version of the engine propelled all Voodoo models except the F-101B.

Fed by enlarged and redesigned air intakes in the wingroots, the P&W engines were expected to be more powerful than other engines tried or considered, but also to offer better fuel consumption. Still, the aircraft was designed with its enormous 2,341 US gal (8862-litre) fuel capacity.

Because of delays in the flight test programme, the USAF's goal of having an airframe able to withstand 7.33 g could not be met in initial production machines. Numerous remedies were pondered but in the end the USAF opted, in June 1956, to take delivery of 6.33-g airframes until structurally improved models could be built: the USAF decreed that the 'A' suffix would denote 6.33-g airframes while the 'C' suffix would identify 7.33-g airframes. This distinction was preserved with reconnaissance Voodoos which had an 'RF' prefix.

The F-101A drew heavily on the F-88 design and was a low/mid-wing aircraft with the familiar elongated fuselage and swept wings and tail surfaces. The F-101A fuselage offered sufficient ground clearance for afterburner cans of reasonable length. The aircraft was a remarkable 67 ft 4 ¾ in (20.54 m) long, some 14 ft (4.33 m) more than the F-88, yet its wing span remained unchanged at 39 ft 8 in (12.09 m). Because of an increase in chord, wing area rose from 350 sq ft (32.52 m²) to 368 sq ft (34.19 m), yet there remained a rather flimsy appearance to the wing structure and,

Above: Proudly wearing its name on the nose, the first F-101A rests on Rogers Dry Lake at Edwards AFB. In this early form the derivation from the F-88 is clearly visible.

Right: The sixth F-101A was part of the trials fleet, seen here with a full load of three external tanks. The F-101's armament was reduced to four M39 cannon from the F-88's six.

indirectly, the pitch-up problem which was to plague the aircraft throughout its career. The most obvious change from the earlier F-88 was a higher-mounted horizontal stabiliser, almost a T-tail.

McDonnell test pilot Robert C. Little remembers that, "without question, the F-101A at the time had the highest thrust-to-weight ratio and the highest wing loading of any fighter aircraft ever built." Little made the maiden flight of the first F-101A at Edwards AFB, California on 29 September 1954. It was the first time a new aircraft went supersonic on its debut and Little outran two chase planes, a T-33 trainer and an F-100, which could not keep up even on full afterburner.

Like the F-101C to follow, the F-101A was armed with four 20-mm M39 cannons aimed through a K-19 gunsight. World War II experience had shown that bombers could not campaign effectively against a nation's military and industrial infrastructure unless

accompanied by fighter escort, provided in Europe by the North American P-51 Mustang. Strategic Air Command's chief, General Curtis E. LeMay, remained unconvinced that 'little friends' were needed. Although SAC fielded squadrons of Republic F-84F Thunderstreak and F-84E/G Thunderjet fighters, LeMay never lost his misgivings.

Flight tests and minor modifications to the F-101A resolved an early problem with engine compressor stalls. The F-101 Voodoo's pitch-up problem was never overcome. As described by Brigadier General Robin Olds, who commanded a

Voodoo wing, "It didn't take much for the F-101 to go into pitch-up, even in cruise. Reason: the angle of attack needed to achieve lift at, let's say, 34,000 ft [10350 m] with full flaps, drop tanks and internal fuel was awfully close to the pitch-up stall point, where the flow of air over the wings created a downflow over the slab, which the slab could not accommodate." On 10 January 1956, Major Lonnie R. Moore, a Korean War ace with 10 MiG-15 kills, was lost in an F-101A Voodoo pitch-up mishap at Eglin AFB, Florida. Installation of an inhibitor, known to pilots as a 'stick knocker', helped some, but not much. Also never resolved was the problem of retracting the Voodoo's nosewheel, designed to be hoisted forward into the airstream. Beyond a speed of about 90 mph (144 km/h), the wheel would not go up.

SAC operated the F-101A, but for a scant two months. On 1 July 1957, two months after the first deliveries of the F-101A began far behind schedule, the 27th Strategic Fighter Wing at Bergstrom AFB, Texas, was transferred to Tactical Air Command and became the 27th Fighter-Bomber Wing. The wing (consisting of the 481st, 522nd and 523rd FBS) had previously operated the F-84F Thunderstreak. The Voodoo's original mission was forgotten and it was assigned to deliver a centreline nuclear bomb to a target. It was capable of little else and, although designated a 'fighter', would have acquitted itself poorly in any air-to-air duel. Some F-101As later served with the 81st TFW in England (as noted in the separate entry on the F-101C).

An F-101A was assigned to Project

Above: The F-101 was destined to never serve in its intended escort fighter role, but was instead used initially as a nuclear bomber. This trials aircraft carries a test 'shape' for a Mk 7 device on the centreline. During Operation Redwing, an F-101A was flown supersonically through an H-bomb mushroom cloud, although the Voodoo was never used to drop a live weapon.

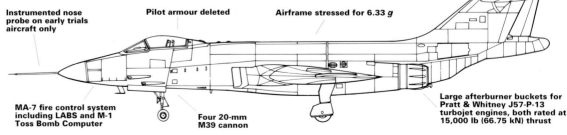

Instrumented nose probe on early trials aircraft only

Pilot armour deleted

Airframe stressed for 6.33 g

Stabilator mounted near top of fin

MA-7 fire control system including LABS and M-1 Toss Bomb Computer

Four 20-mm M39 cannon

Large afterburner buckets for Pratt & Whitney J57-P-13 turbojet engines, both rated at 15,000 lb (66.75 kN) thrust

Above: An F-101A on a pre-delivery flight displays the type's fine lines. An attempt to area-rule the F-101A was made by adding bulges around the afterburner region, but these were unsuccessful.

Redwing, the detonation of hydrogen bombs at Eniwetok Atoll in the Pacific in 1957. By late 1958, however, after less than 18 months of operational service, the 27th FBW began converting to F-100 Super Sabres and F-101As were retired.

NACA acquired two F-101A Voodoos, 53-2434 which was ferried from Edwards to Langley by Jack Reeder on 22 August 1956

Right: F-101As served alongside the strengthened C model in both the 27th FBW and the 81st TFW in England. The latter's aircraft were initially marked with a double fin-stripe in the squadron colours.

and 54-1442 which was taken on charge by NACA on 18 April 1958. Of 77 F-101As accepted by the USAF, 50 reached service and the remainder were used for tests and special projects. Long after their bombing mission was history, 29 F-101As were converted to RF-101G.
F-101A serials: 53-2418/2446, 54-1438/1485.

JF-101A

The sole JF-101A – the 'J' prefix signifying a temporary change in configuration for test purposes — was the ninth F-101A bailed to Pratt & Whitney to evaluate the more powerful J57-P-53 engines chosen for the F-101B interceptor. This required little internal modification, but did require a large extension of the jetpipe to accommodate the much longer afterburner section. The afterburner section of the JF-101A was different to that fitted to production F-101Bs, and incorporated additional air scoops for afterburner cooling.

In Operation Fire Wall on 12 December 1957, Major Adrian Drew of the 27th FBW flew the JF-101A to a world speed record of 1,207.6 mph (1943.43 km/h), taking the record from the British Fairey Delta 2.
JF-101A serial: 53-2426

The 'Fire Wall' aircraft was an engine test-ship, but the chance to shatter the world speed record could not be passed over. After the record run at Edwards, Drew immediately flew to Los Angeles International Airport to receive the DFC from General McCarty, commander of 18th Air Force.

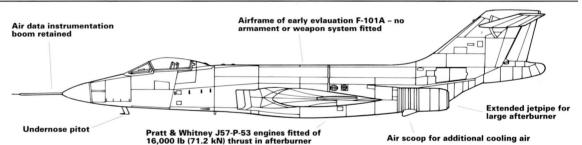

Air data instrumentation boom retained

Airframe of early evluation F-101A – no armament or weapon system fitted

Extended jetpipe for large afterburner

Undernose pitot

Pratt & Whitney J57-P-53 engines fitted of 16,000 lb (71.2 kN) thrust in afterburner

Air scoop for additional cooling air

NF-101A

The NF-101A – the 'N' prefix indicating a permanent change in configuration for test purposes – was the first F-101A bailed to General Electric as a platform for the J79-GE-1 turbojet engine, apparently in connection with design and development work on McDonnell's F4H-1 Phantom II fleet interceptor for the US Navy. The sole NF-101A eventually ended its life as a ground maintenance trainer at Amarillo AFB, Texas, but apparently was not assigned a GF-101A designation as would have been appropriate.
NF-101A serial: 53-2418.

The J79 Voodoo featured a different extended afterburner section to the JF-101A. This aircraft flew trials in support of the Phantom programme.

YRF-101A

The YRF-101A was the service-test prototype for the 'recce' Voodoo, also known to the Pentagon was Weapon System WS-105L. The 'YRF' had the same configuration as the 6.33-*g* RF-101A and 7.33-*g* RF-101C which followed.

On 11 October 1953, the USAF contracted McDonnell to rebuild the 16th and 19th F-101As on the production line and complete them as YRF-101As. The USAF considered but rejected a design with an interchangeable nose to carry guns on one sortie and, after a quick ground change, cameras on the next. On 13 January 1954 during a mock-up inspection it was decided to incorporate the bulky KA-1 camera which dictated the long, wedge-shaped configuration of the camera nose. The first YRF-101A flew on 30 June 1955.
YRF-101A serials: 54-149/150

54-0149 was the first of two YRF-101As converted on the production line and was delivered without cameras. The drag chute was housed in the tailcone behind a hinged cap.

The second YRF-101A was fitted with cameras, a mixture of Fairchild KA-1 and KA-2 units. The large KA-1 which faced obliquely forward through the nose dictated the characteristic chisel-shaped nose.

RF-101A

The RF-101A reconnaissance Voodoo followed the pair of service-test ships. The RF-101A was originally intended for SAC, but years were to pass until the command picked up a dedicated reconnaissance aircraft (the SR-71); in a last-minute change, the RF-101A went to Tactical Air Command. Thirty-five were built.

All reconnaissance versions of the Voodoo could carry up to six cameras. The RF-101A's initial 'fit' consisted of one 12-in focal length Fairchild KA-2 framing camera shooting forward, three 6-in focal length KA-2s in a forward tri-camera station shooting downward, and a pair of larger KA-1s farther astern. A KA-18 strip camera could also be carried. A VF-31 viewfinder allowed the pilot to look through the tri-camera station. The RF-101A offered redundant receptacles for air refuelling (flying boom for KC-97 and KC-135, probe and drogue for the KB-50J).

The RF-101A's nose camera system had a battery-operated elevator to lower the camera to retrieve the film packs. When the cameras were not installed, the forward regions of the wedge nose provided excess stowage space for cargo or personal belongings.

Although the aircraft design was mature, development of camera systems for the RF-101A was still occurring (with the 3241st Test Squadron at Eglin AFB, Florida) when the first aircraft were delivered to the 17th Tactical Reconnaissance Squadron (and, soon afterward, the 18th TRS), 363rd Tactical Reconnaissance Wing, at Shaw Air Force Base, South Carolina on 6 May 1957, replacing the RB-57A/B Canberra.

On 26 November 1957, an RF-101A Voodoo flown by Gustave B. Klatt set a West Coast (Los Angeles to New York to Los Angeles) transcontinental record of six hours 42 minutes 6.9 seconds. On the return leg, Klatt set an east-west record of three hours 34 minutes 8.6 seconds.

RF-101As served briefly with the Air National Guard's 154th TRS (Fort Smith, Arkansas) and 127th TRG (Selfridge ANGB, Michigan).

In Operation Boom Town culminating in October 1959, approximately eight RF-101As were transferred to the Republic of China air force on Formosa (as Americans called Taiwan, then), which used them for reconnaissance operations over the Chinese mainland. Peking claims to have shot down two RF-101As, one of them in March 1965.
RF-101A serials: 54-1494/1521; 56-155/161

Chisel nose containing camera installation

Retractable refuelling probe in upper nose

Airframe based on F-101A – 6.33 *g* stressing

Pratt & Whitney J57-P-13 engines

Above: The first USAF unit to receive the Voodoo was the 363rd Tactical Reconnaissance Wing at Shaw AFB, which acquired its first RF-101A on 6 May 1957. This aircraft wears the marks of the 18th TRS.

Below: RF-101As were all delivered in a natural metal finish, with a dark anti-glare panel on the upper forward fuselage.

Right: During the mid-1960s several RF-101As were tested with complicated camouflage patterns. These were shelved in favour of the standard T.O. 114 three-tone 'Southeast Asia' camouflage.

Below right: The RF-101 fleet was given a light grey paint scheme in the mid-1960s to protect against corrosion. Many aircraft did not wear unit markings, although this machine wears the TAC badge.

Below: A 363rd TRW F-101A flies by at speed. The 363rd controlled the 432nd TRG which, when elevated to wing status, took over control of the four RF-101A squadrons in 1958.

F-101B

The F-101B (originally, F-109) was the two-seat, long-range interceptor. The aircraft was also known to the manufacturer as the Model 36 AT, and to the USAF as Weapon System 217A. Its forward fuselage had tandem pressurised and air-conditioned cockpits under a single clamshell-style plexiglass canopy. With 479 examples built for the Air Defense Command, or ADC (Aerospace Defense Command after January 1968), the F-101B was the most numerous Voodoo model. It was heavier than single-seat variants and employed larger tyres with a beefed-up undercarriage and bulges in the lower gear doors and undersides of the fuselage to accommodate the tyres.
The F-101B was powered by two 10,700-lb (44.47-kN) thrust Pratt & Whitney J57-P-55 turbojet engines, the only Voodoo not using

After service evaluation by the 60th FIS at Otis AFB, the F-101B entered service with 17 Air Defense Command squadrons, all equipped by December 1960. This aircraft flew with the 29th FIS at Malmstrom.

the -13 version of the engine. The F-101B had extended afterburner cans about 24 in (60 cm) longer than those on other Voodoo models. Afterburning raised the thrust rating to about 15,000 lb (66.73 kN).
The F-101B was compatible with the Semi-Automatic Ground Environment (SAGE) system which was the USAF's standard method of ground-controlled intercept in the 1950s. Its Hughes MG-13 fire-control system handled both nuclear and non-nuclear air-to-air rocket missiles and projectiles. Armament initially comprised two Hughes GAR-8 (originally XF-98, later AIM-4) Falcon infra-red air-to-air missiles. The F-101B acquired additional teeth when it was configured in a 1961 modification programme to carry two MB-1 (later AIR-2A) Genie unguided rockets with atomic warheads. The latter was designed to scatter incoming Soviet bomb formations and was tested 'live' on 19 July 1957 when a Genie was fired from an F-89J Scorpion over Yucca Flat, Nevada and detonated a 1.5-kT blast. The F-101B was also configured to carry a number of tow targets, principally the Hayes TDU-25/B. The F-101B's fire control system initially was the Hughes MG-11, replaced in retrofit by the MG-13.

Above: Early F-101Bs were assigned to trials duties and often had metal noses housing test equipment rather than the radar. This aircraft was the fifth B model.

McDonnell F-88/F-101 Voodoo Variants

Above: A common sight on F-101Bs, particularly at Tyndall AFB, was the 'Rummy 8', more formally known as the RMU-8A target system. A centreline mounted pod could reel out a dart target on up to 49,000 ft (14935 m) of cable on 'Super Tow' missions. Different darts could undertake missile or Genie test scoring, and contained radar signature enhancers and infra-red sources.

Above: Another view of 56-0236 portrays the twin carriage of AIR-2A Genies during the early B test programme. At the time the rocket was designated MB-1.

Right: With missile bays empty and airbrakes out, an F-101B of the 437th FIS breaks from the camera. The 437th was based at Oxnard AFB, California.

The F-101B entered service with the 60th Fighter-Interceptor Squadron at Otis AFB, Massachusetts on 5 January 1959 while still testing its compatibility with the SAGE system. Early users of the B model from June 1959 included the 84th (Hamilton AFB, California), 98th (Dover AFB, Delaware) and 322nd (Klamath Falls, Oregon) squadrons, joined before the end of 1959 by the 2nd (Suffolk County, New York), 13th (Glascow AFB, Montana), 49th (Griffiss AFB, New York), and 62nd (K. I. Sawyer AFB, Michigan). By June 1960, a third stage of readiness had been attained when the F-101B reached initial operating capability with the 15th (Davis-Monthan AFB, Arizona), 18th (Grand Forks AFB, North Dakota), 29th (Malmstrom AFB, Montana), 87th (Lockbourne AFB, Ohio), 437th (Oxnard AFB, California), 444th (Charleston AFB, South Carolina) and 445th (Wurtsmith AFB, Michigan). The F-101B was flown by the 4570th Test Squadron, the operational suitability test unit for ADC, at Tyndall AFB, Florida and by the 4756th CCTS (later redesignated the 2nd Fighter-Interceptor Training Squadron) at the same location. ADC F-101Bs were withdrawn from service over the period 1969-72.

The ANG began operating the F-101B

interceptor in November 1969. ANG squadrons included the 111th (Ellington AFB, Texas), 116th (Spokane, Washington), 123rd (Portland, Oregon), 132nd (Bangor AFB, Maine), 136th (Niagara Falls, New York), 178th (Fargo, South Dakota), 179th (Duluth, Minnesota) and 192nd (Reno, Nevada). The final operator of the F-101B was the 111th FIS at Ellington, which operated the F-101B/F briefly as a part of Tactical Air Command after ADC was inactivated on 1 April 1980. In 1981, after the base itself had changed from an AFB to an ANGB, Ellington gave up its Voodoos for the F-4C Phantom. Also in 1981, Colorado State University flew a civil-registered F-101B fitted with special instrumentation as part of a weather research programme.

Production of the F-101B interceptor ended on 24 March 1961. Subsequently, a major update of the fire control system,

The Hughes MG-13 fire control system was integrated with the SAGE system. It was hard to master but was capable of hands-off Genie launches, including automatic launch of rocket, turning the airplane into the escape manoeuvre, and detonating the nuclear warhead at the appropriate time.

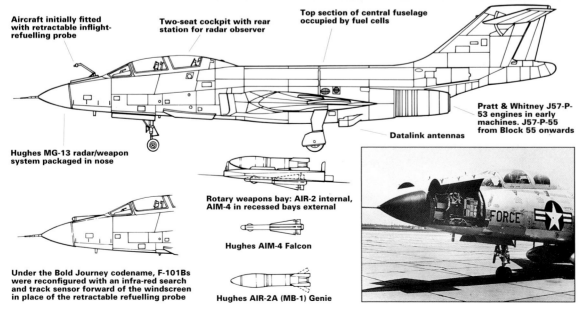

Aircraft initially fitted with retractable inflight-refuelling probe

Two-seat cockpit with rear station for radar observer

Top section of central fuselage occupied by fuel cells

Pratt & Whitney J57-P-53 engines in early machines. J57-P-55 from Block 55 onwards

Datalink antennas

Hughes MG-13 radar/weapon system packaged in nose

Rotary weapons bay: AIR-2 internal, AIM-4 in recessed bays external

Hughes AIM-4 Falcon

Under the Bold Journey codename, F-101Bs were reconfigured with an infra-red search and track sensor forward of the windscreen in place of the retractable refuelling probe

Hughes AIR-2A (MB-1) Genie

Above: After its active-duty days were over, the F-101B served with the Guard. These aircraft are from the 136th FIS, New York ANG. Note the searchlight below the rear cockpit.

Below: An F-101B displays the striking markings of the 437th FIS. Between 1960 and 1964 the F-101 was ADC's most numerous aircraft, but by 1971 all operational aircraft had passed to the ANG.

accomplished in the latter half of 1961 and known by the codename Kitty Car, brought earlier production F-101Bs up to the final Block 120 standard. Other post-production improvements were introduced between 1961 and 1966 in project Bold Journey, also known as the IIP (Interceptor Improvement Program). This long-running programme enhanced the resistance of F-101B airframes to electromagnetic pulse and installed an improved MG-13 fire-control system for use especially against targets flying at low level. The distinguishing feature of Bold Journey was the infra-red detection scanner in the nose space formerly occupied by an inflight-refuelling probe.

Delivered in bare metal, F-101Bs were later painted grey to reduce corrosion. Of 479 F-101Bs manufactured, 79 were completed as 'two-seat dual-control aircraft' and 152 more retrofitted to dual-control configuration. In the first batch of 79, 58 were initially completed as TF-101B aircraft . All dual-control aircraft were eventually designated F-101F. Serials are listed in the F-101F entry.

Some 112 F-101B interceptors were transferred to Canada along with 20 dual-control CF-101Fs.

F-101B serials (including two-seat aircraft): 56-0233/00328, 57-0247/0452, 58-0259/0342, 59-0391/0483

The AIM-4 Falcon was fired from a rail which deployed down from the rotary door. Ahead of the port missile was a baffle to deflect hot air from a cooling exhaust away from the infra-red sensor.

Above: The Tyndall-based Air Defense Weapons Center was the final USAF user of the F-101B, operating the type on target-towing and EW (note ECM pod) duties until 20 September 1982. The final ANG F-101B user was the 111th FIS, Texas ANG, which gave up Voodoos earlier in the year.

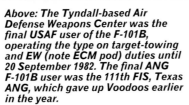

CF-101B

CF-101B was the Canadian designation for F-101Bs supplied from USAF inventory to the Canadians in two batches on separate occasions. Under Operation Queens Row, the US provided 66 Voodoos, including 56 F-101Bs and 10 dual-control ships which were handed over at RCAF Uplands in April 1961. The CF-101B was virtually identical to the USAF F-101B; those in the first batch were turned over with a nose inflight-refuelling probe just forward of the pilot's windscreen even though air refuelling was never used tactically by RCAF Voodoos. It must be assumed that arrangements existed for the US to release to Canada the nuclear warhead for the AIR-2A Genie missile, which the Canadians employed. The first batch was in service on 1 February 1968, the date of integration when the RCAF (Royal Canadian Air Force) became the CAF (Canadian Armed Forces/Forces Armées Canadiennes). The arrival of the bilingual era saw French titles appearing alongside English on Voodoos.

The second batch of 66 Voodoos reaching Canada from US inventory contained a retrofit also found on their American counterparts, namely a nose-mounted infra-red sensor ball used for target detection.

RCAF squadrons operating the Voodoo were Nos. 409 'Crossbow' (later 'Nighthawk') (Comox, Cold Lake), 410 'Cougar' (Uplands, Bagotville), 414 'Black Knights' (North Bay), 416 'Black Lynx' (Uplands, Bagotville, Chatham), and 425 'Alhouette' (Bagotville). No. 410 Squadron at Uplands was the Operational Training Squadron for the type. No. 414 Squadron at North Bay was the final operator of the CF-101B/F.

CF-101B serials from the first batch delivered to Canada (not including 10 dual-control aircraft designated CF-101F in Canadian service, serials of which are listed separately): 59-391/392 (RCAF 17391/17392); 59-394/399 (17394/17399); 59-401/411 (17401/17411); 59-433/436 (17433/17436); 59-438/442 (17438/17442); 59-444/448 (17444/17448); 59-450/453 (17450/17453); 59-445/457 (17455/17457); 59-459 (17459); 59-461 (17461); 57-463/465 (17463/17465); 59-467/471 (17467/17471);

Above: Initial deliveries went to Namao, Alberta, in October 1961, the first Canadian crews having undergone training at Hamilton AFB, California. Squadron colours were carried on the rudder.

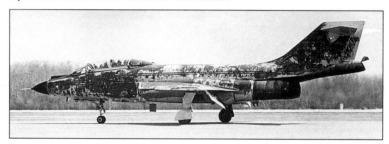

Above: Temporary camouflage was applied to a 425 Sqn CF-101B for a Maple Flag exericse held at CFB Cold Lake. The paint was soluble and easily washed off.

59-475/477 (17475/17477); 59-479/483 (17479/17483).

CF-101B serials from the second batch delivered to Canada (not including 10 dual-control CF-101Fs listed separately): 56-260 (CAF 101002); 57-268, 57-273, 57-286, 57-289, 57-293, 57-296, 57-298/299, 57-303, 57-305/306, 57-314/315, 57-321

(101008/101021); 57-323 (101023); 57-334, 57-340/341, 57-346, 57-351, 57-354, 57-358/360, 57-362/364, 57-366, 57-368/369, 57-373/375, 57-380/382, 57-384, 57-388, 57-391, 57-395/396, 57-398 (101025/101051); 57-418, 57-420, 57-424, 57-426, 57-429, 57-431/434, 57-441/444, 57-451 (101053/101066).

Above: This CF-101B is in the interim scheme, retaining the natural metal but having adopted the 'band-aid' maple leaf flag. Note the datalink under the starboard engine.

Below: From 1 July 1982, 425 Sqn CF-101Bs began Cold Shaft operations, holding at one-hour readiness to augment other squadrons at five-mninute alert. This trio of 425 aircraft includes two CF-101Fs.

McDonnell CF-101B Voodoo
410 'Cougar' Squadron
Royal Canadian Air Force

The Voodoo in Canadian service

Five RCAF squadrons converted at Namao to the Voodoo in the winter of 1961/62, the first being 425 'Alouette' Sqn (black/silver rudder stripes). This undertook the conversion role until October 1962 at Bagotville, where No. 3(AW) OTU took over the role. 410 'Cougar' Sqn was the next to convert, moving to Uplands between December 1961 and March 1964, before moving to Bagotville. Here it eventually took over from No. 3(AW) OTU as the training unit, before becoming the Hornet OCU in 1982. 416 'Black Lynx' Sqn converted to the Voodoo in January 1962, flying initially from Uplands and Bagotville before settling at Chatham. 409 'Nighthawk' Sqn followed before moving to Comox. The fifth and final Canadian Voodoo squadron was 414 'Black Night' Sqn, which flew from North Bay until June 1964. It later flew the sole EF-101B in the 1980s.

The North American Air Defense Command (NORAD) was created jointly by the US and Canada in 1958, with a US commander and Canadian deputy. The organisation controlled a complicated system of radars and interceptors. From 1962 to 1984 the CF-101B was the main Canadian contribution to NORAD's air assets.

Weapon system

CF-101s were fitted with the MG-13 fire control system. The system tracked the target, assigned the missile and provided a steering cue for the pilot. It commanded him to arm the missile, and then automatically launched it at the correct moment.

Navigator cockpit

The rear cockpit was dominated by a large circular display for the radar, situated with its controls on the starboard side of the dashboard. To port were flight and navigation instruments, shaded by a large hood.

Markings

Initial markings consisted of the original Canadian flag on the fin, 'Royal Canadian Air Force' titles and a large maple roundel on the nose on an unpainted aircraft. The legend 'RCAF' appeared ahead of the roundel with the last-three of the serial behind. The 'RCAF' was soon dropped, as shown here. A considerable period of transition then occurred, the first markings to change being the flag, which became the current 'band-aid' maple leaf, and the roundel, which remained large but with the maple leaf becoming much smaller in side the white circle. The second batch of aircraft featured silver aluminium paint with small-size roundels. Fuselage titles reflected the integration of the services with 'Canadian Armed Forces' to port and 'Forces Armées Canadiennes' to starboard. This scheme subsequently gave way to anti-corrosion light grey paint, with 'Canada' fuselage titles and small roundels flanked by 'Armed Forces' and 'Forces Armées'.

Fuel

Five fuel cells in the upper fuselage and three in each wing combined to give an internal capacity of 13,546 lb (6144 kg). This could be augmented by two 450-US gal (1703-litre) drop tanks, which were short large-diameter units on the first batch of aircraft and longer, more streamlined tanks on the second batch. The first batch of aircraft also retained the retractable refuelling probe in the nose but was not used. The second batch replaced the probe with the infra-red search and track sensor.

Alert operations

On air defence alert, the Voodoo was normally held at five-minute readiness. 416 Sqn at Chatham undertook most 'live' intercepts by nature of its geographical location, although other squadrons manned alerts at their bases. In July 1982 Operation Cold Shaft saw 425 Sqn's CF-101s on alert at Loring AFB, Maine, among other bases, although they were held at only one-hour readiness, and were expected to fuel-stop at Gander for a 'live' mission against Soviet patrol aircraft.

Armament

CF-101s carried the same armament as the USAF interceptors: two AIM-4D Falcons and up to two AIR-2A Genies. The Falcons were programmed to launch in salvo, the second firing a half-second behind the first. The improved AIM-26B later replaced the AIM-4s. The Genie was never officially confirmed as a CF-101 weapon, although Canadian crews trained with it often. It is believed a dual-key arrangement existed for the release by the US of the nuclear warheads.

McDonnell F-88/F-101 Voodoo Variants

EF-101B

Canada leased the sole EF-101B, or 'Electric Voodoo', from the US Air Force and flew the aircraft with 414 'Black Knights' Squadron at North Bay. Not among Canada's two batches of 66 F-101B interceptors, the EF-101B served as an electronic target aircraft, simulating the radar signature of an incoming Soviet bomber. Retired in 1987 (and relegated to a museum in Minneapolis-St Paul), the EF-101B was the final Voodoo in service with any air arm.
EF-101B serial: 58-0300 (CAF 101067)

The EF-101B entered service with 414 Sqn in 1983, having been stored at Davis-Monthan. Originally delivered in grey, it was the only Canadian Voodoo to never receive a fuselage cheat line. Note the additional antennas below and behind the cockpit.

NF-101B

The NF-101B was the two-seat prototype for the long-range F-101B/F interceptor series. The aircraft was retained at Edwards AFB, California after its 27 March 1957 first flight (which also qualifies as the first flight by an F-101B). This was the only B model built with an A-model airframe limited to 6.33 g. It remained a test ship because teething troubles demanded a more rigorous flight-test programme than originally foreseen.

A second ship was later given the 'N' prefix, which indicates a permanent change for test purposes. This aircraft had a one-of-a-kind pointed nose configuration and was used to test systems for surface-to-air drones as targets at Tyndall.
NF-101B serials: 56-232, 57-409.

The prototype two-seater was designated NF-101B in respect of its permanent test status. The aircraft had the low-strength airframe, and had test equipment in the nose instead of the fire control system and radar.

Another view of '232 during an early test flight, carrying dummy Falcon missiles. The NF-101B could be distinguished by having much shorter jetpipes instead of the lengthened burner cans of production aircraft.

RF-101B

The RF-101B became the final reconnaissance version of the Voodoo and the only version with a backseat crew member. On their return from Canada, the US Air Force converted 22 ex-CAF F-101B interceptors to RF-101B standard. Under a 30 December 1968 contract, the aircraft had their fire control systems removed and flying boom refuelling receptacle added. The work was accomplished between September 1971 and January 1972 by Ling-Temco-Vought in Greenville, South Carolina. A 23rd RF-101B (57-301), actually the first to be flown, was a developmental test airframe and did not come from Canada.

The reconnaissance package for the RF-101B included three KS-87B cameras in forward, left split vertical, and right split vertical configurations, plus two AXQ-2 television cameras in forward-looking and downward-looking positions. The pilot's panel was equipped with a TV viewfinder control indicator. Most instruments in the rear cockpit were removed during the modification.

The RF-101B was assigned to the 192nd TRS, Nevada ANG, at Reno 1971-72. Upon its arrival, Reno sent its RF-101Hs to Louisville, while the Kentucky ANG transferred its RF-101Gs to Arkansas.
RF-101B serials (all but the first converted from CF-101B): 57-301, 59-391, 59-397/398, 59-402/404, 59-410, 59-434, 59-436, 59-441, 59-447/448, 59-450, 59-453, 59-457, 59-459, 59-463, 59-467, 59-477, 59-481/483.

A total of 23 RF-101B conversions was undertaken for the ANG, and the only user was the 192nd TRG at Reno. The aircrafts' career was relatively short, replacing RF-101Gs in November 1971 and giving way to RF-4C Phantoms in July 1975. The type was produced to cover a perceived shortfall in tactical reconnaissance assets, but proved to be a very costly programme compared to the results achieved, while the aircraft required several fixes in their short lives to maintain an acceptable operational standard.

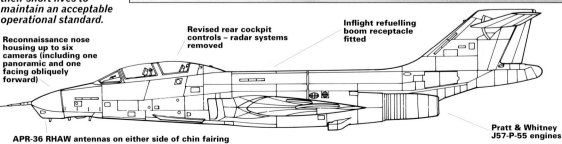

Reconnaissance nose housing up to six cameras (including one panoramic and one facing obliquely forward)

Revised rear cockpit controls – radar systems removed

Inflight refuelling boom receptacle fitted

APR-36 RHAW antennas on either side of chin fairing

Pratt & Whitney J57-P-55 engines

TF-101B

The TF-101B designation was applied at the factory to the first 58 'two-seat dual-control airplanes', all of which (79 from new production and 152 from conversions) were eventually designated F-101F. Serials are listed in the F-101F entry.

F-101C

The F-101C was virtually identical to the F-101A. The variants were used interchangeably, and both relied on the same 'Dash One' (pilots manual) and 'Dash Thirty-Four' (weapons manual). Much of the time, a pilot did not even notice whether his mount was an A model or a C.

The F-101C was, however, 500 lb (227 kg) heavier to accommodate structural improvements which increased its maximum *g* tolerance from 6.33 to 7.33. The F-101C also had different fuel pumps and fuel feed and control systems, increasing its maximum available afterburner time from six minutes (F-101A) to 15. The F-101C had very minor changes in its pressurisation system. The aircraft never had any mission except to fly – probably one way – and to deliver a centreline atomic bomb. Except for tolerance to g-forces which was increased in the C model, the F-101A and F-101C were interchangeable. The F-101C also began its operational career with the 27th FBW at Bergstrom. Fighter-bomber wings were redesignated tactical fighter wings on 7 July 1958, and the first Voodoo operator became the 27th TFW. F-101A/C Voodoos of the 27th deployed to Formosa during heightened tensions in 1958.

In a move in part for economy reasons and largely to bring the Voodoo's striking power closer to targets in the Soviet Union,

the men and equipment of the 27th TFW were transferred to the 81st Tactical Fighter Wing at RAF Bentwaters/Woodbridge. Here, the F-101C replaced the F-84F. The 81st TFW operated three squadrons, the 78th TFS 'Bushmasters', 91st TFS 'Blue Streaks' and 92nd TFS 'Avengers'.

The mission of the F-101C was to fly out to a distance as great as 1,000 miles (1610 km) and drop a single, tactical nuclear weapon on a Soviet or Eastern European target. In the F-101C, field refinements were made of systems built into both F-101A and C models, including the all-weather, low-level nuclear delivery system using the Voodoo's gun-ranging radar which had a ground-mapping mode. The F-101A/C's Low Altitude Bombing System (LABS) and its later Low Angle Drogued Delivery (LADD) systems were a maze of gyros, timers and computers designed to permit the aircraft to drop its atomic bomb after making a run-in top target at an altitude as low as 50 ft (17 m). LABS employed a Mergenthaler Linotype M-1 Toss Bombing System (TBS-1), enabling the pilot to deliver his weapon by lining up the target on the crosshairs of his K-19 gunsight and pushing a button which computed an automatic release. Pilots were briefed that they were flying a one-way mission, and received training in E & E (escape and evasion) techniques to be used after ejecting and parachuting behind Soviet lines.

The 81st TFW operated the F-101C Voodoo until 3 January 1966 when the wing

Seen in 1964, this 81st TFW clutches a pair of fuel tanks to its belly. The tanks were not attached to pylons, but directly to attachments on the fuselage itself. This eased the problem of ground clearance.

finished replacing the type with the McDonnell F-4C Phantom. Forty-seven F-101Cs were built, of which 32 were later converted to RF-101H reconnaissance models. An additional 96 aircraft originally scheduled to be built as F-101Cs were

Nose of F-101C showing refuelling probe extended

completed as RF-101C reconnaissance aircraft.
F-101C serials: 54-1486/1493; 56-001/039

Above: The star-studded fins of this line of F-101Cs identify the aircraft as serving with the 27th TFW at Bergstrom AFB. Fins were marked by colour according to squadron (481st TFS – green, 522nd TFS – red, 523rd TFS – yellow, 524th TFS – blue).

Right and below: When the Voodoos moved to Bentwaters, the markings changed to a double stripe. Again these were in squadron colours (78th TFS – red, 91st TFS – blue, 92nd TFS – yellow).

Nuclear weapon

The F-101 and C both carried a single nuclear weapon on the centreline pylon as their only operational weapon. The pylon was stressed for carrying a Mk 7 bomb weighing in at 3,721 lb (1688 kg). This weapon had a basic yield of 1 MT, and would have been used primarily against large and well-defended military targets such as airfields. Other smaller weapons were also available for carriage by the 'fighter' Voodoo.

Navigation systems

In addition to the mapping radar the F-101 used the ASN-6 dead-reckoning navigation system and ARN-14 nav radio. An MB-1 autopilot was fitted. Defence was handled by an ASP-54 radar warning system.

Strategic mission

Although the 81st TFW practised strafing with the 20-mm cannon, nuclear bomb delivery was the only operational role for the F-101A/C force. The aircraft were assigned targets deep behind the German border, including Soviet airfields. Ingress was made at high speed and very low altitude (less than 50 ft/15m) to punch through ground defensive belts. To deliver the weapon an Immelmann toss manoeuvre was used to launch the bomb upwards. This gave approximately a minute to complete the Immelmann and egress to a safe distance before the bomb came back down. LABS (low altitude bombing system) equipment was used initially, or the TBS-1 system. Later LADD (low-angle drogued delivery) systems with para-retarded bombs aided delivery and escape. Even with a standard LABS toss, accuracy in the region of 300 ft (100 m) was achievable, although this figure was somewhat academic with a 1-MT nuclear weapon.

Markings

When first assigned from Bergstrom to Bentwaters, the F-101A/C force was painted with two fin-stripes in the individual squadron colours. The 81st TFW's dragon badge was often displayed beneath the cockpit rail. In 1962 the wing adopted a central maintenance policy, which resulted in the individual squadrons operating aircraft drawn from a wing pool. A change in markings reflected this, the tails being marked with all three squadron colours. Stars were superimposed, reviving memories of the aircraft's previous use by the 27th TFW at Bergstrom, which had marked its aircraft with stars on a coloured fin.

Powerplant

The J57 was a landmark powerplant, being the first of a new generation of two-spool high thrust-weight ratio engines. In addition to the F-101, it powered the F-100, F-102, B-52, Boeing 707, KC-135 and A-3 Skywarrior among others.

McDonnell F-101C Voodoo
81st Tactical Fighter Wing
United States Air Forces in Europe

With SAC's disbandment of its strategic fighter wings and TAC's desire to rid itself of its single wing of a difficult-to-support type, the F-101A/C was left without a home and a mission. Forced into USAFE, the F-101s nevertheless proved to be a crucial part of the Cold War deterrent, and also provided a cadre of highly experienced pilots for the Southeast Asia war to come.

Cannon

The F-101A/C was initially fitted with four Colt-Browning M38 20-mm cannon, and the Voodoo proved to be a stable gunnery platform. For service in England one of the cannon was removed to make way for a transponder.

F-101A/C in service

The fighter Voodoo served with the 27th Strategic Fighter Wing from May 1957 to 1 July, when TAC took over the aircraft with the 27th Fighter-Bomber Wing. This unit had three squadrons (522nd, 523rd and 524th), and was redesignated 27th TFW on 1 July 1958. In the following December/January the aircraft were ferried to England for the 81st TFW.

Other stores

Although the 'special weapon' was the primary store, the aircraft could theoretically carry conventional stores as well. In practice these were limited to a baggage pod on the centreline or a training 'shape' for the 'Big Boy', with two drop tanks either side.

Fire control system

The F-101A/C featured the MA-7 system, the heart of which was the nose radar. Originally intended for the air-to-air mission, the radar proved remarkably adept at ground mapping after a few 'tweaks'. An MA-2 LABS was integrated with the system.

RF-101C

The RF-101C was the definitive reconnaissance Voodoo, combining the wing structure of the F-101C with the camera installation of the RF-101A. It was the only Voodoo to see combat in American hands. The RF-101C first flew on 12 July 1957 and (corresponding to the F-101C in the 'bomber' world) was improved over the A model in being stressed to handle 7.33 *g* and was modified to carry a centreline nuclear weapon.

The beginning of RF-101 operations at Shaw AFB, South Carolina is cited in the entry for the RF-101A, which served beside the RF-101C for a brief time but was quickly replaced by it. In June 1958, the 4414th Combat Crew Training Squadron became operational with Shaw's 363rd TRW as the RTU (replacement training unit) for Voodoo reconnaissance pilots.

In May 1958, the RF-101C-equipped 17th and 18th TRS were transferred from Shaw AFB, South Carolina to join the 66th TRW at Laon AB, France. The Laon-based wing also

included the 32nd and 38th TRS which relinquished RF-84F Thunderstreaks for the RF-101C. The 38th changed location to Ramstein AB, Germany when Laon grew desperately short of ramp space and facilities, and the entire wing moved in 1965 to RAF Upper Heyford, England, ending RF-101C operations when it was inactivated on 1 April 1970.

The RF-101A/C had a critical role in the Cuban missile crisis: Voodoos from Shaw deployed to Florida and flew 82 combat sorties between 26 October and 15 November 1962.

Only RF-101C models reached Vietnam. Beginning in 1958, the RF-101C Voodoo was operated by the 432nd Tactical Reconnaissance Wing, which initially was responsible for the 20th and 29th TRS and later acquired the 17th and 18th (from Shaw AFB, SC). The wing was formed at Shaw in February 1958 and detached to the Far East two years later. From 1965, the wing operated at Udorn RTAFB, Thailand, where

Above: RF-101Cs were delivered in natural metal, but adopted light grey anti-corrosive paint. Several camouflage schemes were tested before the standard T.O.114 scheme was settled upon.

Below: The RF-101C was the first USAF jet to fly missions in Southeast Asia, the 15th and 45th TRS manning detachments at Saigon (Pipe Stem) and Don Muang (Able Mabel) from November 1961. Camouflage swiftly appeared on these aircraft, and the national insignia were reduced in size.

Right and above right: Operation Sun Run was conducted on 27 November 1957 using six RF-101Cs to shatter US coast-to-coast records. These included a west-east time of 3 hours 7 minutes 43 seconds (Lt Gustav Klatt), east-west of 3:36.32 and round-trip of 6:46.36 (both by Captain Robert Sweet).

McDonnell F-88/F-101 Voodoo Variants

Above: RF-101Cs were delivered to the 432nd TRG at Shaw from the end of 1957. The following year the RF-101s were put under the control of the 363rd TRW, in whose markings this aircraft is seen. The wing controlled two operational squadrons (20th and 29th TRS), and the training unit (4414th CCTS). The Shaw wing flew 82 combat reconnaissance flights during the Cuban missile crisis.

it acquired the 20th TRS, by now nicknamed 'Green Pythons', which carried out the bulk of combat operations credited to the Voodoo. The 15th TRS 'Cotton Pickers' at Kadena AB, Okinawa began operating RF-101Cs in Southeast Asia as early as 1960. These began with temporary deployments to Don Muang airfield in Thailand and Tan Son Nhut in South Vietnam. The 45th TRS 'Polka Dots', originally at Misawa AB, Japan and later at Tan Son Nhut, also joined the fighting.

In Southeast Asia, RF-101Cs were modified to carry photo flash cartridges and TLQ-8 jammers. The Toy Tiger update was a retrofit of cameras introducing a new nose panoramic and 4.5 x 4.5-in format KA-45s on side and vertical gyro stab, including night cameras using flash cartridges, as well as Hycon KS-72 cameras and automatic controls designed for the RF-4C Phantom. The 45th TRS ended a decade of Voodoo combat operations when the last RF-101C Voodoo, replaced by the RF-4C Phantom, departed Saigon on 16 November 1970. The last Tactical Air Command RF-101C was phased out by the 31st TRTS, a replacement training unit at Shaw, on 16 February 1971. RF-101Cs later served with several Air National Guard squadrons alongside RF-101As.

Of 166 RF-101Cs completed, 96 had originally been scheduled for production as F-101C airplanes.

RF-101C serials: 56-40/135, 56-162/231

Above: The RF-101C was the first USAF type to don tactical warpaint.

Right: In Europe the 66th TRW and its four squadrons (17th, 18th, 32nd and 38th TRS) were very active along the German border, flying from Laon and a detachment at Ramstein. Unofficial reports talk of RF-101s employing maximum afterburner turns to escape from MiGs. In the early 1960s the 66th crews were qualified in the delivery of nuclear weapons.

Six ANG squadrons flew the RF-101C in the early 1970s: 154th (illustrated) and 184th TRS/AR ANG, 107th and 171st TRS/MI ANG, 165th TRS/KY ANG and 153rd TRS/MS.

The RF-101C largely replaced the RF-101G/H and RF-84F in Guard service, this being a Kentucky aircraft. Mississippi's 153rd TRS had the distinction of flying the last USAF RF-101 mission on 13 January 1979.

McDonnell RF-101C Voodoo

45th Tactical Reconnaissance
Squadron 'Polka Dots'
Pacific Air Forces

The RF-101C was the USAF's main tactical reconnaissance asset when it entered the Southeast Asia war in 1961, and the type served with distinction until replacement by the slower but better-equipped RF-4C was completed in November 1970. Around 35,000 combat sorties were flown, including 10,000 over North Vietnam and 9,000 over Laos.

Mission profile

When the RF-101C began SEA operations, the type usually flew medium-altitude single-ship missions, although two-ship missions were flown into heavily-defended areas. From mid-1965 the SAM threat dictated a change in tactics, the Voodoos using a low-altitude ingress followed by a pop-up to about 10,000-15,000 ft. About two or three minutes were available at this altitude for the photo-run before SAM operators could lock up and launch. After the pop-up, the aircraft dived back down to the safety of low altitude. This tactic continued until April 1967, when improved ECM equipment (in the form of up to four ALQ-71 pods on each aircraft) allowed a return to medium-altitude operations. However, the pods seriously damaged the RF-101's blistering speed, making them easier to catch by MiGs (which were otherwise not a serious threat). Consequently, fighter escorts became more prevalent.

Cameras

RF-101Cs were initially fitted with a 12-in Fairchild KA-2 camera facing forward, three 6-in KA-2s in a tri-sensor station behind, and two 36-in Fairchild KA-1 cameras facing downwards. In order to give a night capability, some RF-101Cs were reconfigured with four KA-45 cameras in the forward station and two 12-in KA-47s replacing the KA-1s. These 'Toy Tiger' aircraft carried up to 80 M123 photo-flash cartridges in a centreline ejector pod. In 1964/65 many RF-101Cs were given the KA-2 camera installation, which replaced the KA-2 cameras with Hycon KS-72 sensors, and added an automatic control system as developed for the RF-4C. Initial operations were not encouraging, but later proved to be effective after some modification.

Nuclear weapons

Unlike the RF-101A, the C was capable of carrying a single centreline nuclear bomb, principally for European service. McDonnell had originally proposed a quick-change radar nose but this was rejected owing to the complexity of the camera installation.

Cockpit

The instrument panel of the RF-101C was dominated by a large circular scope for the VF-31 viewfinder. This provided a vertical view as seen from the tri-camera station.

RF-101C losses

During the Southeast Asia war, the RF-101C fleet suffered 44 losses. Of these 31 fell to AAA guns, five to SAMs, one to a MiG, one in an airfield attack and six to operational causes.

RF-101C in PACAF

RF-101Cs were initially delivered to the 15th TRS 'Cotton Pickers' at Kadena and the 45th TRS 'Polka Dots' at Misawa. These units manned the initial SEA Pipe Stem and Able Mable deployments on rotation. Aircraft were occasionally drafted in from Shaw, and in 1965 the 20th TRS 'Green Pythons' was moved in to replace the 15th TRS, which converted to RF-4Cs. The 20th operated for most of its career from Udorn, and took the lion's share of northern North Vietnam missions. The 45th TRS was based at Tan Son Nhut, covering the south.

Individual aircraft

This aircraft wears the polka dot fin-cap of the 45th TRS, based at Tan Son Nhut. The 'Luv Bug' nose art was worn only briefly. Earlier the aircraft had achieved fame as one of the six Sun Run record-breakers, painted with the nickname 'Cin Min'. Flown by Captain Ray Schrecengost, it was the first away and briefly held the round-trip coast-to-coast record before being beaten by a following aircraft. The aircraft is now preserved in the Air Force Museum, after 6,604.9 flying hours.

McDonnell F-88/F-101 Voodoo Variants

F-101F

The designation F-101F was assigned on 3 February 1961 to all 'two-seat dual-control aircraft' which were otherwise identical to the F-101B interceptor. Seventy-nine of these were manufactured from the outset as 'two-seat dual-control aircraft' and 152 more were originally completed as F-101Bs but, rather than being upgraded with the rest of the F-101B fleet, were retrofitted to dual-control configuration.

F-101F serials (for the 72 aircraft built as dual-control ships): 56-274/275, 56-277, 56-289, 56-294, 56-299, 56-304, 56-308, 56-312, 56-316, 56-320, 56-324, 56-328, 57-263, 57-267, 57-271, 57-275, 57-279, 57-283, 57-287, 57-292, 57-297, 57-302, 57-307, 57-312, 57-317, 57-322, 57-327, 57-332, 57-337, 57-342, 57-347, 57-352, 57-357, 57-365, 57-372, 57-379, 57-386, 57-393, 57-400, 57-407, 57-414, 57-421, 57-428, 57-449, 58-262, 58-269, 58-276, 58-283, 58-290, 58-297, 58-304, 58-311, 58-318, 58-324, 58-331, 58-338, 59-393, 59-400, 59-407, 59-413, 59-419, 59-425, 59-437, 59-443, 59-449, 59-454, 59-460, 59-466, 59-472, 59-278, and two others.

At the start of 1970 the 11th FIS/Texas ANG adopted the Guard training role for the F-102, and added the same CCTU function for the interceptor Voodoo in May 1971, acquiring several dual-control F-101Fs. The CCTU task was relinquished in April 1976, but the 111th continued as a regular interceptor unit with its original F-101B/F aircraft.

Right: Dual-control aircraft were widespread throughout the fleet, and retained combat capability. A sizeable proportion were concentrated in the training units, with a handful assigned to each operational interceptor unit. Reconnaissance Voodoo squadrons were also assigned a handful of F-101Fs to assist with their conversion/continuation training programmes. This aircraft wears the muted markings of the 154th TRS/Arkansas ANG, based at Little Rock AFB.

TF-101F

Twenty-four 'two-seat dual-control aircraft' based on the F-101B interceptor were initially designated TF-101F. These were later redesignated F-101F and are listed in the entry for the latter.

CF-101F

This designation was applied to the dual-control aircraft supplied to Canada, of which there were 10 in each batch. Serial numbers are as follows:

1st batch: 59-0393 (17393), 59-0400 (17400), 59-0407 (17407), 59-0437 (17437), 59-0443 (17443), 59-0449 (17449), 59-0460 (17460), 59-0466 (17466), 59-0472 (17472), 59-0478 (17478)

2nd batch: 56-0253 (101001), 56-0260 (101002), 56-0262 (101003), 56-0277 (101004), 56-0304 (101005), 56-0324 (101006), 56-0328 (101007), 57-0322 (101022), 57-0332 (101024), 57-0400 (101052)

The rear seat of the F/CF-101F had only rudimentary controls, and could not operate flaps, afterburner, landing gear or brake chute. This CF-101F is from 425 'Alouette' Sqn.

RF-101G

The RF-101G was a conversion of the 29 F-101A airframes to become a single-seat reconnaissance aircraft (corresponding to the RF-101H conversion made from F-101C models). Accomplished by Lockheed Aircraft Services, the modification work entailed removal of integral cannon armament and its replacement by cameras, a revised nosecone featuring camera ports being fitted at the same time.

The first RF-101G conversions went to the Kentucky Air National Guard (165rd TRS/123rd TRW) at Standiford Airport in Louisville. Kentucky received its first RF-101G in July 1965, replacing the RB-57B Canberra. Kentucky Guardsmen were activated during the 1968 *Pueblo* crisis in Korea. While the group did not deploy to Korea, it carried out operations in Alaska, Panama and Japan while on active duty. In 1969, the Louisville unit came off active duty, transferred its RF-101G aircraft to Fort Smith, Arkansas, and converted to the RF-101H model.

The RF-101G was also employed by the Arkansas ANG (154th TRS/189th TFG) from July 1965 as a replacement for the RB-57B, (with a *Pueblo*-era active-duty stint intervening) concluding in 1972 when the unit converted to RF-101Cs.

RF-101G serials (converted from F-101A): 54-1445, 54-1449, 54-1451/1455; 54-1457, 54-1459/1464; 54-1466, 54-1468, 54-1470, 54-1472/1473, 54-1475/1477, 54-1479, 54-1481/1482, 54-1484/1485, plus two other aircraft from among 54-1456, 54-1469, and 54-1516.

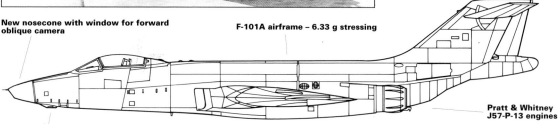

When the F-101As and Cs in England were replaced on the nuclear strike role by F-4C Phantoms in 1965-66, they became available for conversion to the reconnaissance role. The camera fit included a pallet of cameras mounted aft of the front fuselage bulkhead, and a new nose housing a forward-facing camera. The nosecone slid forward on rails to allow technicians to maintain the cameras and load film. Large hinged panels allowed access to the pallet and avionics bay to the rear. Lockheed undertook about half the conversions, with McClellan AFB performing the rest to speed up the process.

New nosecone with window for forward oblique camera

F-101A airframe – 6.33 g stressing

Pratt & Whitney J57-P-13 engines

Camera pallet mounted in forward fuselage with fan mounting and panoramic window

RF-101Gs and Hs initially served alongside each other with the three ANG units, but in 1971 were rationalised into RF-101B (Nevada), RF-101G (Arkansas) and RF-101H (Kentucky) units. This RF-101G is seen shortly after delivery in 1965 to Kentucky's 165th TRS. All three units undertook deployments to Itazuke during 1968/69.

RF-101H

In a conversion similar to the RF-101G, 32 F-101Cs were given reconnaissance systenms to become RF-101Hs. The only difference between the two was the strengthened airframe of the H. The RF-101H was employed by the Nevada Air National Guard from October 1965, and also served alongside Gs with Arkansas and Kentucky Guards. All three units were called to active duty during the *Pueblo* crisis in 1968/69. In 1971 the ANG fleet was rationalised, with all RF-101Hs being assigned to the 165th TRS, Kentucky ANG. These were replaced by RF-101Cs in 1972.

RF-101H serials (converted from F-101C): 54-1486/1488, 54-1491, 54-1493, 56-0001/0004; 56-0006, 56-0010/0012; 56-0014, 56-0016, 56-0018/0020; 56-0022/0023; 56-0025/0027, 56-0029/0036, 56-0039

The H was outwardly identical to the G, and could only be distinguished by serial number.

F-109

The only aircraft ever assigned the designation F-109 by the US Air Force was the ship which was quickly redesignated F-101B and, as a long-range interceptor, became the most numerous Voodoo model. Contrary to published accounts, the F-109 nomenclature was never assigned to the tail-sitter Ryan vertical take-off aircraft (completed as the X-13 Vertijet) or to a Bell horizontal V/STOL proposal. The F-109 concept was redesignated F-101B in August 1955.

Fleet Air Arm 1960-69

In the 1960s the Royal Navy had a two-fold mission. Heavily embroiled in the Cold War, the Senior Service also supported Britain's dwindling colonial interests. Air power had become an important part of the Navy's ability to carry out its tasks, although by the end of the decade this capability was being phased out thanks to misguided political edicts.

No armed force in history can have seen greater changes than those suffered by Britain's Fleet Air Arm in the decade 1960-69. It began the period welcoming the powerful Scimitar and Sea Vixen, and looking forward to the NA.39, later named Buccaneer. With such aircraft, British air power could assuredly be projected to the furthest corners of the globe. It ended the decade facing the imminent elimination of the floating airfields upon which this airpower was based.

To some degree this reflected belated recognition of the fact that the United Kingdom was no longer a great Imperial power. In 1965 it was written that "The carrier must be the backbone of any amphibious task force, and two should operate together to provide a balanced strike/reconnaissance/fighter force as well as an alternative deck to land on. Present plans reduce the number of carriers below the safe minimum, for with only five available (including the obsolescent *Centaur*) it is no longer possible to guarantee two modern carriers east of Suez." Very soon there were to be no modern British carriers either east or west of Suez!

To a considerable degree, the Fleet Air Arm in the 1960s encapsulated the utter failure of the British system of defence procurement. Time after time the sequence was: statement of an operational requirement; placing of contracts with British industry; striving by British companies to meet the demand; political vacillation, repeated changes to the requirement and trickle funding; further changes to the demand, typically down-grading the capability to 'save money'; after years of delay and expenditure of several times the expected budget, cancellation and replacement by an American product. To make the American product more acceptable it would be fitted with British equipment (such as engines), guaranteeing further delay and wild escalation in cost. The process continues to this day.

In the 1950s this procedure had yet to take hold. All that happened in that decade is that, while in the USA and Soviet Union the procurement machine went flat out to obtain the

latest technology at the earliest possible date, in order to save money, in Britain the dead hand of the Treasury combined with an imbecilic air of relaxation to stretch out every programme. This at a stroke multiplied the cost, so that it became standard practice to reduce the number of each weapon procured, and guaranteed that when the item entered service it would no longer be in the front rank technically.

One can trace the evolution of the FAA's major weapon systems of the 1960s, the Scimitar, Sea Vixen and anti-submarine helicopters. The Scimitar single-seat strike fighter stemmed from a 1945 study for a fighter without normal landing gear, to operate from a carrier with a flexible flight deck. This idea proved to be unsound, and when the Supermarine 508 prototype flew in 1951 it had normal landing gear. Unfortunately, it also had unswept wings, so more years were spent sweeping back the wings and tail, resulting in the Type 525 of 1954. Further fiddling resulted in the Type 544 of 1956, which in turn led to the Scimitar which was produced in 1957-60.

As the US Navy was at the same time testing the Phantom II, the subsonic radar-less Scimitar was hardly a competitive aircraft. Moreover, because of escalation in price caused by the long development, the original order for 100 had to be cut to only 76. These gave brief and undistinguished service with four squadrons, the last to go being No. 803 in 1966.

Likewise, the Sea Vixen two-seat all-weather interceptor also stemmed from a specification written at the end of World War II. N.40/46 called for "an advanced carrierborne all-weather fighter," and if this objective had simply been pursued clearly the FAA might have got the resulting aircraft as early as 1952. For comparison, the US Navy's counterpart, the Douglas F3D Skyknight, entered service in 1951 and was soon in action over Korea. Not so in Britain, which needed another nine years.

Part of the delay was caused by the fact that the first two de Havilland D.H.110 prototypes were of the land-based RAF version. This was partly because Their Lordships at the Admiralty

At the start of the 1960s the Sea Hawk was being phased out of front-line service. Its most important task was advanced training, carried out by these FGA.Mk 6s of 736 Sqn at Lossiemouth.

767 Sqn at Yeovilton operated the Sea Venom FAW.Mk 21 as the all-weather fighter training squadron. The Venoms were fully replaced by Sea Vixens in October 1960.

Sea Venom FAW.Mk 22s were in the front-line until July 1961. This aircraft was from 894 Sqn, which served in Albion until October 1960.

wondered whether swept wings could fly from carriers. Further delay was caused by the very public crash of the first D.H.110 in September 1952, which (like the loss of the BOAC Comets) appeared to put the procurement machine into a state of shock, in which it was thought preferable to do nothing.

After wasting two years the decision was

Fleet Air Arm Chronology 1960-1969

1960

15 January 815 Sqn deploys its Whirlwind HAS.Mk 7s to *Albion* for a Far East cruise (shore stops at Hal Far and Sembawang). Returns to Fleetlands 15 December

19 January *Albion* is recommissioned as a commando carrier

21 January 810 Sqn sends four Gannet AS.Mk 4s from *Centaur* to Seletar

27 January 893 Sqn embarks Sea

Venom FAW.Mk 22s to *Victorious*, which return to Yeovilton on 25 February. Joined by 849 Sqn 'B' Flt which dispatches four Skyraider AEW.Mk 1s, returning to Culdrose on 22 February

29 January 820 Sqn moves from Portland to Culdrose with six Whirlwind HAS.Mk 7s

February 737 Sqn (ASW helicopter training with Whirlwind HAS.Mk 7s) at Portland receives two Whirlwind HAS.Mk 22s for SAR duties

1 February 700G Flt (Gannet AEW.Mk 3 IFTU) renumbered as 849 'A' Flt at Culdrose

1 February 824 Sqn moves its Whirlwind HAS.Mk 7s from Portland to Culdrose

1 February 890 Sqn formed at Yeovilton with two Sea Vixen FAW.Mk 1s (subsequent maximum 16)

1 February 894 Sqn embarks its Sea Venom FAW.Mk 22s for a final cruise in *Albion*. Shore operations undertaken from Seletar, Kai Tak and Hal Far. Return to Yeovilton on 15 December

2 February 803 Sqn embarks in

Victorious with 11 Scimitar F.Mk 1s, returning to Lossiemouth on 25 February

5 February 849 Sqn 'D' Flt deploys aboard *Albion* for the Skyraider AEW.Mk 1's final operational cruise (shore operations from Hal Far and Seletar). Returns to Culdrose on 15 December. 806 Sqn embarks its Sea Hawk FGA.Mk 6s for the same cruise, with shore stops at Seletar, Kai Tak, Butterworth and Changi before returning to Brawdy on 15 December

24 February Sea Hawk FGA.Mk 6s of 801 Sqn take part in three-day exercise from *Centaur*, including mock

Demonstrating precision slow flying, this nine-ship of 800 Sqn Scimitars displayed at the 1961 Farnborough air show.

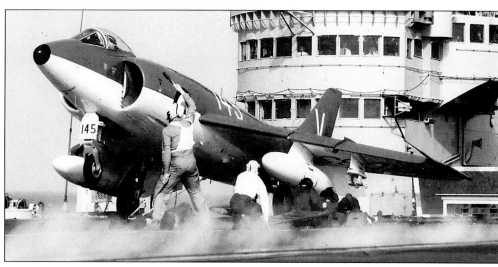

Above and right: 736 Sqn at Lossiemouth operated the Scimitar for advanced training until 1965, the type replacing the Sea Hawk FGA.Mk 6. When 736 converted to Buccaneers, a handful of Scimitars continued to train Airwork pilots on the type as 764 Sqn 'B' Flight, retaining 736's lightning flash markings.

Above: At the start of the decade 803 Sqn flew its Scimitar F.Mk 1s from the deck of Victorious. *It subsequently served on* Hermes *and* Ark Royal *before disbanding in October 1966.*

807 Sqn received its first Scimitars in 1958, and used them until 1962 with Ark Royal and Centaur as the assigned carriers.

A pair of 803 Sqn Scimitars prepares for launch from **Ark Royal** in 1965. Owing to the small carrier decks from which they operated, Scimitars were launched nose up to provide sufficient incidence.

Proudly wearing the squadron badge of a tiger holding a dagger in its mouth, this 804 Sqn Scimitar F.Mk 1 also wears the 'H' deck codes to signify its assignment to Hermes. The Scimitar was used in either an attack tasking with bombs and rockets, or as a fighter with four Sidewinders, unguided rockets or 20-mm cannon.

taken to continue D.H.110 development as a carrier-based interceptor, which is what it had been eight years previously. At last a fully navalised prototype flew on 20 March 1957, named Sea Vixen FAW.Mk 1. Powered by two 11,230-lb (49.95-kN) thrust Rolls-Royce Avon 208 turbojets, the Vixen had a crew of two, AI.18 radar and four Firestreak heat-homing missiles. Where guns might have been expected were two boxes each housing 14 spin-stabilised 2-in rockets. Wing pylons could carry various attack loads.

The FAW.Mk 1 entered service in 1959, and in 1963 production switched at the 115th aircraft to the FAW.Mk 2. This had a totally different missile system, the curve-of-pursuit Firestreak being replaced by the somewhat less unimpressive Red Top, which could make collision-course interceptions from any direction. Visually, the main change in the Mk 2 aircraft was that the front part of each tail boom was swollen, enabling an additional 800 Imp gal (3637 litres) of fuel to be accommodated. Because the revised shape matched the transon-

invasion of Trincomalee
29 February 893 Sqn (Sea Venom FAW.Mk 22) disbanded at Yeovilton
1 March 804 Sqn commissioned at Lossiemouth with three Scimitar F.Mk 1s (subsequent maximum six)
2 March 820 and 824 Sqn Whirlwinds deploy to *Ark Royal* for Mediterranean cruise (shore stops Hal Far, Ta Kali, St Mandrier). 824 returns to Culdrose on 26 August, with subsequent detachments to Dartmouth, *Hermes* and Portland. 820 returns to Culdrose on 3 October
3 March 800 and 807 Sqn Scimitars, with four Gannet AEW.Mk 3s from 849

Sqn 'A' Flt and 892 Sqn 'A' Flt with Sea Vixens join 820 in *Ark Royal* for Mediterranean cruise, calling at Hal Far and North Front. Return to Lossiemouth and Culdrose on 30 September
10 March 848 Sqn deploys from Worthy Down to *Bulwark* with Whirlwind HAS.Mk 7s for a Middle/Far East cruise (shore operations from Sembawang, Pearce, Dhal, Sumail, Kai Tak, Sek Kong and Hal Far) which includes operations during the Kuwait crisis. Returns to Culdrose on 19 December 1962
1 April 814 Sqn formed at Culdrose

with five Whirlwind HAS.Mk 7 (subsequent maximum eight)
1 April 700H Flt formed at Culdrose as the Wessex HAS.1 IFTU
25 April 891 Sqn (Sea Venom FAW.Mk 22) returns to Yeovilton from *Albion*. Its Far East cruise involved shore operations from Hal Far, Khormaksar, Drigh Road, and Seletar
26 April 810 Sqn returns to Culdrose with six Gannet AS.Mk 4s from Far East cruise in *Centaur*
7 May 814 Sqn moves from Culdrose to Portland
17 May 719 Sqn formed at Eglinton as

the Helicopter Development Unit of the Joint Anti-submarine School Flight with three Whirlwind HAS.Mk 7s
12 June 891 Sqn embarks for its final cruise in *Centaur*, involving stops at Bodo, Sola and Lossiemouth. Returns to Yeovilton on 3 October. Short deployments subsequently made to Lossiemouth and Culdrose
13 June 810 Sqn undertakes last anti-submarine Gannet cruise, flying its AS.Mk 4s to *Centaur*
14 June Britannia Flight formed at Roborough to provide air experience and training to Dartmouth Naval College

FLEET AIR ARM ORDER OF BATTLE AT 1 JANUARY 1960

UNIT	SHIP	TYPE	BASE
First Line Squadrons			
800 Squadron	Ark Royal	6 Scimitar F.Mk 1	Lossiemouth.
801 Squadron	Centaur	14 Sea Hawk FGA.Mk 6	aboard ship in the Far East (Brawdy)
803 Squadron	Victorious	12 Scimitar F.Mk 1	Lossiemouth.
806 Squadron	Eagle	14 Sea Hawk FGA.Mk 6	Brawdy
807 Squadron	Ark Royal	8 Scimitar F.Mk 1	Lossiemouth
810 Squadron	Centaur	6 Gannet AS.Mk 4	aboard ship in the Far East (Culdrose)
815 Squadron	Albion	8 Whirlwind HAS.Mk 7	Culdrose
820 Squadron	Ark Royal	6 Whirlwind HAS.Mk 7	Portland.
824 Squadron	Ark Royal	8 Whirlwind HAS.Mk 7	Portland
831 Squadron 'A' Flight	Victorious	4 Gannet ECM. 6, 2 Avenger AS.6B	Culdrose
831 Squadron 'B' Flight	Victorious	4 Sea Venom Mk 21 (ECM)	Culdrose
848 Squadron	Bulwark	13 Whirlwind HAS.Mk 7	Worthy Down
849 Squadron Headquarters		22 Skyraider AEW.1, 4 Gannet AS.4	Culdrose
849 Squadron 'B' Flight	Victorious	4 Gannet AEW.Mk 3	Culdrose
849 Squadron 'C' Flight	Albion	4 Gannet AEW.Mk 3.	Culdrose
849 Squadron 'D' Flight	Centaur	4 Skyraider AEW.Mk 1	Culdrose
892 Squadron	Ark Royal	8 Sea Vixen FAW.Mk 1	Yeovilton
892B Flight (Firestreak evaluation)		4 Sea Vixen FAW.Mk 1	Yeovilton
893 Squadron	Victorious	14 Sea Venom FAW.Mk 22	Yeovilton
894 Squadron	Albion	12 Sea Venom FAW.Mk 22	Yeovilton

UNIT	TYPE	BASE
Second Line Squadrons		
700 Squadron (Trials and Requirements Unit)	3 Sea Venom FAW.21, 2 Gannet AS.1, 1 Meteor TT.20, 2 Whirlwind HAR.3/HAS.7	Yeovilton .
700G (Gannet AEW.3 Intensive Flying Trials Unit)	4 Gannet AEW.Mk 3	Culdrose
700X (P.531 Intensive Flying Trials Unit)	3 P.531 (Wasp)	Yeovilton
705 Squadron (Helicopter Training Unit)	6 Hiller HT.Mk 1, 7 Dragonfly HR.Mk 3/HR.5, 13(?) Whirlwind HAR.Mk 1/HAS.Mk 3	Culdrose
727 Squadron (Dartmouth Air Cadets Training)	4 Sea Prince T.Mk 1, 9 Sea Vampire T.Mk 22, 2 Dragonfly HR.Mk 5, 1 Sea Devon C.Mk 20	Brawdy
728 Squadron (Fleet Requirements Unit)	2 Sea Devon C.20, 4 Meteor T.7, 5 Meteor TT.20	Hal Far
728B Squadron (Fleet Requirements Unit– target drones)	9 Firefly U.Mk 9, 5 Meteor U.Mk 15	Hal Far
736 Squadron (ID Flight, Operational Flying School)	14 Sea Hawk FGA.Mk 6, 4 Scimitar F.Mk 1	Lossiemouth.
737 Squadron (Air Anti-Submarine School)	12 Whirlwind HAS.Mk 7	Portland
738 Squadron (All-weather, Flight Operational Flying School)	12 Sea Venom FAW.Mk 21, 4 Sea Venom T.Mk 22	Lossiemouth
750 Squadron (Observer and Air Signal School)	13 Sea Prince T.Mk 1	Hal Far.
764 Squadron (Air Warfare Instructor Training Squadron)	5 Hunter T.Mk 8	Lossiemouth
766 Squadron (All-weather Flying Training Squadron)	14 Sea Venom FAW.Mk 21, 2 Sea Vixen FAW.Mk 1	Yeovilton
781 Squadron (Communications Squadron)	8 Sea Devon C.Mk 20, 1 Whirlwind HAS.Mk 22, 1 Dominie Mk 1, 1 Sea Vampire T.Mk 22	Lee-on-Solent

Miscellaneous units

Ship's Flights – *Ark Royal* (Dragonfly HR.5), *Centaur* (Dragonfly HR.5), *Victorious* (Dragonfly HR.5)
Station Flights – Abbotsinch (Sea Vampire T.22, Sea Balliol T.21), Arbroath (Tiger Moth, Dominie), Brawdy (Sea Vampire T.22, Tiger Moth, Meteor T.7, Sea Hawk FGA.6), Culdrose (Dragonfly HR.5, Sea Balliol T.21, Gannet T.5, Dominie, Whirlwind HAS.7), Hal Far (Dragonfly HR.5, Sea Hawk FB.5, Sea Vampire T.22, Whirlwind HAS.7, Whirlwind HAS.22), Lee-on-Solent (Hellcat II, Tiger Moth, Sea Hawk FGA.6, Sea Vampire T.22, Meteor T.7, Dragonfly HR.5, Sea Devon C.20), Yeovilton (Dominie, Sea Vampire T.22, Dragonfly HR.5, Sea Balliol T.21, Sea Prince C.2)
Joint Warfare Establishment, Old Sarum (Sea Balliol T.21)
Airwork, Brawdy (Sea Venom FAW.21, Sea Vampire T.22)
Airwork Fleet Requirements Unit, Hurn (Sea Fury FB.11, Sea Hawk FB.5, Meteor TT.20, Dragonfly HR.3)

An important task of the Sea Vixen was inflight refuelling, demonstrated here by an FAW.Mk 2 of 899 Sqn and a Buccaneer of 800 Sqn.

899 Sqn at Yeovilton was the Sea Vixen FAW.Mk 1 headquarters squadron between 1961 and 1964. Here two of the squadron's aircraft demonstrate inflight refuelling using the buddy pod.

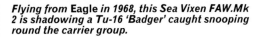

Flying from Eagle in 1968, this Sea Vixen FAW.Mk 2 is shadowing a Tu-16 'Badger' caught snooping round the carrier group.

cadets. Initial equipment was the Dragonfly HR.Mk 5, joined by the Tiger Moth in November. In 1966/67 equipment changed to Chipmunks and Wasps
July 736 Sqn (advanced tactics school) at Lossiemouth dispatched its last Sea Hawk FGA.Mk 6s to 738 Sqn, leaving its complement standing at eight Scimitar F.Mk 1s
1 July 892 Sqn 'B' Flt joins 'A' Flt on *Ark Royal*. Entire squadron returns to Yeovilton on 30 September
1 July 750 Sqn, the Hal Far-based Observer training unit, adds four Sea Venom FAW.Mk 21s for high-level navigation training. The principal equipment is the Sea Prince T.Mk 1
5 July 849 Sqn 'C' Flt embarks with Gannet AEW.Mk 3s in *Hermes* for work with 804 Sqn, including a shore deployment to Lossiemouth. Returns to Culdrose on 15 October
6 July 804 Sqn embarks in *Hermes* for short cruise with Scimitars, returning to Lossiemouth on 1 October. Also on

board is 810 Sqn with Whirlwind HAS.Mk 7s, which returns to Culdrose on 15 October. Sea Vixen FAW.Mk 1s of 890 Sqn remain on board for Far East cruise (shore ops from Lossiemouth, Hal Far and Tengah), returning to Yeovilton on 10 May 1961
7 July Sea Hawk FGA.Mk 6s from 801 Sqn in *Centaur* visit Sweden
12 July 810 Sqn and its Gannet AS.Mk 4s returns from *Centaur* to Culdrose, disbanding the same day
26 July 801 Sqn (Sea Hawk FGA.Mk 6) disbanded following return from Far East cruise on *Centaur*
August 781 Sqn at Lee-on-Solent adds a Tiger Moth T.Mk 2 and a Sea Vampire T.Mk 21 to its inventory, the latter being flown by FONA (Flag Officer Naval Aviation)
9 August 825 Sqn moves from Culdrose to Portland prior to embarcation in *Victorious*
16 August 825 Sqn formed at Culdrose with Whirlwind HAS.Mk 7 (maximum complement eight)

16 August Two Sea Vixen FAW.Mk 1s arrive at Yeovilton for soon-to-be-formed 893 Sqn
29 August 803 Sqn Scimitars deployed briefly to *Ark Royal* and *Hermes*
1 September 893 Sqn reformed at Yeovilton with Sea Vixen FAW.Mk 1s
25 September 803 Sqn sends Scimitar detachment to *Victorious*, which returns to Lossiemouth on 1 October
3 October On disembarcation from *Ark Royal*, 820 Sqn (Whirlwind HAS.Mk 7) disbands at Culdrose
5 October 719 Sqn undertakes a short embarcation in *Hermes*, returning to Eglinton on 14 October
17 October 803 Sqn embarks Scimitar F.Mk 1s aboard *Victorious*, returning to Lossiemouth on 19 December
18 October 825 Sqn Whirlwinds join 803 in *Victorious* for Mediterranean cruise (shore stop at Hal Far). Return to Portland on 9 January 1961. 849 Sqn 'B'

Flt, now with Gannet AEW.Mk 3s, joins cruise from Culdrose, returning on 19 December
22 October Sea Vixen FAW.Mk 1s of 892 Sqn board *Victorious* for Med cruise, stopping at Hal Far and returning to Yeovilton on 19 December
24 October 766 Sqn 'B' Flt (with Sea Vixen FAW.Mk 1s) is disbanded when 766 Sqn's final Sea Venom FAW.Mk 21s are retired, allowing the 'B' Flt to be recommissioned as 766 Sqn as the Sea Vixen FAW.Mk 1 OCU
25 October 824 Sqn deploys Whirlwind HAS.Mk 7s to *Ark Royal* for Mediterranean cruise, during which operations are undertaken from *Victorious* and Hal Far. Return to Culdrose on 28 February 1961
26 October 800 and 807 Sqn Scimitar F.Mk 1s with four Gannet AEW.Mk 3s of 849 Sqn 'A' Flt embark in *Ark Royal* for winter cruise to Mediterranean (calling at Hal Far)
7 November 814 Sqn Whirlwind HAS.Mk 7s board *Hermes* for the Far

892 Sqn was the first front-line user of the Sea Vixen FAW.Mk 1. It was assigned to Victorious for its first major cruise to the Far East.

From late 1963, 892's Vixen Mk 1s were aboard Centaur, staying with the ship until the squadron converted to FAW.Mk 2s in December 1965.

766 Sqn at Yeovilton was the Vixen training unit, equipped with both versions. The Mk 2 (shown) arrived in 1965, the Mk 1 not retiring until 1968.

Above: 893 Sqn re-equipped with the FAW.Mk 1 in 1960, this aircraft seen landing on Victorious.

Vixen training was initially undertaken by 766 Sqn 'B' Flt, although this was reorganised as 766 Sqn when the last Sea Venoms were retired in late 1960. The FAW.Mk 1 marked a significant increase in capability over the Venoms.

An 890 Sqn FAW. Mk 1 buzzes Hermes in 1961. The squadron later served as a fighter trials unit with both versions of the Vixen.

ic Area Rule there was virtually no increase in drag, though the extra weight (from 37,615 to 44,907 lb/17062 to 20370 kg) somewhat degraded performance.

Nevertheless, the basic D.H.110 design of 1949 was so good that even in the 1960s the Sea Vixen was still a useful aircraft. Only 29 were built as FAW.Mk 2s, the last being delivered in 1965, but 67 FAW.Mk 1 Vixens were returned to what had become Hawker Siddeley to be brought up to Mk 2 standard, making 96 in all. These equipped Nos 890, 892, 893 and 899 Squadrons, operating from various shore bases and from HMS *Ark Royal*, *Centaur*, *Eagle* and *Victorious* until the last to go, 899, was disbanded in January 1972. A few Vixens became

red/yellow pilotless Sea Vixen D.Mk 3 drones.

Thanks to the small design team led by W. A. Tamblin at Hatfield and Christchurch (where the Vixens were built), this programme can fairly be termed a success, despite all the procurement machine could do. Most programmes, however, achieved little beyond consuming money, and one such was the fumbling attempt to create a helicopter able both to find and also destroy submarines. This programme was one of the first to succumb to the notion that home industry, and one's own design capability, is of no importance, and that it would be nice always to buy a supposedly proven product from the USA instead. This disease began in 1955 with BOAC, later becoming entrenched

East. After shore stops at North Front, Sembawang and Hal Far the squadron returns to Culdrose on 18 April 1961. AEW detachment provided by 849 Sqn 'C' Flt Gannet AEW.Mk 3s, which remain afloat throughout, returning to Culdrose on the same date
25 November 893 Sqn embarks in *Ark Royal* for Mediterranean cruise (calling at Hal Far). Returns to Yeovilton on 28 February 1961
26 November After a transit to Gibraltar, 803 Sqn joins *Hermes* for its Far East cruise, returning to Lossiemouth on 10 September 1961
15 December *Albion* disembarks its aircraft after Far East cruise. 806 (Sea Hawk FGA.Mk 6) disbands at Brawdy, 894 Sqn (Sea Venom FAW.Mk 22) then disbands on return to Yeovilton, while 849 Sqn 'D' Flt returns from Skyraider AEW.Mk 1's last cruise and is disbanded on same day. Last Skyraider leaves Culdrose on 19 December
16 December After return from the Far East, 815 Sqn (Whirlwind HAS.Mk 7) disbands at Fleetlands

16 December 727 Sqn disbands at Brawdy. It had been the Dartmouth Cadet Air Training Squadron, with two Sea Prince T.Mk 1s and six Sea Vampire T.Mk 22s

1961
12 January 700H Flt (Wessex HAS.Mk 1 IFTU) disbands at Culdrose
21 January 803 Sqn embarks Scimitar F.Mk 1s aboard *Victorious* for Far East cruise, including stops at Tengah and Butterworth and a period in the Persian Gulf during the Kuwait crisis. Joined by 892 Sqn Sea Vixens. 803 returns to Lossiemouth on 19 December while 892 flies to Yeovilton on 8 December
26 January AEW assets for *Victorious* provided by 849 Sqn 'B' Flt which, after stops at Tengah and Seletar, returns to Culdrose on 17 December
27 January 825 Sqn Whirlwinds join 803 Sqn in *Victorious* (operations from Sembawang, *Bulwark*, HMAS *Melbourne*, Port Reitz, Malindi, Lanna Beach)

1 February 899 Sqn commissioned at Yeovilton as Sea Vixen FAW.Mk 1 Headquarters Squadron. Between this date and 1964 detachments are made to *Ark Royal*, *Hermes*, *Centaur*, *Eagle* and *Victorious*
27 February 800 and 807 Sqn Scimitar F.Mk 1s return from *Ark Royal* to Lossiemouth for the summer aerobatic season. 849 'A' Flt disembarks to Culdrose
7 March 700Z Flt forms at Lossiemouth to act as Intensive Flying Trials Unit for the Buccaneer S.Mk 1. No aircraft assigned initially, but two Meteor T.Mk 7s gained in May and four Hunter T.Mk 8s between May and July
1 April 893 Sqn flies to *Centaur* for Mediterranean cruise (shore operations from Hal Far, North Front and Khormaksar). Disembarks to Yeovilton on 1 September
10 April 807 Sqn and 849 'A' Flt embark in *Centaur* for Mediterranean cruise (shore stop at Hal Far) which includes a period in the Persian Gulf in support of the response to the Kuwait

crisis. Joined by 824 Sqn Whirlwinds (also operate from Hal Far and North Front). Return to Lossiemouth and Culdrose on 1 September
29 May 849 Sqn 'C' Flt undertakes cruise aboard *Hermes*, returning to Culdrose on 28 July. 890 Sqn Sea Vixens also on board, returning to Yeovilton on 23 June
6 June 700X Flt (P.531 Wasp IFTU) disbands at Culdrose
10 June 814 Sqn flies Whirlwind HAS.Mk 7s to *Hermes*, disembarking at Portland on 8 August and returning back to Culdrose on 14 August
30 June 890 Sqn returns to *Hermes*, leaving on 10 August
3 July 700 Sqn disbanded at Yeovilton, leaving individual flights to continue IFTU work under their own designations
4 July 815 Sqn reformed at Culdrose with Wessex HAS.Mk 1
11 July 771 Sqn is formed at Portland out of 700 Sqn as a helicopter trials and training squadron with Whirlwind HAS.Mk 7s and a single HAS.Mk 22 for

A Decade of Air Power

Above: A Wasp hovers over the deck of Rothesay. 829 Sqn adminstered all the small ship flights from the headquarters base at Portland.

Below: 825 Sqn Whirlwind HAS.Mk 7s from Victorious were used on flood relief work in Africa in addition to their normal tasks.

700X Flt was conducting trials with the Saro P.531 (forerunner of the Wasp) until June 1961.

The definitive Wasp HAS.Mk 1 was issued to 700W Flt at Culdrose for trials. The type became the standard small ship helicopter.

With Whirlwind HAR.Mk 3s 771 Sqn took over the Portland SAR commitment in 1961. This aircraft is seen carrying minesweeping equipment.

A 771 Sqn Whirlwind HAS.Mk 7 practises SAR work. This version was the Navy's first anti-submarine helicopter.

with British Airways, spread in 1956 to the Royal Navy and is today a cornerstone of the procurement policy of all the British armed forces.

In 1952 the first supposedly capable British helicopter, the Bristol 173, began its flight test programme. It had a long body like a railway carriage, with a piston engine and rotor at each end. In 1953 it carried out sea trials aboard *Eagle*, and in 1954 substantial orders were placed for more powerful derived versions. The latter included the Bristol 191, for multiple shipboard roles with the Fleet Air Arm, including rescue and communications as well as ASW (anti-submarine warfare) and anti-ship attack. Orders were placed for three piston-engined prototypes and 65 production Bristol 191s with two Napier Gazelle turbine engines.

Unfortunately for the British company, the Admiralty were determined to replace the homegrown product by the Sikorsky S-58, made under licence by Westland. The excuses given in 1956 for cancelling the 191 were rising costs and various technical problems, none of which stood up to examination. In its place came a version of the S-58 called the Westland Wessex, powered by a single Gazelle. (That there was little wrong with the Bristol helicopter is shown by its long service as the Belvedere with the RAF, which at that time still bought British aircraft.)

Like the Bristol 191, the Wessex was equipped to carry a dipping sonar and anti-submarine torpedoes, while in the anti-ship role it could carry four primitive Nord SS.11 wire-guided missiles. Other features included a Newmark autostabiliser, folding main-rotor blades and a folding tail. The first flight was made in May 1957, and Fleet Air Arm trials

with 700H Flight at Culdrose began in April 1960. First-line service of the Wessex HAS.Mk 1 began with 815 Sqn in July 1961. Further development led to the Wessex HAS.Mk 3, with more comprehensive avionics to automate the process of searching for submarines from liftoff to the final deck landing. Called 'the Camel' because of its prominent dorsal radome, the HAS.Mk 3 entered service from late 1966, but was destined soon to be replaced by the more capable Sea King.

Another Wessex version was the HU.Mk 5, an assault transport for Royal Marine Commandos. Based on the RAF's HC.Mk 2 version, the HU.Mk 5 was powered by a

Rolls-Royce (originally de Havilland) Coupled Gnome, with two 1,350-shp (1012-kW) power sections giving twin-engine safety. Typically equipped to carry 16 troops with their equipment, the HU.Mk 5 entered service with 848 Sqn in 1964, and subsequently served with 845 and 846.

All the helicopters so far mentioned operated from the large decks of carriers or assault ships, or from shore bases. It was obvious from 1945 that smaller helicopters could operate from the quarterdeck (fantail) of a frigate or large destroyer. Among the duties they could perform were ASW, communications, SAR (search and rescue) and reconnaissance (for

---

SAR duties

13 July 848 Sqn Whirlwind HAS.Mk 7s put 42 Royal Marine Commando ashore in Kuwait from *Bulwark*. The landing is in response to a threat from Iraq to annex the sheikhdom

21 July The first of four Sea Heron C.Mk 2s arrives at Lee-on-Solent to serve with the Communications Squadron (781 Sqn). At the time the fleet comprised five Sea Devon C.Mk 20s, one Dominie Mk 1 and one Whirlwind HAS.Mk 1

27 July 891 Sqn (Sea Venom FAW.Mk 22) disbanded at Yeovilton

3 August 700Z Flt receives the first two (of six) Buccaneer S.Mk 1s for IFTU work

9 August 849 Sqn 'C' Flt embarks in

Hermes for cruise, ending on 10 September

September 849 Sqn HQ takes on charge two Gannet AS.Mk 4 Courier (later known as COD.Mk 4) and three Gannet T.Mk 5s

14 September 814 Sqn (Whirlwind HAS.Mk 7) disbands at Culdrose

15 September 804 Sqn (Scimitar F.Mk 1) disbanded at Lossiemouth

25 September 750 Sqn takes on four Sea Venom FAW.Mk 22s to replace its FAW.Mk 21s. These fly until 1970

October 771 Sqn receives two Whirlwind HAR.Mk 3s for SAR duties at Portland

5 October 819 Sqn formed at Eglinton as Wessex HQ Sqn with two Wessex HAS.Mk 1s (subsequent

maximum seven) and one Whirlwind HAS.Mk 7. Reformation achieved by renumbering 719 Sqn

19 October 824 Sqn embarks on *Centaur* for Far East/African cruise (shore operations from Hal Far, Port Reitz, Malindi, Lanna Beach and Sembawang). Return to Culdrose14 May 1962

20 October 807 Sqn undertakes its final cruise with Scimitars aboard *Centaur*, calling at Hal Far and returning to Lossiemouth on 15 May 1962. Also on board is 849 'A' Flt with Gannet AEW.Mk 3s (shore stop at Tengah), which returns to Culdrose on 14 May 1962, and 893 Sqn (shore stops at Hal Far, Khormaksar and Tengah) which disembarks on 14 May 1962

27 October 819 Sqn deploys to Culdrose, returning to Eglinton on 10 November

13 November 12 Scimitar F.Mk 1s from 800 Sqn deploy to Ark Royal. They return to Lossiemouth on 15 January 1962. Joined by 815 Sqn Wessex HAS.Mk 1, which transfer to *Victorious* on 10 December. AEW coverage from 849 Sqn 'C' Flt, including shore ops from Hal Far. Gannets return to Culdrose on 14 January 1962. Fighter squadron is 890 (Sea Vixen FAW.Mk 1s), which disembarks to Yeovilton on 16 January after a short detachment to Hal Far

20 November 819 Sqn Wessex deploy for short cruise on USS *Essex*, returning to Eglinton on 30 November

22 November Whirlwind HAS.Mk 7s

700H Flt was tasked with intensive trials on the Wessex HAS.Mk 1 in 1960-62 from Culdrose. Here an aircraft is seen 'dunking' sonar.

In 1967 700H Flt was reformed, this time to bring the Wessex HAS.Mk 3 into service. Here a torpedo is being launched.

Anti-submarine squadrons briefly equipped with Whirlwinds prior to the Wessex HAS.Mk 1 entering service. This example of the latter served with 814 Sqn aboard Victorious from August 1963, and is seen winching from the deck.

Above: From 1967 737 Sqn at Portland operated the Wessex HAS.Mk 3 on anti-submarine training duties.

Below: Wessex HAS.Mk 1s began to replace the Whirlwinds of 771 Sqn towards the end of the 1960s. The unit was based at Portland.

814 Sqn operated the Wessex HAS.Mk 3 between 1967 and 1970. Initially assigned to Victorious, the squadron shifted to Hermes in May 1968.

During 1963/64 847 Sqn was at Culdrose with Whirlwind HAS.Mk 7s as an intensive training unit for commando helicopter crews destined for Borneo.

The turbine-powered Whirlwind HAR.Mk 9 was introduced in 1966. This example served with Brawdy's SAR flight.

example, during passage through ice). The 1950s were spent arguing over the US Navy's persistence with small unmanned radio-controlled helicopters in the ASW role, but eventually it was decided to buy a shipboard derivative of the Saro P.531, a conventional helicopter which first flew in July 1958.

The result was the Westland Wasp, powered by a 1,050-hp (783-kW) Rolls-Royce (originally Blackburn) Nimbus engine. Features included folding rotor blades and tail, flotation gear and a unique four-wheel landing gear which could set the wheels diagonally so that the helicopter might rotate but could not travel across the deck. Special sprag (locking) brakes

were also fitted. There were two seats in front and a three-seat bench behind, and in the ASW role two Mk 44 torpedoes could be carried, though no search equipment was provided. Essentially the Wasp acted in this role as a delivery system to hostile submarines detected by the parent ship.

The Wasp entered service in summer 1963, and a total of 93 was delivered. They served on almost all FAA shore establishments, but their main duty was as elements of 829 Sqn aboard some 40 frigates of the 'Leander' and 'Tribal' classes. At the end of the decade it was expected that they would be replaced by the Westland WG.13, but this helicopter (later named Lynx)

did not even reach the FAA trials unit until 1976.

Though both the Scimitar and Sea Vixen were announced as being capable of carrying a nuclear weapon, no such weapons were issued to squadrons equipped with these aircraft. In contrast, the NA.39 was explicitly designed in the mid-1950s as an advanced carrier-based attack aircraft, armed with nuclear weapons just as much as with conventional bombs. It was also designed to carry mines and, when these were available, with guided attack missiles. It was originally designed to a naval requirement – initially concerned with the threat posed by Soviet 'Kirov'-class cruisers – calling for the

of 825 Sqn put ashore from *Centaur* to help with flood relief in Kenya
28 November 814 Sqn reformed at Culdrose with four Wessex HAS.Mk 1 (subsequent maximum eight)
29 November 728B Flt at Hal Far bade the Navy's farewell to the Firefly, when the last U.Mk 9 drone was shot down by the guns of HMS *Duchess*
2 December 728B Flt at Hal Far is disbanded. Remaining with the drone target unit were five Canberra D.Mk 14s (received in May 1961) and a single Meteor U.Mk 16
8 December 825 Sqn's Whirlwind HAS.Mk 1s given to 824 Sqn, which continues flood relief operations in Kenya
18 December 815 Sqn Wessex

disembarks from *Victorious* to Lee-on-Solent, travelling on to Culdrose on 12 January 1962

1962
4 January 706 Sqn is reformed at Culdrose as an advanced helicopter training squadron with eight Wessex HAS.Mk 1s
18 January 750 Sqn adds the Sea Vampire T.Mk 22 to its observer training line-up. These are retired in May 1965
2 February 803 Sqn embarks with Scimitar F.Mk 1s aboard *Victorious* for Mediterranean cruise, including shore-stop at North Front. Return to Lossiemouth 2 April. Joined on board by 849 Sqn 'B' Flt which flies back to Culdrose on 30 March

9 February *Victorious* air group completed by 892 Sqn Sea Vixens, which return to Yeovilton on 30 March
March Helicopter training squadron 705 Sqn at Culdrose retires the Dragonfly HR.Mk 5, although the type continues to see service with station's SAR Flight
6 March 814 Sqn deploys to Portland for a pre-cruise work-up, returning to Culdrose on 11 April
9 March 815 Sqn with Wessex HAS.Mk 1s embarks in *Ark Royal* for Far East cruise (shore stop at Sembawang). Returns to Culdrose on 14 December
10 March 800 Sqn Scimitar F.Mk 1s and 890 Sqn Sea Vixen FAW.Mk 1s join 814 in *Ark Royal* for Far East cruise (shore stops at Pearce and Tengah).

Return to Lossiemouth on 16 December and Yeovilton on 14 December respectively. AEW coverage by 849 Sqn 'C' Flt which puts ashore at Tengah and Seletar and returns to Culdrose on 1 January 1963
2 April 825 Sqn (Whirlwind HAS.Mk 7) disbanded
10 April 845 Sqn formed at Culdrose as a commando assault unit with 12 Wessex HAS.Mk 1s
May During the month 781 Sqn took delivery of a Sea Hawk FGA.Mk 6 for the personal use of Flag Officer Air Home
8 May 846 Sqn formed at Culdrose with six (later seven) Whirlwind HAS.Mk 7s
15 May 807 Sqn (Scimitar F.Mk 1) disbands at Lossiemouth

700B Flt was formed at Lossiemouth in April 1965 to test the Buccaneer S.Mk 2 operationally. Aircraft wore a 'B' badge on the fin.

To undertake initial trials on the Buccaneer S.Mk 1, 700Z Flt was formed at Lossiemouth in 1961. The unit also operated Hunters and Meteors.

736 Sqn took over Buccaneer training in 1965, formed out of 809 Sqn. It added S.Mk 2s to its S.Mk 1s from 1966.

Above: Buccaneer S.Mk 1s were assigned to 800 Sqn from March 1964, flying from Eagle. The Buccaneer had an unusual split tailcone airbrake.

Below: An 800 Sqn Buccaneer S.Mk 2 is seen seconds from launch, a Bullpup precision missile clutched under its wing pylon.

ability to attack at close to the speed of sound at the lowest possible height above the sea.

To the astonishment of many, the contract was won in 1955 by Blackburn Aircraft. Their B.103 design featured the most advanced use then seen of BLC (boundary-layer control) by high-energy blowing with hot high-pressure air bled from the engines. At low speeds, this was expelled in thin transonic sheets from narrow slits ahead of the flaps and tailplane. As a result, these surfaces (especially the tailplane) were remarkably small in relation to the capacious fuselage, which seated the pilot and navigator in tandem ahead of a large internal weapon bay. The result was a brilliant attack aircraft whose

only shortcoming was that, to meet the range demanded, the engines were 7,100-lb (31.58-kN) DH Gyron Junior turbojets. At full load this resulted in an extremely long take-off, though of course on a carrier the aircraft could be catapulted.

In April 1957 Duncan Sandys had proclaimed his belief that the RAF would need no more fighters or bombers, but somehow he overlooked the Fleet Air Arm. As a result this very important programme continued, and the first of 20 NA.39 development aircraft flew on 30 April 1958. The first production Buccaneer S.Mk 1 flew on 23 January 1962, painted in white anti-nuclear flash finish. The first

Buccaneer squadron, No. 801, commissioned in July 1962 and embarked aboard HMS *Ark Royal* in February 1963.

Excluding the preceding 20, a total of 40 S.Mk 1 aircraft were delivered, progressively replacing the Scimitar. In their ability to cruise smoothly and almost buffet-free at Mach 0.85 at wave-top height, and then pull up and toss a 'weapon' in a forward or over-the-shoulder manoeuvre, they had no equal anywhere else in the world. Apart from a nuclear weapon, the internal bay could accommodate four 1,000-lb (454-kg) bombs, and with this load all Buccaneers were faster than any other attack aircraft in the world with the same bomb load.

---

16 May Gannets of 849 Sqn 'B' Flt embark in *Hermes* for cruise including stops at Hal Far and North Front. Return to Culdrose on 2 October
18 May 892 Sqn joins *Hermes* for Mediterranean cruise, stopping at Hal Far and North Front. Returns to Yeovilton on 1 October
25 May 803 Sqn deploys aboard *Hermes* for Mediterranean cruise with stops at Hal Far and North Front. Return to Lossiemouth on 4 October
26 May 814 Sqn joins *Hermes*, later putting ashore at Hal Far and returning to Culdrose on 4 October
June 764 Sqn (air warfare instruction and swept-wing conversion) adds three Hunter GA.Mk 11s to its fleet of eight Hunter T.Mk 8s at Lossiemouth

19 June 824 Sqn Whirlwinds deploy aboard *Centaur*, disembarking at Portland on 5 July
21 June 849 'A' Flt embarks in *Centaur*, returning to Culdrose on 5 July
22 June 893 Sqn takes its Sea Vixen FAW.Mk 1s aboard *Centaur*, returning to Yeovilton on 5 July
July During the month 738 Sqn (advanced training at Lossiemouth) retires the Sea Hawk FGA.Mk 6 in favour of the Hunter GA.Mk 11
4 July The ASW helicopter school at Portland, 737 Sqn, receives its first Wessex HAS.Mk 1 to begin the replacement of the Whirlwind HAS.Mk 7. Subsequent maximum complement is nine aircraft
12 July 849 'A' Flt returns to *Centaur*,

flying back to Culdrose on 25 October. 893 Sqn Sea Vixen FAW.Mk 1s join ship, calling at North Front and Hal Far during the cruise, and supplying a detachment for the Farnborough air show. Return to Yeovilton on 25 October with subsequent deployment to Culdrose
17 July 801 Sqn recommissioned at Lossiemouth with Buccaneer S.Mk 1 (first aircraft delivered 26 July)
20 July 824 Sqn embarks in *Centaur* for Mediterranean cruise (shore ops from North Front). Return to Culdrose on 21 November
August 700Z Flt borrows five Buccaneer S.Mk 1s from 801 Sqn to work up display routine for the following month's Farnborough air show
1 August *Albion* recommissioned

after modifications
September 738 Sqn at Brawdy relinquishes its last Sea Vampire T.Mk 22 as Hunter T.Mk 8s enter service
4 September 705 Sqn receives its first Hiller HT.Mk 2 at Culdrose to replace the ageing Hiller HT.Mk 1s
18 September 845 Sqn takes Wessex HAS.Mk 1s aboard *Albion*, returning to Culdrose on 24 September
2 November 845 Sqn embarks on *Albion* for the Far East. Extended shore operations during the Indonesian conflict include use of bases at Sembawang, Semanggang, Belaga, Nanga Gaat, Kuching, Labuan and Sibu. 846 Sqn's Whirlwind HAS.Mk 7s also on *Albion* (shore operations from Aden, Melindiana, Kuching, Labuan, Sibu,

Above: 801 Sqn was the first front-line recipient of the Buccaneer S.Mk 1, flying initially from Ark Royal. The aircraft were originally delivered in nuclear anti-flash white with toned-down national insignia.

Right: 809 Sqn received Buccaneers in January 1963, and operated as the type conversion unit at Lossiemouth, with occasional forays aboard ship. This aircraft is seen in November 1963 during anti-ship exercises using HMS Tiger as a target. The Buccaneer was in its day the world's finest maritime strike platform.

The Buccaneer was designed with nuclear delivery as the primary mission. Here an 801 Sqn aircraft from Victorious test-drops a nuclear training 'shape'.

809 Sqn reformed as a front-line unit with Buccaneer S.Mk 2s in 1966. Until 1968 it was assigned to the air wing of Hermes.

Their shortcoming, apart from lacking engine power, was in making the backseater rely on a reference gyro and Doppler radar, instead of having inertial navigation.

When the Buccaneer entered service it was stated that a new version was planned with a different engine. The first Buccaneer S.Mk 2, an early prototype converted, first flew on 17 May 1963, and the first production S.Mk 2 aircraft followed the last S.Mk 1 on 5 June 1964. The new engine was the Rolls-Royce Spey, which offered considerable advantages. Its take-off thrust was not 7,100 lb (31.58 kN) but 11,100 lb (49.38 kN). Its specific fuel consumption was so much better that, despite the extra power, it actually burned less fuel, though the greater power enabled fuel/weapon loads to be significantly increased. Not least, it provided air for BLC blowing with less increase in turbine temperature.

A total of 84 Buccaneer S.Mk 2 aircraft were ordered, none of the in-service Mk 1s being converted. New features of the S.Mk 2 included a fixed inflight-refuelling probe above the nose, revised avionics (but retaining the original navigation system), a strengthened wing and four new and repositioned 'universal' wing pylons each able to carry three 1,000-lb bombs, a total of 12,000 lb (5443 kg). The final upgrade, before the axe fell on further development in the Labour Defence White Paper of 1966, was to fit Martel guided missiles, with TV control by the backseater. The S.Mk 2 could also double as a tanker, with a hosedrum buddy pack, but one aircraft showed the capability of these aircraft without refuelling by taking off from *Victorious* in the Irish Sea, making a simulated attack on Gibraltar and then flying back, a total of over 2,300 miles (3700 km).

The 1966 White Paper announced nothing less than the termination of British seagoing airpower. It said, in effect "Oh dear, while the US Navy is adding a gigantic new supercarrier each year, to a total of 14 carrier air groups, we find we cannot afford to have any carriers at all. The present Royal Navy carrier force will run down in the 1970s and will not be replaced. The CVA-01, the new fleet carrier planned since 1953, is cancelled. The Fleet Air Arm's fixed-wing airpower will be transferred to the RAF." The document went on to say that costly carrier-based aircraft could be replaced by "cheaper land-based aircraft." This overlooked the slight problem that the unpredictable future conflict would almost certainly start somewhere where Her Majesty had no land base. For example, nobody foresaw the need to retake the Falklands.

In that conflict of 1982, faced by the small amount of airpower that could be rushed together a key absence was any kind of AEW (airborne early-warning) radar. Back in the 1950s the Fleet Air Arm's fighters had enjoyed the sure guidance of the 'Salisbury' class aircraft direction frigates and the big APS-20 radars carried by the Douglas Skyraiders of 849 Sqn. To replace the popular and effective Skyraider as the FAA's AEW aircraft, orders were placed in 1954 for the Fairey Gannet AEW.Mk 3.

The first order for the original anti-submarine version of the Gannet had been placed in August 1946. It finally entered FAA service in 1954-55 as a three-seat carrier-based ASW aircraft with a unique Double Mamba 101 turboprop engine with left and right power sections. On take-off both were in use, putting 3,035 hp (2264 kW) into two coaxial four-bladed pro-

---

Brunei, Kai Tak and Tawau)
12 November 814 Sqn flies to *Hermes* for Far East cruise (periods spent at Sembawang, in HMS *Albion* and in HMAS *Melbourne*)
13 November 803 Sqn embarks Scimitar F.Mk 1s aboard *Hermes* for Far East cruise (calls at Tengah and Butterworth). Return to Yeovilton on 11 September 1963. Joined by 849 Sqn 'B' Flt from Culdrose and 892 from Yeovilton which all disembark on the same date
14/15 December 845 and 846 Sqns from *Albion* land 40 Royal Marine Commando in Brunei to help quell internal unrest, marking the beginning of the Navy's involvement in the Borneo conflict

1963
15 January 700Z Flt disbands at Lossiemouth as the Buccaneer S.Mk 1 IFTU, becoming 809 Sqn with five Buccaneer S.Mk 1s and one Hunter T.Mk 8 as Strike Headquarters Sqn and Buccaneer OCU
15 January 824 Sqn Whirlwind HAS.Mk 7s move to Portland prior to a short cruise on *Centaur*, departing on 21 January and returning to Culdrose on 14 February
22 January 849 'A' Flt fly to *Centaur* for short cruise, terminating on 12 February. Joined by 893 Sqn, which fly back to Yeovilton on 14 February
4 February 819 Sqn Wessex HAS.Mk 1s undertake short trip in *Centaur*,

before disembarking to new base at Ballykelly on 7 February. Subsequent exercise detachments made to HrMs *Karel Doorman*, *Victorious*, Portland, *Hermes*, RFA *Tidepool*, Yeovilton and HMS *Lofoten*
16 February Five Buccaneer S.Mk 1s from 801 Sqn in *Ark Royal* to make the type's first operational cruise. Return to Lossiemouth on 15 March
18 February 800 Sqn 'A' Flt Scimitar F.Mk 1s embark in *Ark Royal*. Returns to Lossiemouth on 16 March
19 February 890 Sqn provides fighter assets in *Ark Royal*, disembarking to Yeovilton on 14 March
20 February 815 Sqn embarks on *Ark Royal* for Far East cruise (calling at North Front and Sembawang). AEW

coverage by 849 Sqn 'C' Flt (stops at North Front, Embakasi and Seletar) which returns to Culdrose 30 December and 893 Sqn (shore stops at Khormaksar and Embakasi) which returns to Yeovilton on 15 May
21 February 824 Sqn embarks in *Centaur* for final cruise. Also 849 'A' Flt which makes stops at Khormaksar and Embakasi before returning to Culdrose on 20 May
6 March 728 Sqn at Hal Far adds a Sea Heron C.Mk 2 to its Sea Devon C.Mk 20 fleet
May Further expansion for 728 Sqn results in two Whirlwind HAS.Mk 22s being added for SAR duties
1 May 800 Sqn Scimitars embark in *Ark Royal* for a Far East cruise (shore

The Gannet AS.Mk 4 had been largely replaced by helicopters by 1960. 810 Sqn (illustrated) made the ASW version's last cruise in 1960 in Centaur.

Above and below right: At the beginning of 1960, 849 Sqn at Culdrose still had over 20 Skyraider AEW.Mk 1s, allowing it to put up this fine formation. The changeover to Gannet AEW.Mk 3s for the HQ squadron and its four flights began in February and was completed by the end of the year.

This Gannet COD.Mk 4 served with 849 Sqn 'D' Flt aboard Eagle. One COD aircraft was assigned to each carrier operated by the AEW flight.

Left: The Skyraider flew its last carrier cruise with 849 Sqn 'D' Flt aboard Albion during 1960, returning to Culdrose in December.

A handful of surplus ASW Gannets were reworked to serve in the electronic warfare training role as ECM.Mk 6s, serving with 831 Sqn.

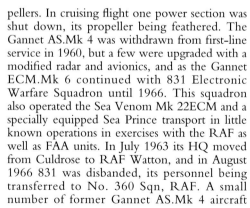

pellers. In cruising flight one power section was shut down, its propeller being feathered. The Gannet AS.Mk 4 was withdrawn from first-line service in 1960, but a few were upgraded with a modified radar and avionics, and as the Gannet ECM.Mk 6 continued with 831 Electronic Warfare Squadron until 1966. This squadron also operated the Sea Venom Mk 22ECM and a specially equipped Sea Prince transport in little known operations in exercises with the RAF as well as FAA units. In July 1963 its HQ moved from Culdrose to RAF Watton, and in August 1966 831 was disbanded, its personnel being transferred to No. 360 Sqn, RAF. A small number of former Gannet AS.Mk 4 aircraft

were also stripped of their operational equipment, painted Midnight blue and served as Gannet COD.Mk 4 carrier on-board delivery transports. They mainly replenished *Ark Royal* and *Eagle*, administered by 849 Sqn B and D Flights from 1964 to late 1974.

Development of the Gannet AEW.Mk 3 was typically protracted. The prototype did not fly until August 1958, and work was then little-helped by the takeover of Fairey Aviation by Westland Aircraft in 1960. The resulting Westland Gannet AEW.Mk 3 reached the first Flight of 849 Sqn in February 1960. Hardly any part of the AEW.Mk 3 resembled previous marks. The weapon bay and retractable

ASW/ASV radar were eliminated and replaced by APS-20 radar – the same old sets which were taken out of the Skyraiders, and which on withdrawal of the Gannet force in 1978 were then bolted on to RAF Shackletons! A new cabin in the rear fuselage housed the two operators, and among many other changes were long-stroke landing gears, a 3,875-hp (2906-kW) Double Mamba 102 engine and enlarged fin and rudder.

Including the prototype, 44 Gannet AEW.Mk 3 aircraft were delivered, and they gave good service with 849 Sqn at Culdrose in 1960-65, at Brawdy in 1965-70 and thereafter in decreasing numbers at Lossiemouth. The

stops at Tengah and Embakasi). Return to Lossiemouth on 31 December
4 May 890 Sqn Sea Vixens join 800 for Far East cruise (shore operations from Embakasi and Tengah), returning to Yeovilton on 28 December
7 May 847 Sqn formed at Culdrose with Whirlwind HAS.Mk 7 (maximum 12)
21 May 824 Sqn (Whirlwind HAS.Mk 7) disbands at Culdrose
25 May 849 'A' Flt embarks in *Centaur*, returning to Culdrose on 6 June
June 1963 831 Sqn receives a single Sea Prince T.Mk 1 at its Culdrose base
4 June 700W Flt established at Culdrose to act as Wasp HAS.Mk 1 IFTU
21 June 700W Flt receives the first of

an eventual five Wasp HAS.Mk 1s
26 July 831 Sqn moves from Culdrose to RAF Watton for closer co-operation with the RAF's Central Signals Establishment. Equipment consisted of four Sea Venom Mk 22ECM, one Sea Vampire T.Mk 22, one Sea Prince T.Mk 1 and four Gannet ECM.Mk 6
30 July 848 Sqn (Whirlwind HAS.Mk 7) disbands at Culdrose
1 August 759 Sqn is formed at Brawdy as an advanced flying training unit with nine Hunter T.Mk 8s (subsequent maximum 13)
12 August 801 Sqn Buccaneer S.Mk 1s deploy aboard *Victorious* for a Far East/African cruise, including shore

deployments to Tengah, Kai Tak, Cubi Point, Changi and Embakasi. Return to Lossiemouth on 22 July 1965
14 August 849 'A' Flt Gannet AEW.Mk 3s join *Victorious* for Far East cruise, calling at Tengah, Embakasi and Seletar, returning to the new squadron base at Brawdy on 22 July 1965. Also on board are Sea Vixen FAW.Mk 1s of 893 Sqn, which operates from shore bases at Tengah, Kai Tak, Changi and Embakasi before returning home on 22 July 1965
26 September 849 Sqn 'B' Flt flies to *Hermes* for short cruise, terminating on 18 October
27 September 892 Sqn Sea Vixens and 803 Sqn Scimitar F.Mk 1s undertake

short cruise aboard *Hermes*, disembarking to Yeovilton on 21 October and Lossiemouth on 22 October respectively
29 October 700V Flt established at Culdrose without aircraft to become the Wessex HU.Mk 5 IFTU
29 November 803 Sqn Scimitar F.Mk 1s embark in *Hermes* for a short cruise, ending at Lossiemouth on 12 December
7 December The Wessex HU.Mk 5 IFTU, 700V Flt, receives the first of six assigned aircraft
18 December On route from Far East, 815 Sqn Wessex HAS.Mk 1s disembark from *Ark Royal* at Khormaksar as the first Navy unit involved in fighting

Above: For type conversion 849 Sqn operated a few Gannet T.Mk 5 trainers (foreground). The AEW.Mk 3 (background) was virtually a new aircraft, however.

Left: Seen in 1966, this Gannet served with 849 Sqn 'B' Flt aboard Hermes. In addition to the pilot, the AEW.Mk 3 carried two radar operators in a central fuselage cabin..

849 Sqn 'B' Flt was aboard Hermes in 1967, supplying airborne early warning coverage. Visible here is the catapult bridle falling away from the aircraft the moment of launch. The Gannet employed both power sections of its Double Mamba engine for take-off and climb-out, but shut one down for patrol.

The Gannet AEW.Mk 3 headquarters squadron moved from Culdrose to Brawdy in December 1964, and remained at the Welsh base until moving to Lossiemouth in 1970. In addition to supporting the embarked flights, the squadron undertook type conversion training and instruction in AEW techniques.

November 1961 Hawker Aircraft hosted a meeting of representatives from aircraft manufacturers throughout Europe and the USA. The result was launch of the Hawker P.1154 to meet the NATO Basic Military Requirement No. 3 for a supersonic strike fighter with V/STOL (vertical/short take-off and landing).

This resembled a stretched Hawker P.1127 or Kestrel, with variable inlets to a Bristol Siddeley BS.100 turbofan engine in the over-30,000-lb (133.45-kN) class with plenum-chamber burning to boost this to 35,600 lb (158.36 kN). It appeared to be a brilliant concept, as simple as a Harrier yet with multi-mode radar, a heavy weapon load and Mach 2 capability. In April 1962 NATO announced that the P.1154 had won the potentially huge NBMR-3 competition. By the summer of 1962 the P.1154 was being developed not only for NATO but also as a replacement for the Hunter in the RAF and the Scimitar and Sea Vixen in the FAA.

There were a few problems. One was that the NBMR-3 contest meant nothing, because it was left to individual countries to take further action, and the only country to do anything (other than the UK) was France, which predictably announced that it was building the rival Mirage III-V. Another was that the Royal Navy did all it could to make the P.1154RN as different as possible from the P.1154RAF. For example, Their Lordships demanded a backseat navigator, a different radar with folding radome, folding wings, different engine inlets and ducts and a totally different landing gear (the official list of conflicting requirements totalled 47 items).

To cut a long and acrimonious story short,

rather cramped cabin restricted the size of the main display and prevented a moving cursor, but the AEW.Mk 3 did have IFF interrogation and a video accumulator, and just before withdrawal at last got AMTI (airborne moving-target indication). Since nobody had the foresight to imagine that such aircraft might actually be needed, the British Task Force in the South Atlantic in 1982 had no AEW capability, with disastrous results.

In the early 1960s the FAA looked wistfully at more capable equipment of the kind fielded by the US Navy. The Grumman E-2C Hawkeye would have offered superior capability in the AEW role, while the Mach-2 North

American (Rockwell) RA-5C Vigilante could confer a previously absent strategic reconnaissance capability with multiple sensors. The planned new fleet carrier CVA-01 was designed to operate both types, but political will was in the same short supply as money, and none of these plans came to anything.

In the early 1960s the FAA had no fighter of a kind that might be expected to win in close combat, for example against a Mirage, F-5 or MiG-21. Development of such aircraft had been prohibited by 'the Sandystorm' of April 1957, but what could probably have been a world-beating combat aircraft was enabled to happen by a roundabout route. On 17

---

rebel tribesmen in the Radfan region of the Aden Protectorate
19 December To avoid congestion at Lossiemouth, the advanced training unit, 738 Sqn, moves to Brawdy with three Hunter T.Mk 8s and 15 Hunter GA.Mk 11s
21 December 892 Sqn embarks in *Centaur* for Far East cruise (shore operations from Tengah, Kai Tak and Embakasi). Returns to Yeovilton on 19 December 1964
22 December 849 Sqn 'B' Flt deploys its Gannets aboard *Centaur* for a Far Far East cruise with stops at Seletar, Kai Tak and Embakasi. Disembarks to Brawdy on 20 December 1964

1964
January 815 Sqn from *Ark Royal* uses Wessex HAS.Mk 1s to put 45 Royal Marine Commando ashore at Dar-es-Salaam to restore order in Tanganyika. The city is under control within one hour and the rebellion falters
7 January 706 Sqn 'B' Flt formed at Culdrose with five Wessex HAS.Mk 1s and two Hiller HT.Mk 2s for trials aboard *Bulwark*. Later absorbed into 845 Sqn
15 January After Christmas in Khormaksar, 815 Sqn and its Wessex HAS.Mk 1s embark in *Centaur* and return to Far East (shore stop at Sembawang), eventually returning to

Culdrose on 22 December
16 January 803 Sqn Scimitar F.Mk 1s board *Hermes* for short cruise, returning to Lossiemouth on 27 February. Briefly joined by 849 Sqn 'C' Flt and 890 Sqn which disembark to Culdrose and Yeovilton on 30 January
29 January *Albion* leaves Far East for the UK, leaving 845 Sqn shore-based at Sibu pending the arrival of *Bulwark*
7 February Buccaneers of 801 Sqn deploy to Embakasi (Nairobi) to reinforce the policing action in neighbouring Tanganyika
14 February 849 Sqn 'C' Flt returns to *Hermes*, arriving back at Culdrose (via Lossiemouth) on 24 February

22 February 814 Sqn Wessex HAS.Mk 1s transfer from *Hermes* to *Victorious* and continue Far East cruise (deployments to Sembawang and RFA *Tidespring*). Return to Culdrose on 26 July 1965
25 February 800 Sqn disbands at Lossiemouth as a Scimitar F.Mk 1 unit
March 829 Sqn receives Wessex HAS.Mk 1 to parent flights on 'County'-class destroyers
4 March 829 Sqn formed at Culdrose from disbanding 700W Flight as small ships flight squadron. Initial equipment of three Wasp HAS.Mk 1s and one Whirlwind HAR.Mk 1
5 March 847 'B' Flt detaches

A Decent of Air Power

759 Sqn was established at Brawdy in 1963 to function as the advanced training unit with Hunter T.Mk 8s.

on 27 February 1964 it was announced that the P.1154RN was being abandoned, and that in its place the American McDonnell Phantom II would be purchased. Had anyone at that time had any inkling that two years later the decision would be taken to run down and eliminate the RN carrier force, this decision would have been recognised as a monumental error – at least from the FAA's viewpoint. The Phantom could never be anything but a big-deck or long-runway aircraft, whereas the P.1154 could have operated from small and simple ships with no catapults or arrester gear, but nobody at the time saw this as important. The inability to continue to fund fleet carriers seemed to come as a genuine surprise.

As always, the government of the day were mesmerised by the idea of buying something 'cheap, fully developed and proven' from the USA. The FAA Phantom was called the F-4K in the USA and Phantom FG.Mk 1 in Britain. To make it more acceptable it was fitted with Rolls-Royce Spey engines, and various parts and some of the equipment were made in the UK. Unexpectedly, the much more powerful British engines actually increased drag so much that performance was degraded, and there were so many modifications that unit price was roughly 60 per cent higher than for the US Navy's F-4J.

The prototype YF-4K flew on 27 June 1966, and the Phantom FG.Mk 1 entered service with 892 Sqn in March 1969. By this time it was known that the FAA's days of fixed-wing warplanes were (it was thought) soon to end, so 892 painted a Greek Omega character on their fins, signifying that they were the last such unit to exist. The Phantom buy was cut from 130 to only 50, of which (lacking suitable decks on which to put them) half were immediately

Above: Hunters of 764 Sqn at Lossiemouth were used for Air Warfare Instructor Training and for swept-wing conversion. This is a GA.Mk 11.

Above: These Hunter GA.Mk 11s are from 738 Sqn, which undertook advanced/weapons training from Lossiemouth. It moved to Brawdy in 1964 to concentrate on weapons instrcution.

Right: Several Hunters served with station flights, like this T.Mk 8 at Yeovilton.

Above: The Hunter GA.Mk 11, with nose-mounted Harley Light, was used by the Airwork Fleet Requirements Unit at Hurn from March 1969.

transferred to No. 43 Sqn, RAF. On withdrawal of *Ark Royal* No. 892 disbanded in December 1978.

In 1967, virtually all Britain's military aircraft programmes having been torn up, plans were made to develop replacements with France. The plan for helicopters was little more than a wholesale adoption of French designs, but it did launch a British machine called the Westland WG.13. The prototype did not fly until March 1971, but as the Lynx this helicopter was to serve the Royal Navy in several versions, at first as a replacement for the Wasp.

Westland had also designed a larger helicopter, the WG.1, to meet the RAF's need for a transport and SAR machine, the Army's heavy-lift requirement and the FAA's need for a hunter/killer ASW machine to replace the Wessex. In true British style, the customers so complicated the programme that, as invariably happened, the homegrown project was abandoned and replaced by a US product. The American helicopter had first flown in March 1959 as the Sikorsky HSS-2 (S-61). Licensed to Westland, it became the Sea King powered by twin US T58 engines made under licence with

---

Whirlwind HAS.Mk 7s to *Bulwark* for a Far East cruise including operations from Sembawang
18 March 800 Sqn reforms at Lossiemouth with the Buccaneer S.Mk 1
April The Fleet Air Arm celebrates its 40th anniversary with a major review at Yeovilton
7 May 700V Flt (Wessex HU.Mk 5 IFTU) disbands at Culdrose and becomes 848 Sqn (maximum complement 18 aircraft)
22 May 815 Sqn Wessex HAS.Mk 1s from *Ark Royal* land 45 Royal Marine Commando in the Radfan area of Aden
15 June 899 Sqn is recommissioned at Yeovilton as the Sea Vixen FAW.Mk 2 Intensive Flying Trials Unit but with front-line status (attached to *Eagle*). Complement is 16 aircraft
3 September 849 Sqn 'D' Flt

reformed at Culdrose with three (later four) Gannet AEW.Mk 3s. Short deployment made subsequently to Lossiemouth
9 September 800B Flt formed at Lossiemouth with four Scimitar F.Mk 1s for air-to-air refuelling trials
23 September 820 Sqn reformed at Culdrose with Wessex HAS.Mk 1 (maximum complement eight)
19 October After brief deployment to *Bulwark*, 846 Sqn (Whirlwind HAS.Mk 7) disbands at Sembawang
30 November 848 'D' Flt embarks on *Albion*
30 November 706 Sqn receives two Wasp HAS.Mk 1s to begin training for small ships flights, a task it assumes from 829 Sqn
1 December Wessex HAS.Mk 1s of 820 Sqn embark in *Eagle* for Far East

cruise (call at Sembawang). Return to Culdrose 25 May 1965
1 December 829 Sqn moves to Portland and is amalgamated with 771 Sqn to become HQ Sqn for Wasp. 771 disbands on the same day
2 December 800 Sqn takes its Buccaneer S.Mk 1s for their first cruise in *Eagle*, returning from Far East to Lossiemouth on 21 May 1965. AEW coverage by 849 Sqn 'D' Flt, which also undertakes shore ops from Seletar and Kai Tak. Returns to Brawdy on 24 May 1965. 899 Sqn provides fighter cover, returning to Yeovilton on 24 June
2 December 847 Sqn (Whirlwind HAS.Mk 7) disbanded at Culdrose
9 December 707 Sqn reformed (out of 847 Sqn) at Culdrose as the commando helicopter training unit with six Wessex HU.Mk 5s (subsequent

maximum 16)
15 December 849 Sqn HQ Flt moves from Culdrose to Brawdy with eight Gannet AEW.Mk 3s and six T.Mk 5s
18 December 849 Sqn 'C' Flt follows the HQ Flt to Brawdy with four Gannet AEW.Mk 3s and a single COD.Mk 4

1965

January 829 Sqn receives Whirlwind HAS.Mk 7 to begin type training
January 848 Sqn adds two Whirlwind HAS.Mk 7s to its Wessex fleet
12 January 890 Sqn embarks in *Ark Royal* for home cruise with shore stop at Lossiemouth. Return to Yeovilton on 18 March
14 January 849 Sqn 'C' Flt flies to *Ark Royal* for home waters cruise, including shore ops from Lossiemouth. Returns to Brawdy on 16 March

*Right: 892 Sqn became the only front-line Phantom user. The aircraft in the foreground is marked with the name of USS **Saratoga**, the first ship the squadron deployed to.*

The Navy's first Sea King HAS.Mk 1s were assigned to 700S Flt for trials in late 1969.

Right at the end of the decade, 706 Sqn (advanced rotary wing training) became the first squadron to receive the Sea King HAS.Mk 1.

The 'Steel Chickens' markings were worn by the Phantoms of 767 Sqn, the type conversion unit at Yeovilton.

700P Flt was formed as the Phantom trials unit, operational between April 1968 and March 1969, at which time it renumbered as 892 Sqn.

Apart from its week aboard Saratoga, 892 Sqn was carrier-based only in Ark Royal. The squadron survived until December 1978.

767 Sqn trained Phantom crews from 1969 to 1972, at which point the task was transferred to the Phantom Post Operational Conversion Unit.

the name Bristol Siddeley Gnome.

The first order was for 60 Sea King HAS.Mk 1 anti-submarine helicopters for the FAA. The last 56 were built by Westland, and the first reached 700S trials unit at Culdrose at the very end of the decade in July 1969. With reasonable avionics, dunking sonar, Ekco radar in a 'Camel' radome and the ability to carry up to four Mk 46 torpedoes, or mines or other loads, the Sea King was to have with the FAA a long career whose end is not yet in sight.

What nobody dared even to consider in the 1960s was that the FAA was eventually to

recover a little of its fixed-wing air power. Before the decade was out Hawker Aircraft at Kingston had sketched ideas for a Maritime Harrier, able to operate from the simple ships and which were eventually to be ordered as 'through deck cruisers' (the notion of an aircraft carrier was still taboo). In 1975 the first order was to be placed for the Sea Harrier. Without it, Argentina would today rule the Malvinas.

Operations

During the 1960s the Fleet Air Arm was involved in a number of campaigns as the

British Empire slowly contracted. The first was the Kuwait crisis of 1961.

Kuwait was one of Britain's main oil suppliers, and a defence treaty was in place. When this commitment was renewed in June 1961, Iraq, which had recently become a revolutionary state, reacted angrily and threatened to annex the territory to which it had long maintained a claim. Troops were rushed into Kuwait to provide a powerful deterrent. A key portion of the plan was the putting ashore of No. 42 Royal Marine Commando from *Bulwark*, a task undertaken by the Whirlwind HAS.Mk 7s of

16 January 803 Sqn takes Scimitar F.Mk 1s aboard *Ark Royal* for work-up cruise, ending at Lossiemouth on 15 March. 819 Sqn brings Wessex HAS.Mk 1s which return to Ballykelly on 16 March. Subsequent exercise detachments to RFA *Olynthus*, RFA *Oleander*, Lossiemouth, Sydenham, RFA *Olna*, RFA *Tidepool*, Bulwark, HMCS *Assiniboine*, Arbroath, RFA *Olwen* and Prestwick
February 846 Sqn begins using Whirlwind HAS.Mk 7 for training purposes
12 March The remainder of 848 Sqn joins 'D' Flt in *Albion* for a major Middle/Far East cruise, involving shore operations from Sembawang, Sibu, Nanga Gaat, Bario, Labuan, Aden, Khormaksar, Kota Balud and Sepulot, with a shipborne detachment to RFA *Sir*

Lancelot. Squadron returns to Culdrose on 7 September
26 March In a reshuffle at Lossiemouth, 736 Sqn (with Scimitar F.Mk 1s) renumbers as 764B Flt to continue the training on the type (for Airwork pilots), while 809 Sqn disbands at Lossiemouth and renumbers as the 'new' 736 Sqn, continuing Buccaneer OCU work with a complement of seven Buccaneer S.Mk 1s and one Hunter T.Mk 8
8 April 849 Sqn 'B' Flt embarks in *Centaur* for Mediterranean cruise (stops at Hal Far and North Front), returning to Brawdy on 27 July. 892 Sqn joins on their final Sea Vixen FAW.Mk 1 cruise which ends at Yeovilton on 27 July
9 April 700 Sqn 'B' Flt commissioned at Lossiemouth as Buccaneer S.Mk 2 Intensive Flying Trials Unit with four

Buccaneer S.Mk 2s (subsequently six) and one Hunter T.Mk 8
8 May 849 Sqn 'C' Flt undertakes short work-up in *Ark Royal*, returning to Brawdy on 25 May
13 May 803 Sqn Scimitars back aboard *Ark Royal* for a Far East cruise, calling at Changi. Return to Lossiemouth on 12 June 1966
14 May Short work-up for 890 Sqn on *Ark Royal*, ending at Yeovilton on 27 May
15 June 890 Sqn Sea Vixen FAW.Mk 1s reboard *Ark Royal* for Far East (including stops at Changi and Butterworth), returning to Yeovilton on 7 June 1966. During the latter part of the cruise the *Ark Royal* aircraft are active on the Beira patrol
16 June 815 Sqn Wessex HAS.Mk 1s join 803 for Far East cruise (calls at

Sembawang and Kuala Lumpur). Return to Culdrose 14 June 1966
17 June 849 Sqn 'C' Flt embarks in *Ark Royal* for a Far East cruise (shore ops from Seletar, Changi and Butterworth), returning to Brawdy on 12 June 1966
23 June 845 Sqn embark on *Bulwark* for the return from Borneo operations, arriving at Culdrose on 3 September
5 July 750 Sqn, the observer school, returns to the UK from Hal Far. It is established at Lossiemouth with nine Sea Prince T.Mk 1s and five Sea Venom FAW.Mk 22s
9 July 766 Sqn (the Sea Vixen OCU) undertakes its first FAW.Mk 2 sortie
27 July 801 Sqn (Buccaneer S.Mk 1) disbands at Lossiemouth and 849 'A' Flt disbands at Brawdy after Far East cruise in *Victorious*

A Decide of Air Power

Above: Wessex HAS.Mk 1s were used to transport troops and resupply outposts in the Radfan area during the early part of the Aden campaign. This aircraft is from 814 Sqn in Centaur.

Below: The Whirlwind HAS.Mk 7 was re-roled as a commando transport, and the variant was heavily involved in the Borneo campaign in the early months.

Above: The Wessex HAS.Mk 1s of 845 Sqn were involved in Borneo from the outset, not returning to the UK until September 1965. This pair is seen at one of the major detachments at Nanga Gaat.

From 1964 Wessex HU.Mk 5 training was undertaken by 707 Sqn. This example displays the carriage of Nord SS.11 guided missiles on the undercarriage struts.

848 Sqn. The Marines secured Kuwait New Airfield, allowing two RAF Hunter squadrons to move into Kuwait from Bahrain. Subsequently *Victorious* and its Scimitars (803 Sqn) and Sea Vixens (892 Sqn) arrived in the Gulf to lend weight to the British deterrent, followed by *Centaur* (893 Sqn Sea Vixens and 807 Sqn Scimitars). The large British force prevailed, with Iraq backing down without a shot being fired.

Protection of Kuwait had been provided at the request of the Sheikh, and another request

was to result in the Fleet Air Arm (and RAF) becoming embroiled in the major conflict of the decade. In December 1962 internal unrest in the Sultanate of Brunei and the neighbouring Crown Colony of Sarawak moved the Sultan to request help from the British. This initially arrived by RAF transports, which staged to the relatively secure island base at Labuan. On 14 and 15 December the Wessex of 845 Sqn and the Whirlwinds of 846 Sqn put 42 Royal Marine Commando ashore from *Albion* at Kuching, in southwest Sarawak, beginning a

long involvement of the Navy's commando squadrons in the conflict.

Borneo was a large island consisting of the Crown Colonies of Sabah and Sarawak, with the Sultanate of Brunei, to the north, and the province of Kalimantan, part of Indonesia, to the south. It was Britain's intention that Sabah and Sarawak should join the Malaysian Federation, threatening Indonesia's dominance of the region. It was very much in Indonesia's interests to train, supply and, on occasion, directly support the rebels to the north. The Borneo conflict soon became a confrontation with Indonesia, although Britain was anxious to keep the conflict confined within the borders of its own territory. Operations were broadly cat-

---

29 July Shortly after its return from a long Far East cruise in *Victorious*, 893 Sqn (Sea Vixen FAW.Mk 1) disbands at Yeovilton
24 August 820 Sqn embarks Wessex HAS.Mk 1s in *Eagle* for Far East cruise (shore operations from Sembawang). Returns to Culdrose 22 August 1966
25 August 800 Sqn embarks in *Eagle* for a Far East cruise (shore stops at Changi). Disembark to Lossiemouth on 14 August 1966. Joined by 849 Sqn 'D' Flt which returns to Brawdy on 21 August 1966 and 899 Sqn which returns to Yeovilton on 15 August 1966 (subsequently deploying to Boscombe

Down). During 1966 the carrier mans the Beira patrol
12 September 849 Sqn 'B' Flt (Gannet AEW.Mk 3/COD.Mk 4) disbanded at Brawdy
30 September 700 Sqn 'B' Flt (Buccaneer S.Mk 2 IFTU) disbanded at Lossiemouth
6 October 845 Sqn re-equips with 16 Wessex HU.Mk 5s at Culdrose (maximum complement 22)
14 October 801 Sqn reforms at Lossiemouth with Buccaneer S.Mk 2
4 November 893 Sqn is reformed at Yeovilton with Sea Vixen FAW.Mk 2s
23 November 764B Flt (Scimitar

F.Mk 1s) is disbanded at Lossiemouth
December 892 Sqn transitions from Sea Vixen FAW.Mk 1 to FAW.Mk 2 at Yeovilton

1966

20 January 849 'A' Flt reforms at Brawdy with three (later four) Gannet AEW.Mk 3s and a single Gannet COD.Mk 4 to act as AEW flight aboard *Victorious*
27 January 809 Sqn reformed at Lossiemouth with Buccaneer S.Mk 2s
18 March 826 Sqn reformed at Culdrose with six Wessex HAS.Mk 1 (subsequent maximum eight)

12 April 814 Sqn undertakes short cruise on *Victorious*, returning to Culdrose on 2 May
18 April 849 Sqn 'B' Flt reformed at Brawdy with two Gannet AEW.Mk 3s (later four plus one COD.Mk 4). Subsequent deployments made to Ballykelly and Yeovilton
2 May 845 Sqn embarks in *Bulwark* for work-up, returning to Culdrose on 6 May. Two subsequent work-up cruises undertaken 19 May – 10 June and 17 June – 7 July
6 May 826 Sqn deploys to Ballykelly with Wessex HAS.Mk 1s. Undertakes detachments to HMS *Lofoten* and RFA

Above: 848 Sqn sent its Wessex HU.Mk 5s to Borneo for the latter phases of the conflict. These used Albion as the main floating base.

Right: A typical scene from Borneo portrays an 846 Sqn Whirlwind HAS.Mk 7 landing in a jungle clearing. The Navy helicopters were a key part of the 'hearts and minds' campaign.

From 1959 to 1966 the ice-ship Protector's flight operated the Whirlwind HAR.Mk 1 (left) in the South Atlantic/Antarctic. The turbine-powered HAR.Mk 9 (above) was introduced in 1967. 829 Sqn took over responsibility for the flight in 1966, which was transferred to Endurance in 1968.

In 1964/65, during the unit's involvement in Borneo, 845 Sqn operated this Hiller HT.Mk 2 on pathfinding and liaison duties for its Wessex HAS.Mk 1s. Later Wasps were used by the commando squadrons for similar purposes.

A few elderly Hiller HT.Mk 1s were still in use with 705 Sqn at Culdrose until early 1963.

Hiller HT.Mk 2s served with 705 Sqn on basic helicopter training from September 1962.

egorised as patrolling and defending the border with Kalimantan, stopping infiltration into northern Borneo by sea and maintaining internal security.

Navy involvement centred around the two commando squadrons, which became heavily embroiled in the 'hearts and minds' internal security campaign. Using *Albion* as a floating base (replaced by *Bulwark* in 1964), or Labuan and Kuching as main operating locations ashore, the Wessex and Whirlwinds flew deep into the jungle to insert Marine patrols and keep them resupplied. Forward operating locations were subsequently established in the jungle to which detachments were regularly made. In April 1964 845 Sqn began using Hiller HT.2s to act as pathfinders for the Wessex, and later that year 846 Sqn retired the Whirlwinds from the fray. In May 1965 848 Sqn arrived with Wessex HU.5s, allowing 845 to leave the theatre in June. 846 Sqn was honoured for its work in Borneo with the award of the prestigious Boyd Trophy in 1963, the honour being bestowed on 845 the following year. The commando heli-

copters finally left Borneo when 848 Sqn rounded up its detachments in August 1966.

Further Navy action in the Borneo conflict concerned the aircraft of the main Fleet carriers, which made many cruises in the area during the campaign. As the war deepened, the British established an ADIZ along the border with Kalimantan, and the FAA helped patrol it, using Sea Vixen fighters and Gannet AEW.Mk 3s for radar early warning. The presence of carriers in the Straits of Malacca (which separates

Singapore from the Indonesian island of Sumatra) and the heavy use made of Singapore's four airfields (Sembawang, Seletar, Changi and Tengah) by both FAA and RAF aircraft averted any major action by Indonesia against Malaya and Singapore, while restricting the opposition in Borneo to a few cross-border landings (which were rapidly mopped up by heliborne forces) and air strikes (which were of limited effect). The Indonesian will to prolong the fight waned dramatically in 1966, leaving

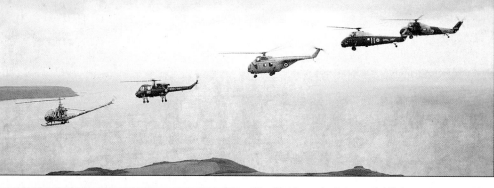

The Culdrose training establishment put up this formation combining the types used by 705 (basic), 706 (advanced) and 707 (commando) Sqns.

The advanced helicopter training unit, 706 Sqn, operated the Wessex HAS.Mk 1 (above) and Wasp HAS. Mk 1 (below) for much of the 1960s.

A single specially-equipped Sea Prince T.Mk 1 was used by the ECM training unit (831 Sqn), co-located with the RAF EW effort at Watton.

750 Sqn was the FAA's Observer (navigator) school, and operated the Sea Prince T.Mk 1 (above) as its principal equipment. Sea Venom FAW.Mk 22s (below) were used for high altitude work. The squadron was based at Hal Far until 1965, when it transferred to Lossiemouth.

Left: 705 Sqn used a mixture of Hillers and Whirlwinds for its basic helicopter training role. This aircraft is a Whirlwind HAS.Mk 7, overflying the ramp at Culdrose with further squadron aircraft including Hiller HT.Mk 2s.

Brunei to enjoy the independent wealth of its oilfields and Sarawak and Sabah to become a peaceful part of the Malaysian Federation.

While the Navy commando squadrons were performing sterling work in Borneo, Britain was increasingly involved in internal security work in another of its colonies. Civil unrest in the southern Arabian Protectorate of Aden had run high since the end of World War II, exacerbated in September 1962 by a coup in neighbouring Yemen. This revolutionary state began supporting the FLOSY rebels in Aden, notably

in the city itself and the mountainous Radfan region in the north. In December 1963 815 Sqn took its Wessex HAS.Mk 1s ashore to the major RAF base at Khormaksar to help in operations against dissident tribesmen, shortly before the major Nutcracker offensive was launched in January 1964. However, in late January the squadron was hastily called away to another crisis which had loomed in Tanganyika. Sailing in *Centaur*, 815 Sqn landed No. 45 Royal Marine Commando ashore to restore order in Dar-es-Salaam, an objective achieved

with great rapidity. To further reinforce British resolve in East Africa, and to deter any further unrest, Buccaneers from 801 Sqn moved to Embakasi in Kenya during February.

With the Tanganyika situation under control, Navy helicopters returned to Aden to support operations there. While RAF Belvederes were the main vehicle for positioning artillery, the task of troop movements fell increasingly to Navy helicopters. On 22 May 1964 815 Sqn landed 45 RMC into the Radfan mountains as part of the final Nutcracker operation, which

Far East. Operations undertaken during this period from Sembawang, Shoalwater Bay, Gemas, Jason's Bay, *Fearless*, Sek Kong, Mersing, Terrendak, Kluang, Kuantan, *Eagle*, *Hermes*, *Phoebe*, Masirah, RFA *Olwen* and Changi. Squadron returns to Culdrose on 20 April 1968
14 August 800B Flt, the inflight refuelling trials unit, is disbanded at Lossiemouth with four Scimitar F.Mk 1s
5 September One Hiller HT.Mk 2 added to 845 Sqn complement
22 September 826 Sqn embarks in *Hermes* for short cruise (including shore detachment to Arbroath), returning to Culdrose on 16 November. Joined by 849 Sqn 'B' Flt from Brawdy, which returns on 20 October, and 892, which

undertakes its first Sea Vixen FAW.Mk 2 cruise ending the same date
27 September 800 Sqn flies its first sortie with the Buccaneer S.Mk 2
October 829 Sqn receives two Wessex HU.Mk 5s for ship's flights of RFA *Regent* and RFA *Resource*
1 October On disembarkation from *Ark Royal*, 803 Sqn (10 Scimitar F.Mk 1s) is disbanded
5 October 849 Sqn 'C' Flt (four Gannet AEW.Mk 3 and one COD.Mk 4) disbanded at Brawdy
7 October 815 Sqn (Wessex HAS.Mk 1) disbanded at Culdrose
7 October 890 Sqn (Sea Vixen FAW.Mk 1) disbanded at Yeovilton
8 October 892 Sqn deploys Vixens to *Hermes*, returning on 30 November

1967

9 January 700H Flt reformed as Wessex HAS.Mk 3 IFTU at Culdrose with one aircraft (subsequent complement three Wessex HAS.Mk 3 and two HAS.Mk 1)
16 Janaury 826 Sqn flies to *Hermes* for Far East cruise (operations from North Front, Hal Far, RFA *Olna* and Sembawang). Returns to Culdrose 30 September
18 Janaury 809 Sqn embarks its Buccaneer S.Mk 2s aboard *Hermes* for Far East cruise (stops at N. Front, Hal Far and Changi). Returns to Lossiemouth on 29 September. Supported by 849 Sqn 'B' Flt (shore operations from North Front and Changi) which returns to

Brawdy on 30 September
19 January 892 Sqn joins *Hermes* to provide fighter assets on Far East cruise (shore stops at Hal Far and Changi). Returns to Yeovilton on 29 September
6 February 849 Sqn 'D' Flt receives single Gannet COD.Mk 4 to add to its four AEW.Mk 3s
March Replacement of 800 Sqn's eight Buccaneer S.Mk 1s by 12 Buccaneer S.Mk 2s is completed
28 March Buccaneers of 736 Sqn and 800 Sqn called in to conduct three days of bombing the grounded oil tanker *Torrey Canyon*
1 May 848 Sqn undertakes short deployment to *Albion*, returning to Culdrose on 5 July
31 May 728 Sqn, the Mediterranean

Dragonfly HR.Mk 5s remained in 705 Sqn service at the start of the 1960s, but were withdrawn in 1962. The type continued in use with station flights for a while after.

Nominally on charge of 781 Sqn at Lee-on-Solent, this 'Admiral's Barge' Sea Vampire T.Mk 22 was the personal mount of Flag Officer Air Home.

Among the elderly aircraft still serving on station flights (which also included the Swordfish and Hellcat) were several Tiger Moth T.Mk 2s, exemplified by this Lossiemouth aircraft.

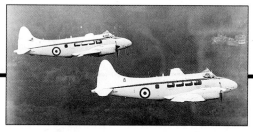

In use by 781 Sqn for communications work were several Sea Devon C.Mk 20s.

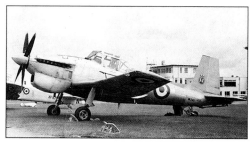

This elderly Whirlwind HAS.Mk 22 wore a smart 'Admiral's Barge' colour scheme for VIP work throughout the 1960s with 781 Sqn.

Two relics which survived into the 1960s in small numbers were the Sea Balliol T.Mk 21 (above), which flew with some station flights, and the Sea Fury FB.Mk 11 (below), which served with the Airwork FRU at Hurn until 1961.

Partnering the Sea Devon was the larger Sea Heron C.Mk 2 and other Heron variants.

781 Sqn received this smart Wessex HU.Mk 5 in 1969 for SAR and VIP transport work.

This short-nosed Sea Prince C.Mk 1 was used by Culdrose station flight in 1964/65.

The Chipmunk T.Mk 10 served with Britannia Flight at Roborough from June 1966, having replaced Tiger Moths with the Royal Naval College's air experience unit. Helicopters assigned were Dragonflies and Wasps (after 1967).

successfully concluded in June. Despite having taken all of the rebel strongholds in the Radfan, terrorism continued unabated in Aden itself, and the decision was made to withdraw in late 1967. In the interim Navy helicopters were involved in several troop lifting operations, notably 820 Sqn's Wessex in 1965/66.

One final major operation undertaken in the decade was the blockade of Rhodesia. On 11 November 1965 Rhodesia proclaimed its Unilateral Declaration of Independence in direct contravention of the British intention of a peaceful transition to majority rule, a policy fully backed by the United Nations.

Within hours Prime Minister Harold Wilson imposed a total trade embargo on Rhodesia, and both RAF aircraft and Royal Navy carriers were dispatched to enforce the blockade. The principal aim was to stop the flow of oil into Rhodesia through the Mozambique port of Beira, which was also the main export harbour for Rhodesian goods. Both *Eagle* and *Ark Royal* undertook spells on the Beira Patrol, the latter being on station for much of 1966. The ship's 849 Sqn 'C' Flight, with Gannets, was heavily involved, and was awarded the 1966 Boyd Trophy in recognition of its work. Subsequently the Beira Patrol became more of an RAF tasking, with Shackletons operating in concert with Royal Navy frigates. Although Beira was no longer effective as a port, the Rhodesians developed many sanction-busting methods and, far from crippling the nation, there was some argument that the embargo increased Rhodesian resolve by strengthening ties with other, less principled, nations.

Fleet liaison and target-towing squadron at Hal Far, is disbanded with five Meteor TT.Mk 20s, one Meteor T.Mk 7 and one Sea Heron C.Mk 2
6 June 849 Sqn 'D' Flt embarks in *Eagle* for four days, returning on 10 June
23 June 820 Sqn Wessex HAS.Mk 1s fly to *Eagle* for short cruise, disembarking to Culdrose on 18 July
23 June 771 Sqn is reformed at Portland from the Whirlwind flight of 829 Sqn with 10 Whirlwind HAS.Mk 7s for fleet requirements work
24 June 899 Sqn Sea Vixen FAW.Mk 2s deploy from temporary base at Boscombe for cruise in *Eagle* which ends on 18 July
26 June 800 Sqn Buccaneer S.Mk 2s and 849 Sqn 'D' Flt Gannets embark in

Eagle for a short work-up cruise, returning to Lossiemouth on 18 July and Brawdy on 17 July respectively
July Whirlwind HAR.Mk 9 received by 829 Sqn to replace HMS *Protector* iceship's flight (from 1968 HMS *Endurance*)
3 July 803 Sqn reformed at Lossiemouth as Buccaneer Headquarters Squadron with one S.Mk 1 (subsequent maximum four aircraft)
4 August 820 Sqn Wessex join *Eagle* for Far East cruise (shore stop at Sembawang). Return to Culdrose 18 June 1968
14 August Gannets of 849 Sqn 'D' Flt join *Eagle*'s air group, operating from Changi, Pearce and Kai Tak during the cruise which ends on 17 June 1968
14 August 890 Sqn reforms at

Yeovilton with two Sea Vixen FAW.Mk 1s as Sea Vixen Headquarters Squadron
15 August Buccaneer S.Mk 2s of 800 Sqn embark in *Eagle* for a Far East cruise, calling at Changi and Pearce before returning to Lossiemouth on 18 June 1968. Joined by 899 Sqn Sea Vixen FAW.Mk 2s from Boscombe Down which return to Yeovilton on 19 June 1968
25 August 848 Sqn adds a single Wasp for Marine liaison
8 September 848 Sqn embarks in *Albion* for Far East cruise (including operations from Sembawang, Mersing, Jason's Bay and *Intrepid*). Return to Culdrose on 29 June 1969
15 September 700H Flt (Wessex HAS.Mk 3 IFTU) disbanded at Culdrose

28 September 890 Sqn receives its first Sea Vixen FAW.Mk 2 at Yeovilton (maximum complement six). Subsequent detachments made to Akrotiri and Lossiemouth
5 October 737 Sqn at Portland receives the first of an eventual maximum of eight Wessex HAS.Mk 3s for the ASW training role
9 October 814 Sqn welcomes first Wessex HAS.Mk 3 to replace the HAS.Mk 1
30 October 892 Sqn embarks in *Hermes* for cruise which ends on 18 February 1968
31 October Wessex HAS.Mk 1s of 826 Sqn embark in *Hermes* for cruise which ends 19 February 1968. Detachment made to RFA *Olwen* during

728 Sqn operated this Meteor T.Mk 7 from Hal Far alongside its TT.Mk 20 target-tugs.

A pilotless Meteor U.Mk 15 target of 728B Flt, seen shortly before it was expended in May 1960. The flight also operated the U.Mk 16 variant.

Above: Target facilities were provided by the Airwork FRU at Hurn. Scimitar F.Mk 1s were on strength from 1965 to 1970.

The Air Direction Training Unit was resident at Yeovilton from January 1961, flying Sea Venom FAW.Mk 22s (illustrated) and Sea Vampires.

EW training was the province of Watton-based 831 Sqn, which operated this Sea Venom Mk 22ECM alongside Gannet ECM.Mk 6s and a single Sea Prince. In 1966 the squadron disbanded, most of its personnel being assigned to the joint RAF/RN ECM training unit (No.360 Sqn).

Above: 728 Sqn 'B' Flt at Hal Far operated the pilotless Firefly U.Mk 9 drones, the last being destroyed in late 1961. Note the damage to the fin of this aircraft caused by naval gunfire.

Right: The Airwork FRU also flew several Meteor TT.Mk 20s from its Hurn base, equipped with Rushton high-speed targets

Towards the end of the decade the Fleet Air Arm began to run down its carrier forces, and there would be no further colonial wars to fight until the Falklands. Two minor events which kept the FAA in the public eye as the decade closed were the bombing of the grounded tanker *Torrey Canyon* in March 1967, and the attempt by the newly-delivered Phantoms to win the Daily Mail Transatlantic air race in

1969. As if to emphasise the miserable end of a decade which had started so brightly for the FAA, the Phantoms were defeated in the race by the 'crabs' of the RAF, which used a Harrier GR.Mk 1, although 892 Sqn did set a west-east Transatlantic record in the process.

Looking back at the 1960s, the Fleet Air Arm could draw some pride from a job well done. At the start of the decade, the British

government was undertaking a policy of handing back its colonial mandate to democratic governments as peacefully as possible, a process accelerated by the Wilson government when it assumed power in 1964. Inevitably, this process was not achieved without some mistakes and fighting, but in their overall aim the British were largely successful and by the end of the 1960s there were few colonial interests left to

cruise, and post-cruise detachments to RFA *Olmeda* and RFA *Olna*
November *Victorious* damaged by fire during refit for a final commission. Ship paid off and scrapped in 1969
1 November 849 Sqn 'B' Flt flies to *Hermes* for winter cruise, ending on 18 February 1968
4 November 809 Sqn deploys Buccaneer S.Mk 2s to join 849 Sqn 'B' Flt aboard *Hermes*. Returns to Lossiemouth on 18 February 1968

1968
24 January 803 Sqn accepts five Buccaneer S.Mk 2s at Lossiemouth to begin replacement of S.Mk 1s
28 February 849 Sqn 'B' Flt (four Gannet AEW.Mk 3 and one COD.Mk 4) disbanded at Brawdy
3 April 819 Sqn receives first Wessex HAS.Mk 3 (maximum four) to replace HAS.Mk 1s. Subsequent exercise detachments made to RFA *Engadine*, RFA *Tidepool*, Arbroath, Prestwick, Tiree, RFA *Olmeda*, Linton on Ouse and Bishop's Court
30 April 700P Flt is established at Yeovilton as Intensive Flying Trials Unit for the Phantom FG.Mk 1

27 May 814 Sqn deploys for a work-up prior to a Far East cruise with Wessex HAS.Mk 3 in *Hermes*, returning to Culdrose on 30 March 1969
29 May Gannets of 849 'A' Flt fly to *Hermes* for short cruise, ending on 20 June
30 May 893 Sqn deploys Sea Vixen FAW.Mk 2s in *Hermes*, disembarking to Yeovilton on 20 June
30 May 845 Sqn deploys aboard *Bulwark* for Exercise Polar Express, returning to Culdrose on 2 August
31 May 801 Sqn takes its Buccaneer S.Mk 2s aboard *Hermes*, returning to Lossiemouth on 20 June
June 766 Sqn, the Yeovilton-based Sea Vixen OCU, retires its last FAW.Mk 1
8 July Far East cruise for 893 Sqn begins with embarcation in *Hermes*. Return after shore stops at Changi is effected 31 March 1969
9 July 801 Sqn and 849 'A' Flt join 814 aboard *Hermes* for Far East cruise (stop made at Changi), returning to Lossiemouth and Brawdy on 30 and 31 March 1969 respectively
29 July 846 Sqn reformed at Culdrose as Wessex HU.Mk 5 Headquarters

Squadron with four aircraft (maximum seven). Subsequent training detachments to *Bulwark*, *Fearless* and RFA *Engadine*
22 August Wessex HAS.Mk 1s of 820 Sqn embark in *Eagle*, returning to Culdrose on 3 October. Subsequent detachments made to RFA *Olmeda*, RFA *Tidepool* and HMS *Blake*
24 August 849 Sqn 'D' Flt Gannets and 899 Sqn embark in *Eagle*, returning to Brawdy and Yeovilton on 2 October. During the winter both units deploy to Decimomannu.
28 August 800 Sqn embarks Buccaneer S.Mk 2s in *Eagle* for short cruise, returning to Lossiemouth on 2 October
2 September 809 Sqn detaches to Yeovilton, returning to Lossiemouth on 23 September
6 September 845 Sqn moves to Farnborough for participation in the SBAC show, returning back to Culdrose on 23 September
1 October 826 Sqn receives first Wessex HAS.Mk 3 (maximum six) to replace HAS.Mk 1
4 October 892 Sqn (Sea Vixen FAW.Mk 2) disbanded at Yeovilton

19 October 10 Wessex HU.Mk 5s from 845 Sqn deploy in *Fearless* for an exercise
7 November 800 Sqn Buccaneer S.Mk 2s undertake short detachment to Luqa, returning to Lossiemouth on 18 November

1969
14 January 767 Sqn is commissioned at Yeovilton as the Phantom Training Squadron with two aircraft (subsequent maximum 11)
9 February 846 Sqn embarks in RFA *Engadine* for cold-weather trials in Norway, the first of many such exercises for the Royal Marines and their helicopter support
14 March 847 Sqn reformed at Sembawang to support Royal Marines with eight Wessex HU.Mk 5s previously operated by 848 Sqn
31 March 700P Flt (Phantom IFTU) disbands at Yeovilton and reforms as 892 Sqn with eight Phantom FG.Mk 1s to become the only RN front-liner user of the type
1 April 826 Sqn makes its first Wessex HAS.Mk 3 cruise in *Eagle*, returning to Culdrose on 30 April

Among the best-known of the FAA's support aircraft were the all-black civilian-flown Sea Hawk FGA.Mk 6s of the FRU at Hurn

A pointer for the future were the deck trials by Harrier GR.Mk 1s during the latter part of the 1960s. This aircraft wears an 'E' for trials on Eagle.

support. Although there were many other political factors at work, ironically it was the Royal Navy's success in implementing this British foreign policy that was a major factor in the demise of the carrier force. With *Hermes* and *Eagle* gone by 1972, the Navy was left with only one carrier (*Ark Royal*) with which to continue an ill-defined Cold War tasking.

Bill Gunston and David Donald

FLEET AIR ARM ORDER OF BATTLE AT 31 DECEMBER 1969

UNIT	SHIP/ROLE	TYPE	BASE
Front line squadrons			
800 Squadron	*Eagle*	14 Buccaneer S.Mk 2	Lossiemouth
801 Squadron	*Hermes*	7 Buccaneer S.Mk 2	Lossiemouth
809 Squadron	*Ark Royal*	8 Buccaneer S.Mk 2	Lossiemouth
814 Squadron	*Hermes*	5 Wessex HAS.Mk 3	Culdrose
819 Squadron	RFA detachments	4 Wessex HAS.Mk 3	Ballykelly
820 Squadron	*Blake*	Wessex HAS.Mk 3	Culdrose
826 Squadron	*Eagle*	5 Wessex HAS.Mk 3	Culdrose
829 Squadron	small ship flights	Wasp HAS.Mk 1, Wessex HAS.Mk 1, HAS.Mk 3, 2 HU.Mk 5, 2 Whirlwind HAR.Mk 9	Portland
845 Squadron	*Albion*	1 Wasp HAS.Mk 1, 16 Wessex HU.Mk 5	Culdrose
846 Squadron	commando HQ	4 Wessex HU.Mk 5	Culdrose
847 Squadron	*Fearless/Sir Galahad*	8 Wessex HU.Mk 5	Sembawang
848 Squadron	*Bulwark*	1 Wasp HAS.Mk 1, 10 Wessex HU.Mk 5	Culdrose
849 Squadron HQ		4 Gannet AEW.Mk 3, COD.Mk 4, 2 T.Mk 5	Brawdy
849 Squadron 'A' Flt	*Hermes*	4 Gannet AEW.Mk 3, 1 COD.Mk 4	Brawdy
849 Squadron 'D' Flt	*Eagle*	4 Gannet AEW.Mk 3, 1 COD.Mk 4	Brawdy
890 Squadron	operational trials/training	5 Sea Vixen FAW.Mk 2	Yeovilton
892 Squadron	*Ark Royal*	8 Phantom FG.Mk 1	Yeovilton
893 Squadron	*Hermes*	12 Sea Vixen FAW.Mk 2	Yeovilton
899 Squadron	*Eagle*	16 Sea Vixen FAW.Mk 2	Yeovilton

UNIT	TYPE	BASE
Second-line squadrons		
700S Squadron (Intensive Flight Trials Unit)	6 Sea King HAS.Mk 1	Culdrose
705 Squadron (Helicopter Training Squadron)	Whirlwind HAS.Mk 7	Culdrose
706 Squadron (Helicopter Advanced Flying Training Squadron)	6 Wessex HAS.Mk 1, 6 HAS.Mk 3, 5 Wasp HAS.Mk 1, 2 Sea King HAS.Mk 1	Culdrose
707 Squadron (Commando Advanced/Operational Flying Training)	12 Wessex HU.Mk 5	Culdrose
736 Squadron (Jet Strike Training Squadron)	7 Buccaneer S.Mk 1, 7 Buccaneer S.Mk 2	Lossiemouth
737 Squadron (Anti-submarine Operational Flying School)	Wessex HAS.Mk 1, HAS.Mk 3	Portland
738 Squadron (Advanced Training Squadron)	3 Hunter T.Mk 8, 8 GA.Mk 11	Brawdy
750 Squadron (Observer School)	9 Sea Prince T.Mk 1, 5 Sea Venom FAW.Mk 22	Lossiemouth
764 Squadron (Air Warfare Instructor Training Squadron)	2 Hunter T.Mk 8b, 4 T.Mk 8c, 8 GA.Mk 11/PR.Mk 11	Lossiemouth
766 Squadron (All-Weather Fighter Training Squadron)	11 Sea Vixen FAW.Mk 2	Yeovilton
767 Squadron (Phantom Operational Conversion Unit)	8 Phantom FG.Mk 1	Yeovilton
771 Squadron (Anti-submarine Fleet Requirements Unit)	8 Whirlwind HAS.Mk 7, 4 Wessex HAS.Mk 1	Portland
781 Squadron (Communications Squadron)	1 Tiger Moth T.Mk 2, 4 Sea Heron C.Mk 2, 1 Heron C.Mk 4, 3 Sea Devon C.Mk 20, 2 Wessex HU.Mk 5	Lee-on-Solent

Miscellaneous units
Ship's Flights – *Eagle* (Wessex HAS.1), *Hermes* (Wessex HAS.1)
Station Flights – Brawdy (Sea Vampire T.22, Sea Prince T.1, Whirlwind HAR.9), Church Fenton (Sea Prince T.1), Culdrose (Whirlwind HAS.7, Whirlwind HAR.9), Lee-on-Solent (Sea Devon C.20), Lossiemouth (Sea Prince T.1, Whirlwind HAS.7, Whirlwind HAR.9), Yeovilton (Sea Prince C.2, Sea Devon C.20, Tiger Moth, Whirlwind HAS.7, Hunter T.7, Hunter T.8, Hunter GA.11)
Air Direction Training Unit, Yeovilton (Sea Venom FAW.22, Sea Vampire T.22)
Airwork Fleet Requirement Unit, Hurn (Meteor T.7, Meteor TT.20, Scimitar F.1, Hunter T.8, Hunter GA.11, Canberra B.2, Canberra T.4, Canberra TT.18)
Britannia Flight, Roborough (Chipmunk T.10, Wasp HAS.1)

---

3 April Short cruise for 849 Sqn 'D' Flt and 899 Sqn in *Eagle*, ending on 29 April
10 April Short embarcation for 800 Sqn Buccaneer S.Mk 2s to *Eagle*, disembarking to Lossiemouth on 28 April
17 April 845 Sqn dispatches 14 Wessex HU.Mk 5s and a Wasp to *Bulwark* for a Mediterranean cruise. Shore ops flown from Dhekelia, Akrotiri, St Mandrier, Cuers and Luqa before returning to Culdrose on 13 August
30 April 846 Sqn Wessex HU.Mk 5 begins Exercise Sparrowhawk to evaluate helicopter v. fighter air-to-air combat
4-11 May 892 Sqn takes part in the Daily Mail Transatlantic Air Race using Phantom FG.Mk 1s. The Navy is just pipped by the RAF flying a Harrier GR.Mk 1
16 May 847 Sqn embarks in *Albion* for short cruise, returning to Sembawang on 28 May
22 May 826 Sqn boards *Eagle* with Wessex HAS.Mk 3s, flying back to Culdrose on 20 July
23 May 800 Sqn Buccaneer S.Mk 2s embark in *Eagle*, returning to Lossiemouth on 18 July. AEW detachment provided by 849 Sqn 'D' Flt

which flies back to Brawdy on 2 June
23 May First Wessex HAS.Mk 3 arrives for 820 Sqn at Culdrose (maximum complement four) to replace HAS.Mk 1
June Wessex HAS.Mk 3s replace HAS.Mk 1s with 829 Sqn's 'County'-class flights
June 781 Sqn at Lee-on-Solent receives its first Wessex HU.Mk 5 to replace two Whirlwind HAS.Mk 22s in use as a VIP transport (and secondary SAR duties)
16 June 849 Sqn 'D' Flt re-embarks in *Eagle*, disembarking on 19 July. 899 Sqn also embarks that day, staying aboard until 18 July
1 July 700S Flt established at Culdrose without aircraft as Sea King HAS.Mk 1 IFTU
14 July 847 Sqn dispatches five Wessex HU.Mk 5s to *Fearless* and the remaining three to *Sir Galahad*
11 August First of six Sea King HAS.Mk 1s arrive for 700H Flt at Culdrose
September 781 Sqn's communications fleet is bolstered by the delivery of an ex-RAF Heron C.Mk 4
3 September 826 Sqn embarks in

Eagle for Mediterranean cruise. Returns to Culdrose on 5 December
4 September 800 Sqn Buccaneer S.Mk 2s, 899 Sqn Sea Vixen FAW.Mk 2s and 849 Sqn 'D' Flt Gannets embark in *Eagle* for Mediterranean cruise (shore deployments to Luqa and North Front). 899 returns to Yeovilton on 3 December, while 800 and 849D return to Lossiemouth and Brawdy on 4 December
4 September 771 Sqn begins replacement of its Whirlwinds with the Wessex HAS.Mk 1. Four are in use by the year's end
8 September 845 Sqn moves its home base from Culdrose to Yeovilton
15 September 848 Sqn embarks in *Bulwark* with Wessex HU.Mk 5s
17 September 814 Sqn embarks in *Hermes* for a short cruise, returning to Culdrose and Lee-on-Solent on 28 October
19 September 845 Sqn begins short deployment to *Bulwark*, returning to Yeovilton on 23 October
25 September 801 Sqn, 893 Sqn and 849 Sqn 'A' Flt undertake short cruise on *Hermes*, flying back to Lossiemouth, Yeovilton and Brawdy on 27, 27 and 28

October respectively
18 October 892's first shipboard deployment is made with Phantom FG.Mk 1s to USS *Saratoga*. Return to Yeovilton made on 24 October
14 November Buccaneer S.Mk 2s of 801 Sqn embark in *Hermes* as strike element, returning to Lossiemouth on 4 December. Fighters provided by 893 Sqn Sea Vixen FAW.Mk 2s which disembark on 3 December. Joined by 814 Sqn Wessex HAS.Mk 3s from Culdrose and Lee-on-Solent, which return to the former base on 4 December. Gannet AEW.Mk 3/COD.Mk 4s of 849 'A' Flt also on board, returning to Brawdy on 4 December
18 November 706 Sqn (advanced helicopter training unit) at Culdrose receives its first Sea King HAS.Mk 1
3/4 December Major pre-Christmas disembarcation date for FAA squadrons
18 December 803 Sqn (Buccaneer S.Mk 2 HQ Sqn) disbands at Lossiemouth
24 December 759 Sqn at Brawdy is disbanded with nine Hunter T.Mk 8s

INDEX

Picture acknowledgments

Front cover: McDonnell Douglas. **4:** Hale via Warren Thompson (WT). **5:** Richard Irving via WT, Orrin Fox via WT, MacClancy Collection. **6:** Ray Ruscoe via WT, Carl Fraser via WT. **7:** Leo Needham via WT, Morris Washatka via WT, George Deans via WT. **8:** Duane Dunklee via WT, D.T. Allred via WT. **9:** Bob Dewald via WT, White via WT. **10:** Russ Rogers via WT. **11:** Bill Williams via WT, Ray Stewart via WT. **12:** Fogg via WT, Jack Jenkins via WT. **13:** Wurster via WT, USAF. **14:** Dewald via WT, Ray Stewart via WT. **15:** James Dennison via WT, Zach Ryall via WT, Frank Clark via WT. **16:** Reeves via WT. **17:** H.I. Price via WT (two). **18:** Wurster via WT, Sonny Bush via WT. **19:** WT, Russ Janson via WT. **20:** Allen Nelson via WT, Marsh via WT, Cothern via WT. **21:** Peter B. Mersky, Ray Bell via WT. **22:** Charles Schreffer via WT, Al Wimer via WT. **23:** via WT. **24:** O'Donnell via WT, John Stanek via WT. **25:** Frank Durkee via WT, Boyd Gibson via WT, Fahlberg via WT. **26:** Allen Nelson via WT, Allen Miller via WT, Don Loegering via WT. **27:** Evans Stephens via WT, Allen Nelson via WT. **28:** US Navy via Peter B. Mersky, Ed Johnson via WT. **29:** Leo Fournier via WT, A.J. Walter via WT. **30:** John Henderson via WT. **31:** Bruce Hinton via WT, John Henderson via WT. **32:** Lawler via WT, John Henderson via WT. **33:** Bill Taylor via WT, James Dennison via WT. **34-35:** Northrop. **36:** Northrop (two), Northrop via Jon Lake. **37-45:** Northrop. **46:** Northrop via Hugh Cowin, Northrop. **47:** Northrop via Hugh Cowin. **48:** UK MoD, No. 56 Sqn. **49:** UK MoD. **50:** No. 56 Sqn, Bruce Robertson. **51:** No. 56 Sqn (two). **53:** No. 56 Sqn, UK MoD. **54-55:** No. 56 Sqn. **56-57:** USAF. **58:** USAF via Jeff Ethell, NAA (two). **59:** USAF, Jeff Ethell (two). **60:** Aerospace (two). **61:** Aerospace (four), Jeff Ethell. **62:** MAP, Aerospace. **64:** Jeff Ethell, USAF, NAA, USAF via Jeff Ethell. **65:** USAF (three), Aerospace, René J. Francillon. **68:** Jeff Ethell, Rolls-Royce, USAF via Jeff Ethell, NAA. **69:** NAA (two). **70:** Jeff Ethell (three), USAF via Jeff Ethell. **71:** MAP. **72:** Jeff Ethell (two). **73:** Aerospace (two), USAF via Jeff Ethell, USAF (three). **76:** Jeff Ethell (three), Imperial War Museum (two). **79:** Jeff Ethell (three). **80:** Jeff Ethell, René J. Francillon. **81:** René J. Francillon (two), USAF. **82:** USAF via Jeff Ethell. **84:** Jeff Ethell (three), USAF. **85:** Jeff Ethell (three), USAF. **86:** Aerospace, USAF via Jeff Ethell. **87:** USAF via Jeff Ethell, Jeff Ethell. **98:** USAF, Jeff Ethell, NAA (three). **99:** NAA (two), Jeff Ethell (two). **100:** USAF, USAF via Jeff Ethell (two). **101:** US Army, USAF via Jeff Ethell (two). **102:** Jeff Ethell. **104-106:** Jeff Ethell. **107:** D. Hughes, Jeff Ethell. **108:** Jeff Ethell, Cavalier (three). **109:** Cavalier, MAP, Piper. **110:** Jeff Ethell, Mike Jerram, Dustin Carter, L.L. Coombs. **111:** Chuck Aro. **112:** John Zawiski (two), Chuck Aro, Peter R. March. **113:** Peter R. March, P.H. Green, Anders Nylen. **114:** Peter R. March (two), Jeremy Flack/API. **115:** Jeremy Flack/API (two), Jeff Ethell, Jim Dunn. **116:** US Navy. **117:** US Navy (two), US Navy via Peter B. Mersky. **120:** US Navy, Peter B. Mersky. **121:** US Navy via Peter B. Mersky, US Navy. **122:** US Navy, Lionel Paul via Robert F. Dorr. **123:** Peter B. Mersky. **124:** US Navy (two). **125:** Peter B. Mersky. **126:** US Navy (two). **127:** McDonnell Douglas via Peter B. Mersky, Robert L. Lawson. **128:** McDonnell, US Navy, Peter B. Mersky. **129:** Peter B. Mersky, McDonnell, Lionel Paul via

Robert F. Dorr (two). **130:** Peter B. Mersky (two), US Navy via Peter B. Mersky, Lionel Paul via Robert F. Dorr, via Robert F. Dorr. **131:** Peter B. Mersky (two), US Navy via Peter B. Mersky, McDonnell. **132:** US Navy (three), US Navy via Peter B. Mersky (two). **133:** US Navy (four), US Navy via Peter B. Mersky. **134:** US Navy, US Navy via Peter B. Mersky. **135:** US Navy (six). **136:** US Navy (two), Peter B. Mersky, US Navy via Peter B. Mersky (two). **137:** Peter B. Mersky, US Navy via Peter B. Mersky (two), US Navy. **138:** Peter B. Mersky (three), US Navy. **139:** Peter B. Mersky (two), US Navy (two), Jan Jacobs via Robert F. Dorr. **140-141:** Nigel Eastaway/Russian Aviation Research Trust. **142:** Aerospace, Bruce Robertson, via John Weal. **143:** JG71 via John Weal. **144:** Aerospace, Bruce Robertson, Imperial War Museum. **146-147:** Bruce Robertson. **148:** Bruce Robertson, BMW, J.W.R. Taylor. **150:** Bruce Robertson (two), JG71. **151:** JG71, Aerospace, Gerd-Günther Voss via John Weal. **152:** JG71, via John Weal. **154:** Bruce Robertson, JG71 via John Weal, Aerospace. **156:** Bruce Robertson (three), Aerospace. **157:** Gerd-Günther Voss via John Weal. **158:** Bundesarchiv (three). **160:** Bundesarchiv (two), Gerd-Günther Voss via John Weal (two), Imperial War Museum. **162:** JG71 via John Weal (three), Stefan Petersen, JG71. **163:** Bruce Robertson (two), JG71 via John Weal. **164:** JG71 via John Weal, Luftwaffe (two). **165:** Stefan Petersen. **166-167:** McDonnell, USAF (two). **168:** Richard Burns via Warren Thompson, Peter R. Foster. **169:** USAF, Robert F. Dorr (two). **170-171:** McDonnell. **172:** USAF (two), McDonnell. **173:** McDonnell (two), USAF, C.A. Johnson. **174:** McDonnell (three), USAF. **175:** USAF (three), McDonnell. **176:** McDonnell (three), Aerospace, Robert F. Dorr. **177:** McDonnell, USAF. **178:** RCAF (two), Aerospace, Peter R. Foster. **180:** Peter R. Foster (two), McDonnell (two). **181:** Robert F. Dorr, McDonnell, Roy Marsh via Warren Thompson, Richard Burns via Warren Thompson. **183:** Aerospace, USAF via Peter R. Foster. **184:** Aerospace, USAF, Robert F. Dorr (two). **186:** Peter R. Foster. **187:** Lockheed, Kentucky ANG, Aerospace. **188:** Fleet Air Arm Museum, Peter R. March. **189:** Peter R. March (three), Fleet Air Arm Museum (two), Royal Navy. **190:** Peter R. March, Fleet Air Arm Museum (three). **191:** Royal Navy, Peter R. March (two), Fleet Air Arm Museum (two). **192:** Westland, Peter R. March (two), Fleet Air Arm Museum (two). **193:** Fleet Air Arm Museum (three), Blackburn, Royal Navy. **194:** Fleet Air Arm Museum (three). **195:** Charles E. Brown Collection/RAF Museum, Fleet Air Arm Museum (three). **196:** Fleet Air Arm Museum (two), Aerospace, Bruce Robertson, Peter R. March. **197:** RNAS Brawdy, Royal Navy, Peter R. March. **198:** Fleet Air Arm Museum (three), Peter R. March (two). **199:** Peter R. March (three), Royal Navy, Jon Lake, Hugh Cowin. **200:** Fleet Air Arm Museum (five), Peter R. March (two). **201:** Peter R. March (three), Fleet Air Arm Museum three. **203:** Peter R.March (nine), Fleet Air Arm Museum (two). **204:** Peter R. March (five), Fleet Air Arm Museum (two). **205:** Peter R. March, HSA via Michael Stroud.